Books by Brenda Maddox

Beyond Babel: New Directions in Communications
The Half-Parent: Living with Other People's Children
Who's Afraid of Elizabeth Taylor?
Married and Gay
Nora: The Real Life of Molly Bloom

D.H. Lawrence

THE STORY

OF A MARRIAGE

BY

BRENDA MADDOX

SIMON & SCHUSTER

NEW YORK   LONDON   TORONTO
SYDNEY   TOKYO   SINGAPORE

SIMON & SCHUSTER
ROCKEFELLER CENTER
1230 AVENUE OF THE AMERICAS
NEW YORK, NEW YORK 10020

DESIGNED BY EVE METZ
MANUFACTURED IN THE UNITED STATES OF AMERICA

10 9 8 7 6 5 4 3 2 1

LIBRARY OF CONGRESS CATALOGING-IN-PUBLICATION DATA

MADDOX, BRENDA.
    D. H. LAWRENCE, THE STORY OF A MARRIAGE / BY BRENDA MADDOX.
        P. CM.
    INCLUDES BIBLIOGRAPHICAL REFERENCES AND INDEX.
    1. LAWRENCE, D. H. (DAVID HERBERT), 1885–1930—MARRIAGE.
    2. LAWRENCE, FRIEDA VON RICHTHOFEN, 1879–1956—MARRIAGE.
    3. AUTHORS, ENGLISH—20TH CENTURY—BIOGRAPHY.   4. AUTHORS' SPOUSES—
    GREAT BRITAIN—BIOGRAPHY.   I. TITLE
    PR6023.A93Z6758   1994
    823'.912—DC20   94-28960
    [B]   CIP

ISBN: 0-671-68712-3

TO BRONWEN

CONTENTS

Contents

PART FOUR

INTRODUCTION

^{66}B*ut Why, Mr. Lawrence?" asked a headline in the* New York Herald Tribune*'s Sunday book section on March 8, 1925.*

A reviewer was puzzled, even angered, by a small book on the French Foreign Legion, carrying an introduction by the internationally known D. H. Lawrence. Not only was Lawrence's essay almost half as long as the undistinguished memoir it introduced, but he had used it to call the author (identified only as "a certain M.M. now dead") a human rat, a contemptible sponge, and a loathsome rascal.

But why? So much about Lawrence, who died in 1930 at the age of forty-four, raises the same question. Seen from the end of the century he did so much to unsettle, D. H. Lawrence does not add up. He gives to the sexual act a weight it will not bear. His own sexuality remains ambiguous; he is accused of being both a repressed homosexual and a heterosexual sodomite. He is both sympathetic and offensively hostile to women. The canon of his utterances can be mined to yield opinions for and against almost any subject close to his heart: mothers, the working class, education, England and the English, the United States and Americans, Jews, Italians, war, sunshine, his pets. He was an infuriating friend—one minute, full of understanding, amusing, and generous; the next, angry, preachy, disloyal, and ungrateful.

Blessed with great narrative and descriptive gifts and uncanny psychological insight, Lawrence insisted on writing philosophy as well. Much of it is, and was in his time, incoherent even to his most devoted followers. In his fiction and poetry too, he allowed himself to produce a great deal of bad work. "Few celebrated writers," Noel Annan has said, "even Wordsworth, have ever written worse."

It is partly Lawrence's own fault that he is caricatured so often as a solemn bearded prophet. He saw his life as exemplary and in many ways sought the effect he achieved: a latter-day Jesus. He attracts believers and imitators as well as readers. In New Mexico particularly, Lawrence-worship is out of all proportion to the short time he spent there.

But why another book about Lawrence? Because he wants capturing between two covers; his life is often sliced into fragments of time, place, or topic, as if his forty-four years on earth were too extraordinary to be squeezed into a single volume. Because, for all his contradictoriness, he is not a spent force like George Bernard Shaw or H. G. Wells; he enters the twenty-first century with fresh things to say to an age more worried about the environment and health than about sex. And because he retains his ability to disturb; his name appears in today's newspapers more often than that of Lloyd George or other political leaders of his day. What was there about this frail, coughing man that gives him such power from beyond the grave?

The justification for adding to the Lawrencian mountain is to cut through it. I hope my book will interest not only those who cannot read Lawrence but also those who love him too much to face the flaws in his personality and his work.

I have chosen to examine his life through the greatest contradiction in it: his marriage, taking it not as just another aspect of Lawrence but as the encompassing whole. His maturity did not really begin until he met the German aristocrat Frieda von Richthofen Weekley. Her influence on his work can scarcely be exaggerated. To an acquaintance asking what his message was, Lawrence wrote: "You shall love your wife completely and implicitly and in entire nakedness of body and spirit. . . . This that I tell you is my message as far as I've got any."

Theirs was a mismatch made in heaven. Few couples have been so spectacularly unsuited. Frieda, as Mrs. Lawrence, appears to have lacked the wifely virtues of fidelity and a desire to comfort. Lawrence's complete love included throttling her and covering her with bruises. But their rows were not the whole story. I have tried to capture the living quality of this marriage, in which both were unfaithful in their fashion but which lasted until the end of his life—a life in which, he told Frieda, "nothing has mattered but you." Or so she claimed.

As I worked on this book, three questions were put to me again and again. The answer to them all is yes.

"Is there new material?" There are masses of it, emerging continually, like lava from the ocean floor, as if to prove that the boundaries of a life are never fixed. The newly translated love letters from the Austrian psychoanalyst Otto Gross to Frieda, along with the many still unpublished letters between Frieda's elder sister, Else Jaffe, and Otto Gross's wife, reveal the swamp of central European erotic ideology into which Lawrence unwittingly walked in the spring of 1912 when he met Frieda.

Newly available, too, are the private papers of certain of Lawrence's close friends. It was 1991 before the daughter of the English artist Rosalind Baynes thought it right to release her mother's memoir of a love affair with Lawrence in 1920. Many unpublished letters of Frieda's are still coming to light, and even some of Lawrence's. One of his letters, found among the Norman Douglas papers at the Beinecke Library at Yale, sheds new light on the background of the brilliant, scathing introduction to the Foreign Legion memoir of the "certain M.M.," the homosexual Maurice Magnus, for whose suicide Lawrence bore an ill-defined guilt.

The major new source of biographical material is the Cambridge University Press edition of *The Letters of D. H. Lawrence,* of which Volume VII appeared in May 1993. The majority of the letters in this volume, covering the last fifteen months of Lawrence's life, were previously unpublished. Indeed, about forty percent of the entire collection—5,534 letters in all—consists of such letters, notably many Lawrence wrote to his sisters, his nieces and nephews, and his German in-laws. The result is the most vivid and engaging self-portrait left by any English writer since Keats.

The store of new biographical information in the letters lies waiting to be presented to the nonacademic reader. So too does the new perspective on Lawrence and Frieda offered by the Lawrence novel first published in 1984, *Mr. Noon.*

The appearance of *Mr. Noon* wiped clean the slate of Lawrence biography, for the novel's second half appears to be a factually accurate and barely fictionalized account of Lawrence and Frieda's early sexual relations. Reviewing the book and taking it as biographical fact, the critic Diana Trilling was so shocked by its revelations of Frieda's casual promiscuity that she accused Lawrence of artistic dishonesty. To Mrs. Trilling, Lawrence's acceptance of a woman who shared her body freely proved that "so ardent a student of the sexual emotions, Lawrence never dealt with this elementary challenge to the stability of the relation between a man and a woman but continued, in everything he wrote, to deceive us that he wrote from within the boundaries of monogamous marriage."

Did Lawrence deceive us? Or does the evidence show that his marriage was held together by a bond deeper than monogamy?

The persistence of another question shows how little is generally known of a supposedly overfamiliar life story. I was often asked, with some astonishment, "Did Lawrence really go to Australia?" Far more interesting is the question of what he actually did while he was there for three months in 1922. Chapter 12 examines the controversial allegations that the political plot of Lawrence's Australian novel, *Kangaroo,* reflects his involvement with supporters of secret right-wing armies of "Diggers"—returned war veterans. I suggest also that the novel, with its brilliant parallel of the wars of politics and marriage, deserves more attention. I am at one with the late Philip Larkin, who wished there were fewer term papers on the "turgid and hypertensive" *Women in Love* and more on *Kangaroo.*

The final question that dogged me was "Do you really like Lawrence?"

No one could read Lawrence's letters and not like him.

MY own questions were different. How did Lawrence deal with his longings for a strong male bond? He was not homosexual in any accepted meaning of the term. But he was troubled much of his life by yearnings for manly love which his marriage, against his hopes, failed to dispel.

Also, why did he not acknowledge his tuberculosis and seek a cure? Why in his last faltering years did he not return to New Mexico, a haven for consumptives? And can he really be described as impoverished? Lawrence the businessman is one of the surprises to emerge from the newly published letters.

As an author, why did he collaborate so often? Most writers are insanely jealous of their own words. Lawrence co-authored, translated, and borrowed endlessly. It is tempting to wonder, considering the reckless literalness with which he put real people and places into his fiction, whether he made *anything* up. A close reading of his work and letters, however, shows that the search for real-life counterparts of even female Lawrence characters inevitably leads back to the complex personality of the author himself.

Why did he work so hard? Almost every day of his adult life—and his letters show that there were few periods when he felt really well—he committed thousands of words to paper, and if not words, pictures.

When not writing or painting, he made bread, cakes, gardens, furniture, clothes. The nature of this compulsion to organize experience and to fight off the fear of extinction by making marks on any available medium is too little examined by a world in sentimental awe of "genius."

My main questions center on his marriage. Why should a freethinker and the product of a mismatched mother and father have so idealized the bond of husband and wife? Why should such an idealist so calmly tolerate being a cuckold? Then there is the matter of children. Lawrence was wonderful with children. How could he have been so unsympathetic to Frieda's loss of hers? In their own marriage, were they childless by choice? His letters seem to shout that they were not, that both were greatly distressed by their infertility—a disappointment which may explain why Lawrence seems to understand everything about women except their fear of becoming pregnant.

Why did Frieda not force him to seek treatment for his illness? Why did she remain with him to the end? He was probably the least skilled of her lovers; he told her she was a fool, when she was not; he hit her and swore at her. She did not lack for alternatives. She remained, in spite of weight and age, powerfully attractive to men most of her life.

In trying to solve the puzzle of Lawrence, I have tried to avoid judging Lawrence by today's standards. No man was more a prisoner of his time, with its sexual hypocrisy, its disorientation in the wake of Darwin, Freud, and a pointless World War, its slow travel, its unreliable contraception, and its clumsy medicine.

I CAME to Lawrence chiefly through James Joyce, whose wife, Nora, was the subject of my previous biography. Lawrence and Joyce are the English and Irish sides of the same coin: twentieth-century exiles who, from within the safety of marriages to strong women, liberated the English printed word and who acquired unjustified reputations as pornographers and libertines. Both writers utterly rejected the First World War, turning their backs on it to write their masterpieces about the wider war, between men and women. Ghostly mothers haunt their works. So do anal preoccupations, which their followers were very slow to recognize.

Each in his way has had a powerful posthumous effect on the young. Joyce helped many who struggled as he had against a harsh, repressive form of Roman Catholicism. Lawrence helped many others by releasing them from puritanical guilt about the body.

There the resemblance ends. Joyce and Lawrence are as Catholic to Protestant, Irish to English. Nothing characterizes their differences more than their attitudes toward money. In *Ulysses,* Joyce mocks "the Englishman's proudest boast . . . *I paid my way.*" That *was* Lawrence's proudest boast—one reason he produced so much uneven work. Unlike

Joyce, he had no patron. Apart from the bleak period following the suppression of *The Rainbow* in 1915, when he was unpublishable, he paid his way, and his wife's, with his pen.

Joyce was the quintessential urban man. A biographer following his footsteps is led to the heart of Trieste, Zurich, Paris, Dublin, and London. Lawrence loathed cities. His trail is largely unpaved, leading down dirt roads from Surrey to Cornwall, from Tuscany to Taos. In New South Wales, to get a look at the bungalow where he wrote *Kangaroo,* I had to walk along Pacific sands and trespass over a seawall.

Lawrence, unlike Joyce, has had many biographers. The nationality difference helps to explain that too. Joyce left Ireland when he was twenty-two and disappeared for eleven years into the obscurity of Trieste. His fame was swiftly followed by notoriety. After *Ulysses,* few in Ireland, even his own sisters, wanted to admit they knew him. And Ireland itself, in the throes of rebellion and civil war, was not in an archive-gathering mood.

Lawrence, in contrast, was famous almost from the start of his career. The London literati who took him up when he was twenty-four recorded their impressions of the young working-class genius almost the day they met him. They saved his letters and those written about him. They put him in their fiction. His early death gave them a chance to say it all again. Then came decades of interviewers and scholars eager to capture the memories of almost everyone in England who had ever laid eyes on him. The consequence has been the overrecording of Lawrence the Englishman at the expense of the deracinated man he became.

Two other earlier books of my own also led me to this one. In *The Half-Parent: Living with Other People's Children,* I wrote about Lawrence as a stepfather. In *Married and Gay* I inquired into the attractions that the institution of marriage holds for those with homosexual and bisexual desires.

It is time for a fresh eye on Lawrence if only because he looks very different from the end of the century than he did in the years immediately after his death or in the postwar era when the main adulatory biographies were written. I have tried to explain his misogyny without clobbering him with it. From the far side of feminism, we now know more than Lawrence or even Freud did about the dark truth that underlies misogyny: man's fear of woman.

New approaches to literary criticism have also changed the look of Lawrence. They have revealed an ironic, even comic writer whose narrative voice, not at all the same as that of his characters, speaks over and above them. His loose, incantatory style, moreover, so antithetical to Joyce's "scrupulous meanness" and T. E. Hulme's "dry hardness," is now seen as a way of expressing the consciousness that exists beyond language and of giving the inarticulate a place in fiction. What is more, Lawrence the poet is only now coming into his own.

Frieda too changes as she recedes in time. No longer can she be dismissed as the Bolter, the woman who abandoned her children. John Worthen's 1993 biography of Lawrence's early years makes clear that it was Lawrence who, from terror that she would leave him, tricked her out of them. Then, too, Frieda's three books of translation, published before she met Lawrence, have been unearthed. They testify to an attempt, however fitful, to do something in her own right, and they help to explain the injured insistence on her own importance that so annoyed Lawrence's English circle.

If his attitudes toward sex are dated, there is nothing dated about Lawrence's courage. A new generation obsessed with health can admire the Lawrence who, with half-eaten lungs, wandered the world, determined, like Keats and Stevenson (of whose fates he was well aware), to live to the full a life he knew would be short.

I hope the man that emerges from these pages is not the glowering preacher with baleful eye and sunken chest, but a likable Lawrence: a devastating mimic, an inspired teacher, a handy householder, a hardworking journalist, a loyal brother and generous uncle, a good cook, an eager traveler and brilliant travel writer, a dogged, dreadful painter, an ecological visionary and, above all—as he saw himself—a married man.

Alas, whither shall I climb now with my longing? I look out from every mountain for fatherlands and motherlands.

But nowhere have I found a home; I am unsettled in every city and depart from every gate.

Friedrich Nietzsche,
Thus Spake Zarathustra, 1883–1892

God knows he is a fool, and undeveloped, but he is so genuine, a genuine force, inhuman like one also—and such a strain.

Frieda Lawrence to E. M. Forster, 1915

We are fearfully fond of one another, all the more, perhaps, when it doesn't show. We want remarkably the same thing in life—sort of freedom, nakedness of intimacy, free breathing-space between us. You don't know how fine it is between us—whatever either of us says.

D. H. Lawrence to Edward Garnett, 1912

Part One

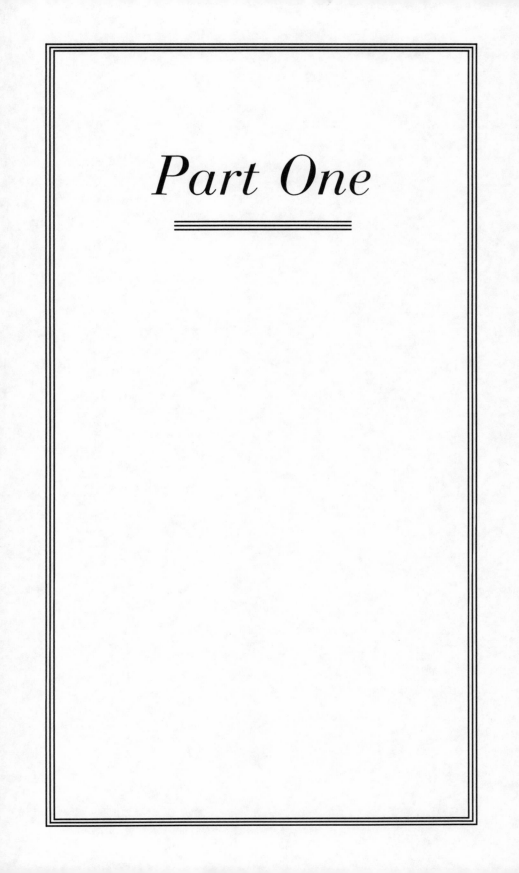

PROLOGUE
Born Again Again

---

*R*ail *travelers approaching London from the south see suburbia with* its back turned. Mile after mile they roll through an ocher sea of sheds, lavatories, chimneypots, garden walls, and flower beds jealously hidden from all but the passing trains.

Late in November 1911, in the back bedroom of "Sunnybrae," one of these citadels of the lower bourgeoisie, David Herbert Lawrence lay dangerously ill. A coal fire glowed in the grate. Lights flashed through the blinds from the Woodside and South Croydon line at the bottom of the garden. Lawrence's younger sister, Ada, who had taken leave from her teaching job in the Midlands to nurse him, sat by the bedside, not knowing whether he would live or die.

It was the year of the coronation of King George V. Lawrence was twenty-six. He was a bachelor and a schoolmaster, snub-nosed, with wide-set bright blue eyes and a mat of light brown hair. For three years since leaving his home in the mining town of Eastwood near Nottingham, he had taught twelve-year-olds at the Davidson Road School in Croydon outside London. The whole time he had been lodging with a family on Colworth Road, about a mile from the school. Only that spring he had remarked to a friend, "I wouldn't be ill in digs, not for any money." His words tempted fate. On Monday, November 20, he awoke with a high fever and could not get out of bed. The school was telephoned, the doctor summoned. It was double pneumonia. For weeks Lawrence was confined to his small room on the first floor, flat on his back, forbidden to sit up or even to turn on his side.

Pneumonia in that era was often fatal, especially when it invaded both lungs. It was a dramatic illness, marked by severe shortness of breath, a harsh cough, a high fever, and hallucinations. Over a fortnight the disease slowly built to a climax whose outcome, even for the strongest, was impossible to foretell. As Lawrence approached the crisis, he received two injections of "morphia," as the sedative was ambiguously called, fueling his delirium. As he lay there, with his mind wandering and loud fragments of phrases tumbling out, a corner of his mind watched the tiny spark of life that was himself flicker and fade and threaten to go out.

Nearly dying was nothing new for him. Born on September 13, 1885, the fourth of five children in a Nottinghamshire mining family, he had virtually entered the world with bronchitis. Bert, as his family called him, survived infancy against the doctor's expectations and struggled through a sickly childhood until stricken by pneumonia when he was sixteen.

That illness had come in early winter, barely six weeks after his older brother, Ernest, had died suddenly from a swift attack of pneumonia and feverish inflammation of the skin. Mrs. Lawrence had been summoned to Catford in South London, where Ernest was working as a clerk, but by the time she arrived, there was no hope; she brought her twenty-three-year-old son back to Eastwood in his coffin. The family was stunned by grief—Ernest, tall, clever, and handsome, had been the favorite—and waited for the delicate Bert to die too. His father stood weeping quietly by his bed.

To general astonishment, the weakling survived. But from then on he lived as one who had as good as returned from the dead. Lawrence accepted that he would live on the precipice, with what was called "a weak chest"; the family doctor told Mrs. Lawrence flatly that her youngest boy was tubercular. But his close encounter with death, rather than turning him depressed and hypochondriacal, left him with a heightened awareness of the physical world, and with a messianic tendency to preach. One of his Eastwood friends later called him Jehovah Junior, while another marveled that "he saw colours always three shades brighter than any of the rest of us." As Lawrence grew to manhood, he counted himself able to come back from death's door again and again. But, fighting for life in Croydon in late 1911, he was trying the trick for the first time without his mother.

Lydia Lawrence had died just a year before, at home, in the month of December. Then it had been Bert and Ada, both on leave from their respective schools, who had kept vigil by the bedside, and there was no uncertainty about the outcome. Mrs. Lawrence's cancer was incurable. She was buried in time for Lawrence to return to his classroom in Croydon before the Christmas break.

All during the following year, 1911, the suffering of his mother's last days haunted him. Passionately attached to her, he had written to her from Croydon every week. With her gone, he was disoriented. She was so near and so absent. He was ill even more than usual and missed much school. Ada, back home in Eastwood, was the only one to whom he could confide his unhealing grief. "When one is a bit off in health, how it all comes back, worse than ever," he wrote her in the spring of 1911. "No one understands but you." He suffered from nightmares that people were trying to kill him. The world around him seemed unreal, and when pneumonia struck in November it came almost as an invitation to join his mother in death.

Ada's arrival in Croydon put her firmly in her mother's place. As the baby of the family, she had clung to Bert in childhood, holding his hand as he led her to school. But she knew how dependent he was on the women in the family, and with their mother gone and their sister Emily married with a family of her own, the duty of nursing Bert had naturally fallen to her. If the worst happened, it was she who would break the news to their father, to their brother George and Emily, and to Louie Burrows, the girl to whom Bert had been engaged for a year.

By November 28, ten days into his illness, with the doctor calling at least once a day and a nurse in attendance, Ada at last dared write hopefully to Louie. Headmistress of a Church of England school in Leicestershire, Louie had not seen her fiancé since the end of October. All three of them had trained together as teachers at the Ilkeston Pupil-Teacher Centre near Eastwood, and it was Ada who had introduced Louie to her brother.

Frugally squeezing her important message onto a postcard which would reach Leicestershire by morning for halfpence, half the price of a letter, Ada told Louie:

Doctor says that Bert is no worse—tomorrow or next day is the crisis and please God all may be well—the disease in the left lung has not spread further. Last night he had a morphia injection and therefore had a fairly good night. . . . We are all fighting hard for him. . . . You know he will be in bed for weeks & weeks if he gets through so I shall make arrangements for you to spend Xmas here with us.

Your Sister Ada

To Louie, Ada's message was not entirely welcome. She wanted to dash to Croydon but was being held at bay. Ada was letting her know that a sister was privileged to care for an invalid in ways unthinkable for a fiancée. "We mustnt be too venturesome," Ada wrote, relaying the doctor's veto on Louie's intended visit. Helpless at a distance, Louie could only send flowers, fresh eggs for a custard, and infuriating letters advising the immobilized Lawrence to rest.

But Lawrence was not helpless. Once again he fought hard for himself and once again he won. With his first ounce of strength, he summoned a bit of paper and a pencil and scrawled an apology: "Did I frighten you all? Never mind, I'm soon going to be all right."

Watching the spectacle unmoved was the landlord, John William Jones. In the tiny house, the sickroom, with its slops, soiled linen, and night noises, lay only six feet away from the Joneses' bedroom and the adjoining room shared by their two little girls. Jones had had enough of his coughing lodger, who, at the best of times, was all too fond of his wife. He heartily wished Lawrence a speedy recovery in order that he might pack up and go.

1

NEW AGE, OLD ADAM

1908–1910

A new house, a new school, a new century: Lawrence, arriving from Eastwood at the Joneses' three years earlier, in October 1908, could scarcely believe his good luck. His first real job had landed him in the heart of South London modernity.

Croydon was an important railway junction and since 1888 a county borough in its own right: a temple of Edwardian self-satisfaction, with heavily ornamented new buildings and three hundred trains a day to London. In the distance, high on Sydenham Hill, the Crystal Palace gleamed like a vision of the future. Double-deck trams plowed down the middle of the roads, with passengers hanging from the sides beneath signs advertising the products of imperial prosperity: Heinz 57 Varieties, Dewar's Whisky, Lipton's Tea, Beecham's Pills, Bird's Custard.

Lawrence had found what he described in chirpy letters home as "excellent digs" with John Jones, superintendent of Croydon's school-attendance officers; his wife, Marie; and their two small daughters. "My landlady is a splendid woman—my landlord is affable and plays chess worse than I do—What more can I want?" Lawrence asked. He might have wanted something cheaper. Room and board cost eighteen shillings a week, nearly half his pay, but he thought it was worth it.

The Joneses had just moved into one of eighteen houses on a short new road built in 1903. The size of Croydon had increased nearly ten-fold in sixty years as people seized the new opportunity the railway provided to live in the country while working in town. The Joneses' semidetached villa, with its stained-glass decoration and mock-Tudor gable end, delighted Lawrence, along with its East Croydon neighbor-hood, Addiscombe, "a smart, quiet quarter." Savoring the luxury of a room all to himself, he did not mind that the hallway was narrower than the span of his outstretched arms or that the Joneses in their room over the front door could hear every time he came in or went out.

The location gave him easy access to London, by tram (the terminus was around the corner), train, or motor bus. In the capital itself, he felt remarkably at home. He wandered through the galleries, the public buildings, and the big department stores, such as Selfridges, and enjoyed writing postcards to his friends, whom he now regarded as "buried" in the provinces: "Dear Gert, Here I stand with all London rumbling round me, thinking of you. I wish you could see the shops and the folks here—." To the south of Croydon, the unexpected large stretches of open commons and rolling countryside inspired more glowing postcards home: "Dear Lou, Now I've seen sweeter country than Quorn and Woodhouse. Down here it is wonderful."

Above all, he counted himself lucky in his school. The Davidson Road School, with nearly a thousand pupils, had been opened only the year before. It was one of the new local government–supported "board" schools offering free education up to the secondary level. Sherlock Holmes describes them admiringly to Dr. Watson: "lighthouses, my boy, beacons of the future, capsules with hundreds of bright little seeds in each, out of which will spring the wiser, better England of the future."

Lawrence, who was being paid ninety-five pounds a year, had written to Louie Burrows, whose annual salary in her new post in Leicester was twenty pounds less, that at Davidson Road everything was "up to date, solid and good." "Everything" included the red brick exterior, the shiny brown wall tiles, the high vaulted windows that brought light streaming into the large classrooms, the double desks, and the blackboards that ran continuously around the walls.

A sense of the twentieth century's limitless possibilities of change filled the pages of *The New Age,* a weekly journal to which Lawrence began subscribing for six shillings a year. He even got his mother to read it. Founded in 1907, *The New Age* provided a steady infusion of pungent, stylish essays on politics, medicine, science, art, and morals. Its pages were spattered with the names of the social crusaders and secular priests of the day—Beatrice and Sidney Webb, George Bernard Shaw, H. G.

Wells, and Havelock Ellis; hardly an issue appeared without a reference to the German philosopher Nietzsche, who rejected Christian morality, proclaiming that the human race owed its survival and ascendancy to its lower instincts.

On issues of the day, *The New Age* was socialist and radical. It supported a national health service, unemployment insurance, Home Rule for Ireland, literacy for India, eradication of tuberculosis by slum clearance, and abolition of the House of Lords. It was intrigued with the promise of eugenics—vigorous breeding for good stock. Its radicalism most emphatically extended to sexual politics. Marriage was slavery; easier divorce was essential. So were votes for women, and sex education. There should be an end to prudery and shame. "We should be taught to regard our bodies not with horror, but with some admiration," declared its principal writer on science, psychology, and medicine, Dr. M. D. Eder, who within a few years would play an important part in Lawrence's life.

For all his radical reading, Lawrence was the ideal lodger. He was tidy. He was delighted with the food. He drank (but not too much) with Mr. Jones and stood his round when the two of them went for a drink at the Greyhound Hotel, a respectable, popular meeting place in central Croydon. He warmed to Mrs. Jones ("I like the missis best," he confided to Louie). In the evening he sat by the fire writing, on a pad on his knee— poems, stories, and a novel. He smoked a cigarette a day, if that.

The Joneses, who were just settling into their new home, found that they had also acquired a resident handyman. Lawrence was full of practical skills learned from both his father and his mother, and he tackled small jobs with extraordinary dexterity. He hung pictures and arranged books. He never dropped or broke anything. He actually enjoyed housework, from scrubbing floors and washing dishes to peeling onions. He was a genius in the garden, such as it was. He was never underfoot. He did his morning exercises in the bathroom but otherwise got out of the house. Saturdays he went for fifteen- to twenty-mile walks. On Sunday mornings he painted lovely copies of flowers or landscapes, and on Sunday afternoons, in common with most of his countrymen, he took a nap.

The Joneses were charmed by the lively blue eyes and the amusing stream of talk. Lawrence had opinions on everything and delivered them well. He was a wicked mimic too, able to reproduce any accent and imitate any gesture in a way that left his listeners helpless with laughter. He loved games and card tricks. His capacity for fun was infectious; when he was happy, everyone around him was happy.

Lawrence, unlike most good talkers, was also a good listener. He drew confidences as salt draws water. Utterly absorbed in what was being said to him, he fastened his intense gaze on the face of the speaker, who, flattered, opened up as never before. (When these innermost thoughts later appeared in a story or novel and there were cries of betrayal, Lawrence was genuinely surprised. He did not draw people out to exploit them. He had a genuine curiosity about their lives. That they claimed subsequently to recognize "themselves" in characters created out of his imagination and wide-ranging observation had nothing to do with him, although occasionally he did acknowledge that he had recreated a person "*faithfully* from life.")

At Colworth Road, the little Jones girls responded to Lawrence's charm. He played with them endlessly, inventing games, chasing them around the garden, dancing them around the room. Winifred, aged five, was soon besotted with him, while he was even more enchanted with the baby, Hilda Mary. He let her maul and mash his face. His letters home are rhapsodic: "We have the jolliest fat baby, eight months old. You cannot tell how fond I am of her; her fine hazel eyes laugh at me so brightly." He was fascinated by the rapid changes of the first year of life, and recorded them in a remarkable series of poems. "Baby Running Barefoot" conveys the exultation of the child who has learned to run, while "A Baby Asleep After Pain" captures the exhausting misery of teething:

> As a drenched, drowned bee
> Hangs numb and heavy from a bending flower,
>   So clings to me
> My baby, her brown hair brushed with wet tears
> And laid against her cheek . . .

At twenty-three, Lawrence had an intuitive sympathy for young children that is rare among the childless. But he did not think of himself as childless, for he had quickly grown to speak of Hilda Mary as "my own baby."

CONTENTMENT with his new circumstances did not prevent agonies of homesickness. Lawrence had never lived away from home before, apart from a month with an aunt in Skegness. Yet he had had no choice but to leave Eastwood. It had taken him the entire summer after obtaining his teacher's certificate from Nottingham University College to find a job. There was, he noted ruefully, a glut of certified teachers. He had landed the post at Croydon after a rejection by Stockport, the only other interview he had been granted after his innumerable letters of application.

When he had said his good-byes in Eastwood, there was weeping almost as if he were going to war. For his family and his friends, Croydon was the same as London, the alien metropolis that had killed his brother Ernest. In leaving Eastwood, Lawrence was also wrenching himself from his closest friend, Jessie Chambers, two years his junior. Her large and literate family, which discussed books by the fire, provided the second and happier home of his youth, and his walks through the woods to their home at Haggs Farm took him out of the industrial present into the bucolic past. It was at "the Haggs" that he had recovered his health after the attack of pneumonia when he was sixteen. The Chambers family was sad that he was leaving, but felt that the move was a good one and that his brilliance deserved London polish.

In Croydon, in keeping with his new professional status, Lawrence joined the National Union of Teachers. But union membership did not impress a classroom full of tough city lads. He was not inexperienced. For several years from the age of seventeen, he had been a "pupil-teacher," one who taught part-time in exchange for training, in an Eastwood school, where he was so well-liked that when he left the pupils raised half a crown to buy him a mechanical colored pencil. He was unprepared, therefore, for the insolence he encountered in Croydon as an assistant master with a class of his own. Nor was he prepared for the seething hatred that welled up inside himself.

All his life, Lawrence had the habit of picturing himself as an animal or bird. As he stood uncertainly behind his desk in Standard IV at the Davidson Road School, he saw himself as "a quivering grey hound set to mind a herd of pigs." Since his own school days he had loathed aggressive males. Now he found himself facing forty-five of them. He knew he was no leader. There was only one recourse: the rod. There were days when he caned and caned, resenting that he was required to enter in the punishment book the number of strokes given each boy. He poured his wrath and disillusion into an angry, guilty poem, "Discipline." He had tried meekness and forbearance; the boys had responded with "a blindness of fury against me." The result was sullen force: "Over them all the dark net of my discipline weaves."

Reviewing some of Lawrence's poems the following year, his union magazine, *The Schoolteacher,* reprinted "Discipline" in its entirety. The editor (the N.U.T.'s general secretary) said in his review, "Thousands of teachers have felt like that before a class, once or twice in their lifetimes at least, but no other teacher has expressed it." He hailed his union brother as a "true-born poet."

Yet Lawrence had been given to violent outbursts long before he reached Croydon. At Haggs Farm, where he sometimes helped the Chambers family to get in the hay, he would suddenly fly into a rage at one of the older boys and lay him out flat with a blow on the back of the

neck. David Chambers, youngest of the brothers, felt there was something "incalculable and uncontrollable" about Lawrence.

Lawrence recognized the failing in himself. During much of 1908 he
had been conducting a long, self-analytical correspondence with an unmarried older woman in Liverpool, Blanche Jennings. His weekly letters
to his mother have not survived, but they can hardly have been more
personal than the thoughts he confided to Blanche, a post office worker
and feminist. Lawrence looked up to her as a middle-class professional
woman, a good critic of writing, and a social superior. In that first
troubled term in Croydon, he confessed: "I have an irritable temper, but
generally it's cushioned down—except when I'm not well, or when I'm
screwed up to a new pitch—as I am here."

His irritability had a deeper source. At twenty-three, Lawrence was
still a virgin; he had not even kissed a girl on the mouth. He seemed to
come closest to women through his letters. He wrote regularly to another woman of socialist and suffragist views, Alice Dax. Born in Liverpool, Mrs. Dax was an outsider in Eastwood, where she had moved
upon her marriage in 1905 to a local chemist. She was a plain, animated
woman, a member of the Congregational Literary Society and founder
of the Eastwood Nursing Association—the very model of the New
Woman of her day: perceptive, brusque, indifferent to appearances. After she and Lawrence became friends, they conducted a bookish flirtation based on their mutual interest in social policy, literature, and
agnosticism, and their disdain for Eastwood. Before her marriage, she,
too, had been employed by the post office, where her radical ideas had
gotten her in trouble. It was she who had introduced Lawrence to
Blanche Jennings, after a women's rights rally in Nottingham.

With these older women Lawrence could express on paper what was
troubling him. His chastity was not only a burden but an embarrassment. The novel he was writing, ever on his mind, told of men struggling
to reconcile their physical desires with their wish for stability. Yet what
was the woman's point of view? Although he trusted his intuitions, he
kept sending bits of his manuscript to his female mentors for comment.
His purpose was ostensibly literary, but he also wanted guidance in
growing up.

He was searching, so he wrote Blanche, for great love in the manner
of *La Dame aux Camélias*. Yet what would happen if he found it? Seeing
the Dumas play, performed in Nottingham by Sarah Bernhardt in June
1908, threw Lawrence into such a panic that he ran out of the theater.
Describing the experience later to Jessie Chambers, he did not allude to
the heroine's fate, death from consumption, but rather blamed his terror
on a sudden vision that he too might become enslaved to a woman. He
warned Blanche Jennings: "Take care about going to see Bernhardt.
Unless you are very sound, do not go. When I think of her now I can still

feel the weight hanging in my chest as it hung there for days after I saw her."

He did not try to disguise his wish that the great love he dreamed of would have healing powers: "If there were any woman to whom I could abandon myself," he wrote Blanche, "I should find infinite comfort if she would nurse me, console me, soothe me, and tell me that I should soon be better."

This correspondence (discovered some years after Blanche Jennings's death in 1944 when Lawrence's letters to her were found intact in her brother's woodshed) was as touching as it was extraordinary. The two were near strangers: a thirtyish postal clerk worried about becoming an old maid, and a novice teacher in his twenties. Lawrence's letters to Blanche helped him clarify a great deal in his own mind, yet they were at once filial and sexually charged—perhaps actually masturbatory, as when he wrote:

> As I was rubbing myself down in the late twilight a few minutes ago, and as I passed my hands over my sides where the muscles lie suave and secret, I did love myself. I am thin, but well skimmed over with muscle; my skin is very white and unblemished; soft and dull with a fine pubescent bloom. . . . I like you because I can talk like this to you.

So full of doubts about his own sexual nature, Lawrence felt very exposed as he submitted himself daily to the merciless scrutiny of a roomful of pubescent boys. As an adolescent, he himself seems to have been warned against masturbation with the conventional "leave-yourself-alone" wisdom of the day. His earliest poems show that he knew well about the temptations of the solitary bed and the penis with a will of its own. In "The Body Awake" (later renamed "Virgin Youth"), written when he was twenty, he had addressed his penis as if it were a superior male: "He stands, and I tremble before him." He apologized to it for his protracted virginity: "Thy tower impinges / On nothingness. Pardon me!" And, with anatomical frankness and religious fervor, he prayed to his own organ in words he would never have spoken aloud: "Thou proud, curved beauty! I / Would worship thee, letting my buttocks prance."

Such was the confessional honesty of Lawrence's approach to his poetry that he did not shy from the homoerotic element in the relation between master and pupil: "And do I not seek to mate my grown, desirous soul / With the lusty souls of my boys?"

In Lawrence's contradictory personality, nothing was more split than his attitude toward schoolmastering. For all that he claimed to loathe the boys and to wait for the bell as impatiently as any of them, part of him loved teaching. After a shaky start, he was very good at it. The headmaster, Philip Smith, later had nothing but praise for Lawrence's time at Davidson Road. Voluntarily Lawrence took on the duties teachers will avoid if they can, such as organizing the library and painting scenery for school plays. He liked supervising the playground, with the boys crowding around and saying, "Please, Mr. Lawrence, Mr. Smith says, will you blow the whistle?" And he laughed when they shot imaginary arrows at him during the lessons. He listened eagerly when they excitedly babbled out news—that the Cherry Blossom Boot Polish Company, for example, was offering a free day at the Crystal Palace to anybody producing the lid from a can of the polish.

Lawrence was the kind of teacher who is remembered for a lifetime. Under his direction, his boys fought the battle of Agincourt in the classroom. He had them reciting robust poetry so loudly that the school inspector in the corridor had to knock on the door to see what was making the noise. He gave interesting writing assignments, like "An Event in a Newspaper." He would help out scruffy orphans from a nearby children's home with the gift of a shilling, and he encouraged his pupils to send their stories and essays to a boys' magazine, introducing them to a thrill he had himself known for only a short time—writing for money.

He wrote a series of powerful poems whose very titles—"A Snowy Day in School"; "Afternoon in School"—evoke the classroom: the experience of sitting indoors on a fine day with the blinds drawn against the sun; of pupils working hard, lifting their heads to stare blindly at the teacher, then turning back to their books. Lawrence could not have hated teaching the day he wrote "The Best of School":

> And very sweet it is, while the sunlight waves
> In the ripening morning, to sit alone with the class
> And feel the stream of awakening ripple and pass
> From me to the boys. . . .

The subject he taught best was botany. It had been his favorite subject at Nottingham University College, one of the five in which he had achieved distinction. ("Never anything in English—is it not a joke?" he wrote Louie Burrows.)

Lawrence never received an academic degree. As a boy he was very bright and prodigiously well read. At twelve he won (in a rare achievement for a miner's son) a scholarship to Nottingham High School, an excellent secondary school, where, during three years of arduous commuting by train from Eastwood, he achieved a fair but undistinguished record. He never played sports because his family could not afford the uniforms.

After leaving school in 1901, he worked for a brief period in a surgical-goods factory in Nottingham, but left when he was struck with pneumonia. He began as a pupil-teacher in Eastwood but after two years enrolled as well at the Ilkeston Pupil-Teacher Centre in a nearby town. There he began formal preparation for the national—King's—examination required for a place at a training college, the best way to gain the teacher's certificate without which no teacher could expect to rise very high in the profession. Taking the examination in November 1904, he did better than pass; he reached the top division for the whole country. Even after a later examination won him a place at Nottingham University College he had to postpone his enrollment in order to work full-time for a year to save up the entrance fee of twenty pounds.

When at last he entered Nottingham in 1906, at the age of twenty-one, he faced a choice between the Normal, or two-year, course, leading to the teacher's certificate, or the three-year course leading to a bachelor of arts degree from the University of London. Lawrence rejected the degree course because he wanted more time for his writing and because he did not have sufficient Latin. By choosing the shorter program, he won the chance to take an optional course in botany.

After he left college, his lack of formal academic credentials sometimes bothered him. Without a degree he could not aspire to teach in a secondary school. Yet, for better and for worse, the less rigorous form of his higher education left its mark on his writing style. Like W. B. Yeats and George Bernard Shaw, he managed to achieve greatness without a university degree.

He may not have known much Latin, but he did know botany. Well before he reached college, he was an intent naturalist, thanks to his father. Arthur Lawrence, who began work underground in the coal mines when he was seven and was barely literate, knew the name of every animal and plant in the region of Eastwood and taught them to his youngest son on their long walks together. When Lawrence went to college, the botany lectures added a scientific dimension to this vast store of knowledge, and they awakened him to the sexual explicitness of plants, with their swollen ovaries and thrusting stamens.

College botany, taught by one of the few professors at Nottingham University College whom he respected, forced Lawrence to consider the philosophical implications of evolution. Darwin's *The Origin of Species,* first published in 1859, had a firm hold on the popular imagination by the turn of the century, and Lawrence was overwhelmed by the obvious truth of its theory of natural selection. By the time he left college with his certificate in July 1908, he had rejected not only the chapel Congregationalism of his youth but Christianity and religion altogether. Life on earth, he quickly came to believe, was a continuous stream. There was no Creator who crafted individually every slug and

snail. All forms of life, man included, were just drops in "the big shimmering sea of unorganised life we call God."

Loss of faith heightened Lawrence's sense of the importance of the
relations between men and women. Evolution might be impersonal, he
had decided, but it was purposeful. Human beings might be no more
than comical creatures in "the menagerie," he wrote Blanche Jennings,
and the physical attraction between the sexes no more than a trick of
nature to propagate the species. Life, all the same, was "a great procession" that keeps on "marching, on the whole, in the right direction," and
love was the force which kept the whole menagerie on the move. Accordingly, human beings had no more important task in working out
their destiny than to find the right mate.

MUCH of this personal Darwinism was being poured into his novel.
Although he was still working on it when he reached Croydon, he had
largely completed the first version during his first impressionable year at
University College, the year when the deep religious faith of his boyhood
slid from him.

The novel, published two and a half years later as *The White Peacock,*
is ostensibly a rural idyll, yet it exudes the German philosophy Lawrence
was absorbing: Schopenhauer reinforced by Nietzsche, whom he read
(in translation) in *The New Age* and at the Croydon Public Library. He
took much to heart their warnings of the danger of overestimating the
conscious forces of the personality at the expense of the instincts. Christianity, they argued and Lawrence came to believe, had destructively
split human nature into warring opposites and wrongly elevated the
spiritual over the passional.

This theme—that Christianity has alienated humankind from nature
and destroyed pagan wisdom—appears in the very second sentence of
The White Peacock, as the narrator, Cyril (Lawrence's counterpart),
watches shadowy gray fish slide through the gloom of a millpond: "They
were descendants of the silvery things that had darted away from the
monks, in the young days when the valley was lusty."

As the novel's plot evolved through many rewritings, Lawrence's
young heroine, Lettie (for "Laetitia," the book's original title), is shown
to make the mistake of resisting her desire for the virile if wayward
George Saxton and following the dictates of her supposed higher nature
by marrying a safe, dull businessman. Thus Lawrence, at the very start
of his writing career, was declaring war on the ethos that rejected sexual
attraction as "merely" physical.

The White Peacock is a Nietzschean text, rich in images of a nature
red in tooth and claw. It shows the precariousness of animal existence;
indeed, the animals in the book are more real than its people. They are

not only burned in a fire, they are dropped to drown in a pond, killed in traps, and beaten for disobeying their human masters. Yet the humans hardly fare better—one man is even killed in a "man-trap" in the forest, and the children suffer most of all: bruised, battered, crowded out in the struggle for food.

The novel draws vividly the scramble for life. In the Saxton farmhouse, George's mother puts the weakest of a brood of baby chickens on the fender "to coax it into life." But the chick totters into the fire "and gasped its faint gasp among the red-hot cokes." There is a smell of "singed down and cooked meat." Mrs. Saxton is not bothered at all. " 'There goes number one!' said the mother, with her queer little laugh." In nature's teeming menagerie, one life more or less makes no difference, and it is the weakest who are most expendable. And while the characters struggle to make the right choices, they struggle in vain; they are caught in the traps of their natures.

Yet nature will not be mocked. The message of the book is delivered almost as a sermon, by a curious peripheral character called Annable— Lawrence's first gamekeeper. Described as a man with a magnificent physique, great vigor and vitality, and a swarthy, gloomy face, Annable is patently an idealized version of Lawrence's own father. Annable's advice to Cyril is clear and tough: "Be a good animal, true to your animal instinct." For "when a man's more than nature he's a devil."

Cyril says that Annable treats him "as an affectionate father treats a delicate son." Appropriately, Annable gives Cyril a fatherly warning about the dangers of the female of the species. He tells Cyril the bitter story of his first wife, now dead. She used him for the insatiable demands of her "beak" (Lawrence's word for clitoris), then discarded him, drained and humiliated, when she had no further use for him. She was, Annable boasts, a titled woman, with the name of Lady Crystabel: "a lady in her own right"; "fine and frank and unconventional—ripping."

The setting for this exchange is a country churchyard. As the two men speak, a white peacock flies down and excretes on a gravestone. Annable, infuriated, declares that the bird, "which seemed to stretch its beak at us in derision," was "a woman to the end, I tell you, all vanity and screech and defilement." He rounds off his lurid sexual tale with the details of Lady Crystabel's death.

Lawrence, as if to make certain that the reader has grasped the message, has Cyril exclaim, "So she's dead—your poor peacock!" And then, as Annable allows that he may have been too harsh in his judgment of his late wife, Cyril suggests, "A white peacock, we will say."

The Lady Crystabel whom Lawrence conjured up for this book was his first "Lady C." His attachment to this form of name suggests that the demanding female sexual organ beginning with "c" and containing the sharp letter "t" held a terrifying and permanent grip on his imagination.

But which kind of woman is worse—she who is obsessed by her desires or she who denies them? Lawrence the bachelor was surrounded by the second sort, those who found it all too easy to be spiritual. His heroine, Lettie, senses her mistake. The sight of a bank of snowdrops strikes her like a reproach; the little white flowers remind her of "something out of an old religion . . . They belong to some knowledge we have lost, that I have lost and I need." For Lawrence, flowers, moist, open, and odorous, carried heavy female sexual significance; he did not confine his thoughts to his novel but poured them into the young heads in the Standard IV classroom at Davidson Road, where he taught his boys to color gynaeceous flowers red and androgynous yellow.

CONQUERING his homesickness in the autumn of 1908, Lawrence warmed to London. He wrote poems about the prostitutes in Piccadilly and about the huddled tramps on the Embankment. He took little Winnie Jones up to the London shops to meet Father Christmas. He loved showing friends from the provinces around the capital, and in arch and boyish letters catalogued in advance the delights he would show them: Covent Garden, Drury Lane, the Royal Academy, the Tate, the Tower, St. Paul's. He looked forward to the visit of both parents the following summer.

Lawrence also explored the southern Thames Valley by foot, bicycle, and train. He went to Hampton Court, to Wimbledon Common (where he liked the old windmill), and to Richmond Park, and he also traveled south to the coast. The sight of Brighton released a torrent of adjectives for Blanche Jennings. The Regency town was "big," "stately," and "magnificent"; the sea was "like pale green jewels," "lapis lazuli green," "wavering, shimmering, intermingling with purple," and ultimately, "inexpressible."

Above all Lawrence distanced himself from thoughts of illness. To Blanche, he scoffed at the poet A. E. Housman for writing melancholy poems about death. He declared rhetorically, "Life is the fact, the everything: Death is only the 'To be concluded at the end of the volume.' " He had no use for what he saw as Housman's morbidity. "I believe he comes of a consumptive family," he wrote. "I believe he himself is consumptive. Bah!"

Yet Lawrence had to confess to Blanche how unadaptable he himself was on account of his health. "Very rarely have I been able to enjoy the first weeks of anything, even a holiday, because I am always a bit sick as a result of the change." Revealingly, later in the same letter he allowed himself a seductive image of death. The painting *Love and Death*, by the Victorian artist G. F. Watts, he said, owed some of its beauty to "the blurred idea that Death is shrouded, but a dark, embracing mother, who stoops over us, and frightens us because we are children."

AT the Davidson Road School, Lawrence made one good friend, a fellow teacher, Arthur McLeod, a lanky Scottish bachelor who lived with his mother and who loved literature. In time, the headmaster, Philip Smith, also became a social acquaintance. But the other men at school avoided Lawrence, suspicious of his reserve and lack of interest in sports. They saw him as the rebel on the staff, the one who wore soft collars when the others wore stiff, who refused to say "Sir" to the old Scottish master, and who dramatized plays when others read them aloud by rote. They did not see his amusing side.

Jones, Lawrence's landlord, an officious school bureaucrat, noticed with disapproval that Lawrence had too many women friends and apparently no men friends at all. Blanche Jennings had noticed the same thing from his letters, and charged him with it. "You tell me I have no male friends," he shot back. "The man I have been working with in the hay is the original of my George." The man in question was Jessie Chambers's handsome brother Alan, whose virile good looks were at the heart of the novel: "His black hair was moisted and twisted into confused half-curls. Firmly planted, he swung with a beautiful rhythm from the waist."

Lawrence was fond of Alan Chambers, the only one of his childhood friends to become a farmer, an occupation he idealized for its physicality. The attraction Lawrence never felt for Jessie, although she was a pretty girl with dark brown curls, seemed to flow toward her brother. But, Lawrence confessed to Blanche, as if to support the charge that there was something unmanly about him, "It seems my men friends are all alike; they make themselves, on the whole, softmannered towards me; they defer to me also."

Blanche's sharp observation had touched a nerve. Lawrence's isolation from the society of men, like his admiration for the well-developed male physique, had begun early—perhaps as soon as he watched strong, muscular Arthur Lawrence washing off the pit dust in a tub by the fire, and saw in his father everything he was not. Writing his novel, he was acutely conscious that he was the antithesis of his virile George. Just as he was trying to settle into Croydon, he wrote to Blanche Jennings a letter that has become notorious, saying how he would deal with "all the sick, the halt and the maimed":

I would build a lethal chamber as big as the Crystal Palace, with a military band playing softly, and a Cinematograph working brightly; then I'd go out in the back streets and main streets and bring them in . . . , I would lead them gently, and they would smile me a weary thanks; and the band would softly bubble out the "Hallelujah Chorus."

From the far side of the Holocaust, these lines seem to ally Lawrence with Nietzsche's wish to breed a master race by exterminating the weak. But written in October 1908 by a young subscriber to the *The New Age*, which two months earlier had completed a thirteen-part series by M. D. Eder on "Good Breeding or Eugenics," the vivid lines express nothing so much as the fear and self-loathing of a sickly young man all too aware that he was the runt of the litter.

MANY men of great achievement have been eldest sons. Lawrence was the fourth child out of five. Not for nothing did he identify with the small creatures of the English farm and field. He had been, moreover, according to his college friend George Neville, an unwanted child: the fourth in ten years of marriage and the first after a three-year gap. Although Arthur Lawrence earned a decent wage (between a pound and two pounds ten shillings a week, depending on the weight of coal dug) as a miner's butty—a kind of foreman who assigned work to other men belowground—there was little to spare. Lydia Lawrence tried to earn a bit extra by keeping a shop for ribbons and sundries in the front room of the tiny two-bedroom terraced house where Lawrence was born, but after a few years the shop failed. For such luxuries as the family enjoyed—a piano and paints for the children, for example—she scraped and saved from her meager housekeeping money and her Co-operative Society dividends; she also looked to her well-married sisters, particularly her sister in Leicester, Ada Krenkow, who was married to a German scholar of independent means and had two maids.

Lydia Lawrence was a stimulating mother but a bitter woman. Small, neat, and well-spoken, once a pupil-teacher herself, she felt she had married beneath her. In her grandfather's time her family, the Beardsalls of Nottingham, had been fairly well-to-do. However, a slump in the lace industry and an injury to her father, an engineer, tumbled them into poverty. To help out, as young women Lydia and her sisters were turned into cottage-workers for the lace factories, forced to labor at home, pulling the draw-threads out of strips of machine-made lace.

Her sisters recovered the family's lost social status by marrying well, but Lydia chose a collier. Arthur Lawrence was a handsome, vivacious man, a wonderful dancer and an amusing mimic and raconteur, whom she met at a dance in Nottingham. Devastatingly, when she reached Eastwood as a bride in 1865, never having even visited a mining village, she found that her new husband was lower on the social scale than she had been led to believe. He did not work in the mining office; he worked in the mines. He did not own the house to which they moved soon after their wedding; he was a tenant. The persistent theme in Lawrence's work of the well-born woman in the clutches of an earthy, low-bred man had its roots in his mother's disillusion.

Lydia Lawrence created for herself an existence largely separate from that of her unlettered husband. She wrote poetry, headed the Women's Co-operative Guild, and was an ardent Congregationalist. She believed this variant of Nonconformism to be a cut above crude Methodism. The Eastwood Congregational chapel, with its small but impressive Gothic Revival building and well-read clergymen, was her intellectual and emotional refuge, and so it became for her son.

Going to chapel twice on Sundays and often in the evenings, stimulated by the Congregational Literary Society (to which Jessie Chambers also belonged), he absorbed utterly its Nonconformist creed—that conscience is the touchstone of truth. Although he quickly lost any formal belief at college, he remained a Dissenter, a passionate Puritan, with a religious outlook, an uncompromising steadfastness, an instinct for hard work, and a deep feeling for the Bible and the never-seen Holy Land. And all his life he continued to sing the strong hymns of his childhood, whose incantatory rhythms and unashamed emotion were the joy of his early years:

> Sun of my soul, thou Saviour dear,
> It is not night if Thou be near.

Lydia Lawrence dedicated her life to her children. She was determined that they would advance in life and, above all, that the boys would not follow their father "down the mines." Over the years, she made her husband, black with coal dust, an outcast in his own home. When he came in, as one of Lawrence's childhood friends remembered, "the family would all tell him, even if he had a lively story to tell them, to go on up to bed."

To be sure, Arthur Lawrence was not defenseless. His tongue was, for all its dialect, as sharp as his wife's, and he would round on her for cossetting the children. The father in the fairly autobiographical *Sons and Lovers* does not mince his words: "Look at the children, you nasty little bitch! . . . they're like yourself; you've put 'em up to your own tricks and nasty ways—you've learned 'em in it, you 'ave."

The hostility between husband and wife was compounded by tension about money. Like many English workingmen, Arthur Lawrence gave his wife only what he chose out of his variable earnings and considered the rest his own. He was by no means an alcoholic, but rather a man who liked to relax at the pub and drink more than was good for him while Lydia, a confirmed teetotaler, waited at home, seething at the thought of the money wasted on intemperance.

Food in such a household was doled out as carefully as money; arguments over who got what were common. In 1900 when Lawrence was fifteen, his paternal uncle Walter, who also lived in Eastwood, accidentally killed his own teenage son in a family row over which of them should have an egg for tea. After a trial (fully reported in the local newspapers) Walter Lawrence spent fourteen weeks in jail. Thus the adolescent Lawrence was no stranger to the murderous tensions of domestic life—or to the humiliations of the press. His grades at Nottingham High School at that time showed a sharp drop.

IF Mrs. Lawrence had not wanted a fourth baby, she certainly did not want a fifth. The real crisis of Lawrence's early life could well have been the birth of Ada in June 1886, when he was twenty-one months old. It is a demographic axiom that in poor families the arrival of a second baby within two years after the mother's last delivery reduces the older child's chances of survival. The mother loses her milk during pregnancy; the newborn then consumes her strength and attention, while the once-cherished older child turns into an irritating toddler, whining and tugging at her knees. For Lawrence, with his wheezy chest, streaming nose, and fragile hold on life, his mother's pregnancy when he was just over a year old (especially if she was still nursing him at the time) might have been sufficiently life-threatening to account for the murderous rage against women that later filled his work. He undoubtedly bore the brunt, too, of her exhaustion. His lifelong passion for washing and scrubbing, accompanied by a guilty delight in the dark smells and crevices of the body, may reflect the pressure to be "clean" put on the elder of two babies by a mother who had to do all the family laundry by hand.

That there were no more pregnancies following Ada suggests that Lydia Lawrence, at the age of thirty-six, took the form of prevention most readily available to her, and refused intercourse with her husband. In an early poem, "Discord in Childhood," Lawrence describes, with images of blood, thong, and lash, the terror of young children huddling under the blankets, hearing the angry voices in the parents' bedroom, wondering if their father will hit their mother again. But neither the poem nor Lawrence's many later analyses of his parents' marriage hint at any awareness of an insoluble conflict between sexual desire and fear of another mouth to feed.

Yet Ada's arrival gave Lawrence an ally, and the two grew up together, pets of the family—Ada her father's, Bert his mother's. The older three left the nest early. Lawrence's alienation from the older men in his family was intensifed by his mother's overprotectiveness. Years later, his eldest brother, George—another member of the family not averse to animal metaphor—said of their mother: "She looked after Bert like a sick monkey."

Lawrence did not begin school at the usual age for Eastwood children. In May 1889, four months before his fourth birthday, he made an abortive start, but cried so much that he was sent home. There he remained until he was seven, enjoying the company and conversation of his mother, reading, playing and inventing games, and learning the household arts. He began school again in 1892, when Ada did, but even then he found the other boys rough, and he cried a lot. Irritably, his mother would say, "Bless the child—whatever is he crying for now?" But he would sob, "I don't know," and continue to cry.

The misery of his early school days was deepened by the shadow of his older brother Ernest, good at everything from books to sports. The headmaster of Beauvale Primary School told Lawrence that he would never be fit to tie Ernest's bootlaces. He was unpopular with the other boys too—a rejection that, along with his alienation from a father who was surrounded by jovial mates of pit and pub, left him with an incurable longing for male companionship. (In *Kangaroo*, written in 1922, the narrator says of the main character, Lawrence's alter ego Richard Lovat Somers, "All his life he had secretly grieved over his friendlessness.")

LAWRENCE was a painter before he was a writer. His siblings were on their guard against his sharp tongue, but they genuinely admired his talent for copying pictures. Thanks to their mother, they were the only children in the neighborhood to have paints, and it was Bert who made the best use of them. When he was in his teens, they would crowd around the table to marvel at how close to the original he could get. His technique was to work square by square, in the manner of the young draper in *Kipps,* H. G. Wells's novel published in 1905. (Kipps, as the first step toward self-improvement, takes an evening class "in that extraordinary routine of reproducing freehand 'copies,' which for two generations has passed with English people for instruction in art.") It took Lawrence a day to copy the kind of paintings he fancied; when done, they made nice gifts.

His creative urge (which he called, with echoes of Goethe, his "demon") did not shift from paint to pen until he was nineteen, and was then to express itself in a highly visual way, with vivid word pictures for everything from physical objects to inner states of mind. Writing, in contrast to painting, was a private activity, as furtive as masturbation— and he described it as such. "I remember perfectly the Sunday afternoon when I perpetrated those first two pieces [poems]," he later wrote. "They seemed to me to come from somewhere, I didn't quite know where, out of a me whom I didn't know and didn't want to know, and to say things I would much rather not have said." He tore up many and would have destroyed more had not Jessie Chambers prevented him.

Even as a writer, however, he had a penchant for copying and collaborating, intensified by his schoolmasterly wish to correct, tinker with, and improve the work of others, and an utter lack of possessiveness. His first published work, in December 1907, appeared under Jessie Chambers's name. He had submitted three stories to the *Nottinghamshire Guardian*'s Christmas competition and, hoping for three prizes, had used three different names. Enlisting Louie Burrows as well, he gave her a manuscript to send in, saying, "I make the story your property. If you have scruples, do not hesitate to say so." In the end it was Jessie's entry that took the prize, which was well worth having: three guineas, more than his father earned in a good week.

In June 1909, as Lawrence's first school year at Croydon was drawing to a close, Louie Burrows sent some of her own writing for him to judge. "I'm glad you are writing stories," he replied. "I can't do 'em myself." "Send me them, please, and I'll see if I can put a bit of surface on them and publish them for you. We'll collaborate, shall we?" Although he claimed no competence, he gave her some excellent advice on how to write a short story: select a few striking details, use vivid words, explain as little as possible, keep the pace swift, avoid sentimentalizing or moralizing, and base characters on real acquaintances. Also, he warned her, be wary of slang: "A little is as much as most folks can stand."

That November, hoping to try again for the *Guardian* prize, he asked Louie to send in a story they had written together about Nottingham's annual Goose Fair. "You will also have to swear that the story is yours," he told her, "but what does it matter?"

"Goose Fair" (published elsewhere early in 1910) is a smoldering tale of hatred between the sexes, the generations, and the social classes. It tells of the courtship between Will, a young man with "a short face and a curling lip" (genetic features indicating underbreeding by eugenic theories of the day), and his socially superior girlfriend. Hearing of a fire at Will's father's mill, the girl fears that Will has died in the fire, or, worse, has set it. Rushing to the scene, however, she is greeted by Will and her own brother. They are safe indeed, having spent the night in jail; they were arrested for bullying a country girl and her geese on the way to the fair. Relieved but angry, the young woman righteously tells Will that everyone thinks that he started the fire. "Aye, well, they made a mistake for once," he replies.

Then comes Lawrence's conclusion. Written when he was twenty-four, it is as bitter as anything he was ever to write about the war between the sexes and shows the deep antagonism toward the righteous female that underlay his search for a bride:

> They walked side by side as if they belonged to each other. She was his conscience-keeper. She was far from forgiving him, but she was still farther from letting him go. And he walked at her side like a boy who has to be punished before he can be exonerated. He submitted. But there was a geniune bitter contempt in the curl of his lip.

The name of the conscience-keeping young woman was Louisa. If Louie (baptized Louisa) Burrows, accepting Lawrence's proposal of marriage the following year, had any illusion that she would lead him like a goose to the altar, she had not read their joint story very carefully.

As the months turned to years in Croydon, Lawrence found that once again he was living with a husband and wife who did not get on. Once again he was the woman's confidant; Marie Jones complained bitterly about her husband just as his mother had done about hers.

The close quarters made Lawrence acutely aware of Mrs. Jones's soulful eyes and large breasts. They would have had to work hard not to brush against each other as they squeezed between the stove and the table in the narrow kitchen, sat before the coal fire in the tiny parlor, or waited their turn to use the single bathroom. Marie Jones and Lawrence were alone together a great deal: "en famille," as he called it. He read his work to her, and she poured out all her grievances—her husband's drinking; his mysterious absences from home and his late returns. Lawrence summed up what she told him as "things marital . . . and faintly horrifying."

At home, Lawrence had heard only the woman's side of the marital horrors. At the Joneses', however, he was treated to the other side as well. John Jones complained to Lawrence that his wife had "no more use for him than for a bag of mud"; he drew Lawrence's attention to the barmaids at the Greyhound and implied that if Lawrence were a real man, he would know how to take advantage of what was on offer.

The two men began to get on each other's nerves and to invade each other's territory. Lawrence taught himself to type on Jones's new typewriter while Jones began to copy paintings, and found, to his surprise, "that I was better at it." Lawrence did not think so. He sniggered to himself at his landlord's brush technique, "like a bird pecking crumbs off the doorstep." And he came to loathe the way Jones walked around the house singing "Miserere Domine."

Jones disliked the way Lawrence spoke of his own father, and soon saw himself cast as the unwanted parent in the little family on Colworth

Road. "Mrs Jones mothered him," Jones later said. "I bossed him. No one else seemed to."

As Lawrence grew more and more part of the household, he portrayed the little girls in increasingly sexual terms. He told Louie how Hilda Mary sipped his beer and looked for his reaction: "wicked little sinner that she is." He spoke often of "larking about" with the children in his bedroom—games which he said left him at the end collapsed, breathless, dizzy, careless. He described also how he caressed them and admired them in "their combinations." His phrases today would be suspect— "how I feel my soul enlarged through contact with the soft arms and face and body of my Hilda Mary"—but must be read as the only unfettered sensuality open to him.

Lawrence felt no guilt for his attraction, although once he did confess that he had dusted the house to make up to Marie Jones for the time he wasted with the children. Guilt was an emotion he thrust from him. He sought relief instead in fiction in which he could arrange the events and emotions of his life into a pattern that satisfied him.

In the first part of the twentieth century, English society clung to its faith in the innocence of children, untroubled by and almost totally unaware of Freud's *Three Essays on the Theory of Sexuality* published in 1905, the second of which declared the ubiquity of a sexual drive in childhood. Knowledge of Freud's work was slow to trickle through to Britain, and largely unwelcome when it did. In the summer of 1911, when M. D. Eder, psychoanalyst and contributor to *The New Age*, described to a section of the British Medical Association his successful treatment of a case of hysteria by the "Freud method"—he had released the patient's hidden childhood memories of lying in bed naked at the age of three, stroking his sister—the audience got up and walked out without a word.

But Lawrence, writing that same summer, described infantile sexuality and oedipal rivalry in terms almost as explicit as Freud's, in a short story with the stark simplicity of a fable—a fable that, incidentally, tells all that anyone could wish to know of the steamy atmosphere of life at the Joneses'.

"The Old Adam" takes place in a London suburban house with a garden and a railway at the back. The fictional family differs from the Joneses only in employing a maid, rather than a charwoman, and bearing the Welsh name of Thomas, not Jones. The Thomases have a lodger too—"tall and thin, but graceful in his energy"—Edward Severn, educated in France. (The name Severn bristles with clues to its significance for Lawrence. The Severn is the river dividing England from the dark land of Wales; Joseph Severn was the friend who accompanied the tubercular Keats on his last journey to Italy and in whose arms Keats died.)

In Lawrence's story, a seductive three-year-old called Mary—"a laughing rogue," "wild as a bacchanal"—leads the lodger on a wild chase into the garden. She darts out her tongue and licks his cheeks shamelessly in lieu of a kiss, and demands that he take her clothes off as she prepares for bed. Severn obeys, but feels that "she was getting too old for a man to undress her."

The seductive child is finally bundled off to bed by her mother, who is embarrassed and envious at the sight of the unchaste kisses. Alone together, she and her lodger cast sultry glances at each other while he reads aloud sonorous French poetry. When a thunderstorm strikes, both are "panting, and afraid, not of the lightning but of themselves and of each other." But the husband returns. Thomas, thickly built, ruddy-faced, aggressive, full of lies about where he has been, invites the lodger to help him carry a heavy metal trunk down the twisting stairs. The lodger chuckles to himself; "a subconscious instinct made the risk doubly sweet when his rival was under the box."

Lo and behold, only one step from the landing halfway down, "Severn did slip, quite accidentally." The heavy box flings the landlord against the banister post. "You ———, you did it on purpose!" shouts Thomas, and lunges for Severn. Miraculously, although the older man is a former footballer and a boxer, the poetical young man suddenly manifests the strength of ten—"his rare intelligence concentrated, not scattered; concentrated on strangling Thomas swiftly"—and wins the struggle. Severn is then overcome with remorse, gentleness, and shame; he "would . . . have given his right hand for the man he had hurt." He utters a Nietzschean apology: " 'I didn't know we were such essential brutes,' he said. 'I thought I was so civilised . . .' "

The title Lawrence gave his story, "The Old Adam," declared just as confidently as any theory emerging from Vienna that the current of sex throbs through every man, woman, and child, and that so, too, does the son's wish to kill the father. Lawrence's three-year-old Mary Thomas, "a little bright wave of wilfulness, so abandoned to her impulses," deserves a place with Freud's Dora and Little Hans among the children who mark the twentieth century's grudging acceptance of infantile sexuality, and is, moreover, based on longer, closer observation than Freud gave any of his patients.

But Freud developed his theories as a married man and a father. Lawrence, when he wrote "The Old Adam," was a lonely bachelor schoolmaster living in digs, nowhere near attaining a wife and child of his own.

2

IN WANT OF
A WIFE

1910–1911

*L*awrence was fascinated by marriage and marriages. His stories, like the novel he was writing, explored the classic theme of the search for a mate and the terrible consequences of choosing the wrong one, as he believed his mother had done. His characters inhabited the moral universe of his parents. Marriage was indissoluble; Congreve's warning "Marry'd in haste, we may repent at leisure" was clear as a commandment. There was no reprieve from a life sentence of regret.

Yet the deterrent was as ineffective in Eastwood as everywhere else. Pregnancy before marriage was not unknown, nor were births out of wedlock. In 1897 Lawrence's oldest brother, George, was forced into a marriage; the subsequent birth of his son, William, six months later made Lawrence an uncle at the age of twelve.

Lawrence, however, remained innocent of the ways of the flesh longer than most boys, perhaps because he was slow physically to mature. When he was twelve or thirteen, a neighbor calling at the Lawrences' home was shocked to find Bert sitting on his mother's lap. Over the next years of adolescence, he never played sports or went swimming with other boys. Rather, he kept company with girls—but never flirted or tried to kiss them. They treated him as one of themselves and took him with them when they shopped, letting him choose their hats and frocks. The other boys noticed, of course, and taunted him, calling him a "mardy-boy" (soft) or worse, with its suggestions of effeminacy, "mard-arse." His nephew William noticed that if someone trod on a flower during their walks in the woods, Lawrence would cry "Vandal," or "Murderer," and try to straighten it up.

As he grew older, however, he developed a friendship with an old schoolmate, George Neville. Neville, lively, bright, and mischievous, was a neighbor, and like Lawrence a miner's son good at his books. After Beauvale Primary School both became scholarship boys commuting to Nottingham High School (where they were fellow victims of the prevailing snobbery). Neville, like Ada and Louie Burrows, had trained at the Ilkeston Pupil-Teacher Centre, and was one of the band of Eastwood student-teachers who called themselves the Pagans, priding themselves on their discussions of advanced ideas.

Neville and Lawrence had special names for each other—Lawrence was "Billy" and Neville "Teufel" (German for devil). Together they tramped over the Derbyshire dales, collecting natural specimens. Neville laughed at Lawrence for leaving him to get the insects. He laughed, too, when Lawrence blushed at the way the facts of animal mating were casually discussed at Haggs Farm.

According to Neville, Lawrence was in college before he learned that women had pubic hair. He claimed that he himself had broken the bad news, by making fun of one of Lawrence's drawings for lacking this realistic detail, and that Lawrence had leaped out of his chair, pummeling him and crying, "It's not true!" If so, it is no wonder that Lawrence was so entranced by the bodies of the little girls at Colworth Road: they were the smooth and sculpted female forms of his young dreams.

Another reason for Lawrence's ignorance of the female anatomy was sheer terror. At sixteen, while at work at Haywood's surgical-appliance factory in Nottingham, he had been set upon by some raucous factory girls. Cornering him in the storeroom, they tried to remove his trousers. They failed—at least, he told Neville that they had failed—because he had fought them off. His claim is hard to believe, for he was outnumbered and he was never known to defend himself even in the school playground. Whether or not the hoydens did manage to glimpse his secret parts, the shock of the assault was severe—so severe, Neville believed, that it led to the pneumonia which nearly killed him not long after.

Lawrence never overcame his dread of the female but he made good use of it. In 1918 he drew on his adolescent trauma in a fine short story, "Tickets, Please," in which aggressive girl tram conductors, doing men's jobs because of the war, set upon a young male passenger. In a later novel, *The Boy in the Bush,* he portrayed a young Australian—as strong-bodied as can be, and yet "with girls and women he felt exposed to some sort of danger—as if some were going to seize him by the neck, from behind."

Yet Lawrence always expected to marry. He told a girl playmate in Eastwood that when he grew up, he would "marry a pretty lady, not like you. She will have blue ribbon in her hair, not wool." As he grew older and became the constant companion of Jessie Chambers, even at chapel, it did not trouble him that local people considered them engaged and that Jessie seemed to do so too. It troubled his mother and sisters, however, and in 1906, when he was twenty-one and entering college, they urged him to break with her. Jessie believed that they were being possessive about their Bert, which was true. But they could also recognize the depressive personality reflected in the way she walked, with heavy, clumsy gait, head held down and thrust forward. To the Lawrence women, accustomed to close-knit family circles, the fact that the Chamberses considered Jessie the odd one out among the four brothers and three sisters at Haggs Farm was proof that she was not the right wife for their Bert.

Lawrence himself was puzzled by the absence of any physical desire for Jessie. Being blunt, he told her in 1906: "I've looked into my heart and I cannot find that I love you as a husband should love his wife." A year later, he spelled it out again: "You have no sexual attraction at all, none whatever."

By the summer of 1909, as he approached his twenty-fourth birthday and the end of his first school year at Croydon, he was oppressed by what he called "the stunting bonds of my chastity." His desire to marry became a near panic. Continuing his heated correspondence with women, he tried to puzzle out the mystery of the sexes. He tried to reconcile his ideas of Woman: shy and resisting, on the one hand, bold and voracious on the other. He sounded out Blanche Jennings: "By the way, in love, or at least in love-making, do you think the woman is always passive . . . enjoying the man's demonstration, a wee bit frit [upset]—not active? I prefer a little devil—a Carmen—I like not things passive."

He also badgered Neville for information. Neville had grown into a handsome rakish type with rippling muscles and a roving eye, and he had narrowly escaped a forced marriage in 1906 when a nineteen-year-old girl whom he had made pregnant (after a Methodist camp meeting, to Lawrence's disgust) was thrown out by her father. "Thank God," Lawrence told Jessie at the time, "I've been saved from that . . . so far." His own mother had warned him about how a man could ruin his life in a few thoughtless minutes.

Lawrence was short of experience but not of imagination. His writing was savagely sexual and angry. He could not see his way out of the impasse. While half hating women for their strength and control, he clung at the same time to conventional Victorian romantic notions of the powerful man sweeping the reluctant virgin off her feet—his view of his own parents' courtship. In the novel he was working on, he made his handsome George admire the well-known picture *An Idyll,* by the Victorian artist Maurice Greiffenhagen, which shows two figures: a ruddy-skinned half-naked man of the woods, clad in skins and leaves, roughly clasping a pale pre-Raphaelite maiden. "Wouldn't it be fine?" George muses. "A girl like that—half afraid—and passion!"

Alice Dax, to whom he sent the manuscript for comments, called it "coarse." But Alice had just had a baby and Lawrence blamed maternity for depriving her of her critical powers. "She has no mind left; she has no interest in anything but 'Son,' " he told Blanche. (Blanche had warned him that his nose would be out of joint when Alice became a mother.)

Among his correspondents, Louie Burrows and Jessie Chambers were free to travel, and separately they visited him in Croydon. There was a perennial problem of where his women visitors were to stay. Louie solved it decorously by returning to Leicester the same day, but Jessie boldly accepted a bed at the Joneses', probably in the dining room at the back. Her family was scandalized by the impropriety and wrote to remind Lawrence of his moral responsibilities.

In November 1909, on Jessie's second visit, he took advantage of the unorthodox arrangement by keeping her up, long after the Joneses had gone to bed, to discuss the philosophy of love and sex. He also wanted to tell her that he had almost decided to marry a Croydon teacher named Agnes Holt whom he had been seeing. The frustration of life alone, he said, was more than he could bear. Besides, he needed someone to look after him. "You know, I could so easily peg out," he said. But how, he mused, could he marry with no money?

What he asked from Jessie was her opinion on whether a young woman would give him sex without marriage and whether it would be wrong. Sleepily and unhappily, she replied that "the kind of girl who would, I think you wouldn't like" but that, no, in her view, it would not be wrong.

Sadly for Lawrence, Agnes Holt showed no interest in releasing her animal instincts; she only made him angry for forcing him to repress his own. Within two months Lawrence had dropped her, dismissing her to Blanche as sham, superficial, sentimental, and mid-Victorian. "She pretends to be very fond of me; she isn't really; even if she were, what do I care!—but if she were, she wouldn't be the timid duffer she is."

So much for Agnes Holt. She married someone else not long after.

Lawrence gave her copies of *An Idyll* and another painting for a wedding present.

LAWRENCE'S protracted virginity was not altogether his own fault. The sexual frustration among sensitive well-brought-up men of that time was widespread and real. The young T. S. Eliot, living in Paris in 1911, was tormented, according to his biographer Peter Ackroyd, by "the women who stood uncorsetted in doorways" and by "sexual longings upon which he would not act." Yeats remained a virgin until the age of thirty-one and Shaw until twenty-nine. Shaw's sexual excitement before that time, says Michael Holroyd, his biographer, expressed itself in "an ejaculation of words." Such men, if they disdained prostitutes, had to find partners in the form of obliging wives with complaisant husbands, or single women of an independent cast of mind. But Lawrence took no consolation from the ordinariness of his predicament. The world of passion seemed determined to exclude him personally, as he realized once again when in the autumn of 1909 he became privy to the secret details of yet another sexual melodrama.

Helen Corke, a tiny, pretty woman of twenty-eight, with red hair, sharp features, and pale skin, was a teacher at another Croydon school. With her decided opinions, musical ability, and strong interest in Nietzsche, Helen was a discovery, far more sophisticated and stimulating than most of the people he met in and around Croydon. When they met during his first term, at the home of Alice Mason, senior mistress at Lawrence's school, Helen liked him immediately. She was impressed by a highly attractive habit of his which she saw as "that momentary complete concentration upon the individual contact which is a mark of good breeding." Lawrence was also, Helen swiftly saw, the life of the party. He told fortunes and kept up a steady patter, embellished by words from several languages, which entertained young and old alike. When later, during a walk on Wimbledon Common with her and Alice Mason, he stopped and read Swinburne aloud, Helen knew that she had found a kindred soul, someone like herself "in love with beauty."

In the summer of 1909 Lawrence learned that he and Helen were both going to the Isle of Wight for the first week in August. He was planning to meet his parents for a holiday (a sign that Arthur and Lydia Lawrence were not entirely averse to each other's company) and suggested to Helen that they might travel together on the train down to Southampton. But she had her own arrangements.

Returning to school in the autumn of 1909, he learned what they were. On the island, Helen had kept an assignation with the married man, thirty-nine-year-old Herbert Macartney, who had been her violin teacher for several years. They became lovers, briefly, and spent five days together. Then Helen left, to meet Alice Mason and another woman friend in Cornwall. The lonely adulterer returned to his southwestern London suburb (New Malden, near Wimbledon) and hanged himself from a hook on the bedroom door.

Helen learned the news from a newspaper placard when she returned to London. The suicide of a well-known professional musician and teacher was news: "Violinist's Tragic End. Member of Covent Garden Orchestra Terminates His Life." For the details, Helen had only the account given by the widow to the coroner's court, and the coroner's conclusion that "so far as was known, the deceased had no worries, and no reason could be assigned for his act."

The shock sent Helen into an almost speechless depression. As autumn turned to winter, Alice Mason asked Lawrence if he could help. He was more than willing. "Can I see her? Do you think she would see me?" he asked. Mason, an older teacher with whom Helen had a long (and probably lesbian) friendship, took him to Helen's home and introduced him to her parents.

From then on Lawrence was excited by Helen, a genuine femme fatale, and visited her often. (Her mother was glad to see him but worried about his constant cough, especially as he always insisted on walking, even in the cold and wet, the five miles or so from Addiscombe to the part of Selhurst where the Corkes lived.) And his kindness did help. He got Helen out of the house for long walks on the North Downs and the Weald of Kent. He consoled her with more Swinburne: "Content thee, howsoe'er, whose days are done / There lies not any troublous thing before." He persuaded her to read aloud with him classical tragedies that put her own story in an epic light.

With that enthusiasm for things German which flourished in England until the First World War, they read Goethe—he helping her with her German. He gave her poems: and his translation of "Über allen Gipfeln"; she introduced him to Wagner's *Ring*. She saw herself leading Lawrence's imagination with hers to "the plane of supermen, gods and heroes," far from the petty life of humanity driven by "the economic whip."

Helen had become a passionate devotee of Wagner (and Nietzsche) under Macartney's tutelage. With him playing among the first violins, she had attended the *Ring* cycle at Covent Garden and loved it all, particularly *Die Walküre*. It had required little effort for her to see herself and her teacher as the guilty lovers of the operatic plot, and privately they referred to each other by the names Siegmund and Sieglinde.

To aid her recovery, Lawrence daringly took Helen away for a platonic overnight outing to the Channel coast, where they stayed in a lodging house, in separate rooms at opposite ends of the corridor. The intrepid Helen could not resist tiptoeing to Lawrence's door and listening to him muttering in his sleep. When she told him later, he made the incident into a poem which he called, pointedly, "Coldness in Love."

He had absorbed Helen's tragic experience entirely, yet in his heart he blamed her for her "Siegmund's" death. If she had not rejected Macartney's further embraces on the Isle of Wight; if she had not left him to join her preferred female companions . . . Macartney's fate confirmed Lawrence's fears that women, with their icy self-control, had life-or-death power over the hopelessly instinctual male.

BUT by late November in 1909 Lawrence owed a special debt to Jessie Chambers. Thanks to her, he had become a published writer. As he walked over the muddy waste ground and builder's rubble that separated his school and his lodgings, he felt "rather daft" to think of his name in print. Jessie, who had admired his poems about the school and the Jones baby, had sent four to the *English Review*, explaining to the editor that their author was too shy to send them in himself.

The *English Review* was for new writing what *The New Age* was for social reform. When Ford Madox Ford,* Joseph Conrad, H. G. Wells, and others founded "the *English*" in the summer of 1908, Wells was so excited that he exclaimed, "It's IT this year!" and chose it for the four-part serialization of his new novel, *Tono-Bungay*.

Excitement over the *English Review* had reached Haggs Farm, for Lawrence had been urging all his friends to buy it. When Jessie took her gamble and won—all four of Lawrence's poems were immediately accepted—the Chambers family was as surprised and delighted as Lawrence himself. To make his debut in such august company—Henry James, Thomas Hardy, John Galsworthy, and W. H. Hudson all had appeared in its pages—meant that Lawrence was starting at the top.

Soon Lawrence was summoned to meet Ford. They met at the *English*'s office, which was also Ford's living quarters, above a fishmonger's at 84 Holland Park Avenue, and it was then that Ford realized that he had caught something rarer than a new poet: a miner's son. Ford was entranced. He and his new mistress, the handsome and successful novelist Violet Hunt, like all their literary circle, were people with a highly tuned social conscience who aspired to raise the cultural sights of the English working class. In Ford's words, "In the early decades of this

---

* Ford, born in Merton, Surrey, in 1873, the son of a musicologist, editor, and writer who had immigrated to England from Germany, and grandson of the pre-Raphaelite painter Ford Madox Brown, was then known under his original surname, Hueffer. After World War I he changed it by deed poll to the less Teutonic Ford. He will be referred to in these pages, as he is in the 1990 biography by Alan Judd, as Ford.

century, we enormously wanted authentic projects of that type of life which hitherto had gone quite unvoiced."

Ford was not referring to the lower middle classes. These were being delivered to English literature very nicely by Wells and Arnold Bennett. He meant, rather, "the completely different race of the English artisan— and it was a race as sharply divided from the ruling or even the mere white-collar classes as was the Negro from the gentry of Virginia."

In one heady day, Lawrence found himself summoned to Kensington to lunch at South Lodge, Violet Hunt's villa on Campden Hill; then borne off, like a trophy, to Hampstead, to be exhibited first at tea with Ernest Rhys, an editor of literary classics, and then, later, at the home of the great Wells himself. There Lawrence, with frank curiosity, observed the manners of the middle classes as Wells's two little boys came out in blue dressing gowns to kiss the visitors good night.

Lawrence, who tended to a cheeky, chip-on-the-shoulder approach to his social superiors ("This isn't my idea, Sir, of an editor's office" was his opening remark to Ford), could not have been as nervous as Ford was before their first meeting. "If he was really the son of a working coal-miner," Ford asked himself, "how exactly how was I to approach him in conversation?" Ford was no snob but, as he later wrote, "a working man was so unfamiliar as a proposition that I really did not know how to bring it off."

Ford's apprehension, which Violet shared, gives some idea of the barriers Lawrence faced in English society. He was a professional teacher, fluent in French, competent in German, prodigiously well-read in English and European literature, and a writer as well, of poems and stories that Ford considered remarkable, yet his father's occupation marked him as a horny-handed son of toil. Lawrence was well aware that suddenly he had been led to the ladder of social advance—"I'll make two thousand a year!" he predicted to Jessie—but he also could see that he was a curiosity: "What will the others say? That I'm a fool. A collier's son a poet!"

Lawrence's intuition was correct. From the beginning, said the writer Richard Aldington, who met him in London in 1914, "an odious class snobbery came into action." Even Aldington, who considered himself immune, believed it a tribute to a mother's dedication that the son of a barely literate workingman had received enough education to become a schoolteacher in a London suburb.

This sudden, early, and condescending fame blighted Lawrence's artistic development almost as much as lack of recognition has hurt other great writers. He was taken up, typecast, and caricatured. Some of the memoirs written at the time gave him a rough accent and rustic manners he could not have had as a London schoolmaster.

By most accounts, Lawrence had a cultured voice with Midlands traces; how strong these were depended on the hearer. Willie Hopkin, Eastwood's chief socialist intellectual and Lawrence's early mentor, summed up Lawrence's accent, saying that from boyhood Lawrence always spoke correctly but that he could lapse at will into the local mixture of Nottinghamshire-borders and Derbyshire.

In other words, Lawrence, like many people of humble origins and good education, took care with his speech and was, in a sense, bilingual; he was fluent in both his mother's standard English and his father's dialect. Besides, if Lawrence had wanted to change his voice, he certainly could have done so. With his gifts, he soon could do a wicked imitation of Ford, screwing an imaginary monocle into his eye and reproducing perfectly the fluffy plummy speech that emerged from "fat Fordie's" walrus-mustached mouth.

At Ford's suggestion Lawrence brought Jessie with him to a second lunch at South Lodge. She found it an uncomfortably glamorous occasion. She had to contend with servants, with champagne served as an accompaniment to the meal, and with the eccentricity of one of the guests, Ezra Pound, a young American poet who lived nearby. Pound had a growing reputation in London, where he was a prolific contributor to *The New Age,* but he was already showing signs of bizarre behavior. Jessie, with little experience of Americans, was puzzled when he bowed stiffly from the waist, then barked out questions like an interrogator. The decor of South Lodge must also have been a shock to her, with its white woodwork and William Morris wallpaper: hallmarks of avant-garde taste.

Their hostess watched the two young Midlanders as if they were creatures from outer space. At forty-seven (to Ford's thirty-five), never married but having had a string of lovers, Violet Hunt was sophisticated, elegant, and acidly brilliant. When she observed Jessie softly asking the maid whether or not to keep her gloves on while eating, she seized on it as an anecdote to tell her friends. To Jessie's face, however, Violet was kind. She assumed that the couple were engaged, and promised Jessie that Ford would do all he could for Lawrence.

As Lawrence's discoverer, Ford tried to nudge him back to the provinces in his writing. But scenes from industrial life, full of dialect and coal dust, were not at all what Lawrence wanted to do; the kind of truth he was struggling to capture was not social but sexual and emotional. All the same, almost dutifully, Lawrence began to think of writing a Midlands novel, the story of his mother's life, in which the psychological and sociological elements could be combined.

In his new circle, Lawrence's charm soon won out over class. When he ran into Pound at one of Violet Hunt's "at homes" at the Reform Club, Pound took him out to supper and back to his room in Kensington. To get home Lawrence had to catch the underground to Charing Cross, a train to East Croydon, and then a tram car to the Addiscombe terminus.

Back at Colworth Road, Lawrence wrote breathlessly to Louie Burrows: "He knows W B Yeats & all the Swells."

The two young poets became friends and Lawrence enjoyed Pound's idiosyncratic hospitality in what Aldington, a near neighbor, considered "an awful slum courtyard" behind St. Mary Abbots Church. Pound liked to burn incense, give his guests dried apricots to eat, and sing Hebridean songs. One night, when the party ran late, Pound let Lawrence have half his bed. But Lawrence could not sleep, kept awake by the sound of Pound's snoring and the insistent bells of St. Mary Abbots.

Pound assisted Lawrence's upward mobility by introducing him in late November 1909 to Grace Crawford, the pert, sharp-tongued daughter of wealthy American expatriates; her father was manager of Buffalo Bill's traveling Wild West Show. She was probably Lawrence's first American woman; he was intrigued by her directness and by her enthusiasm for art. In a neat barter, he let her read the dialect play he had written, *A Collier's Friday Night,* while she taught him Italian and etiquette. ("How do you pronounce 'Chianti'?" he wanted to know.)

He sparred with Grace, at tea with her parents and in letters, but always in formal terms. Although she and Pound had been "Grace" and "Ezra" from the day they met, she and Lawrence never addressed each other as anything but "Miss Crawford" and "Mr. Lawrence." But Grace joined the circle of women correspondents to whom he wrote with great care—in her case, to be amusing. One day after a visit to the Crystal Palace ice rink he compared the tiny Burmese gentlemen he had seen there to "sprigs of golden privet, skating like bits of yellow machine round and round."

To Grace, an outsider like himself on the London scene, Lawrence could speak frankly, as he did in a self-mocking account of a summer party at South Lodge in July 1910. He had run up the stairs, only to fall into the open arms of a waiter, who barked his name to the crowd. Inside, Lawrence recounted, it was "like a bargain sale." He did not know a soul. He talked to Ford's uncle, then to Ford's secretary, then eyed eagerly an attractive woman seated at the piano in a short red satin dress; she looked like a Christmas cracker, he told himself. But Ford carted him off and introduced him to others instead, singing his praises, to Lawrence's intense embarrassment:

> I wish Hueffer [Ford] wouldn't introduce me as a genius. When a fellow hasn't enough money to buy a decent pair of boots, and not enough sense to borrow or steal a pair, he's ticketed "genius" as a last resource: just as they call things "very desirable" when nobody on earth wants them.

In the end Lawrence fled the party without saying good-bye to Violet Hunt in her lace dress and feathered hat because he did not know how to interrupt. "Was that criminal?" he asked his American mentor.

The friendship broke up when Grace's parents took her to Rome, possibly to get her away from Lawrence, whom she had begun seeing frequently. Her father had already warned her away from the handsome Pound, who had taken to wearing an open-necked black shirt, a straw hat, and a single dangling turquoise earring.

By early 1910 Lawrence had at last rid himself of his unwanted virginity. Jessie Chambers had martyred herself to the cause when Lawrence, rebuffed by Agnes Holt and Helen Corke, abruptly told her that he had changed his mind: he was suddenly full of physical desire for her. Desperate, devoted thing that she was, Jessie put aside the religious scruples of a lifetime and surrendered her body.

It was a terrible introduction to sex for her, and perhaps for him, although he may well have managed his formal initiation elsewhere. He and Jessie had to make love outdoors, Lawrence fumbling with condoms (which, at five shillings a packet, one-eighth of his week's pay, were not cheap). Lines from his poem "Scent of Irises," probably written that spring, give some hint of the scene: "You upon the dry, dead beech-leaves, once more, only once / Taken like a sacrifice, in the night invisible; / Only the darkness and the scent of you!" Lawrence could not disguise the association he made between the odor of flowers and that of female genitalia; the poem begins with the nauseous admission: "A faint, sickening scent of irises / Persists all morning."

Another flower poem was almost more explicit. In "Lilies in the Fire" he compares Jessie to a "stack of white lilies, all white and gold!" but the sensations he describes are far from radiant. "Is it with pain, my dear, that you shudder so?" the poem asks. "Why even now you speak through close-shut teeth. / Was this too much for you?" For Lawrence it was intolerable that his performance of the sexual act ("all my best / Soul's naked lightning") was for Jessie "a burden of dead flesh / Heavy to bear." At the end of the poem, hardly surprisingly, the lilies are "flagged and sere / Upon the floor."

For Jessie, the seriousness of the commitment—tantamount to an engagement—compensated for the clenched teeth, the chilly ground, and the ruptured hymen. At the start Lawrence seemed to interpret their lovemaking that way, too. He thanked her in a letter for "the great good" she had done him; he wanted her near him, he said, and he wanted them to have a little house together. But then his anger grew. That he could not arouse her was a deep humiliation. In revenge as well as frustration he threw himself simultaneously at Alice Dax and Helen Corke.

He concealed from Jessie his increasing attraction to Helen Corke but he did report candidly that Alice Dax had come to London to see him, that they had gone together to hear Richard Strauss's *Elektra,* and that they had stayed in a hotel, in separate rooms. In the morning, he told Jessie, Alice had come into his room, but he had refused her offer of sex. "I told her I was engaged to you," Lawrence said, adding that "it is all finished now with her." (Whether by "all" he meant a sexual relationship is unclear.)

More important to Lawrence was his progress as a novelist. Ford had liked his book, which now bore the name "Nethermere," and had passed it along to the publisher William Heinemann. In January 1910, Heinemann accepted it for publication and promised an advance on royalties of fifteen pounds. Lawrence began to believe that he was not doomed to be a schoolmaster forever.

HELEN Corke would not give herself to Lawrence, although he began making advances. But early in 1910, visiting him when he was bedridden with flu, she gave him her book of herself instead: "The Freshwater Diary," named for the little town on the Isle of Wight where she and Macartney had their five stolen days. She said demurely that she had not meant the diary for other eyes. "But writing pre-supposes a reader," Lawrence said, terribly excited, sensing a subject for his second novel, "and human experience is the property of humanity."

That spring, with "Nethermere" more or less finished, he turned his attention to Helen's diary. He made her three promises: to consult her throughout the writing; to allow nothing to appear without her consent; and to refrain from publishing the book for five years. Then he got to work. He kept her sequence of events, as well as many of her details and actual phrases. Inspired by the Wagnerian love-death theme, he also kept Helen's name for her hero and called the new book "The Saga of Siegmund." But for the name of the girl who led her lover to his death, he rejected "Sieglinde" for the more English "Helena."

Reading the early draft, Helen did not complain. She was stunned at Lawrence's perceptiveness in sensing the voluptuous love between the main women characters, to which the doomed Siegmund's desires run a poor second. She had acknowledged the lesbian longings within herself and had taken much comfort (for what she called "my problem") from the thesis of the homosexual writer Edward Carpenter, in *Love's Coming of Age,* that sex was a spectrum of responses and intuition ranging from masculine to feminine.

The resulting novel, *The Trespasser,* shows how Lawrence could take over other people's material yet make it entirely his own. The last pages of the book are pure invention; they recreate the anguish and despair of Macartney's last hours, which Helen could have known nothing about: the adulterer's lonely return to his suburban home, and his suicide.

Lawrence clearly drew on what he imagined as the feelings of his own father, excluded from the warm family circle. He describes a man driven to self-destruction by the coldness of his mistress, of his wife—and even of his beloved small daughter. When the trembling, unsatisfied Siegmund returns home and sees his little Gwen, he wonders: "Would the child speak to him?—Would she touch him with her soft hands?" When Gwen turns away, Siegmund's fate is sealed.

When *The Trespasser* was published in 1912, one of its reviewers, Constance Garnett, the English translator of the great nineteenth-century Russian writers, found the last fifty pages, describing the husband's humiliation, mental agony, and delirium, as clear and strong in their psychological intensity as "the best Russian school."

But the novel did not solve the problem of Lawrence's own rejection by Helen. His anger was fierce even though he recognized her bisexuality; rather, it was all the greater as he knew she was no virgin. But Helen's obsession with the dead Macartney touched another raw nerve as well. From his mother's unending grief for his lost brother, Ernest, he knew that the dead are unvanquishable rivals. He wrote Helen a letter saying he wanted to strangle her: "You see, I know Siegmund is there all the time. I know you would go back to him, after me, and disclaim me. . . . I feel often inclined, when I think of you, to put my thumbs on your throat."

Lawrence was never content merely to have a number of women in his life. He had to bring them together, manipulate them, scheme, and play one off against the other in ways that often hurt them greatly. At college he had made a triangle of Jessie, himself, and pretty Louie Burrows. Now he drew Helen into his relation with Jessie.

Helen and Jessie, however, to his surprise, got along all too well. He had told Helen all about Jessie, how his family was pressing him either to become engaged or to give her up, preferably the latter. And, of course, he told Jessie all about Helen's ill-fated love affair. When Jessie came to London in July 1910, the three of them went for a walk on Hayes Common.

Helen's admiration for Jessie in her dark red dress was instant and physical: "dark silky hairwaves . . . a slightly gypsy tan. . . . Her brown eyes, even when she smiles, are sorrowful." Like Jessie, Helen had no physical desire for Lawrence, but found their intellectual intimacy irresistible and irreplaceable. Soon the two women were writing to each other—about him—and writing like him. Lawrence was doomed to attract women with literary ambitions, who poured out lush imitations of his own writing style. Jessie, for example, eagerly described to Helen what it was like to be Lawrence's half-wanted girlfriend:

Times and times without number he has left me to walk over a wet meadow with water on one hand and black woods on the other, and all heaven and earth shaken in my soul. And every time before I reached home I had fought and wrestled with the intangible, and found a heaven in my heart, a fighting heaven—a regular Valhalla except for the feasting.

Helen was not to be outdone. She too saw herself as a writer, and was inclined to the florid: "Your letter gives me to feel so poignantly the breadths of the Downs and the silence of the larchwood that I am moved to reply on the instant."

Together they enjoyed calling him by his rarely used first name, David.

As he wrote "The Saga of Siegmund" in the spring and summer of 1910, Lawrence's life was an intricate interweaving of his women and his work. John Worthen, reconstructing the complicated chronology of those turbulent months, concludes that Lawrence's sexual relationship with Jessie "ended within a fortnight of the ending of 'The Saga,' and may actually have been ended *by* it, as Lawrence began to dread the power of the loving woman and the helplessness of the frustrated man." "The Saga," in other words, was not only the story of Helen and Macartney but of Jessie and Lawrence.

By summer, Lawrence was virtually enlisting Helen's help in breaking with Jessie, as when he wrote:

She is very pretty and very wistful. She came to see me yesterday. She kisses me. It makes my heart feel like ashes. But then she kisses me more and moves my sex fire. Mein Gott, it is hideous. I have promised to go there tomorrow, to stay till Thursday. If I have courage I shall not stay. It is my present intention not to stay. I must tell her. I must tell her that we ought finally and definitely to part; if I have the heart to tell her.

By that time Lawrence's mother and sisters had begun to suspect that Jessie was using the sexual snare to try to capture Bert. The Chambers family may also have suspected that she was "fallen." Jessie was living in digs in Nottingham, and when she asked her family if she could return to live with them, they refused. Her isolation made her all the more dependent on Lawrence and desperate that he should marry her.

Once school was out, Jessie expected to go on holiday with Lawrence. Instead he came to see her to declare that their informal engagement was over. If so—Jessie gambled on his dependence on their intellectual companionship—their friendship was finished, too. She gave him an ultimatum: marriage, or nothing. The reply was inevitable: "Then I am afraid it must be nothing." Lawrence could not bear any woman to have such power over him.

*   *   *

ALL the while Lawrence kept up his friendly correspondence with Louie Burrows, and it was to her that he confided one trouble with his publishers. "They [Heinemann's] are worrying me for another title for the first book—let them go to blazes." By then he had finished "The Saga" and was well into a third novel, which he referred to as "Paul"—the story of his mother, and also of himself, thinly disguised as a painter with the name of Paul Morel.

Lawrence wrote with extraordinary speed. Not that he turned out a steady stream of finished work; he revised extensively, often producing highly different versions of the same book, story, or poem. The first draft of the second novel had gone like a breeze, nonetheless, owing to Helen's raw material and his gift for lavish language, which he had indulged to the full. Titles were another matter.

Lawrence was hopeless with titles for his novels. His was not a classifying imagination: he could not put a label to what was, in effect, a whole separate universe of his own creation. Working on them, he made them his children—"Laetitia" was often "that young lady" or "my little girl." When the reality of publication loomed, he tried hard to find better labels for his wares. By the time the long-nurtured "Nethermere," *née* "Laetitia," was at the proof stage, he tried to help out the unhappy Heinemann. "Lapwings"? he suggested to his editor. "Peewits"? "The Cry of the Peacock"? "The Talent in the Napkin"? "The Talent, the Beggar and the Box"? Or (because his hero George kept stretching out like bindweed for things beyond his reach) perhaps "Tendrils Outreach" or "Outreach of Tendrils"? He kept on trying. His projected titles, he told Heinemann's, would fill a curio shop. A few days later he was writing in despair, " 'Crab-apples' seems to me as good as any."

Finally, the publishers took the image central to the meaning of the book and decreed *The White Peacock*.

As he began to look for a publisher for "The Saga of Siegmund," to Helen he cursed the fates that had "stigmatised me 'writer.' It is a sickening business." Eighteen bitter years would pass before he found a way to circumvent the arguments, the deals, the editorial nitpicking, the politicking and self-censorship of the hated literary world.

HAD Lawrence a premonition of the coming breakup of his childhood home? In early August he sat at the table in Eastwood and wrote Grace Crawford an almost photographic description of the scene:

> My father is a coal miner: the house has eight rooms: I am writing in
> the kitchen, or the middle parlour as it would be called if my mother

were magniloquent,—but she's not, she's rather scornful. It is cosy enough. There is a big fire—miners keep fires in their living rooms though the world reels with sunheat—a large oval mahogany table, three shelves of study-books, a book-case of reading books, a dresser, a sofa, and four wooden chairs. Just like all the other small homes in England.

Writing this passage also served as a warm-up exercise for his new novel, the story of his mother's blighted hopes and disastrous marriage.

In mid-August Lawrence went with George Neville for a roistering week at a boardinghouse in Blackpool on the Lancashire coast, then on to Leicester to visit his maternal aunt Ada Krenkow. In an instant his world shattered. He found his mother, who had been staying there, desperately ill. A Leicester doctor had diagnosed an incurable tumor of the stomach. Lawrence took her back to Eastwood and concluded his holiday by sitting with her.

When he returned to Croydon, more bad news followed. Ford had read the second novel and found it one-quarter masterpiece, the rest "rotten"—phallic, dreary, moralistic—although (small consolation to Lawrence, who wanted to be paid) "a rotten work of genius." Ford piled on the scolding. To raise a dreary commonplace incident from a penny paper to Wagnerian proportions was a cheap stunt; the novel was not a worthy successor to *The White Peacock*. Moreover, it was "erotic—not that I, personally, mind that," said Ford, "but an erotic work *must* be good art, which this is not." The letter effectively ended their friendship. When Heinemann, although willing to go ahead with publication, agreed with Ford, Lawrence, hurt and furious, withdrew the book.

Lawrence should not have been surprised at their reaction. With the rise in literacy, there was widespread concern among the English educated classes about the moral danger to the masses. News agents such as W. H. Smith's, which enjoyed the monopoly of bookstalls in railway stations, were held to have a special duty to keep noxious literature from defiling readers' minds. So were other national chains, such as Boots Chemists, whose lending libraries catered to the reading appetites of the general public. Just a year before, in November 1909, representatives of Smith's, Boots, Mudie's Library, *The Times* Book Club, and others met to form a Circulating Libraries' Association, at which they undertook "that, in future, we will not place in circulation any book which, by reason of the personal, scandalous, libellous, immoral, or otherwise disagreeable nature of its contents, is in our opinion likely to prove offensive to any considerable section of our subscribers." They therefore requested all publishers to submit to them, at least one clear week before the date of publication, any book "about the character of which there can possibly be any question."

When William Heinemann, Edmund Gosse, and the Society of Authors protested against this censorship—or "dictatorship," as Heinemann called it in a letter to *The Times*—their protests were dismissed in a wonderfully sarcastic *Times* leading article the same day, as the "familiar outcry from the too familiar throats." The newspaper itself applauded the association's "sensible and business-like decision."

Any censorship, declared "The Thunderer," came from the customers: the "unregenerate" bourgeoisie, whose taste was

> on the whole, a wide and liberal taste, but it is not wide enough to tolerate the extravagances and the indecencies, not to say the obscenities, which some youthful writers mistake for proofs of originality, and to which some older writers resort in a desperate attempt to season matter which they shrewdly suspect to be essentially insipid.

It would still be "open to bold spirits," *The Times* declared scathingly, "whose immortal productions transgress the bounds of convention accepted by their neighbours, to find publishers for their works when they can. They may still revel in their own improprieties and invite their admirers to share the fearful joy with them." They might even, *The Times* sneered, advertise their books as "rejected by the Circulating Libraries' Association."

Letters to the editor of *The Times* tended to the same view. As a reader, H. D. Rawnsley, who joined the debate on December 10, observed:

> There is no doubt that the British public that cares for the sanctities of home life, for a manhood with high ideals, and a pure womanhood, will be profoundly grateful to the Circulating Libraries' Association for the step it has now taken in the direction of safeguarding readers from the contamination of the nasty novel. . . . But what about the free libraries?

DURING the autumn, as Lydia Lawrence's condition worsened, Lawrence went home to Eastwood every other weekend. He would return to London at three or four o'clock on the Monday morning, walk across the silent city from Marylebone Station to Charing Cross, and be at his desk at Davidson Road when school opened. Once Helen went with him, to visit Jessie. By December, with the end near, he took leave from school to be with his mother. His brother George felt that Lawrence should have done more to help out but, in the event, it was the younger two, Lawrence and Ada, who kept the night vigil. Mrs. Lawrence was gray and shrunken. She looked like a fish, Lawrence thought. She refused water, had a mouth and throat infection, and could not even turn over. He put into her hands a copy of *The White Peacock,* which had just arrived, to hold so that she might see that he had written a book. Ada read her the inscription: "To my Mother, with love, D. H. Lawrence." She did not react.

IT is just as well. The novel is a horrendous indictment of the destructiveness of mothers. Those in the book who defy the gamekeeper's maxim—"When a man's more than nature he's a devil"—are the women. They are cruel. In the name of civilization, they fight nature, burn their chickens, beat their children, and enfeeble their sons and husbands.

Chiefly because of the oedipal plot of *Sons and Lovers*—son and mother allied against the father, son crippled by his mother's possessiveness—Lawrence has often been described as Freudian. But the primitive rage against mothers displayed in *The White Peacock* fits much better the schema of Freud's successor Melanie Klein, who placed the formative conflict much earlier, in the first year of life when the infant is driven to sadistic rages against the all-powerful mother and takes them out on her objectification, the breast.

It would be hard to find a better illustration of Klein's concept of the "damaged breast"—the angry infant's attack on the mother who pulls away when he most needs her—than the passage in *The White Peacock* where George strikes the cow "like a beaten woman" for withholding her milk. For good measure, George adds—almost as if Klein were prompting from the wings—"I should like to squeeze her until she screamed."

By the same light, the book's rejected title, "Nethermere," taken from the name of a dark pond in the story, carries overtones not only of the dank and dangerous nether regions of the body but also, in French, of the mother and the sea. All considered, "Nethermere" may not have been such a poor choice of title for a book which suggests that the maternal embrace is a sucking swamp from which men must struggle to escape.

LAWRENCE steeled himself for his mother's death in two ways. He copied pictures, and he asked Louie Burrows to marry him. When he first arrived at Eastwood in December to give full attention to his mother, he was copying a watercolor, *The Orange Market,* done by the English artist Frank Brangwyn in 1901. He found the activity beautiful and soothing but recognized that there was something odd about his reluctance to paint anything original. "Ada says I shall have to begin to paint for myself," he wrote Louie. "That seems very strange. I have no acquisitive facility. To possess property worries me."

The proposal came five days before his mother's death. He was sitting with Louie on a train from Leicester to Quorn when suddenly he asked her if she would marry him. Just as spontaneously, she accepted. A strong, pretty girl of twenty-three, with a snub nose, full flattish lips, a firm rounded chin, and a thin line of hair on her upper lip, she was, unlike Jessie, extroverted and cheerful. About six weeks before, on one of his weekends home, as she walked him to his train, he had quietly realized that she might do as a wife. When he got home, he tested the idea on his mother. Would it be "all right" if he married Louie? Mrs. Lawrence said, "No, I don't—" and then, after half a minute, "Well—if you think you'd be happy with her—yes." It was not exactly a blessing, more a sigh of relief that he had found someone other than Jessie.

He was detached enough from the event to write an account to "Mac," his bachelor colleague Arthur McLeod at the Davidson Road School, telling it with dialogue as if it were one of his own stories. Louie had asked him what he would like to do after Christmas and he said he did not know.

> "What would you like to do?" she asked, and suddenly I thought she looked wistful. I said I didn't know—then added, "Why, I should like to get married." She hung her head. "Should you?" I asked. She was much embarrassed, and said she didn't know. "I should like to marry you" I said suddenly, and I opened my eyes, I can tell you. She flushed scarlet.—"Should you?" I added. She looked out of the window and murmured huskily "What?".—"Like to marry me?" I said. She turned to me quickly, and her face shone like a luminous thing. "Later" she said. I was very glad.

Lawrence concluded the romantic tale with a wrenching account of his mother's agony, also reported with dialogue. When he turned her over, " 'Bert'—she said, very strange and childish and plaintive—half audible. 'It's very windy.' " She had just been able to discern that the house was banging and shaking. It was terrible to see her gray and sunken, approaching death by degrees.

To Louie he could not have made the connection between his impending loss and their engagement more clear. He apologized to her for not sounding happier. "I must feel my mother's hand slip out of mine before I can really take yours. She is my first, great love. She was a wonderful, rare woman—you do not know; as strong, and steadfast, and generous as the sun." And his mother had always liked Louie, Lawrence added, just as (small compliment to Louie) she had hated Jessie and would have risen from her grave to prevent him marrying her.

The proposal was almost as if timed to coincide with the death. Yet in terrible pain, moaning, Mrs. Lawrence hung on. What was the point of such suffering? Why had his father given his mother such a miserable life? Looking out of the window, he asked the landscape for an answer, and got none. Every day he wished she would die. Every morning she was still there. Misery turned to impatience. He waited for a week—at night he slept on the floor by her bed—then could bear it no longer. His brother, George, heard him beg Gillespie, the family doctor, "Can't you give her something to end it?"

"I can't," Gillespie replied. However, he did the kindness of leaving the sedative bottle behind. That night, taking turns, Lawrence and Ada fed their mother an overdose in her milk. That night, too, he began for the first time to sketch out a copy of the picture which played such an important part in his novel: Greiffenhagen's *Idyll,* the sensual representation of his fantasy of his parents. By morning—December 10, 1909— Lydia Lawrence was dead. Dr. Gillespie signed the death certificate; the informant was listed as "D. H. Lawrence, son, Present-at-the-Death."

The next step was to cut free of Jessie once and for all. Lawrence had already written her a letter telling her that he was betrothed to Louie. The day before his mother's funeral, he took Jessie for a long country walk, and delivered himself of one of the blunt declarations she knew too well. He began, "You know—I've always loved mother," and when Jessie protested that, of course, she understood, he cut in, "I don't mean that. I've loved her, like a lover. That's why I could never love you."

His attachment to his mother was not what upset Jessie but, rather, his choice of Louie, their mutual friend, who was undoubtedly ignorant of their sexual relationship. To Jessie's reproaches, Lawrence responded with a statement of his moral philosophy that she, in her subsequent writings, gave to the world: "With *should* and *ought* I have nothing to do."

These were strong words from someone who had just committed euthanasia. Yet guilt in the Christian sense was something he refused to accept. As he had told Jessie in the letter breaking the news of his engagement, "I can't help it, I'm made this way."

What was done was done. He organized his mother's funeral and began to think of the future. Marriage, now that he was committed to it, did not mean passion so much as money. The day after burying his mother, he wrote to Violet Hunt, asking how he might sell some of the short plays he had written. "Do tell me," he implored. "I want some money to get married. If I can't stick my head in some hole—c'est a dire, a woman's bosom—I soon shall be as daft as Dostoieffsky."

He signed off with an apology: "I'm afraid I'm incorrigibly ill-bred."

3

WAITING, PUZZLED

1911

*This eternal cultivation of the habit of going with-
out what one wants—needs—is very damnable.*
—D. H. Lawrence to Louie Burrows,
November 3, 1911

*B*ack at school the following week, just before the Christmas break,
Lawrence felt wretched, "physical, I suppose," he wrote Louie. But she
was never to worry about his health. If he were sick, she was to scold
him, because any illness would be only a ploy to luxuriate in her sympathy. He could hardly expect her to understand. "You are sane and
strong and healthy," he said enviously. He confessed, with a vampire
image that startled him, "Some savage in me would like to taste your
blood. Oh dear, you'll have to burn this."

He sketched vague plans for reorganizing his life so that they might
marry—teaching in a country school in Cornwall, perhaps? When Louie
vetoed this, he tried again and said that if he got the Cornwall job—it
paid £115 a year—she would have to come with him or go to the devil.
("I don't mean it," he continued nervously. "I'm on paper you see.")
Then he cheered himself by going up to London for Christmas shopping,
buying presents for all the children he knew, laughing to himself that the
shopgirls must think him the father of a large brood.

He and Ada spent the Christmas immediately following their mother's death at Brighton. He felt a duty to cheer his sister up. "She & I are very near to one another," he told Louie. "I would give a very great deal to make her even a bit happy," adding, "And I want comfort myself, like a kid, and cheering, like a tearful girl."

At Brighton he saw a sight new to him, dark skin. Three Indians at the boardinghouse were like "lithe beasts from the jungle." It was all very well for Louie to talk about the brotherhood of man, he wrote her two days after Christmas, "but a terrier dog is much nearer kin to us than those men with their wild laughter and rolling eyes. Either I am disagreeable or a bit barbaric myself: but I felt the race instinct of aversion and slight antagonism to those blacks, rather strongly."

While at Brighton Lawrence and his headmaster, Philip Smith, who was staying at another hotel, went for a day's tramp over the South Downs and stopped at a pub for lunch. The chance remark of another customer suddenly caused Lawrence to explode with rage. Smith was almost as cowed as the unfortunate stranger by the fury of the lightning attack.

Then Lawrence entered 1911, the year that may have been, as Jessie Chambers later said, the most arid of his life, but that was also one of the most important. He went north to see in the New Year with Louie at church, then resumed his Croydon life, outwardly enjoying himself, with opera and concerts, tea parties and dinners, walks over Richmond Park and Wimbledon Common, often accompanied by Helen Corke. But he was depressed, or, as he saw it, "dull, sleep-heavy, unwell." Since his mother's death, he had been overwhelmed by the meaninglessness of life. In a letter to the Congregational minister in Eastwood who had been his mother's good friend and to whom he wrote because Ada was having trouble with their father—"he's old, and stupid, and very helpless"—Lawrence described his own cold creed: man was just another organism in the indifferent march of evolution. "We crawl, like blinking sea creatures, out of the Ocean, onto a spur of rock, we creep over the promontory bewildered and dazzled and hurting ourselves, then we drop in the ocean on the other side: and the little transit doesn't matter so much."

His engagement did nothing to cheer him. It was an epistolary affair, with Louie 150 miles to the north, in a new post as headmistress of a school in Gaddesby, Leicestershire. Lawrence wrote her regularly, as he had his mother, working hard to convince himself that he would become a respectable English paterfamilias. But the correspondence did not bring out the best in him. Although Louie was highly intelligent (holding the college "distinction" in English that had eluded him) and a dedicated campaigner for women's voting rights, she was also conventional, highly religious, and easily shocked. His letters to her were forced and matey; rich in detail, low in feeling.

It was to Ada that he confided his darker thoughts—his hatred of Eastwood, his worries about their father, and his own unshakable gloom. "Sometimes I have a fit of horrors which is very hard to put up with. It is often a case of living by sheer effort." And to Ada he could admit his reservations about Louie. Louie, the daughter of a wood-carver and crafts teacher, had grown up in the peace of a lovely rural English village where her large and happy family lived in an ivy-covered house next to the church. Louie therefore knew nothing, Lawrence told Ada, of the "horror of life, and we've been brought up in its presence: with father." He told his sister that she need never be jealous of Louie, who did not understand one bit. "You are my one, real relative in the world: only you. I am yours: is it not so?"

Sexual frustration added to his burden. No relief was in sight. He was physically attracted to Louie, and had been even at college, but knew that she would not allow herself to act as Jessie had done. Legitimate sexual satisfaction would have to be purchased through careful saving. The equation was clear: no sex without marriage; no marriage without money. His only recourse was to convert his passion into industry. "Work is a fine substitute for a wife," he wryly told Louie.

In some respects he understood himself very well. He had no patience. What he wanted he had to have immediately; this was a dangerous single-mindedness, to be sure: "I go straight, like a bullet, towards my aim . . . I am a nuisance and a trouble to everybody." But (his guiding philosophy) "it doesn't alter me what I am." All men were like that, he told Louie. Having so swiftly applied the balm of betrothal to the wound of his loss, however, he did not notice how his impatience had increased since his mother's death.

Lawrence's real vices were ambivalence, grandiloquence, and irascibility. Torn so many ways within himself, he could blast off in any direction, with vivid expressions that stuck in the mind. This facility led him to talk about his friends behind their backs, mocking one to the other, or giving highly different accounts of the same event. Inevitably the varying versions collided. It was a sure way to lose friends and gave Lawrence, wherever he went, a reputation for duplicity.

But poor Louie Burrows, stuck in her little Church of England school in Leicestershire, took her fiancé's words at face value. When he wrote that he longed to see her, she came to London for a weekend (refusing to stay with the Joneses, so that Lawrence had hastily to arrange accommodation with a woman teacher in Croydon). Yet as soon as he saw her, he wanted to run away—an impulse that he disloyally related to Jessie Chambers, with whom he was still corresponding. Yet no sooner was Louie back in the Midlands than he again wrote her to say that he really wanted her very badly indeed. He swore that he would be a good husband.

He talked against Louie also to Helen, with the ulterior motive of seduction. He explained to Helen that while Louie had "the common everyday rather superficial man of me," she, in contrast, was privileged to know "the open-eyed, sad critical, deep-seeing man of me." In other words, Helen—who unlike Louie was passionate, sexually experienced, intellectually combative—ought to be willing to give their "soul-intimate" companionship physical expression.

Helen was unpersuaded, and Lawrence was furious. She kissed him readily enough, and put her arms around him: "Now if you can tell me any difference between this and the ultimate, I shall thank you."

This sexual charade took place in the spring of 1911. By then, if not on her visit to London the previous year, Alice Dax had got him to bed. This cocky Liverpudlian freethinker, with her wispy hair, angular face, and bold eyes, had survived Eastwood by shocking it. A milkman was said to have seen her once without stockings. She refused to decorate her home like the rest; she wanted everything stark, hygienic, and simple. She disdained carpets in favor of bare floors; her furniture was oak instead of mahogany. She owned no knickknacks or glass vases—nothing to catch the dust—and her insistence on drapes instead of the traditional Nottingham lace curtains so offended the populace that there were threats to break her windows.

After five years of marriage and one child, Alice knew what she needed to know about sex and contraception. She knew, too, that there was more to passion than she enjoyed with her dull pharmacist husband, Harry; she had married him when he asked her because everybody assured her that with her looks it was the only chance she would get. Her close friend in Eastwood was Sallie Hopkin, the wife of Lawrence's friend and mentor Willie Hopkin, and it was to Sallie that Alice reported, "I gave Bert sex. I had to. He was over at our house, struggling with a poem he couldn't finish, so I took him upstairs and gave him sex. He came downstairs and finished the poem."

Louie, who was jealous of Jessie's continuing relationship with Lawrence, seems to have known nothing about the Dax affair, nor about the pursuit of Helen Corke. John Jones probably did. Jones took a very dim view of his lodger's sexual activities. These may have included other women still undiscovered, either because they did not save his letters or because he did not send them any (even Lawrence did not write letters to everybody). What is indisputable is that, by the time he was twenty-five, his sexual experience was slight and his confidence slighter still.

BUT there was nothing lacking in his self-assurance as a writer. His fault, as all his critics, from his teachers at Nottingham to Ford Madox Ford, had told him, lay in being too lush, too descriptive. He tried to tone himself down. Poems, stories, reviews continued to pour out in an un-stoppable flow, even though after his mother's death he found himself unable to resume his new novel and was ill much of the time.

The colds went on longer than the intervals between them. What he later called "his sick year" began in January 1911 with a cold that made him sound like "a croaking crow." March saw another, "a damned cold which hangs on abominably. I'll really have a go at shifting it this week," he promised Ada. But in April he still had it, or perhaps it was a new one, and with it low spirits that led him to curse the English climate, which he began to blame not only for his health but for his troubles with women. He dreamed of the warm south: "I swear I'll flee to the tropics first opportunity," he wrote Louie, telling her she would look well in a scarlet bandana. With May came more misery: "I've got a grinning skull-and-crossbones headache. The amount of energy required to live is—how many volts a second?" He was tired, lacked the strength "to get my muscle up". He took to his bed; in fact, he swore to Louie, "I do nothing to the detriment of my physical well-being: I go to bed early, eschew pleasures of all kinds, I keep a cheerful frame of mind; I do nothing in excess, nor work, nor read, nor think, nor eat, nor drink, nor smoke."

Four furies were tearing him apart: sex, grief, illness, and the compulsion to write. Sometimes he could not tell which was which. Ironically, it was at school that he felt safe and secure. He warmed to the sound of the boys singing in the hall; he laughed as they acted out *As You Like It* in the classroom, jostling and bumping into the desks. "While I am at school," he told Louie, "I never wish myself anywhere else, " adding, "There's nothing so decent and amiable as boys."

Those were the rare good moments. Sometimes he was so unhappy he could hardly eat. By then he recognized that he simply could not adjust to the loss of his mother. Every day he wore his black mourning suit to school. The sorrowful poems poured forth, changing from immediate grief ("To My Mother—Dead"; "My Love, My Mother") to (in "In Trouble and Shame") the wish to cast off his own body—"Like luggage of some departed traveller"—to fantasies of joining her ("Call into Death"; "Troth with the Dead").

Even to Helen, writing to her when he was home at Eastwood for Easter in April, he allowed himself uncharacteristic morbidity. He had become so indifferent to life, he said, that death seemed to be "the one beautiful and generous adventure left." His phrase echoed J. M. Barrie's Peter Pan, who, abandoned on the pirates' island, says bravely: "To die will be an awfully big adventure."

As so often when Lawrence felt low, his picture-copying intensified and pushed writing into second place. Obsessively, he copied four times the Greiffenhagen picture that he had first begun the night his mother died. "Strange," he remarked in a letter to Louie, "when I can write I can't paint, and vice versa." When it went well, the painting had a soothing effect. Sometimes he painted for an entire day. But painting, too, could go wrong. One day after copying a Corot, he felt he had spoiled the picture and tore it into thirty pieces.

It was mid-March before he could bring himself to work on the autobiographical "Paul Morel" again. As with his first novel, he personified it: he was going to do "a bit of Paul" or "a scrap of Paul." As for his painting, he told Louie, as he had told Ada, "I would do original stuff—but it is impossible."

Yet the warm living world seemed to recede. He put it starkly in a closing sentence in a letter to Louie: "Goodbye—this room's as cold as the grave. I guess you're nice and warm ... Addio—I can hear Sammarco in *Traviata* 'Addi-i-i-o'." (Mario Sammarco was a popular baritone of the time.)

Fearful of his own frailty, he admired a big strapping girl like Louie. In June, writing to her about the performance at Covent Garden of Nellie Melba as the consumptive Mimi in *La Bohème,* he was not changing the subject as much as he thought when, a few sentences later, he begged Louie, "Don't get thin—I like you to get fat—dont get any thinner. I am a Turk—like my houri plump."

WAS Lawrence even in 1911 secretly afraid of tuberculosis—the "wasting disease," which cruelly attacked the young, and doomed them to early death? The symptoms were common knowledge. Keats, medically trained at London's Guy's Hospital, described them with clinical accuracy in "Ode to a Nightingale": "Youth grows pale, and spectre-thin, and dies."

The belief that consumptives were more passionate than other mortals made them staple characters of nineteenth-century operas and novels. With dark, burning eyes, chalky pallor, flushed cheeks, with wild outbursts of frenzy and bizarre fantasies, the victims exuded heightened sexuality. The last odes of Keats, with their feverish ecstasy and despairing pursuit of unconsummatable love, are full of these signals of terminal tuberculosis, as are the arias of the dying Violetta and Mimi in *La Traviata* and *La Bohème,* two cautionary tales of unmarried women punished by tuberculosis for breaking the sexual conventions.

The romance of consumption was heightened by its supposed predilection for genius. The fates of Chekhov, Chopin, Poe, Robert Louis Stevenson, Emily Brontë, and Shelley (drowned in Italy, where he was seeking a cure for his lungs) were part of popular legend, the poignancy of early death heightened by the desperate race to cram a life's work into a few short years. No wonder Lawrence did not like Ford calling him a genius.

No wonder, either, that he was worried about the rages that swept

over him, like fires, out of nowhere. He warned Louie that "my temper is so sudden and impetuous, I am astonished. Not irritability—
inflammability." But his internal fire, he insisted, was caused by the
"accumulation of dissatisfied love" in his veins—a condition for which
he held Louie responsible. "I should like to suggest all the—you would
say wicked—plans in the world. I say, only that is wicked which is a
violation of one's feeling and instinct." Another day, longing to feel
her body close to his, he described himself as a "black coal bubbling
red into fire."

For Lawrence, the cold, in and out of the house, reminded him fright-
eningly of the tomb, a word that appears in his letters again and again.
His room was "cold as the tomb"; the June nights were "cold as the icy
tomb." He assured Louie that he would be recovered by the following
week when she came to London for a women's suffrage parade (which
was to attract forty thousand people and stretch for five miles). The
week after that he would return to Eastwood for the week's holiday to
celebrate the coronation of George V.

LOUIE, for her part, was more worried about Lawrence's habits than his
health. Her parents were unhappy about the engagement and saw Lawrence as an irreligious rascal. As if to prepare her defense, Louie badgered him with questions—Did he smoke? Did he drink? Would he go to
church with her when they were married? He kept reassuring her that he
did nothing to excess, that he only drank enough to chase away the
blues, smoked very lightly and had, in short, "no vicious tendencies, I
believe: save an inclination to blundering forwardness."

Now that he was engaged, Lawrence was more worried about the
balance of power in marriage. Like many of his time, he was wrestling
with the apparent irreconcilability of sexual equality with the husband's
traditional position as head of the family. There was nothing equivocal
about his own firm support of voting rights for women. His best women
friends were active campaigners for enfranchisement, as well as being
(apart from Alice Dax) what were called bachelor women—unmarried,
self-supporting. Even Ada earned her living, and paid many of their
father's bills (Lawrence helped, too) on her salary of seventy-five pounds
a year.

Yet Lawrence was not immune from the contemporary male fear of
sexual anarchy, the biggest obstacle to women's enfranchisement. The
social order was seen to be founded on a sharp division of the sexes into
breadwinners and homemakers. If the distinction collapsed, the family
might decline; the underpopulation of Britain might even result. Men
would scold "suffragettes" passing out votes-for-women leaflets on street
corners, telling them they should be at home looking after children

instead. Accordingly, when Louie boasted to Lawrence that she was learning to cook and bake, he was patronizingly approving. In their marriage, as he envisaged it, "I'd be the 'captain bold' and you could be all the rest."

But no date was set. Lawrence and Louie both agreed on the sensible course followed by Ada and most engaged couples of their time. The wedding was postponed until a decent sum of money had been saved up. But when Lawrence began to increase the size of the stipulated sum, from one hundred pounds to one hundred and fifty, plus a nest egg of one hundred more, Louie began to be uneasy. He was spending, not saving. The goodly sum of ten pounds which the *English Review* paid for the story "Odour of Chrysanthemums" went toward supporting his father, which Louie could hardly begrudge, but also on a totally unnecessary gift of five pounds to a friend whose wife needed a gynecological operation. Louie's hopes for the necessary extra infusion of capital were now fixed on the new novel, "Paul," and she nagged Lawrence to get on with it.

He snapped back. "Am I a newspaper printing machine to turn out a hundred sheets in half an hour?"

He still intended to go through with the marriage, but seethed at the price men were expected to pay for socially sanctioned sex. Helen Corke bore the brunt. They were still seeing each other regularly—arguing all the time. He had some condoms—"little articles of temptation that Jones gave me months back"—but to no avail. When Helen said no yet one more time, Lawrence disconsolately threw the little articles over St. James's railway bridge and then exploded in an angry letter.

With a frankness he never accorded Louie, he told Helen that, although he could never completely love either her or Louie, Louie at least would leave him free. "And I *cannot* marry save where I am not held." By now marriage and money were so firmly entwined in his mind that, in a vow written at nearly one o'clock in the morning, he spat out his acceptance that women had their "market price": "I will never ask for sex relationship again, never, unless I can give the dirty coin of marriage: unless it be a prostitute, whom I can love because I'm sorry for her."

He continued to see Helen all the same, and introduced her to his brother George, who came to London for a visit. George thought Helen a tartar. A highly religious man, he rounded on her for making caustic remarks during an organ recital. Lawrence was delighted. "There, you bloody little cat, that settles you," he told Helen.

Lawrence's seething anger against reproving women spilled over into a bitter narrative poem in dialect. In "Whether or Not," a young woman cries to her mother that her fiancé has made his landlady—a widow of forty-five—pregnant. How, the girl asks, shuddering at the thought of the widow's dry yellow skin, could he have done it? Back comes the sour answer: "My gel, owt'll do for a man i' th'dark." Yet the girl wants to marry her Timmy nonetheless. She tells him that she forgives him, and hints that her father might get him a job in a bank. But he is on the spot; the widow, too, demands marriage. The poem ends with Timmy rejecting them both: the old one is too possessive, the young one too righteous. "Talk about love o' women!" he says. "Ter me it's no fun." And he walks away a free man.

Lawrence, in spite of his ease in talking with and writing about women, did not understand them. He attributed their sexual inhibitions to an innate, controlling coldness. He had only contempt for the way Louie placed parts of her body out of bounds. In "Hands of the Betrothed" he scoffed, using images of commerce:

> . . . yet if I lay my hand in her breast
> She puts me away, like a saleswoman whose mart is
> Endangered by the pilferer on his quest.

He mocked Louie's fear that she had flung herself too much at him. "I only wish you flung yourself a bit farther," he said dryly. His simmering anger at Louie's tenacious virginity that summer produced the powerful poem "Snap-Dragon." A girl in a white dress teasingly invites her lover into the garden, where she makes sport of the snapdragon's bifurcation. The young man takes up the game, but more roughly:

> I pressed the wretched, throttled flower between
> My fingers, till its head lay back, its fangs
> Poised at her. Like a weapon my hand was white and keen . . .

The girl pleads "Don't!" and tells him to stop. He does, but exults:

> . . . I bade her eyes
> Meet mine, I opened her helpless eyes to consult
> Their fear, their shame, their joy that underlies
> Defeat in such a battle.

He did not see the poem as a metaphor for rape; he saw no excuse for women holding back, especially as he fervently believed that the balance of power lay in the woman's favor. "When a man & a woman are together—the man is always the younger," he wrote Louie (twenty-two to his twenty-five). The supremacy of women, to him, was a natural injustice.

In his fiction, marriage, rather than death, was the "awfully big adventure." His two finished novels and "Paul Morel" were about the terrible choice between heart and head, or, as he put it, between "sex sympathy" and "soul sympathy." A harmonious resolution seemed an impossible ideal, its pursuit the most important goal in life. In 1911 he also wrote the first version of a long story of two sisters, eventually published as "Daughters of the Vicar," a stark moral fable illustrating the wrong way (a sensible, loveless marriage) and the right (abandoning all for love).

But how to achieve "soul sympathy" if the sexes were fundamentally incompatible? As he had once tried to persuade Blanche Jennings:

> Now a woman's soul of emotion is not so organised, so distinctly divided and active in part as a man's. Set a woman's soul vibrating in response to your own, and it is her whole soul trembles with a strong, soft note of uncertain quality. But a man will respond, if he be a friend, to the very chord you strike, with clear and satisfying timbre, responding with a part, not the whole, of his soul. It makes a man much more satisfactory.

Fondness for the little Jones girls began to turn into a desire for children of his own. Reproaching Louie, he told her how Hilda Mary "removes my bracelet, wipes my nose, and kisses me thrice. That's one better than your two." He thought her "the prettiest youngster in all England" and wished that "she were my own and thine." Ill in bed late in May, he had one of the vivid early-morning dreams that had begun to plague him. He had to break into French to describe it to Louie, it was so personal. She was giving birth to their first child, and suffering such great pain that he could feel his own insides dissolving. Then out came a boy, with blue eyes. But when Louie showed him the child, Lawrence turned into a black shadow and Louie into his sister Emily. (Emily's first child had been stillborn.)

Waking, he could still recapture the sound of Louie's moaning and his joy on seeing the child. He told Louie: "To be your husband is my supremest wish." But one accompaniment to marriage was intolerable. "It seems to me inconceivable that I should own property: a house," he warned his bride-to-be. "It will have to be yours." Yet he was never less than affectionate, and signed his letters with little phrases in German, such as "Gut Nacht, meine lieben Schatz. (Brahms)."

THE *White Peacock* was published in January 1911, shortly after their engagement, and Louie proudly showed it around to her friends as the work of the man she was to marry.

The reviewers were remarkably acute; their judgments on Lawrence's first novel would stand for his completed work. They saw a startling mixture of genius and eloquence with aimlessness and banality. *The*

Observer called the book "strange and disturbing with elements of greatness."

The critics also spotted sexual uncertainty. "To begin with, what is the sex of 'D. H. Lawrence'?" asked the *Morning Post,* suspecting that another George Eliot might be disguised behind the initials; "the particular way in which physical charm is praised almost convinces us that it is the work of a woman."

They noticed the social ambiguity as well. "In what milieu does the author live? . . . Do they really discuss Ibsen and Aubrey Beardsley in the farmhouses of the Trent Valley?" And what was Lawrence trying to say about marriage with "these pictures of wasted lives and ill-matched marriages"? Was he a new prophet of "the old fallacy of returning to Nature"?

No one could deny the formidable powers of physical description exhibited in *The White Peacock.* The *Daily News*'s reviewer declared,

> At its best, it is eloquent—intolerably so. Its cloying descriptiveness is varied by incidents of . . . "brutality." D. H. Lawrence is fond of that word. On page 18 a cat is caught in a trap by both forefeet. . . . In *The White Peacock* the sick thoughts are always there although the day be spring and the clouds high.

Lawrence, as his first novel made immediately apparent, was no logical thinker. He relied instead on simile and metaphor to establish relations between things. This addiction infuriated one reviewer, who noted sourly: "D. H. Lawrence does not seem to be able to conceive of anything without making it 'like' something else."

The White Peacock, an uneven early work obscured by Lawrence's later books, retains the beauty and power that so impressed E. M. Forster not long after its first publication:

> There is [a passage] in *The White Peacock* which is no more than a catalogue of the names of flowers yet it brings the glory of summer nearer to me than could pages of elaborate poetry. That [book] is altogether a remarkable product—so very absurd and incompetent as a novel, the narrator recounting conversations that he could never have heard, and the characters changing not only their natures but their outward appearances at the author's whim. Yet how vivid the impression it leaves!

The critics of that pre-Freudian era were not as blinkered on sexual matters as a later age imagines. They understood that the scene of the peacock defiling a gravestone represented a dark association of the female sex with excrement. "The White Peacock metaphor smears the whole book," said the *Daily News.* "Life itself, as well as woman, would appear to be all vanity, screech, and defilement."

Yet none remarked on the love that all but shouts its name in the relationship between the novel's virile hero, George, and the narrator, Cyril. The two young men plunge into a millpond for a June morning swim before haying. When they emerge, they rub themselves dry, and Cyril admires George's "handsome physique, heavily limbed." Then comes the first of the often-quoted homoerotic passages in Lawrence's novels that still puzzle those trying to understand the nature of his sexuality.

> He saw I had forgotten to continue my rubbing, and laughing he took hold of me and began to rub me briskly, as if I were a child, or rather, a woman he loved and did not fear. I left myself quite limply in his hands, and, to get a better grip of me, he put his arm round me and pressed me against him, and the sweetness of the touch of our naked bodies one against the other was superb. It satisfied in some measure the vague, indecipherable yearning of my soul; and it was the same with him. When he had rubbed me all warm, he let me go, and we looked at each other with eyes of still laughter, and our love was perfect for a moment, more perfect than any love I have known since, either for man or woman.

The writer Compton Mackenzie many years later recalled Lawrence saying that he had never known perfect love except with a young miner. If Mackenzie mistook, for understandable reasons, the word "farmer" for "miner," the loved one would have been Jessie's brother Alan Chambers, whom Lawrence acknowledged to be "the original of my George."

The good folk of Eastwood seem not to have noticed any hint of unnatural love. But they did recognize themselves. Lawrence pulled a very thin disguise over local people and places. Felley Mill—a well-known landmark on the way to Haggs Farm—appeared as "Strelley Mill," while Lawrence's old school friend Alice Hall was easily identified as the outspoken "Alice Gall." Alice's new husband talked of suing: Lawrence's first brush with the law.

IN the summer of 1911 the threesome of Louie, Lawrence, and Ada, plus five others including Alice "Gall" Hall, went on their carefully planned holiday to Prestatyn on the North Wales coast. Lawrence was quite fed up with the persistent demands of Louie's family for information about the sleeping arrangements on the holiday. In fact, they all lodged chastely with the relatives of a Methodist minister, and when Lawrence later visited the Burrowses at Quorn, he was able to swear that the proprieties had been kept.

But his virtue was feigned. In the interval between Prestatyn and Quorn, he had taken his bicycle (because a national rail strike had halted the trains) and pedaled to visit the Daxes, who had moved to Shire-brook, about eight miles from Eastwood. He told Louie that he found the Daxes "very well." In all probability it was only Mrs. Dax who was the object of the visit. The scenes in *Sons and Lovers* of Paul making love in a field to a married woman called Clara, as peewits circle overhead, may be snapshots of unrecorded moments of Lawrence's 1911 summer holiday.

Back at Colworth Road in September, Lawrence found that the lease on number twelve had expired and that the Joneses had decided to move just two doors away to number sixteen. Lawrence was enlisted to hang pictures and put up shelves. So much was he part of the family that the Joneses even took into the household Lawrence's new dog; the warden at the nearby children's home had given it to him. The dog's name was Fritz and Lawrence reported to Louie, "He is such a jolly little chap, black, with white paws and very frisky. I like him very much. He is weeping on the hall-mat because Mrs Jones has gone out."

But domestic life was no less tense at number sixteen than at number twelve. The new house, Sunnybrae, was not very sunny, although it was at the end of the row. They all lived in the kitchen—"small, bare and ugly, because the electric isn't connected up—all too poor to have it done," Lawrence reported. And John Jones, far from being impressed with Lawrence's growing literary success at having two short stories ("Odour of Chrysanthemums" and "A Fragment of Stained Glass") published in the *English Review,* pompously lectured him on how to make a fortune in literature. To Lawrence his landlord looked ugly. Jones had shaved off his mustache, and a small mean mouth emerged—"like a slit in a tight skin." He had liked Jones before; he did not like him now. As Lawrence hammered and sawed away, he was full of wistful dreams—that he would not be lodging with the Joneses in two years' time, that he could give up schoolteaching for writing, and as he told Louie (contradicting his views on property), "I wish, in some little country house of our own, you were lighting the lamp for me. *Mein Gott!*"

Back at school for the autumn term he felt heavy and listless. With dull pupils and two days of visits by school inspectors, what he called his "breathing apparatus" hurt worse than ever. Images of fire flamed. In spite of the unseasonably warm September, he had "a cold like hell—feel as if my long pipe were a stove chimney got red hot."

As usual, the worse he felt the harder he worked. "Oh my dear Lord I am so tired," he wrote Jessie Chambers's sister. ". . . But I shall work it off." Thoughts of death encroached. He dreaded a social evening in which he would be required to help entertain a Frenchman who "speaks such glutinous French I have to struggle like grim death to make a grain of meaning out." He feared that marking blue exercise books would be the death of him. When news reached him that a woman novelist who had admired *The White Peacock* had, as he put it, "gone away into Death," he was very upset, as if she were somehow taking the book along to show his mother, who, he recalled, had never read it. He promised Ada that the two of them would go somewhere "seaside" at Christmas.

IN September 1911 Lawrence sent the *English Review* two more short stories. One appeared the following February, but the other, which was returned, Lawrence judged to be "wicked" but "clever."

Selected for publication was "Second Best," a story of two sisters in which the elder, the beauty of the family, hearing that the young man she is in love with is engaged to someone else, decides to marry an amiable bumpkin of vulgar speech. It shows how, despite his relative inexperience at the age of twenty-six, he was looking at the man-woman relation from very close range and writing with more irony than he is generally given credit for. The girl, Frances, deliberately decides to marry Tom as she cannot have Jimmy. "But, in her deeper self, she knew her own understanding far exceeded his; that he would not, could not, pioneer her into the inner, half-dreadful intimacy and experience, for which she yearned."

But she takes second best: something is better than nothing. To meet his dare, Frances kills a mole—and scares Tom with her boldness. She laughs in his face, which is suddenly "helpless and wistful."

"Do you care for me?" he asked, in a low, shame-faced tone.
She nestled her face on his bosom, with a shaky laugh. She badly wanted fondling, caressing, soothing. He caressed her very tenderly.

Chalk up another victory for the scheming woman.

THE autumn was brightened by an exciting new friendship. Lawrence's literary career had blossomed to the point where he was under pressure to produce. The London publisher Martin Secker offered to publish a collection of his stories. Lawrence could foresee his income from writing rising so that not only might he get married but he might leave teaching. He wrote every spare minute, in school as well as at home.

In August, thinking perhaps he might break into the American market, he had started a correspondence with the well-known publishers' reader Edward Garnett, who was searching for good short stories for the

Century Company in New York. Lawrence sent along a story called "Intimacy" and Garnett was frank, calling it slow and rough. Far from taking offense, Lawrence showed him another, "Two Marriages," with apologies for its length and slow bits. "I tried to do something sufficiently emotional, and moral and—oh American!" he said, and not only offered in advance to revise it but to dash up to London at lunchtime to see Garnett at his office at the publishers, Duckworth, so that Garnett could get a look at him. But, explaining "I teach school, in Croydon," he warned Garnett, with apologies, that he would have to keep strictly within the bounds of an hour if he were to be able to get to Charing Cross and back to his classroom on time.

Garnett was as delighted as Ford had been with his find. He was on the lookout for new work and had an astute but not infallible eye. When Garnett saw Lawrence he was instantly taken, as he later said, with his "lovableness, cheekiness, intensity and pride." He also recognized Lawrence's great talent (of which new examples were soon arriving by post, including a play, *The Widowing of Mrs. Holroyd*). Unhesitating, Garnett invited Lawrence to spend that very weekend at his country house not far from Croydon, and Lawrence accepted.

Garnett's house, called the Cearne, was set in a wooded beauty spot on the Surrey-Kent border inhabited by a colony of Fabian socialists—believers in free love, fresh air, and coeducation. Getting there was half the fun: a three-mile walk from Oxted station through wooded lanes overlooking the Weald of Kent, with the last half mile down a dusty cart track.

The house had been built by a disciple of William Morris, an architect called Cowlishaw, whose aim was to achieve medieval rusticity with modern techniques. The Cearne was Cowlishaw's first house, and what it lacked in convenience—the staircase rose at an odd angle from the living room, the stone corbels over the fireplace projected so far that people struck their heads as they ducked into the inglenook, the toilet was outside the back door—it made up in ideology. Cowlishaw, who worked in an artisan's smock, was so committed to recreating the spirit of a nobler yesterday that he designed an open space in the roof to let out the smoke over the fire. Garnett and his wife, Constance, a woman of independent means, crassly insisted on a chimney instead. Otherwise, they gave Cowlishaw his head. The Cearne had hand-hewn beams, hand-wrought iron hinges and door latches, hard window seats of unpainted wood. Everything was handmade and unpainted, and the furnishing was austere: oak table, thick plates, stone jars. Lawrence was enchanted.

It was his first country weekend spent with the English upper middle classes, and he arrived clutching a batch of poems desperately polished during the evenings of the preceding week. "Garnett" for him was a name to be reckoned with. His boyhood reading in Eastwood had been shaped by the twenty-volume *International Library of Famous Literature,* edited by Garnett's father, which stood on the family shelves. (Lawrence at first thought that Edward, rather than his father, Richard, Keeper of the Printed Books at the British Museum, was responsible for the vast work, published in 1899.) As a boy Lawrence reverentially had devoured nuggets of the world's great books from the green-bound set, bought by his brother Ernest from his earnings as a clerk.

The weekend was a great success. The two men, seated in the inglenook, drank red wine and talked until the small hours. Garnett was delighted to see Lawrence's pleasure in the house and the landscape, and Lawrence soaked up the praise of his work.

Lawrence gave a full report to Louie, describing Garnett's flattery— "He praises me for my sensuous feeling in my writing"—as if he had not recognized it himself. He also gave Louie a sketch of the Garnetts' fond but highly unconventional marriage. Garnett lived most of the week at the Cearne and had a long-standing mistress, cheerfully tolerated by Mrs. Garnett, who was six years older than her husband and led a largely separate existence in London, translating Russian books and raising their young son, David. It was another lesson for Louie, who had already heard about Ford Madox Ford and Violet Hunt, in how progressive-minded couples ordered their affairs.

That weekend moved Edward Garnett to the top of the list of correspondents to whom Lawrence poured out his inner thoughts and sent regular bulletins on his deteriorating health. Something was very wrong with him, and he blamed the central heating at Davidson Road: "This last fortnight I have felt really rotten—it is the dry heat of the pipes in school, and the strain—and a cold," he wrote Garnett. "I must leave school, really." At the same time he reproached himself for a writing block. He resolved to begin his novel for the third time although he felt heavy and sick—as if "I'd got lead in my veins." He warned Louie that his career was wrecking his health and his writing: "I am really very tired of school—I can*not* get on with Paul. I am afraid I shall have to leave—and I am afraid you will be cross with me . . . and I loathe to plead my cause."

In November Garnett, aware that Lawrence was extremely run-down, invited him for a second weekend at the Cearne. Lawrence, worried as usual about his Christmas shopping, as well as his failure to progress with "Paul," much looked forward to it. An added attraction was the promised fellow guest: Rolfe Scott-James, literary editor of the *Daily News.* Lawrence was not disappointed by this visit. He listened while Garnett, warmed by wine and the fire, spoke expansively to Scott-James on the theme of Lawrence's genius—how Lawrence's mining background led to "that fearless exposure of body and soul which was the reality of creative art."

Instead of restoring Lawrence, however, the country weekend nearly killed him. He caught a cold as he walked in the rain from Oxted station to the Cearne; then he chopped wood in wet clothes, and finally, on his way home, had a long lonely wait on the station platform. It was a situation in which a young man could easily feel motherless. When he got back to Croydon, he fell into bed.

The next morning, Monday, he could not get up. Jones sarcastically diagnosed a bad hangover from "drinking with the big wigs of the literary world." The school was telephoned, the doctor called. It was no hangover. Lawrence had caught the pneumonia which was to break his life in two.

Years later, he looked back at the illness in November 1911 as the culmination of his "sick year," in which "everything collapsed, save the mystery of death, and the haunting of death in life." "From the death of my mother," he wrote, "the world began to dissolve around me, beautiful, iridescent, but passing away substanceless. Till I almost dissolved away myself, and was very ill."

Only two days before the pneumonia struck, however, he described his impending collapse more concretely. "My mouth," he wrote Louie, "seems to be lifted blindly for something, and waiting, puzzled."

It was the cry of an abandoned suckling—waiting, puzzled, for a mother who would never return.

4

NOT YET CONSUMPTION

November 1911–Spring 1912

> *'Tis not yet Consumption I believe, but it would be*
> *were I to remain in this climate all the Winter; so I*
> *am thinking of either voyageing or travelling to*
> *Italy.*
>
> —John Keats, August 1820,
> six months before his death in Rome

*T*wo weeks from his collapse, Lawrence had traveled to death's door and back. "The only thing to fear now is a relapse," Ada wrote Garnett on December 2. But Lawrence willed himself a swift recovery. One day, egg on toast. Another, reading (flat on his back) two books for review; then, propped up against pillows, writing a short story and, through Ada, extracting the manuscript of "The Saga of Siegmund" from an unenthusiastic Heinemann and having it sent to the Cearne for Garnett to look at.

The doorbell at 16 Colworth Road rang constantly. The stream of visitors who trooped up to the bedroom found the invalid sitting in a chair wrapped in a shawl, apparently his old self apart from a fuzz of red beard. Soon the beard went, when his jolly nurse, having let him admire it in the glass, lathered him and handed him the razor so that he could shave.

Still, it was almost a month before Lawrence was able to walk to the bathroom. Ada sent the news delicately to Louie: "Mr Garnett is upstairs with Bert so I've seized the opportunity to get off a few letters. Bert actually made a short journey down the passage this morning hanging onto my shoulder." To Bert, however, the spectacle was rather less pathetic. "This morning I strolled into the bathroom," he wrote Louie, "prancing like the horses of the Walküre, on nimble air."

The visitors included his sister Emily, Garnett, and twin brothers from the school. Louie wanted to come down from the Midlands but the doctor, William Addey, a Croydon general practitioner, still ruled it out, perhaps on the sound medical ground that the sight of a fiancée would be too exciting. Lawrence promised the disappointed Louie that she could come with him and Ada when they went, as the doctor ordered, to Bournemouth. He could not wait to leave the house; suddenly he wanted to get away from the Joneses, even the children.

Ada did not welcome the women visitors who did come. On sight she disliked Helen Corke, with her pale face and sharp features, and thought to herself that "Nell Corke was the vampire type of female." She was hardly pleased either to see Jessie Chambers, who accompanied Helen, but she did concede that, with her dark hair and eyes, Jessie was beautiful—from the shoulders up.

For her part, Jessie, in London ostensibly to see Helen Corke, found her "David," whom she had scarcely seen for a year, a sad sight as he sat by his little fire, wiping his mouth with linen scraps and dropping them onto the coals. She observed that he was still obsessed with his mother.

For John Jones, Lawrence's illness was the last straw. With both Ada and the nurse in residence, his family could hardly call the house their own. Tempers frayed, the charwoman gave notice, and Lawrence coughed constantly. Dr. Addey took away a sputum sample for analysis.

Tuberculosis? The very hint was enough to make Lawrence persona non grata, not only at the Joneses' but at the Davidson Road School, where his poor health had been noticed soon after his appointment. Jones's official duties as superintendent of school attendance officers included monitoring local illnesses and epidemics for their effect on school attendance, and it would not have escaped his notice that Lawrence, even at his best, presented the classic picture of the consumptive: narrow shoulders, concave chest, and a thin high-pitched voice suggesting bellows too weak to pump the organ. For that matter, with all his doxies around, Lawrence fitted the bill of frenzied sexual passion as well.

Consumption was the great killer of the day, the cause of one in eleven deaths in England and Wales. It carried enormous stigma and threat of blackmail, spoiling chances of marriage, of promotion, and even of life insurance for the victim's whole family. The stigma thrived on the disease's association with illicit sex. During Lawrence's Croydon years, the English medical profession was campaigning to have consumption made a "notifiable" illness under the Contagious Diseases Act, passed in 1864 to curb the rampant venereal infections brought back by the British armed forces returning from the Crimea and India. (The law required compulsory treatment of prostitutes but not of the men who frequented them.)

Compulsory notification of cases of consumption was achieved in 1912 (after Lawrence left Croydon), and was highly unpopular. Patients shied away from doctors known to be sticklers for the law and sought instead lenient others, who would avoid the diagnosis if they could, and who would record a death as caused by "bronchitis" or "pneumonia" for the sake of the family. This widely practiced subterfuge concealed the true prevalence of the disease.

The shame attached to consumption was all the greater because of the disease's association with poverty and dirt. Although autopsies showed that most of the population carried the tuberculosis bacillus in their lungs, those who succumbed to it were mainly the poor who lived in unsanitary, overcrowded conditions—conditions that were considered somehow their own fault. This message was preached at them in no uncertain terms. In 1909, opening the Whitechapel Exhibition of Tuberculosis in London's teeming East End, John Burns, a member of Parliament and head of the Local Government Association, ringingly declared, "Generally speaking, consumption is the child of poverty, the daughter of ignorance, the offspring of drink, the product of carelessness."

The real terror of tuberculosis, of course, lay in its incurability. The only recourse for admitted sufferers was a long stay in a sanatorium or clinic in a climate considered restorative. The favored "fresh air" cure was harsh. Patients were forced to live in wooden huts or to lie out on balconies or in wards with open windows. Compulsory rest alternated with strenuous exercise for those who were able to do it, and all patients were virtually force-fed good, wholesome food. One sanatorium in Bavaria made its patients eat twelve eggs a day. Known consumptives too poor to afford private institutions were locked up by force, while even the wealthy felt themselves to be prisoners in the remote high-altitude clinics then fashionable from the Alps to the Rockies, where they accepted the Spartan regimes as a punishment for the sin of having fallen ill.

Lawrence was all too aware of the fate of so many of his Eastwood friends and neighbors. Two of his college friends had been sent away with consumption: Gertie Cooper, one of his student-teacher circle of "Pagans," and Hilda Shaw. Gertie was a former neighbor in Eastwood. All the women in her family seemed to be dying of the disease, one by one. Hilda, who was in the Ransom sanatorium at Mansfield, drew Louie a typical picture of life in "the San." A young patient who had received word that her mother was dying could not go home "unless she signs a paper that she goes against the Doctor's orders & so will be received in no other Sanatorium. Oh! Lou, I *can't* write more for everyone is crying."

Lawrence, who wrote long letters to Hilda, knew that in 1901 his mother had been warned by an Eastwood doctor that he was tubercular. From his Croydon sickbed in December 1911, therefore, he castigated himself repeatedly for his lingering invalidism. To Grace Crawford he wrote, "It *is* stupid to be ill—almost unpardonable," and to Edward Garnett, "If I am ever ill again, I shall die of mortification."

AWAITING the results of the sputum test, Ada and Lawrence conspired like children to ward off bad news. With Dr. Addey on the alert for the well-known symptom of persistent fever, Lawrence drank cold water day and night. Before he took his temperature, he gave his mouth an extra cold rinse. If the thermometer registered above normal, as on December 13, Ada did not record it. They would wait, Lawrence would swallow more cold water, "then lo, it is normal—a huge joke—the doctor gets so jumpy if I'm high," he wrote Louie. She wrote back scolding him.

All the same he did not husband his energies. His mind was racing with ideas. He had "The Saga of Siegmund" to revise—Garnett wanted to offer it to Duckworth, provided that it was rewritten and given a different title—and he had begun thinking about a collection of short poems. Somehow he felt compelled also to sketch an *Idyll* for his friend McLeod. He apologized to McLeod for not doing it in oil, "but the lumbering drawing-board was too much for me, damn it."

The combined efforts of brother and sister were rewarded when, eight days before Christmas, Dr. Addey reported that the test had proved negative. As Ada informed Garnett,

> My brother is now able to sit up for a short time each day, but is very weak. . . . The report concerning the expectoration was very satisfactory. No germs were discovered and since then both lungs have almost completely cleared up.
>
> Of course my brother will be very liable to consumption and as the doctors say will always need great care. He has to give up school too.

Lawrence said the same himself to Garnett: "The doctor says I mustn't go to school again or I shall be consumptive." (This was one of the few times in Lawrence's life that he mentioned himself and the disease in the same breath.) The meager evidence does not make it clear whether Dr. Addey, in telling him to give up teaching, was protecting Lawrence or the Davidson Road School. The Croydon school authorities were unlikely to have wanted him back if there was a hint of consumption. Yet Lawrence himself wanted to leave; with the prospect of publishing "The Saga," he believed he had a chance of making a living by writing.

In any event, the negative sputum test was no guarantee that Lawrence did not have pulmonary tuberculosis. A negative result occurred in many indisputable cases. Robert Louis Stevenson, seriously ill with the disease, tested negative in the winter of 1887–1888 when he turned up at Dr. Edward Trudeau's famed sanatorium at Saranac Lake in the Adirondack Mountains of New York State in the course of his global wanderings in search of a cure. A certain diagnosis, according to the best medical practice of the day, required an X ray of the chest.

Whatever his own thoughts about Lawrence's prognosis, Dr. Addey gave him the standard instruction to consumptives: not to marry for a long time, if ever.

ON Christmas Eve, at long last, Louie Burrows was allowed to approach Colworth Road, full of health and hope and carrying a plucked bird for their Christmas dinner. Lawrence went downstairs for the first time and, happy that the noisy Jones family had gone away, the two pairs of betrothed—Lawrence and Louie, Ada and her fiancé, Eddie Clarke, who had joined them—had the house to themselves. For propriety's sake Louie retreated for the night, as usual, to a woman teacher's home.

As before, after anticipating a visit from Louie, Lawrence was not glad to see her in the flesh. She irritated him with the way she kept rubbing her cheek against his, asking "Are you happy?" He was not. In his trembling state, still in the grip of what today would be called a near-death experience, he could only sense that somehow he had altered a great deal and that nothing could be the same again. Except Louie. She was the mixture as before—"passionate as a gipsy," he wrote Garnett, "but good, awfully good, churchy."

He and Louie had only about twelve days together. Expecting to come along with him and Ada to Bournemouth, when Ada withdrew because of the expense Louie had no choice but to do the same, and return to the Midlands. Before they parted, Lawrence impulsively invited her to marry him at once. Louie later claimed that she accepted without hesitation. But the proposal was unreal. Lawrence was in no position to carry it out. He left Croydon alone, with some bitter words to speed him on his way; Jones told him to take all his things with him and to get out for good.

IF the diagnosis was not yet consumption, Lawrence from January 1912 onward lived his life exactly as if it were. Short of consigning himself to a sanatorium, he followed all the instructions laid down in popular books such as *Advice to Consumptives* on how to behave. He sought the sun, the fresh air of sea or mountains; he stuffed himself with butter, eggs, and milk; and as far as he could, he avoided cities, especially the city known as "The Smoke."

In the late seventeeth century, Dr. Thomas Sydenham, author of *De Phthisi*, a medical textbook on consumption, observed, "By a peculiar infelicity of our air none are more subject to it than the inhabitants of London." In the early twentieth century, with the rise in population and the advent of coal-fired trains, London's air was less felicitous than ever. Dr. Addey told Lawrence that on no account was he to go into London en route from Croydon to Bournemouth; he was to make his way to the south coast direct.

The bracing but sheltered air of Bournemouth, near Southampton, was the nearest that England offered to the warmer climes favored by those with "chests." Once there, Lawrence entered into the spirit of the place and pushed himself hard. The legs that would not carry him downstairs in mid-December were soon taking him on long walks, and within days of arrival, he could boast on a postcard to Louie: "Can walk 1 1/2 miles like a bird." He had a rash, he said, but it went away.

He plunged, with his usual speed, into rewriting "The Saga of Siegmund," according to the instructions of Garnett, who wanted the florid language of the book toned down before showing it to Duckworth. He needed money. Having asked for a leave of absence from Croydon and always careful to avoid debt, he calculated that he could support himself for six months at home with the fifty pounds still owing him from *The White Peacock*. He did not want to take an advance from Duckworth for the new book; he would wait until it was published—in the spring, he hoped. However, it seemed sensible to put aside "Paul Morel," on which he had been working hard just before his illness, in order to get his second novel ready for the market.

But the threat of consumption was ever on his mind. In a casual letter to a Croydon friend, he recalled that Stevenson had also gone to Bournemouth as an invalid. To Jessie, so often a repository for his darker thoughts, he summed up the Bournemouth atmosphere:

> The place exists for the sick. They hide the fact as far as possible, but it's like a huge hospital. At every turn you come across invalids being pushed or pulled along. Quite a nice place of course, everything arranged for the comfort of the invalid, sunny sheltered corners and the like, but pah—I shall be glad when I get away.

Once he had settled in, Lawrence began to enjoy himself. Always interested in new faces, he found plenty to study at his large boarding-house. There was "a little Finn," and other "delightful folk, men and women," with whom he went out to tea and on excursions. He had to be on his guard against getting mixed up in other people's problems. As he told Garnett, "I run to such close intimacy with folk, it is complicating." He enjoyed being fussed over by the old ladies. He played games and cards in the recreation room—"the rec." In the evening he drank gin and bitters with his fellow boarders. During the day he worked hard on his book, either in the billiard room or in his bedroom, where he was pleased to find he had a fire. He ate, so he reported to Louie, as much as was decent, four meals a day, and drank hot milk, morning and night "like a good un." He particularly liked "the very prolific breakfasts—bacon and kidneys and ham and eggs."

In spite of all his precautions, only a month after his lungs had cleared, he caught a vicious cold that would not go away. He filled letter after letter with curses on it: "a damned cold," "such a rotten one," "a fierce and fiendish cold which lingers." He longed for news from the school, and his vivid, troubling dreams persisted, curiously making sense of the jumbled thoughts of his days.

After Bournemouth, he planned to return briefly to Croydon and to visit the Cearne; then, he told Garnett, "I shall go home to the midlands." He would bring the revised manuscript of the book that was now called *The Trespasser*. This title was finally agreed on after Garnett rejected Lawrence's other suggestions—including "Trespassers in Cythera" and "The Levanters"—and Lawrence had implored, "Help me out."

Lawrence had not forgotten his sometime mistress from Eastwood. He asked Helen Corke to send Alice Dax an article on evolution from the *Hibbert Journal,* a religious quarterly. (With the voracity of an autodidact, Lawrence read everything he could get his hands on.) The article in question, "Creative Evolution and Philosophic Doubt," by the statesman and humanist A. J. Balfour, examined the theories of the French philosopher Henri Bergson in a way much in accord with Lawrence's own thinking—that life struggles on, blindly but in a forward direction, toward the vague but discernible goal of more diverse forms of life. That Lawrence so much wished Alice to read it was a sign of their closeness; with his former self sliding off like an outworn skin, he nonetheless wanted to share with her this provocative reformulation of the purpose of life.

In mid-January 1912, halfway through his Bournemouth retreat, there arrived the invitation that changed his life. It came from Germany, from Hannah Krenkow, the German sister-in-law of his aunt Ada Krenkow in Leicester. Hannah was in her late thirties and married, recently but not happily, to the brother of Lawrence's German-born uncle by marriage, Fritz Krenkow. Hannah, having heard of Lawrence's illness, and probably of his charm and literary success as well, suggested to his aunt that he might like to spend the spring at Waldbröl near Cologne.

Instantly Lawrence fixed on the idea. He had never been abroad. Germany suggested health. He could speak a bit of German, although he was not as fluent as in French. Perhaps if he could acquire a living knowledge of both languages—so he rationalized to the long-suffering Louie, who was trying to make wedding plans—in the future he could go into secondary school teaching "at any time." Above all, he told Louie flatly, almost defiantly, "I want to go over sea."

With this new incentive and, as ever, writing like the wind, he redid the three hundred or so pages of *The Trespasser* by the end of January. He had thrown out a good deal of the beginning, including some of the cloying literariness and sentimentality that had so dismayed Ford Madox Ford. He had kept comparatively unchanged the strong ending—the part of the book that derived least from Helen Corke.

Helen, one of the recipients of the barrage of letters he sent from Bournemouth, read the revised manuscript and was appalled. She accused him of totally changing his personality, of abandoning all his former values, and of mauling her spontaneous love story. The reply was haughty and pedantic: "The Saga is a work of fiction on a frame of actual experience. It is my presentation and therefore sometimes false to your view. The necessity is not that our two views coincide but that it should be a work of art."

ON February 3, 1912, heavier, and strong enough to walk six miles, he left Bournemouth and headed for the Cearne.

In the silence and snow, Lawrence suddenly missed the bustle of the boardinghouse; he did not know what was the matter with him. Images of blood—the last sight that anyone threatened with tuberculosis wants to see—were in his mind. The day after his arrival, he wrote the letter so long overdue:

My dear Lou:
    You will be wondering why I am so long in writing. I have been thinking what the doctor at Croydon & the doctor at Bournemouth both urged on me: that I ought not to marry, at least for a long time, if ever. And I feel my health is so precarious, I wouldn't undertake the responsibility. Then, seeing I mustn't teach, I shall have a struggle to keep myself. I will not drag on an engagement—so I ask you to dismiss me. I fear we are not well-suited.
    My illness has changed me a good deal, has broken a good many of the old bonds that held me. I can't help it. It is no good to go on. I asked Ada, and she thought it would be better if the engagement were broken off; because it is not fair to you.
    It's a miserable business, and the fault is all mine.

                                                          D H Lawrence

He turned back to Helen. Almost immediately he wrote from the Cearne to ask her to meet him on Limpsfield Common one evening for a walk down to see the house. She might even, he suggested (hope springing eternal), stay the night; Garnett would not mind. Helen took the invitation as an ultimatum. "I could enjoy a walk over the snow-covered common with David," she confided to her memoirs, "but not a casual introduction by night to the house of the unconventional Garnett." She declined the offer, and never saw Lawrence again.

Lawrence was a changed man: flippant, bitter, angry. He blamed the transformation on his illness and, in a sense, he was right. The damage to his chest had left him under a permanent, if suspended, sentence of early death. The world would thenceforth look hostile to him. Yet his new personality was also a belated growing-up. Ada did not like the result. She consoled the devastated Louie, "I wouldn't marry a man like him, no, not if he were the only one on the earth."

THE return to Eastwood was hardly a homecoming. Ada and his father (now sixty-six) had moved from the house where Lydia Lawrence had died and were living in a crowded ménage with Emily, her husband, Samuel King, and their two small daughters. The windswept hilltop mining town itself, grimy with smoke and dust, its vistas scarred with the black paraphernalia of ten coal pits, was not at its best in February—particularly not in February 1912, when there was gloom over an impending national miners' strike.

The appearance of a novel had won him no glory in his old hometown. Apart from the mutterings over recognizable local characters, it had been greeted with laconic amusement. His best male friends were married and gone—Alan Chambers to Nottingham, and George Neville to Staffordshire, exiled to a remote headmastership for the shame of being the father of a son born only three months after the wedding. Lawrence's own family was upset at the broken engagement with Louie. Even Ada was no longer a comfort. On her home territory, she became bossy, nagging as badly as his mother ever had about what time he came in.

Lawrence was cutting his ties with the past one by one, but he chose an odd way of doing so: he threw himself at every woman in sight, Louie excepted, as if he were afraid of going to Germany alone. At a dance at a mining village near Eastwood, he shocked Ada by his unseemly public embraces with a friend of hers ("and we were kissing like nuts," he confessed gleefully to Garnett). He began to see Jessie again. He held her close and suggested that, in a year or so, after he returned from Germany, if nothing else had turned up, they might marry.

Jessie was incredulous. If Helen Corke had been dismayed by the revised *Trespasser,* Jessie was shattered by what she read of the new "Paul Morel." The third and (she had every reason to think) final

version of his novel of their youth demoted her. Far from being represented as Paul's muse and his partner in a prodigious program of self-
education, Jessie found herself—as "Miriam"—pared down to a naïve,
passive onlooker at Paul's solitary efforts to free himself from his mother
and establish himself as an artist. Jessie had felt quite diminished enough
by Lawrence's decision, made in an earlier version, to make Paul Morel
a painter rather than a writer—a metamorphosis that had, at a stroke,
removed her considerable contribution to his artistic development. She
declined the offer.

Lawrence braced himself to see Louie face-to-face, to negotiate the
details of ending their engagement. They had an excruciating visit to the
museum, of a type familiar to many feuding couples. They snapped at
one another, disagreed over the most casual observations about what
they saw, and contradicted each other on facts. It made matters worse
for Louie that Lawrence obviously had an evening appointment. In
midafternoon he was already dressed in evening clothes and kept his
overcoat buttoned up to conceal them. "Is there another girl?" Louie
asked. "Yes, if you'd *call* her a girl," Lawrence answered. He then took
her for tea at a café where, he recounted unchivalrously to Garnett,
"When she began to giggle, I asked her coolly for the joke: when she
began to cry, I wanted a cup of tea." Just after five o'clock he put her on
the train.

Lawrence did want to remain friends, however, and when Louie wrote
him amicably later and offered to send back the brooch he had given her,
he refused. It was not nice, he said, to send back "small things that were
given in such good spirit." He would keep the waistcoat and the ring she
had given him.

What Lawrence would have become, had he married either Jessie or
Louie, is one of the great might-have-beens of English literature. Many
have speculated, including Rebecca West and, more recently, the English
literary biographer Claire Tomalin:

> There could have been a different story, in which Lawrence married
> someone like the intelligent Louie; in which he settled in England and
> lived a quiet, healthy—and longer—life, cherished by his wife and
> family; in which his novels continued more in the pattern of *Sons and
> Lovers* and *The Rainbow*, social and psychological studies of the coun-
> try and people he knew best.

But those marriages were never in the cards. Jessie was too depressed
and dependent, ill-suited by temperament to stand the buffeting Lawrence gave her during the six years of their informal engagement. Louie,
an active suffragist and school administrator, was made of stronger stuff,
but she also was too much a part of the familiar fabric of his early life

to provide the challenge and sense of difference Lawrence craved. Perhaps nobody should marry the boy or girl next door.

The other "girl," who was not really a girl, was Alice Dax. At some point during those desperate weeks in Eastwood Lawrence asked her to leave her husband and run away with him. Alice was sorely tempted. Their affair had been a sexual awakening for her. But she could neither leave her four-year-old son behind nor foist him on the jobless Lawrence. And she was honest with herself. She foresaw a great future for Lawrence and felt that she was too unattractive, too unidealistic, and too provincial to hold him. There was one other obstacle: she was pregnant.

Was it Lawrence's child? Probably not. But it is a wise lover that knows his own child. The first time Lawrence saw Alice after his terrible illness seems to have been their visit to the theater on February 13; it was she for whom he was wearing evening dress the afternoon he saw Louie. Alice's baby was born eight months later, on October 6, and eight-month pregnancies are relatively rare.

Alice many years later said that the child was her husband's and "would never have been conceived but for an unendurable passion which only *he* [Lawrence] had roused and my husband had slaked." If, however, the child (later much loved) indeed had been conceived in January while Lawrence was in Bournemouth, Alice would not have been sure in mid-February whether she was pregnant or not. What is more, something happened between her and Lawrence on the evening of February 13 that was too personal for him to put even in his confessional letters to Garnett. After relaying to Garnett in great detail the highly personal scene of parting with Louie, he added intriguingly: "The sequel—which startled *me*—I will tell you personally some time. It shall not be committed to paper."

Was the "sequel" Alice's announcement to Lawrence that she might be pregnant? Or was it the experience of making love to a possibly pregnant woman? Either way, the ambiguous sequence of events left both Lawrence and Alice free to dream that the child she was carrying might be his.

The feelings of a young man on hearing that his mistress is pregnant surfaced in the autobiographical *Mr. Noon*, which Lawrence wrote in 1920–1921. The "facts" in the novel reflect the predicament of his friend George Neville, a teacher forced into marriage and professionally embarrassed by an unwanted pregnancy. But they convey equally Lawrence's situation in February 1912.

In *Mr. Noon*, Gilbert Noon, a young teacher in a small English Midlands town, is caught in flagrante with his girlfriend by her angry father, who proceeds to drag him before the school committee and demand his resignation on the grounds of "criminal commerce" and getting the girl "into trouble." Gilbert asks himself: "Did that mean she was going to have a baby. Lord save us, he hoped not. And even if she was, whose baby was it going to be?" Nonetheless, he sits down, writes his resignation to the Knarborough Education Committee, and decides to leave England and go to Germany.

Several years later Gilbert returns from abroad and encounters on the street his old girlfriend, now a married woman, holding by the hand "a little girl clad in a white curly-wooly coat and white woollen gaiters." Gilbert greets "Mrs. Whiffen" politely and shoots a quick sharp look at the child, whose bright blue eyes stare at him. He hurries on. What's past is past and does not bear thinking about. His own eyes, as the novel has already made clear, are blue.

Alice Dax did not wait nine years to link her little daughter to Lawrence. When the baby was born in October, she called her Phyllis, the name Lawrence had chosen in 1908 when he hoped that Alice's firstborn would be a girl. It is clear, however, that when Lawrence asked the pregnant Alice to run away with him early in 1912, he was willing to take on the burden of two young children at the very time when he had become unemployed and when he was simmering with rage about George Neville's entrapment into fatherhood.

The burdens of paternity were much on his mind when, early in March, visiting Jessie Chambers, her sister, and her brother-in-law, he shocked them all with a staccato stream of declarations: "Fatherhood's a myth" and "The average man with a family is nothing but a cart-horse, dragging the family behind him for the best part of his life. I'm not going to be a cart-horse." Hardly a fortnight later, to the six weeks pregnant Alice Dax, Lawrence broke the most momentous news of his life. He had found the wife he had been searching for.

On a morning early in March, in Nottingham, he had fallen in love. Within days, he was writing passionate letters in unequivocal phrases new to him. "You are the most wonderful woman in all England," he declared.

But the wonderful woman was also encumbered with a husband and children, and she was not English.

5

THE GIANTESS

Frieda's Life to Spring 1912

> *All women in their natures are like giantesses.*
> —D. H. Lawrence to Ernest Weekley,
> May 7, 1912

*I*n the spring of 1912 the secret life of Mrs. Ernest Weekley of Nottingham was out of control. Her lover was facing jail in Zurich for bombing the barracks of the canton police; she was sending money for his assistance. A former lover, whose love letters were her secret treasure, was also in trouble with the Swiss police for abetting a suicide.

Erotic melodrama made endurable a staid life as the wife of a professor of modern languages at Nottingham University College. Her three children were growing up and no longer ran to her as they had when they were small and they thought she was a kind of god. Her Nottingham home, Cowley, on Private Road, Mapperley Hill, a prosperous and wooded area of stuccoed classical and High Victorian villas, ran itself. A young girl from the Rhine Valley looked after the children, and a tyrannous cook excluded her from the kitchen.

Between her dramatic Continental adventures, conducted while her husband thought she was visiting her parents and sisters in Germany, Frieda Weekley fitted in love affairs closer to home. Her first adultery was committed with Ernest Dowson, a Nottingham businessman and neighbor, godfather to the Weekleys' youngest child; proximity and family friendship made this liaison in many ways the boldest of them all.

Frieda conducted her affairs not only out of boredom but also from conviction. She believed in Eros—the liberating power of sexual love—a doctrine taught her by a lover, the Austrian psychoanalyst Otto Gross, and reinforced by her emancipated sister Else Jaffe and by her favorite philosopher, Nietzsche. Gross's motto was "Repress nothing!" Frieda needed little persuading that conventional Christian morality was the source of society's ills and that erotic pleasure, free from the constraints of patriarchal monogamy, was the cure. She also believed that women should use their strength to nurture male genius and that in giving her body she was also giving her mind.

It was a dangerous double life, and it cost money. To finance it she relied on Else, who was rich and moved in avant-garde intellectual circles in Heidelberg and Munich, where defiance of the bourgeoisie was the prevailing creed. Only five months before, Else had sent a hundred marks to the Swiss anarchist Ernst Frick, so that he could travel from Switzerland to England to continue his affair with Frieda.

The cuckolded husband was ostensibly blind to his wife's activities. He was busy—writing, lecturing, teaching workers' classes in the evening, traveling to Cambridge every Saturday. Even so, he cannot have ignored her drives into the countryside with Dowson, owner of one of Nottingham's few motorcars.

The thirty-two-year-old Mrs. Weekley, therefore, was one of the few people in England who would have agreed with Lawrence that "with *should* and *ought* I have nothing to do." And she—unlike Lawrence—had no trouble putting the maxim into practice. Born Baroness Frieda von Richthofen at Metz in Germany in 1879, she had alert pale-green eyes and a wide, confident smile that suggested that nothing human was alien to her. She was a very pretty woman, with a sharp nose, high cheekbones, well-shaped chin, and symmetrical features. Her broad form was much admired in an age that equated ample curves with voluptuousness, health, even wealth. She bore her weight proudly, with the confident carriage of the aristocracy to which in every fiber of her being she felt she belonged. And, with her light hair and fair complexion, she radiated untroubled Teutonic sensuality.

A life of sexual intrigue was fed by fantasy. Alone much of the time, Frieda sustained herself by reading the lovers' letters, furtively concealed in letters from Else or Else's husband, Edgar, or by dancing around her bedroom nude, draping herself with a shawl like the notorious Isadora Duncan and imagining how shocked the good burghers of Nottingham would be if they only knew.

*   *   *

By March 1912 Frieda had lived in Nottingham nearly thirteen years. To his mother-in-law, describing the birth of their second child in September 1902, Weekley had joked, "Immediately on its arrival, it said 'My name is Frieda Elsa Agnes, and I despise Nottingham.' " It sounds like a complaint he had heard often. But he himself had none. "If the little girl grows up like her mother then I consider myself a happy man."

Frieda had come as a bride from Metz. The former French fortress city, in Alsace-Lorraine, had been part of the new German empire since the Franco-Prussian War of 1870–1871. She was the second of three spirited daughters of a minor Prussian aristocrat, the Baron Friedrich von Richthofen. The family name had been Praetorious until 1661, when the fine-sounding "von Richthofen" was added to accompany the acquisition of a Bohemian barony from Frederick the Great. But what money or Prussian land still attached to the title by the nineteenth century was lost by Frieda's grandfather; her father, who succeeded to the barony, was directed to a military career in the Prussian army, which he entered at the age of seventeen in 1862. It was not to be a brilliant career. The war with France cost the young baron the use of his right hand and any chance of military advancement. Invalided out at twenty-five, he was compensated with a post in the administration occupying Metz, which became the second-biggest garrison town in the newly united Germany. He married a bright, strong-minded woman from a solid Black Forest professional family and they lived unhappily ever after.

All three of their daughters were born in Metz. As daughters of a baron the girls were properly styled *Freiin*. (The usual translation of this word is "baroness," a word that connotes a more august rank in English than it does in German.) The title *baronin* belonged to their mother, Anna, the wife of a baron. Frieda suffered more than most from the low self-esteem of the middle child, for she was neither the brains of the family—Else, five years older, was the cleverest—nor the beauty, a title awarded by general agreement to Nusch (formally, Johanna), three years younger. Frieda carved out her own distinction by making herself the most unmanageable. In her memoirs, she recalls her mother calling her "ein Atavismus"—a primitive, a throwback. Indifferent to reprimand, Frieda went her own way. She played with dolls, banged out Beethoven on the piano, and worshiped her father, whose maimed hand and nervous disposition left him far more insecure than the Iron Cross on his uniform suggested.

Frieda was undisciplined but not unintellectual. She was educated by nuns in Metz and later at a finishing school in the Black Forest. She read a great deal. When seventeen, she had spent a year with Nusch in court circles in Berlin, thanks to their uncle, Oswald von Richthofen, who was minister of foreign affairs for the first Reich. In the social whirl of the imperial capital, Frieda flaunted her title, to the amusement of

Uncle Oswald, who felt that she exaggerated the importance of the family's modest baronial credentials. By then, however, while she was never to achieve the head-turning sultriness of Nusch or the serene dignity of Else, Frieda had blossomed into her own provocative good looks. She and Nusch made a striking pair in Berlin and it was said that Kaiser Wilhelm II himself had observed that the foreign secretary had very beautiful nieces.

From Berlin Frieda returned to the military gaiety of Metz, where there was no shortage of handsome straight-backed young men with whom to flirt. She enjoyed falling in love and having men fall in love with her—"a nice entertainment," she told her bookish elder sister. Else had chosen a different course in life and become a schoolteacher in order to earn money to go to university. But pretty a trio as they were, the von Richthofen sisters had a signal disadvantage: the lack of a fortune. This presented an almost insuperable obstacle to becoming the wife of an officer—and officers were the only men they met.

The family's financial straits were worsened by the baron's habits. What he did not waste at the gaming tables he spent on his mistress. His wife, sorely tried, was keen to marry her daughters off as soon as possible. When Ernest Weekley, a tall, handsome, graying Englishman on holiday in the Black Forest, fell in love with Frieda and proposed marriage, Baroness von Richthofen did not hesitate at the difficulties that the disparity in age or a life of exile might hold for her headstrong middle daughter. He was accepted.

Ernest Weekley had excellent prospects. He was a Cambridge graduate in modern languages who had studied in Berne and in Paris and spent a year in Germany as *Lektor* in English at the University of Freiburg; he now had an appointment waiting at Nottingham University College. Although Frieda and Else were grieved at the thought of being parted, Else saw that Frieda was genuinely fond of her Englishman.

Weekley may have suspected that he was marrying trouble. From Freiburg in August 1899, where he had been courting Frieda (under chaperonage), he wrote to Else, describing his happiness and adding:

> The more I see of her the more I admire her noble and unspoilt character; may God grant that I may show myself in some measure worthy of such self sacrificing love as she has for me. I only wish, for her sake, that I could offer her a more brilliant future than that of being the wife of a plain English professor: she ought to be an empress.

He also sensed Frieda's hidden fires. To Else, whom he recognized as older and wiser than her sister, he confided, "I think it is really better for us to be separated for a little while."

In the event, there was a year's separation. Weekley returned to England and installed himself in Nottingham. Frieda and her parents crossed the Channel to get a look at England and to meet the Weekleys, a large, upright, religious, middle-class family who lived in Hampstead in London. The one who was to matter most in Frieda's life was her future mother-in-law, Agnes, mother of nine, fiercely proud of her oldest son, who by his own efforts had risen from a grammar school background and an external degree from London University to become a scholar at Trinity College, Cambridge. Mrs. Weekley was not pleased with the *fräulein* she saw on the dock at Dover; she thought Frieda "a washed-out looking thing." But the wedding went ahead, in Freiburg on August 29, 1899. The groom was thirty-four, the bride twenty.

Frieda approached her wedding night an impatient virgin. The tale of what ensued in a hotel in Lucerne was one that she told often in her late life. In one of its franker versions she said: "I went to the bedroom first and climbed up by the door and when Ernest came in, I threw myself naked into his arms. He was horrified and told me to put on my nightdress at once." In all the accounts, the sexual initiation that followed was "a horror."

That was not the whole truth of the marriage. The handsome and witty Weekley was a passionate man who adored his lively young wife and startled her with the force of his adulation, and in time, to judge from Lawrence's autobiographical *Mr. Noon,* with his dark, and satisfying, sensuality. By the time Frieda began her affair with Otto Gross in Munich in 1907, she was so awakened a woman that Gross, an expert on human sexuality, found her the erotic partner of his dreams. Some credit must be due Weekley.

AT first Frieda despised neither Nottingham nor her husband. She became pregnant the first month of the marriage and, settled in Nottingham, wrote home just before Nusch's wedding in 1900 that she was happier every day. So much did Weekley love his wife, whom he affectionately called Fritz, that, as the pregnancy advanced, he feared he might be jealous if the baby was a boy. Charles Montague Weekley was born on June 15, 1900.

Frieda's own jealousy was directed at her sister Else. The same summer that "Monty" arrived and Nusch married, Else became one of the first women ever to receive a degree from Heidelberg, with a doctorate in social economics, summa cum laude, and a dissertation on worker protection written under the direction of the eminent sociologist Max Weber. Else capped her distinction by securing an appointment, equally rare for a woman, as factory inspector for the state of Baden, with a special interest in the working conditions of women. From Nottingham

Weekley wrote to congratulate Else: "We shall now expect the publication of some great work on political economy."

Frieda was inspired to do something modestly comparable. In 1901,
in spite of her new baby, she edited, in collaboration with a colleague of
Weekley's, an English translation of Schiller's ballads for Blackie's *Little
German Classics* series. When the book was done, she proudly accepted
her payment, telling Else: "It fills me with great pride to produce something 'brainy.' A little exercise does my rusty brain good. I receive 100
M. for very little work! I can easily use a few hundred." She dreamed of
what the money might be put toward—a villa "for all of us" in the Black
Forest, perhaps, or a dowry for Monty. But above all, she told her sister,
"my little book about Schiller has given me tremendous pleasure. It is
mean that people try to keep us women away by force from everything
'brainy,' as if one didn't need it just as much when one is married!" She
followed the Schiller with another book, *Bechstein's "Märchen,"* "selected and edited by Frieda Weekly."

Frieda envied Else's independence and told her to be satisfied with her
single state. At the same time, somewhat defensively, she told her sister
that it was quite possible to be an educated woman and yet enjoy cleaning, sewing, and child-rearing: "What surprises me is the assertion that
educated women are poor housekeepers is very seldom proved true.
They have a more over-all view, to manage a household successfully is
no small thing."

She was delighted with her son's progress and also with her place at
the center of his life: "It is wonderful for me that no one is above his
'Momamo.' "

She kept up her reading all the while. At Christmas 1902 the gift from
a friend in Germany of a calendar of Nietzsche's sayings inspired her to
ask Else if she could borrow her copy of *Thus Spake Zarathustra*. Frieda
became, if she was not already, devoted to Nietzsche. In later life she
referred to him as "my old friend" and from a Lawrence poem she took
as the title of her own autobiography a Nietzschean phrase, "not I, but
the wind," implying that her own powerful personality was nothing but
the life force that blew through her.

The sisters liked Nietzsche for the same reason that writers such as
Shaw, Yeats, and Wells were attracted to him: he was aphoristic, full of
memorable, scientific-sounding nuggets of wisdom. Phrases such as "the
collapse of all values," "the Will to Power," and "the Eternal Return,"
and ringing statements such as "The human animal . . . is *the* sick animal" and "A thing is the sum of its effects" were far more attractive to
the literary imagination than long pages of philosophy. Yeats's lines
"How but in custom and in ceremony / Are innocence and beauty
born?" (from "Prayer for My Daughter") can be read as a direct expression of Nietzsche's ideas on obedience and authority, and Shaw's

"Superman" as an anglicized *Übermensch*. In 1908 Shaw so far followed the Nietzschean example as to allow the publication of *The G.B.S. Perpetual Calendar* ("Made to hang on the wall . . . There is nothing to equal it as a daily companion or as a propagandist of new faith") containing a Shavian quotation for every day of the year.

In those early years, life at the Weekleys' continued tranquil. Frieda sang in a women's choir. She gardened. She and Ernest studied Italian together in the evenings. They did not quarrel. Occasionally she accompanied him to Cambridge. Certainly Weekley thought they were happy. When their little girl was born, he described the accouchement in a glowing letter to his father-in-law, whom he addressed as "Dear Papa," reporting Frieda's delight as the newborn sucked eagerly at her breast—or, as he delicately put it, "the source of nourishment." And to "Dear Mama," Frieda's mother, Weekley declared, "We despise people who do not have children, we are arrogant."

From her domestic contentment in Nottingham, Frieda was dismayed to hear that the beauteous Nusch, at eighteen, was to be married to Max von Schreibershofen, a brusque army officer twice her age, from the German general staff in Berlin. But there was worse to come. Two years later Frieda was devastated when Else, then twenty-eight, having rejected several suitors, decided to marry without love and, apparently, for money. Frieda stormed that the marriage was "an Iphegenie sacrifice"—as if Else, like Agamemnon's daughter, were being sacrificed for the sake of her father.

Unquestionably, Else's choice promised to make life much easier for the von Richthofens. Dr. Edgar Jaffe, a tiny, mild-mannered economist and professor of political economy at Heidelberg, came from a rich Jewish family of Hamburg textile manufacturers. He had considerable wealth in his own right. Ten years spent in England with the Manchester branch of the family firm gave him the independence to leave commerce for academic life. Their marriage on November 18, 1902, gave Else comparable freedom. To the disapproval of some of her feminist circle, she gave up her factory inspector's job in favor of life as a powerful intellectual hostess reigning from a four-story villa in Germany's foremost university town.

Yet Jaffe's personal attractions were greater than Frieda at first realized. He had been one of Else's teachers at Heidelberg and was a patron of modern art; he was also a friend of her own good friends, the pioneering sociologists Max and Marianne Weber. Else had hopes of using her own gifts to help Jaffe to rise higher, as he did when in 1904 he bought and edited, with Max Weber and another scholar, the *Archiv für Sozialwissenschaft und Sozialpolitik,* turning it into a distinguished journal in the new field of social science.

Frieda Weekley could not appreciate the influence this marriage would have on her own life. It was clear, however, that Jaffe would present no barrier to the beautiful Else's pursuit of love, for he too believed that women needed emancipation from the European authoritarian ethos and that, in the conflict between reason and feeling, feeling should win.

The cultural historian Martin Green, in his influential book *The von Richthofen Sisters,* says that in marrying Jaffe, Else "married Heidelberg—that is, she entered the active centre of liberal, reformist, resistant Germany, one of the two great nodes of the anti-Bismarck movement." The other node was Munich, where Jaffe had a flat and where he and Else, together and separately, spent a great deal of time.

Else's elevation to high priestess of the German counterculture spelled the doom of Frieda's marriage. Stuck in Nottingham, she saw herself fallen way behind her sisters. Nusch, in spite of her unpleasant husband, was living a glamorous life of romantic intrigue and haute couture in Berlin, while Else, shuttling between Heidelberg and Munich, was at the heart of all that was new in art, philosophy, and psychology.

In December 1904, with the birth of her third child, Barbara, Frieda's childbearing stopped. She began to spend long periods of time visiting her parents and sisters. On a trip to see the Jaffes in Munich in the spring of 1907, at the Café Stephanie in Schwabing, Munich's artistic and bohemian quarter, she was introduced to the dazzling Otto Gross. With a forthrightness that delighted him, she summoned him to be her lover.

WHAT followed has been called an important event in the history of the erotic movement and, considering its consequences for literature and censorship, perhaps it was. Gross, then thirty, had been trained as a neurologist and psychiatrist in Graz in southern Austria, but since 1900 had become a follower of Sigmund Freud and a practitioner of the new psychoanalysis. In those early years of the movement, Freud found Gross and Carl Gustav Jung of Zurich to be the two most original of his disciples. Ernest Jones, the British doctor who was to introduce psychoanalysis into Britain and who was studying under Gross in Munich in 1907, considered Gross to have an extraordinary ability to penetrate people's inner thoughts and feelings; he was, said Jones, "the nearest approach to the romantic idea of a genius I have ever met."

Gross was certainly Frieda's first genius. Although Ernest Weekley was gaining recognition in linguistic studies, his field was narrow and his subject dry. Gross, in contrast, had published highly original work on the kinds of ideas that excited Frieda: the libido, sexual symbolism, the harmfulness of repression, and the psychological difference between male and female. Besides, as all who knew him testified, Gross was superbly charismatic: tall, with intense blue eyes and tousled blond hair, so hyperactive that he talked all the time, even (to judge from *Mr. Noon*) during sexual intercourse. He virtually lived at the Café Stephanie, where he received his mail and saw his analysands. He hardly ever changed his clothes or went home.

Gross was also addicted to morphine, and had been since before his marriage in 1903. (Drugs presented an even greater temptation to the medical profession then than now, for there was virtually no regulation of supply and prescription.) Frieda did not seem to mind the addiction, if indeed she was aware of it. Imperturbable herself, she did not object to instability allied to greatness. Having been persuaded by Gross's doctrine that "only out of decadence . . . a new harmony in life creates itself," she was quite ready to interpret sickness as health.

Even in 1907, Gross was taking analysis far beyond Freud's cautious medical conception and down the road to open rebellion against all patriarchal restraints, sexual inhibition above all. It was a campaign for which he was well-qualified. His own large, overbearing father, Hanns Gross, Austria's foremost criminologist, was the punishing patriarch personified; to get away from his father had been one of Otto's reasons for moving to Munich.

March 1907 was an eventful month in the life of Otto Gross. He and his wife signed a pact giving each other complete sexual freedom. He met Frieda Weekley. And, almost as a parting gift to mark the end of their own affair, he made her sister Else Jaffe pregnant. To the three women, it was irrelevant that, in the same year, Frau Gross also presented Gross with a son and that one of his patients was also expecting his child. They all believed in the Magna Mater, the strong matriarch who took many lovers and bore many children, and believed their behavior a return to the superior form of social organization of pagan life which European civilization, based on patriarchy and Christianity, had destroyed.

A slight complication in their relations was that Gross's wife was also named Frieda. Frieda Gross, born Schloffer, was a school friend of Else's. When Frieda von Richthofen was young and gawky, with unmanageable hair, she was immensely impressed by the older girl from Graz, with her soft Austrian accent and thick dark-blond coil of hair, which, when loose, reached her waist. And the younger Frieda remained in awe of her sister's friend: in her maturity, Frieda Gross easily found new lovers; with her heavy hair, ivory skin, and melancholy passivity, she was very attractive to men.

In the ideological sisterhood and continuing friendship of the two Friedas and Else Jaffe, says Martin Green, Gross saw his "Welt-Frühling," his world-awakening. In the spirit of the Magna Mater, Frieda Weekley soon began to hope that she, too, would have a child by Gross. That summer, to celebrate their love, she gave Gross a ring with the figures of three women carved on it; and she told him, "You won't find 3 people like the 3 of us on every street-corner."

Where he would have found far more than three women like them was in early twentieth-century literature. Nineteenth-century heroines who defied the patriarchy with their passions, even if they escaped consumption, paid with their lives: Isolde, Carmen, Aïda, Tosca, Emma Bovary, and Anna Karenina. But by the time Otto Gross reached Schwabing, the death penalty had been lifted and the sophisticated world was full of women ready to follow the example of Ibsen's Nora and Shaw's heroines, and to slough off the domineering male and survive.

Among his own three New Women, Gross gave the prize to Frieda Weekley. She was, he told her, the woman of his dreams—totally uninhibited, careless of reputation, erotically innovative—the woman who embodied all his hopes of a new world sexual order.

I *know* now what people will be like who keep themselves unpolluted by all the things that I hate and fight against—I know it through *you,* the only human being who *already, today,* has remained free from the code of chastity, from Christianity, from democracy and all that accumulated filth—*remained free through her own strength*—how on earth have you brought this miracle about, you golden child—

Once he had made love to Frieda, Gross realized how melancholy, cerebral, and duty-bound her sister Else was, and how repressed was his own wife. By comparison, his beloved Frieda Weekley was careless and carefree. He loved the way she wore a blue dressing gown with nothing beneath it but her golden body; he called her, for reasons that can only be imagined, "my Turkish horse" (*Turkische Pferde*).

If Frieda Weekley showed him the farther shores of female response, he taught her Freud. In 1907 the Oedipus complex was hardly known outside Freud's circle. (Freud had mentioned it for the first time only ten years earlier, in a letter to his friend Wilhelm Fliess.) His theory of the unconscious had been in circulation for only eight years—and only in German. *Die Traumdeutung*, published at the end of 1899, did not appear in English as *Interpretation of Dreams* until 1913. Through her affair with Gross, therefore, Frieda had every reason to think that she was in at the beginning of a revolution based on the only principle that made sense to her.

Gross, moreover, related Frieda's beloved Nietzsche to Freud, as reinterpreted by himself: the act of sexual love was a sacrament and if the sacrament were freely given and taken, the ills of society would disappear. As Frieda Weekley had showed him a dimension of physical joy that he had not dreamed existed, Gross thanked her for rescuing him from Freud's shadow and turning his own course down the road to sexual revolution. His future work, he assured her, would be their children.

THE actual period of the affair was pathetically brief: one week together in Munich, followed later that spring by another week in Amsterdam. On her way to Amsterdam, Frieda stopped in Heidelberg to visit Else. Nothing in their ideological sisterhood saved them from ordinary sibling rivalry. For each of the sisters, the affair with Gross had been overwhelming, almost a religious experience. Each woman saw herself reborn through the touch of this gifted lover. (The phrases that both used to describe how Gross had awakened them to "their true natures" sound like euphemisms for orgasm.)

When they met, therefore, each sister was horribly jealous of the other, for good reason. Else was in the queasy early months of pregnancy, still smarting at her younger sister's success in snatching Gross away from her. Gross, moreover, had let her know that she was by no means as uninhibited in bed as her sister; in fact, he told her frankly that she was not cut out for erotic emancipation. Frieda, for her part, fiercely envied Else's pregnancy. She alone among Gross's sexual partners that year seemed unable to conceive; she hoped to achieve her wish during their forthcoming week in Holland before she returned to what now seemed a living death in Nottingham.

The sisters reverted to their childish relationship: Else superior and cutting, Frieda oversimple and blunt. The result was a colossal row in which, Frieda reported to Gross, she and Else had fought "like Brünnhilde and Krimhilde." Then Frieda left for Amsterdam and her idyll with Gross.

When the time came for them to part, to snatch a few last hours of passion Gross followed Frieda onto the night ferry for England and crossed the Channel with her. Memories of that Wagnerian voyage were to fill their letters in the months that followed; they quoted Nietzsche to each other and dreamed of the child that she might produce and the great works of psychology he would write: "yours and mine together." In the morning, she left him with the words "I go away only to return."

GROSS returned immediately to the Continent. He was preparing a paper for the First International Congress of Psychiatry and Neurology, to be held in Amsterdam in September. He hoped that Frieda would join him.

Back in the safety of England, Frieda began to think that Gross should come to her. What would be more ideal than a meeting at the seaside in Lincolnshire, where she was taking the children without Ernest? She began her holiday; she swam, she clambered over the rocks in her bath-ing costume, she admired her beautiful blond children, and she waited. "Are you frightened by your fierce Teutonic woman?" she challenged him. Gross did not appear. Her menstrual period did.

When she wrote to Gross to break the sad news, he replied that "the fact that our hope has not been fulfilled is hard for me to bear . . . not *only* for your sake." He wanted their love to bear fruit, children as well as deeds. But could they not try again?

Frieda began making excuses, with sound justification. She did not have the money for another Continental trip; she was worried about Gross's "health"—perhaps his drug addiction. In the end, neither obliged the other and Gross went to Amsterdam instead with his wife, who, he acknowledged with satisfaction, was at last taking an interest in his professional work.

His hope of making a life with Frieda Weekley remained bright. The intensity of his frenzied letters of passion and philosophy increased in 1908 with her hint that she might travel to the Continent in the spring. He begged her to leave her husband. "Come, Frieda, come to me!" he implored. "I love you as I love this age and its prophetic signs of the future." He asked her to take her children and flee to her mother's house, arguing (with some foresight, as things turned out) that unless her chil-dren were with her and out of England, she would not have the freedom to decide her course.

Their letters continued at fever pitch, opening with "My Beloved" and "O You Beloved" and closing with "Thy Frieda" and "Thy Otto," as they swore undying love for each other and their ideals. Gross recalled how she had come to him "like a greeting from the future." He cherished the memory of "when you chose me in your wonderful aristocratic way." That Frieda was a baron's daughter was important to him, for Gross believed, and spelled out for a highly receptive Frieda, that natural law required "the absolute separation of the aristocracy from the peo-ple." (This was another borrowing from Nietzsche, who considered democracy as pernicious as Christianity.)

The deathblow to the relationship seems to have been struck by Else. She and Gross had an argument about his affair with Frieda. Gross professed astonishment. How could Else, so great and noble, so fond of her younger sister, be hurt by the affair? "What cause for *suffering* can there be in the sunny happiness of two people, both of whom you love? I cannot understand it—." But they fought also over Else's new lover, a man their letters do not name but who, because of his belief in democ-racy, was anathema to Gross. Gross psychoanalytically interpreted Else's choice as an unconscious act of revenge for his affair with her sister.

Else took it upon herself to write and tell Frieda to abandon any thought of Gross. On no account must she think of leaving her husband for a penniless psychotic. Said Else, in the scornful, scolding tones of an older sister:

Can't you see that he's almost destroyed Frieda's [Gross's] life? that he's not able to constrain himself even for a quarter of an hour . . . ?

As a "lover" he's incomparable, but a person doesn't consist of that alone. God, it's useless to say anything. You are under that tremendous power of suggestion which emanates from him and which I myself have felt.

Else concluded by reminding her younger sister to think of her husband's great love for her.

Frieda obeyed. Without Else's financial help, she could not leave Ernest Weekley. She told Gross flatly that she did not have "the right to gamble with the existence of a good fellow." Furthermore, she as much as told him that she had a new lover, for she boasted of having converted a Nottingham friend, Madge Bradley—and Madge's fiancé as well—to Gross's erotic creed. "I hope I will experience something beautiful with him," Frieda wrote. "I have the rage of 'giving' upon me."

Gross finally accepted what was happening, with effusive resignation:

My love for you will live as before, and more strongly than before, and should you return, even after many years—and should my hope be alive or dead—you know, I am yours. . . . And unchanged too—indeed, heightened—is the *capacity* of love with you—if *you come to me.* Whenever you come. Whether now, or in the distant times to come—*for ever.* Whenever a new day and a new dream recalls me to your desire. For ever, Beloved, Otto.

When she had left Munich, her brother-in-law, and coconspirator in the affair, Edgar Jaffe made Frieda promise to burn all Gross's letters. But she could not do it. "I must still have something," she wrote Edgar. "I am nonetheless *very* careful." Perhaps she realized even then that her contribution to world-awakening would begin with her hoard of love letters covered with Gross's wild scrawl and crazed underlinings.

ON Christmas Eve 1907 Else gave birth to a son, and Edgar Jaffe registered the boy as his own (under the name of Edgar Peter Behrend Jaffe). In keeping with the Magna Mater's belief in the interchangeability of males, Else gave her child the same name, Peter, as Frieda Gross's son, born on January 31, 1906. If Frieda Weekley had succeeded in her wish to become pregnant by the incomparable lover, Otto Gross might have been blessed with three sons close in age called Peter.

But Gross was falling apart, his mind clouding, his addiction out of control. Had Frieda Weekley gone to Amsterdam, she would have seen that Gross's extremism was pushing him out of the psychoanalytic movement. Jung reported sadly to Freud, who had not attended the Amsterdam conference, that Gross was seducing his patients:

> Dr. Gross tells me that he puts a quick stop to the transference by turning people into sexual immoralists. He says the transference to the analyst and its persistent fixation are mere monogamy symbols and as such symptomatic of repression. The truly healthy state for the neurotic is sexual immorality. . . . I feel Gross is going along too far with the vogue for the sexual short-circuit, which is neither intelligent, nor in good taste, but merely convenient, and therefore anything but a civilising factor.

Freud began to distance himself from Gross the following April at Salzburg when they met at the First International Conference on Psychoanalysis. It was a historic occasion, the first public recognition of Freud's work and the gathering of such subsequently celebrated names as A. A. Brill from New York, Alfred Adler from Vienna, Karl Abraham from Berlin, and Sándor Ferenczi from Budapest. Freud enthralled his followers by relating, without notes and in a conversational voice, the case of obsessional neurosis now known as the Rat Man. However, when Gross rose and, enthusiastically comparing Freud to Nietzsche, declared him a fellow revolutionary and destroyer of old values, Freud icily rebuked him. "We are doctors," he declared, "and doctors we will remain."

Beyond a doubt, Freud was building his new method on the concept—so dear to Gross—of the harmful consequences of repressing the sexual instincts. Yet Freud was steering psychoanalysis away from a Dionysian glorification of ecstasy and unfettered instinct (for which Nietzsche had originated the term "id") and toward a recognition of the importance of the ego in controlling the forces of the unconscious. Max Weber was later to distance himself from Nietzsche on the same grounds: the need for self-discipline. All the same, Freudian psychoanalysis has not yet been cleared of Gross's charge that its theory and practice are built upon the cultural values of fin-de-siècle European patriarchy.

Frieda Gross attended the Salzburg conference as she had the one in Amsterdam, and is listed among the main participants. At Salzburg or shortly afterward Gross asked his pupil Ernest Jones (a psychiatrist himself highly inclined to sexual dalliance) to take his wife into analysis. Jones was most reluctant because of the patent instability of both husband and wife, but Gross was, as usual, phenomenally persuasive.

In consequence, bulletins on Gross's deteriorating mental condition in the summer of 1908 reached Freud in Vienna, along with details of the Gross marriage. Jones reported to Freud that Frieda Gross was deeply in love with another man but that she was concealing it from Gross, as the two men disliked each other. Ordinarily, as Jones told Freud:

> Gross gets great delight in getting other men to love her—no doubt a perverse paranoid development of his free love ideas. This she doesn't like, as she says it is her own business; in addition she has been very jealous about his relations with other women. All this I know you will treat as strictly private, but I thought you ought to know it. I should be grateful for any advice you have to send me.

Jones thus knew that Frieda Weekley was one of Gross's other women, and this knowledge was to prove useful when he met her years later in London.

In May 1908 Gross seemed determined to be cured himself. He committed himself to Jung's Burghölzli Asylum in Zurich, to be taken off drugs completely and to undergo analysis with Jung. The treatment lasted one month. In June he escaped from the clinic, jumping over the wall, and made his way back to Munich, pronouncing himself cured. Jones, who saw him there, advised Freud that Gross was "much worse, quite paranoiac—shut off from the outside world," and that he was also taking cocaine.

Thus, Frieda acted wisely when she decided not to leave Ernest Weekley for Otto Gross. Within the year she had known him, Gross had undergone a precipitous and irreversible decline into what Jung diagnosed as schizophrenia and Freud as paranoia. But she had not been deluding herself about Gross's gifts. At his best, he was brilliant. When Jones later told Freud that he had learned more from Gross than he ever had from Jung, he was referring to the very period of Gross's affair and correspondence with Frieda Weekley.

WITH Gross out of her life, Frieda was trapped in Nottingham, expressing as well as she could her "rage of 'giving.'" She watched enviously as Else and Frieda Gross plunged back into *la ronde*. By 1909 Else had formed a lasting liaison with Alfred Weber, a cultural sociologist, Max Weber's younger brother, and probably the man of whom Gross so strongly disapproved. Alfred had long been in love with her and, with Jaffe's acquiescence, became virtually Else's second husband. Frieda Gross, meanwhile, had left Otto for Ernst Frick, a gauntly handsome Swiss painter and committed anarchist, by whom she had a daughter. They lived at Ascona, a hotbed of free love, modern dance, and vegetarianism at the Swiss end of Lake Maggiore.

Else and Frieda Gross kept up an intense correspondence about their complicated parallel lives. Frieda Gross mused idly to Else—the rules of the new matriarchy being so uncertain—whether it would be incestuous if her daughter by Frick and Else's son by Gross were to love each other, as, in a manner of speaking, they were brother and sister through their mother.

For Frieda Gross the new relationship was hardly progress. Frick was rational enough: a working-class intellectual and editor of an anarchist journal. But he was a fearless radical and in trouble with the Swiss police, who connected him with two terrorist attacks: a bomb explosion at the barracks of the Zurich canton police in 1907 and the derailment of a tram in November 1908. Frick even resembled Otto: wiry, intense, fair, hawk-nosed but handsomer; his long face, with deep-set, penetrating eyes, strong chin, and firm lips, conveyed a dark, brooding sensuality. Frieda Gross loved him very much—so much, she told Else, that in spite of the pain Frick caused her with his other women, she stayed with him because he drew strength from her. But she had to recognize, as she wrote Else, "that my second great love has fallen upon another impossible man." Sadly she added: "It's going rather like it did with Otto only quite differently in that Ernst has a place in my world-view and perhaps will always stand there, as he did during our best hours. (Unfortunately they were never days.)"

It did all go with Ernst rather like it did with Otto. Before long, from Nottingham, Frieda Weekley swooped in and helped herself to Frieda Gross's new man. The older Frieda put up with the new affair ("If he can experience something good with another, that's all right with me") in the hope that it might steady Ernst's nerves. They were all, even Ernst, distraught because Otto, who also had been living in Ascona, had committed a new outrage: he had given his latest mistress, Sophie Benz, poison with which to commit suicide—the second suicide he had assisted in Ascona within five years. Frick said he wished he had killed Otto. All in all, it was a bad time for Friedele, as Else and Frieda Gross referred to Frieda Weekley, to be arriving for a spell of erotic liberation. As Frieda Gross told Else, who was being kept informed of her sister's every move:

> Friedele should come tomorrow but if she follows my advice she will leave Ascona completely and only travel with other people. Here is in any case a great deal of confusion and unpleasantness. In many things Friedele is a complete sheep. For example, when she quite charitably writes to Ernst that she wants to be together with me because I will enjoy it, I've really got as little inclination towards that as possible.

Ernst Frick, for his part, may have expected actually to run away with Frieda Weekley as a result of the visit, for the day before her arrival in

April 1911 he wrote to the Zurich police telling them that he intended to move abroad. However, the Easter meeting was turbulent; the two lovers fought much of the time. They decided to meet again, however, in England, in the summer.

Frieda Weekley was so eager for the reunion that she sent Frick money to pay for his ticket; unfortunately, she did not send enough. Frieda Gross had to intercede and ask Else's help:

August 6, 1911

Ernst is soon going back to England by boat. Since he needs much more money for this journey than Friedele sent him I've unfortunately got to ask you straight away for 100 MK. His health has been so bad recently that I would like without any hesitation for him to stay on the sea voyage. Poor Friedele had only a very few happy hours here for he really can't love at all any more, and not just only me.

There was one new problem. Frieda Gross was pregnant by Frick once again (another sign of the Magna Mater's disdain for contraception). How could she cope with a new baby? She had so many other worries. Otto had been admitted to an asylum to save him from arrest for Sophie's death. Otto's father, the criminologist, was suing for custody of his grandson Peter Gross, and the boy himself, now about four, was not easy. "He is entirely Otto's child," Frieda Gross told Else. "In good and bad. The charm. The complete instability."

No sooner had she received the hundred marks for Frick than she pleaded with Else for three thousand more, for herself. The three thousand marks duly arrived. Frieda Gross's next trauma was a miscarriage—or just possibly an abortion. What she wrote Else in early September was "The child did not want it. Perhaps it was the excitement of the whole time or a cold bath—that's neither here nor there now. I'm healthy again but I'm feeling weaker than if I had a child." She had to remain in bed for two weeks, thinking how, as she wrote Else, "our Ernst has got so nicely away from it all":

He must have arrived in Southampton two days ago. I don't suffer from any jealousy although I know that it is going much better for him now than when Friedele was here, and how much better since I am away and that they therefore have a far far better life together than when they were here, when they had only rows together.

All in all Frick spent more than a month in England with Frieda, meeting a few friends who knew about the affair, practicing his English. When he returned, he continued to write to Frieda in Nottingham, with the ever reliable Else providing safe cover for his letters.

October 9, 1911

Please, Frau Else, send this letter to Friedele. We haven't as yet managed to arrange any better connection by letter. Frieda must have told you about the adventure of the journey to England. It was sometimes comic, especially with the modern permissiveness of the respectable classes in England. I am very happy to have been there and I have returned from that country missing the culture and the respect. On the surface we understand each other most wonderfully but one's just got to be a great enemy [*Feind*] of the English.

As a prose stylist Frick was no Otto Gross, but he had more on his mind that autumn than writing world-shaping love letters. The case against him mounting, the Zurich police closed in and locked him up on charges of violating the Explosives Act. His future correspondence with Frieda Weekley was conducted from the Regensdorf jail.

In her later writings about her life, Frieda omitted any mention of Ernst Frick, who was eventually found guilty and sentenced to a year in prison. In her fictionalized memoirs, moreover, she transformed Otto Gross, who died as a derelict drug addict in Berlin in 1921, into a heroic doctor who had been killed in the First World War. ("How he must have suffered! He, who had dreamed of a glorious coming day for all men, saw before him the torn bodies and broken spirits of the young that he had dreamed his dreams of happiness for!")

In her highly romanticized autobiography, *Not I, but the Wind . . .*, she reduced the whole morass of her life in early 1912 to the simple declaration: "I had just met a remarkable disciple of Freud and was full of undigested theories. This friend did a lot for me. I was living like a somnambulist in a conventional set life and he awakened the consciousness of my own proper self."

To call Gross a friend was poetic license, as was "just met." In 1912 her affair with Gross had been over for four years. The affair with Frick was still fresh, only five months distant, even if much of it had been spent discussing how to evade the police. It was also untrue that she had led the life of a zombie in Nottingham in the years after she parted from Gross. She had new love affairs. She produced another book: a cotranslation, with a Nottingham University College academic, of Yeats's *The Land of Heart's Desire*, published in Düsseldorf in 1911. To a later generation, which takes seriously women's tendency to disclaim seriousness, the Yeats book looks important. "If she did indeed engage in this challenging intellectual exercise in partnership . . ." said a letter to the *Times Literary Supplement* in 1985, "the view of those years as 'sleepwalking through the days' may have to be modified." But as an emotional record Frieda's memory is accurate. It was Otto Gross who gave her the theoretical justification for her sexual temperament and who convinced her that her destiny was to be an erotic muse for the comfort and liberation of the creative male.

Such was the woman lying in wait for the lonely, ailing, directionless D. H. Lawrence when he came to lunch at the Weekleys' house on Private Road, Nottingham, early in March 1912. He never had a chance.

Part Two

6

UNENGLISHED

March–December 1912

Within twenty minutes of meeting him, Frieda had Lawrence in bed. Lawrence told his Eastwood mentor, Willie Hopkin, what had happened and, in his transparently autobiographical *Mr. Noon,* he tells how. When the revealing passage in *Mr. Noon* was first published in 1984, fifty-four years after Lawrence's death, the novelist David Lodge declared, "Nowhere else in Lawrence's fiction is the allure of an unashamedly sexual woman so powerfully communicated."

Mr. Noon, written in 1920, eight years after the dramatic events it describes, shows an experienced seductress trapping her quarry literally on the way into the dining room. In the scene, transposed to Germany, the woman is "Johanna Keighley," the German wife of an English doctor, on a visit home to Germany. The guest is an ill-at-ease young Englishman; the host is a professor, the woman's brother-in-law, who carries all the marks of Frieda's own brother-in-law Professor Edgar Jaffe, to the life.

In the drawing room before dinner, the professor complains that he has a headache. Johanna (who bears one of Frieda's middle names as

well as the first name of her younger sister) tells him to go and wash his
face in hot water. Gilbert Noon, the English guest, stirs awkwardly, not
knowing what to do next. He passes Johanna

> hovering in the doorway of her room as he went down the passage. A
> bright, roused look was on her face. She lifted her eyelids with a
> strange flare of invitation: for the first time passion broke like light-
> ning out of Gilbert's blood: for the first time in his life. He went into
> her room with her and shut the door. The sultriness and lethargy of his
> soul had broken into a storm of desire for her which shook and swept
> him at varying intervals all his life long.

From behind the closed doors, Johanna and Gilbert hear the professor's voice calling them to dinner. Johanna trills loudly that she is coming: "And in two more minutes she appeared, bright, a little dazzled and
very handsome." Gilbert takes longer, but nonetheless manages, as the
soup plates are being cleared away, to walk "in a dignified manner into
the dining-room, wearing a neat bow tie."

It is a prettied-up version of a shocking event, a sexual tour de force.
The likelihood that it was performed in a sedate Nottingham household
on a spring morning in 1912 is bolstered by the known facts: that Willie
Hopkin, a scholar and editor with a strong social conscience, was a most
reliable source; that Mabel Dodge Luhan many years later in New Mexico heard the same story from Frieda; that Frieda was expert at the swift
seduction and believed—"fanatically," she confesses in her autobiography—that "if only sex were 'free,' the world would straight-away turn
into a paradise"; and that Lawrence always drew heavily on crucial
personal experiences for his fiction. In any event, it is known that Frieda
had Lawrence to herself for a half-hour before lunch in her own room
and that their first meeting was dramatic enough to alter the course of
their lives.

The fictional scene, with its compulsive repetition of the phrase "the
first time" accompanied by images of thunder and lightning, suggests
that Lawrence, stumbling into Frieda's arms after a miserable and un-
satisfying sex life, discovered at last "wonderful desire: violent, genuine
desire!"

BEYOND a doubt, Frieda was expecting a genius to lunch that day.
Weekley had described Lawrence as a genius when he had him in class,
and by 1912 Lawrence was known in Nottingham as a promising author. As soon as she saw the thin, intense, agile figure striding into her
house, moreover, she could tell at a glance that he was like Otto and
Ernst—only nicer.

Lawrence had never met a woman like Frieda, nor, for that matter, heard a voice like hers. She spoke with the deep rasp of a German-speaking heavy smoker. If in those days smoking advertised a woman's emancipation, Frieda was a veritable Mrs. Pankhurst. She was seldom without a cigarette in the corner of her mouth and kept it there while she talked, and she talked constantly, in fluent English. After more than a dozen years in England, she was bilingual and she did not say "v" for "w." Her idiom, however, was often Germanic, as were her sexual theories, and when she passed them on to Lawrence, she was translating.

The theories came fast. By Frieda's own euphemistic account, on that first day "we talked of Oedipus and understanding leaped through our words." She could not have known that she was talking to a young man who was working on a novel about a son in love with his mother.

That Lawrence had not actually read Freud was no barrier to their conversation. He was well acquainted with the Oedipus myth and admired Gilbert Murray's verse translation of Sophocles' *Oedipus* and other Greek plays. Had he needed any reminder, the same February 1912 issue of the *English Review* that carried his short story "Second Best" also contained a glowing review of Covent Garden's new production of the tragedy of the king "destined by God to slay his father and live in incest with his mother."

The dialogue in *Mr. Noon* so parallels Frieda's own account of what she and Lawrence said to each other that day that it is like a tape retrieved from a time capsule.* Lawrence, according to Frieda's recollection, complained that he was finished with women. He appears to have gotten a swift diagnosis: mother-love. "There isn't a man worth having, nowadays, who can get away from his mother," says Johanna in the book. "Their mothers are all in love with them, and they're all in love with their mothers, and what are we poor women to do?"

Then, if *Mr. Noon* is any guide, Frieda quickly gave Lawrence two important bits of information: that she was habitually unfaithful to her husband and that no lover could expect to match up to Otto Gross. The profile of the incomparable lover presented in *Mr. Noon* matches that of Gross in every detail: a doctor and philosopher who lived in Munich, a

*John Worthen, in *D. H. Lawrence: The Early Years, 1885–1912* (Cambridge University Press, 1991), judges *Mr. Noon* to be a more accurate source of biographical information than Lawrence's letters of the time.

Michael Black, the Cambridge University Press publisher who inspired the collective re-editing of Lawrence's letters and works, described *Mr. Noon*'s Part II as "essentially a miraculously fresh and almost total recall, subtly rendered into fiction, of Lawrence's and Frieda's relationship between May and September 1912. It seems amazing that he should, eight years later, remember so much in such vivid details—but then it was the most important passage in his whole life." (*D. H. Lawrence Review*, vol. 20, no. 2; summer 1988).

former lover of her sister's who was the husband of her sister's best friend, and a writer of inspiringly passionate letters. Johanna credits this man with teaching her the sacredness of love, the repressiveness of marriage, and the selfishness of jealousy: in sum, that love *is* sex and can never be wrong; that the only wickedness is "sex in the head, like the saints."

Gilbert Noon is very much like Lawrence; he does not appreciate being lectured. He challenges Johanna for a definition of sex, and gets it: "the kind of magnetism that holds people together, and which is bigger than individuals." Still he will not give in: "But you don't have sexual connection with everybody." Again she shoots straight back: "Not directly—but indirectly." Gilbert grows depressed, and no wonder. The erotic paragon from her past was "a genius—a genius at love . . . and far more brilliant than Freud."

This lover's name was Eberhard—almost identical with that of Johanna's puritanical husband, Everard. The similarity of names is the only hint that Lawrence knew that before he met her Frieda had had a lover whose first name was the German equivalent of her husband's: Ernst Frick, Ernest Weekley.

That Lawrence should adorn the fictional counterparts of his two main rivals in Frieda's life with variants of a virile-sounding "ever-hard" suggests a realization that he had formidable predecessors to live up to. *Mr. Noon* is quite clear on the point: whatever the failings of the husband from whom Mrs. Keighley wants to escape, sexual inadequacy is not among them. What Johanna says of Everard is what Frieda probably told Lawrence about Ernest Weekley—that, in spite of his fierce sense of shame, he was "a highly sensual man, well able to satisfy a woman."

Lawrence always made the most of the creator's power to name his characters. His choices bristle with clues, often anagrammatic, either to their counterparts in real life or to their private significance for him. Johanna's surname, Keighley, clearly derives from Weekley, and its suffix was to surface again years later in the form of "Chatterley." The components of the name "Gilbert Noon" point to three sources: an old schoolmate of Lawrence's, whose name it actually was and who had died before the book was written; George Neville, who had the same initials and the same sexual predicament; and Lawrence himself, who is present in the form of "-bert."

Lawrence also used his authorial powers to reduce the scale of his troubles. The German Johanna in *Mr. Noon* has two children, not three. Her English husband practices his profession in Boston, Massachusetts, not in Nottingham, England. And Gilbert Noon, the schoolteacher who escapes to Germany, suffers a physical weakness, but in his heart, not his lungs. In the book, however, the intractable problem is as it was in Lawrence's life. How to pry the woman free?

* * *

BUT Lawrence was no immoralist. He knew, as his desire flooded toward his professor's wife, the enormity of what he was doing. He was betraying one of the two professors he had admired at college and a man who was trying to help him. The tall, handsome Weekley was an excellent and witty teacher. Lawrence had admired the way Weekley used to sit, feet on desk, lazily pointing at the blackboard and addressing his students—sarcastically, Lawrence thought—as "gentlemen." Lawrence missed the signs that showed Weekley to be a London grammar-school boy from a large working-class family, who, by force of intellect and maternal pride, had become a scholar of Trinity College at Cambridge— the great university to which Weekley had high hopes of returning one day as a professor.

If he had wanted to be discouraging, Weekley could swiftly have told Lawrence that no one without an academic degree could aspire to a post as lecturer at a German university. Instead, out of kindness and perhaps as a favor to Lawrence's uncle Fritz Krenkow, an Arabic scholar, Weekley invited Lawrence to lunch. When Lawrence declined the invitation, Mrs. Weekley sent another in her own name; he accepted because he felt it would be rude to refuse a lady. Subsequent legend in the Weekley family holds that, on the fateful day, Weekley actually forgot that there was a guest coming to lunch and stayed too long at his office; by the time he got home, his marriage was over.

IMMEDIATELY after meeting Frieda, Lawerence spent a week in Shire-brook with the pregnant Alice Dax and her husband, then returned to Eastwood and made plans to visit George Neville, now exiled by his shotgun marriage to the headmastership of a remote Staffordshire village school.

But first he had to see more of Mrs. Weekley. Visiting her at her home one day, Lawrence gave her a taste of his bluntness. He ridiculed her for being unable to turn on the gas ring when the servants were not there. He scolded her for her indifference to her husband: "You take no notice of him," he said. (She felt this was an observation he should have kept to himself.) And on one occasion when Weekley was away and she invited him to spend the night, he refused because it would dishonor her husband's house.

For all his concern for correctness, Lawrence began to see Frieda so often that Weekley reproved her. Lawrence took her out in public, escorting her to the Nottingham Theatre Royal to see a performance of Shaw's *Man and Superman*. They must have been noticed. Frieda at that time was an elegant and striking young matron who had not yet begun to dress like a woman of the counterculture, wearing what H. G. Wells's hero Kipps calls "those picturesque loose robes . . . usually associated with sandals and advanced ideas." Rather, photographs show her in the clothes appropriate to the wife of a professional man: tailored suits; soft blouses trimmed with lace; white gloves and smart hats. The dress worn to the theater in *Sons and Lovers* by Clara, Paul Morel's married mistress, was (so Jessie Chambers later believed) Frieda's: "a sort of semi-evening dress . . . a simple thing of green crape. . . . She looked quite grand he thought. . . . Her beauty was a torture to him."

He also took her to see Jessie's sister May Holbrook and her husband at their farm outside Nottingham. Like many paying court to a parent, Lawrence put himself out to be good with the children. When Frieda brought Elsa, aged ten, and Barby, eight, to the farm, he placed a plate of rock cakes on the kitchen table where they would see them, with a sign: "Take One." He then took them to a stream and made a game of setting paper boats on fire. With his schoolmaster's voice, he challenged, "This is the Spanish Armada and you don't know what that was."

"Yes, we do," contradicted Elsa, with a hostility that would last all her life. Neither she nor Barby liked Lawrence at first sight; they found him pale and tense.

When Lawrence finally took himself to see George Neville, he gave no inkling that he had met the woman of his life. With Neville's new wife and baby living elsewhere with her parents (to dampen the scandal), the two young men were free to tramp the hills and crawl around the pubs as they had done since college days. (Neville later believed that Lawrence was about to flee to Germany because he felt abandoned by his old friends, by him particularly.)

Lawrence devoted a week to Neville—a long time for a man who has just met the most wonderful woman in England. The visit inspired him to write a quick play about a lothario trapped into marriage. He called it *The Married Man*—a dig at the philandering Neville, who, two months married, was already chasing girls again. Lawrence portrayed himself as "Billy" (Neville's pet name for him), a bank clerk with a German fiancée called Elsa who is large, blond, handsome, and about thirty. Elsa appears briefly in the third act to preach the free-love gospel according to Otto Gross. A married man ought to offer his love for just what it is—"the love of a man married to another woman"—for it is love all the same, and "with a little love, we can help each other so much." Elsa exits with a sunny "Don't make sorrow and trouble in the world; try to make happiness."

Lawrence, even at that early stage, seems to have taken Frieda's lectures on Freud to heart. With Neville, he visited a farm run by a mother and her sons and wrote to May Holbrook: "Mrs Titterton is the masterful sort. . . . She mothers her own three great sons to such an extent that they will never marry."

Yet he himself, committed at last, suddenly confronted his stark terror of the female sex. Women seemed to him entirely powerful and self-sufficient. To the depths of his being, he felt that men did not have the strength to get free of them, or even to redress the balance of power. He now saw the miners' strike then in progress in a new light. A union ballot had been distributed to the strikers, his father among them, to decide whether or not to go back to work pending a pay settlement. As Lawrence made the rounds with a friend delivering tickets for relief payments from the union's strike fund, he sensed that the women would settle for the pay packet over principle any time.

EDWARD Garnett continued to act for Lawrence not only as father confessor but as literary adviser and agent. Lawrence, despite the upheaval in his life, was working as hard as usual. That month he sent Garnett a new short story, "Strike Pay," and corrected the proofs of *The Trespasser*. (The sight of his florid prose in type made him vow to Garnett "to wage war on my adjectives.")

The decision to run away with Frieda, as is clarified in John Worthen's biography of Lawrence's early years, was no decision at all. Rather, as March turned to April, a vague idea was forming in the back of Lawrence's mind, set off by a convenient conjunction of plans, and he was so intent on working it out that he hardly noticed that the world around him was in shock over the sinking of the *Titanic* on April 14–15. He was going, as arranged, to Waldbröl, east of Cologne, to stay with the Krenkow relatives. Frieda, he learned, was going to Metz at about the same time, to celebrate the fiftieth anniversary of her father's entry into the Prussian military service. If their departures could be synchronized, they might snatch at least a week together.

Dreaming of Germany, Lawrence was at the same time flooded with nostalgia. When his old colleagues at Davidson Road sent him a farewell present of books, he nearly wept. Suddenly he missed the school, the boys, even the playground: "such a space of view," he wrote his old headmaster, Philip Smith, "and a lot of sky." "Sometimes," he went on, "I think I should like to come and take my Nature lessons—cool and jolly, with the boys happy."

Yet he avoided Croydon when he went back to the Cearne, where he had nudged Garnett into inviting him and Frieda for the weekend. The Cearne, he reminded Garnett, was "the nearest place to a home I've got." Bringing Frieda there was tantamount to bringing her home to meet his parents, and, nervous that Garnett might disapprove, he gave her formidable advance billing: "She is ripping—she's the finest woman

I've ever met—daughter of Baron von Richthofen, of the ancient and famous house of Richthofen—but she is splendid, she is really. . . . Oh but she is the woman of a lifetime."

He did not add that Mrs. Weekley was the mother of three children, aged twelve, ten, and eight.

Garnett obliged. Unreproving himself, he was only concerned about what his housekeeper might say. The Saturday night that Frieda and Lawrence spent at the Cearne in late April may have been their first night in a bed together, and a rare interlude of peace. Frieda read through the manuscript of "Paul Morel"; Lawrence worked in the garden and wrote a poem, "At the Cearne," comparing the start of their love to the springtime. "On the little bank our two souls / Glow like blossoms astart / With gladness." Yet even in the poem, he is in the supplicant position: "I / Shy of your face, still bend to woo / Your feet . . ."

Lawrence was hooked. But what about Frieda? He pressed her to tell Weekley about their affair and formally declare that she was leaving for good. The next week he confidently told Garnett, "She is going to tell him today." Yet he knew that Weekley had a fierce temper and had, Lawrence later told Jessie, threatened to murder Frieda for sending money to socialists in Switzerland (presumably to Ernst Frick). At twenty-six, Lawrence could not believe that an old man like Weekley entertained any sexual passion for his wife. As he explained it to Garnett, Weekley was forty-six, "getting elderly and a bit tired. He doesn't want a wife like Frieda, not to monopolise her."

Frieda did not tell Weekley, however—at least not what Lawrence wanted her to tell. Instead, she confessed two past affairs, most likely those with Gross and Dowson; then, having prepared the girls to go to London to stay with their grandparents, she went, without any sense of finality, to take leave of her son. The boy was spinning tops on the lawn outside the house when she came out. "Come and say good-bye to me, Monty," she said (pronouncing his name, as she always did, as if it had an umlaut: "Muenty"). Then she was gone, out of his childhood, except for the briefest of encounters, forever.

The lovers still had no plan. Lawrence was not even sure what day Frieda was leaving, let alone by what train and boat. Forced to communicate by letter, they did not agree on a date until four days before departure. He went through the motions of packing—collecting his laundry and getting his suit from the tailor—in a state of vague terror which seemed to lodge in his chest. "I feel as if I can't breathe while we're in England," he wrote Frieda.

Nothing did stop them. They met, on Friday, May 3, at two o'clock outside the First Class Ladies' Room at Charing Cross Station, and caught the train to Dover, connecting with the night boat to Ostend. Only a very few people, Garnett and Ada among them, knew that Lawrence was not traveling alone. With him Lawrence had a scant eleven pounds. His flight was cushioned, however, by the expectation of fifty pounds from Duckworth, to be paid upon the publication later that month of *The Trespasser:* a tale of lovers drawn together by *Die Walküre*, the saga of Siegmund, the young stranger who repays an act of hospitality by stealing his host's wife.

As they sat out on deck and Lawrence for the first time watched England recede, he and Frieda were not as unlikely a pair as they might have seemed to Garnett. Both had grown up bossed about by older sisters. Both were, perhaps in consequence, dogmatic and preachy. Each admired Nietzsche and knew Yeats—Lawrence in person, Frieda from translating his work. Each was an infuriating mix of common sense and wildness. Neither cared about wealth or possessions; what they did admire was the written word. In his luggage was the manuscript of "Paul Morel," in hers, the letters of Otto Gross. In their contempt for the stultifying hypocrisy of England, with its concern for appearances and its deep shame about the body, they were as one, and in their odd alliance they were refusing to collaborate in it any longer.

WITHIN a day of arriving in Metz, Lawrence was in culture shock. He had met, and been overwhelmed by, Frieda's two beautiful sisters, especially by Else (described in *Mr. Noon* as "a very beautiful woman, with grey eyes, soft coiled hair, warm colouring and a chiselled face," and also as "very rich"). Else had in tow two little boys, one of whom, Lawrence knew, was Gross's son. As for Johanna, he found her as flirtatious as a courtesan, making up for her lack of English with skilled use of her eyes. The sisters, experienced appraisers of men, had a good look themselves, and approved. Nusch pronounced Lawrence trustworthy; Else found him quiet, but not shy.

Baroness Anna von Richthofen was another revelation for Lawrence: a mother perfectly at ease with the adulteries of her daughters. She was "utterly non-moral, and kind," he wrote Garnett. "Lord—what a family. I've never seen anything like it."

His astonishment was genuine. In allying himself with German aristocrats, Lawrence was, anthropologically speaking, marrying not only up, but out. Exogamy is a major theme in all his writings, a projection of the vast social distance he perceived between his parents. Artistically and personally, he found in the mixed marriage a way to slough off the past and allow a new man to emerge.

The von Richthofens were more concerned about taking their Friedele back into the family circle. They swept her off to their house in a suburb outside Metz, obliging Lawrence, with his schoolboy German, to find himself a hotel. He skulked around his first foreign city in cap and raincoat, and did not like what he saw: an untidy jumble of "new town, old town, barracks, barracks, cathedral." He recoiled at the signs of military occupation. There were German soldiers everywhere, and signs in the public parks forbidding the speaking of French—visible reminders to the French population to abandon dreams of retaking the lost province of Alsace-Lorraine.

Lawrence never knew when he would see Frieda. Twice he bumped into her in the street—once to be brushed away, because her father was coming. The tightness in his chest continued.

They did manage to make love, but erratically. In *Mr. Noon* Johanna Keighley turns up unannounced at Gilbert's hotel room door, and it is then up to him to demonstrate that he can meet the standards of his predecessors. "Do you know," she says condescendingly, "I was rather frightened that you weren't a good lover. But it isn't every man who can love a woman three times in a quarter of an hour—so *well*—is it—?"

"How should I know?" is Gilbert's dumbfounded response.*

The implication is that he has won unexpectedly high marks from an exacting judge but that his performance will continue to be monitored.

Gilbert is more impressed with Johanna's performance *out* of bed. Once when they are interrupted making love by a knock on the door, the totally nude Johanna flies behind a screen and emerges almost instantly in gray silk stockings, rosebud garters, and cambric chemise. Then on go "her lacey-white knickers, her pretty, open work, French stays, her grey silk petty and her reddish dress." With a few more lightning moves, the dress is fastened, shoelaces tied, hair tucked under a feather toque, scarf flung over the shoulders—and she is out the door. A few minutes later Gilbert descends and finds Johanna in the lobby, chatting animatedly to her sister.

While the celebrations for the baron's anniversary progressed, with hordes of von Richthofen relatives arriving from Prussia and Silesia, and Metz *en fête,* with banners flying and bands playing, Lawrence had little to do but brood and send Frieda notes. He felt very foreign. He was inhibited about saying "I love you," and apologized: "I always have to bite my tongue before I say it. It's only my Englishness." Frustration made him overcome it. He wrote a declaration of love, which he wanted Frieda to send along to Weekley as proof that she was leaving him, and dispatched it into the von Richthofen stronghold. "Don't show this

---

*In *Human Sexual Response,* in 1966, Masters and Johnson published their finding that many males below the age of thirty, but "relatively few thereafter," have the ability to ejaculate frequently, with only slight intervals in between. One study subject was observed to ejaculate three times within ten minutes "from the onset of stimulative activity."

letter to either of your sisters—no!" he commanded in a covering note.

These sisters, Lawrence rightly realized, were dubious allies. They had made their own accommodations with monogamy, and expected Friedele to do the same: have affairs, stay married. In principle, they did not object to Frieda's leaving her husband and throwing in her lot with a jobless young English writer six years her junior. They could even accept that Lawrence might, as Frieda promised, turn out to be a great writer. But why rush? She should seek an orderly arrangement with Weekley in the English courts, one which would provide for the children and her own future financial support. Then she could decide where and how to live.

But such reasoned arguments came too late. When Lawrence found that Frieda had not sent his letter to Weekley, he sent it himself. It was short and powerful, well worthy to be the first published letter of D. H. Lawrence, although he cannot have intended it to appear, as it did the following year, on the front page of the *News of the World*. In it he said:

> I love your wife and she loves me. I am not frivolous or impertinent. Mrs. Weekley is afraid of being stunted and not allowed to grow, and so she must live her own life. All women in their natures are like giantesses. They will break through everything and go on with their own lives. The position is one of torture for us all. Do not think I am a student of your class—a young cripple. In this matter are we not simple men? However you think of me, the situation still remains. I almost burst my heart in trying to think what will be best. At any rate we ought to be fair to ourselves. Mrs. Weekley must live largely and abundantly. It is her nature. To me it means the future. I feel as if my effort of life was all for her. Cannot we all forgive something? It is not too much to ask. Certainly if there is any real wrong being done I am doing it, but I think there is not.
>
> D. H. Lawrence

Yet sending this letter without Frieda's consent was selfish and destructive. It cost Frieda her children. Once it was in Weekley's hands, on May 10, a week after they had left England, he held proof that his wife was actively cohabiting with another man. She thereby forfeited all her rights to support or visits with the children, and became totally dependent on her wronged husband's mercy.

Lawrence's action was additionally unfair because Frieda had not agreed to marry him. Indeed, she had sworn that she did not wish to marry again. In leaving her husband, she was only seeking freedom. She fully intended to return to England and to see her children again. A more cautious woman would have calculated the danger, but Frieda was not in the habit of anticipating dire consequences to her spontaneous actions. As Monty observed many years later, "Mamma was a great cake-eater and cake-haver."

Any dispute they might have had over the letter, however, was over-shadowed by a more immediate crisis: Lawrence's arrest as an English spy. He and Frieda had been lying on the grassy ramparts of the town when a German soldier came up to them. Only military personnel were allowed on the fortifications. Lawrence was a foreigner. Frieda's rank and nationality made no difference. Orders were orders.

The incident, comic in retrospect, was grave enough to warrant in-troducing Lawrence to Frieda's father. The baron interceded to get the charge dropped, but angrily. He did not like the way his daughters carried on; he liked Weekley and did not like Lawrence, whom he as-sessed as a common low-bred lout. It was decided that Lawrence had best remove himself from Metz. In *Mr. Noon,* the wealthy sister supplies seventy marks to assist.

Lawrence was apoplectic. To Garnett he stormed, "They vow I am an English officer—*I*—*I*!! The damn fools. So behold me, fleeing eighty miles away, to Trier. Mrs. Weekley is coming on Saturday." The scene of the arrest, recreated in *Mr. Noon,* shows the couple lying in the grass, deep in an argument about fidelity. "But why love *all* men?" Gilbert asks Johanna. "You are only one person. You aren't a universal."

She disagrees. All women are like herself. "And I *do* understand some-thing in every man I meet—I *do.* And in nice men I understand such a *lot* that I feel *forced* to love them."

Gilbert cannot accept this sweeping endorsement of promiscuity from the woman he loves. She might as well, he says sarcastically, call herself Panacea. That label is fine with Johanna; she will distribute her love remedies wherever they are needed.

Gilbert fights back. He insists, "I want exclusive physical love.—There may be aberrations. But the real fact in physical love is the exclusiveness once the love is really *there.*"

As the argument was the essence of the ideological conflict between them—an argument that Lawrence lost then, and all his life with Frie-da—it is not surprising that the lovers did not notice the soldier creeping up on them until they heard a curt "Was machen Sie hier!"

The incident gave Lawrence an instant and fierce antagonism to Ger-man militarism. Many of his countrymen had felt the same way for several years. At the time when Lawrence set out for Germany, relations between the two countries were exceedingly tense. Britain considered war inevitable. It saw Germany increasing its military might with the obvious intention of marching through small and neutral Belgium to launch an assault upon northern France. That very month the British Liberal government's first lord of the Admiralty, Winston Churchill, had announced an increase in spending on naval forces in order to counter Germany's growing sea power; the navy was the only branch of the services in which Britain held numerical superiority. For the rest, Ger-man forces outnumbered Britain's by twenty to one.

In Trier, Lawrence found himself alone, and he never liked being alone, even on the Moselle in a lovely town once the second city of the Holy Roman Empire. He felt the first stirrings of anger. What if Frieda did not come on Saturday as promised? "By Jove, if you don't!" he threatened, then added sweetly, "We shall always have to battle with *life*, so we'll never fight with each other, always help."

She came—but on Friday, for only half a day, and, at her father's insistence, with her mother as chaperone. Then she returned to Metz. Lawrence was left disappointed, and embarrassed. The chatty hotel-keeper in *Mr. Noon* is very inquisitive about the unseen "wife" for whom Gilbert has taken a double room, with matrimonial bed.

Frieda was in Trier long enough, however, to send Ernest Weekley a telegram. Even before receiving Lawrence's letter, Weekley had begun to suspect that Frieda was not alone. He wrote demanding that she wire him a straight answer. Evading the request would have been easy, but Lawrence would not permit it. He marched her straight to the telegraph office and forced her to wire Weekley that his suspicions were correct.

Lawrence, although he had rejected Christianity, remained a puritan. He believed in plain truth, plainly spoken. Any form of compromise—so he argued to Frieda—any deliberate ambiguity or half-truth was a lie. To a sophisticated European, like Else Jaffe with her Heidelberg doctorate, that attitude was simplistic nonsense. "The truth is never true," the elder sister in *Mr. Noon* observes as if to a child.

But Ernest Weekley lived by the same absolutes as Lawrence did. Since Frieda's departure, Weekley had been on the verge of a breakdown. He feared that his reputation in Nottingham would be ruined by the disgrace of a runaway wife. He might lose his job. By the time Lawrence's shattering letter arrived, Weekley had decided what to do. He spelled it out in a letter to Frieda, stating, "All compromises are unthinkable. We are not rabbits . . . Have some remorse for all your deception of a loving man." He would move the children to London, where they would live with his parents and his sister Maude; he would buy a new house for them all in a neighborhood where the children could go to school, make new friends, and once more live in the atmosphere of a family home.

Weekley's fears were hardly groundless. He was a man with no private income. The British establishment did not like scandal, and the scandal of a divorce could be considerable, for divorces were rare and shocking. Only 587 were granted in 1912 in England and Wales.

Yet he was not bitter. Just like many people in a far more permissive age, Weekley approached divorce reasonably at first, only to turn vindictive later under pressure from lawyers and his own increasing anger. At that early stage, he told Frieda: "I bear him no ill-will and hope you will be happy with him." He wrote generously and emotionally (in German) to her parents. To "Dear Mama," he said: "Today I had to lecture for four hours and take part in a long session of the Senate. I have

desperately to stretch every nerve in order not to cry out hysterically."
To "Dear Papa!" he declared that his only goals were to provide for
Frieda's happiness and the children's future, and to keep news of the
divorce from getting into the newspapers. If there were any risk of
publicity, he would call the whole thing off. His own parents were
already suffering: "It is unjust that in their old age they must again suffer
so, for them it is ten thousand times worse than death."

The decision was entirely his. Under the harsh English law as it remained until 1969, divorce was a gift of the injured spouse to the guilty.
Innocent parties could not be divorced against their will. If Weekley did
not choose to divorce Frieda, she would remain his wife, just as Mrs.
Ford Madox Ford refused to divorce Ford in order to prevent him from
marrying Violet Hunt.

Lawrence, meanwhile, hung around Trier, enjoying the absence of
soldiers, thinking of Frieda and how pretty she was ("At this moment, I
seem to love you, because you've got such a nice chin"), having nightmares about Weekley, and working. Then he moved on to his original
destination, the Krenkows' home in Waldbröl. On the way, he wrote a
fine poem at Hennef am Rhein, where, as he changed trains, he felt
soothed by "the little river twittering in the twilight."

"Bei Hennef" sums up their state of imperfect bliss after one week
abroad:

> You are the call and I am the answer,
> . . . .
> What else? it is perfect enough.
> It is perfectly complete,
> You and I,
> What more——?
>
> Strange, how we suffer in spite of this!

Less ambivalently, he assured Frieda on a postcard: "I know I only
love you. The rest is nothing at all." Less poetically, he wrote another
postcard, to Flossie Cullen, an Eastwood family friend and nurse, who
had looked after Mrs. Lawrence in her last illness, to report that the
weather in Germany was "hot as H."

FRIEDA was suffering, too. The family was in an uproar. Warnings were
shouted at her from all sides. From Nottingham, her neighbor Lily Kip-
ping implored: "Don't spoil your own life and the lives of all the others—the little girls without a mother, no mother's love, and Monty, he
must have a mother to protect him." And from London her sister-in-law

Maude Weekley wrote, devastated that her splendid brother, pride of the family, should be so cast aside: "I cannot be fond of a person for thirteen years and then suddenly cease to think them dear. What does all this mean, what are you doing and why! . . . I do love you still but oh! that you had chosen any other life than his to smash."

Poor Weekley. Just as his private world was falling apart, his new book, *The Romance of Words,* was attracting excellent reviews. *The Times Literary Supplement,* which accorded it half the front-page review on May 30, called it "so amusing that we could not put it down."

LAWRENCE, ever perceptive, joked to Frieda that he and Weekley were like allies: "See the men combining in their free masonry against you. It is very strange." Indeed it was. Both men were determined to push Frieda, against her wishes, into marrying Lawrence. Lawrence congratulated himself on Weekley's decision to divorce Frieda. "That is the result of *my* letter to him. I will crow my little crow in opposition to you."

From Waldbröl, Lawrence began to send Frieda a barrage of sermons on marriage: "Remember you are to be my wife." "We are going to be married respectable people." At the same time, he refused to join her in Munich, where she was going with Else after Metz. He would not budge. He wanted time to himself, to prepare, like a monk before taking vows. "My next coming to you is solemn, intrinsically—I am solemn over it—not sad, oh no—but it is my marriage, after all, and a great thing—not a thing to be snatched and clumsily handled."

Frieda fought back in her own fashion. On successive days, she delivered two hammer blows. First, she wrote that she thought she was pregnant. Lawrence did not even flinch.

Never mind about the infant. If it should come, we will be glad, and stir ourselves to provide for it—and if it should not come, ever—I shall be sorry. I do not believe, when people love each other, in interfering there. . . . I want you to have children to me—I don't care how soon. I never thought I should have that definite desire.

Even so, he would not join her.

A little waiting, let us have, because I love you. . . . I seem to want a certain time to prepare myself. . . . Because it is a great thing for me to marry you, not a quick passionate coming together. I know in my heart, "here's my marriage" . . . it is a great thing in my life—it is *my* life.

If he seemed hesitant, she would have to forgive him. "You have got all myself . . . It's a funny thing, to feel one's passion—sex desire, no longer a sort of wandering thing, but steady, and calm." "I shall love you all my life," he concluded. "That also is a new idea to me. But I believe it."

Then came Frieda's second blow. She had a new lover. She had run into an old friend in Metz, an officer, Udo von Henning. Learning that he was unhappily married and feared that he was impotent, she naturally was doing what she could to reassure him.

Lawrence was equally unperturbed. "If you want Henning, or anybody, have him," he replied equably. "But I don't want anybody till I see you. But all natures aren't alike." He was more worried about her health. "Only my dear, because I love you, don't be sick, do will to be well and sane." He stuck to his insistence on a period of solitude before they came together again—"to start living. It's a marriage, not a meeting."

For a man so easily angered, Lawrence accepted with astonishing calm that he was a cuckold before he was a husband. It shows how maternal was the role in which he cast Frieda. Like the baby of a family, he did not mind what she did for others as long as she was mainly his. He used the imagery of the nursing mother to describe her affair with von Henning; he scolded her for making von Henning "babyfied":

> You make me think of a Maupassants [*sic*] story. An Italian workman, a young man, was crossing in the train to France, and had no money, and had eaten nothing for a long time. There came a woman with breasts full of milk—she was going into France as a wet nurse. Her breasts full of milk hurt her—the young man was in a bad way with hunger. They relieved each other and went their several ways. Only where is Henning to get his next feed?

The idea of sex as a form of maternal sustenance persists in *Mr. Noon,* where Udo von Henning is translated into "Rudolf von Daumling," who fears that he has lost his virility:

> Johanna, of course, who took her sex as a religion, felt herself bound to administer the cup of consolation to him. . . .
>   She found occasion to draw her old Rudolf to her breast, and even further, restoring to him his manliness.

Gilbert Noon addresses the reader: "Would it have been more noble, under the circumstances, to give him the baby's dummy-teat of ideal sympathy and a kind breast?" The answer implicit in the question is no; sexual intercourse is a more honest and direct form of sympathy than listening and talking.

Sheer fiscal prudence, if nothing else, kept Lawrence in Waldbröl for nearly two weeks. While he enjoyed himself in the small village, flirting with his cousin Hannah, learning German, going to a local fair, and drinking beer in the *Gasthaus,* he also worked exceedingly hard.

Lawrence, when he needed money, wrote something. Short stories and bits of journalism came easily to him. While in Waldbröl, a spectacular storm, with hailstones, the size of chicken eggs, smashing roofs—vividly reported in the *Waldbröler Zeitung*—gave him an easy article, which Garnett promptly sold to the *Saturday Westminister Gazette.* That month, apart from his journalism and his poems, he applied himself to revising "Paul Morel" for the third time and beginning a new novel, based on Flossie Cullen, the Eastwood nurse.

Lawrence was determined to support Frieda by his writing. When he promised her that they were going to be "married respectable people," he meant, among other things, people who paid their bills. He loathed muddle and debt. "One *must* be detached, impersonal, cold, and logical, when one is arranging *affairs*," he lectured her by letter. Still defending their separation as a kind of religious fast before a feast, he said: "In our marriage, let us be business-like. The love is there—then let the common-sense match it."

His love was there. But hers? In her memoirs, Frieda conceded that there had been no grand passion between herself and Lawrence when they went away together. All the same, she was under his formidable spell. He seemed to understand her and to make the world fresh and new. And he needed her. She wrote Edward Garnett, whose good opinion she very much wished, "I love him with 1000 different loves. I want everybody to love him he deserves it. There is no fight between us, we want the same thing, and our fighting will be against other people *never* with each other."

Frieda had complete faith in Lawrence as a writer. It was a vocation for which she and her culture held the greatest respect. In allying herself with the young Lawrence, moreover, she was overtaking her sister Else as the muse of genius. If she glimpsed immortality, she would not have been wrong.

ON May 24, the day after *The Trespasser* was published in London, Lawrence reached Munich at last. He found their "honeymoon"—as he insisted on calling it—had been organized by the Jaffes. Frieda's eldest sister and her husband were bound by common interests and by his money, if not by love; together they played a great and underrecognized part in the success of the elopement. The Jaffes offered Lawrence and Frieda advice, encouragement, free housing, and cash in those difficult early years.

Jaffe, satirized in *Mr. Noon* as an aging, diminutive German-Jewish professor of economics, seems to have viewed his sister-in-law's wild escapade with indulgent amusement. In the novel, when the young Englishman finally turns up in Munich, the little professor greets him with the English accent acquired during his years in England, "Ha-ha! Ha-ha! . . . The return of the truant! The return of the Bad Boy! Well I never! Well I nevah!" The professor takes it upon himself to warn the truant about the formidable family of sisters into which he has fallen: "These women have no conscience—AT ALL." "I married one," he says, laughing, "so I know."

Under the Jaffes' guidance, Frieda and Lawrence traveled south, into the Bavarian countryside where the meadows meet the foothills of the Alps. There, within easy reach of each other, in villages strung along the same (now suburban) railway line, Else and her children lived in a villa in Wolfratshausen; her lover, Alfred, had a holiday flat in Icking; and Jaffe was building a villa of his own in Irschenhausen.

For Lawrence and Frieda's "honeymoon" the Jaffes suggested the Gasthaus zum Post in the slightly more distant village of Beuerberg. They chose well. Beuerberg was, and remains, an idyllic cluster of a few rustic houses and a village green where cattle graze in front of a twelfth-century cloister and onion-top church.

Lawrence and Frieda arrived by train, crossed to the *Gasthaus,* and registered as man and wife. Lawrence then learned what it was like to accompany Frieda into a public drinking place full of men. The Bavarian farmers in *Mr. Noon* are handsome, and look over their pot lids at Johanna with a "half-hostile, challenging mountain stare."

Alone at last, they were happy at last—much of the time. Lawrence accepted Frieda's sexual tutelage and recorded his awakening in a series of confessional love poems, later published as *Look! We Have Come Through!* The poems, full of dialogue and self-reference in the manner of Wordsworth and Walt Whitman, disclose Frieda's sexual technique. True to her word, she could find something lovable in any man, even in the scrawny Lawrence. She felt all over his thin body with her experienced hands. "Why shouldn't your legs and your good strong thighs / be rough and hairy?—I'm glad they are like that."

She laughed at his shame and reassured him:

> And I love you so! Straight and clean and all of a piece is
> the body of a man,
> such an instrument, a spade, like a spear, or an oar, such a
> joy to me—"
> So she laid her hands and pressed them down my sides,
> so that I began to wonder over myself, and what I was.

But Frieda was undergoing a conversion, too, from mistress into muse, as they walked in the countryside, bathed in mountain streams, and talked about their lives and his work. Honeymoon or not, Lawrence kept up his rate of production. In addition to the poems, he revised three short stories and rewrote "Paul Morel" during those early weeks in Bavaria. As Frieda gushed in a letter to Garnett, "Lawrence is a joy in *all* moods and it's fearfully exciting when he writes and I watch while it comes and it is a thrill."

Lawrence's powers of sensual description were stirred by the unfamiliar varieties of wildflowers. Architecture rarely moved him, and to his stern Protestant eye, the interior of the Beuerberg Pfarrkirche, a baroque effusion of white and gold with a vast gold altarpiece, was "gaudy, wildly, savagely religious." But the meadows inspired him to word paintings, which he sent back to England, to his less fortunate friends who had never seen

> primulas, like mauve cowslips, somewhat—and queer marsh violets, and orchids, and lots of bell-flowers, like large, tangled, dark-purple harebells, and stuff like larkspur, very rich, and lucerne, so pink, and in the woods, lilies of the valley—oh, flowers, great wild mad profusion of them, everywhere.

One of his finest love poems to Frieda that summer compares her Rubenesque golden breasts to full-blown yellow "Gloire de Dijon" roses.

Each of them felt liberated, Lawrence not only from his landscape but from his national identity. It was his first sense of the expanse of Europe; he felt he could walk to Russia. The passage in *Mr. Noon* expressing this exhilaration could serve, like the last movement of Beethoven's Ninth Symphony, as a hymn for Europe:

> . . . the sense of an infinite multiplicity of connections. There seemed to run gleams and shadows from the vast spaces of Russia, a yellow light seemed to struggle through the great Alp-knot of Italy, magical Italy, while the north, from the massive lands of Germany, and from far-off Scandinavia one could feel a whiteness, a northern, sub-arctic whiteness. Many magical lands, many magical peoples, all magnetic and strange, unite to form the vast patchwork of Europe.

Europe also gave him a new perspective on his native land:

> For the first time he saw England from the outside: tiny she seemed, and tight, and so partial. Such a little bit among all the vast rest. Whereas till now she had seemed all-in-all in herself. Now he knew it was not so. . . . And he became unEnglished.

* * *

H<small>E</small> and Frieda had no plans. They awaited the next move from Weekley. Else, needless to say, had communicated the whole drama to her good friend in Ascona, and Frieda Gross wrote back with her own doubts. Was it wise of Friedele and her lover to live together so openly?

> Now as to how this Lawrence ["dieser Lawrence" in the German] might be. The one of whom you all speak quite good things in such remarkably impersonal tones. He appears to me rather like a hero out of a novel. Even Friedele seems to have put him on this earth without a word . . . she simply wrote that he is rather like Otto and Ernst. I assume that he is an Englishman who is going to live in Germany and that they are going to live together. That they are now together makes me terribly happy for Friedele but I am also surprised that she is doing this during the period of her divorce.

Frieda Gross knew nothing at all about Weekley; perhaps he was sympathetic.

> But otherwise I would think it is usually fairly provocative for a man to think that his wife is going to set up a household with someone else—one in which he would also have to allow the children to make visits.

Perhaps, Frieda Gross concluded philosophically, "one can never quite see the reality of the rest of life when in a state of erotic happiness."

Erotic happiness, possibly, but not bliss. The fights started almost immediately. There were two causes. In spite of Lawrence's early stamina and Frieda's encouragement, they were sexually ill-matched. From the honeymoon poems (so explicit that W. H. Auden later said they made him feel like a Peeping Tom) and from the couple's private comments to friends, it is not hard to understand why. Lawrence's clumsiness and eagerness were no match for Frieda's appetite and experience. She achieved orgasm easily and insistently, after Lawrence had finished his own. The man who had written of the terrors of the beaked woman in *The White Peacock* was now bound to a woman who clung to him until she had achieved her own satisfaction. He felt used.

Then there was the problem of the children. As the weeks turned into months, Frieda was learning the price that would be exacted for jettisoning her Nottingham life—not only the loss of her children, but Lawrence's rage at any mention of their existence. So tolerant of her sexual infidelity, he demanded that she suppress both the most powerful loyalty in her life and any sign that she was sick with grief. The mere sight of her eyes clouding over drove him to a frenzy. In a long and bitter poem written in Beuerberg, "She Looks Back," he sees himself deceived as she makes love to him while the mother in her, "fierce as a murderess," yearns toward England. He ends with a curse "against all mothers."

On the first of June the honeymoon ended and domestic life began. Their first home was Alfred Weber's flat in Icking. Weber, who was impressed with Lawrence, lent it rent-free. Lawrence got down to work again, bemused by having a beautiful woman at his side. As he wrote to Edward Garnett, "Frieda is awfully good looking. . . . She's got a figure like a fine Rubens woman, but her face is almost Greek." He loved to see her in a scarlet pinafore, leaning over the balcony against a backdrop of the blue Alps. He liked less seeing her out on the balcony wearing only her nightgown; she refused to follow his example and put on a dressing gown.

But the peace of bucolic Bavaria was marred by the signs of Germany readying for war. Below their flat the German cavalry thudded by. Lawrence was frightened. The massed troops—in *Mr. Noon,* "the strange, dark heavy soldiery"—reminded him that he had no comrades, no family, no ties to life even, nothing except his writing and his love for Frieda.

And she was by no means tied to him. Her old lover Ernst Frick had been writing to her from his prison cell, and she suddenly thought she might like to go to Zurich to attend his forthcoming trial. Frick discouraged her. "I know that you would like to see me here," he wrote that June, "but it is not really right for me to meet you in prison. . . . What could we do here except have a conventional conversation as in England?"

Frick wrote affectionately. He knew Frieda had a new lover, one around whom she might build a new life, and, he told her, he sympathized with her restless suffering and her wish for freedom. But he warned her not to underestimate the price that strong people had to pay for it. "You can see," he concluded, "that you are being consoled by a prisoner about your freedom." But he promised (optimistically, as it turned out: he got a one-year prison sentence for the barracks bombing) that he would very soon be with her to talk it all over in person.

In Ascona, Frieda Gross was appalled at the suggestion that Frieda might drop in during the height of their crisis. She begged Else to tell her sister to stay away.

Frieda took the opportunity of their interlude in Icking to instruct Lawrence in the ways of Ascona—the joys of nudity, for one thing. She would bathe in a mountain stream and then spread herself bare in the sun while he (comically, as he saw himself in *Mr. Noon*) crouched, hunched up on the rocks. *Mr. Noon* also recounts a lesson in eurythmics. In the lovers' borrowed flat Johanna floats naked from room to room, wafting her hands in waving motions and inviting him to copy her. "Dance," she orders Gilbert Noon. "Dance!" And the Englishman, "ashamed to be ashamed, danced in correspondence, with a jerky, male stiffness." In that scene even their body hair speaks the difference between them: hers, like her body, is soft and golden, but his is a ruddy brown, an obscene contrast to his dark hair and chalk-white skin. (As a writer Lawrence wasted very little. The proud dance of a naked pregnant woman appears in *The Rainbow,* one of the shocking scenes that were to get the book into trouble with English law.)

Frieda was a proud, heavy nude, but she was not pregnant. "If the infant should come," Lawrence had said in May, "we will be glad . . . and if it should not come, ever—I shall be sorry." It was an unequivocal wish for fatherhood. As the months went by, Lawrence waited, just as Otto Gross had exactly five years earlier, for Frieda to give him the good news. Else Jaffe and Frieda Gross waited too. "Friedele must have new little children," wrote Frau Gross to Else. "Not only to replace the ones she has lost but because she must have some." The matriarchy expected no less.

But Frieda did not conceive. Lawrence probably believed, as have many since, that, with his poor health, the failure was his. As Frieda had so swiftly proved to Ernest Weekley after their marriage, she was a very fertile woman. Yet the trouble could equally well have been hers. At the time of her elopement with Lawrence, she had not become pregnant for eight years; and, with Gross at least, it is certain that she had not used contraception. She may have become infertile, like Constance Garnett, Lady Ottoline Morrell, and many women of her time, from complications following childbirth. It is also quite possible that from one of her various lovers Frieda had caught a venereal disease. Syphilis, rampant at the time, was the cause of infertility in Violet Hunt and the writer Katherine Mansfield. In any event, Lawrence and Frieda slowly came to realize that they would have to resolve the conflicts between them without the salutary shock of parenthood.

Their rows were phenomenal, and brought out the worst in each. Lawrence had not seen himself so violent since childhood, while Frieda would retreat into the defiant defensiveness of her girlhood, when she felt herself insignificant, squeezed in between Else and Nusch. In one letter she confessed, "I am feeling so small today, like a small cat I want to crawl under the bed and miow" and in another, "I don't believe I have anybody who can put up with me."

Living with Frieda revealed to Lawrence the fact of life that in many ways the sexes are incompatible. They do not see things the same way. For his part, he could not love any woman more than he loved Frieda. He wanted no other, could not even flirt with others. Yet she would not accept his views.

He accepted the perpetual battle between them by declaring it universal. The real tragedy in life, as he explained to Garnett, was not premature death or love for a forbidden person, but rather "the inner war which is waged between people who love each other." Or, as he put it in the facetious *Mr. Noon*, "No, damn it all, what was the good of love that wasn't a fight—."

Yet their real tragedy was probably their childlessness. Seeing his own child at Frieda's breast might have lifted Lawrence out of the infantile solipsism celebrated in one of the most impassioned of the honeymoon poems, "Song of a Man Who Is Loved": "Between her breasts is my home . . . So I hope I shall spend eternity / With my face down buried between her breasts."

He had always expected to have children. He had rejected Jessie Chambers four years earlier by telling her that he wanted "a woman I can kiss and embrace and make the mother of my children." He once had told Helen Corke, "You know, when I'm middle-aged, I shall probably be married and settled, and take my family to church every Sunday." He believed that procreation was the purpose of sex, that the urgent will of nature explained the sexual drive. The act of sexual congress itself, as he wrote in another of that summer's poems, "Rose of All the World," was a "heave of effort / At starting other life." In it he marveled "that my completion of manhood should be the beginning / Another life from mine! For so it looks." Yet "Rose of All the World" ends with quiet resignation, almost as if the menstrual period they hoped not to see had arrived. Perhaps, the poem says, their love may have to be its own justification, "without an ulterior motive."

Another poem in the series, "Wedlock," is just as plain:

> And think, there will something come forth from us,
> We two, folded so small together,
> There will something come forth from us.
> Children, acts, utterance,
> Perhaps only happiness.
> Perhaps only happiness will come forth from us.
>
> . . . .
>
> But that is all I want.
> And I am sure of that.

The failure to start a family of their own was compensated for in part by the new ties Frieda brought him. Lawrence was to find a second mother in Frieda's mother even though their relationship got off to an unpromising start. The day the stout old lady had chaperoned Frieda to Trier, she had delivered the von Richthofen case against him: a penniless young man had no right to take a mother away from her children or a wife away from a learned professor, let alone to make the daughter of a cultured nobleman live the life of a tramp. Later that summer the old baroness turned up unexpectedly at their flat in Icking to say it all again. Lawrence took the tirade in silence. When she was finished, he politely escorted her to the station—and won a friend for life.

Lawrence was also fond of Else, but recognized her as a controlling woman, "the sort who organises other people's affairs." When Else took Frieda to Wolfratshausen for four days, he nearly went out of his mind. He knew that Else was telling her sister to go back to England and that Frieda was increasingly vulnerable to the suggestion. She missed her children so much she ached. She could not sleep, and in the middle of the night Lawrence would find her huddled under the window, staring blankly out. Sometimes she simply lay on the floor and cried. To Garnett, Lawrence boasted that Frieda was free to make up her own mind; he would not beg her to stay for his sake.

Not in so many words, perhaps. But Frieda above all wanted to be needed, and Lawrence had convinced her that he needed her more than her children did. As he told Garnett, "If she left me, I do not think I should be alive six months hence."

A constant theme in their marriage began on their "honeymoon": a desperate plea for visitors. "Come and see us" runs through all their letters, a hope for relief of the strain between them and also for the recognition as a couple that a visitor from England would give. Only a month abroad, they began urging Garnett to join them in Bavaria. Instead, he sent his son.

David Garnett had not met the Lawrences, although he had admired *The White Peacock*. At twenty-one he was a younger version of his father, a tall, shambling, genial figure. He was traveling around Munich when Lawrence's invitation came; he happily went down to Icking, where Lawrence met him at the station and took him on a walk through the woods to Wolfratshausen to meet Frieda. "Lawrence," David wrote home, "is very very alive."

The junior Garnett was a fitting heir to a literary dynasty. His description of the famous runaways as he saw them that summer has achieved the historic status of a wedding photograph. With his Fabian upbringing, David Garnett was highly sympathetic to the working class, but also alert to its genetic manifestations. He said Lawrence's hair was

> of a colour, and grew in a particular way, which I have never seen except in English working men. It was bright mud-colour, with a streak of red in it, a thick mat, parted on one side. Somehow, it was incredibly plebeian, mongrel and underbred.

Lawrence's nose, as well, was eugenically wanting. It was too short and lumpy and the chin was too large and round, while the mustache was short and scrubby. At the same time David liked Lawrence's marvelous blue eyes, his constant self-mockery, and his smile that said "Come on, let's have some fun." In sum:

> He was the type of the plumber's mate who goes back to fetch the tools. He was the weedy runt you find in every gang of workmen: the one who keeps the other men laughing all the time, who makes trouble with the boss and is saucy to the foreman; who gets the sack . . . the type who provokes the most violent class-hatred in this country: the impotent hatred of the upper classes for the lower.

In contrast was Frieda:

> Her head and the whole carriage of her body were noble. Her eyes were green, with a lot of tawny yellow in them, the nose straight. She looked one dead in the eyes, fearlessly judging one.

With her swift lazy leap, Frieda was, to David, a lioness. He fell in love with them both.

And they with him. He became their substitute child. They admired his strong swimming, roared with laughter at his jokes, and got him to play charades, which they loved. (Lawrence, David said later, was "a natural copy-cat, the only great mimic I have known.") After one giddy evening, improvising ballets, David whirling about, draped in Frieda's scarves, Lawrence wrote almost enviously to Edward Garnett, "By Jove, I reckon his parents have done joyously well for that young man."

Life was not all games. Working hard during the day, Lawrence completed another rewriting of "Paul Morel" and sent it off to William Heinemann, confidently saying that it was his best book. On July 1 Heinemann sent it back. The new book, said the publisher of *The White Peacock*, was a disappointment. It lacked unity, sympathetic characters, and "reticence." The last was the fatal flaw, for it meant that Heinemann judged the book unacceptable for the circulating libraries and therefore unpublishable.

It was as well that William Heinemann was not there when his rejection letter arrived. Lawrence let fly a torrent of insults impugning the manhood of all Englishmen: "the blasted, jelly-boned swines, the slimy belly-wriggling invertebrates, the miserable sodding rotters, the flaming sods." What was more, he continued to Garnett (revealing that the specifics of male fertility were much on his mind), "their spunk is that watery its a marvel they can breed."

Frieda had assured him that Garnett would stick by him. Garnett did more. He got Duckworth to accept "Paul Morel" immediately and sent his own detailed advice on reshaping it.

But they had to move on. Alfred Weber needed his flat. Nothing was decided in London. In fact, Weekley had now changed his mind and was refusing divorce. Every day was spoiled by the arrival of the post as Weekley stormed to Frieda's helpless parents, who passed the letters on, that Lawrence was no gentleman and that he would beat her when the going got rough. In stepped Else. She had been won over by Lawrence, and he by her. "Have you never been to Italy?" asks her counterpart in *Mr. Noon.* "Oh but it is lovely! Why not go there? Why not go, and walk some of the distance!"

But the cost? "Ach money! Money will come." This statement, coming from a forceful and wealthy elder sister—*Mr. Noon* places the income of this sister's husband at about twenty thousand pounds a year—was as good as an insurance policy.

THE long march over the Alps took a month. For Frieda it was the moment of decision. When she put a rucksack on her back on August 5, 1912, and turned south, she effectively abandoned thoughts of returning to London or settling in Munich. "I have at last nailed F.'s nose to my wagon," Lawrence boasted to Garnett, and they set out.

The route Lawrence chose was doubly significant. It followed, as Lawrence describes in *Twilight in Italy,* "the imperial road to Italy . . . from Munich across the Tyrol, through Innsbruck," and over the Brenner pass to Verona. It was also the road to health, for the high, sheltered, windless Alpine valleys had been favored sites for health spas for consumptives since the 1890s. (In the late spring of that same year, Thomas Mann visited Davos in Switzerland, which was to provide the sanatorium setting for *The Magic Mountain.*)

With their trunks sent ahead to Bozen (Bolzano), Frieda hiked with a happy air of slumming; she liked the idea of the baron's daughter on the open road, cooking on a little portable stove, sleeping—and making love—in hay huts.

For Lawrence it was his first ascent into the ice-blue mountains that had glittered at him since he arrived in Bavaria. If flowers for Lawrence carried the heavy allure of female sexuality, mountains were Woman in another aspect:

> The great slopes shelving upwards, far overhead: the sudden dark, hairy ravines in which he was trapped: all made him feel he was caught, shut in down below there. He felt tiny, like a dwarf among the great thighs.

It is hard to reconcile Lawrence's frail health with strenuous walking, but he could and often did walk seven or eight hours at a stretch, perhaps by taking his time. On their nuptial trek, he and Frieda covered at best twenty miles in three days; they did long stretches by train and broke their journey with a fortnight's stay at a village farmhouse. In all, they walked eleven days out of thirty-one.

He worked as he walked, turning their march into myth. His essays about the journey in which they forged their life together were the first of his travel writing, a genre in which he has few peers; full of personal and practical information, the essays tell how the new couple evolved the kind of plain meal they both enjoyed—bread, ham, butter, and eggs, or, in Lawrence's parlance, "good black-rye bread," "thin raw ham," "thick firm Alp-grass butter," and "orange-golden" scrambled eggs. Frieda's hefty appetite—a sign of her robust health—never ceased to amuse Lawrence and, within their budget, he indulged it.

In his various accounts, Lawrence recorded again and again the excitement (in *Mr. Noon* he called it the "flame of male ardour") that Frieda aroused among strange men, as if he felt them jeering because they could see he was no match for her. In these Alpine settings, Frieda is often portrayed dressed in bright Bavarian costume, with its full skirts, laced bodice, and puffed sleeves. They both agreed that she looked marvelous in it. In *Mr. Noon*, at the sight of Johanna in "a Bavarian peasant-dress, tight at the breasts, full-skirted, with a rose silk apron," a lusty villager asks her to dance. She accepts, with a "bright, excited face," leaving Gilbert on the sidelines to watch the peasant throw her into the air, stamp his feet like a bull, and to hear Johanna give "a cry of unconsciousness, such as a woman gives in her crisis of embrace."

Johanna, Lawrence wrote with sacrificial honesty, "legitimately was the bride of the mountaineer that night." The same concession to defeat appears in his short sketch "A Chapel Among the Mountains," in which the wanderers enter an inn in a rainstorm: "ruddy joyous peasants, three of them handsome, made a bonfire of their hearts in honour of Anita [Frieda], whilst I sat in a corner and dripped."

David Garnett represented no such threat and, after a week, they were begging him to catch a train and join them on their walk. He agreed. While they waited for him in the Tyrolean village of Mayrhofen, Lawrence allowed himself some uneasy thoughts of home. He knew that Ada was furious with him and would not mention him to anybody, aware too that Alice Dax's baby was nearly due and that it had been a difficult pregnancy. "I am sorry for her, she is so ill," Lawrence wrote to Sallie Hopkin. "At any rate, and whatever happens," he said, dismissing all thoughts of Alice and the coming child, "I do love, and I am loved—I have given and I have taken—and that is eternal. Oh, if only people could marry properly. I believe in marriage."

LAWRENCE's claim to love Frieda "whatever happens" was soon put to the test. A few days after David arrived, he was joined by a tall, handsome, sun-tanned, young and amusing friend, Harold Hobson, on his way back to London from Moscow.

Before two days were out, Frieda had seduced Hobson. Lawrence and

David had gone off together to look for wildflowers, leaving her and Hobson alone together. Hobson, who had discovered in Frieda a sympathetic listener to his romantic troubles, suddenly announced that he wildly desired her. A hay hut was handy. Ergo . . .

David, when he learned about the encounter later, was not surprised. Frieda made no secret of her sexual adventurousness. She had boasted to David that she had got her revenge on Lawrence after a row by swimming across a river and giving herself to a woodcutter. She had regaled David also with the Chaucerian tale of her wedding night with the prudish Weekley. She had even offered herself to David. One day, walking together in the woods, they had come to a clearing with soft pine needles, and she suggested they take advantage of it. When he declined, she good-naturedly bore no hard feelings.

Lawrence did not learn of the seduction for two days, not until, after more hard hiking, David and Hobson had returned to Munich. Alone together once again, Lawrence and Frieda plodded on toward Italy, with Frieda begging to stop and Lawrence threatening to leave her behind. At eight-thirty in the evening, after a steep climb that took them near the summit of a very high pass, with cold rain and icy wind blowing around them, Lawrence, who was in charge of the map, announced that they had missed the path. It was then that Frieda chose to break her news. To judge from *Mr. Noon,* which (with Hobson renamed "Stanley") corroborates the details given in David Garnett's memoir, her words were "Stanley had me the night before last."

Lawrence's reaction was catatonically blank. Describing it in *Mr. Noon,* he says that Gilbert's world went into a blur: "Night, loneliness, danger, all merged." Then Gilbert says: "Never mind, my love. Never mind. Never mind. We do things we don't know we're doing." He kisses her, and in one of Lawrence's repetitive passages that rock like a child seeking comfort, he says, as much to himself as to Johanna:

> And they don't signify. They don't signify really, do they? They don't really mean anything, do they? I love you—and so what does it matter?

It was these lines that so staggered Diana Trilling when *Mr. Noon* appeared in 1984. For generations D. H. Lawrence had been understood to be preaching the religious seriousness of sex and to offer his own life with Frieda as an example. Yet to accept casual coupling as a matter of no importance was to betray not only his readers but his tradition. In English literature, from Thomas Malory to Harold Pinter, adultery is betrayal. The sexual act is the ultimate personal commitment—not what it is for Johanna in *Mr. Noon,* just another form of conversation.

Another critic shocked by *Mr. Noon,* and for the same reason, was the

English writer David Holbrook. Before he met Frieda, Lawrence, said Holbrook, had believed in the ideal of marriage held by William Blake, Jane Austen, and Charlotte Brontë, that of a union combining sensuality with trust and fidelity. In *Mr. Noon,* Gilbert first praises this kind of marriage as "the secret of English greatness," only to mock it later in despair as a broken-down ideal, a cul-de-sac. This disillusion, said Holbrook, was "the catastrophe that overtook Lawrence," the reason why he could not finish *Mr. Noon* and why his later novels took a nasty turn into misogynism. Lawrence was unEnglished by Frieda's promiscuity.

Why did Lawrence put up with it? The answer favored by some Lawrence scholars, and most complimentary to Lawrence, is that he respected Frieda's freedom to do what she wanted. But a truer answer may lie in the sad poem "Humiliation," written on that terrible journey: "Do not leave me, or I shall break. / . . . And, God, that she is *necessary! / Necessary,* and I have no choice! / Do not leave me."

The most memorable literary legacy of that legendary journey is not *Mr. Noon* but the travel essays, such as "Christs in the Tirol," later published in *Twilight in Italy.* Lawrence, with his Nonconformist eye accustomed to the stark clean cross of English Christendom, gazed with fascinated horror at the sensual sadism and morbidity displayed in the wayside crucifixes that dotted their path, hung with Christs thin and fat, fair and dark, elegant and vulgar, serene and angry, with bleeding gashes, bound feet, and slipping-down loincloths. Sometimes, blasphemously, he would taunt the unfortunate effigy: "Come down! Come down and have a drink," and "Never mind. It'll be worse yet, before you've done."

Lawrence's poem about an angry Christ glaring at him with eyes "black and helpless with hate" seems a projection of the hate he felt emanating from Ernest Weekley. Yet the intensity of the observation lavished on the young male corpses, particularly on the angry Christ— with "the heavy body defiled by torture and death, the strong, virile life overcome by physical violence, the eyes still looking back bloodshot in consummate hate and misery"—suggests that they are Lawrences all.

YET there are ways and ways of punishing. Lawrence was, to put it mildly, careful with money. ("You are quite wrong about Lawrence," David wrote home to his mother. "He never spends a penny.") He kept Frieda on very short rations. A sign of his forgiveness after the Hobson crisis was a loosening of the purse strings; he halted the walk and decided that they could complete their journey to Italy by train. In *Mr. Noon,* Gilbert goes so far in indulging Johanna as to buy second-class rather than third-class tickets and to allow them the supreme luxury of eating in the dining car. ("And Gilbert paid, and begrudged the money, and begrudged the tip he had to leave for the superior waiter.")

Mr. Noon also chronicles the defrocking of Frieda. The elegant towns-woman who had been wearing "dull smoke-coloured gauze" and wide-brimmed hats of "delicate black" reaches Italy in a dark green Burberry, mud-spotted dress, and Panama hat whose sodden red ribbon is stream-ing color into the straw. Frieda still wore elegant clothes when her sisters bought them for her, and Lawrence liked seeing her in them, just as in his fiction he dressed his women in opulent fabrics and wondrous colors. Yet a fierce part of himself was edging her into submissive garb. As he declares in his poem "Lady Wife":

> Queens, ladies, angels, women rare,
> I have had enough.
> Put sackcloth on, be crowned with powdery ash,
> Be common stuff.

Before long Frieda was complaining that Lawrence forbade the silky lingerie she loved (and he loved to write about), and was forcing her instead to wear long underdrawers of coarse plain cambric.

There was one other way in which he exerted his domination. Sexual behavior is ordinarily unknowable unless one of the partners chooses to reveal it. Even then, most others would prefer the curtain to remain drawn; as Bertrand Russell famously joked when *Look! We Have Come Through!* was published, "I am glad they have come through but why should I look?" But Lawrence intended the poems to be read autobio-graphically. He put them in chronological order, sometimes with place names, so that his readers could trace the parallels of his emotional and geographical journeys with Frieda.

He did not intend, as far as is known, that the second half of *Mr. Noon* should be published at all, although it tells the same story. That it was too close to life has been suggested as one of the reasons he never pressed on toward its publication. Now that it is available, *Mr. Noon* clarifies some of the sexual references that the poems (published in 1918) left ambiguous, for Lawrence tended to metaphor when he got into anatomical territory. In the poem "New Heaven and Earth," he says that one night he touched "the flank of my wife" and was carried over to a "new world." But what part of the body is the "flank," and where does it lead?

> Ah no, I cannot tell you what it is, the new world.
> I cannot tell you the mad, astounded rapture of its discovery.
> I shall be mad with delight before I have done,
> and whosoever comes after will find me in the new world
> a madman in rapture.

Mr. Noon gives more information. Before the novel breaks off abruptly, it shows the couple lying in bed the night after having arrived at

Lake Garda on the far side of the Alps. Suddenly, Gilbert feels passion once again breaking like lightning out of his blood. For the second time, he is born again—but with a difference:

> Something seemed to come loose in Gilbert's soul quite suddenly. Quite suddenly, in the night one night he touched Johanna as she lay asleep with her back to him, touching him, and something broke alive in his soul that had been dead before. A sudden shock of new experience . . . his soul broke like a dry rock that breaks and gushes into life. Ach richness—unspeakable and untellable richness. Ach bliss— deep sensual, silken bliss. It was as if the old sky cracked, curled and peeled away, leaving a great new sky.

Unspeakable, untellable; her back to him; shock, rock, crack . . . What Lawrence had discovered was the anus as erogenous zone: a new world, a place of discovery, away from the viperish vagina, the greedy womb, the monstrous thighs, the insistent clitoris, and the safe breasts.

To Holbrook this passage from *Mr. Noon* is evidence of the "sodomitic solution," and its discovery just after the couple had come through the crisis over "Stanley" suggests that Lawrence was using hostile sodomy as a way of punishing Frieda for betrayal.

By that light, some of Lawrence's lines in the *Look!* series reveal a punitive thrust: "If only I am keen and hard like the sheer tip of a wedge / Driven by invisible blows, / The rock will split, we shall come at the wonder . . ." Even in punishment, however, there can be connivance. Equal evidence can be mined from the poems to suggest that it was Frieda who led the way into the forbidden region:

> Ah, with a fearful, strange detection
> She found the source of my subjection . . .

She also appears as the instigator in the brutal poem "Rabbit Snared in the Night," written late in 1912:

> It must have been *your* inbreathing, gaping desire
> that drew this red gush in me;
> I must be reciprocating *your* vacuous, hideous passion.
>
> . . . .
>
> Come, you shall have your desire,
> since already I am implicated with you
> in your strange lust.

A fair guess is that Frieda led the way. With her mastery of the amatory arts, she may have recognized that the reason for the unsatisfactoriness of their embraces lay in Lawrence's longing for a touch "on the root and quick of my darkness." With the confidence that Otto Gross so admired, she would have had no hesitation in introducing him to "Something unexplored: a place of loneliness . . . Lovelier than Paradise." On the next-to-last page of the never finished *Mr. Noon* the narrator observes that "If he [Gilbert] had married some *really* nice woman . . . then he would never have broken out of the dry integument that enclosed him."

Anal sex seems to have been the Lawrences' resolution to the conflict between them. Their mutual pleasure in the forbidden zone was part of their strange bond. There was even a perverse logic about it, a defiant abandoning of the procreative position just as they were beginning to suspect that the infant might not come, ever.

Yet it also tightened the bond into a snare. Frieda's belief that nothing in the name of love could be wrong liberated Lawrence, as a man and as a writer. Yet it obliged him to stay with her, the only woman who could satisfy him.

ITALY was the country in which they were to spend more time than any other and Lawrence, with his acute sense of place, sized up its dolce far niente at a glance: "The indefinable slackness, nobody is on the spot, and nobody cares, and life trails on." That nobody cared whether there were bugs on the walls or whether the lavatories were clean, however, was less pleasing to their northern sensibilities. The filth and stench drove Frieda to tears.

By mid-September, in Gargnano on the western shore of Lake Garda, they were installed in the first real home of their own: an enormous flat on the ground floor of a pink villa with windows overlooking the lake, for a rent of three guineas a month.

The couple were rarely as poor as he claimed them to be. "I only talk about my poverty so as not to seem swank," he admitted to his Croydon friend Arthur McLeod. Like many thrifty people, he *felt* poor unless he had something put by for a rainy day. Nor, when complaining about the state of his finances, did he record the financial assistance from Else, which, if anything like her generosity to Frieda Gross, was considerable. In any event, at Gargnano he could see their way through the winter because Duckworth had paid him the fifty pounds owing for *The Trespasser*, in cash.

(Lawrence by then hated the book. Not so the *New York Times* reviewer, who said it was "not only the frankest of serious contemporary novels; it comes near to being the best.")

At their Villa Igéa, the Lawrences threw themselves into housekeeping. They shared a passion for cleanliness. Lawrence scrubbed the floors by hand. Frieda learned to wash sheets and cook macaroni. Settled at last, Lawrence dashed off a play, "The Fight for Barbara," turning his elopement into a comedy about an English aristocrat, Barbara (conveniently childless), who leaves her professor husband to run off with the miner's son she loves. Lawrence took much of the dialogue from real life, including Baroness von Richthofen's taunt: "You have not got even enough money to keep her. She has to have money from her sister."

The campaign for visitors intensified. In place of sunny Bavarian meadows and ice-green glacial streams, they now filled their letters with visions of olive groves, orange and lemon trees, figs, peaches, dark blue grapes, and a dark blue lake, "clear as a jewel." They invited most everybody they knew: Ada, Sallie Hopkin, Arthur McLeod, Else, and all three Garnetts.

They found a local schoolmistress to tutor them in Italian and romantically compared themselves to Anna Karenina and Count Vronsky, defying society for the sake of their love. "She finds Anna very much like herself," Lawrence wrote Garnett, "only inferior." However, he might have added, Madame Karenina was not such a heavy smoker that she had to keep a spittoon under her side of the bed.

Contrary to Lawrence's expectations, however, time was no healer of the maternal instinct. Frieda wandered around the flat like a cat without her kittens, wondering where, if the children came, they would sleep. Agitated letters continued to arrive from Weekley, who kept changing his mind about divorce. Now he made a new offer. Frieda could have her own flat in London, where she might live as a separated wife, with the children—on the condition that she renounce all the free-love ideas she had gotten from Otto Gross (whose letters she had foolishly sent him to read). From Munich, Else advised acceptance. On December 2 Lawrence answered for Frieda, fear of losing her increasing his eloquence. "If Frieda and the children could live happily together, I should say 'Go'—because the happiness of two out of three is sufficient." But if she were not going to be happy herself, she would only be making herself a martyr, and thereby a curse to the children. "The worst of sacrifice," he declared sagely, "is that we have to pay back."

Temperamental, moral, and even physical opposites, they soldiered on. Once Frieda ran away from the villa for two days; at other times he told her to get out. Yet they came back together and enjoyed each other's company. In the best of times, he made life seem fresh and new to her; she made him sure of himself. As he describes in *Mr. Noon,* after a horrible row in which she sobbed that he was cruel to her, he enfolded her "as a tree enfolds a great stone with its roots."

*　　*　　*

IN the land of the Madonna, living with a mother grieving for her children, Lawrence got control of his novel about the crippling power of mother love. Frieda helped him conceptualize and universalize it. "Can I call it *Sons and Lovers?*" Lawrence asked Garnett in mid-October. Those who regret Frieda's influence should consider whether the book would have had the same impact as "Paul Morel."

Frieda threw herself into the rewriting. As Lawrence worked, he read bits aloud to her and sought her opinion as to what his mother might have said. They had furious arguments. He had missed the point, she told him. He had really loved his mother more than any other woman— not only his tragedy, she said, but all men's.

Their joint labors resulted in a tauter book, less flowery and metaphorical. The older brother as well as the younger was now a victim of the mother's possessiveness. But in the process of making a starker oedipal opposition between wife and husband, the father became less sympathetic—meaner, more bullying, less kind to the children.

In no sense was Frieda a coauthor. Her own writing is direct and readable, but amateurish and often unintentionally parodic in its Lawrencian touches. Yet she saw herself as an active partner. To Garnett, she claimed credit for bringing out the oedipal theme of *Sons and Lovers* and declared that, if Garnett still found the book formless, he was exhibiting an English fault. "That's what I love Lawrence for, that he is so plucky and honest in his work, he dares to come out in the open and plants his stuff down bald and naked, really he is the only revolutionary worthy of the name that I know."

After repeated reworkings, *Sons and Lovers* had moved in many emotional as well as factual details far from the reality of Lawrence's early years. After six months with Frieda, Lawrence had a clearer grasp of the damage done to him by his mother's possessiveness. Unfortunately for Frieda, he turned this insight against her and hardened his heart against her anguish. Cutting her children loose, he now believed, was the finest thing a mother could do.

Sons and Lovers, as a classic of English literature, is often read as a paean to mother love when it is a story of matricide. Paul Morel kills his mother. Lawrence is quite explicit on the point. Milk is used symbolically in *Sons and Lovers* to flow in reverse and unnatural direction, from son to mother, and to kill her. As Mrs. Morel lies dying, Paul first waters her milk so that it will not nourish her, then uses it as the medium in which to slip the fatal draft of morphia. ("Morphia," incidentally, was one of Lawrence's words for the sexual relief that Frieda gave her Metz lover, von Henning.)

Yet *Sons and Lovers* contains a far more savage enactment of matricide than the mercy killing of Mrs. Morel. In an earlier scene the young Paul destroys his sister's doll. Having (accidentally, he says) broken it,

Paul persuades his sister to let him conduct a funeral sacrifice. He makes a pile of bricks, he pours on paraffin, and watches as (Lawrence is unrivaled at this kind of physical description) "the drops of wax melt off the broken forehead of Arabella, and drop like sweat into the flame." At the end, "he poked among the embers with a stick, fished out the arms and legs, all blackened, and smashed them under stones. 'That's the sacrifice of Missis Arabella,' he said. 'An' I'm glad there's nothing left of her.' "

One of Lawrence's best-known statements is "one sheds ones sicknesses in books." Novelist, heal thyself. If his proposition were correct, *Sons and Lovers* should have cured him of his unhealthy attachment to his mother. But as therapy, the book was a flop. In November 1912, even as he finished it, he was writing poems to his dead mother as if she were watching him, and thinking that he saw her face in crowds. He told Frieda frankly that not even she could have pulled him loose had his mother been alive.

Neither did the novel cure his simmering rage against all women. It did not help him to fathom why he was so furious with "Miriam," Jessie Chambers's counterpart. Perhaps the theories of Melanie Klein or the existentialist Jean-Paul Sartre go further than Freud's toward clarifying the source of the anger: an infant's fear of the powerful mother whose embrace threatens to annihilate the self. (Paul accuses Miriam: "You want to put me in your pocket. And I should die there, smothered.")

The effect of writing *Sons and Lovers* was to deepen Lawrence's longing for the love of a father. Guilt for the unfairness of the portrait of Arthur Lawrence in *Sons and Lovers* was to remain with him. But Lawrence was right when, posting the manuscript off on November 19, he declared to Garnett: "I tell you I've written a great book." It *was* a great book—an epic account of a young man's journey in search of himself, and the finest picture of proletarian life in the modern English novel.

Duckworth offered one hundred pounds for it. Lawrence termed the offer "quite gorgeous," accepting, willingly or not, that Garnett would do considerable cutting and that he himself would not see the result until the proofs came. He knew the book was too long.

As their first Christmas together approached, the stricken Frieda tried to send her children ten shillings each. Lawrence, unwisely and perhaps deliberately, sent the money in a postal order under his own name. Weekley sent the money back, with a letter threatening to come and kill them both for insulting his children with the name of "that filthy hound."

Weekley now promised a divorce—on the condition that Frieda cease contact and be as good as dead to the children. He sent their photograph to twist the knife. In future, he said, he would communicate with her only through lawyers. Under the adversarial divorce law of the time, any direct communication between the guilty and innocent party constituted collusion and made the divorce unobtainable.

More than ever, the runaways needed friends. To an admirer he hadn't met, the artist Ernest Collings, whose letter praising *The Trespasser* pleased him greatly, Lawrence urged, "If ever you are within reach, will you come and see me?" (He also confided to Collings, a complete stranger, à propos of some illustrations, that "women are more passionate than men, only the men daren't allow it.") To McLeod, still teaching in Croydon, he implored early in October: "Why can't you ever come? You could if you wanted to, at Christmas." And, later that month, "Will you come and spend Christmas here?—do, *do*—I should love it so."

As Frieda moaned that she had not received even one card from any of her friends, one person responded to their call for visitors: young Harold Hobson. Lawrence assured Garnett, who obviously had heard from David about the seduction in the hay hut, that everything would be all right. "We get on really awfully well, we three together. . . . No, I can trust H. as my friend now."

On Christmas Day, Lawrence rose from his sickbed, just as he had the year before. Suffering from a "venomous cold," he sat up, writing to Sallie Hopkin another declaration that would become famous: "I'll do my life work, sticking up for love between man and woman. . . . I shall always be a priest of love, and now a glad one, and I'll preach my heart out." Yet at his side, the woman he loved was basking in the admiration of her erstwhile seducer.

There is no hint that the affair between Frieda and Hobson resumed during this visit. However, Lawrence muttered darkly in a poem written that December:

> . . . When I sit in the room,
> here in my own house,
> and you want to enlarge yourself with this friend of mine,
> such a friend as he is,
> yet you cannot get beyond your awareness of me . . .

Lawrence insisted that he did not mind. When Frieda boasted to David Garnett how splendid she had looked at the opera in Gargnano, in her best velvet dress and hat, flanked by her two escorts, and then went on to claim that Lawrence was jealous of the sailor who delivered parcels to the house, Lawrence wrote over her words: "balls-aching rot."

In his everyday speech, Lawrence was by no means puritanical. He swore freely, and Frieda's heavy banalities were often more than he could bear. In the same letter to David, where he saw that she had written, "in Lawrence I discovered abysses of elusive, destructive spiritual tragedy," he wrote "Balls!" Elsewhere he added "Shit!" and "Bitch!" and "Arse-licking." Over the place where she had innocently used the words "come off" (his slang for "orgasm"), the priest of love drew a coarse two-fingered salute.

To Edward Garnett, they sent a politer, joint letter, looking forward to 1913. There would be a divorce. Frieda would come to England at Easter to try to see the children. They would get married. "Fancy me marrying again," she wrote, "it gives me the creeps." "Stinker" added Lawrence.

Undaunted, Frieda assured Garnett that she was a reformed character. She, who had felt unloved, now had so much love that she had put her wild theories aside; she would be faithful from now on. As for the future of her children, she said sanctimoniously, "I must trust in the Lord."

"Who's he?" scrawled Lawrence in large black letters across the page, circling "Lord." "Some new bloke?"

7

THE WEDDING RING

January 1913–August 1914

*E*arly in April 1913, Constance Garnett got a shock. Just as a houseful of guests was about to descend on the Cearne for the weekend, a letter from Italy announced the Lawrences' imminent arrival. Immediately she put her friends off. The Lawrences took top priority. "Frieda will probably prefer *not* to meet people," she wrote Edward in alarm. "I gather . . . that she's rather at a crisis, poor darling. . . . People so often don't mix."

But the Lawrences never turned up. Abruptly Ernest Weekley had vetoed the Easter visit with the children that Frieda had been counting on for months. Frieda was shattered, and Lawrence, who was depressed and had a bad cold, became even more depressed by Frieda's depression. They changed their plans from day to day. First, at Else's suggestion, they decided to abandon thoughts of England and instead join her in Rome. (Else traveled to Italy twice a year with her Alfred Weber.) But as they were about to leave the Villa Igéa, Frieda balked. They had to go to England immediately. She had to see the children; she would waylay them as they came out of school if Ernest would not allow a proper visit.

The luggage was readdressed for England, but abruptly they decided to stop in Verona on the way and catch Else there.

Frieda begged Garnett not to be cross with their chopping and changing. It was mostly her fault, but also Lawrence's health; he was "seedy." With their repeated nonarrivals, they were, she said, like the "ewige Wieder Kehr" [Eternal Return] of Nietzsche. "We feel awfully at present as if nobody would have anything to do with us, quite outcasts we feel!"

Lawrence thoroughly disliked her plan, which was to try to persuade the children, when she met them, to ask their father if they might visit their mother in Germany. He disapproved, he said, of drawing children into a conspiracy against a parent. He was also aware of Weekley's instructions that anything to do with the children had to go through the solicitors.

In anguish, Frieda wrote Garnett: "For the first time really in my life, I am undecided, I *don't know what to do*. Of course I don't think it's desirable that I should see the children in the street, but what can I do?" They were, she felt, "slipping away into nothing from me and I simply can't stand it and *won't* stand it!" Her in-laws, she was sure, were telling them that their mother had left them, and she wanted to explain to them, face to face, "I left your father, not you."

Traveling north, they got only as far as Bavaria. When Edgar Jaffe offered them his new summer house at Irschenhausen, near Icking where they had spent the previous summer, they settled in. The Villa Jaffe was the most luxurious accommodation they had ever enjoyed; set in a corner of a pine forest, it was furnished with Persian carpets, Dürer engravings, and Bavarian pottery, and warmed by an old green tile stove. Lawrence immediately went to bed with a new cold. He dared not move. He blamed his fresh illness on the snow-covered Bavarian ground, the moral climate (after Italy, he found Germany narrow, cruel, and "domestic"), and the uprooting from the Villa Igéa. "I take badly to places. . . . I'm the sort of weedy plant that takes badly to removal." There were other reasons, too, for staying put: his dread of Frieda seeing her children again, his reluctance to give up their rent-free quarters, and his unwillingness to interrupt the momentum of a new book.

In sickness and in health, Lawrence poured out words. In their luggage ("an unwieldy mass," he grumbled) were all sorts of manuscripts, including an abandoned novel about Robert Burns, two hundred pages of the novel about an Eastwood nurse ("The Insurrection of Miss Houghton"), and more than a hundred pages of a newer novel, called "The Sisters."

"The Sisters," he told Garnett, was "a novel in a foreign language," and in a sense it was. The plot was based on the unmarried life of Frieda

and Else, and although the novel was set in England, the highly theoretical conversation of the two young women bore the stamp of the von
Richthofen sisters' Germanic feminism. And it was hardly an English
touch to have the sisters' pet rabbit named Bismarck.

"The Sisters" went through many evolutionary stages before splitting
into *The Rainbow* and *Women in Love*. Lawrence's laborious method of
working—extensive revision, with hundreds of pages discarded, plots
and characters often changed beyond recognition—should not disguise
the speed with which he wrote, rapidly, in pen, in a clear legible schoolmaster's hand. In essence, he wrote several books in the time most
novelists take to complete one.

With a speed impossible to exaggerate, Lawrence also responded instantly to changes of place. Overreaction and hypersensitivity were his
genius and his curse. He captured the essence of new surroundings as a
photographic plate picks up light. The early pages of "The Sisters" thus
absorbed the heavy atmosphere of the German avant-garde in which
they took shape. In the Jaffe circle, full of intellectuals such as Max,
Marianne, and Alfred Weber, preoccupied with defining culture and the
relation between society and personality, the conversation was anything
but frivolous. As Lawrence noted wryly, "We sit by lamplight and drink
beer, and hear Edgar on Modern Capitalism. *Why* was I born?"

The return to Germany immersed Lawrence in a world of strong
women just as he had begun his new novel in the first person and in a
woman's voice. Frieda and her sisters had much to say and write to each
other. They were very protective of their mother (now living with her
retired husband in Baden-Baden) and admired the strong spirit with
which she had fought against the harsh realities of her own marriage.
Else even used some of her money to pay off her father's mistress.

Indeed Else dispensed largesse in all directions: to Nusch in Berlin,
married to a gambler like their father; to Frieda, trying to live with the
impecunious Lawrence; and to Frieda Gross, to whom she gave five
thousand marks. Waiting for Ernst Frick to get out of jail, Frieda Gross
was involved in a custody battle of her own with her father-in-law,
Hanns Gross, who was trying to win control of Peter, her son by Otto
Gross, on the grounds that she was an unstable and amoral mother.
How well she sympathized with Friedele! Frieda Gross exclaimed to
Else. "To surrender a child must be wrenching," she wrote, but added
cattily, "Friedele can probably bear the loss better than you or I."

The lively correspondence flowing along this female network centered
on Else cannot have escaped Lawrence's notice. Else was a source of
strength for him too. They had much in common, from a love of walking
(Else was a great Alpine hiker) to the rigors of schoolteaching. They had
a mutual interest in probing the changing role of women in marriage, in
education, in the labor force, in art. Lawrence tried to enlist Else to write

an article for the *English Review* on "The Woman-Poets of Germany Today":

> *Do* write about the women—their aims and ideals—and a bit about them personally, any you know—and how they'd rather paint pictures than nurse children, because any motherly body can do the latter, while it needs a fine and wonderful woman to speak a message. Didn't somebody tell you that? Did she have red hair? Put it all in.

Else was one of the very few women close to Lawrence of whom Frieda was jealous.

Six months' semi-isolation on Lake Garda had left the runaways closer than ever. They had read a great deal and observed the Italians with admiration and condescension. They laughed at a fat Hamlet in *Amleto,* declaiming "Essere—o non essere." They walked in the hills, stuck their noses into little churches for whose atmosphere Lawrence found the perfect phrase—"hot spiced darkness"—and talked endlessly of their pasts: their families, their teachers, and their lovers. From what she heard from Lawrence, Frieda decided that Jessie Chambers was "sex in the head" incarnate.

But the war between them raged unabated. Frieda's children remained the main cause—"the drawn sword between us," said Lawrence—but there was more. They disagreed on how life should be lived. They argued constantly, about everything. "We live so hard on each other one day like the lions that ate each other, there will be nothing but two tails left," Frieda wrote David Garnett. There seem to have been a lot of climactic rows of the "if you're going, leave now" variety, with money being slammed down on the table. In February Frieda took off for Munich alone—"careering and carousing," Lawrence complained to Else. The very titles of his lengthening sequence of honeymoon poems testify to the alternating faces of their relationship: on the one hand, "Song of a Man Who Is Loved"; on the other, "Song of a Man Who Is Not Loved"; one day, "Misery," another, "Paradise Re-entered."

Their rivalry extended to letters. They finished each other's, adding long postscripts contradicting what had gone before. They even fought over space on the paper. "Frieda scrawls so large I must squeeze myself small," Lawrence complained to Edward Garnett. He told her off for writing too much to Ada—trying, he charged, to get his sister to take her side against him. As indeed she was. Frieda told Ada, whom she had never met, that Lawrence was driving her to think that she was unfit to be a human being. Even the blurb for the book jacket of *Sons and Lovers* became a bone of contention. Lawrence wrote his version; then Frieda wrote her own and demanded he send it to Garnett. Lawrence told her it was no good but sent it anyway.

The rows had an uglier dimension. Frieda had a masochistic streak that played into his uncontrollable rage. She would provoke him, then whimper and cringe when he flailed at her. When in his play *The Fight for Barbara* the aristocratic mistress finally threatens to walk out on her low-born lover, he grows angry and, according to Lawrence's stage direction: "They struggle. He forces her backward, flings her with a smash on to the couch."

In their real fights Frieda was not always the victim. In Irschenhausen one day while washing up, she broke a plate over Lawrence's head and ran away to Else's. Friedel, Else's worldly-wise ten-year-old son, scolded her, saying, "Tante Frieda, now you will get tired of this man and 3 uncles from one aunt are too much."

DURING their time in Italy Lawrence shot off a series of philosophical dicta that have become famous. Yet, except perhaps when he wrote to Garnett, he was not writing self-consciously for posterity. Just as often he dashed off momentous lines for the benefit of strangers or nonliterary friends, such as his old Croydon colleague Arthur McLeod, who he had no reason to think were hoarding his letters. He did it—so he wrote to Ernest Collings, whom he still had not met—because "I love people who can write reams and reams about themselves: it seems generous." To Collings he gave his thoughts about the place of women in his life: "It is hopeless for me to try to do anything without I have a woman at the back of me."

Love for a woman, Lawrence said, kept him in touch "with the unknown, in which otherwise I am a bit lost." He also gave Collings what is perhaps his most celebrated statement:

> My great religion is a belief in the blood, the flesh, as being wiser than the intellect. We can go wrong in our minds. But what our blood feels and believes and says, is always true.

It was a rendering of Nietzsche ("There is more reason in your body than in your best wisdom," says Zarathustra. "And who knows for what purpose your body requires precisely your best wisdom?") but deeply felt. He went on to put it in plainer English: "The real way of living is to answer to one's wants. . . . I want that liberty, I want that woman, I want that pound of peaches. . . . I want to insult that man."

But what did he want? Not hedonism, Lawrence was always to insist, but rather a trust in the rightness of natural instinct. Yet the dividing line is difficult to detect, and it is not clear, considering his admiration of

Frieda's self-indulgence, that he was aware of the possibility that he might be deceiving himself.

The atmosphere of Bavaria that spring elicited a short story about an army officer who beats his orderly. It was, Lawrence claimed with justice, the best he had ever done. Garnett must have agreed, for he later made it the title story in *The Prussian Officer and Other Stories*. "What 'Prussian Officer'?" fumed Lawrence when he saw the title Garnett had appended to the story and book, discarding his own title, "Honour and Arms," in the process. But the answer seems obvious: Baron von Richthofen, whose experiences, relayed to Lawrence through Frieda and the baron's diaries, gave him searing details, such as "I whipped an artillery officer with my sabre." But the story's intimations of the latent homosexuality of military life came from Lawrence himself. To Garnett, Lawrence amplified his thoughts, saying that "cruelty is a form of perverted sex. I want to dogmatise. Priests in their celibacy . . . Inquisitions, soldiers herded together, men without women."

A lesser story with a German background, which he wrote around that time, is interesting because he himself described it as both "autobiographical" and "too hot." It tells of a one-night stand of an aristocrat's daughter with a dashing German officer she encountered at a hotel. Appropriately titled "Once," it reveals Lawrence to have been attracted to the conventions of pornography: anonymous sex in titillating attire and exotic situations.

"Once" is set in a hotel room where Anita, a Frieda look-alike, tells a tale from her rich past to her new, highly serious, inexperienced young lover. As she speaks, Anita is wearing high boots, a transparent lacy chemise, and a feathered hat. The listening lover displays an even more curious blend of clothing: nothing but a top hat and a pair of gloves. And the grand night of passion that Anita recollects is described as taking place on a bed strewn with roses (a variety apparently without thorns):

> All that night we loved each other. There were crushed, crumpled little rose-leaves on him when he sat up, almost like crimson blood! Oh, and he was fierce, and at the same time, tender!

Such erotic fantasies notwithstanding, in his correspondence Lawrence kept up his protestations of faith in love between one man and one woman. It was the subject of his new book. "I can only write what I feel pretty strongly about: and that, at present, is the relations between men and women. After all, it is *the* problem of today, the establishment of a new relation, or the re-adjustment of the old one, between men and women."

Yet, in the same letter: "It is queer, but nobody seems to want, or to love, *two* people together. Heaps of folk love me alone—if I were alone—and of course all the world adores Frieda—when I'm not there. But together we seem to be a pest."

LAWRENCE, expecting the second fifty pounds of his advance from Duckworth for *Sons and Lovers,* was both bitterly resigned to cuts in the text—"It's got to sell," he told Garnett; "I've got to live"—and grateful. Much has been made of the alleged damage done the book by Garnett, but Lawrence was able to write with such speed in part because he counted on being edited. As a writer he was less concerned with the *mot juste* than with passion, spontaneity, and force.

And he professed to like the book he saw in print. "You did the pruning jolly well," he told Garnett, "and I am grateful. I hope you'll live a long time to barber up my novels for me before they're published. I wish I weren't so profuse—or prolix, or whatever it is." When he got his author's copy of the finished version of *Sons and Lovers,* he said, "I hope to God it will sell," and had Garnett send out five copies: one each to his sisters and his brother, one to McLeod at the Davidson Road School, and the last—a sign of their former closeness—to Mrs. Marie Jones of 16 Colworth Road, Croydon. *Sons and Lovers,* he told Garnett, was "quite a great book," but it marked the end of his youthful period. "I shall not write quite in that style any more."

At the same time Lawrence had noticed that Garnett had not reacted to the pages of "The Sisters" he had been sent. Lawrence braced himself, with the good temper he usually accorded Garnett's judgment, for the verdict. "Never mind, you can tell me what fault you find, and I can re-write the book."

Lawrence was right: no news was bad news. Garnett eventually wrote to say he did not like what he had read. He particularly disliked the "remarkable women"—by which he meant the central characters, the ponderous, theorizing, dogmatizing sisters. Into battle swung Frieda. She addressed Garnett as one critic to another. The wooden characterization was her fault: "They are *me,* these beastly, superior, arrogant females!"—and she knew the reason: "Lawrence *hated* me just over [*sic*] the children" and had taken his revenge in caricature. Then she theorized some more, borrowing liberally from Otto Gross (and giving some idea of the ideological barrage Lawrence had to live with day after day). She gushed to Garnett about the "amazing brutality" of *Sons and Lovers:* "How that brutality remains in spite of Christianity, of the two thousand years; it's better like that, than in the civilized forms it takes!"

She told Garnett to trust her; the new book would be all right after revision. Her main worry was Lawrence's health. When sick, she said, he just kept on working; he was "a writing machine." For his part, Lawrence, too, promised Garnett that the book would be all right after rewriting and a shift into the third person. All the same, it had done him good to get Frieda's "God Almightiness" onto the page.

Garnett was unpersuaded. But, after nine months together, Lawrence and Frieda were mutually convinced that their imperfect union had catalyzed his gift and was turning a good writer into a great one. In any event, they promised Garnett that they would stop stalling and see him in England soon. "It depends on L's health now," wrote Frieda. "Not true," interpolated Lawrence. "It depends on Frieda's will."

SONS *and Lovers,* published on May 29, 1913, confirmed Lawrence's arrival in the first rank of writers. It drew superb reviews in London, and later in America, where the *The New York Times Book Review* pronounced it a "human document" and "a novel of rare excellence."

As with *The White Peacock,* the reviewers got the oedipal point without the benefit of Freud. (The English translation of Freud's *The Interpretation of Dreams* appeared that same year.) In London, the critic of *The Ladies' Field,* under a flattering photograph of the author, "Mr D. H. Lawrence," neatly summed up the consequences of Mrs. Morel's marriage to a miner, a man unworthy of her:

> Her second son, Paul, is over-sensitive and full of a shrinking self-consciousness. He adores his mother, whose whole happiness becomes wrapped up in him. She waits for his home-coming in the evening to unburden herself of all that she has thought of during the day, and he sits and listens with intense earnestness. The two "share lives."

The gentle readers of *The Ladies' Field* were told that "Paul's life as a son has been embittered by his failure as a lover." As for "Miriam": "in her the sex-instinct is over-refined, so that, lacking that confidence on his part that could alone encourage her, she thinks of marriage with him as self-sacrifice."

The clever *Manchester Guardian* got straight to the heart of the paradox, of the book and of the author. "A simultaneous passion of love and hatred is, of course, a well-known psychological fact," declared the poet Lascelles Abercrombie. Yet it was a fact one could easily have too much of. The constant juxtaposition of love and hatred looked like an obsession. *Sons and Lovers* would be "merely dull and clever" were Lawrence not also "one of the most remarkable poets of the day."

> Indeed, you do not realize how astonishingly interesting the whole book is until you find yourself protesting that this thing or that thing bores you, and eagerly reading on in spite of your protestations. The

brutish father catches your sympathy; the heroic mother is at times downright disagreeable. You think you are reading through an unimportant scene; and then find that it has burnt itself on your mind.

In sum, said Abercrombie, Lawrence was *contrary*—"in the sense of the word which rhymes with Mary. Life, for Mr. Lawrence, is a coin which has both obverse and reverse. . . . His unusual art consists in his surprising ability to illuminate both sides simultaneously."

The Psychoanalytic Review was gleeful at the appearance of a novel embodying the new theories from Vienna. In *Sons and Lovers,* said its reviewer Alfred Kuttner, Lawrence had managed,

> though unknowingly, to attest the truth of what is perhaps the most far-reaching psychological theory ever propounded[;] he has also given us an illuminating insight into the mystery of artistic creation. For Mr Lawrence has escaped the destructive fate that dogs that hapless Paul by the grace of expression: out of the dark struggles of his own soul he has emerged as a triumphant artist. In every epoch the soul of the artist is sick with the problems of his generation. He cures himself by expression in his art. And by producing a catharsis in the spectator through the enjoyment of his art he also heals his fellow beings. His artistic stature is measured by the universality of the problem which his art has transfigured.

Lawrence was always to distance himself from the reductionist theories of psychoanalysis. Yet he did not mind being considered a healer. In June 1913, returning, after his first absence, to his native land, he knew exactly how he could help it: "I do write because I want folk—English folk—to alter, and have more sense."

SOON after their arrival in England, Frieda played the scene she had so long rehearsed in her mind. She went to Hammersmith in West London, to Colet Court, the preparatory school for St. Paul's, entered the dark corridors of the turreted red-brick Victorian building and, amid the scrum of gray flannel trousers and blue blazers, picked out her son. Monty, just turned fourteen, stopped in his tracks. "You," he said slowly. "You."

She spoke conspiratorially. "Can you come with me now for half an hour without anybody knowing?" she asked. Monty said he would have to ask permission. "Tell him," said Frieda the experienced deceiver, "it's your aunt."

They went to a tea shop. Monty gave her news about the girls, how Elsa was clever and Barby could draw. Frieda wept and borrowed his handkerchief. They walked around the school together and Frieda snatched a guilty moment of maternal pride from the tall boy at her side.

Monty was conscious of a man lurking in the distance. He knew at once who it was.

Another day Frieda intercepted her daughters. They were on their way to school in Chiswick, near the house Weekley had bought for them and his parents. They danced around her and cried, "Mama, you are back, when are you coming home?"

The Weekley children, since she had left, had undergone the change of regime found in Victorian children's novels. Frieda had been a merry and indulgent mother. She had played games with them, splashed beside them in the surf, taken them with her on holidays to Germany, indulged their whims. When Monty had fallen in love with a new pair of boots with buttons on the side, she let him wear them to bed.

Once their mother had gone and their Nottingham home was broken up, the children were doubly deprived, for their young German nurse, Ida, also left. Any German-speaking stopped. The only German word Elsa used was that for chamber pot. The Weekley family were so determined to stamp out any memory of Frieda that the children were not allowed even to mention her. But they were shattered by her disappearance; Monty could scarcely eat for six months. Frieda took comfort from the fact that they had grown so close together after she went away.

LAWRENCE'S return to London allowed him to capitalize on his new fame. He calculated that he and Frieda could live on two hundred pounds a year—half earned from his novels, the rest from reviews, articles, and other bits and pieces. As well as going to the tailor's and the photographer's, he renewed his literary contacts. He looked up Ezra Pound. He went to a party at H. G. Wells's; he visited the editor of the *English Review*, Austin Harrison, and met his likable assistant, the cosmopolitan, witty, and outrageous Norman Douglas.

With Frieda, he went to Chancery Lane to meet the New Zealand writer Katherine Mansfield and her lover, John Middleton Murry, who together edited the magazine *Rhythm* and its successor, the *Blue Review*. The rapport was instant between the two couples who saw themselves as defiantly and proudly living in sin.

LAWRENCE'S success did nothing to make them easy guests at the Cearne. Again, arriving in June, they had invited themselves at a bad time. David Garnett was about to take a botany examination for the Royal College of Science; his mother was trying to finish her translation of Dostoyevsky's *The Possessed*. Edward Garnett was away; so was the housekeeper. Muttering "Bless those Lawrences!" Constance changed her plans, got the house ready, and looked after them herself.

Constance Garnett thus had ample opportunity to witness the

Lawrences' phenomenal rows—and to record them. By coming back to London, the Lawrences had moved into the sights of the literati, from whose memoirs and correspondence their posthumous reputations would mainly be drawn.

To her husband, Constance immediately wrote her diagnosis: she thought Lawrence cruel and cold to Frieda's suffering, while she found Frieda tactless, dense, and insensitive. When there was peace, she observed, Frieda would start the fight afresh. Just after the Lawrences arrived, a telegram from a friend in Nottingham warned them that Ernest Weekley might appear over the hill to shoot Lawrence, and perhaps himself, on the spot. Constance, quiet but outspoken, told Lawrence that she did not believe his relationship with Frieda could survive such anger. He should leave Frieda, Constance declared, before he made her life any more miserable.

As was his way, Lawrence opened his heart. The problem, he told his hostess, was that while his love for Frieda was permanent she only half loved him. He was determined to make her love him altogether. "This," Constance commented dryly to Edward, "apparently involves her forgetting the past."

But Mrs. Garnett soon was as charmed by Lawrence as her son had been in Bavaria. She watched him throw himself into the gardening. He netted the raspberries, thinned the new carrots, and offered to snare the rabbits. From her fear that he would have a bad influence on her son, she moved wholeheartedly into the family enterprise of launching Lawrence. She put his money through her own banking account, as Lawrence did not have one in England. Her sister and her nephew typed his short stories for him, and David, fond of Frieda as ever, accompanied her on several trips to St. Paul's school.

In July, waiting for Ada's wedding and working intensively on his short stories, Lawrence rented a flat in Kingsgate, near Broadstairs in Kent. The sea air, he thought, would be the best they could get from the English climate.

The Channel coast, with its tea shops and bathing tents, was decidedly bourgeois, the aristocracy preferring moors and hills to salt air and damp sand under gray skies. Kingsgate, with its little villas, boarding-houses, and tram lines, was a Croydon-sur-mer. The grandly named Riley House, in which the Lawrences had their flat, was one of a row of identical semidetached villas with fake timbers, bow windows, and tidy front gardens. At the end of the road, a steep flight of stairs led down from the grassy clifftops to a tiny bay. (John Buchan's *The Thirty-Nine Steps,* written in a house nearby, took its title from a similar staircase.) Frieda and Lawrence loved bathing at the small beach under the chalk cliffs. Frieda, as Lawrence knew from Bavaria, was a strong swimmer; he contented himself with hopping up and down in the waves and clowning in the water.

For a time, perhaps because she had seen her children, they were content. They felt healthy and sleepy, kept track of the tides, and found the place pleasantly boring, full of "fat fatherly Jews and their motor cars and their bathing tents." (Lawrence spoke with the casual anti-Semitism common to his day. There is no disguising that he saw Jews as very alien—but, ugly as some of his remarks appear to later generations, his was in no sense a blind bigotry, as some of his enduring friendships prove. Frieda's prejudices were deeper-seated; the von Richthofens never forgot Edgar Jaffe's Jewishness, although they appreciated his money.)

WHILE back in England, Lawrence was eager to sell as much work as possible in order to see him and Frieda through the coming winter in Italy. Both Ezra Pound, who was trawling for an American magazine, *Smart Set,* and Austin Harrison of the *English Review* were pressing him for stories. Harrison promised fifteen pounds apiece. Lawrence, always careless with his manuscripts, began rounding up bits and pieces he had left with Garnett and Arthur McLeod in Croydon with a view to polishing them, getting them typed by Garnett's sister-in-law and nephew, Katharine and Douglas Clayton, and leaving them behind in salable form before he and Frieda returned to the Continent at the beginning of August. The project required him to push his formidable production capacity to the limit, and with his habitual rapidity he succeeded. He polished off about a dozen stories, mainly during the three weeks in July at Kingsgate. The revisions were generally to the good, bringing confidence, control, and detachment to youthful work.

It was a prodigious effort, especially considering the new friendships and social engagements he and Frieda packed into just under seven weeks. His letters vividly express the pressure he was under. On July 8, still at the Cearne, he wrote to Henry Savage, the writer, "I am very poor and in tight circumstances all round." To Katharine Clayton, apparently the same day (the precise dates in July 1913 are conjectural, taken mainly from postmarks): "Did McLeod send on the other two stories? Let me have the type copies as soon as you can, please—they ought to be going out." To David Garnett on July 11: "Oh, I can't find a little story of mine, in MS. called Intimacy. You might see if it's kicking round at the Cearne." To Constance Garnett, on July 13, he reported the lost story found, "mingled up with Frieda's underclothing." To Katharine Clayton the same day: "Here's another story." To Edward Garnett on July 14: "I am drudging away revising the stories. How glad I shall be when I have cleared that mess up! I *will* keep a list." Two days later he described himself to Garnett as still "swotting away at the short stories—and shall be so glad to get them done." "You don't know how nice they look," he told his mentor, "and how convincing, now I have revised them and they are type-written."

By July 20 Lawrence had informed Garnett of at least eight stories completed and either sent or ready to be sent to potential publishers: "A Sick Collier" and "The Christening" had gone to the Northern Newspaper Syndicate, and three others ("Once" and two unidentified) to the *North American Review.* He held three short ones for the *New Statesman:* "The Fly in the Ointment," "The White Stocking," and "The Witch à la Mode" (the renamed "Intimacy"). He also sent Garnett "Love Among the Haystacks" and promised to forward as soon as it was typed, "Two Marriages" (later "Daughters of the Vicar"), a long and powerful story which he had rewritten a good deal. He mentioned also having in hand "two more little things" which he did not name. On July 22, still at Kingsgate, he moaned in a letter to McLeod: "I have been grubbing away among the short stories. God, I shall be glad when it is done." On July 28 he sent Douglas Clayton another story, "The Primrose Path," and said that one or two still remained and would "come filtering in." At the end of the month Lawrence returned to the Cearne, and on August 7 he left to return to Germany.

When Lawrence was in a hurry, when he was in unfamiliar territory, or when he was not deeply committed to the text in hand, he could be a careless borrower. The wind that blew through him carried a lot of other people's words upon it. Collaboration with less skilled writers was always attractive to him, as two of his novels testify: *The Trespasser,* made out of Helen Corke's "Saga of Siegmund," and later *The Boy in the Bush,* from Mollie Skinner's "The House of Ellis." He also liked translating.

His gift for mimicry and intense involvement in his reading, moreover, led him easily to simulation. His *Movements in European History,* produced in haste in 1918–1919 because he needed the money, drew liberally on Gibbon's *Decline and Fall of the Roman Empire.* When in 1990 one of his previously undiscovered poems, "Death-Paean of a Mother," was found, excitement was tempered by the uncertainty over whether it was composed by Lawrence or translated by him from a German poem. And no one will ever know, the original manuscript having disappeared, how much of his first published story, "Goose Fair," was the work of Louie Burrows.

One of the stories he remodeled during the summer of 1913, "The Shadow in the Rose Garden," shows, according to Lawrence scholar Émile Delavenay, signs of hasty revision. Haste, and also considerable expansion. The expanded story is more than three times as long as "The

Vicar's Garden," on which it is based, and presents an entirely new plot wrapped around the original core, which describes a young woman and her fiancé exploring a churchyard garden and discovering a lunatic.

"The Shadow in the Rose Garden," as rewritten, captures the moment of crisis in the marriage of a smug young husband and his auburn-haired wife. What should have been a romantic interlude away from home is spoiled by his discovery of an unsuspected love in her past. The husband interrogates his wife closely about this supposed rival, only to be silenced by her tale of hearing of her lover's death. The story's ending is bleak: the conjugal outing is ruined; there is no lovemaking, no reconciliation. The husband is left realizing that he does not know his wife at all; indeed, he does not know himself.

T. S. Eliot, among others, remarked upon the similarity of the Lawrence short story to the final episode in James Joyce's "The Dead." Indeed, although the two stories differ in essential respects, certain textual resemblances are so close—in dramatic and descriptive detail, in dialogical rhythm, and in word sequence (what the language of information technology calls "word strings")—as to appear to defy coincidence. In 1913 Joyce's *Dubliners,* a collection of stories of which "The Dead," written in 1907, forms the finale, was wandering through London in the sixth year of its long and frustrating search for a publisher. In his letters, Lawrence never mentioned reading Joyce until 1922, when he tried, and failed, to read *Ulysses.* Yet he could have done so all the same. In either manuscript or proof form, *Dubliners* was in London during much of the time that Lawrence was. It is not impossible that somewhere in the untidy studies and offices of the London publishing world—conceivably at the Cearne—Joyce's unpublished, and apparently unpublishable, pages fell under his eye, and the powerful scene of confrontation between husband and wife imprinted itself on his magpie mind. (See pages 511–515 for the bibliographical history of both stories.)

Lawrence's story was first into print. In November 1913 Pound sold it to *Smart Set,* which published it the following March. Yet "The Shadow in the Rose Garden" made its first appearance before an English audience in November 1914, five months after the publication of *Dubliners.* By then, when the story appeared as part of Lawrence's collection *The Prussian Officer,* published by Duckworth, Lawrence had completely revised the ending.

The resemblances to "The Dead" in *The Prussian Officer* are fewer than in the *Smart Set* version. But even the revised "Shadow in the Rose Garden," as it now appears among Lawrence's stories and tales, contains many ingredients in common with "The Dead." Both stories, for example, deliver a strong signal to the reader that the self-satisfied husband is about to confront his true self.

In "The Dead":

As he passed in the way of the cheval-glass he caught sight of himself
in full length, his broad, well-filled shirtfront, the face whose expression always puzzled him when he saw it in a mirror.

In "The Shadow in the Rose Garden":

He caught sight of his own face in a little mirror. . . . He was not
ill-favoured. . . . A look of self-commiseration mingled with the satisfaction he had derived from the sight of himself.

In each story, the young married couple is away from home, in "The
Dead" at a hotel, in "The Shadow in the Rose Garden" at a seaside
boardinghouse. There is an early clue to the coming estrangement between the pair as the husband, looking upward, sees an auburn-haired
woman lost in reverie and fails for an instant to recognize her.
In "The Dead":

He was in a dark part of the hall gazing up the staircase. A woman was
standing near the top of the first flight, in the shadow also. . . . It was
his wife. She was leaning on the banisters, listening to something.

In "The Shadow in the Rose Garden," the husband is standing in the
garden under an apple tree and looks up at the bedroom windows:

He started, seeing a woman's figure, but it was only his wife. She was
gazing across the sea, apparently ignorant of him. . . . Her rich auburn
hair was heaped in folds on her forehead. She looked shut off from
him and his world, gazing away to the sea. It irked her husband that
she should continue to be so in ignorance of him, so he pulled poppy
fruits and threw them at the window.

In "The Dead," the signaling device thrown against an upstairs bedroom
window from the garden is gravel. In both stories the wife is then described as if in a chiaroscuro painting. First, Joyce:

If he were a painter he would paint her in that attitude. Her blue felt
hat would show off the bronze of her hair against the darkness and the
dark panels of her skirt would show off the light ones.

And Lawrence:

She went slowly, stopping at length by an open doorway, which shone
like a picture of light in the dark wall.

Later the husband joins her in their bedroom and tries to fathom her curious mood. In "The Dead," Gabriel Conroy says to Gretta:

—You look tired . . . You don't feel ill or weak? . . .
He was trembling now with annoyance. Why did she seem so abstracted? . . . Was she annoyed, too, about something? He longed to be master of her strange mood.

In "The Shadow in the Rose Garden," after the husband demands that his wife unlock the bedroom door:

"What's the matter?" he asked, a tinge of impatience in his voice. "Aren't you feeling well? . . ."
His hands began to twitch. He could not bear it that she was no more sensible to him than if he did not exist.

In each story the man extracts from the woman the admission that she is thinking of someone in her past. Then, in "The Dead":

A dull anger began to gather again at the back of his mind and the dull fires of his lust began to glow angrily in his veins.

In "The Shadow in the Rose Garden": "His anger rose, filling the veins in his throat."
This anger grows as the husband learns that the figure from the past is a former lover. In "The Dead" he is a boy from the wife's home region, the West of Ireland; in "The Shadow in the Rose Garden" he is a young man from the very seaside town where the couple is staying, the place where the wife lived as a girl.
Furiously, in each story, the husband accuses his wife of secretly wishing to revive this romantic association of her girlhood. In "The Dead":

—Perhaps that was why you wanted to go to Galway with that Ivors girl, he said coldly . . . to see him perhaps?

In "The Shadow in the Rose Garden" (*Smart Set* version):

"So you've been looking at your old courting places!" he said angrily. "That was what you wanted to go out by yourself for this morning."

Tension mounts as the wife defensively crouches on the bed and the husband throws a string of questions at her, extracting detail upon detail from the buried past: the age of the lover, his occupation, the extent of the affair, and the young man's sorry fate. When she hesitates, he prods her to get on with the story. In both stories there is a strong element of social embarrassment arising from a working-class connection with modern industry. In "The Dead" Gabriel is humiliated to find that his wife's great love was a boy from "the gasworks." In "The Shadow in the Rose Garden," the husband feels inferior to his wife because "he was only a laboring electrician in the mines." Both wives thereupon gain the upper hand by telling their husbands of the shock of receiving the news that the old lover was dead.

Gretta Conroy says:

He was very fond of me. . . . And when I was only a week in the convent he died. . . . O, the day that I heard that, that he was dead!

The wife in "The Shadow in the Rose Garden" says:

He was awfully fond of me . . . and almost the very day I first met you I heard from Miss Birch he'd got sunstroke—and two months after, that he was dead—.

During the questioning, Joyce has Gabriel grow gentler:

—And what did he die of so young, Gretta? Consumption, was it?
—I think he died for me, she answered.

In the *Smart Set* version of Lawrence's similar scene, the husband also softens his tone:

"He shouldn't ha gone, then, [to Tripoli]," said the husband, almost sympathetic now.
"He wouldn't if it hadn't been for me," she said.

In both stories, there comes the moment of revelation in which the husband faces the ruins of his marriage. In "The Dead":

It hardly pained him now to think how poor a part he, her husband, had played in her life. He watched her while she slept, as though he and she had never lived together as man and wife.

In "The Shadow in the Rose Garden":

Though he had not known it, he had never really had her: she had never loved him and given herself up to him.

In the *Prussian Officer* version of the story, this line reads: "Though he had not known it, yet he had never really won her, she had never loved him."

In both the *Smart Set* version and Joyce's story, the husband turns to the window and sees a storm coming. In "The Dead":

A few light taps upon the pane made him turn to the window. It had begun to snow again.

In "The Shadow in the Rose Garden":

He went away from the door to the window. A yellowish dimness was coming over the sky. There was going to be a storm.

The sky is yellow in the Joyce story as well, although a few pages earlier: "A dull yellow light brooded over the houses and the river, and the sky seemed to be descending."

Then, in each story, confronted with the indifference of the vast forces of nature, the husband feels his own self blurring into nothingness. In "The Dead":

His own identity was fading out into a grey impalpable world: the solid world itself, which these dead had one time reared and lived in, was dissolving and dwindling.

In "The Shadow in the Rose Garden":

The suffering was greater than he was. It was queer, to him, to find himself submerged.

Lawrence made his revisions to the story the following summer, in 1914, working once again in great haste at the Cearne, in order to get the collection ready for publication in book form. It is generally agreed that his revisions made "The Shadow in the Rose Garden" more powerful, more sexual, and more tragic. It is also evident, however, from both versions of the story, that Lawrence's revisions, made three weeks after the London publication of "The Dead," gave it a new ending less like Joyce's. He cut out the "yellowish dimness" of the sky. He deleted also the approaching storm and the reference to submerged identity; also the wife's dramatic line "He wouldn't if it hadn't been for me." As the story now appears in *The Prussian Officer and Other Stories,* it ends with the couple aware of the distance between them: "shocked so much, they were impersonal, and no longer hated each other."

However, if Lawrence, under great pressure, did derive one of his inferior stories from Joyce's finest, it was like Chaucer drawing from Boccaccio; he made something entirely his own. His story, both as it appeared in *Smart Set* and as it appears now in *The Prussian Officer and Other Stories,* has an extra twist, as the wife learns that her old lover is not really dead, but mad. She has seen him that very day in the rectory garden. Husband and wife, moreover, are locked into a Lawrencian marriage of warring opposites. The man is in the Lawrencian mold— married above his station, not beneath it, unlike Gabriel Conroy in the Joyce story. Rougher and angrier, he is able to indulge (in the final version of the story) in the freedom of coarse speech to force the sexual truth out of his wife:

> "Do you mean to say you used to go—the whole hogger?"
> "Why, what else do you think I mean?" she cried brutally.

He is left to realize that the woman he married was sexually awakened, and acquainted with sorrow, to a degree of which he was unaware: "At last he had learned the width of the breach between them." The story, for all its inelegance, states Lawrence's great theme of human isolation, even in marriage, which was to find its finest expression in *The Rainbow:* "He had lain with her but never known her." The final version, written with the experience of two full years of life with Frieda, leaves Lawrence's fictional couple, if not with their conflict resolved, at least with a way of continuing. They no longer hate each other: "The thing must work itself out."

IN Kingsgate as in Italy, the Lawrences invited everyone to come and see them and to stay in their spare bedroom, but this time with more success. Lawrence even sent Middleton Murry and Katherine Mansfield a pound to help with the train fare when he learned that they were short of money, and he scolded them for not saying so. He may have been thrifty but he was also generous. When Katherine agreed to act as a go-between for Frieda and her son, Lawrence gave her a sovereign (a coin worth one pound) to give to Monty as he came out of school. "I am not poor, you know," he told Murry. "But I didn't know you were really stoney. . . . Only I have to watch it, because Frieda doesn't care."

As they became closer, the couples could see that the parallels between them extended far beyond the lack of a wedding certificate. Both women were older than their lovers, and more worldly. Katherine, like Frieda, had a cast-off husband who played a game of offering and refusing divorce. Katherine, moreover, had had affairs with both sexes, and an abortion. Both were foreign and socially superior to their men. Katherine enjoyed a decent income of £130 a year from her father, a wealthy banker in Wellington, New Zealand. Jack Murry, to whom Lawrence warmed, was also a man from the common people—and "only a lad of

23," said Lawrence (at twenty-seven). Unlike Lawrence and Frieda, how-ever, whose physical appearance was a study in opposites, the "Mur-ries," as Lawrence called them, looked alike: small, neat, elegant figures with dark eyes and bony sculpted heads.

Lawrence was, for a professed reformer, self-conscious about his anomalous marital status. In his letter inviting to Kingsgate the writer Henry Savage, one of the reviewers of *The White Peacock* and a subse-quent close correspondent although they had not yet met, he said: "My wife was (or is—one gets so mixed up)—the legal wife of another man." But Savage was not to fear that they were "bookish": "I am the son of a coal-miner, and very ordinary. I should probably pass as a 30/ clerk."

During his visit Savage walked along the cliffs with Lawrence, and, as they lay on the grass talking about their frustrations and dreams, Law-rence struck his chest and told Savage that there was something inside which would kill him if he could not get it out. Savage knew Lawrence was talking about his work, not his health. Yet Savage also believed him to be suffering from tuberculosis, or "phthisis," as he called it, and felt that Lawrence's intensity concealed a race against time. Lawrence had told him, when he admitted that he was discouraged about ever getting his poetry published, that a writer must push on regardless.

"It's hellish," Lawrence wrote, "but it's worth it. Death is all right in its way, but one must finish one's job first."

Lawrence never let up from scolding Savage. He could not understand how a man could be glum if, like Savage, he had a pub to run. (Savage and his brother had inherited the pub from their father.) Visiting it, Lawrence said that he, too, would like to run a pub. He looked around the bar eagerly and said, "Look at the variety of people with whom you are in personal contact!" Above all, he professed to be mystified as to how Savage could be despondent when his wife was expecting their first baby.

I think if I had a child coming, I think I should be happy too. Because if one is careful—I think all the world starts again, right clean and jolly, when a child is born. One should be happy, I think, when a child is coming, because the mother's blood ought to run in the womb sweet like sunshine. Because we must all die, whereas we *mightn't* have been born. And when a child comes, something is which might never have been[.] And if it was my child I should be glad, whoever died, being old, or being in a cul de sac.

The success of *Sons and Lovers* gave the Lawrences a boost up the social ladder. He was delighted to be welcomed into the ranks of those considered "in society." Although there were many who felt that Law-rence was more of a snob than Frieda, that he lost no chance to drop the fact that she was born a baroness, he used Frieda as an excuse for pursuing the high life. "I don't want to bury Frieda alive," he had told Garnett. "Wherever I go with her, we shall have to fall into the intelligent, as it were upper classes."

Among the famous names who accepted their invitations that summer (although just for tea) was Edward Marsh. Marsh as editor of *Georgian Poetry,* which had published Lawrence's "Snap-Dragon" in its first issue, stood at the center of a wide and distinguished artistic circle. He was a member of the Apostles' Society at Cambridge and a friend of the philosophers G. E. Moore and Bertrand Russell. But the forty-year-old Marsh was more important than that. He was private secretary to Winston Churchill, first lord of the Admiralty. Frieda, who had never learned that the English consider personal remarks rude, on meeting Marsh (who, with waistcoat and monocle, was the very model of a buttoned-up civil servant) told him that he did not look like a man who would be interested in poetry. Marsh was hurt. His private impression was that as a couple they got on well together, but that Lawrence looked terribly ill.

As luck would have it, they invited Marsh the very weekend that he was coming down from London to Kingsgate to stay with the Herbert Asquiths, who had a house facing the sea. Herbert Asquith was the son of the prime minister, Herbert Henry Asquith, and his wife, Cynthia, was a well-born beauty. (The following year she became Lady Cynthia when her father succeeded to the title of Earl of Wemyss.) Marsh (whom they now called "Eddie") introduced them, and Lawrence was fascinated. Cynthia Asquith presented a vision of the road not taken—alliance with an English, rather than a German, aristocrat—and she was the kind of woman he admired: tall, fine-featured, with sharp curving lips, masses of dark-gold hair, and a dignified, questioning manner. Her voice was lovely and low, with precise diction and upper-class vowels.

The Asquiths' uneasy marriage was one to excite Lawrence's imagination. Herbert ("Beb") Asquith had all the disadvantages of a second son of a famous man; he lacked confidence and his career had never crystallized, which left his beautiful wife discontent, without the wealth appropriate to her station. An added attraction was their child—a year-old boy named John whom the entranced Lawrences dubbed the Jonquil.

The fascination was mutual. After a few hours under the spell of the formidable charm, the Asquiths, a rather depressed pair, fell for Lawrence like converts to a new religion. Indeed, Cynthia told her diary, "He is a Pentecost to one." He was so perceptive she would not have been surprised if he could see in the dark. To take a walk with him, as she later recalled, "made you feel that hitherto you had walked the earth with your eyes blindfolded and your ears plugged." As for his talk:

"Words welled out of him. He spoke in flashing phrases, at times colloquially, almost challengingly so, but often with a startling beauty of utterance. His voice was now harsh, now soft. One moment lyrically, contagiously joyous, the next sardonic, gibing."

Cynthia's admiration extended to Frieda as well: "exuberant, warm, burgeoning, she radiated health, strength and generosity of nature." In sum, she found the Lawrences "the most intoxicating company in the world."

The captivated Asquiths showered invitations upon the Lawrences, and not they alone. So full was the Lawrences' social calendar that by the time they were ready to return to London, writing with a new formality appropriate to his higher social position, Lawrence declined Henry Savage's offer of a room because they already had a place to stay in Kensington, had a dinner engagement in the evening, and were fully booked for the following day.

New friends in high places did not blunt Lawrence's double-edged tongue. To Garnett, he said, "Thank Mrs Garnett for her letter—she's awfully good to us!" And five days later, to Else Jaffe, "Garnett was awfully nice, but I don't like Mrs G and I hated her cold-blooded sister from Ceylon." Yet within a fortnight he was trying to get Mrs. Garnett to promise to visit them in Italy.

The welcome he received that summer left Lawrence with a different impression of his country. The qualities he despised were still there, but Englishness, he appreciated as never before, also had its virtues: gentleness, kindliness, and civility.

Late in July Frieda paid the price for the stolen moments with her children. Weekley took out a court order to prevent her from even attempting to see them. Defeated, she returned to Germany alone, leaving Lawrence to stay on for a busy week. He attended Ada's wedding in Eastwood and saw the Hopkins (making sure that Alice Dax, with her new baby, did not know he was in town). In London at dinner he met the celebrated society hostess Lady Ottoline Morrell. Yet within a week he was back with Frieda on the balcony of Villa Jaffe, overlooking the pine forest: "together again—for which I am thankful."

IN Irschenhausen, however, the couple argued so much that they decided to make their separate ways back to Italy. Undaunted, Lawrence wrote to Savage, reaffirming his faith: "My whole working philosophy is that the only stable happiness for mankind is that it shall live married in blessed union to woman-kind—intimacy, physical and psychical between a man and his wife." He added that his own state of bliss was by no means perfect.

But first he asked Savage about his wife's pregnancy. "Is she all right?

You might have the decency to mention her." Within a fortnight he was writing again to Savage, and in a rare direct reference to the precarious state of his "crocky" lungs, he suggested that his emotional problems might be physical in origin:

> I am not really afraid of consumption, I don't know why—I don't think I shall ever die of *that*. For one thing, I am quite certain that when I have been ill, it has been sheer distress and nerve strain which have let go of my lungs. I am one of those fools who take my living damnably hard. And I have a good old English habit of shutting my rages of trouble well inside my belly, so that they play havoc with my innards. . . . Not that I've anything so tremendous and tragic in my life, any more than anybody else. Only I am so damnably violent, really, and self destructive. . . . I am just learning—thanks to Frieda—to let go a bit.

From Irschenhausen he and Frieda then headed in different directions before making their way to the Ligurian coast south of La Spezia, where Edgar Jaffe was looking for a house for them. Frieda went to see her mother, while Lawrence walked—faster, without Frieda to slow him down—via Lake Constance over to the Rhine, down to the falls at Schaffhausen, then to Lucerne and Zurich, and up into the terrifying mountains. He saw the white peaks, as he recounted in *Twilight in Italy:* "bright with transcendent snow . . . like death, eternal death . . . The very pure source of breaking-down, decomposition, the very quick of cold death."

On his way into Italian Switzerland, Lawrence did an odd thing. At a villa by the lake, while he enjoyed honey cakes with jam, the two women who served him asked him if he was from Austria. In response, "I said I was from Graz; that my father was a doctor in Graz. . . . I said this because I knew a doctor from Graz who was always wandering about, and because I did not want to be myself, an Englishman, to these two old ladies." Such were his powers of impersonation, he found himself trapped more deeply in the false character than he had intended, shedding tears like an Austrian. He felt he had to leave, even though he had wanted to stay, and took himself away, to spend the night at "a detestable brutal room at an inn in the town."

Lawrence was intimately acquainted with the details of only one doctor from Graz: Otto Gross. He must have known, from Else Jaffe's letters to Frieda, that Gross's father had put a warrant out for his son's arrest and that from Ascona, Frieda Gross had warned her unstable estranged husband, then in Berlin, not to cross the Swiss border. In declaring himself a doctor from Graz, therefore, Lawrence was playing the part not only of Frieda's incomparable lover, but of a psychopath wanted by the Swiss police.

Coming to the end of this journey, as he headed down out of the St. Gothard pass, he made an unnecessary detour to the west to go to Locarno. It is possible that he may have continued on an extra few miles to get a look at Ascona. If so, he did not record it. By the end of September he had rejoined Frieda. They met in Milan, a city of which Lawrence formed a swift and venomous impression: "with its imitation hedge-hog of a cathedral and its hateful town Italians all socks and purple cravats and hats over the ear."

EDGAR Jaffe had found them a small pink house at Fiascherino near Lerici, south of Genoa and La Spezia, a stretch of mountainous coast popular with Germans as well as English. Frieda's Bohemian friend from Munich, Countess Fanny von Reventlow, spent time there in October 1912; and Frieda Gross took Ernst Frick to La Spezia to recuperate when he got out of jail in November 1913.

The view from the Lawrences' house was dramatic, with jagged black cliffs like pincers protecting their little turquoise cove from the wide bay of La Spezia. The house itself, perched just above the seawall edging the beach, was dark, low-ceilinged, and damp and could only be reached by rowboat or a steep scramble down a stony path from the road above.

After a year Lawrence well understood the Italian attitude to *bella figura*. Beauty, fashion, art were to be shown off in the open, in public places. As he explained to Cynthia Asquith, who was to become one of his valued correspondents: "But the Italians don't consider their houses, like we do, as being their extended person. In England, my house is my outer cuticle, like a snail has a shell. Here, it is a hole into which I creep out of the rain and dark."

Eagerly he and Frieda scrubbed their extended person until its floor tiles showed red through the grime. They laughed at their unhygienic Italian neighbors, a captain and his wife, who threw their scraps on the tile floor for the animals to eat. Lawrence marveled, "Lord, but how Italy can stink."

From that dark sooty cave emerged *The Rainbow*, which opens with Lawrence's idyllic evocation of unspoiled rural Nottinghamshire: its fields of golden corn, its lines of geese strutting to the pond, and the white dot of the village church clock showing distant above the horizontal land. When they first arrived in Lerici, however, the book was still "The Sisters," and with the original manuscript lost in the post somewhere between Munich and Lerici, he began again.

Otherwise, he and Frieda lazed about, ate the figs falling in the garden, and wrote long philosophic letters. Henry Savage had written to them the news that an English writer, Richard Middleton, had committed suicide. The Lawrences had read Middleton's essays critical of the female sex and agreed with each other on the real cause of his death: hatred of his own body. Lawrence's diagnosis was that "it is so much more difficult to live with one's body than with one's soul. One's body is so much more exacting: what it won't have it won't have." Frieda chimed in, implying that it was Middleton's misfortune not to have met her. Echoing Zarathustra's condemnation of "Despisers of the Body," she told Savage:

> I get so *cross* with Middleton when he hates his body, God made it and even if it was'nt Apollo like it *must* have been a lovable one—What this really means that no woman ever loved it, if a woman had, he would not have killed himself and he would have been a very great man—It was really sex—unsatisfied sex—that killed him.

Tutored by Frieda, Lawrence had embraced the fashionable Asconan idea that sexual frustration led to illness. He was not, however, sympathetic when she was ill, as she was with a cold that autumn. Frieda barked, he complained in a letter to Cynthia Asquith, "like a dog fox. It's sickening." He blamed his own constant weariness on his Englishness and his repressed upbringing. And he seemed unable to get Middleton's suicide off his mind. "Perhaps there was something obstructing him, in his soul—and probably it was his sex . . ." he wrote Henry Savage. "Most poets die of sex—Keats, Shelley, Burns."

In fact, Keats and Shelley had consumption—the reason they had come to Italy—and Shelley probably would have died of it, like Keats, had he not drowned in the Bay of La Spezia first.

Shelley was much on their minds in Lerici, for San Terenzo, the village where he lived and from which he had set sail on his last voyage, was just an hour's walk away on the other side of the bay. As Lawrence joked to Eddie Marsh, "I don't swim more than a dozen yards, so am always trying to follow the starry Shelley, and set amid the waves."

On November 9 Hanns Gross achieved his wish when, on his sworn statement that his son was a dangerous psychopath, Otto was arrested in Berlin and taken to an asylum in Austria. It became a cause célèbre—the archetypal father's vengeance on his son ("le créateur de la psychoanalyse," as the French poet and columnist Apollonaire called the martyr.) In Vienna admirers circulated ten thousand handbills, demanding "Free Otto Gross."

By then Lawrence and Frieda had made headlines of their own. On Saturday, October 19, 1913, the second page of the London *Evening*

News carried "The Author's Lament," a report on the Weekley divorce. By Sunday the divorce was national news, sharing the front page of *News of the World* with Austria's ultimatum to Serbia to withdraw its troops from Albania ("If the Belgrade Government fails to comply war is practically certain"); with Mrs. Pankhurst's detention at Ellis Island as an undesirable alien because she was on her way to address a suffragists' meeting in Washington; and with the newspaper's boast that its circulation was more than two million. Equally prominent were the cabinet's decision to press ahead with Home Rule for Ireland and a juicy sexual scandal of the kind then as now essential to the British Sunday: "Romantic Tragedy. Sensational Discovery in West-End Hotel. Young Couple Locked in Dying Embrace." For Lawrence notoriety was tempered by a typographical error in his name, given as Mr. B. H. Lawrence.

It was not over by Monday, when *The London Standard* fastened "Curious Analysis of Women's Nature" above the story. What had caught the paper's eye was Lawrence's statement in his letter to Weekley that "women are in their natures like giantesses." News indeed. Only the day before, the British press baron Lord Northcliffe had declared in a speech in Chicago that if women were given the same freedom as men they would dominate the Empire: "No self-respecting man is going to be dominated by women."

The full story of the divorce also appeared—so much for Ernest Weekley's hopes of privacy—the same day in the *Nottinghamshire Guardian*, with extra details about Lawrence having become a visitor to the Weekley house and Weekley having had to remonstrate with his wife "about being too much with the co-respondent."

All the papers reported the same facts: that on October 18, 1913, Ernest Weekley was granted a decree nisi (final in six months, barring reason to the contrary) with custody of the children, plus costs. Lawrence, therefore, owed Weekley a considerable sum. Constance Garnett feared that he would be in financial straits "unless Frieda's people are prepared to help. They really ought to, for it's quite as much her responsibility."

The press attention was not extraordinary, considering the rarity of divorce and the professional prominence of the parties involved. The Church of England resisted all attempts at reforms that would make divorce easier. Pillorying in the press was welcomed as part of the penalty to be paid for breaking the code of a society that held sexual desire to be a subversive force.

THE press reports left Lawrence with some explaining to do. Now his friends in Eastwood, and his family—his father, his religious older brother, George, and his sister Emily—knew of the secret he had kept hidden when he came home for Ada's wedding. Lawrence feared that the revelations had also blackened his name in higher circles. He wrote to Cynthia Asquith, apologizing for the fact that "we had appeared before you as if we were a perfectly respectable couple. I thought of the contamination—etc., etc.—and I really was upset."

Lawrence did not realize at first that the English in Italy were a more tolerant lot. For generations, Italy had been a haven for lovers, divorcés, homosexuals, and others fleeing the English moral climate. When he and Frieda went to spend several days with a wealthy couple, the Cochranes, who lived at Rezzola above Lerici and made their home a rendezvous for English people in Italy, he was uneasy in the extreme. He concealed it during the first evening; he was extremely entertaining at dinner, and everyone liked him enormously. Next morning, however, there was a knock on the door of Helen Cochrane's private apartment, and the maid showed in Signor Lawrence. Without any preamble, he blurted out that he and Frieda were not married and that he felt they could not abuse her hospitality any longer. His hostess laughed merrily and said that it could not matter less. Thus reassured, he and Frieda stayed on.

In late 1913, Lawrence decided to abandon the thousand pages of manuscript he had written since March and begin again. He sent the rewritten first half—the beginning of what is now *The Rainbow*—to Garnett on January 6, 1914.

As he reshaped his book, Lawrence jumped back two generations. His Ursula Brangwen, a modern young woman who taught school and took lovers, could not, he realized, just come out of nowhere; she needed a family background from which to emerge as a young woman who dares to break free. Into the family saga of the Brangwens of Nottinghamshire, Lawrence mixed bits of the long history of the von Richthofens of Silesia and also of Louie's family, the Burrowses of Leicestershire.

The book's new sweep allowed him to portray the change in the nature of marriage—the equation between the sexes that, as he saw it, must be balanced in a way that leaves women free of dependence on men, and men free to feel brotherhood for each other—and his own search for a way of life in which people lived in harmony with nature. That he had the energy, let alone the imagination, for such swift and drastic reconstruction is a measure of the intensity with which he worked. "I am a slow writer really—I only have great outbursts of work," he told Garnett.

Garnett did not like the new version any better than that of the previous spring. The news landed like a bomb in Fiascherino. Constance Garnett, who had just arrived to visit and was staying nearby in Lerici, was at the Lawrences' cottage that day, and witnessed Lawrence's white face when he got her husband's letter. Later when the couple appeared together, she felt that both looked as if they had been crying.

Writing to Garnett, Frieda accepted full responsibility. Once again, she said, she had made the mistake of ignoring the new novel, but she had done so only in order to spite Lawrence for the pain he was causing her:

> Over the children I thought he was beastly; he hated me for being miserable, not a moment of misery did he put up with; he denied all the suffering and suffered all the more, like his mother before him; how we fought over this. In revenge I did not care about his writing. If he denies my life and suffering I deny his art, so you see he wrote without me at the back of him. The novel is a failure but you must feel something at the back of it struggling, trying to come out. . . . I am going to throw myself into the novel now and you will see what a *gioia* it will be. There is one triumph for us women, you men can't do things alone.

As he doggedly began afresh ("for about the seventh time"), Lawrence wrote McLeod at the Davidson Road School that he did not regret what he had to throw away: "You know that the perfect statue is in the marble, the kernel of it. But the thing is the getting it out clean."

Sending off the re-revised "Wedding Ring," Lawrence defended it in terms that Garnett was hardly happy to hear as their joint production of a big and beautiful work. The struggle between him and Frieda, he admitted, had spoiled the first version, making it flippant, vulgar, and jeering. Now, Garnett was told, "you will find her and me in the novel, I think, and the work is of both of us."

Garnett dug in. He liked the book no better, and said so in terms which (with echoes of his son) implied that Lawrence was an underbred mongrel—or, as Lawrence recapitulated it, that "I am half a Frenchman and one-eighth a Cockney."

Almost unbelievably, Lawrence began the book yet again, at the same time writing to Jack Murry, who was having difficulties with Katherine Mansfield, that they should stick to the love they had for each other the way he and Frieda had done. "Frieda and I are really very deeply happy."

Deep happiness, as before, did not mean peace. No subject was too trivial for disagreement—certainly not how to row a boat: "Frieda and I fell out so frightfully—we were rowing one oar each,—that the boat revolved on its axis. . . . So today Madam must walk, whether she will or no." They did not see eye to eye even on the weather: "It's still gorgeous here," Frieda wrote Cynthia Asquith just before Christmas. "It isn't," interjected Lawrence, "—it's cold and dark."

*　　*　　*

In Fiascherino the Lawrences had been more than ever in their come-and-see-us mode. In addition to Constance Garnett, their English visitors included Eddie Marsh and an Old Etonian, James Strachey Barnes, who had been on a walking tour in Spain. Barnes's later view of Lawrence was probably formed on the spot: "a genius but his genius was warped by the fact that he was a very sick man, and only half-educated."

They also had as a guest for six weeks a twenty-four-year-old novelist from London named Ivy Low. Lawrence met her at the station at Saranza, and was taken aback to to find a plump, dark-haired young woman in a Balkan peasant dress of the type affected by the intelligentsia. "Why, the girl's a swell!" he exclaimed by way of greeting. And when he followed it with the corollary "Do you think I look like a working-class man?" he was cross to get the answer he did not want: "Yes."

Ivy's aunt, Barbara Low, and an uncle by marriage, Dr. M. D. Eder, the *New Age* writer, were psychoanalysts. That year, with Dr. Ernest Jones, they had founded the London (later the British) Institute of Psycho-Analysis (spelled with a hyphen cherished to this day). Ivy had read *Sons and Lovers* at one sitting, straight through to the end, where Paul Morel turns his back on his dead mother and chooses life:

> "Mother!" he whimpered—"mother!"
> She was the only thing that held him up, himself, amid all this. And she was gone, intermingled herself. He wanted her to touch him, have him alongside with her.
> But no, he would not give in. Turning sharply, he walked towards the city's gold phosphorescence.

Ivy was so excited that she sent postcards to all her friends, full of girlish extravagance: "Be sure to read *Sons and Lovers*!" "This is a book about the Oedipus complex!" "The most marvellous novel I have ever read." "Discovered a genius." "I've found a classic by a living author." And "Don't talk to me about Joseph Conrad."

Ivy had written to Lawrence, care of his publishers. She was twenty-four, dark-eyed, dark-haired, and plump. While she was in the habit of writing to authors, seeking meetings, she had hardly expected to receive from Italy an invitation to come and spend several weeks with her idol.

Her account of the visit, a wonderful piece of reporting, captures the extreme contrariness of Lawrence's personality noted by the *Manchester Guardian* in its review of *Sons and Lovers*. The first five days in Fiascherino, she said, were the happiest in her life. Lawrence hung on her every word; he took her on walks in the woods, he gave her advice about being true to herself. They made marmalade together. Ivy, although a virgin, was so smitten that she would have gone to bed with

Lawrence had he not been closeted with Frieda in the room across the corridor.

Suddenly the magic was gone. Lawrence turned critical, mocking, disapproving; he scolded her for running around the garden in her bathing dress and washing her hair in the open. Walking with her in Lerici, he would turn without warning into narrow streets, making her (deliberately, she felt) bump into him, whereupon he told her she had no rhythm. He ridiculed her opinions. She liked Bach? Pretending to like Bach was a symptom of the ills of "cultured people"; they had to say they liked Bach, but they didn't really. He introduced her to a visiting poet and later mocked what she had said during the conversation, imitating her voice and her manner of drawing out vowels.

Then he went for the jugular. Ivy's father, Walter Low, an editor and socialist intellectual, had died of pneumonia when she was five, leaving her mother with three small daughters. Lawrence attacked him nonetheless. "Your father shouldn't have died," he said (expanding on his favorite theme of illness as moral weakness). It had been cowardly of him; he should have lived to help Ivy on in life.

Frieda, confident and lazily lying on her bed reading, looked up occasionally to deliver her own form of the cheerful put-down. As Ivy prepared to go out with Lawrence, Frieda remarked, "Lawrence can't bear walking alone! He'd ask the dullest person in the world, just so's not to walk alone!" Ivy cattily noticed in turn how Frieda always brightened when a new man came into the room.

By the end of six weeks, not surprisingly, they had all had enough of one another. The Lawrences took Ivy to the station, but she was still smitten. As the train moved out of Saranza, her eyes were streaming with tears.

By June, after another visit from Else, "The Wedding Ring" was done, an enormous manuscript, typed personally by Sir Thomas Dacre Dunlop, the British consul at La Spezia, and retitled by Frieda: *The Rainbow.* Lawrence had engaged a London literary agent, J. B. Pinker, who secured an excellent offer of three hundred pounds from Methuen. Frieda's divorce having become final in April, they prepared to return to England to marry.

But Garnett's reaction to the completed book arrived before they left. He still was unhappy about it. He still felt that the novel was shaky and the psychological development of the characters unrealistic.

With new and magisterial confidence, Lawrence explained why Garnett was wrong and he was right. He had a new conception of character and plot. He no longer saw characters in a novel as individuals confronted with moral choices.

You mustn't look in my novel for the old stable ego of the character. There is another ego, according to whose action the individual is unrecognisable, and passes through, as it were allotropic states which it needs a deeper sense than any we've been used to exercise, to discover are states of the same single radically-unchanged element.

He compared the two kinds of self to diamond and coal, both forms of carbon. He did not care, he amplified, what a woman *felt*; he cared what she *was*. The nonhuman element in humanity—its material essence—interested him more than the personal or moral element.

But, of course, the old forms were what Garnett, and most readers, were looking for: characters facing decisions, plots that developed and led to a resolution. His rejection was a sign of his discomfort with new modernist abstract writing, and *The Rainbow* was not his only stumbling block. In 1914 he also rejected for Duckworth Joyce's *Portrait of the Artist as a Young Man,* as "too discursive, formless, unrestrained" with "ugly things, ugly words" too prominent and "a complete falling to bits" at the end. (See page 513.) But in turning down *The Rainbow* Garnett was also signifying that his protégé had grown beyond him and needed him no longer, whether as critic, agent, or counselor.

LAWRENCE is widely thought to have been impervious to Frieda's anguish over the loss of her children. Hard-heartedness is consistent with his infantile streak; having lost his mother, he stole another and demanded that she be nobody's mother but his.

Yet just as he harbored dreams of fatherhood, he had hidden inside himself a secret stepfather, a kindly man who knew exactly what Frieda's children were going through and how he would comfort them. In all literature there may be no finer picture of a stepfather and stepdaughter than that of Tom Brangwen and Anna in *The Rainbow*. In a famous passage, it is the stepfather who knows how to solace a child screaming (as the Weekley children had never been allowed to do) "I—want—my—mother!" And Lawrence shows, in a brilliant touch, as Tom feeds the cows with one arm, while holding Anna in the other, how parents willingly handicap themselves for love of a child.

Tom has married Anna's mother, Lydia, a Polish widow. Lydia becomes pregnant, and when she goes into labor, little Anna is not allowed to see her. All this has been explained to her, but she repeats: " 'I want my mother, I want my mother—' and a bitter pathetic sobbing that soon had the soft-hearted Tilly sobbing too. The child's anguish was that her mother was gone, gone."

Tom, as stepfather, tries to intervene. The girl will not listen. She refuses to go to bed; she will not have a drink; she will not stop sobbing.

Tom is at first angry, then indifferent, then inspired. "Nay," he says. "It's not as bad as that." He wraps Anna in his mother's shawl and takes her out to the barn while he feeds the cows.

> He opened the doors, upper and lower, and they entered into the high, dry barn, that smelled warm even if it were not warm. He hung the lantern on the nail and shut the door. They were in another world now. The light shed softly on the timbered barn, on the whitewashed walls, and the great heap of hay; instruments cast their shadows largely, a ladder rose to the dark arch of a loft. Outside there was the driving rain, inside, the softly-illuminated stillness and calmness of the barn.
>
> Holding the child on one arm, he set about preparing the food for the cows, filling a pan with chopped hay and brewer's grains and a little meal. The child, all wonder, watched what he did. A new being was created in her for the new conditions. Sometimes, a little spasm, eddying from the bygone storm of sobbing, shook her small body. Her eyes were wide and wondering, pathetic. She was silent, quite still.

Tom's remedy works. A bond forms between them. Anna puts her arm around his neck.

> And they two sat still listening to the snuffing and breathing of cows feeding in the sheds communicating with this small barn. The lantern shed a soft, steady light from one wall. All outside was still in the rain. He looked down at the silky folds of the paisley shawl. It reminded him of his mother. She used to go to church in it. He was back again in the old irresponsibility and security, a boy at home.

Tom has won—taken Anna out of herself, brought her into contact with a world beyond her mother, shown her other forms of love and life. The passage shows Lawrence at his best. With vivid particularity and intense sympathy, he creates a scene which, powerfully and unobtrusively, preaches a message that transcends anything he wrote about sex. In the rain, in the darkness, Tom Brangwen humbly senses that beyond human beings, beyond even the plant and animal kingdom, "there was the infinite world, eternal, unchanging, as well as the world of life."

IT seemed possible, as they headed for England, that the regularization of their union might persuade Weekley to allow Frieda access to her children. Lawrence himself really wanted to make progress on solving the problem.

On the way back to England, while Frieda visited her mother in Baden-Baden, Lawrence stopped in Heidelberg. Listening to Alfred Weber expounding the latest theories on the German political economy, he got a mental picture once more of himself as a bird: "like a little half fledged bird opening my beak *Very wide* to gulp down the fat phrases. But it is all very interesting."

In London they stayed with Murry's friend the Irish barrister Gordon Campbell (later Lord Glenavy), in his small house at 9 Selwood Terrace, South Kensington. Lawrence, fortified by Methuen's advance for *The Rainbow,* opened a bank account with the Aldwych branch of London County and Westminster. Trying to round up still more missing manuscripts of short stories, they went to the Cearne for the weekend. They saw Cynthia Asquith, who was expecting her second child, and marveled at how well she looked.

Through Ivy Low, Lawrence made two staunch friends: the young Scottish novelist Catherine Carswell (then Jackson) and Dr. M. D. (David) Eder, Ivy's uncle by marriage, her spiritual father and hero. Eder called on Lawrence several times at Selwood Place to discuss the Freudian implications of *Sons and Lovers.* Eder, as Carswell's son, John, later observed, "found in it confirmation of the theories which he was one of the few men in England at that time to espouse." Eder, who had translated Freud's *Traumdeutung* into a short English version, *On Dreams,* had met Freud in Vienna that year and returned to help Ernest Jones in the introduction of Freudian analysis to Britain. Twenty years older than Lawrence, he was a large, warm, and kindly man with whom Lawrence could easily discuss the new theories about psychology and the unconscious.

FROM Selwood Terrace, on the very hot morning of Monday, July 13, Lawrence and Frieda set out for the Kensington Register Office on Marloes Road. Belatedly for a man writing a book which had until two months before been called "The Wedding Ring," he realized that he ought to buy one. He stopped on the way and made his purchase, whereupon Frieda, in a splendid spontaneous gesture, pulled off the ring Weekley had put on her finger fourteen years before and gave it to Katherine Mansfield. It was an appropriate hand-me-down, from one woman who had cast off a husband to another. (Lawrence had dealt with the problem differently in *The Rainbow,* where Lydia Brangwen insists on wearing two rings to show that she has had two husbands.)

Their witnesses, according to their marriage certificate, were Murry and Mansfield and a J. D. Fergusson. Their first choices had been Eddie Marsh and Arthur McLeod. But Marsh was detained by urgent work at the Admiralty that morning. McLeod was stuck, as Lawrence had been less than three years before, in his Croydon classroom.

After the brief ceremony Lawrence and Frieda posed in the garden of

Selwood Terrace with the Murrys. Frieda was the least well-turned-out of the quartet, in flowered jacket and skirt, with a straw hat plonked on the back of her head, and scarves amateurishly tied to form a belt and hatband. Katherine was smart and jaunty, with her hat at a rakish angle. Both men, with hats and straight backs, looked very dapper, Murry the more so with a wing collar. That evening David Garnett gave them a wedding dinner. "I don't feel a changed man," Lawrence wrote Sallie Hopkin, "but I suppose I am one."

Marriage gave them the confidence to redouble their efforts to gain access to Frieda's children. Lawrence's letters in his first week of marriage show how acute "the trouble about the children" had become, and reveal at the same time a poignant preoccupation with the imminent arrival of Cynthia's new baby. But their hopes were swiftly crushed by lawyers who told them that their new status made no difference; Ernest Weekley absolutely refused to let the children see their mother.

His hardness of heart was not excessive in the moral climate of his time. It was twenty-four years since adultery with Mrs. Kitty O'Shea had brought the downfall of the Irish leader Charles Stewart Parnell, and only nineteen since the trials and imprisonment of Oscar Wilde. Weekley had to protect his reputation and his livelihood; the scandal of his divorce had probably cost him any chance of academic advancement. What is more, Frieda's moral offense—open adultery and cohabitation—was considered grave, on a par with a later age's opinion of drug addiction or child abuse. The prevailing wisdom, moreover, held that the best interests of children lay in making a clean break with a miscreant parent rather than in trying to keep the tie alive.

As before, therefore, Frieda had to resort to furtive glimpses, but even these were now to be denied her. Elsa and Barby went to school accompanied by their aunt Maude. When Maude spotted Frieda, she shouted, "Run, children, run!" and they ran. Monty, too, was under strict orders. When Katherine Mansfield tried to deliver a message from Frieda, Monty sent word by another boy that he was not allowed to talk to people who approached him at school.

Despairingly, Frieda wrote to her mother in Baden-Baden to come and help. Lawrence encouraged the idea. He hoped that the admirable *Frau Baronin,* now his mother-in-law, would turn up and throw one of her splendid fits of indignation. "Then we shall see sparks fly round the maggoty Weekley house," he promised Garnett.

But Anna von Richthofen did not come to England, then or ever again.

8

THE WIDER WAR

July 1914–December 1915

> *It is very difficult for a sick man not to be a scoundrel.*
>
> —Dr. Johnson

*A*t the height of the London season in the summer when the Lawrences married, Eddie Marsh, still Winston Churchill's secretary, twice invited them to lunch at smart restaurants with the poet Rupert Brooke. Frieda found Brooke, Marsh's young protégé, so good-looking it took her breath away. Between these two lunches fell the assassination at Sarajevo. Austria, enraged by the death of the imperial heir apparent, the Archduke Franz Ferdinand, and his wife at the hands of Serbian nationalists, determined to annihilate Serbia. Germany readied itself to assist its ally, Austria—a move certain to draw Russia into battle on Serbia's side. For his second engagement with the Lawrences, Marsh arrived late and excited. "I believe Sir Edward Grey has just prevented war with Germany," he said.

Marsh was wrong. The German Kaiser refused the mediation conference that Grey, foreign secretary in Asquith's Liberal government, had pressed Germany to accept. Russia accordingly invaded Serbia, while Germany set its huge military might rolling—not to the east, as expected, toward Russia, but westward, toward its old enemy France.

Britain was under no obligation to intercede on France's behalf. It was bound by treaty, however, to defend the French ports on the English Channel (in order to allow the French navy to remain in the Mediterranean), and bound also to protect the neutrality of Belgium. When the Germans chose a corner of Belgium as their route to northern France, Britain was dragged into war. The rapid sequence of events took place over the English bank holiday weekend at the beginning of August 1914. Crowds thronged into London to await the declaration of war.

Lawrence was not among them. He was walking in the Lake District with three men friends, on what was to have been an eight-day holiday. They did not learn of the expiration of Britain's ultimatum to Germany at midnight on August 4 until they came down off the moors and into Barrow-in-Furness the following day. Lawrence returned to London immediately. From what he had seen of the Bavarian army in training the summer before, he foresaw the new kind of industrialized war that lay in store. Never one to waste his perceptions, he quickly turned them into an article for the *Manchester Guardian,* in which he envisaged "a war of machines, and men no more than the subjective material of the machine ... My God, why am I a man at all, when this is all, this machinery piercing and tearing?" The paper rewarded him with two guineas and one of its characteristic misprints; the name of the writer of "With the Guns" appeared as "H. D. Lawrence."

War cut Lawrence and Frieda off from the German half of their lives and from their pink house in Italy. It imprisoned Lawrence, moreover, in a country that he believed (probably correctly) to be harmful to his health and that was exhibiting a new and ugly jingoism. The consolation, for him and Frieda as for everyone, was the certainty that the war would be over by Christmas—if not sooner; the Kaiser told his troops during the first week in August that they would be home before the leaves had fallen from the trees. Neither side, conditioned by the short Franco-Prussian war of 1870, had stockpiled food or equipment for more than six months.

Half the Liberal cabinet had opposed fighting to aid France. But the atrocities committed upon the Belgian civilian population quelled their neutralist sentiments, as did the prospect of living just across the Channel from a pan-European empire more powerful than Napoleon's. With the cabinet dissidents united behind the prime minister, Britain sent an expeditionary force of a hundred thousand men to help block the German advance on Paris, and when, in the Battle of the Marne in early September, the Germans were forced to retreat, expectations of a swift victory were reinforced and the high cost in casualties accepted as a fair price.

Asquith may have taken a united cabinet with him into war, but not a united country. Against the patriotic tide were many who did not believe the war essential to Britain's self-defense and who saw instead secretive and war-happy leaders drawing Britain needlessly into the old conflict between France and Germany.

The war brought out the worst in Lawrence. It invaded his personality and released his darkest fears: of debt and death and disintegration. It forced him to confront the strains in his marriage and his fantasies of the unspeakable possibilities of men herded together. It accelerated the wild vacillations of his mood. A pattern of smashing relationships and abusing hospitality set in.

The friendship with Henry Savage, for example, which had so flourished in correspondence, did not survive a lunch in London. Sitting at the table Savage watched in helpless dismay while Lawrence lashed out in indiscriminate attacks upon the writer Anatole France and, more awkwardly, upon a woman guest. Savage left, convinced that Lawrence had reached the point where he wanted only listeners and disciples, not friends. They never met again.

Katherine Mansfield and John Middleton Murry remained friends—for the time being. When Lawrence and Frieda found the younger couple living on the top floor of a charmless, insect-infested house on the Chelsea-Fulham border, they persuaded them (after rebuking them for tolerating squalor) to leave London and join them in the Buckinghamshire countryside.

The war reduced the Lawrences to living in country cottages, those rustic retreats of the English intelligentsia for whom privacy, natural beauty, and cheap rent were more important than dry walls and indoor plumbing. But neither Lawrence nor Frieda minded discomfort or constant uprooting. In the twelve months following their return to the Continent in the late summer of 1913, they had lived at five different addresses and, determined as they were to avoid the encumbrance of possessions, had become adept at installing little personal touches wherever they went, to make themselves feel at home.

In the autumn of 1914, for ten shillings a week, they rented a brick-and-slate house amid an artists' colony in and around Chesham, Buckinghamshire, about twenty-five miles northwest of London. The Gordon Campbells and the Murrys had shared a house nearby the previous year. At the heart of the colony was an old mill where the novelist Gilbert Cannan wrote his highly regarded novels. He and his wife, Mary—an elegant woman seventeen years his senior, whom he had stolen from J. M. Barrie—lived in a modern house at the other end of the garden from the mill.

Lawrence and Frieda happily fell into their domestic routine; the quiet times of painting, decorating, and hanging curtains seemed to soothe the tensions between them. They whitewashed their own cottage, and the Murrys' as well, Lawrence impatient with Jack's laziness. "Get it *done!*"

he would say, splashing on with the brush. He and Frieda picked black-berries from the hedges, and such was Lawrence's mastery of the house-hold arts that they made the berries not into jam, which is easy, but into jelly, which is not.

Homemaking could not shut out the war. Lawrence wrote Eddie Marsh, "I can't get away from it for a minute: live in a sort of coma, like one of those nightmares when you can't move. I hate it—everything." He thanked Marsh for a welcome check from *Georgian Poetry* royalties, adding: "Come and see us if you ever have time."

Marsh did not have time. Churchill, who was still first lord of the Admiralty and to whom he was "dear Eddie," was pursuing the war with gusto. Alone among the cabinet, Churchill foresaw that the high rate of casualties would soon create a shortage of men; he advocated conscription. (Britain was the only country among the Allies to depend on voluntary enlistment; hence the urgency of Lord Kitchener's recruit-ing poster, "Your Country Needs YOU.") Such was the hostility to the war—not only from pacifists but from Little Englanders opposed to foreign entanglements—that at the start compulsory military service was politically unthinkable.

Marsh, who had even crossed the Channel with Churchill to discuss strategy with French generals, had, not surprisingly, swiftly acquired the prevailing hatred of all things German. The war was widely seen as the consequence of the German national characteristics of subservience and aggressiveness, which led its population docilely to follow the dictates of Prussian militarism.

All the same, Marsh continued to be warm toward the Lawrences. Hearing that Lawrence wanted to write a book about Thomas Hardy, he sent him Hardy's complete works, as well as ten pounds and a letter expressing his confidence in Lawrence's genius. Lawrence was so touched he nearly wept. "Frieda has always got money from Germany when we have been badly reduced before," he wrote back. But, he declared candidly, the hatred of all Germans nearly broke his heart. He knew that they should not win and were incapable of doing so. "But they are a young, only adolescent, nation and they don't know what to do with themselves."

Frieda weighed in with her usual blend of common sense ("I think the *women* ought to kick and say, we *wont* [sic] have our men killed, it's such a job to bring up a child and then after all the bother, he is shot—no, it's *not* glorious") and nonsense. She scoffed at all the fuss that was being made about rapes in Belgium; after all, only two cases had been reported. And she commanded Marsh, "You *are* not to hate the Ger-mans. . . . —We are frightfully nice people," but she despaired of the English capacity to understand anything outside themselves.

The Lawrences had heard of Marsh's anti-Teutonic sentiments from

Mark Gertler, a young painter and Buckinghamshire neighbor. Gertler, an East End Jew of immigrant parents, had been taken up by Marsh, who bought a great deal of his work and gave him a room in his flat in Lincoln's Inn, an evening suit, a purple dressing gown, and an allowance of ten pounds a month. To Marsh, writing to Rupert Brooke, Gertler was "a beautiful little Jew, like a Lippo Lippi cherub," and so he was: slim, with high cheekbones, wide-spaced black-lashed eyes, aquiline nose, bow lips, and with a great gift of draftsmanship and a wicked sense of humor. Gertler was not homosexual, but, like the bisexual Rupert Brooke, he played up to Marsh's interest in young men.

But Gertler could not stomach the war, and although a true Londoner who always preferred the capital to the country, had fled to Buckinghamshire to get away from it all. Living at the Cannans', he had swiftly become a fast friend of the Lawrences. Himself a brilliant mimic, he soon could do a wonderful Lawrence, massaging his head and shrieking, "You lie! You lie!" or dropping the casual aside, "She's a *Baroness,* you know."

The Cannans, Gertler, and the Murrys made a solid nucleus for a lively country social life: eating around the kitchen table with wet gumboots drying by the fire, playing charades, drinking too much red wine, and talking late into the night about subjects unacceptable in town. There was a constant stream of guests. Lawrence's new friend Samuel Koteliansky, a Russian Jew and translator who had been one of the walking party in the Lakes, thought nothing of traveling up on the train from London's Marylebone Station and walking three and a half miles over country lanes just for Sunday lunch.

Koteliansky, or Kot, as all called him, believed Lawrence to be a great man, and was the most steadfast of the very few whose friendship with Lawrence stood the test of time and temperament. Kot had come to London from Kiev to study law and had remained, working as a translator in the scruffy, ambiguously named Russian Law Bureau in Holborn. An austere bachelor, he exuded an uncompromising intensity, with fierce eyes and an awesome corona of wiry black hair. On his visits to Buckinghamshire, Kot was pleased to act as courier between the Lawrences' rural retreat and the shops of London, and brought with him on various visits a lapis lazuli necklace for Frieda, which Lawrence had admired in the window of a secondhand-jewelry shop in Soho; bottles of Chianti; a small jar of fish paste; and a typewriter ribbon.

A typewriter was advanced technology for authors of the day. Lawrence owned one thanks to the American poet Amy Lowell. At Marsh's suggestion, Lowell had invited Lawrence and Frieda to a dinner with other young poets identified with the movement called Imagism: Ezra Pound, Richard Aldington, and Hilda Doolittle. Hilda, an American who wrote as H.D., was Aldington's new wife and Pound's former girlfriend. (The two Americans had known each other at the University of Pennsylvania.) Lawrence was unsure that his highly personal, unrhymed verse fit any better among Miss Lowell's Imagists than among Marsh's Georgians, but he liked her and welcomed the prospect of publication with royalties.

The portly, cigar-smoking Lowell, a Boston Brahmin and sister of the president of Harvard, edited several anthologies of Imagist poetry and shuffled her contributors and their tiny payments with the skill of a State Street banker. Not long after accepting seven of Lawrence's poems, she heard that the war had placed him in financial difficulties. Deciding (wrongly) that he was too proud to accept gifts of cash, she wrote that she was sending him her cast-off typewriter instead.

Lawrence was delighted. "My wife and I are already pushing each other off the chair and fighting as to who shall work it," he wrote to Lowell in Boston. The typewriter would enable him to finish work faster, and he hoped that Kot would type his Thomas Hardy book on it. Oddly, he seemed less grateful for a more substantial gift: fifty pounds from the Royal Literary Fund. Even though he had formally applied for some assistance, he resented having to accept the fund's "tame thin-gutted charity." Nonetheless, he now had enough to see himself and Frieda comfortably through the winter.

But first he had to get through the autumn. The change of environment had, as usual, affected his health, and he spent many days in bed. Maintaining that it was for the good of his throat, he grew a beard. It might look hideous, he wrote Catherine Carswell (who, like Kot, was becoming a loyal friend and correspondent), yet "it is so warm and complete, and such a clothing to ones [sic] nakedness that I like it and shall keep it."

And he did. He was never clean-shaven again. Although the beard made no discernible improvement in his health, it possibly gave him strength in other ways. Married for only a few months, he may have wished to display the gravitas befitting a husband; his father had a heavy beard. Or, deep into the new work on Hardy he called "my philosophy," he may have wished to look the part of a prophet. The "nakedness" he wished to hide was probably his mouth. He had disliked the "mean slit" that had emerged when Jones, his Croydon landlord, had shaved his beard. He also was undoubtedly aware of the "consumptive mouth," a protruding boney feature associated with the disease—which had claimed the life of his Eastwood friend Hilda Shaw in spite of her stay in a sanatorium. With the outbreak of war, moreover, Lawrence had every wish to flaunt a thick mask of facial hair, an outward proclamation that he was the very antithesis of a soldier. Men in uniform had to be clean-shaven.

*   *   *

DINING together twice a week, the men doing the cooking, the tight foursome of the Lawrences and the Murrys spoke freely about their sex lives. They all knew that Katherine was growing dissatisfied with Jack (she had been writing farewells to him in her journal). Lawrence told Jack that often when he wanted Frieda she did not want him at all, while Frieda complained loudly about Lawrence's gracelessness in bed. Murry put it all in *his* journal, along with an analysis of the Lawrence marriage in which Frieda came out very badly:

> There is no high degree of physical satisfaction for him. That is all wrong between them. F. accuses him of taking her "as a dog does a bitch." . . . Sincerely I do not believe she loves *him* at all. She is in love with the idea of him as a famous and brilliant novelist—and that's all. And the idea that she should have been allowed to tyrannize over him with her damnably false "love" for her children is utterly repulsive to me.

Murry, utterly smitten with Lawrence, could hardly be civil to Frieda. He felt she was stupid, "and stupid assertiveness is hard enough to bear." He could not understand why Lawrence put up with her; he told his journal that Katherine, Gordon Campbell, and Kot felt as he did.

Stupid assertiveness was particularly hard to bear in 1914 when it came with a German accent. Frieda was combative, sententious, and infuriating, but she was not stupid, nor was her love for her children feigned. Not everyone disliked her. Amy Lowell found Frieda a woman of vivacity and breeding. Wherever they went, the Lawrences as a couple tended to produce divided feelings among their friends, and by no means was he always the favorite. Murry was later dramatically to switch his own affections from one to the other. But never was Frieda more hated than in England during the First World War.

The English writer Compton Mackenzie, for example, has left a memoir of meeting Frieda which has the subtlety of a cartoon of the Kaiser. In the autumn of 1914, he and some friends visited the Lawrences in Chesham on a Sunday afternoon and found Lawrence scrubbing the cottage floor. Lawrence, seeing visitors, called upstairs (in a Midlands accent, Mackenzie observed), "Will you get off that bloody bed and come down?" Then the presence of Frieda filled the room "like a genial goddess of Plenty"—a Germanic goddess, in a floppy dress, "her knot of fair hair collapsing, blue eyes dancing" and "white teeth glittering in a wide smile."

There is no doubt where Mackenzie's allegiance lay. He admired the "quiet light grace" with which Lawrence made and served tea, while

Lawrence's wife sat on a stool, legs apart, conducting a "rollicking guttural monologue" on the superiority of German courage, German culture, even German trees. Finally, Lawrence told her to shut up. "You don't know a damned thing about the English," he said.

"How can I not know them?" Frieda demanded. "I have been married to two Englishmen, I think I know a huge lot about the English." She would have told them too, had not Lawrence made her stop.

Katherine Mansfield certainly found Frieda tedious at times and recorded the feeling in her journal. But she did not always tell her journal the whole truth. That autumn she eagerly confided in Frieda, and she had much to confide. She was deliberating whether or not to go to Paris to have an affair with Francis Carco, a French writer to whom Murry had introduced her. She must have welcomed a confidante, too, for a medical problem, a vaginal discharge from which she was suffering and did not then recognize as a sign of gonorrhea. Then there was the rich subject of pregnancy.

Like Frieda, Katherine wanted a child. Not knowing that the venereal infection had made her sterile, she had forced Murry to take a fertility test in 1912. For neither couple, in the autumn of 1914, had the possibility of parenthood been ruled out.

Over Christmas they all entertained each other, Lawrence and Frieda boiling hams and roasting chickens, the Cannans preparing a suckling pig which no one, not even Lawrence, knew how to carve. The Cannans' evening ended with a disastrous game of charades in which the drunken Gertler, at Murry's invitation, pretended to be the drunken Katherine's new lover. Both threw themselves so passionately into their parts that Gertler finally burst into tears at having taken another man's woman and Lawrence scolded Murry for exposing himself to humiliation. The parties, Gertler concluded, "were really fun," but he had to take himself back to London to recover.

Over the whole Chesham scene hovered the baleful presence of Kot. He had fallen hopelessly in love with Katherine, a passion only exceeded by his loathing of Frieda. He felt—as all the Buckinghamshire crowd did—that the genius had chosen the wrong woman.

LAWRENCE managed to get through the New Year without his usual Christmas collapse. But blaming the Chesham cottage for his sickly autumn, he joyfully accepted the offer of another in Sussex. Any move to the south seemed progress, and by mid-January he and Frieda were on their way, pausing for a few days in London, where they stayed with David Eder and his wife.

Lawrence was in the grip of a new obsession. He would gather a band of like-minded souls and sail away from the evil industrial world of greed and slaughter to a remote island where he and his band would found a purer society based on trust and cooperation.

The dream of a remote utopian community where all are equal runs through English literature. At the end of the eighteenth century Samuel Taylor Coleridge and Robert Southey gave it a name: Pantisocracy. Their Pantisocracy would be, in Coleridge's words, "a small Company of chosen Individuals . . . trying the experiment of human Perfectibility on the banks of the Susquehannah." Lawrence gave his dream a name too: Rananim. He took the word from one of Kot's Hebrew songs, although the actual idea of starting a community of his own probably came from his Zionist friend, David Eder.

Planning Rananim, Lawrence was like a boy organizing a club. He even designed a Rananim badge: a phoenix on a black background. Such were his narrative gifts, all his friends were drawn into the venture. "Dined at the Lawrences," Katherine Mansfield wrote in her journal the day after New Year, "and talked the Island."

In Eder, his host, Lawrence had before him a man who had actually undertaken a quest for a place in the sun in a more elemental society (and who was later to find it: Eder was one of the founders of the state of Israel, and his ideal communities blossomed in the form of kibbutzim.) As the First World War began, Eder was convinced, as were many nonreligious Jews after the Dreyfus trial in France, that the only solution to the "Jewish problem" was a homeland. And he was prominent among those Jews who did not believe that the only possible place was Palestine. When Lawrence and Eder met in late 1914, Eder had made three trips to South America on behalf of the Jewish Territorial Organisation, which was looking for sites for a permanent Jewish homeland. (Some people thought it might then become part of the British Empire.) Lawrence immodestly hoped that Eder, his wife, Edith, and his two stepsons would join *his* colony instead, and perhaps even provide, through their connections, its location.

The Eders were the epitome of progressivism. Both divorced, they were ardent Fabians. Their home in the Hampstead Garden Suburb (an ideal community in its own right, designed as a *rus in urbe*, free of signs of commerce) was a center for socialists, feminists, psychoanalysts, and Zionists. Edith Eder, Ivy Low's aunt, epitomized the New Woman. She was a vegetarian who wore flat heels and an Egyptian jibbah, and who had had both an analysis with Jung and an affair with H. G. Wells.

The Murrys, as was their way, made fun of Lawrence's "Freudian entourage," but Lawrence felt very much at home with the Eders. He told Edith that she was the perfect hostess; he felt free and simple living in her house. In the sparse correspondence that survives from this underrecorded close friendship there is no hint of him ever saying anything against either of them.

Eder's travels had filled him with exotic tales of journeys up the Amazon, into the Andes, and to remotest Paraguay, of life in an atmosphere of revolution, tropical rains, and remote tribes. One of his published stories prefigures some of Lawrence's later Mexican and New Mexican works. "My Cannibal Nurse" describes a young native woman with shaved eyebrows and armpits in a straight simple shift, who nursed Eder through a tropical fever. When the nurse pre-chewed his food to help him digest, Eder feared that she was feeding him to turn him into a good meal. Only upon his return to England, on reading a German anthropological text, did he realize that in his nurse's tribe human flesh was eaten by men only, and only on festival occasions.

NEARER the heart of London was another tight community of like-minded souls: Bloomsbury. On January 15 the Lawrences attended a dinner party at the Bedford Square home of Lady Ottoline Morrell, wife of the Liberal M.P. Philip Morrell and half-sister of the Duke of Portland. Lady Ottoline (who pronounced her Christian name "Ottoleen" and her surname "Murrell," with the stress on the first syllable) introduced them to her lover, Bertrand Russell, and also to the painter Duncan Grant and the novelist E. M. Forster.

Forster swiftly fell victim to the famous charm. He was raised out of his deep gloom about the war, as he wrote a friend, "by D. H. Lawrence: Not the novels, but the author, a sandy haired passionate Nibelung . . . He is really extraordinarily nice." Lawrence had done all the talking and Forster, a good listener, did not even mind that his answers were disregarded, so refreshing was Lawrence's intense commitment to his own ideas.

It was Lawrence's first real encounter with the Bloomsbury set: the creative, self-satisfied, and well-bred coterie who regarded him as a prize bull in their china shop. When Ottoline's dinner party reassembled the following day for tea at Duncan Grant's studio, Lawrence took one look at the canvases and, overreacting either to Grant's abstraction or his homosexuality, launched into a tirade so fierce that Frieda could not calm him down and the shy Forster made his excuses and left. But in the author of the highly successful *Howards End,* and recipient of a small private income, Lawrence had spotted a potential recruit for his Pantisocracy and moved to sign him up.

The vision of Rananim was so vivid in Lawrence's mind that his letters that month were virtual travel brochures. To Willie Hopkin: "I want to gather together about twenty souls and sail away from this world of war and squalor and found a little colony where there shall be no money but a sort of communism as far as necessaries of life go, and some real decency." To Ottoline Morrell: "We will bring house and church and shop together." And to Forster: "people to come without class or money, sacrificing nothing, but each coming with all his desires, yet knowing his life is but a tiny section of a Whole." But, he added mournfully: "I can't find anybody." That was quite true. The bit about coming without money was not. Lawrence expected his Pantisocrats to pay their way.

VIOLA Meynell's cottage was at Greatham near Pulborough in Sussex, just over the South Downs from the sea. Viola was another young novelist, a friend of Ivy Low's, and like Ivy, was an intense admirer of Lawrence's work. Lawrence, settling in, braced once more for the shock of the new. He felt, he wrote Forster, inviting him for a weekend in Greatham, "as if I'd just come out of the shell and hadn't got any feathers to protect me."

Lawrence had landed himself in yet another utopia. The Meynells, a large and literary Catholic family, even called it "the Colony." At its head were Wilfrid Meynell and his wife, Alice, poets and dedicated Catholic journalists. They had rescued the Catholic poet Francis Thompson from dereliction and looked after him until his death in 1907. In 1912 they had bought the rambling Sussex estate of eighty acres and renovated its numerous cottages and outbuildings to house their growing collection of books, papers, and grandchildren. The Catholic designer and medievalist Eric Gill had been the first guest; the Irish writer Padraic Colum and his wife had spent their honeymoon there. The Meynell colony was, all in all, a self-conscious and beautifully appointed private world built around a family and a religion. Lady Cynthia Asquith, after a visit that spring, said that she had never seen anything so pretentious in her life.

The main house, where the patriarch reigned, was the original of what the Cearne was aiming at: a beautiful old English farmhouse with steep red-tiled roof, timbered walls, and oak beams. Meynell had added a dark-oak library which, lined with family portraits and books, made an ideal environment for the English gentleman who likes to read by the fire with a rug thrown over his knees and a view of the garden.

A stone's throw from the main house, by the front gate, was the cottage allotted to Viola. The Lawrences were delighted when they walked into the long low building, with its monastic white walls, black beams, and brick fireplace. The smell of damp rose to greet their nostrils, but they were not perturbed. Lawrence thought any form of heating other than an open fire was immoral. Nor did they mind that the cottage was a converted string of cowsheds, although they never used its name, Shed Hall, on their letters. It had three bedrooms, a kitchen, a long, imposing sitting room and—real luxury—a bathroom with hot water. Viola would not hear of them paying rent; she even paid for the cleaning woman herself.

*   *   *

"DEAR Lawrences: Until you think it worthwhile to function separately, I'd better address you as one." Thus E. M. Forster thanked the Lawrences for the miserable weekend he had spent at Shed Hall. Forster was objecting strongly to the couple's habit of writing joint letters, but he had far more to complain of than that. He had been looking forward to his Sussex weekend, but had made the mistake of arriving with bad news: that the Boots Lending Library would refuse to circulate *The Prussian Officer* on grounds of indecency. Almost in retaliation, Lawrence gave his guest the same hot-cold treatment that had so devastated Ivy Low in Fiascherino.

The visit began well, with an idyllic walk over the downs, with Lawrence warm and confidential, talking about his Eastwood family, picking catkins and pointing out birds. Next day Lawrence worked on *The Rainbow* and Forster wrote letters until teatime. Lawrence then emerged to attack. He lit into the faults of Forster's novels, then of Forster the man. Forster was vulnerable. At thirty-six, with sloping shoulders, a receding chin, and the face of a morose pixie, he was a homosexual and a virgin. He had even written a secret novel (*Maurice,* published in 1971, after his death) about a homosexual love affair, but had not yet achieved any consummated sexual encounter.

Lawrence was not naïve. He seems to have recognized Forster's homosexuality. What he railed against, however, was Forster's recoil from passion and intimacy. Politely captive, Forster sat and listened, as Lawrence ranted on, to intemperate calls for the immediate nationalization of industry, agriculture, and the press. Lawrence began to shout. At one point he even, Forster later reported to a friend, "said '——— ———.' " (Forster decorously deleted the expletives.) The whole exhibition so offended Forster that he took his candle and went to bed without saying good night. Next morning he rose very early, before the Lawrences were up, and walked four miles in the dark over frosty fields to catch the 8:20 A.M. train back to London.

The visit left both men shaken. In a letter to Bertrand Russell, Lawrence implied that homosexuality could be "cured" by marriage. "He sucks his dummy—you know, those child's comforters—long after his age. . . . But why can't he act? Why can't he take a woman and fight clear to his own basic, primal being?" For his part, Forster believed Lawrence blind to his own impulses. Recommending to a friend the nude bathing scene in *The White Peacock* ("a beautiful poem of male friendship"), Forster commented that Lawrence "has not a glimmering from first to last of what he's up to."

In his thank-you letter, Forster made so bold as to tell Lawrence that he was a divided man. "I like Mrs Lawrence," he wrote; "I like the

Lawrence who . . . sees birds and is physically restful and wrote *The White Peacock,* he doesn't know why; but I do not like the deaf impercipient fanatic who has nosed over his own little sexual round until he believes that there is no other path for others to take."

Frieda was not one to remain silent in such a contretemps. Forster's complaint about getting letters from the "firm" had touched a sore spot: "poor little author's wife, who does her little best and everybody wishes her to Jericho." She herself told Forster what ailed him: "The trouble with you modern men is that you place too high a value on consciousness." She also told Forster, whom she trusted because she liked his novels, what was wrong with Lawrence: "God knows he is a fool, and undeveloped, but he is so genuine, a genuine force, inhuman like one also—and such a strain; but you ought to help him, he is really very inarticulate and *unformed.*" Frieda scolded Forster for summing up Lawrence as "customs beastly, manners none." "Think," she said, "*I* have to put up with them, and they have improved!"

The friendship was irrecoverable. Forster, a supremely fair man, never ceased to support and defend Lawrence as a writer. However, as he confided to his secret diary that year, "he makes me feel that I am in a bad state and have no friends. . . . I regret I cannot know him."

BUT Lawrence had made a more distinguished catch. Ottoline Morrell had brought Bertrand Russell to Greatham. The lovers made an incongruous couple—the stately Ottoline, six feet tall, with flamboyant clothes and bright red hair that looked as if it were dyed although it was not, towering over Russell, small, brisk, and ugly, with prominent forehead and bright eyes. But they were hardly a more unlikely match than the miner's son and the son of an earl. The two men, however, got along, in Russell's later words, "merrily as a marriage bell."

Many other visitors answered Lawrence's summons. He tried to make sure they did not overlap. Murry came, and collapsed with flu and heartache. Katherine had run off, as threatened, to her affair in Paris. When she returned to London abruptly while Murry was with Lawrence and he bounded back to meet her, Lawrence, who had enjoyed nursing his sick friend, was hurt. The psychoanalyst Barbara Low, Eder's sister-in-law, was a guest who came more often and stayed longer.

Any visitor arriving at Pulborough station had to decide whether to walk the four miles to the Meynell colony or whether, like Ottoline, who arrived in pearls and purple velvet when she came with Russell, to indulge in hiring a "fly": a horse-drawn carriage. Kot, of course, would cover the distance on foot, and Lawrence wrote explicit directions before his first visit. Coming out of the station, he was to turn left at the high road, look for the bridge in the meadows, cross the bridge, and keep straight on. Then, unless Lawrence had intercepted him, he should look for "The Labouring Man" pub. Then:

> Next to that is an old house below the level of the road. At the end of the land of the house is a path going across the fields on your left. Take that. It crosses the railway and brings you to our road. Turn to the left again and you come straight to Greatham. At the red house in Greatham turn to the right down the lane and the first house is ours. So—a blind man could walk here without asking a question.

The Honorable Bertrand Russell, aged forty-three, author of *Principia Mathematica,* lecturer at Trinity, grandson of a former prime minister, godson of John Stuart Mill, and lover since 1911 of Ottoline Morrell, fell upon Lawrence as upon a lost part of himself. Many had told Russell that he was too much of a slave to reason to be capable of an intuitive understanding of unconscious forces such as Lawrence possessed. He met Lawrence at a time when, fiercely opposed to the war, he was trying to draw up a scheme for the social reconstruction of the postwar world. In Lawrence, then twenty-nine, he found a man passionately convinced that a fundamental change in society was needed to put the world right. And at Greatham, with Lawrence basting the roast lamb and making onion sauce the while, the two men saw how they might bring it about together.

It was not apparent to either of them, in the first flush of collaboration, that they worked in entirely different spheres, virtually in different languages. Russell found Lawrence's irrationality "vivifying." He ought to have been alerted to a profound indifference to realpolitik when Lawrence wrote him describing the coming social revolution as one "between individual men and women, not between nations and classes. And the great living experience for every man is his adventure into the woman. And the ultimate passion of every man to be within himself the whole of mankind . . ." For Lawrence, the state began with marriage, society when two individuals came together as one.

As if Lawrence were a disciplined political thinker who would benefit from an exchange of ideas with other intellectuals, Russell invited him to Cambridge to meet the economist John Maynard Keynes, the political scientist Goldsworthy Lowes Dickinson, and the philosopher G. E. Moore. Lawrence was apprehensive at approaching the great university for the first time. He asked Russell whether he should bring a dinner jacket. He confessed his fear that he would be overly impressed and asked Russell not to force him to meet too many people at once. He did not like groups of any sort. "Truly I am rather afraid," he said. The disaster that followed is a set piece in the memoirs of those who witnessed it.

Dining at Trinity, Lawrence sat next to Moore and had nothing to say. Next morning he met Keynes, either at Trinity or at King's, and sat by the fire with his head bowed while Russell and Keynes, two of the cleverest Englishmen of their day, talked at and around him. He was infuriated by their brittle banter and even more offended by the spectacle of Keynes still in his nightclothes.

Keynes, frail and in precarious health since childhood, had a lifelong habit of working mainly in bed in the morning, and not getting dressed until lunchtime. To Lawrence the puritan and outsider, Keynes's dishabille represented something quite different: cynical indifference to convention, or, quite simply, homosexuality.

In early 1915, Keynes, who the following year was to register as a conscientious objector, had not begun to think seriously about his own relation to the war; according to his biographer Robert Skidelsky, the fascination of his work at the Treasury was justification enough to him. This detachment appeared to Lawrence as arrogance. And in Keynes's moist red lips, mischievous eyes, and languid posture, Lawrence spotted a vigorous predator for whom his own "greatest living experience"—the adventure into the woman—was of not the slightest interest. Keynes, as Lawrence well knew, was a leader in the Cambridge homosexual circle in which young David Garnett, Lawrence's beloved "Bunny," had begun to travel.

THE war had released in Lawrence a terror that he might be homosexual. He could not hide from himself his attraction to Murry's neat trim body, handsome square face, dark eyes. That this panic coincided with his obsession with Rananim suggests that what he really sought to escape was a despised part of himself. Now that he had reached his new-found-land in Frieda and found it wanting, his quest became geographical rather than personal; the long search for the right woman transformed itself into the search for the right place. But neither the one nor the other satisfied his real longing.

Back in Greatham, Lawrence poured out a flood of letters to vent his misery and rage about his Cambridge visit. They are full of images conveying, fairly undisguised, his horror of buggery. He complained of dreams of bugs—black beetles. He told Russell he could not bear Cambridge's "smell of rottenness, marsh-stagnancy." And to David Garnett, who had defended "men loving men," "I simply can't bear it. It is so wrong . . . as if it came from deep inward dirt—a sort of sewer." David upset him deeply by bringing to Greatham a flippant homosexual friend, Francis Birrell. Afterward, and after a recurrence of the beetle nightmare, Lawrence wrote David an almost hysterical plea to forswear homosexuality.

But you, my dear, you can be all right. You can come away, and grow whole, and love a woman, and marry her, and make life good, and be happy. Now David, in the name of everything that is called love, leave this set and stop this blasphemy against love. . . . Go away, David, and try to love a woman.

But Lawrence was not, like Forster, a suppressed homosexual who did not have the courage of his desires. He is not so neatly categorized. Rather, he was a hypersensitive man unable to bring together the male and female components of his personality, and in the grip of a terror of losing the boundaries of self. In those weeks of collapse after Cambridge, Lawrence drew an almost psychotic picture of loss of identity: "But all the time I am struggling in the dark . . . cut off from everybody and everything . . . walking in a pale assembly of an unreal world." Like a child, he begged Russell not to let him go. But with his genius for compression and association, he linked this death of self to homosexuality. He saw himself as a victim of the war: it unhinged him by forcing him to face daily the hovering specter of his own death. In "New Heaven and Earth," the long and powerful poem completed at Greatham that spring, he says:

> When I heard the cannon of the war, I listened with my own ears
>   to my own destruction.
> When I saw the torn dead, I knew it was my own torn dead body.

The images are of gang rape. He has been "trodden quite out," his body piled with "horrible reeking heaps" of other mutilated youths and men, burned and "consumed in corrupt thick smoke," and then, in almost a pun on sodomy, "trodden to nought in the smoke-sodden tomb."

Rescue, in the poem, comes in the form of his wife, with her "strange green eyes." He says, "my hand / touched that which was verily not me." He is "new-risen, resurrected, starved from the tomb, / starved from a life of devouring always myself," and he rejoices in his discovery of "she who is the other" and who "has strange-mounded breasts and strange sheer slopes, and white levels."

Homosexuality, for Lawrence, threatened more than the criminality and social ostracism of the time. It meant being locked in the tomb of himself and his own sex, shut off from Woman, the unknown and the current of life. Scolding Kot for his continuing dislike of Frieda, Lawrence had explained that Kot's mistake was to think of woman as a man of a different sex when she was a completely different world.

Curiously, he felt no revulsion from sodomy with a woman. In *The*

Rainbow, which he was finishing that spring, Will Brangwen one night suddenly rediscovers Anna, his wife of many years. Anna senses a new wildness in Will and together, like strangers, they "abandoned in one motion the moral position." Will, "as if he were a marauder," begins to explore "the dark half of the moon." Night after night the dark adventure continues. No love, no words, no kisses:

> She, separate, with a strange, dangerous, glistening look in her eyes received all his activities upon her as if they were expected by her, and provoked him when he was quiet to more.
>
> All the shameful, natural and unnatural acts of sensual voluptuousness which he and the woman partook of together, created together, they had their heavy beauty and their delight. Shame, what was it?

This foray into violent, forbidden sex frees the public man in Will Brangwen. He suddenly finds himself able to speak on education and the improvement of the working class.

Lawrence added these passages of dark sensual adventure to *The Rainbow* just as he was most tormented with thoughts of male sodomy, and also just as he prepared to join Russell to give a series of public lectures on the spiritual regeneration of society. The reclusive writer, who hated groups of any sort, was ready to hire a hall.

CAMBRIDGE was an interlude in bouts of illness. "I *hate* having influenza!" Lawrence said in March, but by April he had it again: "My old cold that I have had so long never really gets better . . . it feels like a sore throat in the middle of one's belly." Frieda was ill, too.

Fed up with a surfeit of Meynells and blaming his environment for his illness, he wanted to move. Ottoline Morrell had offered him a cottage at Garsington Manor, the Oxfordshire estate she was renovating with her husband, Philip. At first Lawrence was excited at the prospect. He had come to idealize the aristocratic Ottoline; he told her she was "a special type . . . like Cassandra in Greece, and some of the great women saints." But the plan fell through after an unseemly row about the cost of renovations. Ottoline thought Frieda was behind it, but Lawrence was as much the cause. He did not wish to invest heavily in any property, much less in one he was to have only on loan from wealthy landowners. In a vituperative letter to Philip Morrell, Lawrence tried to deflect his wrath about the expenses he was being asked to pay onto the builders— "The miserable miscreant vermin, with their prices!" Yet by the time the Lawrences paid their first visit to Garsington Manor in June, relations between artist and patron were strained.

As were those between husband and wife. A month after Lawrence finished *The Rainbow,* his majestic hymn to marriage, he and Frieda were temporarily living apart. She had left Greatham for London, where she stayed in Hampstead with Dollie Radford, a kindly older woman poet who was a friend of the Meynells. On Radford's shoulder she could weep about the children. She determined to find a flat of her own. Just how she intended to finance her burst of independence is hard to see. Although she had frequent letters from Else and her mother, thanks to Frieda Gross in Switzerland, who acted as a forwarding agent, there is no evidence that any of the Jaffe money got through to London. Lawrence had little money to spare because he was in the throes of court proceedings that followed his defiance of the order to pay Weekley's divorce costs.

Frieda felt herself surrounded by hate and contempt, cut off from those she loved. Her father had died in February and she wept bitterly at not being able to go to her mother. The least she could do, she felt, was to show herself to her children from time to time or they would forget her.

She was reminded of her nationality on all sides. She had an unpleasant exchange with Violet Hunt one day over Belgian refugees and also over Ford being in uniform. Lawrence was away when Violet came to tea in Greatham with Ford and Mrs. H. G. Wells. At the end of the visit Frieda, who made a habit of covering darkness with light, said, "Good-bye. You are very charming and I do hope we shall meet again." To which Violet replied acidly, "Good-bye. It is you who are charming but I hope we shall *never* meet again." There seems to have been an even less pleasant consequence of the visit. Ford was there, by his own later admission, to report on Frieda "to Authority." When later "Authority" turned against Frieda, Ford cannot be absolved of having used the visit as a guise for investigation and filing a report in which all Frieda's impassioned pro-German remarks were used against her.

Hatred of Germany reached a new pitch in England when the passenger liner *Lusitania* was sunk in the North Atlantic on May 7, drowning almost as many as had gone down with the *Titanic.* The slaughter in the trenches continued. Any hope that the war might be short was ended at Gallipoli when Britain failed to take the Dardanelles and lost the hope of opening a supply route to Germany's enemy Russia. Such was the national mood that German music could not be played, dachshunds were put to death for the crime of their breed, and a statue of Prince Albert was smashed by soldiers when they discovered that he was a cousin of the Kaiser. A Polish Society helped immigrants, like Mark Gertler's German-speaking family, born on Germany's eastern border, to be reclassified. "My people have now turned Poles!" Gertler crowed. "No more are we alien enemies!"

There was no reclassifying Frieda. Even Lawrence, when it suited him, treated her as the enemy. Mrs. Lawrence, he wrote Forster, was gone from Greatham. She was in London, hunting for a flat, "unless a bomb has dropped on her—killed by her own countrymen—it is the kind of fate she is cut out for." He made the same joke the same day to Ottoline Morrell, whom he was using (in letters) as an English foil to Frieda. (But he made it clear that he expected to join Frieda soon.) He even put a racial cast on the murderous fantasies to which he was increasingly prone. To Ottoline, he wrote, "I am mad with rage myself. I would like to kill a million Germans—two million." Or at least one.

But a permanent separation was impossible. Too much bound the Lawrences together, not least their allegiance to German philosophy. Arguing with Kot, Frieda declared, "You think I do not count besides Lawrence, but I take myself, my ideals and life quite as seriously as he does his."

It is hard to tell the extent to which Lawrence actually got his ideas from Frieda. He justified their constant fights to Catherine Carswell, for example, by using Frieda as an authority: "Frieda's letter is quite right, about the *difference* between us being the adventure." Their fights for supremacy were an expression of the Nietzschean phrase *Wille zur Macht,* Will to Power.

Frieda drank deep from the Nietzschean spring when she scolded Russell for misunderstanding her, saying, "You have left out the impersonal me . . . the impersonal thing is in everybody." She had cast off so much of what had formed her life and personality that she believed that she was no longer "very individual." Russell, she charged, liked to confuse people—especially women—with his intellect: "It's your form of *Wille zur Macht.*" This sounds very much like the philosophy Lawrence was hard at work explicating in his new book on Thomas Hardy, which then bore a title, *Morgenrot,* taken from one of Nietzsche's own works. In it Lawrence was arguing that life is essentially impersonal and that in Hardy's novels he found "a great background, vital and vivid, which matters more than the people who move upon it."

In the study, he also blamed the Will to Power for causing the war and went on to link the male instinct for domination to fear of the female. Rape and war were man's response to this innate inferiority. Lawrence said: "He feels full of blood, he walks the earth like a Lord. And it is to this state Nietzsche aspires in his *Wille zur Macht.* It is this the passionate nations crave."*

Thus on the relation of character and environment Lawrence and Frieda preached as one. Their English friends could not see that the

*Colin Wilson, in *Lawrence and Nietzsche,* argues that in 1915 Lawrence well understood that Nietzsche's "Will to Power" was far subtler than a naked lust for bullying, and that *Macht* is more fairly translated as vitality or life force.

genius and the Valkyrie, alone in the confines of their various cottages, did more than throw plates at each other. They talked.

THE intensity with which Lawrence consumed friendships is shown by his brief association that year with Ottoline Morrell. Theirs was an important friendship but not a sexual one, and largely epistolary. Lawrence in fact visited Garsington only three times, for no more than a total of ten days, all of them in 1915. The relationship has possibly been overrecorded because each was a passionate writer of long letters, which were kept and published. Lawrence is also permanently associated with Garsington Manor, Ottoline's Jacobean home in Oxfordshire, because of his memorable description: "It is England—my God, it breaks my soul—this England, these shafted windows, the elm-trees, the blue distance—"

The Morrells had moved to Oxfordshire from London for the sake of the health of their young daughter, who had a "chest." The house stood on fields that had once belonged to Chaucer's son. There Lady Ottoline brought her friends, her dressing-up box, and her bland, neurotic husband, Philip. Lawrence thought the Liberal member of Parliament a buffoon, perhaps because Morrell tolerated Ottoline's affair with Russell on the condition that the two never spend a night together.

Gertler was a frequent guest there, as was the painter Dorothy Brett, a shy, gawky aristocrat, the daughter of Lord Esher. Gertler, like Lawrence, never forgot the class difference between him and his hosts; he felt he could not scrub his face hard enough to look as well washed as the gentry.

It was an environment well suited to Lawrence. He saw Garsington as a staging post for Rananim: "like the Boccacio [*sic*] place where they told all the *Decamerone*." He felt close to Ottoline, moreover, because her family came from Derbyshire and he could talk to her in the local dialect. On their first weekend there, when the Morrells had been in residence for only two months, he left his mark by designing and building the summerhouse and planting the iris bed. Frieda, however, was quite out of place.

There was trouble between the two women almost from the start. During the spring Frieda had been kindly disposed to Ottoline for having interceded with Weekley to ask him to let the children see their mother. But Frieda did not like the grande dame she saw at Garsington, with her shawls, her servants, and her coterie of grateful artists. Neither did she appreciate Lawrence's strolls around the garden in intimate conversation with his towering hostess, and she was indifferent to the fey redecoration of the manor house; she would sit on a table, swinging her legs and making rude comments.

The others could not bear Frieda's tedious insistence that she was just as important as her husband. When they would ask the great Lawrence a question, his wife would answer. After the second night, when the whole house could hear the sounds of battle emerging from the Lawrences' room in the main house, Frieda left in a rage. Ottoline pitied Lawrence standing disconsolately by the luggage in the hall, and Philip urged Lawrence to leave Frieda. "Of course he didn't," Ottoline commented sourly. After their third visit, in December, when Lawrence and Frieda quarreled about Nietzsche at the dinner table, Ottoline told Russell, "If only we could put her in a sack and drown her." The Morrells shared the general view that Lawrence had ruined his life with his choice of wife.

If Lawrence was mischievous in arousing Frieda's jealousy, so he was also unfair in ignoring Ottoline's wider interests. Ottoline was a great and generous hostess, who worked hard at her hospitality, sending taxis and carriages to meet trains and bringing together interesting people: "Come to tea tomorrow afternoon. Bakst is coming & I *think* Nijinsky. Do come." She did more than anyone to try to help Lawrence realize his dream of Rananim. While there may have been a sexual element in her fascination with him, so there was in her relations with many of the other artists she befriended. The time when she was closest to Lawrence was, according to her biographer Miranda Seymour, the most physically satisfying period of her affair with Russell; it was also when she became deeply involved in antiwar activities. (She and Philip, despite their varied infidelities, worked together courageously to make Garsington during the war a refuge for artists and pacifists.)

It was the Morrells' fate to have their kindness repaid with satire by many of those they helped. Aldous Huxley, another beneficiary of Garsington, described her as "arty beyond the dreams of avarice." Ottoline, flamboyant in clothes and manner, certainly courted ridicule, but she did not deserve the caricaturing Lawrence gave her as the horse-faced Hermione Roddice in *Women in Love*.

LESS attention has been paid to a more flagrant abuse of hospitality the same year, one that led the playwright Herbert Farjeon to observe that "Lawrence never forgot nor forgave a good turn" and his sister (the writer Eleanor Farjeon) to sum him up as "a man who colours existence very strongly when you're with him. . . . He tells you anything, with a most winning gentleness and sincerity; but afterwards he would relate anything you had told him to anybody."

Lawrence was a welcome addition to the Meynells' colony. He was an avid gardener, and the whole clan liked him. He was brilliantly entertaining, too. At a family party in May 1915 he played cricket and croquet with them during the day, then led them in charades and songs at night, performing a ballad about the murder of President McKinley ("Mrs McKinley she hollered and she swore, / When she heard her old man wasn't comin' back no more"). In short, he was the ideal impoverished artist for whom to do a good turn. Viola even typed *The Rainbow* for him.

He endeared himself all the more by volunteering, when Frieda left Greatham for London, to stay behind to tutor Viola's ten-year-old niece, Mary Saleeby. With the breakup of the Saleebys' marriage, Mary and her mother, Monica, had moved to the Colony. Monica planned to teach Mary herself. But she suffered a breakdown in early 1915 and was under the care of a nurse and a doctor. Mary, a bright little thing, ran free on the farm on the estate—anarchy that could not be allowed to continue if Mary was to take up the place waiting for her that autumn at St. Paul's Girls' School in London.

Mary's plight brought out the generous strain in Lawrence's character. "I do it for the child's sake, for nothing else," he told Kot. But his motives were never entirely unmixed. He needed to remain at Greatham to finish his philosophy and his Italian travel sketches. Tutoring Mary gave him a chance to repay the Meynells for the rent-free accommodation and also to get back at Frieda—his "child" against hers. He had complained to Ottoline that Frieda "only cares about her children now."

He worked hard at tutoring, as he did at everything. (And succeeded. Mary Saleeby went on to St. Paul's and later became a doctor.) Every morning for three months he crossed to the Saleeby cottage and gave three and a half hours of lessons. He taught Mary about Sir Francis Drake and *la plume de ma tante*, about Julius Caesar's arrival in Britain in 55 B.C., and about the number of inches in a meter. He was a hard marker, taking many points off for mistakes like "ment" for "meant." To improve Mary's handwriting and spelling, he gave her dictation, and it cannot have harmed the lessons that the passages she dutifully wrote down came from his own heart. (One was "Jack Murry is a bad boy because he does not stay here long enough.") There was also a literal description of one of the Meynells' cottages nearby in the woods:

> The building is very old, it dates back about three hundred years, but some new parts have been built on it, a nursery for the children, and a bedroom, a bathroom, and a boxroom. There are three children living there, with their mother, father and nurse. The children's names are Sylvia, Christian and Barbara Lucas. Their father is a soldier. He came home yesterday to see his garden which he has made himself.

Lawrence knew Rackham Cottage well and had worked in its garden himself. In the cottage lived the Meynells' married daughter, Madeleine, her husband, Percy Lucas, and their three little girls. The eldest, Sylvia, as Mary recorded in her dictation, "cut her knee on a fag-hook nearly two years ago."

There indeed lay a tale—in fact, a tale that was on Lawrence's typewriter at that very moment. Wilfred and Alice Meynell had been delighted when Madeleine and Percy Lucas with their three children came to live at Rackham Cottage on the Greatham estate. Their happiness was swiftly blighted when five-year-old Sylvia fell and cut her knee on a rusty sickle in the grass. The wound refused to heal and the child's desperate suffering and screams were a terrible experience for the Meynell family, one of whom wrote a poem about it:

> O come away,
> It is too horrible to stay!
> Come into the next room, and close the door . . .
> But now you only listen more,
> And still you hear the whispering voice complain,
> The sudden scream of terror, and pain . . .

The child was eventually taken to a hospital. Amputation was threatened; for a time even her life was in danger. Alice Meynell tried to cheer up her granddaughter with jolly letters addressed to "dear dear priceless Mrs. Badleg." But Sylvia returned to Rackham Cottage, handicapped for life with a stiff knee that would never bend. Two years later, Lawrence caught just fleeting glimpses of the hobbling girl. But for him a glance was enough.

When Lawrence's short story "England, My England" was published in October 1915, the Meynells were horrified that he had used every detail of Sylvia's accident, then gone on to give a highly unflattering portrait of the Lucas marriage: how Percy Lucas had never worked; how he dabbled in Morris dancing and crafts and gardening, and lived lazily off his wife's father.

Worse, as so often when he borrowed literally from real life, Lawrence added a bizarre twist entirely out of his own imagination. In "England, My England" he chose to make the father responsible for his favorite child's mutilation: "Daddy! Daddy! Oh—oh, Daddy!" she screams after falling on "that sickle thing" he has left lying in the grass.

In fact, Percy Lucas was in Italy at the time of Sylvia's accident; it was a visitor who had left the sickle in the field. But Lawrence drenched his tale with reproof of the father: "He had taken his handkerchief and tied it round the knee. Then he lifted the still sobbing child in his arms, and carried her into the house and upstairs to her bed. In his arms she became quiet. But his heart was burning with pain and with guilt."

Was Lawrence, one wonders, using the accident once more to vent his buried thoughts about the injury he had done the Weekley children? He also added another bit of hurtful invention: the story ends with the guilt-ridden young father killed on the battlefields of France.

These distortions apart, Lawrence drew an almost photographic portrait of the Meynell clan, their house, their Catholic faith, their children plagued by nervous breakdowns. The name changes are among his laziest. He altered "Meynell" no further than "Marshall" and turned Rackham Cottage merely into "Crockham" Cottage. The very description of its location—a mile through the pine woods from the main house—was taken from reality, and the family compound was also accurately placed, four miles from the nearest village.

The story nonetheless is one of Lawrence's finest. It allowed him, for a start, to create one of his best little girls. The injured "Joyce" lies "in her little summer frock, her face very white now after the shock"; then later, she is shown "looking pale and important in bed," eating tapioca pudding, haughtily correcting the doctor who talks to her as if she were a baby. The doctor in the story too is one of Lawrence's classics: pompous, confident, and wrong.

"England, My England" is, above all, an indictment of war, a story of men mechanically sending other men like robots to their deaths. Lawrence makes his tale a fable of the fall of England, a once idyllic country corrupted by war into turning its young men into machines to be slaughtered by machines. He establishes the young couple, the Marshalls, as beautiful, almost fairy-tale figures: Winifred is "out of the old England," "with nut-brown eyes and nut-brown hair . . . ruddy, strong, with a certain crude, passionate quiescence and a hawthorn robustness," while Egbert is "tall and slim and agile, like an English archer," with "fine, silky hair that had darkened from fair, and a slightly arched nose of an old country family."

Egbert's garden too is an English Eden, "scooped out in the little hollow among the snake-infested commons . . . So old, so old a place! And yet he had re-created it!" But it is a flawed paradise. Egbert has no profession; he earns nothing. He thinks he may make money from Morris dancing and folk music. And the passion has gone out of his marriage; his wife has thoughts only for the children. He resents her dependence on her father, he resents the patriarch who ruins his daughters' marriages by not letting them go, and he smarts from the unspoken charge that he is lazy. "He was *not* idle—he was always doing something . . . little jobs—the garden paths—the gorgeous flowers—the chairs to mend." Almost to recover his manhood and expiate his guilt about his daughter, Egbert goes off to war.

The title is apt. Lawrence, so bad with titles for his novels, had a much surer touch with his stories, and with the ironic "England, My England," he condemns the exercise of power, in marriage as in war. Weaving his narrative out of two disparate halves, domestic and military, he illustrates all that he meant when he defended publishing in wartime stories from the ordinary life of men and women: "After all, this is the real fighting line."

The two parts of "England, My England" are unified by images of blood. The vivid description of the injury to the child's knee is painful to read; perhaps Lawrence's greatest gift was to convey physical sensation: "bleeding profusely—it was a deep cut right to the joint." And as Egbert suffers the mortal wound to his head, he asks impersonally as his consciousness fades: "Was there blood on his face? Was hot blood flowing? Or was it dry blood congealing down his cheek?"

At the story's end Lawrence, as powerfully as anywhere in his work, allows himself once more to imagine the moment of death: "The soul like the tiniest little light out on a dark sea, the sea of blood. And the light guttering . . ."

"England, My England" is another reminder that every day during the First World War Lawrence lived his own death, the news from the front combining with the reminder from his ever sore chest to convince him that staying alive was an act of will.

To compress so much psychological, political, and personal truth into one powerful short story might justify any work of art. But why—the question will forever remain—did Lawrence have to put on permanent exhibition the suffering of a real and identifiable little girl? For the Meynell family, injury was piled upon insult when, the July following the story's publication, life imitated art, and Percy Lucas was actually killed in France.

Even Lawrence himself, when he heard the news, said, "I wish the story at the bottom of the sea." But he never allowed himself guilt for long. "No," he corrected himself in the same letter, "I *dont* wish I had never written that story. It should do good, at the long run."

For the Meynells, however, Lawrence was the sickle in the grass, the cause of a wound that would never heal. Within the family nearly a century later, long after Sylvia Lucas had married, raised children, and grown old, his name remained taboo, and any visitor who uttered it became persona non grata.

In contrast, Lady Cynthia Asquith got off lightly. That year Cynthia vied with Ottoline as Lawrence's English counterbalance to Frieda; he played the titled trio off against one another, much as he had the young teachers of his Croydon years. Cynthia was chastely flirtatious and exceedingly lovely to look at. Lawrence, admiring also her blend of reserve and directness, put her into a short story, "The Thimble," in which her worst vice is self-absorption. He had, however, cast a close eye on her relations with her husband and her children. When Cynthia, her children, and their nurse were staying on the coast nearby, Lawrence and Frieda were riveted by the uncontrollable older boy, John, then four. They insisted on taking both John and year-old Michael out for the whole afternoon until bedtime and then visiting the children next day at breakfast. Lawrence then told Cynthia what was wrong with John and why it was her fault. Throwing food on the floor was Descartian, the denial of all authority. The boy should never be bullied, but neither was his mother's passive tolerance correct. The boy needed simple positive handling.

Cynthia was heartbroken; she was just coming to realize that her beloved firstborn was incurable, but she accepted that Lawrence had extraordinary insight. He left her quite alarmed about John, depressed about herself, and no wiser about autism, a rare abnormality occurring mainly in boys, marked by withdrawal and disordered speech and behavior, and not properly recognized until 1943.

Some weeks later, Lawrence cast his baleful eye on the Asquiths' marriage. Cynthia's husband, known to his intimates (with the English upper-class fondness for retaining nursery names in adult life) as Beb, was home on leave from the front, with three teeth knocked out. Lawrence, who had spent much time that spring with the great English beauty with the turquoise eyes, resented his intrusion. When, as the two couples sat on the sands and talked about the war, Lawrence saw Beb throwing pebbles at a bottle bobbing in the waves, he accused him of having the Will to Destroy.

It was hardly a tactful thing to say to the battle-scarred son of the prime minister just after Britain's humiliating defeat at Gallipoli. Beb, who admired Lawrence inordinately, did not complain, but he did allow himself to tell his wife that he did not like "the Hun."

Lawrence's own will to destroy the husbands of women he admired continued strong. To Ottoline, he declared that Beb Asquith was not even aware of his wife's existence, so spellbound was he "by the fighting line. He ought to die."

CLINGING to one woman, in marriage, was Lawrence's own war effort, his own expression of his manhood. He rejected conscientious objection as a kind of Christian turning-of-the-cheek, an outmoded asceticism. But he saw himself as one of the architects of the new social order that must emerge after the war.

However, his own political views were changing, under the influence of the war, of his internal struggles, and of his reading of Heraclitus in an anthology of early Greek philosophy. The shift precipitated a break with Russell. After a short visit to Greatham to plan the lectures they intended to give at Caxton Hall in London—they had agreed that Russell would talk on ethics, Lawrence on immortality—Russell drafted a twenty-two-page outline and sent it to Lawrence. Lawrence exploded. Russell's proposals were too liberal and socialistic, concerned with the workingman. They did not concern themselves enough with what Lawrence called "the Boundless, the Infinite, the Eternal." He scrawled angrily across the outline, as if Russell were a slow pupil: "No! No! No! No! No!!" and "Why do you use 'moral' when you mean 'well-behaved'?"

The war had blurred the outlines of society. Women were doing men's jobs, wearing men's clothes. Edwardian frills had gone forever, and, with so many women as well as men living away from home, so too had the old morality. The war had also softened rigid class divisions and aided the rise of the Labour party and trade unionism.

Lawrence, the miner's son, abhorred the anarchic power of the unions. He particularly disapproved of the Welsh miners' defiance of a government order not to strike. He now rejected democracy as well as political equality of the sexes. He wanted, rather, an elected aristocracy, headed by an elected king "something like Julius Caesar." In a letter to Cynthia Asquith he called the leader a Dictator; the Dictator would control the industrial and economic side of life, while a Dictatrix would lay down rules for private life, "marriage, custody of children etc." Equal power for the sexes, he maintained: "Women shall vote equally with the men, but for different things."

"It isn't bosh," he explained to Russell, "but rational sense." He did not wish to introduce tyrants, but rather a hierarchy, in which the common people voted only for those just above them in the social pyramid. "Above all there must be no democratic control—that is the worst of all."

Another point of disagreement was marriage. In his social reconstruction, Russell, a worldly man at home with his lusts, saw that there might have to be some changes in the institution of marriage. "Successful monogamy," he wrote urbanely, "depends on the successful substitution of habit for emotion in the course of years." Lawrence, furiously if confusingly, retorted: "The desire for monogamy is profound in us. . . . It is still true, that a man and wife are one flesh. A man alone is only fragmentary—also a woman. *Completeness is in marriage.* But State-marriage is a lie."

Soon after, Lawrence switched his allegiance to John Middleton Murry, and his reformist zeal to a new magazine which they and Katherine Mansfield would write and to which his friends could subscribe. Murry would expound on personal freedom, Lawrence on "impersonal freedom." Generously Lawrence invited Russell to contribute, and Russell obliged with an article.

Back came the verdict of Lawrence the editor: "I hate it." But he did not stop there. He hated Russell too. He accused him of not wanting peace but using his antiwar activities to satisfy a "lust to jab and strike." When Lawrence got going, he almost always went too far, but hitting a nerve of truth on the way: "I would rather have the German soldiers with rapine and cruelty, than you with your words of goodness. . . . It is *not* the hatred of falsehood which inspires you. It is the hatred of people . . . a perverted, mental blood-lust."

Russell, who had come to see Lawrence as a kind of Old Testament prophet with superhuman powers of perception, was shattered. He said later that he had contemplated suicide. But he recovered in a day, and dismissed Lawrence's ideas as morbid rubbish. The men remained on cordial terms, but distant, and each was scarred by the encounter.

Both men took their revenge, Lawrence with the fictional portrait in *Women in Love* of Sir Joshua Malleson, a desiccated professor who lounges around his mistress's country house, laughing at his own jokes. Russell got his revenge by living longer and using the benefit of octogenarian hindsight to say that Lawrence's ideas of blood-consciousness led straight to Auschwitz.

Each man nonetheless found followers for his personal religion. Russell's lectures, "Principles of Social Reconstruction," given in Caxton Hall in early 1916, were a great success and launched a long and distinguished public career of opposition to war, culminating in his leadership of Britain's Campaign for Nuclear Disarmament when he was in his nineties. Lawrence continued to preach about the danger of the wider war—between men and women—and to call for revolution in thinking about sex.

It is left to posterity to decide which man had the greater influence on the twentieth century.

LAWRENCE'S dependence on Frieda overrode his antipathy to London. By August they were installed in a ground-floor flat in Byron Villas in the Vale of Health, a small enclave of brick houses within Hampstead Heath. The move placed him in the heart of his Freudian entourage, in Hampstead, London's Schwabing, full of psychoanalysts, writers, and artists. Gertler had his studio nearby; so did Dorothy Brett. The Farjeons and the Carswells lived nearby. Lawrence found himself also closer to the war, and was not immune to its glamour:

In 1915, autumn, Hampstead Heath, leaves burning in heaps, in the blue air, London still almost pre-war London: but by the pond on the Spaniards Road, blue soldiers, wounded soldiers in their bright hospital blue and red, always there: and earth-coloured recruits with pale faces drilling near Parliament Hill. The pre-war world still lingering, and some vivid strangeness, glamour thrown in. At night all the great beams of the searchlights, in great straight bars, feeling across the London sky, feeling the clouds, feeling the body of the dark overhead. And then Zeppelin raids: the awful noise and the excitement.

The war between himself and Frieda also retained its awful excitement. One night Frieda burst into the consulting rooms of Ernest Jones, weeping that her husband was trying to murder her. "From the way you treat him," said Jones the analyst, "I wonder he has not done so long ago." Jones, having studied with Otto Gross in Munich in 1907 and analyzed Frieda Gross in 1908, was one of the few in London to know of Frieda's colorful past.

Jones had observed with clinical interest the sadistic frenzy with which the Lawrences goaded each other in public, and that night he talked with Frieda for a long time about "the dark forces that drove them into such tempestuous situations." That their marriage survived, he judged, showed that "some elements of wisdom and self-control must have played their part. And she was a charming as well as an intelligent woman."

Jones admired Lawrence's assertive, penetrating intelligence, but politely declined the invitation to Rananim. Any community with Lawrence at the head, he judged, was not going to live in harmony and brotherly love for long.

RANANIM temporarily had taken the form of a little center in London where Lawrence and Murry would hold weekly meetings and publish their magazine to expound their own views. Called *The Signature*, it would be a vessel for the ideas stirred up by Lawrence's work with Russell. To help with publication, Murry and Mansfield moved to nearby St. John's Wood.

All outsiders in the British establishment, they advertised the magazine as "a series of six papers on social and personal freedom by D. H. Lawrence and J. M. Murry." Their good friends subscribed: Ernest Jones, Barbara Low, Arthur McLeod, even Alice Dax (to whom Lawrence had decided not to write personally "after so long a silence," he told Sallie Hopkin, asking her to solicit on his behalf). The price was half a crown for six issues, but the magazine lasted for only three.

Lawrence engagingly allowed that the Infinite had taken second place to buying chairs, a desk, and other used furniture at the Caledonian Market. He and Frieda enjoyed, as they always did, fixing up their new home from bits and pieces—enjoying possessions for their very temporariness and scrappiness. Eddie Marsh loaned them money to buy a blue Persian rug. And for Frieda the move had worked; on her birthday, September 11, Weekley—mysteriously, she thought (in fact, after consulting his children)—had given his permission for a formal visit between her and them at his solicitor's office. "I am in *bliss*," she wrote Dollie Radford.

The early war years were a time of suspicion and vigilance, when neighbor reported neighbor. The police were worried by the bearded foreign presence of Koteliansky and, making inquiries, called on the Murrys, his neighbors on Acacia Road, who had also caused alarm by leaving the lights on while admiring a Zeppelin.

It was at the Murrys' flat that Lawrence sat in a chair and watched them read the review of the Irish writer Robert Lynd savaging *The Rainbow*. The Murrys hardly knew what to say. Murry disliked the heavy sexuality of the book. Katherine hated it, especially the scene where the pregnant Anna dances naked before the mirror. They agreed that the ponderousness and over-obvious sex were Frieda's fault. Whenever Frieda boasted that something that Lawrence wrote was magnificent, or worse—that she herself had written part of it—their hearts would sink.

The war then ripped into their own circle. Katherine Mansfield's brother—the adored only son in a family with five girls—was killed in France only a month after visiting her in London. The news made Katherine feel that she must leave Acacia Road immediately, and she fled to the south of France, taking Murry with her. Cynthia Asquith's brother was killed in action only three weeks after reaching the front; Rupert Brooke had died on his way to Gallipoli. And from Else Jaffe in Germany came the sad news that Frieda's little nephew Peter, Otto Gross's son, had died. Lawrence wrote movingly to Else that in the sacrilege of war, she should be comforted to know that she had one child at least at peace: "eternal, beyond anxiety."

ON November 3 London's Bow Street Magistrates' Court, acting on the basis of a single complaint, issued a warrant to Methuen and Company to surrender all copies of *The Rainbow*. No books could be sold; all copies had to be handed in to the police. Methuen, to the firm's eternal shame, offered no defense but pleaded guilty to obscenity without even telling Lawrence, who did not learn about it until nearly two weeks later. Methuen then piled on further punishment by demanding that Lawrence return the three-hundred-pound advance on royalties. Lawrence at a stroke became a pauper, at least in his own strict terms. His main source of livelihood was cut off. It also made him hate his country as never before.

Yet he chose to ignore how offensive the book was by the standards of the age and the war. It contained scenes of lesbianism, nudity, and violent and open-air lovemaking. Its inspiration (as reviewers noted) was Germanic; Lawrence had defiantly dedicated it in German: "zu Else." War had made the English national prudishness worse; libertinism, in the face of the sexual temptations of war, seemed positively subversive. Britain's troops, alone among those of the Allies, were not given condoms—or even instructed on protection from venereal disease. And *The Rainbow*'s sexual scenes were more explicit (the anal intimations entirely ignored) than anything in print. Lawrence's agent in New York doubted that the book could even be published in the United States, extinguishing Lawrence's hopes for some royalties from that quarter.

Many who might have stuck by him simply disliked the book. Eddie Marsh and Cynthia Asquith were scornful, while Aldous Huxley, still at Balliol, thought its suppression silly, "particularly when the book is so dull that no one would under ordinary circumstances read it." E. M. Forster would say nothing about the book's merit. Nonetheless, in spite of his lambasting by Lawrence that year, Forster wrote to the barrister and author Sir Henry Newbolt to deplore the confiscation of the new novel by Lawrence, "whom I regard as a man of genius and a serious writer." Forster, leaving England for Red Cross work in Egypt, hoped Newbolt could do something: "Some people would say 'Oh but *this* isn't the time to make a fuss'; I feel myself that the right to literary expression is as great in war as it was ever in peace, and in far greater danger, and I write on the chance of your being willing and able to protect it."

Even before *The Rainbow* came out, Lawrence had been trying to organize his escape to a warmer country before the winter. He applied for a passport. He complained of the fog that ate his lungs, and Ottoline Morrell feared he might not survive until spring. She offered thirty pounds of her own and passed the hat among her friends. George Bernard Shaw gave the substantial sum of five pounds—not because he had ever heard of Lawrence, he later explained, but because it was "the smallest sum I [could] decently offer to Lady Ottoline without forfeiting her regard."

The book's suppression determined Lawrence on one course: flight. He would get out of England—to some warm place where a new society would grow around him and his followers. Perhaps because he did not expect the ban to be permanent, Lawrence retained his sense of humor. Cynthia Asquith brought her sister to tea at the Lawrences' and he walked them back to the tube. "When one sees him again," she marveled to her diary, "one can scarcely connect the man with his writing. There is so much delicious laughter in him which he entirely extinguishes on paper."

His pantisocracy gained in number. At Ottoline's suggestion he invited Aldous Huxley to tea at Byron Villas. The tall, nearly blind Balliol student was passionately opposed to the war, and accepted instantly.

Huxley had no illusions about the success of the idea. "But," as he wrote to his brother Julian, then studying in the United States, "Lawrence is a great man, and as he finds the world too destructive for his taste, he must, I suppose, be allowed to get out of it to some place where he can construct freely and where, by a unanimous process, the rest of his young colony, might do the same." Huxley would at least spend a little time in this "eremitic colony . . . which, I am sure, would be quite particularly medicinal to my soul."

Lawrence, just turning thirty, wanted young followers (a response to his childlessness, Murry later said). One of the most committed, however, was slightly older than he: the painter Dorothy Brett, whom he knew from Garsington. Awkward and shy (partly because of severe deafness), she was eager for some sense of direction in life. Brett (who liked to be known by her surname) was, Lawrence said caustically to Ottoline, "one of the 'sisters' of this life."

ANOTHER firm recruit was a young musician and composer, Philip Heseltine (Peter Warlock). He suggested that they all go to the estate in Florida owned by the composer Frederick Delius. Then he put the idea to Delius, confident in the persuasive power of Lawrence's fame:

> He can stand this country no longer and is going to America in a week's time. He wants to go to Florida for the winter, since he is, I am afraid, rather far gone with consumption. I write this hurried note to ask whether it would be possible for him to go and live in your orange grove. He has nowhere definite to go in Florida and is very poor. His last book—a perfectly magnificent work—has just been suppressed by the police for supposed immorality.

Delius advised California instead: the Florida house was in ruins, isolated, and expensive. Anyway, he was mystified why an artist like Lawrence would want to waste his gifts planting potatoes and tobacco.

Lawrence was undaunted. Twice he booked passage and gave his friends his sailing date, but he did not budge. The ostensible reason for the delay was the need to fight for *The Rainbow*. He visited Philip Morrell at the House of Commons to talk about a campaign and Morrell indeed twice raised the matter, to no avail. A Home Office memorandum suggests that it was Lawrence's German wife as much as anything in the text that caused the book's suppression.

While he delayed, he dreamed of Fort Myers, a little town on Florida's west coast that had become very real to him: "5,000 people, many niggers—9 miles from sea, on a big river one mile wide: many fish, and quails, and wild turkeys; land flat, covered with orange groves and pine trees: climate perfect." He hoped to sail direct so as to avoid "that cursed New York," and he made Frieda a Russian toque out of bits of fur for the voyage.

Why "cursed New York," when he had never been there? Because David Eder had advised him that New York in winter might be bad for his chest. From that time on New York joined London at the top of Lawrence's list of urban deathtraps and for the rest of his life he tried to avoid even passing through.

But he made an error that cost him his chance to escape. To leave the country, he needed a "misfit"—a certificate exempting him from service on grounds of health. They were not hard to get. Murry had obtained one in order to join Katherine in Bandol, in the south of France, and Ernest Jones seems to have given Lawrence the necessary doctor's letter. Accordingly, on December 11, 1915, Lawrence presented himself for a medical examination in Battersea Town Hall. After waiting for hours with hundreds of men in a queue, he got within sight of the registration table, only to run out and jump on a bus heading toward Westminster.

This precipitate act left him with some explaining to do. He told Ottoline, "I *hated* [underlined five times] the situation almost to *madness.*" He told Hilda Doolittle that he had been forced to stand in the pouring rain. The consequence was, as Hilda informed Amy Lowell, "the Lawrences are postponing Florida" or, as Lawrence told Ottoline, "I shall not go to America until a stronger force from there pulls me across the sea."

Perhaps he did not really want to go. Uncontrollable anxiety overwhelmed his wish for the exemption. The fervid images he used for Ottoline to describe his terrible day in the line of men—his sense of their "slumbering strength" and of his own escape from "the underworld of this spectral submission"—suggest once again that, as a conspicuous weakling, he feared homosexual attack. He also may have recoiled from hearing the diagnosis of consumption called out loud and clear. He had, as Aldous Huxley was later to note, a phenomenal fear of the medical profession.

In any event, they needed a cottage somewhere in England. Murry was delegated to find it, and he obliged. As the terrible year of 1915 turned to 1916, the Lawrences found themselves on the shores of the Atlantic, not facing east as he had hoped but on the rocky coast of Cornwall, still yearning westward. It was, said Lawrence, summoning his colonists, the first step to Florida.

9

THE YEARS THE DAMAGE WAS DONE

"Awful years—'16, '17, '18, '19—the years when the damage was done." Kangaroo

Porthcothan St. Merryn
Padstow Cornwall

Dear Mr. Russell,

I am so worried about Lawrence. He isn't at all
well. I really don't know what to do. If you have a
few days to spare it really would be kind of you if
you came down. I know he would very much enjoy
seeing you, and to me it would be a help. I feel it
such a responsibility, it's too much for me. He
might just die because everything is too much for
him. But he simply mustn't die. . . .

Yours very sincerely,
Frieda Lawrence

*B*y *New Year's Day of 1916 the Lawrences were installed in a big*
bare house in Padstow on the north coast of Cornwall. The house, which
had been lent to them, faced the sea, and with a local unwed mother to
cook and look after them, Lawrence watched the rain, thought of King
Arthur and Tristan and Isolde, and read *Moby-Dick*. The remote peninsula jutting out into the Atlantic left him feeling exposed ("on the
brink of existence, and there remains only to fall off into oblivion") and
exhausted ("absolutely run to earth, like a fox they have chased till it
can't go any further").

Then he collapsed. It was far more than his usual turn-of-the-year
illness; for two weeks he could not get out of bed. He was paralyzed on

the left side, with burning chest and trembling stomach. He thought he was dying; at times, he imagined he was already dead. Frieda despaired, seeing Lawrence full of ideas and too ill to write them down. "Do come," she begged in her letter to Russell. "There are so few people Lawrence can bear the sight of."

Russell did not oblige. He had problems of his own. Trying to go to America to give some lectures at Harvard, he found that month that the Foreign Office had blacklisted him for his antiwar activities and denied him his passport. In a matter of weeks, he was also stripped of his lectureship at Trinity College, classified as a suspicious person, and forbidden to travel to any coastal area.

Yet even without the stimulus of Russell, Lawrence once again rose from what he thought was his deathbed. His recovery was much helped by Dr. Maitland Radford, who came down from London especially to see him. The only doctors Lawrence trusted were personal friends, and the diagnosis that Dollie Radford's son gave him was music to his ears. As Lawrence recapitulated it for Kot, Radford said that "stress on the nerves sets up an inflammation in the lining of the chest, and the breathing passages and the stomach, and that I must be very quiet and very warm and still, and that I mustn't think about anything." But he was a darker, sicker, more irritable man.

The crisis took place, like so many in the Lawrences' lives, before houseguests. Milling around at Padstow for two months was the composer and Rananim stalwart, the twenty-two-year-old Philip Heseltine, and for about a month Heseltine's pregnant girlfriend, Minnie Lucie Channing, an artist's model whom they all called Puma. Another arrival, even younger, was Dikran Kouyoumdjian, a Bulgarian who Lawrence believed would be a great writer. (Kouyoumdjian later became known as Michael Arlen, author of *The Green Hat*.)

Heseltine and Kouyoumdjian, although arguing noisily between themselves, liked Frieda. Heseltine, thinking to mend the rift between her and Ottoline, wrote to Ottoline, "I have come to the conclusion that Mrs L has been most unjustly maligned, behind her back, in several quarters." He made the mistake of telling the same to Frieda, who herself wrote to Ottoline: "You have been very unfair to me, I think, you have tried to put me down as of no account—I could understand that as you must have had to put up with some terrible artists' wives." Ottoline told Russell that Frieda must be mad.

Lawrence did not much like Kouyoumdjian but he was fond of Heseltine, a hero-worshiping Old Etonian who had ideas for publishing *The Rainbow* by private subscription and who had money of his own to invest in Rananim. For a while Heseltine's loyalty held fast. He wrote to Delius in Florida that Lawrence's autocratic views were hard to bear, but the man himself remained "an arresting figure, a great and attractive personality, and his passion for a new, clean untrammelled life is very splendid."

A few weeks later Lawrence appeared less attractive. He and Frieda were much intrigued by Heseltine's complicated love life. Trying vainly to pair him off with another Rananim recruit, Ottoline's niece Dorothy Warren, they were thwarted by Heseltine's news that, although Puma was pregnant, he had fallen in love with, and proposed to, Juliette Baillot, a wonderfully pretty Swiss girl employed at Garsington as governess to Ottoline's daughter. Lawrence tried to persuade Heseltine that he might keep both women. He lectured the young composer about the dangers of rejecting the dark sensual "blood connection" (the promiscuous brunette Puma) in favor of "the white consciousness" (the decorous blond Swiss). In a letter to Ottoline, Lawrence expanded his theory. Some men, like Heseltine, might need two wives because they were divided within themselves. But luckily, not he. "For myself, thank God, I feel myself becoming more and more unified . . . And Frieda and I are becoming more truly married—for which I thank heaven."

When Heseltine found out that all the secrets of his personal life were being chewed over by Lawrence and Ottoline, he had had enough. Having gone up to London on business, he refused to return to Cornwall. Lawrence, he wrote a friend, "has no real sympathy. All he likes in one is the potential convert to his own reactionary creed . . . personal relationship with him is almost impossible." Heseltine did not then realize how unwise it was to make an enemy of a novelist who wrote from reality. By withdrawing abruptly from Rananim that spring, Heseltine catapulted himself and Puma into the pages of *Women in Love.*

At the end of February their Padstow benefactor wanted his house back, and the Lawrences had to move on. With the American publication of *The Rainbow* shelved, Lawrence announced to all and sundry that he and Frieda were going to be very poor. He kept his real financial situation to himself, but there was certainly no large payment in the offing, and he was terrified. His loathing of debt went deeper than Protestant thriftiness: it touched his fears of dissolution, degradation, dirt, and shame—"letting go," in the crudest sense.

The solution was to take an unfurnished cottage farther out on the Cornish peninsula, at Zennor, about seven miles west of St. Ives. The little house, half of an eighteenth-century pair, was nothing but a fourteen-foot-square stone box, with its main room only six feet four inches high, with a bedroom above and a lean-to kitchen at the back. There was no water supply, even from a pump or a well. He and Frieda had to fetch water in buckets from a spring a hundred yards uphill. There, tucked into the moors, just below a dirt farm track, with the sea visible in the distance, Lawrence burrowed in like a fox under a hill and thought they might live there forever.

The cottage was part of a cluster called Higher Tregerthen—"higher" because it overlooked Lower Tregerthen, a farm run by a family named Hocking. Its juxtaposition at right angles to a larger cottage with a small tower suggested a monastic community to Lawrence; he immediately summoned John Middleton Murry and Katherine Mansfield from Bandol. He calculated that Katherine, with her good annual allowance from her father, could easily afford the rent for the tower house—sixteen pounds a year.

In the many letters he wrote that spring, Lawrence sounds more like an accountant than an author. Almost every one mentions a money sum. He boasted to all his friends about his own low rent. He talked so much about his poverty that his friend and typist Katherine Clayton sent stamped envelopes to save him the cost of replying to her letters. He told her to stop, claiming that it was an insult. Yet when he asked Dollie Radford to pack up all the furniture they had left behind at Byron Villas—the Persian rug, the kitchen table, the china, the fireplace fender, and the blankets—he told her not to send the things on to Cornwall if the cost was more than eight shillings. They themselves could not afford to come to London, he said, as the round-trip rail fare to London from St. Ives was two pounds ten shillings (half a year's rent).

For the rest of their needs, he and Frieda went to St. Ives, traveling by horse-drawn cart, with the mists blowing around the black crags and menhirs. The Cornish were accustomed to having bohemians and dubious couples in their midst; their long tapering county was, according to a local joke, "a stocking in which all the nuts go to the toe." Even so, the Lawrences, picking their way about the auction rooms and market stalls of St. Ives, must have been as inconspicuous as Mickey and Minnie Mouse: he, thin and darkly bearded, with his white canvas hat jammed down over his ears and his rucksack on his back, and she, large and pretty, with her loud, hoarse German voice and red stockings.

Frieda wore colored stockings because Lawrence insisted on it. He ordered them for her himself, not only in red, but in rose pink, yellow, orange, and bright green. Frieda loved her bright legs and was much amused when the woman who kept the shop in Zennor came around from behind the counter to take a better look at them.

He lavished his color sense on their cottage too. As usual, making as much as he could with his own hands, he proudly made a dresser himself and painted it royal blue. He painted the cottage walls pink and the ceiling white, and instructed the landlord on the color scheme for the redecoration of the tower cottage: the dining room was to be red, the large bedroom a pale pink, and the downstairs tower room cream. Coconut matting was laid on the floors. When it was done, and he had also planted two vegetable gardens and arranged to get their milk, eggs, butter, and meat from the farm at Lower Tregerthen, he sent delighted letters to the

Murrys describing the happy life in store—communal meals in the tower cottage's dining room and indeed "a Blutbruderschaft between us all." Frieda chimed in with an assurance that they all would live together like lilies in the field.

WHEN Lawrence turned on the charm, he was irresistible. The Murrys arrived the first week in April, Katherine riding elegantly on the cart atop the luggage in a little black-and-gold jacket. Jack was convinced that Lawrence was the greatest man he had met in his life and, fortified with a military rejection slip on grounds of health, wanted somewhere cheap in England in which to lie low until the war was over. Frieda had warned them, however, that they might find Lawrence changed by his terrible illness.

They were not prepared for what they found. Not the jolly group leader of the enthusiastic letters, but an ill, obsessive, and angry man, seething with hate for all humanity. Katherine's disillusion was instant. She loathed Cornwall; its desolate beauty was dismal after the south of France, and she had not recovered from her brother's death. She resented the time Jack spent walking with Lawrence. Her old intimacy with Frieda vanished to the point where they were not speaking. Soon Katherine was sending a stream of maliciously witty letters to friends such as Gordon Campbell's wife, Bici:

> I want to talk about the L's. But if I do don't tell Kot or Gertler for then it will get back to L and I will be literally murdered. He has changed v. much. He's quite "lost." He has become v. fond of sewing, especially hemming, and of making little copies of pictures. When he is doing these things he is quiet and gentle and kind, but once you start talking I cannot describe the frenzy that comes over him. He simply *raves*, roars and beats the table, abuses everybody. . . . F is more or less used to this. She has a passion for washing clothes. . . . They are both too tough for me to enjoy playing with.

Lawrence had begun to batter Frieda. Shocked, the Murrys watched it happen right in front of them. One day when Frieda had disparaged Shelley, Lawrence told her she did not know a damned thing about Shelley. She picked up the cue: "*Now* I have had enough. Out of my house—you little God Almighty you. I've had enough of you. . . ." He followed with, "I'll give you a dab on the cheek to quiet you, you dirty hussy," whereupon he began hitting her with the full force of his outstretched arm.

The Lawrences' rows had a histrionic quality, as if staged before literary people who they knew would write it all down, with dialogue.

The Murrys did not fail them, Katherine particularly. The carefully crafted accounts sent to Kot, Bici Campbell, and Ottoline repeat the same details and phrases almost as if Katherine were writing from notes or copies, as indeed she may have been.

According to her report of the Shelley fight, she and Jack retreated to their own house convinced that they had witnessed the end of the Lawrence marriage. That evening Lawrence came to eat with them alone. There was no sign of Frieda, which was a relief, as he swore, "I'll cut her throat if she comes near this table." Suddenly through the window Frieda appeared, walking around and around the cottage, until (Katherine to Kot) Lawrence "made a blind rush at her . . . He beat her—he beat her to death—her head and face and breast and pulled out her hair. . . . He was so white—almost green and he just hit—thumped the big soft woman." Or (Katherine to Ottoline): "He kept his eyes on her . . . he stood back on his heels and swung his arm forward. He was quite green with fury. Then when he was tired he sat down, collapsed and she, sobbing and crying sat down too."

The aftermath was more surprising still. Half an hour after the fight ended, said Katherine, Lawrence and Frieda glided into small talk with each other about some "very rich but very good macaroni cheese" and returned to their own cottage, arm in arm. Next morning the startled Murrys saw Lawrence taking Frieda breakfast in bed and making her a hat while she wove flowers into her hair.

Katherine told Ottoline she never imagined anyone could so relish a beating as Frieda. "I hate them for it—I hate them for falsity," she stormed. "Lawrence has definitely chosen to sin against himself and Frieda is triumphant. It is horrible. You understand—don't you—," her letter added conspiratorially, "that I could not write like this to anyone but you."

The many witnesses to such scenes from the home life of the Lawrences searched for explanation. Some assumed that they were observing the rough ways of a working-class man with his woman; Lawrence was just imitating his father, they thought. Many others found the answer in the well-known phenomenon of consumptive rage. Indeed, when Katherine came down with tuberculosis not long after, she observed the same wild outbursts of violence in herself and declared that she and Lawrence were "incredibly alike." (Her biographer Claire Tomalin suggests that she may have caught her tuberculosis from Lawrence.)

But the two couples were nothing alike. The Murrys were professional rivals, while Frieda was a worshiper of Lawrence's genius; she thought him superior to Nietzsche and Dostoevsky, even though her power had been necessary to make him so. And the Lawrences stuck together. By the end of 1916, the Murrys had split up yet again, but the Lawrences remained (when not in active combat), sitting cozily by their Cornish hearth, reading Italian together, painting bowls, and comparing their needlework. Their pretense of happy marriage may have been transparent, yet they made no serious effort for some years to live apart.

So how to explain the savagery of their fights? Something happened to Lawrence between *The Rainbow* and *Women in Love*. Weighed down by the war, the suppression of his book, and his poor health, he lost his faith in the healing power of married love. He was grieved that after four years together, he and Frieda could not achieve what he believed all-important: simultaneous orgasm. He began to dream instead of a kind of triangular marriage, in which his partnership with his wife would be supplemented by the close friendship with a man, a blood brother.

The struggle against homosexual longings might in itself account for his almost insane irritability. During the first month of Murry's stay, Lawrence wrote a long essay, intended as the prologue to the new novel that became *Women in Love,* describing the feelings of the novel's central male character, Rupert Birkin: "Although he was always drawn to women, feeling more at home with a woman than with a man, yet it was for men that he felt the hot, flushing, roused attraction which a man is supposed to feel for the other sex."

Lawrence made it clear that such a man should never surrender. Rupert Birkin is a man with a special and handsome friend, Gerald Crich. Between Crich and Birkin, the prologue says, there was at first sight "a subterranean kindling" and a "trembling nearness." Birkin tries to submerge this dangerous feeling by engaging in violent sexual excesses with his mistress.

> For he would never acquiesce to it. He could never acquiesce to his own feelings, to his own passion. He could never grant that it should be so, that it was well for him to feel this keen desire to have and to possess the bodies of such men.

"Such men" fell into two types: one, like Crich, tall, blue-eyed, and handsome, and the other "dark-skinned, supple, night-smelling." For one "strange Cornish type of man" with "dark, fine, rather stiff hair and full, heavy, softly-strong limbs," Birkin felt overwhelming desire: "to know this man, to have him, as it were to eat him."

> So he went on, month after month, year after year, divided against himself, striving for the day when the beauty of men should not be so acutely attractive to him, when the beauty of woman should move him instead.

As a description of the inner torture of a man who knows he is homosexual but does not want to be, the prologue could not be finer. As a picture of the kind of handsome Cornish man that Birkin would like to eat, the prologue is an almost photographic likeness of William Henry Hocking, thirty-three, unmarried, of Lower Tregerthen Farm. It is small wonder that Lawrence suppressed the prologue when he sent the novel to seek a publisher and that it did not appear in print until long after his death.

THE Murrys stuck it out for about six weeks. Jack soon came to agree that the move to Zennor had been a disaster. He realized that he was drawn to Lawrence only when he felt inadequate with Katherine. He enjoyed (as who did not?) walking with Lawrence, but did not really like the outdoor life; he kept losing his glasses when they went over stiles. Moreover, while he could concede that their friendship might be a kind of love, he recoiled from Lawrence's invitation to perform a German blood rite on the moors. And from his all-too-close quarters next door, he could hear Lawrence crying to Frieda that "Jack is killing me" and that Jack was "an obscene bug" sucking his life away. And their own cottage was a misery; Lawrence's loving name, "Katherine's Tower," could not disguise that the walls ran wet with damp.

Finally the Murrys announced that they were taking themselves to the sheltered south coast of Cornwall, where the climate was milder. Lawrence was shattered. He could not see any reason for their leaving. He really believed that he and Jack had made a little enclave of sanity. He helped them pack but would not say good-bye as Katherine mounted the cart with the luggage and Jack rode up the lane on his bicycle, leaving the Lawrences in a Rananim of two.

LAWRENCE was in despair. Everything was wrong. Publishers were rejecting his poems. England was desecrating itself in a meaningless war on Germany. In Ireland, "windbags and nothings" (Lawrence's words for the poets and martyrs of the 1916 Easter Rising) were wreaking needless further damage upon the fabric of his country. Conscription of all able-bodied men between eighteen and forty-one years old was imminent. There was nothing outside himself in which he could believe— certainly not Christianity or democracy, not marriage. He felt constantly unwell. In this state of mind, he sat in his damp bedroom, with the view of Lower Tregerthen Farm and the sea in the distance, and plunged into his new novel.

He had no hope of publishing it, so wrote what he liked. It was the second half of "The Sisters," the sequel to *The Rainbow,* which ends with Ursula Brangwen liberated, by her own force of spirit, on the brink of marriage to the wrong man, Anton Skrebensky, and saved by a miscarriage from bearing his child. As the story resumes, she meets Rupert Birkin, a school inspector. Birkin is having an affair with Lady Hermione Roddice, a Derbyshire aristocrat and a *Kulturträger* (Lawrence loved putting foreign words into his texts; he translated this one as "a medium for the culture of ideas").

The opening scene is one familiar in the conventions of English literature—two young women discussing the possibility of marriage—but their clothes are hardly traditional. Ursula's sister, Gudrun, wears bright stockings (emerald green, in her first appearance) to show that she is an artist and a young woman of advanced ideas. Nor is the dialogue in an English mode. "Don't you find, that things fail to materialize?" Gudrun asks Ursula. "*Nothing materializes!* Everything withers in the bud."

Lawrence thus instantly states his belief that individuals are the product of impersonal forces. They do not understand why things happen to them nor how they can shape their destinies. All they can do is try to express their sense of the universal sexual charge that throbs through them, and try to communicate with each other. More deeply than ever, Lawrence felt that there was no such thing as the individual personality: "I refuse to see people as unified Godheads anymore," he told Kot. "They are this and that, different and opposing things without any complete identity."

The result is what many consider Lawrence's most controlled, complex, and ambitious work. He wrote the first version in six weeks, much of it during the Murrys' stay. Yet Murry said that during his weeks at Tregerthen he never saw or heard of the book. That Lawrence wrote most of it while they all fought and shopped and dined and drank together and while in his spare time he read voraciously through the classics of American literature is a measure of his prodigious energy and concentration. He did revise the book extensively over the next two years, but there was much of the original, he told Richard Aldington, he could not have improved.

Women in Love is an architectural structure, designed to reveal the disintegration of Western industrial society through the interplay of two sisters; two couples—Birkin and Ursula, Gerald and Gudrun; and conflicting cultures, agricultural and industrial, English and Continental, civilized and primitive. The plot moves from England to the Continent just as Lawrence and Frieda had done, setting a pattern that he would use in his next three novels. *Women in Love* is not set firmly in historic time like *The Rainbow,* but rather is out of time, like a dream. "The book frightens me," Lawrence said, "it is so end-of-the-world."

Women in Love is full of those swaying repetitions that characterize Lawrence's prose. Whether such passages echo the hypnotic refrains of the chapel hymns of his boyhood, the rocking of an anxious infant, or, as Lawrence maintained, the rhythmic thrust of the sexual act, they were deliberate. In the chapter "Snowed Up," he wrote: "The darkness seemed to be swaying in waves across his mind, great waves of darkness plunging across his mind." And in the chapter called "Flitting" Gudrun wonders:

> What was she short of now? It was marriage—it was the wonderful stability of marriage. She did want it, let her say what she might. She had been lying. The old idea of marriage was right even now—marriage and the home. Yet her mouth gave a little grimace at the words. She thought of Gerald and Shortlands—marriage and the home! Ah well, let it rest!

Lawrence, in the foreword to *Women in Love* (an essay written later than the prologue and distinct from it, but also unpublished until after his death), allowed himself a rare acknowledgment of the hostility expressed to the "continual, slightly modified repetition" in his writing. "The only answer," he declared unapologetically, "is that it is natural to the author." He added: "Every natural crisis in emotion or passion or understanding comes from this pulsing frictional to-and-fro which works up to culmination."

The book blazes with murderous aggression between the sexes. Hermione brings down a stone paperweight on Birkin's head. Gerald attempts to strangle Gudrun, crushing her throat between his hands: "What bliss! Oh what bliss, at last, what satisfaction at last!" And Birkin's dislike of mankind is savage—as intemperate as Lawrence's own that year, which he expressed in a letter to Kot saying that he would like to exterminate the whole human race: "Oh, if one could have but a great box of insect powder, and shake it over them." (This notorious passage should perhaps be read in the context of Lawrence's association of beetles with homosexuality.)

In *Women in Love* Lawrence brought his hate under artistic control. Yet once again he failed to shed his sickness in a book. The story ends inconclusively. Gerald dies in the icy embrace of a Tyrolean mountain peak; Birkin enters a marriage with Ursula that leaves her subdued and him unsatisfied, the issue of his sexuality unresolved. Grieving for Gerald, Birkin tells Ursula that he had wanted eternal union with a man as well as with a woman. In the novel's last line, they reach a stalemate. Ursula says:

> "You can't have two kinds of love. Why should you!"
> "It seems as if I can't," he said. "Yet I wanted it."
> "You can't have it, because it's false, impossible," she said.
> "I don't believe that," he answered.

Yet it is not an impossible dream. You can have two kinds of love—when you are a child. Lawrence's yearning for a man he could eat was less homosexual than infantile; it was the desperation of a frail and hypersensitive boy to incorporate a father to fend off the devouring mother. Such intense self-absorption may seem inappropriate, even immoral, when the world is at war. Lawrence saw the anomaly: "When one is shaken to the very depths, one finds reality in the unreal world. At present my real world is the world of my inner soul, which reflects on to the novel I write."

But grief and loss were the realities of his inner soul. His Birkin struggles to make some sense of his grief—even of love itself—in the face of the terrifying blankness of nature:

> Either the heart would break or cease to care. Best cease to care. Whatever the mystery which has brought forth man and the universe, it is a non-human mystery, it has its own great ends, man is not the criterion.

These were no inappropriate lines for the terrible summer of 1916, when twenty thousand British soldiers died in a single day of the Battle of the Somme. *Women in Love* was Lawrence's war novel.

IN his weakened and highly charged state, he had to face the coming into force of the Second Military Service Act; general conscription—the dreaded "Compulsion"—was on its way. Accordingly, Lawrence was ordered to present himself for medical examination at Bodmin, a rail-junction town in mid-Cornwall. He had little to fear. He had no wish to plead conscientious objection, even though pacifists as young and strong as David Garnett were passing themselves off as farmers in order to avoid the harsh treatment meted out to "conchies"; Garnett performed his duties at Garsington, where, in Osbert Sitwell's words, "some of the best brains in the country were obliged to apply themselves to digging and dunging, to the potato patch or the pig-sty." Lawrence was no pacifist; he believed in violence even if he did not believe in the war with Germany. But his physical condition patently disqualified him from soldiering.

The examination was an ordeal nevertheless. At the station they were lined up and marched through the streets to a barracks and, to Lawrence's dismay, made to stay overnight. He had not brought any pajamas. Incarcerated, he thought of Oscar Wilde on his first night in prison, and he had to put up with teasing from the young men who saw his beard and called him "Dad." The horror of it all he summed up to Dollie Radford as "a sticky male mess. I should die in a week if they made me a soldier. Thirty men in their shirts, being weighed like sheep, one after the other—God! They have such impossible feet."

He got a complete exemption, of course, but he credited his talent for acting rather than his health. He told Barbara Low that he simply summoned a great air of authority, and without even producing the medical certificate he held from Ernest Jones, simply told them that he had consumption. If so, it was another of the few occasions when he used the dreaded word in reference to himself.

Back in Zennor he announced more widely than was wise that he had no will to fight to defend his country or even his house. If the Germans wanted it, they could have it. He would not kill them. He had no sense of patriotism nor of duty. "And what duty is this," he asked Catherine Carswell, "which makes us forfeit everything, because Germany invaded Belgium?" Nor did he believe in helping his neighbor. Christianity was based "on the love of self, the love of property, one degree removed." His supreme value was "the truth of my spirit"; this could not require him to kill anybody.

Frieda, too, flouted the mandatory patriotism of the hour. When enemy submarines were sunk off the Cornish coast, to general jubilation, she pitied the drowned men and told people that they might have been boys she had played with as a child.

By the spring of 1916, Frieda's family name was known the length and breadth of the land. The star of the German war in the air, Baron Manfred von Richthofen, was her cousin. The British press dubbed him the "Red Baron" and *The Times* reported, almost with admiration, his mounting score; on April 30 the Berlin government had announced that Baron von Richthofen had brought down five Allied planes in one day, bringing his aerial victories to a total of fifty-two. There were two other flying von Richthofens, Wolfram and Lothar, who racked up their own neat tallies of direct hits. Zennor had little doubt that Frieda's origins were aristocratic as well as German. The Hockings found her pretty but patrician. The farmworkers noticed the couple's social incongruity. "Where the hell did she find him?" one of them asked the Hocking brothers, William Henry and Stanley. Frieda was often unconsciously patronizing. One day when Lawrence was dressed in the old trousers and shirt he wore for working on the Lower Tregerthen farm, she tactlessly told Mrs. Hocking that her husband was getting to look "more like one of you every day. I don't know what I'm going to do with him."

The Hockings did not know what to make of Lawrence, who knitted sweaters and wove tapestries—things men never did. He was always poorly, which they put down to bronchitis, and they indulged him by making him feel indispensable on the farm. They knew about the rows up at the higher cottage and many evenings, when Lawrence sat in the Hockings' farm kitchen, they assumed he was taking refuge after he and

Frieda had had a fight. They saw, too, how she hated being left alone; she would come down over the fields, shouting at Lawrence to come home.

Lawrence spent much time with William Henry Hocking, who had the kind of untutored, questioning, rural intelligence that makes tempting prey for city people. William Henry, as they called him, did not fit in well with the others in his family; both Lawrence and Frieda began writing to their Hampstead friends about him. They wished to send him to London once the harvest was in. Frieda wanted to marry him off to a lady who would "take an interest in him," and Lawrence wanted the Eders and other kindly agnostics to enlarge his horizons. For his part, William Henry was eager to see the great searchlights he had heard so much about.

By late June 1916, working at his usual breakneck speed, Lawrence decided that his book was publishable and that he would type it himself—a major commitment to one version over another. It was then that the prologue was suppressed. He only took seriously what to put in and leave out when he committed himself to typing it. But Amy Lowell's typewriter was causing him grief by printing double. Also, it required a half-inch ribbon and from London Kot, his source of supply, kept sending him the one-inch size. (The difficulty writers had in getting their manuscripts copied is as hard for a later age to appreciate as are the chronic illnesses of the time. Typists' fees were considerable, and to obtain a copy even of a printed article meant either having it expensively retyped or written out by hand. For an author to be able to retain a copy of a manuscript while its original went off to the publisher was a luxury.)

Lawrence asked his agent Pinker for an advance on the book, and although no publication was in sight received fifty pounds, with which he rented the tower cottage for himself, removed the dampness that had bothered Katherine, and put into it as guests the cadre of Hampstead friends with whom he did not fight, such as Catherine Carswell, Dollie and Maitland Radford, and Barbara Low. He continued to be close to Low, although he told her he found psychoanalysis "irreverent and destructive." He was pleased with his world and hoped to live in his Cornish fastness until he was seventy.

In fact, he found he could not leave. A strange lethargy, a kind of agoraphobia, can come over people in Cornwall; some call it Land's End syndrome. Lawrence, there for a year without a break, tried to stir himself to go up to London with Frieda but, as he told J. D. Beresford, owner of the Padstow house, he was so frightened of the outside world that he could not even get onto a train without terror.

Lawrence's dread once again focused on London's foul air. "I dare not come to London, for my life," he wrote Kot. "It is like walking into some horrible gas, which tears one's lungs." However, he urged Beresford to do just what he himself could not—go to London—because Beresford's wife was expecting a baby. "I don't think one should [trust] these country doctors, when a child is born," he said, perhaps thinking back to Emily's loss of her firstborn. "I do hope you have plenty of money, to do the thing without anxiety."

Frieda braved the smoke and fog and kept an arranged appointment with her children at the lawyers' office. At last her right to see them was being recognized. The possibility of having a day with them, or even longer, was under discussion. The children now were full-grown and good-looking. Monty, at sixteen, was nearly six feet tall; the girls, too, were tall, with fair hair, brown eyes, and delicate coloring. The girls were obviously longing for her approval. "Do you like our dresses?" Elsa asked her plaintively during the visit. "What do you want us to wear?"

Upon her return, Frieda found Lawrence seedy and depressed, persuading himself that she was at last beginning to realize that the mother-child relation was not so important. He had no idea how much the children were on her mind. Sad that she could not shop for them herself, Frieda sent Catherine Carswell ten shillings to buy the girls some jerseys and specified the shop on Oxford Street she wanted, and the color. Catherine was to pretend that the gifts came from their grandmother in Germany, as the children were forbidden to receive anything from their mother. Frieda also wrote to Amy Lowell in Boston and asked outright for money. Lawrence was embarrassed, but only slightly, and the generous sixty pounds that Lowell sent, with Pinker's fifty, gave them a fair-sized nest egg.

Lawrence now began to wonder if he should let Ottoline read his new novel. He had whetted her appetite—it was "a real book," he said, in which he had created a world which he passionately loved. (He was having title trouble again, however. He thought he might call it "The Latter Days," and Frieda was suggesting "Dies Irae.") Offering Ottoline a look at the manuscript meant confronting her with the character of the tall, rich Lady Hermione, with her long blanched face and feathered hats, who "drifted along with a peculiar fixity of the hips . . . impressive, in her lovely pale-yellow and brownish-rose, yet macabre . . . repulsive." Yet Lawrence concluded, in one of his breathtaking acts of self-deception: "It is probable that she will think Hermione has nothing to do with her."

To Catherine Carswell he maintained that he despised fiction drawn too literally from life. For example, *Mendel*, a new novel by Gilbert Cannan, their Berkshire neighbor, was openly based on Mark Gertler. "It is a bad book—statement without creation—really journalism," Lawrence declared. "Gertler, Jew-like, had told every detail of his life to Cannan, who, lawyer-like, wrote it into a novel." Some people also claimed that the character of Mrs. Lupton was based on Frieda; Lawrence frankly could not see it.

Frieda could. In her most sweetly aggrieved tone, she wrote Kot that she was saddened that Cannan had made her so horrid and vulgar. But, she gushed to Kot, "I am *so* nice in L's new novel, anyhow I *think* so." Feeling constantly unappreciated, she loved seeing herself immortalized in Lawrence's fiction; it was part of the unspoken bargain that made it worth being his wife. In any event, she saw the two of them as allies against a hostile England. It made her sick, she continued to Kot, that nobody in England would do anything to help Lawrence get published: "One day they will come, the wretches, but then I will kick them downstairs."

Ottoline did not need to read *Women in Love* to know that she was in it. Gertler had already told her the worst. Unwilling to accept that she could be so betrayed by a man she loved, she wrote to Lawrence, blaming Frieda. She was probably right. Originally the character of Lady Hermione bore strong traces of Jessie Chambers, but became more like Ottoline as Lawrence worked on it, and the voice of Frieda, breathless, nagging, repetitious, can be heard when Ursula denounces Hermione to Birkin:

> And *I, I'm* not spiritual enough, *I'm* not as spiritual as that Hermione—! . . . Then *go* to her, that's all I say, *go* to her, *go*. Ha, she spiritual—*spiritual*, she!

When Ottoline finally got a look at the manuscript some months later, she threatened to sue for libel. It was the end of another friendship. Their intense correspondence stopped, and they did not renew contact for ten years.

However pitilessly Lawrence may have exposed her in the book, he did worse by himself. Ursula, again sounding like Frieda, tells Birkin that he is morbid, inverted, and narcissistic:

> What you are is a foul, deathly thing, obscene, that's what you are, obscene and perverse. You, and love! You may well say, you don't want love. No, you want *yourself,* and dirt and death—that's what you want. You are so *perverse,* so death-eating.

Ursula delivers this verdict after a sexual encounter in which Birkin

> had taken her as he had never been taken himself. He had taken her at the roots of her darkness and shame—like a demon, laughing over the

fountain of mystic corruption which was one of the sources of her being.

This passage occurs in the chapter curiously named "Excurse." Murry, writing after Lawrence's death, said that it could make no sense to "anyone who reads the novel in isolation, and without the necessary clue." Murry proceeded to give it: Birkin's demand of Ursula is the same demand that Lawrence makes upon the woman in the poem "Manifesto." That demand, which Murry delicately avoided quoting, is: "I want her to touch me at last, ah, on the root and quick of my darkness / and perish on me, as I have perished on her."

An anal caress from the female, in other words, in exchange for sodomy by the male. Murry allowed himself to guess why Lawrence wrote it. "To annihilate the female insatiably demanding physical satisfaction from the man who cannot give it her—the female who has thus annihilated him—this is Lawrence's desire . . . to re-establish his own manhood: this is the secret purpose of *Women in Love*."

ON December 5, 1916, Asquith resigned as prime minister after violent criticism in the press for the slaughter at Gallipoli and the Somme. He was replaced by his war secretary, David Lloyd George. Lawrence, stolidly English, thought no more of the Welsh than he did of the Irish. He mourned the loss of Asquith's "old English *decency,* and the lingering love of freedom," and told Amy Lowell that the new prime minister was "a clever little Welsh *rat* . . . capable only of rapid and acute mechanical movements."

The change of leader revived his determination to go to America—the land of his reading, washed by two great oceans, its great open spaces inhabited by Indians who retained the forgotten, dark, sensual mode of life. The contradiction of falling in love with America while scorning American democracy did not trouble him. He resolved it with a series of essays deploring mass identity and extolling individualism.

America was on Britain's mind for another reason—the desperate hope that the United States would come to the Allies' aid. "Mr Wilson Proceeding Warily," reported *The Times* on February 16, adjacent to the news of the second Battle of the Somme. But Lawrence, idealizing America's isolation from Europe's contagion, said that if America declared war, "I think I shall die outright." He meant it literally. "I can't live in England any more," he wrote Kot. "It oppresses one's lungs, one cannot breathe."

He was willing even to brave New York: "One's psychic health is more important than the physical." By psychic, he also meant financial. He wanted to be out of danger of debt. That America looked likely to become his main source of income, he reasoned, would secure them a renewal of their passports despite the drawback of Frieda's birth. He planned to write a series of essays on the American writers he had been reading: Melville, Hawthorne, Poe, and Fenimore Cooper; he would open the heart of the meaning of American literature, which he felt had never been fully appreciated.

Two American guests at Christmas also warmed his expectation of a newer, better world. A handsome unmarried couple, Robert Mountsier, aviation editor of the *New York Sun*, and his girlfriend, Esther Andrews, a freelance writer working on a book about women and the war, had come out from St. Ives to stay with them. Lawrence found them "a queer, gentle couple" but, in their earnest American solemnity, "so old-old, that they are more innocent than children." When Mountsier returned to America early in the New Year, Lawrence promised to follow. Appealing to Eddie Marsh, Gordon Campbell, and Cynthia Asquith to help with the passport problem, he wrote Mountsier that he and Frieda would sail from Falmouth on March 1. Frieda was so eager to go she began stitching what she called her "American trousseau."

Now the mistake of not clearing out in 1915 when they had their documents hit home. Their application to have their passports renewed and endorsed for travel was refused. The terse reason given was "in the interests of National Service." Frieda's origins were the more likely cause; that she had long held British nationality by marriage was of little account in the bitter heat of the war. Lawrence pronounced a biblical curse on his country: "Let the seas swallow it, let the waters cover it, so that it is no more," he told Catherine Carswell. Again, his fear was as much physical as political. The atmosphere of England and the English was "poisonous to an incredible degree: to me at least. I shall die in the fumes of their stench. But I *must* get out."

To the dismay of Frieda, ill with colitis, the winsome Esther Andrews favored them with a return visit. She moved into the tower cottage and hung on Lawrence's every word. She confided in Lawrence her troubles with Mountsier. Lawrence was not so drawn to the male body that he did not respond to female beauty or invitations to intimacy; possibly he even had an affair with his guest. He put her on his list for Rananim. Frieda later referred to Lawrence's relationship with the American as "une passade." She maintained that sometimes he had wanted to go away with other women and that she had encouraged him, for it would have been a relief to her. Nevertheless, Lawrence, preparing his honeymoon sequence of poems for publication, styled them as he saw himself, "Poems of a Married Man."

In April America entered the war and Lawrence abruptly switched his allegiance to Russia. He, like Kot and many antiwar intellectuals in London, fell in love with the idea of the new Russian Revolution. Tsar

Nicholas II had just abdicated and the new provisional government, which would be headed by Alexander Kerensky, was preparing the first parliament. Fleetingly Lawrence envisioned Russia as the only country where he could plant his hopes. America was now "a stink-pot in my nostrils, after having been the land of the future for me."

That month Lawrence wrenched himself from Cornwall to visit his sisters in the Midlands; braving London on his return, he called on Cynthia Asquith. Immediately he picked up his old theme. Her autistic son, John, was the logical conclusion of generations of frustration and "conforming to an unreal plane." John's state was spiritual, not mental; she could cure him by getting off the "false unreal plane" she was on. Two days later, with Cynthia, he took her other child, two-year-old Michael, to the zoo. This kind of intimate flirtation without seduction suited both him and Cynthia very well. She was pleased that the toddler liked Lawrence, and Lawrence obviously enjoyed playing the father, pushing the pram himself.

After about a week away, however, he collapsed "with sickness and diarrhoea"—"the evil influence of aggregate London"—and returned to Cornwall with relief. The seeds had come up in his garden, the mustard and cress were ready to cut, and he settled down to read *Culture of Profitable Vegetables in Small Gardens*.

Not everything was against him. He was, in a modest way, still being published. When *Amores*, a small volume of his poems, appeared in July, the reviewer in *Bookman* praised his gift of rendering sensations in language; Lawrence was "an impressionist, and a wonderfully successful and vivid one." At the same time the reviewer admired *Twilight in Italy*, a collection of his travel essays, for its "pages of description of unsurpassable vividness."

Four of Lawrence's essays on the postwar world appeared in the *English Review* in mid-1917, under the title of "The Reality of Peace." In these he argued, with eloquence if not clarity, the distinction he saw between mass democracy (under which he included communism) and individualism (his own creed). His book of love poems was finished and on its way to the press. Also, Pinker, his agent, was having *Women in Love* typed. (*"I wish I could have a copy,"* he told Pinker. "I would like to look at Ottoline Morrells [*sic*] imaginary portrait again.") A new military service act, calling for the reexamination of rejects, clouded his horizon, but when his turn came to re-present himself at Bodmin, he got away with only a two-hour examination and a 3C classification: able to perform light nonmilitary service but unlikely to be called to do any.

DURING 1917 Lawrence grew closer to William Henry Hocking. In the strapping, tanned, dark-eyed farmer, he clearly saw a useful recruit for

Rananim, and something more. What he thought he was looking for he defined, drawing from Nietzsche's *Thus Spake Zarathustra,* as "friendship with a man ... the friend in whom the world standeth complete." Hocking, too, was looking for something he could not quite place. As Lawrence quoted him to Dollie Radford: " 'Yes, there's something one wants, that isn't money or anything like that—But shall I ever get it?—I want it—' he puts his hand to his chest with a queer, grasping movement—'I can feel the want of it here—but shall I ever get it?' "

It is possible (and, two of Lawrence's biographers have concluded, more than probable) that in the fine summer of 1917, lying in the bracken and talking about sex, Lawrence and Hocking consummated their love. Lawrence invited this conclusion in his novel *Kangaroo,* written five years later. In its most famous chapter, "Nightmare," a seemingly literal re-creation of his war years, Lawrence describes lushly and lovingly how his alter ego, an English writer in Cornwall, and a handsome young farmer lie in the bracken or heather and talk "about the sun, and the moon, the mysterious powers of the moon at night, and the mysterious change in man with the change of season, and the mysterious effects of sex on a man."

To the Cornish, *Kangaroo* implies, homosexuality was no cause for anxiety; their pre-Christian outlook placed them outside conventional ethics and morals. "Only one thing was wrong—any sort of *physical* compulsion or hurt. . . . But for the rest of behaviour—it was all flux." More revealing, perhaps, was the name the novel gives to the handsome farmer: John Thomas, the English vernacular name for the penis, which later, in *Lady Chatterley's Lover,* Lawrence was to use directly as a fond name for the organ itself.

Frieda never denied the Hocking episode. To Murry she later said, "I think the homosexuality in him was a short phase out of misery—I fought him and won." Yet closer to the Cornwall years, she told a woman friend that she thought there had been physical love between Lawrence and Hocking and that it had made her dreadfully unhappy.

IN the depths of the country, the city does not exist. As summer came, Lawrence and Frieda gathered armfuls of pink foxgloves and filled the cottage with them, every table and windowsill. Their lives were brightened also by a new neighbor, a young composer, a friend of Philip Heseltine. Cecil Gray was twenty-two and exempt from service because of a bad heart. He had moved to Cornwall in disgust after some friends threatened to wreck the hall in which he and Heseltine planned to give a concert of the music of Béla Bartók, an enemy alien. Deciding to get as far away from the war as he possibly could, Gray rented an old mine manager's house at Bosigran Castle near Zennor. There was no castle nearby; the name referred to an ancient Briton cliff fortress, part of a line of defensive walls and ditches built across the headland that runs unbroken between St. Ives and Land's End. The house itself was substantial, square and double-fronted, with a deserted tin mine just behind. Standing alone in the middle of the misty moor, between the jutting rock and the sea, it was eerie and exposed. A cliff path connected it to Zennor, three miles away. Gray, like Lawrence, took great satisfaction in the fact that nothing but sea separated him from the New World, and saw himself living as a hermit, in a desolate, black-magical landscape, with no companions apart from the Lawrences.

The three of them met almost every day. They all loved to sing, and Gray liked the same Hebridean songs Lawrence had first heard from Ezra Pound. They talked, of course, of Rananim; Lawrence, knowing of Gray's wealthy father, hoped that Gray would contribute a thousand pounds to the cause. He also enjoyed helping Gray settle into his house and on his behalf bought ten pounds' worth of used furniture at Benney's in St. Ives. He even scrubbed Gray's floors himself. Gray was grateful, although he did notice "a certain streak of mystical self-abasement" in the way Lawrence threw himself into the chore.

In the late summer afternoons of 1917 while Lawrence harvested hay with William Henry, Frieda formed the habit of walking along the cliff path and visiting Gray alone. They probably made love; indeed, it is inconceivable that they did not. Gray was fair, sleek, and charming, a habitué of the Café Royal and, before the war, of the fashionable German spas. He was highly attractive to women and, his daughter later said, he was "immune to none": he had innumerable mistresses and was always madly in love with someone.

The effect on local people can be imagined: a married woman, a German, spending several hours in the house of an unmarried young musician. Her solitary walks would hardly have escaped notice even if she had not been wearing red stockings.

The summer of 1916 was unusually fine—"halcyon days without intermission," Gray remembered later, and he congratulated himself on having "escaped from the world of men into a paradisal existence in which the War and everything connected with it had no place." Yet he, like the Lawrences, indulged in a false sense of isolation. Cornwall was hardly untouched by the war. With German submarines prowling the sea and ships being sunk so close to shore that people in Zennor could see survivors clinging to the wreckage, the Cornish were in a high state of nerves. They feared invasion, or, at very least, secret assassins landing from German submarines to steal into their homes at night and cut their throats as they slept.

All over the British Isles suspicious people were being evacuated from coastal areas. The father of the future Irish prime minister Garret Fitz-

Gerald was forced to leave his seaside home in County Kerry for the duration of the war simply because as an Irish nationalist he opposed Irish men serving in the British army. As Murry later observed, another man, even Lawrence himself at another time, "would simply have removed inland." For Lawrence to remain in Zennor was an act of defiance as well as denial.

Lawrence and Gray chose also to ignore the prevailing hostility to any able-bodied man not in uniform. There was widespread public anger that monks in monasteries were exempted from the fighting, and shock and grief at the pitiful state of the survivors returning from the front. There were so many wounded trying to adjust to civilian life that newspapers carried, in addition to the daily casualty lists, advice to amputees on how to live happily though maimed.

The Lawrences, in any case, had done little to ingratiate themselves with the inhabitants of Zennor. The vicar did not like them because they did not go to church, the center of village life. The postman, making his daily round on his bicycle, was not happy to deliver as part of the Lawrences' voluminous mail the *Berliner Tageblatt* with its alien Gothic lettering, and a great many letters with suspicious-looking foreign postmarks as well.

Frieda's notorious family name, moreover, had moved into the headlines. On August 13, *The Times* reported that "the German Airman Richthofen," who had brought down fifty-seven planes "with the air of an officer and a gentleman," had received two bullet wounds in the head in aerial combat over the German lines. But the Red Baron seemed to be invincible. Soon the papers carried the news that he had climbed back into his cockpit, shooting down his fifty-eighth plane on August 18 and his sixtieth on September 2.

If the Lawrences did not read *The Times*, others did. It is still unclear whether Whitehall or Cornwall was to blame for what happened next. First, the police pounced on Gray for breaking the blackout. According to the *St. Ives Times* of October 5, Cecil W. Gray, musician, of Bosigran was fined twenty pounds for "Unobscured Light at Zennor":

> Norman E. Cooke, deputy coast-watching officer, said numerous complaints had been made of unobscured lights at defendant's house. Defendant showed him a window where lights had been seen. There was a heavy curtain, but the window had been left open. The wind had apparently blown the curtain and produced an intermittent light.

As the house was situated where a light could be a guide to a hostile submarine, the bench had taken a serious view of the offense and accordingly levied the punitively heavy fine.

That was in early October. On Thursday, October 11, William Henry drove his horse and wagon two hours over the moors to the farmers' market at Penzance, as he did every Thursday. His sister and Lawrence went along. When the time came to return, however, the passengers had to wait two hours for William Henry, a lazy, unpunctual man, to turn up. Frieda, who had spent the afternoon with Gray at Bosigran, therefore got back to the cottage before Lawrence did. The place clearly had been searched. Lawrence's letters had been rummaged through, Frieda's workbasket thrown on the floor. Men in uniform had been seen going up the lane.

Next day four officials appeared—an army major, a St. Ives policeman, and two detectives—to read an order from the military commander of the southwest. Mr. and Mrs. Lawrence had three days to get out of Cornwall. They were not to go to any coastal region; they were to report to the police where they did settle.

Lawrence, blinding himself to what was staring everybody else in the face—his German wife—asked, puzzled, "What have I done?" "You know better than I do," answered the captain. Then the four went through the cottage, helping themselves to whatever looked suspicious; they took away the words to a Hebridean song, some letters to Frieda from her mother, and Lawrence's college botany notebook.

There was no choice but to obey. Packing up, Lawrence wrote to Cynthia Asquith that a bolt had fallen from the blue. They were as innocent "as the rabbits of the field outside," he protested.

He has been accused of protesting too much. It was a savage, brutal time. Frieda's passport application bore an inflammatory German name in a year when even the British royal family changed its name (from House of Saxe-Coburg-Gotha to House of Windsor) to disguise the German connection.

Yet Lawrence suffered bitterly from the expulsion from his home; it was a turning point in his life and in his relation to England. He saw it, moreover, as a demonstration of the absolute and vindictive power of the state over the individual—the lesson with which the First World War prepared the world for the rest of the century.

PAINFULLY leaving his two cottages, on which the rent had been paid until the following year, Lawrence hoped that he and Frieda might be allowed to return. They left their books and furniture. On October 15 they shut the door behind them. The Hockings gave them milk and sandwiches for the journey, and William Henry drove them in his cart to St. Ives. A policeman and a military officer watched to make sure they got on the train.

"I always feel doomed when the train is running into London," says Birkin in *Women in Love* as he travels to the dreaded capital in the company of his beloved Gerald Crich. Lawrence felt much the same to be heading for London as winter approached. He was never again to see Cornwall or the farmer who had been briefly his closest friend.

William Henry married two years later, had a family, and lived until 1955. He made little mention thereafter of his brush with genius. His only written record was a diary entry for October 15, 1917: "To St. Ives—Lawrence."

THE capital was at war but having a good time. During the earsplitting air raids, with shrapnel falling, people would drop in on each other, to "spend the raid." The parties ended when the all clear was sounded by a Boy Scout riding a bicycle through the streets with a bugle. Violet Hunt, escorted by Ford Madox Ford, who was home on leave, appeared at one party wearing his soldier's tin hat tied by a broad pink satin ribbon under her chin.

The Lawrences were soon housed, and able to entertain, in Hilda Doolittle's bed-sitter, a handsome room with apricot-colored walls and dark-blue curtains, in Mecklenburgh Square. Cynthia Asquith came to call, and considered that she dined well on an excellent omelette Lawrence cooked by the fire, supplemented with sardines and pears. She worried at how unwell he looked. "His health doesn't allow of his living in London," she told her diary, "and all the money he has in the world is the *prospect* of eighteen pounds for the publication of some poems all about bellies and breasts which he gave me to read."

Hilda Doolittle, who had lent them her room and moved into smaller quarters while her husband, Richard Aldington, was away at officers' training school, was also concerned about their finances. She sent a report to the ever generous Amy Lowell: the Lawrences were in a pickle, "as they can't afford digs in London—and he is pretty ill."

Lawrence was not quite as poor as his friends believed. Living frugally in Cornwall, he had not only the sixty pounds from Amy Lowell and fifty from Pinker but also lesser sums for other work, including thirteen pounds from the *English Review*. Upon his return to London David Eder had also given him money—enough for him to be able to send Cecil Gray five pounds to repay the four he owed, saying, "Now you are short and I am not." Besides, he could always look to Ada, who, with her husband, Eddie Clarke, owned a tailoring business in the Midlands and was able and eager to assist her favorite brother. Their uncle in Leicester, Fritz Krenkow, moreover, also remained a source of subsidy. But Lawrence could not earn, and dependence on charity made him feel poor.

And pushed about, like a refugee. No sooner had they settled in at Mecklenburgh Square than Aldington came home on leave and Hilda reclaimed her room. The Lawrences then had to accept the loan of

Gray's mother's flat in Earl's Court Square: a glisteningly clean set of rooms in which their visitors felt Lawrence looked out of place with his corduroy jacket and faded canvas shoes. That was no more than he felt; he thought the flat too bourgeois for him. His unease was not lessened by the knowledge that the flat was under surveillance by the Criminal Intelligence Department. So much were the Lawrences still under suspicion that the CID had interviewed Ernest Weekley for information about his ex-wife.

In November even their friends found out more about the Lawrences than they wished to know. The passionate love poems Lawrence had been accumulating since 1912 appeared under the exuberant title *Look! We Have Come Through!* Two of the most shocking, "Song of a Man Who Is Loved" ("I hope that I may spend eternity between her breasts") and "Meeting Among the Mountains" ("Christ on the cross!—his beautiful young man's body / Has fallen dead upon the nails"), had been removed before publication at the request of the publisher, Chatto.

For Lawrence and Frieda, the honeymoon was long over. Frieda was preoccupied with Gray, and while they were in London Hilda Doolittle fell in love with Lawrence. From Cornwall, Gray, who heard from Frieda what was going on, wrote Lawrence a stinging letter, accusing him of making himself the center of a cult of worshipful females.

Lawrence did not deny that he had a circle of women. He countered, acknowledging Gray's affinity with Frieda and their mutual hatred of him: "You want an emotional sensuous underworld, like Frieda," while he and "my 'women,' Esther Andrews, Hilda Aldington etc," represented a new world, or underworld, of knowledge and being.

Tension at Mecklenburgh Square was compounded by Aldington's infidelity. He began an affair with Dorothy Yorke, an elegant American model known as Arabella, who was living in the same house. Hilda confided her unhappiness to Lawrence. She had had a stillborn child two years earlier. He, she felt, was the only one who understood her continuing depression over the loss.

The drama at Mecklenburgh Square was messy enough to work its way into four novels: Hilda's (written under her pen name, H.D.), *Bid Me to Live; Miranda Masters,* by John Cournos, Dorothy Yorke's previous lover; Aldington's *Death of a Hero;* and Lawrence's *Aaron's Rod.* All suggest that Hilda was sexually drawn to Lawrence but that he recoiled from her advances.

Frieda was unperturbed. She used the occasion to tell Hilda of her friend, an older man, who had told her that if love is free, everything is free. This would seem to have been wifely permission to a woman trying to seduce her husband. But Frieda spoiled it with the rider: "but Lawrence does not really care for women. He only cares for men. Hilda, *you have no idea of what he is like.*"

Frieda spoke with confidence; her position was unassailable. An Irish friend, Brigit Patmore, watched one night at Mecklenburgh Square while Lawrence sewed and molded Frieda into a piece of black-and-gold brocade so that they could accompany Cynthia Asquith to the opera. Brigit thought Frieda looked magnificent, and she marveled at the bond between the two of them.

IN London, with its good communications and transport (they all traveled by Underground), Lawrence began gathering friends to go to the east slope of the Andes, to the estates in Colombia owned by Eder's relatives. Lawrence was sure that 1918 would be the last year of the war and that they could all sail away the following spring. The roster for Rananim had swelled to include Gray, Hilda, Dorothy Yorke, and possibly the Carswells. Catherine's pregnancy was a complication, but, he told her, "It will make you happy and I want it to be a little girl."

Once again Lawrence placed his faith in the wise, fatherly Eder: "Something *right* in him. And he knows all that—Brazil, Paraguay, Colombia." Eder was not one to be put off by Lawrence's extremes of mood, if indeed he witnessed them. He was one of a band of neurologists who had founded a clinic for the treatment of shell-shocked soldiers, using methods ranging from hypnotism to psychoanalysis. A forerunner of R. D. Laing, moreover, Eder believed that the mad were often saner than the sane. Yet he could not wait for Lawrence. In February he set off in the other direction, to Palestine, as part of the Zionist Commission's delegation to prepare for the Jewish national homeland promised by the British government's Balfour Declaration four months earlier.

The Lawrences' next move took them out of London but no farther than Dollie Radford's cottage in Hermitage, Berkshire, although Ada was offering to pay for a cottage in the Midlands. Settled temporarily, Lawrence suggested to Cynthia Asquith that she might let him and Frieda take her son John for a time. "I think I might be, in some sort, a psychic physician," he told her, "—not doing anything direct, but merely as a presence—especially Frieda and me together." It might be conceited of him to suggest it, he conceded candidly, but he wished he could do something to help.

The offer shows Lawrence, as in his subsequent essays on the unconscious, mimicking Eder's psychoanalytic role. He disdained psychoanalysis just as he had mocked the *Psychoanalytic Review*'s essay on *Sons and Lovers*. "When you've said *mutter complex*, you've said nothing," he sneered. But he kept three analysts—Eder, Low, and Jones—among his good friends throughout those difficult years and tried vainly to get them to use his own theory of the primal unconscious, as expounded in *Studies in Classic American Literature,* to modify their own. Jones, he reported to Benjamin Huebsch, his American publisher, "has gone to Vienna, partly to graft some of the ideas on to Freud and the Freudian theory." "You see I've told Ernest Jones and the Eders the ideas," he said in frustration. "—But they don't know how to use them."

In February, his finances were solid enough to allow him to decline Kot's offer of ten pounds and to renew, after some haggling, the lease on both Cornwall cottages; he hoped to sublet them, perhaps to Virginia and Leonard Woolf. In March there was another two hundred dollars from Amy Lowell, plus royalties for his poems. His health was not in such a good state; he had a constant sore throat.

The Radford cottage had a drawback. Dollie insisted on repossessing it from time to time as a refuge for her husband, who was suffering from a depressive illness. At short notice, therefore, the Lawrences had to get out of the way and to take rooms in the village or on a nearby farm. Grimsbury Farm, and the two young women who ran it, thus fell under Lawrence's eagle eye. He was intrigued especially by Violet Monk, who wore leather boots, jodhpurs, a man's shirt and tie, and a little felt hat. She did the "man's" chores around the place and was very possessive toward her more feminine cousin, Cecily Lambert.

But the observation went two ways. Cecily noticed, when Frieda sprawled carelessly in a chair, that her plump legs were encased in coarse calico bloomers. When he saw Cecily making silky underwear for herself, he pronounced the delicate fabric "prostitutey." Cecily was bold enough to ask Frieda why the Lawrences asked to occupy separate rooms when they came to stay; she answered blithely that she did not wish "to be too much married." This surprised Cecily, who had heard Frieda say how much she wished to have a child by Lawrence. Cecily, however, assumed that as Frieda was on the verge of forty, pregnancy was impossible.

IN May 1918 Lawrence did what he might have done at any time since the war started: he went home to the Midlands. Ada wanted them to move in with her and her little son (her husband, Eddie Clarke, was away in the service) but he declined. "Frieda and I have lived so much alone," he wrote Willie Hopkin in Eastwood, "and in isolated places, that we suffer badly at being cooped up with other folk." But the cottage they took not too far away was spacious and beautiful, on the side of a steep valley in Middleton-by-Wirksworth, Derbyshire. Ada paid the substantial rent of sixty-five pounds a year and gave them twenty pounds to spend. Although they felt exiled from London, and windswept, they stayed at Mountain Cottage for nearly a year. Lawrence saw the place as the "navel of England." Frieda liked the phrase so much she borrowed it herself for a letter to Amy Lowell which shows how well, for all her posturing, she understood her husband's work:

> To understand D. H. Lawrence, one must know that he belongs to the Midlands, that navel of England. It is a strange black country with an underworld quality that is rather frightening. In *Sons and Lovers* the life of the miner[,] the life of the common people[,] has perhaps for the first time been written from the *inside*, not from the point of the intellectual. . . .
>
> At the present moment the world is despairing for this lost reality and trying to regain this Paradise . . . one may admire or not admire D. H. Lawrence's art but the absolute genius and freshness of it nobody can deny.

Their usual plea for visitors brought Dorothy Yorke north to see them. She was very upset, probably about her affair with Aldington, and returned to London in tears, but Lawrence said they were both very fond of her. In *Aaron's Rod*, the novel on which he was working, however, he portrayed her as an elegant, darkly exotic beauty who licks her "full dry red lips" with "the rapid tip of her tongue . . . suggesting a snake's flicker." Lawrence's habit of assigning viperous qualities to women suggests that the fearful fascination of snakes lay not in their slithering shape but in their biting mouths. He did not like kissing, nor did he like nagging; he hated the way his sisters snapped at their children like "jaguars of wrath."

His nephew, Ada's three-year-old son, and his sister Emily's daughter, Peggy, then six, came to stay with him and Frieda: "I was very glad of their presence," he remarked at the end of the visit, saying that the children stopped him from thinking too much. He was of two minds about family life. It was a distraction—"a kind of swamp, in which meals are islands"—but also "a kind of drug, or soporific, a sort of fatness; it saves one."

Mountain Cottage brought the rest of Lawrence's family to visit, even his father. Arthur Lawrence was puzzled at his son's choice of wife— such a big woman, he thought—and, like his son, was conscious of women's mouths. "When 'er oppens 'er mahth," he said of Frieda (according to his grandson's reconstruction of his accent), " 'aif room's dark. 'Er's like a damn girt cart-oss."

Frieda escaped the claustrophobia of Mountain Cottage for occasional visits to London to see her own children, and in August, when Lawrence was cheered by another gift of fifty pounds from the Royal Literary Fund, they both left for a trip to Ross-on-Wye and the Forest of Dean with the Carswells and their newborn infant, who had turned out not to be the girl Lawrence had wanted, but a boy, John. Lawrence, as ahead of his time in child care as in dress (he wore espadrilles and no socks on the holiday), was delighted to help Catherine carry around the infant, for whose birth he had written a poem, "War-Baby." ("The child like mustard seed / Rolls out of the husk of death / Into the woman's fertile, fathomless lap.") And after their return, he told Donald Carswell how much he had enjoyed holding the baby: "One has the future in one's arms, so to speak: and one *is* the present."

In September, still in Derbyshire, working on his American essays and (for another fifty pounds) a school textbook on European history, he turned thirty-three. Shortly after, his papers from Cornwall caught up with him and he was summoned for his third medical examination. It took place in a schoolroom in Derby; he was back at Mountain Cottage the same day, but it was his most traumatic experience of the war. He did not recover—if he ever did—until he had recreated the scene in *Kangaroo* four years later.

The novel describes how the very sound of colliers singing war songs on a bus reminds Richard Lovat Somers (Lawrence's alter ego in *Kangaroo*) of the long, long trail a-winding to death itself. Somers hates the false cheeriness of the singsong, drawn-out vowels: "Good-bye - eeee / Don't cry - eee / Wipe the tear, baby dear, from your eye - eee -."

The examination was all the more humiliating to Lawrence for being conducted in the accents of his native region. The barked commands were intolerably supercilious. "You describe yourself as a writer"; "What doctor said you were threatened with consumption?" He had to walk about naked and when he heard the doctors laughing, he assumed it was at his scarecrow physique. Then came the dreaded command: "Put your feet apart. . . . Bend forward—further—further."

He was thus forced to expose his most sacred and shameful place, the base and back of his loins, and he never forgave "them"—a collective pronoun which included England and everyone in it. Adding insult to injury, the doctors raised his classification by a notch, making him eligible to be called up for nonmilitary service.

As with the expulsion from Cornwall, his reaction may seem disproportionate to the event. Inspection for hemorrhoids was a routine part of the army medical examination. Yet he was not alone in perceiving that the military doctors abused their powers and humiliated the unfit. There were so many complaints against the roughness of the reexaminations of discharged and rejected men that in 1917 a select committee of Parliament was set up to investigate.

The deliberate and needless exposure and ridicule of his physical weakness by those with absolute power over him was the final blow of the war. His old cheery, English self was dead. "Those were the years," he wrote in *Kangaroo*, "when the damage was done." Photographs show the damage. The alert young man of 1915, with his engagingly insolent glare, gives way by 1920 to a slumped figure with emaciated cheeks and listless, sunken eyes.

Lawrence's terrible bitterness at his treatment during the war has been much criticized. He had good grounds for anger: the pointless slaughter, the suppression of *The Rainbow,* and the persecution of himself and his wife as spies. Yet he reacted as if it had been directed at him personally when he suffered less than almost any man of his generation. During the terrible years when British conscientious objectors were being imprisoned, tortured, and even maliciously sent to the front to be killed, and when, for opposing the war, Bertrand Russell was held in solitary confinement in Brixton Prison for over four months, Lawrence endured no more than one night in a military barracks in the course of three medical examinations he had no chance of passing.

Yet a man at the bottom of a well does not worry about forest fires. A writer's task is to convey the world through one pair of eyes. During the war Lawrence suffered more than the war. His marriage—the bulwark of his existence—was flawed in a way that cadenzas of pseudo-philosophy could not conceal. His health deteriorated markedly; he scarcely drew a painless breath. The passionate wish to destroy humanity, expressed in vivid phrases of hate that will forever darken his name, reflects a rage directed more at the state of his lungs than at society.

Not the least of his frustrations was childlessness. Now that a full range of his letters is available, the pitiful attention with which he followed the pregnancies of his women friends can be seen. He had always expected that he would be a father; it was during the war years that he faced the truth that he never would be. Hence his sad joke to Cynthia Asquith when she was expecting her third child: "I had your letter prescribing childbirth—or rather childbearing—as a cure for all the ills: sorry it is denied me: must find a substitute."

Yet during the war, he poured out, with the ease and speed of Mozart, a stream of his greatest work, including *Women in Love,* "The Fox," and the critical masterpiece *Studies in Classic American Literature.* It was a war record to be proud of.

WITHIN seven weeks, however, the war was over, and Lawrence was alive—luckier than his fellow poets Rupert Brooke, who had died on the way to the Dardanelles in 1915, and Wilfred Owen, who was blown up near Compiègne a week before the armistice; luckier too than the Red Baron, who was shot down in April 1918 near a village on the French coast.

Yet death was much on his mind. In London he had seen Katherine Mansfield, now with diagnosed consumption of the lungs. She and Murry had married but she refused to listen to the doctors' warning that unless she went to a sanatorium she would be dead within two to four years. Instead, she demanded that Jack ignore her illness even though her cough shook the bed at night. Soon the Murrys, like the Lawrences, were sleeping apart.

Lawrence commanded Katherine to stay alive. "Be damned and be blasted everything, and let the bloody world come to its end. But one does not die. Jamais." But Katherine, to the contrary, was daydreaming about dying; she chronicled her symptoms for herself and when lying in her bath would compose herself as if she were lying in a coffin. To Lawrence such morbidity was self-indulgence, and he wrote Katherine an ugly letter accusing her of "stewing" in her consumption.

He had just witnessed another of the Coopers, his consumptive neighbors from Eastwood, die of the disease. In the many letters of condolence he wrote during those years, he described his sense that the dead are not really dead. To an aunt in Eastwood, whose son had died in France, he wrote, "They are not lost: they come back and live with one, in one's soul." Their presence helped one through, he told his aunt, something he felt very much about his own mother.

In this mood, knowing how ill she was, Lawrence wrote Katherine, almost as a valedictory, one of the most important letters of his life. He wanted to set down "a few little things I have on my mind." The "mother-incest" idea, for one thing, contained a modicum of truth: "At certain periods the man has a desire and a tendency to return unto the woman, make her his goal and end. . . . He casts himself as it were into her womb, and, she, the Magna Mater, receives him with gratification. This is a kind of incest." Jack had used Katherine in this way, Lawrence declared; he himself had done it with Frieda, and he was now struggling to extricate himself: "In a way, Frieda is the devouring mother. —It is awfully hard, once the sex relation has gone this way, to recover. If we don't recover, we die." He believed, he told Murry, that men must lead and women must follow unquestioningly. Frieda disagreed: "Hence our fight."

THE confusion of sexual roles in wartime society caused by women doing men's jobs and wearing men's clothes disturbed Lawrence deeply. At what point did they become lesbians with no need of men? He certainly did not find woman-to-woman friendship as beautiful as a bond between men. His unease during the months at Hermitage in 1919 went into his haunting short story "The Fox," based on the women at Grimsbury Farm.

Studies in Classic American Literature contains Lawrence's famous remark, "An artist is usually a damned liar. Never trust the artist. Trust the tale. The proper function of a critic is to save the tale from the artist who created it." If so, "The Fox" takes some saving, for the artist does not seem to have understood the tale he was creating. The feminist critic Kate Millett, writing in 1970, argued that in "The Fox" Lawrence represents marriage as not only the taming of woman, but her extinction. "The Fox," she said, shows how a man should anesthetize his bride.

In the story, two young single women, known by their surnames, March and Banford, run Bailey Farm by themselves. Their self-sufficiency is disturbed by the presence of a fox with red bush and bright eyes. March even has a dream in which the fox "whisked his brush across her face," searing her mouth.

Along comes Henry Grendel, a soldier back from the war, looking for his late uncle who had owned the farm. Henry, too, has bright eyes. March is attracted to Henry; Banford sees him as a threat to their union. Henry shoots the fox; then he takes his ax and cuts down a tree, which kills Banford. His competition thus eliminated, Henry plans to sweep March off to Canada, where, in Millett's words, her "drugged loss of self shall give him that total control over her he requires." As Lawrence wrote:

> He did not want her to watch any more, to see any more, to understand any more. He wanted to veil her woman's spirit, as Orientals veil the woman's face. He wanted her to commit herself to him, and to put her independent spirit to sleep. . . . He wanted to make her submit, yield, blindly pass away out of all her strenuous consciousness. . . . And then he would have her, and he would have his own life at last . . . his own life as a young man and a male.

It is a tale of man as the hunter pursuing his mate as prey. It escapes few readers that the fox is like Lawrence, a creature with triangular face, bright eyes, and red hair.

At Mountain Cottage, there was a danger more immediate than tuberculosis: the great influenza epidemic that was sweeping through Europe in the wake of the war. People in the Midlands, Lawrence reported to London, where Kot and Donald Carswell had fallen victim to it, were "horribly frightened, all of them." None more than Lawrence himself. With Frieda away for ten days and with a bad cold, he felt sorry for himself but hopeful that with each ache and pain he had got off with a mild touch. By Christmas he was well enough to stuff a rucksack full of tangerines and gifts and, with Frieda, go off to Ripley for Christmas dinner at Ada's. Ada hired a motorcar to meet them on the way and they had a good time, all generations together, with much food and games and dancing.

*		*		*

THE Lawrences could not leave England until peace was signed and travel became possible, but they did not want to wait a minute longer. Lawrence looked for direction to Eder, or rather to Eder's wife, to whom he wrote on January 2, 1919: "Is Eder coming home? *I must get out.* I must get out of England. . . . I like best to imagine my Andes. But if the Andes are impracticable and if Palestine be practicable, then I'll go to Palestine. I want to see Eder. I *will* get out of Europe this year."

Bavaria also tempted him. Frieda had been left some money by her godfather, if only they could get hold of it. Also, Else's husband, Edgar Jaffe, had just been made minister of finance in the new republic of Bavaria. To friend after friend, Lawrence boasted of this political connection—"my brother-in-law . . . a rich Jew and Professor"—almost as much as he had been wont to do of Frieda's aristocratic birth. When they went to Bavaria, he said, "I suspect we shall be in the midst of things."

This alliance with greatness was short-lived. After two months in office, Jaffe fell victim to melancholic depression and was confined to a clinic. Else, still far closer to her lover, Alfred Weber, than to her husband, anguished over whether her visits to the clinic made Edgar better or worse.

In February Lawrence came down with another cold (at least, to him it seemed like a fresh one) which kept him in bed for a week. Recovered, he got up, took his niece Peggy for a walk in the high ground above Mountain Cottage, then went with Frieda to visit Ada in Ripley. There he collapsed. It was influenza this time, the real thing.

It was his worst illness since the pneumonia in Croydon in 1911, and strangely similar. For two days the doctor thought he would not live. Ada was at his bedside. He took no solid food for a fortnight; it was a month before he went downstairs. Once again, he survived. "My mother never wanted me to be born," he wrote to Cynthia Asquith, who had written of her unexpected third pregnancy, "yet am I not a gem of life?" Any speculation about the true state of Lawrence's lungs during the war years must take into account his survival of this killer epidemic which took millions of lives across Europe in 1918–1919. While recovering, as in 1912, he worked, producing two articles for Murry's magazine, *The Athenaeum,* and copying several pictures as well.

Gifts and sympathy poured in from all his well-wishers: champagne from Fritz Krenkow, grapefruit from Kot, plus port and brandy; butter from the Campbells in Ireland, wine from the Carswells. Eder came himself. Back from Palestine and about to return, he, his wife, and one of his stepsons journeyed all the way to Ripley, bringing a bottle of claret, cake, and sweets. Lawrence found him, as usual, "very nice indeed" and promised to go to Palestine in September.

Recuperating, Lawrence, who was afraid of dominant women, found himself caught between two. Ada decided that she, with her small son, had better accompany her brother as nurse when he was well enough to return to Mountain Cottage. Lawrence's uncharacteristically fierce denunciation of Frieda in a letter to Kot sounds as if he were quoting his sister:

> My sister goes with us to Middleton. I am not going to be left to Frieda's tender mercies until I am well again. She really is a devil—and I feel as if I would part from her for ever—let her go alone to Germany, while I take another road. For it is true, I have been bullied by her long enough. I really could leave her now, without a pang, I believe. If this illness hasn't been a lesson to her, it has to me.

Frieda was jealous of the closeness between the pair. Once, when she came into the room at Middleton and found Lawrence and Ada sitting together, painting a lamp, she accused them of being more than a brother and sister to each other. Lawrence was furious. But Frieda's unbridled insistence on speaking her mind was part of the woman he married. Despite their antagonism, Ada and Frieda together also made a powerful combination. As Lawrence, through the window of his cottage, watched them shaking the heavy snow from the branches of the trees, he felt "like a dazed and sick monkey."

By April he was well enough to leave Ada and return to the uncertain refuge of the Radford cottage in Berkshire, yet it took him five days to recover from the modest journey. Undaunted, he was ready "to tramp off," he wrote Mark Gertler, "to the end of the world." And in a letter to Eder, who had left England on April 3, he now implored: "Oh, do take me to Palestine, and I will love you for ever. . . . Can't I come and do the writing up?"

He had the title ready: "The Entry of the Blessed into Palestine." He could see himself riding on an ass from Jerusalem to Jericho. He did worry about being surrounded by Jews, but was confident that Eder's vision would see him through and that his own ideas of social reorganization, ready since the Russell days, would now be useful for the new Jewish state. He laid down the outline for Eder: there would be no laws—each man would be answerable to his own soul—and each man and woman would have "the right to mate freely." "And so our State begins."

Palestine certainly seemed preferable to Chapel Farm Cottage. Dollie Radford once more, "with stinking impudence, wants us to clear out," as Lawrence put it. He was even angrier with her daughter Margaret, who simply moved in with them when it suited her.

Yet his rage against women was combined with awe and curiosity at the way they reproduced themselves. Before Catherine Carswell's son was born, he wrote her, "I know exactly how it feels. I feel as if I had a child of black fury curled up inside my bowels. I'm sure I can feel exactly what it is to be pregnant." To Amy Lowell, reporting that Hilda Doolittle had moved to Cornwall with Cecil Gray and was expecting a baby: "perhaps the child will soothe her and steady her." When Maitland Radford's wife had a daughter, Lawrence sent warm congratulations, saying, "She is the *real* younger generation."

For Cynthia Asquith, as her pregnancy advanced, he sent almost a prenatal lullaby: "I hope your new little 'Colombe' sleeps softly before her coming: I have decided that it is a girl." Frieda played her part in their couvade rituals by embroidering an endless stream of coverlets and buying toys and baby clothes for the various newborn.

Like many childless couples, the Lawrences enjoyed having other people's children to stay. Next door to Chapel Farm Cottage lived the Brown family, with their eight-year-old daughter, Hilda. Frieda would invite Hilda in to have dinner with her when Lawrence was away and they both would dress up, pretending it was a great occasion. When Lawrence was at home, he helped Hilda with her homework, taught her the "Marseillaise" in French, and let her thread the needles when he sewed (he made blue denim outfits for himself and Frieda, and a gown for Ada). He also took her with him to round up the goats at Grimsbury Farm, shouting to her, "Hilda, don't let the damn things go even if they pull you in half!" She lived with them during her entire summer holiday in 1919.

As before, these scenes from domestic life were only half the story. Who was devouring whom? The young women at Grimsbury Farm watched with terror the way Lawrence seemed to relish humiliating Frieda. One day when she said something to offend him while he was stirring a pan of hot potatoes on the stove, they feared he was going to hurl one at her. Even worse was the day that she had a small accident with Violet Monk's sewing machine. Lawrence exploded and issued a punishment: she was to scour the farmhouse's brick floor. To the onlookers' amazement, Frieda obeyed. With tears streaming down her face and insults from her lips, she fetched a pail of water and sloshed around the floor with a cloth, only infuriating Lawrence more. He told her she was useless and doing it all wrong, bending from the waist instead of kneeling down.

On June 28, 1919, the peace treaty of Versailles was signed at last. With the Lawrences' passports nearly ready, only their destination remained unclear. His American publisher proposed a lecture tour and he sounded out Amy Lowell. She reacted with terror and tact:

Now here is the only difficulty with your plan. I cannot have people stay in the house with me. I am not at all strong, and I find it makes me very nervous to have guests, even delightful and intimate guests like yourself. Therefore, I have to make a rule of not having anyone stay.

In fact, Lowell did not want him in Boston—"not a good place for your purpose." She promised introductions in New York or even Chicago: but "really, to be strictly honest, I do not advise you to come at all." The English attitude toward "letters" was very different from the American, and "the Irish question" put all Englishmen under a shadow.

Even without this dash of cold water, Lawrence was beginning to change his mind about America and to think of returning to Italy instead. As Frieda desperately awaited the moment when she could set out for Germany, Lawrence acquired a new interest.

Rosalind Thornycroft Baynes, with three little girls and a husband who was divorcing her, was a beautiful woman in distress. If feminine strongmindedness and independence in a gentle guise were what Lawrence liked—and an opportunity for surrogate parenthood into the bargain—Rosalind was heaven-sent. She was the estranged wife of Dr. Godwin Baynes, a friend of Maitland Radford, and had had a child by another man. That summer she was living in a cottage called The Myrtles, in Pangbourne near the Lawrences. Nearby too, at Spring Cottage in Bucklebury, lived her sister Joan Farjeon and Joan's husband, the drama critic and playwright Herbert Farjeon.

Rosalind was a freethinker, brought up in artistic and socialist circles in London and the Home Counties, educated at the progressive coeducational King Alfred's School in Hampstead, then at the London School of Economics and the Slade School of Art. Her father was a well-to-do and well-known sculptor, Sir Hamo Thornycroft, R.A.; her mother was quietly feminist and Fabian. Her friends included many known to Lawrence, such as Maitland Radford and David Garnett.

Lawrence was concerned because Rosalind was allowing herself to play the guilty party in her forthcoming divorce in order to save Godwin Baynes's promising medical career from scandal. Guilty of adultery Rosalind certainly was, but her husband had been far more unfaithful than she. Godwin's own father blamed the breakup of the marriage on his son's "free and easy ways with both sexes" and the "H. G. Wells atmosphere" of the couple's home.

Rosalind and the dashing Godwin Baynes had been lovers and had traveled together well before their marriage in 1913. Their love did not survive the early years of the marriage and Godwin's many affairs. The strain between them was worsened when in 1915, while Rosalind was expecting her second child, Godwin volunteered for the army as a medical officer. She was opposed to the war, and her family and friends were passionate pacifists. While Godwin was away for more than a year in the Middle East, Rosalind took a lover, Kenneth Hooper, an old Hampstead friend and conscientious objector, who had been in prison for refusing to serve. Their union produced Rosalind's third daughter, born in 1918, giving Godwin grounds for divorce when he returned to England in January 1919 after long absence overseas.

Lawrence knew and liked the charismatic Godwin and that summer tried to talk him out of the divorce. He warned him that the destructive publicity would outweigh any imagined advantages; the better solution, Lawrence advised, was a kind of triangular marriage—to stay with his wife but to find a man whom he could love and trust. Lawrence, still preaching the brotherhood to which he had tried to convert Murry, told Godwin that what he needed was a new adjustment, to Walt Whitman's ideal of "manly love": "the real implicit reliance of one man on another: as sacred a unison as marriage: only it must be deeper."

At the same time Lawrence found the breakup of the Bayneses was so interesting that he suggested to Herbert Farjeon that together they write a play about it. Farjeon was shocked. "I can't write a play about my own sister-in-law!" he protested. Nonetheless, the Farjeon circle all liked Lawrence, much preferring him to Frieda, and they were always happy to see him coming across the fields alone, bearing bunches of wildflowers.

Rosalind was fascinated by Lawrence and became yet another of the well-brought-up women of artistic tastes irresistibly drawn to him by his uncanny perceptiveness, his dextrous graceful hands, his fascination with children, and his very male ability to take charge.

Lawrence made himself at home at Rosalind's. He startled her young nanny, Ivy Knight, one day when he went into the kitchen to wash up; Ivy had never seen a man do that before. He was not shy, either, in disciplining Rosalind's children. Out walking one day, when the obstreperous oldest girl, Bridget, began banging her mother's legs with a thistle and Rosalind implored her to stop, Lawrence grabbed the thistle and whacked Bridget across the legs with it. As in Greatham, he could not bear the wheedling English middle-class way with children.

By the time Lawrence saw Frieda off to Germany on October 15, he had decided (although he had assured Else only a few months before that he was looking forward to seeing them all again) to go straight to Italy. He was delighted, therefore, to learn that Rosalind, with the help and advice of her father, had decided to take her little girls and move there as well to escape the publicity of the divorce.

Lawrence returned to Hermitage and worked. He was an earning author once again. He had finished the American essays, the first eight of which had been published in the *English Review,* and was confident that they would reveal new truths about the workings of the unconscious as well as of the American mind. He also made each of the little Baynes girls a sheepskin coat for their Italian journey.

Money was rolling in: fifty-five pounds from Pinker, followed by thirty pounds for "The Fox" and twenty pounds for translations of Russian philosophy in collaboration with Kot. In London Martin Secker was offering to bring out *Women in Love* in the spring and was thinking of reissuing *The Rainbow*. American editions looked likely. He also pocketed five pounds from selling Amy Lowell's old typewriter to Catherine Carswell's brother and realized the proceeds from the sale of much of the Cornwall furniture. He gave his piano to William Henry Hocking, but asked for the Persian rug and the dishes and table linens to be sent to him.

On November 14, 1919, more than five years after he had returned to England for what was to be a short visit, and cheered by the arrival of an unexpected twenty pounds from Huebsch on the eve of departure, he headed back to Italy.

Part Three

10

LEGIONNAIRE'S DISEASE

1919–1920

*T*he brave talk of leaving Frieda without a pang disappeared the instant Lawrence reached Florence. The stream of postcards he sent back to England—pictures of the Piazza della Signoria, the Ponte Vecchio, the Uffizi Gallery, the Piazzale Michelangelo—all bore variations on the same theme: "Am here in the rain, waiting for Frieda, of whom I hear nothing yet." "Here am I waiting for your Auntie Frieda." "Here am I on my lonely-o, waiting for Frieda." "Am waiting for Frieda—had a wire from her." "Here I sit in my room over the river Arno, and wait for Mrs Lawrence."

The days dragged on; he poured out the same refrain. To Ada on November 24, "Hope she won't be long"; to Secker the same day, "I hope she will be here quickly"; to Cecily Lambert on November 26, "She is coming this day week"; to the poet Max Plowman, "My wife arrives on Dec 2nd"; to Rosalind, "Frieda will come next Wednesday"; to Ada on November 29, "Frieda is coming"; and, at last, to Kot on December 6, "Frieda is here."

The Frieda who returned was thinner. To Lawrence it was not an improvement and he blamed impoverished Germany's diet, for forcing her to live off carrots. They soon left for Rome, then moved farther south, to a mountain village near Naples, which turned out to be intolerably bleak and primitive (but provided a good setting for the last part of *The Lost Girl,* the unfinished manuscript of a novel which had just reached him from Else in Bavaria, where it had spent the war). Their house was freezing. This was not the Italy of which he had dreamed for five years.

Lawrence wrote to Compton Mackenzie, who had once offered him his cottage on Capri. By Christmas, they were there, happily installed in a small apartment on the second floor of the Palazzo Ferraro, with a chatty English colony around them. To Cecily Lambert back at Grimsbury Farm, Lawrence wrote on Christmas Day, "I really think we shall stay here a while."

ON a February morning in 1920, two months later, Lawrence arose before dawn in their Palazzo Ferraro flat, made himself some coffee, and, leaving behind Frieda, with whom he had already argued about his trip, rode the funicular down the steep hillside and caught the morning steamer to the Italian mainland. Ahead of him lay a three-hour rail journey north of Naples, to the sprawling hilltop Benedictine monastery of Monte Cassino where he was to visit a frequent guest there, a Catholic convert down on his luck.

Lawrence had little personal interest in Roman Catholicism. Yet he had asked to be invited to the monastery, and when the invitation came, he went like a fish reeled in. He went alone, as instructed. His host, Maurice Magnus, an effeminate, cosmopolitan homosexual, was a rabid woman-hater.

Magnus was the *amico* and errand boy of the British writer Norman Douglas, who was a fixture in the Anglo-Florentine literary scene. Magnus was small, plump, and impeccably dressed, American-born but, he claimed, with Hohenzollern blood. He had lived extensively in Russia, from St. Petersburg to the Crimea, had knocked about all the capitals of Europe, and had served as manager for Isadora Duncan. When Lawrence met him, he was a charming freeloader and professed journalist, always about to receive a check from some distant magazine. He was also determined, he assured one and all, to become a Benedictine monk (an order he chose, Norman Douglas liked to comment, because the Benedictines lived better than the rest).

Douglas, in contrast, was a tall and portly Austrian-born Scot, beetle-browed and acidly witty, widely known for his sardonic novel *South Wind,* and less widely for his outrageous habits. Richard Aldington pronounced him "a most masculine pederast" and David Garnett said,

"My father would not leave me alone with Douglas for one minute." Douglas had fled to Italy in 1917 while awaiting trial for molesting a young boy in the Natural History Museum in South Kensington, charges for two similar offenses having been dropped. In Florence he carried on as before. His preference was for boys between ten and twelve—he usually had one in tow—and, fond of boasting that he had syphilis of the throat, he would open his mouth for inspection. Douglas's speech was as shocking as his behavior, but relieved by wit, kindliness, and Foreign Office manners. He had not always been homosexual. His tenure as commercial attaché in the British embassy in St. Petersburg ended when he had to leave to escape the wrath of his pregnant mistress's husband.

Both Magnus and Douglas had been married, Magnus's wife misplaced somewhere, Douglas's killed in Munich in a fire caused by her smoking in bed. Although Douglas and his wife had long been divorced, he liked to tell friends that he had burnt her to death, adding sweetly, "but she *deserved* it, my dear." Magnus and Douglas had met in Capri in 1909 and when Magnus encountered Douglas in Rome in the summer of 1917, they formed a close friendship. Although often separate, in Florence they lived in the same pensione, fond of and dependent on each other, but on the prowl.

Douglas knew Lawrence from the *English Review,* where he had been assistant editor before the war, and he was delighted when he appeared in Florence in late 1919. Lawrence's description of their reunion brings alive not only Douglas, but Lawrence taking off Douglas—a performance said to have been one of his best imitations.

> Isn't that Lawrence? Why of course it is, of course it is, beard and all! Well how are you, eh? You got my note? Well now, my dear boy, you just go on to the Cavelotti—straight ahead, straight ahead—you've got the number. There's a room for you there. We shall be there in half an hour.

"We" were himself and Magnus. Lawrence spent a lot of time with them over the next few days. Magnus admired the color of Lawrence's hair and asked him what he dyed it with. "It's got no particular colour at all" was the reply. "So I couldn't dye it that."

But Lawrence, who at that time was by himself in Florence, was happy to have the pair as amusing dining companions. The table was their stage. Both considered themselves gourmets, with palates too refined for the coarse fare of the modest pensione in which they were obliged to lodge. As recorded by Lawrence, in a fine, and nonfictional, comic scene, one evening Douglas ordered Magnus to go to the kitchen to make sure that the turkey they had ordered was being roasted, as specified, with chestnut stuffing. Magnus protested that it was too late to intervene.

"It's *never* too late. You just run down and absolutely prevent them from boiling that bird in the old soup-water," said Douglas. "If you need force, fetch me."

Unwillingly Magnus went, and came back with the bad news: the turkey was being roasted, but without chestnuts.

"What did I tell you! What did I tell you!" cried Douglas. "They *are* absolute ———! If you don't hold them by the neck while they peel the chestnuts, they'll stuff the bird with old boots, to save themselves the trouble.—Of course you should have gone down sooner, Magnus."

When the dinner came, even though Magnus picked out the nicest bits for him, Douglas poked and pushed around his plate, then gave up in disgust: "Oh, holy Dio I can't eat another thing this evening—."

Lawrence had none of the revulsion for this camp pair that he had felt for Keynes and his homosexual circle at Cambridge. He watched and listened entranced at the way Magnus was "queer and sensitive as a woman" with Douglas. He was, Lawrence wrote later, "just the kind of man I had never met."

Indeed he was. Lawrence had never known anyone who lived so defiantly beyond his means, and he felt that Magnus sneered at his parsimony. He pleaded domestic responsibilities; he had a wife to support, and an uncertain income. Magnus scoffed, "Oh, why that's the very time to spend money, when you've got none." Douglas chimed in, "Precisely . . . Spend when you've nothing to spend, my boy. Spend *hard* then."

Lawrence could not let that pass. "No," he said. "If I can help it, I will never let myself be penniless while I live. I mistrust the world too much."

Unfortunately, Magnus did not mistrust the world enough. Shortly afterward, he left for Rome, first-class, and very soon got into trouble at Anzio by writing a bad check at a good hotel. He immediately thought of Lawrence in Capri. He wrote appealing to him, and to his amazement received in answer the quite princely gift of five pounds.

Frieda was furious, but Lawrence was feeling flush because Amy Lowell had sent him a hundred dollars (about twenty pounds). That he should give away a quarter of this windfall when his earning power was only just beginning to recover was astonishing. Hardly a year before he had sworn to Cynthia Asquith, "Oh my dear sweet Jesus, if I had even £100 a year I would never write another stroke for the public." Yet Lawrence felt a strange obligation to the fluttery con man. It rose in part from his sense that he had to repay the hospitality he had enjoyed in Florence and in part from a wish to dispel Magnus's opinion that he was miserly. But he also felt sorry for Magnus.

*   *   *

WHEN he accepted Magnus's invitation to visit Monte Cassino, Lawrence knew very well that he would be touched for more money. He went anyway. Magnus had sung the monastery's praises strongly. He had been using it as a retreat since 1917 in his periodic bouts of religiosity. On his first visit, he wrote to Douglas that he was sorry that Douglas was lonely but "I am in Paradise—what more can I say—the only life! I only pray that I may be able to settle my affairs soon & be permitted to stay always. The peace—the quiet—the services—the monks and work—it is that 'which passeth understanding.' "

From early mass to compline, the day was ideal: work, prayers, good simple meals of soup, meat, vegetables, fruit, and wine, reading, research, and writing, then vespers, a walk in the garden, more prayers, and "heavenly unbroken sleep."

There is little doubt why Magnus was so eager for Lawrence to come. Not only for more handouts. Lawrence was a big fish in the literary world and Magnus desperately wanted his help in selling his only significant asset: his memoir of life in the French Foreign Legion, in which he had rashly enlisted in 1916. Douglas had helped him write it and for two years Magnus had been peddling the manuscript, entitled "Dregs: Experiences of an American in the Foreign Legion." Grandiosely he hoped to realize about three hundred pounds from it. Just a few weeks before Lawrence's visit he was trying a new tack and looking for magazine serialization.

Canny Magnus, consciously or not, knew that he had struck a chord with Lawrence—indeed, more than one. He sensed Lawrence's fascination with homosexuality; and he, like Lawrence, had never recovered from the death of his mother. Magnus considered her loss (in 1912, when he was thirty-six) to be the tragedy of his life.

Arriving at Monte Cassino, Lawrence played into Magnus's hands. He allowed Magnus to button him into his silky black sealskin jacket against the chill of the sixteenth-century stone. He followed obediently as Magnus led him around cloister, tower, and garden, and with him he went to mass. That night, retiring to his room, he took with him the typescript of Magnus's great work. When he read it, he must have known why he had come.

All his nightmares of the "sticky, male mess" of military life were true, and by the evidence of the pages in his hands, had been endured by his fastidious little host.

Magnus's book told of the young soldiers who were the "jeunes filles" of the regiment—public property so painfully used by their rough lovers at night that they could hardly march during the day. It described the Arab public baths where the attendant gave "one of those massages in the hot room which only an Oriental can give, a massage that awakens every sense in one's body." Worse was Magnus's description of the

barracks baths where, as he had bent down to wash his lower half, a big
Armenian from Egypt tried to assault him "in the face," believing that
"all Englishmen liked that sort of thing."

"Dregs" gave a good reason why a fragile-looking man might wish to
wear a mustache: to distinguish himself from the "*tapettes*" (male prostitutes); in the Legion only they were clean-shaven. The memoir also
spelled out the dangers of life in the barracks, where to go out to the
lavatory in the night was to risk robbery or murder and where the
enforced rituals of cleaning were carried to sadistic extremes. It ended
with Magnus's escape into Italy after the Legion transferred him to
Lyon. He had risked arrest as a deserter, realizing that his sanity and
survival were at stake and that he could no longer bear the society of
Legionnaires, their stench, their vile language, their stealing of everything stealable. In sum, Magnus wrote (in a passage suppressed until
1987),

> their evil mindedness which attributed every action to the lowest mo-
> tives, their physical filth, and finally their drunkenness and sodomistic
> habits revolted and disgusted me to such an extent that life became an
> unbearable burden.

Lawrence was not blind to the homoerotic undercurrents in the scene
around him. The monks, as he saw them, scurried around in a motherly
or schoolboyish manner; he observed Magnus's special friend at the
monastery, a good-looking young Maltese named Don Mauro, at whom
Magnus smiled "with a wistful smirking tenderness." He took in every
detail of Magnus's "cell"—a sumptuous chamber with curtained bed
and bottles of pomade—and he understood Magnus's scarcely veiled
approaches to himself: the ecstatic whispers in his ear, the gentle little
touches on his arm.

Lawrence stood it for three days, then, even though he had planned to
stay a week, went home to Capri. But he did not disappoint Magnus. He
told him to rewrite the last five chapters of his book and then he would
offer it to a publisher. And he was as good as his word. On April 2 he
wrote to the London publisher Stanley Unwin, for whom he was writing
a short book, *Education of the People,* and asked him if he would
consider a manuscript on the Foreign Legion—not war experiences, just
home life in the Legion: a shocking and horrible tale, which would have
to be cut for the English public but was a good straightforward story all
the same.

BY then Lawrence had moved to Sicily. Almost as soon as he returned
from Monte Cassino, he and Frieda headed south and rented for a year
a fine square villa, the Fontana Vecchia, on the outskirts of Taormina on

Sicily's east coast. It was really a move from a small English colony to a larger one, with many of the same friends, among whom was Mary Cannan, living apart from her husband, Gilbert, who had had a mental breakdown. Lawrence shifted south because he was uneasy with the political unrest developing between fascists and socialists on Italy's mainland. Sicily, like Cornwall, seemed as far away from the trouble as he could get. "It is where Europe ends: finally," he wrote Rosalind Baynes, now in Florence with her three daughters; Lawrence was hoping she would follow. And to his new American publisher, Thomas Seltzer, "Italy feels shaky—but Sicily won't change much till Etna erupts again." He made a number of new friends, including a young South African painter, Jan Juta.

Suddenly one morning in late April Lawrence heard a noise on the lower terrace of the Fontana Vecchia. He investigated, and there was Magnus with a terrible tale to tell. One morning, while he was working on his book in his room at Monte Cassino, Don Mauro came to warn him that the police were after him for the Anzio fraud. Scrambling over the wall with 150 lire from Don Mauro (and carrying, to his chagrin, only one change of linen and a toothbrush), Magnus plummeted down the hill and after seven hours' scrambling over pathless rocks and gulleys came to a railway line and caught the train to Naples. He had one thought: Lawrence, who would help him turn his book, now revised and ninety thousand words long, into the money that would clear his debts. He reached Taormina on April 26, only to find that the Lawrences were away for several days on a visit to Syracuse in southern Sicily. With less than two lire left, Magnus checked into a hotel and awaited his savior's return.

From this point Lawrence's and Magnus's accounts of their encounter vary. Both agree that Magnus asked Lawrence to go back to Monte Cassino for him and retrieve his belongings and remaining manuscripts. According to Lawrence (writing two years later, in an essay published in 1925) he was frosty, scolding Magnus for moving into the most expensive hotel in town and telling him that he should have done what Lawrence himself would have done: found a cheap room and lived on bread and cheese. But at the time, according to Magnus's report to Norman Douglas, however, Lawrence was far more sympathetic than Frieda. Lawrence, Magnus wrote Douglas, had been most "willing & most nice" when he discovered Magnus at his villa. However: "She, the bitch, met me. . . . In the afternoon I got a note from Lawrence enclosing 50/ [fifty shillings] saying he had been thinking about it & could not help me!"

> I rushed to see him—my mouth was dry—he was out —she was in—I asked her if she knew what he had written me—she said "more or less"—of course—I knew it was her doing. . . . She looked like nails,

but asked me to come later—I did and repersuaded him—he would let me know the next day.

The next day, so Magnus reported to Douglas, brought more indecision but Lawrence was still being "very nice." However, the following day he received a note from Lawrence enclosing two hundred lire and refusing to have any more to do with him as his wife was angry.

Lawrence's version was that he was stern throughout. He says he paid Magnus's hotel bill on the condition that he move out and find humbler lodgings.

Either way, Magnus was as angry as Frieda was. "Finis," he wrote to Douglas from the small pensione to which Lawrence had nudged him, "Lawrence never asked me for a meal or offered a room in his most commodious house." At his wit's end, Magnus said that he had decided to go farther south, to Malta, then on to Egypt (both places under British rule), where he hoped to find a job on a newspaper. However, he added lugubriously, if anything happened to him, Douglas was to have all his manuscripts and papers, and their proceeds.

Magnus had been right about Lawrence's niceness. Lawrence had been genuinely sympathetic to Magnus's plight and willing to help. Even though he was deep into his new novel, *The Lost Girl,* he intensified his efforts on Magnus's behalf. Even while Magnus was still in Taormina, he posted half of the Foreign Legion opus to Unwin in London, with a strong endorsement. He respected the work, he told Unwin, for its stark simplicity, even for its amateurishness. He followed up this move a week later, writing again to Unwin to say that the second half of the Legionnaire memoir was on its way, and that he hoped to have word about it.

By mid-May, traveling either on Lawrence's loan or on money elicited by telegram from a friend in London (or both), Magnus had made his way south to Syracuse to catch the boat from Sicily to Malta. On or about May 5 Lawrence finished *The Lost Girl,* having written in Magnus as the likable Mr. May, the stage manager for the traveling "Red Indian" troupe, who acts the part of an Indian squaw. On May 7 Lawrence decided to go to Malta himself. "Don't know why it sounds so thrilling," he wrote to Compton Mackenzie in Capri. The reason he gave for the spur-of-the-moment junket was that Mary Cannan had been set on seeing the British island naval base in the middle of the Mediterranean, and, not wishing to travel alone, had offered to pay all their expenses. It was not an important trip, Lawrence assured Mackenzie. They would stay in Malta only two days.

That was not how things turned out. Lawrence, Frieda, and Mary got as far as Syracuse only to find that a steamer strike was on and there were no sailings. They checked into a hotel on the front, whereupon the porter brought Lawrence a note. It was from Magnus. He was waiting for the same steamer and staying at another hotel along the front. Might he borrow ninety lire for his hotel bill?

Reluctantly Lawrence met him, and after much hesitation caved in once more, giving Magnus another hundred lire. Exasperation turned to farce when the Lawrences and Mary Cannan, on board the steamer, saw Magnus, in gray coat, gray hat, and gray suede gloves, coming up the gangplank at the very last minute, followed by a porter with a barrow of luggage, soon after to appear on the first-class deck chatting to a British naval commander.

Once on the much smaller island of Malta the Lawrences and Mary Cannan could hardly avoid Magnus, especially as, like most English visitors, they conspicuously headed for the Great Britain Hotel in Valletta. However, Lawrence did not even try to ignore Magnus. In the week before they could get a return steamer to Sicily, Lawrence spent a fair amount of time with his little friend. The two of them went for a drive around the island with two young Maltese whom Lawrence found pleasant if very religious. Together they also went to the tailor. As the weather was baking hot, Lawrence allowed Magnus to talk him into investing six pounds in a pongee suit. He wrote a friend in Capri, "I'm having a silk suit! Knock-out!" And they talked a great deal, particularly one day at Magnus's hotel when they sat together in his bedroom, consuming whisky and soda. On this occasion, Lawrence's essay says, they talked of manuscripts and publishers. However, according to a private and never-published letter Magnus wrote to Douglas much nearer the time, they talked of Lawrence's own homosexual longings. Magnus passed this confidence on in the last letter Douglas ever received from him and in words that suggest that Lawrence had enjoyed some form of sexual act with William Henry Hocking:

> Don't worry about Lawrence writing nasty. He opened his "heart" (!) to me here accidentally. He is looking for bisexual types *for himself.* Spoke of his innocence when he wrote "Twilight" and "Il Duro." Evidently innocent no longer. Didn't like Malta because he thought that the religion or something prevented their sexual expression! I didn't educate him as I could have done even after a few days' stay! He revels in all that is not just within his reach. He wants it to be within his reach. Arrived too late—regrets it. Never speaks of it unless bored to tears by women as here by Mrs Gilbert Cannan & his wife.

Whatever their actual words to each other, Magnus was writing privately in what was a desperate hour, with no reason to lie, while Lawrence was writing for the public about a man who was two years in the grave.

* * *

"No, I don't like him—shall not bother with him any more." So Lawrence, upon returning to Sicily, dismissed Magnus to the painter Jan Juta. In his later essay on Magnus, Lawrence recorded that he had been happy to think of Magnus "shut up in that beastly island" and complained that Magnus kept sending him letters which he did not answer.

In fact, after his return Lawrence told Thomas Seltzer that the purpose of his visit to Malta had been to see a friend, and he continued to correspond with Magnus. Magnus, in turn, sent him postcards inviting him to return to Malta and spend a month. He reminded Lawrence how attractive the Maltese were: "Such good-looking fellows too, and do anything you want."

Lawrence had a heavy load of work; he had resumed *Aaron's Rod* as well as begun *Mr. Noon,* and he was polishing up other writing. Yet he pressed on with his efforts to get "Dregs" published. His enthusiasm intensified even though Unwin had rejected the book. Trying Martin Secker on July 20, he said, "Magnus is going to send you his *Legion* MS. I thought it *awfully good."* He also put in a good word for Magnus with the *English Review.*

Keeping Magnus in touch with his movements, Lawrence wrote him that he had refused a chance to go to the South Seas on Compton Mackenzie's new yacht. ("I'd love a trip to the South Seas," Magnus reported enviously to his "Dearest Norman.") Instead, Magnus informed Douglas, "Lawrence is going north—his buxom wife going to Germany."

Lawrence was going north—but not out of Italy. Instead, he got in touch with Rosalind Baynes at her villa near Florence. "F. thinks of going to Germany second week in August . . . ," he wrote. "I might come & see you."

11

WHERE THE CLIMATE'S SULTRY

September 1920–1922

Here's to the thorn in flower!
"Figs," D. H. Lawrence, September 1920

*L*awrence *followed his interlude with Magnus with his only recorded* act of adultery. The passage in the woman's diary documenting it was kept private until more than a half century after his death.

When Frieda went to Germany in August 1920, Lawrence made excuses to his mother-in-law, whom he had not seen since 1914, for not coming as well. He ought to have gone, considering how fond he was of the old *Baronin* and his sisters-in-law. Instead, after accompanying Frieda as far as Milan and then traveling to Como and Venice with friends, he went to visit Rosalind Baynes.

Rosalind was happy to see him. The previous year in Berkshire he had provided her with much-needed sympathy, strength, and practical support. Then, from Italy, he had sent her meticulous instructions for her own forthcoming difficult journey with a nanny and three small children. He told her to bring an extra photograph for each visa, to be sure to stand near the passport gangway when the boat drew near the dock at Dieppe ("near the Lower deck 1st class cabins, in front") and to remember that "facchino" was the word for the porter that she must instantly seize.

Rosalind and her family had reached Italy in January 1920, two months after Lawrence did. Before leaving England, she had generously helped Godwin Baynes gather the evidence he needed to file a petition to divorce her. Her lover, Kenneth Hooper, admitted paternity of her third daughter, Jennifer Nan, born in 1918, and it was agreed that the child was probably conceived during a night at the Savoy Hotel in October 1917 after Hooper's release from wartime detention. Then with her children and young nanny, Ivy, Rosalind took herself to live abroad for several years until the scandal would have died down. (That there would be scandal was indisputable. Lawrence and Rosalind's father had been quite right in foreseeing the glee with which the British national press would greet the divorce of a prominent London doctor and the free-thinking daughter of a well-known sculptor and Royal Academician. When the case reached court the following April, the *Daily Mirror*'s headlines were "Decree Nisi Against R.A.'s Daughter" and "Feminist Divorced.")

Once in Italy Rosalind was very much in the mood for a new life. She began studying the mandolin and Italian embroidery. She sent the older girls to local schools. She assured Godwin that she had no intention of marrying Hooper, who, she said, now saw her as an "awful feminist" because she refused him any voice in the education of their child and would not accept any money for support. She had chosen Florence as her destination largely on Lawrence's recommendation, and he directed her, too, to the pensione where Norman Douglas lived, although he had misgivings about putting her in proximity to the disreputable Scot. Shortly after, Rosalind found a beautiful villa, Canovaia, in San Gervasio, a tiny village on the way to Fiesole above Florence.

San Gervasio was reached from Florence by a tram line. Rosalind's daughter Chloe later remembered the tram poster advertisements for huge bottles of castor oil, under which were scrawled threats by Mussolini's fascist supporters of the uses to which the product could be put.

The family settled in the Villa Canovaia until the summer heat drove them to the mountains. While they were away an explosion at a nearby ammunition dump blew out all the windows at the Canovaia, forcing them, when they returned, to resettle in Fiesole. For Lawrence, however, arriving for a few weeks in warm September and disliking his own pensione, where he was glared at by English females, the empty villa was ideal. He had eleven (if windowless) rooms all to himself, as well as a romantic hillside garden with a view overlooking the Duomo and the panorama of Florence.

He had not seen Rosalind in nearly a year, although they had corresponded and he had tried to persuade her to bring the girls to visit him and Frieda in Sicily. He now became a frequent visitor to her new home, the Villino Belvedere, and liked climbing up through olive groves along the steep track that passed both villas. He always brought something for the girls—a salamander, perhaps, or a duck—but the main attraction was Rosalind.

At twenty-nine, she was at the height of her beauty—a blend of pre-Raphaelite brown hair, rich coloring, and large brown eyes. (Her mother, Agatha Thornycroft, had been described by Thomas Hardy as the most beautiful woman in England and had been the model for his Tess of the D'Urbervilles.)

On the evening of Lawrence's thirty-fifth birthday, September 11, 1920, Lawrence and Rosalind had supper on the terrace of her villa. They ate mortadella and drank marsala, then walked up the hills behind the house and looked down on the lights of Florence, and talked. Suddenly he said abruptly: "How do you feel about yourself now without sex in your life?"

Rosalind acknowledged that, of course, she missed it. "Well, why don't you have it?" he asked. She answered candidly that she was "damned fastidious." She wanted more "than a few pretty words and then off to bed."

"Yes, damned fastidious!" he replied. "Yes, most people one can hardly bear to come near, far less make love with." Yet he was contemptuous of so-called Love—personal, possessive, and egotistical. Rather, he suggested, "let us think of love as a force outside and getting us. It is a force; a god. The Ancients had it and for them there were no personalisms, and they were men and still had pride."

Then he said, "I do not see why you and I should not have a sex time together." If it was all too complicated, she had simply to say so. The choice was hers.

As Rosalind told her diary, she was astounded at her own happiness. "Yes, indeed I want it," she said, unable to believe that this remarkable man desired her. Shyly, she told him that she had no idea that he felt that way about her. When he laughed but did not answer, she boldly asked him how he reconciled personal fastidiousness with the impersonality of sex. He had a ready answer: "Oh yes," he said, "there must be understanding of the god *together*."

It was the kind of declaration for which she found him, as she later said, a "source of acceptable and exciting wisdom of a kind unheard of until he came." Then he said, "Let's go back," and they scrambled, laughing, down the mountain. Yet when at her villa he asked: "Tonight you won't have me?" she said no, although she knew that she longed to fall into his arms. (Perhaps she did not want to risk another unwanted pregnancy.)

The next day she was elated and prepared her bedroom in anticipation, but when Lawrence came to visit, he made no move. The following day was a Sunday and he came to lunch. They cooked it together—roast beef and Yorkshire pudding—and he played with Nan, the baby. In the afternoon the two of them walked in Fiesole and bought some small brown Italian sorb apples, sucked them, and spat out the skins. They went home, cooked again, and ate out on the terrace. At last he spoke the words she had hoped for: "How good it is here. It is something quite special and lovely, the time, the place, the beloved."

"My heart jumps with joy," wrote Rosalind, recording the scene in the historic present, much in the style of one of Lawrence's earlier women, Helen Corke. "We sit there until it is quite dark, our hands held together in union. And so to bed."

And then? Rosalind's memoir discreetly draws the curtain.

Her family believed that Rosalind and Lawrence had had a genuine love affair—"proper sex," according to her niece Annabel Anrep. The literary evidence is strong. That month in Fiesole Lawrence produced a stream of highly sensual poems in which fruits are a metaphor for the female body; among these works are "Pomegranate," "Peach," "Medlars and Sorb-Apples," and "Figs."

"Figs" is as unambiguous as one of the botany diagrams Lawrence used to draw for his pupils:

> The Italians vulgarly say, it stands for the female part; the fig-fruit:
> The fissure, the yoni,
> The wonderful moist conductivity towards the centre.

The same poem contains a pun on Rosalind's family name, Thornycroft, and a reference to the rose in her first name as well:

> *Here's to the thorn in flower! Here is to Utterance!*
> The brave, adventurous rosaceæ.
>
> Folded upon itself, and secret unutterable . . .
>
> And then the fig has kept her secret long enough.
> So it explodes, and you see through the fissure the scarlet.

More evidence of Lawrence's physical appreciation of Rosalind Baynes can be found in his description of Lady Chatterley: "a ruddy, country-looking girl with soft brown hair and sturdy body, and slow movements, full of unusual energy. She had big, wondering eyes, and a soft mild voice." (His word-sketch also fits exactly Rosalind's portrait by Sir George Clausen.) Constance Chatterley's background, moreover, is Rosalind's: "Her father was the once well-known R.A." She and her sister have been brought up "between artists and cultured socialists." Her husband has studied at Cambridge. Rosalind Baynes has been little recognized as a model for the outline of Constance Chatterley, but the explicit descriptions of her body suggest that, Frieda apart, she was probably the main one. Like Cynthia Asquith, Rosalind (and later Connie Chatterley) marked Lawrence's return to endogamy, the choice of a deeply English woman, rather than a foreigner, as love object.

Rosalind's own romantic account, like the celebratory female imagery of Lawrence's poems, allows the possibility that, in his long battle with sexuality, as wretched as that with his health, Lawrence may have enjoyed a few weeks—or at least one night—of quiet sensual happiness. Rosalind's diary's discreet wording does not rule out the possibility that Lawrence may have been impotent. On the other hand, the sex between them may have been adventurous and liberating. At the time he was working on *Aaron's Rod* and was stuck halfway through. "But where the other 1/2 is coming from, ask the Divine Providence," he wrote Compton Mackenzie.

In *Aaron's Rod,* Aaron Sisson, who has left his English wife and children and fled to Italy, is invited to bed in Florence by a *marchesa,* the American wife of a rich Italian. After making love, they fall asleep. Then (in a scene expurgated from the text and not restored until 1979), Aaron tries a different position: "He slept for a very little while, and woke suddenly, and his desire had an element of cruelty in it: something rather brutal. He took his way with her now, and she had no chance now of the curious opposition, because of the way he took her."

Whatever passed between Lawrence and Rosalind, he hung about at the Villa Canovaia during most of September, resisting Frieda's appeals that he come to Germany. He wrote and apologized again to his mother-in-law, this time with the excuse that it was late in the year: "With the leaves falling it would be sad." He promised to come in the spring. He also let her know that he was making over to her the royalties from the German publication of his books (for the marks would be no good to him out of Germany). Then, having ruled out Germany, he joined Frieda in Venice at the end of September, as planned, and they made their way back to Sicily.

The letters and postcards he sent to Rosalind over the next year confirmed his words about the impersonalism of love; they were the breezy greetings of a married ex-lover who has most decidedly gone back to his wife.

Rosalind (who remarried happily in 1925 to A. E. Popham, the ex-husband of one of her cousins), must have found parts of *Aaron's Rod* singularly apt when it was published the following year. In the novel, Aaron runs over in his mind how he will tell the fond *marchesa* that he will never see her again. He feels slightly guilty.

She had been generous, and the other thing, that he felt blasted afterwards, which was his experience, that was fate, and not her fault. . . .

The years of marriage had made a married man of him, and any other woman than his wife was a strange woman to him, a violation. . . . When a man is married, he is not in love. A husband is not a lover. . . . Well, I am a husband, if I am anything. And I shall never be a lover again, not while I live.

There were other relevant words, too. When the *marchesa* hears Aaron deliver his farewell, she understandingly tells him that she is sure he loves his wife. Not quite love, Aaron responds. "But when one has been married for ten years—and I did love her—then—some sort of bond or something grows . . . some sort of connexion grows between us, you know. And it isn't natural, quite, to break it."

In the autumn of 1920, Lawrence was not only irretrievably married but also had a lot of work to do. The affair with Rosalind coincided with one of the most productive periods of his prodigious working life. At that time he was not only writing *Aaron's Rod* and enough new poems for two volumes, he was also finishing *Studies in Classic American Literature, Education of the People,* and a short story, "The Blind Man," as well as preparing the manuscript of *The Lost Girl* for his typist in Rome and publishers in London and New York.

THE enigma of Lawrence's preoccupation with homosexuality must be weighed against his unswerving wish to get right the relation between male and female. Or even just between himself and Frieda. He was still deeply disturbed by their (or, as he saw it, his) failure to achieve simultaneous orgasm. He even confessed the problem to Compton Mackenzie.

He also demanded submission in some undefined form from Frieda, and she absolutely refused it, whatever it was. She would not consider herself less important than he, nor detached in any way from his ideas or his writing. There is little doubt, however, that she found sexual solace when and where she wanted it. Her pale hair, daring eyes, wide mouth, and full figure retained their power. Now able once more to spend much time in Germany, she had ample freedom, and it was not long before her sister Else and Frieda Gross (who was still living in Ascona, although under strain, with Ernst Frick) were clucking to each other once again about Friedele's behavior.

The full list of Frieda Lawrence's lovers, it has been said, would fill a small telephone book. Unfortunately, the book has not been found. (One lover, who declared himself somewhat belatedly, was an elderly Italian immigrant living in Pittsburgh, Pennsylvania, in 1990. Just before he died, Peppino D'Allura announced that he had been Frieda Lawrence's lover in Taormina in the early 1920s. At the time a mule driver for a wine merchant, D'Allura claimed that one day when he was visiting the Fontana Vecchia, Frieda appeared suddenly, in the nude. She offered him the gift of herself, which he accepted.)

In any event, Lawrence's works of that period shout disillusion with the idea of marriage. *Mr. Noon,* which he had begun the previous May, looks back with facetious objectivity at his mythic honeymoon journey with Frieda. *Aaron's Rod* presents the case of a man abandoning his wife and then finding adultery to be less interesting than submission to a charismatic male leader. *Studies in Classic American Literature,* as misogynistic as it is brilliant, blames Hawthorne's adulteress, Hester Prynne, for seducing the minister, Dimmesdale, with the "very possessive love" that led her to wear the Scarlet Letter. And *The Lost Girl* is a fantasy of how a woman ought to behave: a well-brought-up Midlands bourgeoise, Alvina Houghton, exchanges her profession and her country for life in a remote Italian farmhouse, with a primitive, passionate husband who is uncommunicative except in bed.

But the power struggle between himself and Frieda was unresolved. Almost in revenge, Lawrence had to plunge on in a bitter, angry search for a political correlative to his marriage in the so-called leadership novels.

Aaron's Rod, like its successors *Kangaroo* and *The Plumed Serpent,* could equally be described as a flight-from-Woman novel. Considered Lawrence's lesser works, too autobiographical and polemical, all three are psychologically revealing, for they show him making the transition from his old faith in "true marriage" into an ideal of leadership born of anger at the female.

Aaron's Rod opens with a scene for which later feminists would not forgive Lawrence: a man walks out on his wife and children on Christmas Eve, with two little girls decorating the Christmas tree, and the smell of mince pies baking in the oven. It should be a time when home is most attractive, but as Lawrence makes clear, it is also when home is most claustrophobic to a man who feels trapped by women and who lives in a household full of them. (Aaron's third child, the baby, is also a girl.) When the eldest daughter aggressively plays with his favorite tree ornament, a blue ball, and, predictably, breaks it (Lawrence gives no sign of intentional double entendre in this chapter, entitled "The Blue Ball"), Aaron goes out into the night to buy Christmas candles, and keeps on going.

Aaron's wanderings with his flute—he is a musician—take on a dreamlike quality. He suppresses thoughts of the females left behind; he sends them money; that is enough. He wants to be alone. In London, taken up by a fashionable literary set, he meets a small thin dark man with a blond Norwegian wife. Aaron feels strangely kin to this wise sardonic man (whose odd name, Rawdon Lilly, echoes Lawrence's own) and who is the kind of Nietzschean alter ego described in Yeats's poem "Ego Dominus Tuus":

> I call to the most mysterious one who yet
> Shall walk the wet stands by the edge of the stream
> And look most like me, being indeed my double,
> And prove of all imaginable things
> The most unlike, being my anti-self.

Lilly's mystical role in Aaron's destiny is revealed when Aaron collapses in Covent Garden and Lilly appears from out of the crowd to rescue him and take him home to his flat. Aaron, it seems, has influenza. Lilly, nursing him like a mother, gives an oil massage which must rank on any list of the most embarrassing passages in Lawrence—not only for the unconsciousness of its homoeroticism ("quickly he uncovered the blond lower body of his patient") but also for its emetic intent. Lilly rubs every inch of Aaron's body "as mothers do their babies whose bowels don't work."

(As a bedridden child, Lawrence must have endured the full range of home remedies an overworked Victorian mother had at her command. A brighter legacy of his long battle with illness is, in *Aaron's Rod* as in "England, My England," the voice of the doctor. Curt and tired, the practitioner who is called in examines Aaron impatiently: "What's the matter with you, man! . . . Can't you pull yourself together?")

As Aaron recovers, he and Lilly discuss the sorry facts of life: primarily, that women will sacrifice eleven men for one baby. Aaron pours out his discontent with marriage—"I hate married people who are two in one—stuck together like two jujube lozenges." Lilly, however, appears to have solved the problem; he and his foreign wife, whose name is Tanny, are childless, and her long trips home to Norway to visit her mother give them long periods apart, "free of each other and eternally inseparable."

Tanny wants children badly, Lilly says, but he himself is glad to be without them. Children would give her a new battlefield on which to fight him. Aaron can only agree: conception is entrapment, a trick played by the woman upon the man to get the children for whom she will forsake him, and whom he must support at the risk of becoming a criminal. It is no debate, because both men are on the same side. Lilly, however, has a vision of a new and better order: "Men have got to stand up to the fact that manhood is more than children—and then force women to admit it."

Aaron, recovered, takes himself off to Italy, making *Aaron's Rod* the third Lawrence novel in a row in which the leading character abandons England—"death's other kingdom"—to be reborn on the Continent. He goes to Florence, where his grievances mount against his abandoned wife. He thinks back to her fierce sexual demands ("oh God, the agony of her desire for him") and the way he punished her. In spite of giving her all the passionate sex she craved—he was a passionate lover, he insists—he withheld "the central core of himself." He also beat her, then added adultery to his brutality. He is not sorry: "She had asked for all she got."

Yet his brief affair with the American *marchesa* teaches Aaron that he can have no other woman. The solution? Rawdon Lilly, deus ex machina, turns up (giving Lawrence the chance to write a comic scene of English expatriates in Florence in which Norman Douglas stars as "James Argyle") and tells Aaron that he must find a heroic male to whom he can submit. "And whom shall I submit to?" Aaron asks Lilly at the end of *Aaron's Rod,* looking into Lilly's face. Lilly answers, dark and remote, "Your soul will tell you."

The real answer, said Lawrence's old friend Richard Aldington, writing a preface to the novel in 1950, is "David Herbert Lawrence."

The Lawrences were in Rome when the news reached them that Maurice Magnus had committed suicide. In Malta, on the morning of November 4, 1920, two detectives had come up to Magnus in the street and asked him to accompany them to the police station. Willingly, was the reply, but as he was only in his sandals, would they allow him to change? The pair accompanied Magnus back to his house and waited while he went in. He did not come out. When they broke the door down, they found him on the bed with a bottle of cyanide at his side and just enough life left in him to receive extreme unction from a priest.

He was three days short of forty-four. Just before he took the poison, he had dropped his last letter to Norman Douglas out of the window in the hope (justified, as it turned out) that someone would post it. His meager personal effects, attested to by two American citizens and the American consul in Malta, included a pince-nez, a silver card case, two pairs of white duck trousers, and an old leather suitcase containing manuscripts.

"*En voila fini,*" said Lawrence curtly, breaking the news in a letter to Norman Douglas, having heard it from Don Mauro at Monte Cassino. "Here it rains hard and I get rather sick of it."

Ghosts were very much on his mind, however, when two months later, in January 1921, he broke off *Aaron's Rod* and pushed on with *Mr. Noon,* now called "Lucky Noon." He hoped to finish the new book that month. Writing a retrospective on his early months with Frieda gave him a chance to pay off an old score against Udo von Henning, the lover with whom Frieda had betrayed him in their first week together in Metz. Lawrence knew that Henning had been killed at the very start of the war, and the narrator of *Mr. Noon* allows himself somewhat guiltily to rejoice:

Fortunately the war came in time, and allowed him to fling his dross
of flesh disdainfully down the winds of death, so that now he probably
flies in all kinds of comforted glory. I hope really he's not flying in our
common air, for I shouldn't like to breathe him. That is really my
greatest trouble with disembodied spirits. I am so afraid of breathing
them in, mixed up with air, and getting bronchitis from them.

For "bronchitis," read "tuberculosis"; for "disembodied spirits," read
"Mother." These thoughts, floating so persistently in the back of
Lawrence's mind, became so allied that he believed that "mothers who
love their sons too much give them tuberculosis."

The pent-up yearning to be a parent, a psychic healer, and a preacher
produced *Psychoanalysis and the Unconscious,* the first of two psychology books he wrote in Italy. The success of Barbara Low's *Introduction
to Psychoanalysis* convinced him that subject was "in the air now." With
his engaging limitless audacity and energy, he believed his mind was the
measure of all things, even human anatomy. He sounded off on the birth
of consciousness, a phenomenon which he located in the solar plexus.
Passionately he criticized what he saw as the Freudian reductionist view
of the unconscious as the source of neurosis and repressed incestuous
desire: "the cellar where the mind keeps its own bastard spawn." To him
the unconscious was nobler, the seat of the natural impulses, which were
"the well-head, the fountain of real motivity" and better expressed without being cerebralized. He had immersed himself in the ideas and con-
cepts of analysis while arguing with his Freudian friends, and when he
produced what he called "six little essays on the Freudian unconscious,"
he commented to Evelyn Scott, a literary critic in London, "Oh what a
jew-jaw it will seem to you."

IF he had not been so restless, they might have stayed at Taormina
forever. Frieda loved it. The Fontana Vecchia had a view of Mount Etna
and the sea, and was very cheap—only two thousand lire (ten dollars) a
year. At the beginning of 1921, Lawrence took it for another year, but
almost instantly pronounced himself weary of expatriate social
Taormina and went to a fancy-dress ball wearing his old gray jacket.
"To hell with them," he said. He dreamed of buying a sailing boat with
his friend Robert Mountsier, who had become his American agent, and
cruising the world, but that would take organization. For the moment,
he decided to explore a stranger environment closer to home. On January 5, he and Frieda left for Sardinia. Perhaps, Lawrence thought, they
might move there.

Few travel writers can have wrung so much out of an eight-day trip.
Sea and Sardinia, finished one month later, swiftly serialized, then pub-

lished in America in book form the following year, is his most popular piece of travel writing. A model of its genre, unashamedly personal, preoccupied with food, discomforts, casual conversations, and irrelevant associations, it captures the place and people more sharply than a documentary film. Casting Frieda as the "Queen Bee" or "q.b." and describing how they carried in their luggage a little portable stove which they called their "kitchenino," it shows them as a comfortable pair of married wanderers for whom the movements of packing are as familiar as those of making love.

In Sardinia Lawrence suffered his usual problem, the initial flush of enthusiasm fading the first time he was crossed. He began by loving Sardinia because it was not Italian, only to be swiftly enraged by the Sardinians because they were more stupid than the Italians. He would have to find somewhere else. Perhaps the run-down Connecticut farmhouse an admirer was offering to lease him cheaply might be a better idea. He was so tempted—he thought he might grow peaches in Connecticut—that he borrowed two hundred pounds from Mary Cannan, even though, as he told Mountsier, "I am terrified of borrowed money, but prepared to take risks. . . . I want to live on my English money, if possible, without touching the American." His American income was swelling; he received an advance of five hundred dollars on *The Lost Girl* in January and fifty dollars for "Tortoises" in March, and the quick sale of *Psychoanalysis and the Unconscious*—due for publication in 1921—gave him more evidence that America appreciated him. Above all, he needed to move. Italy was on the verge of tearing itself apart between the *socialisti* and the *fascisti*. There would be nothing like the Russian Revolution, "no one smash," just genuine Italian "Guelph and Ghibelline business," and he wanted to be out of it.

LATE in the spring of 1921 he began his long-postponed trip to Germany. Frieda had gone to Baden-Baden in March, in response to a telegram saying her mother was very ill. He had fought against joining her, even reopening his offer to David Eder to come to Palestine for a couple of months and write it up. (The book he now proposed to Eder was "Sketch Book of Zion.") He wondered if there was a radical gulf in consciousness between Jew and Gentile. Scolding the writer Louis Golding for writing a novel that was not sufficiently Jewish, Lawrence said that he liked to think there were deep-rooted differences between the races as between men, but he was not sure. He could not really see any great difference even between himself and Zionists, he told Golding: "They seem like one of us English just doing a Zion stunt."

Yet to non-Jews he did not speak so sympathetically. Growing discontented with Mountsier as his American representative, Lawrence seemed to see Mountsier's chief virtue as his not being Jewish. "I hate Jews," he wrote Mountsier, referring to his avant-garde New York publisher, Thomas Seltzer, who was going to bring out *Women in Love,* "and I want to learn to be more *wary* of them."

On the way to join Frieda in Baden-Baden, he stopped in Capri, where Compton Mackenzie introduced him to some very un-Jewish American expatriates about his own age, Earl and Achsah Brewster. Earl, born in Ohio, and Achsah, born in Connecticut, looked like New England Puritans—neat, austere, quiet—but were painters, who used their modest private incomes to live abroad with their small daughter, pursuing their passions, painting and Buddhism. Tenants of the Fontana Vecchia a decade earlier, they were instantly drawn to Lawrence, as he was to them, even though they personified the earnest seriousness he mocked in Americans.

Earl Brewster in particular was bowled over. Nothing in his expectations of the famous writer prepared him for the impact of Lawrence's physical presence. He saw before him a "tall delicate man . . . carelessly dressed in a pale homespun jacket."

> His face was pale; his hands long, narrow, capable; his eyes clear-seeing and blue; his brown hair and red beard glowing like flames from the intensity of his life, his voice flexible, medium pitch, with often a curious, plaintive note, sometimes in excitement rising high in key.

It was a changed Germany that Lawrence saw on his first visit since the war—tired, very sad, with not a uniform in sight. The old order had gone, he wrote Seltzer: "Hohenzollern and Nietzsche and all. And the age of love and peace and democracy with it. There will be an era of war ahead." Jesus had given way to Mars, but Lawrence was not unhappy. He had come to believe that men should make war, not love.

He was happier when he and Frieda had settled (in separate rooms) in a country inn outside Baden-Baden, where her mother lived in a gentlefolks' retirement home. Germany was a welcome, cool, and orderly refuge from Sicily—"the little children never beg"—and cheap, too: about six or seven shillings a day, eight including wine, for "good food—good German sausages and beer, *good* Rhinewine, *good* whipped cream, and the first strawberries." In many ways, he and Frieda were much more at home there than in Italy. They sent toys to Catherine Carswell's little boy and tried to find a German family to take Eder's stepson, Stephen Guest. Lawrence hoped also to bring Ada to Germany, uniting the two halves of his family, and he asked his sister to send him a raincoat.

Hardly had Lawrence arrived when Else's husband, Edgar Jaffe, died in a sanatorium in Munich at the age of fifty-five. There seems to have been little grief among the von Richthofens, and no harking back to Jaffe's brief days in power. Yes, Jaffe was his brother-in-law, Lawrence admitted to Koteliansky; the death had been reported in *The Times* of London (which described Jaffe as professor of economics at the Munich Academy of Commerce). "But he had gone cracked after being Bolshevist Minister of finance for Bavaria." Lawrence told Else he was glad Edgar was dead: "Better death than ignominious living on. Life had no place for him after the war." Anti-Semitism may have contributed to Lawrence's lack of sympathy for Jaffe. His native prejudices had been roused by his return to Germany where he saw "moneyhogs in motorcars, mostly Jews" among those profiteering from the postwar collapse.

Jaffe's death left Else comfortable for life. Still the steady companion of Alfred Weber, she was forbidden by Jaffe's will from selling any of his valuable furniture, jewelry, paintings, or objets d'art. But his money, apart from the bequests to the children, was at her disposal, and she spent freely. She continued to send money to Frieda Gross in Ascona, giving her some jewels as well, and contributed to the support of Peter, the son of Otto Gross; Gross had died on March 13 in an asylum in the Pankow district of Berlin. (As the years went by, Else would be troubled by dreams of a reproachful Jaffe, crying, "Else, Else! What have you done with the money?")

Lawrence, in contrast, was still watching his pennies. He instructed Mountsier, who was arriving from America and passing through London on his way to visit them in Germany, to bring two pairs of cotton underpants for summer, not to cost more than three shillings sixpence per pair, and "*not* to come below the knee." He added tea and three tubes of Kolynos toothpaste to the American shopping list and promised to pay for it all when Mountsier arrived.

Immersed in Frieda's family—Else with her three children had arrived from Munich, and his mother-in-law was recovering from a severe illness—he decided that "relatives are a mistake, and that's the end of it. One should never see one's relations—or anybody else's." The constant speaking of rapid imperfect German affected his English idiom. His sister Emily must have been astonished to get a postcard from him saying "On Friday comes Else from Munich here to this hotel." Mountsier got much the same: "On 1st July comes my sister-in-law from Munich: but speaks good English."

In June *Women in Love,* Lawrence's most ambitious (and most Germanic) work, reached the English literary world. (It had been published in New York the year before and thus appeared just ahead of the two main landmarks of literary modernism, *Ulysses* and *The Waste Land,* both published in 1922.) Critics of the day did not have the benefit of Lawrence's advice to his old friend Arthur McLeod—"Don't look in my novels for the old stable ego of character." Even so, reviewers noticed

Women in Love's revolutionary spirit and its use of characters as mere vehicles for the ideas of the author.

Women in Love, said a reviewer in *The Dial,* an avant-garde American magazine, fell into the category of confessions rather than of a novel. "Having written it, Lawrence might turn philosopher or priest. It is the last word of his living truth. Anything further in this nature, would necessarily be mere exposition." In London, in *The Nation and Athenaeum,* John Middleton Murry put paid to any vestige of friendship when he blasted the book: "It may be that we are benighted in the old world, and that he belongs to the new . . . [but] by the knowledge that we have we can only pronounce it sub-human and bestial."

But Lawrence looked forward, not back. He asked his London publisher to send a copy of the book to Frieda Gross in Ascona, and settled back to work—outdoors under the trees, as was his habit—on his myriad unfinished projects. These included *Fantasia of the Unconscious,* the sequel to his early psychology book, in which, chattily apostrophizing the reader, he makes many of the harsh political and sexual points of *Aaron's Rod:* "Leaders—this is what mankind is craving" and "Fight for your life, men," and *"The great mass of humanity should never learn to read and write—never."* As if recognizing the outrageousness of some of his statements, he begs in *Fantasia:* "Help me to be serious, dear reader."

He used this same disconcerting archaism—the address to the "gentle reader"—in *Mr. Noon.* Whatever its other uses to him—to convey flippancy or to distance himself from highly personal material—talking to the reader was a way of writing fast, and his engines of production were running at full speed.

So quick was Lawrence with his pen that he continued to make little distinction between writing and rewriting. Promising Kot that he would help him polish up some stories translated from the Russian, Lawrence said, "I shall depart into the woods to write the stories when they come." (The editor of the collected correspondence of Lawrence and Koteliansky corrected this statement with a footnote: "Lawrence means, of course, 'rewrite the stories.' ")

Lawrence was honest and straightforward in his financial dealings with his collaborators. He did not object to making quick money by helping out—his adept brushwork quickly transformed pedestrian translations into lively tales—but he tried not to overshadow his co-authors. When *The Dial* published Ivan Bunin's "The Gentleman from San Francisco," describing it as "translated from the Russian by D. H. Lawrence and S. S. Koteliansky," Lawrence was furious—"impudent people, I had told them not to put my name"—and he scolded Kot for sending him half of the thirty dollars they were paid for it.

In August, far from being tired of relatives, he and Frieda sought out more. They left Baden-Baden and, walking part of the way, crossed the

Black Forest and Lake Constance to Austria to join Frieda's pretty younger sister, Nusch, her husband, Max von Schreibershofen, and their son and daughter at a villa on a lake near Salzburg. There they enjoyed themselves, climbing, swimming, and rowing. There too they had separate quarters—perhaps because of Lawrence's cough. He complained of feeling unable to breathe.

FINISHING *Aaron's Rod* and the *Fantasia* in the bosom of Frieda's family, Lawrence faced the incomplete *Mr. Noon* with its recognizable portraits of his in-laws, including the just-dead Jaffe. He decided to withhold the second part, with its German setting, from publication. It was "dangerous," he said.

Until then, whenever Lawrence called some of his writing dangerous, he was thinking of sex, the censors, and the lending libraries. But that summer he learned that authors have one other natural enemy: lawyers. Following the English publication of *Women in Love* it did not take long for Lawrence's former disciple in Cornwall, Philip Heseltine, to recognize himself and his wife, Puma, in the characters of Halliday and Pussum, nor to contact his solicitors, who threatened Lawrence's London publisher, Martin Secker, with a suit for libel.

On their way back to Sicily, the Lawrences got their passports renewed in Florence. Frieda's photograph shows her gone native, costumed as if for *Cavalleria Rusticana,* with a head scarf worn low over her brow and tied behind. It describes her as five feet, four and a half inches tall, with gray eyes and light-brown hair. Lawrence, according to his passport, was five feet, nine inches tall, with blue-gray eyes and light-brown hair. Making their way down to Siena and Rome, and stopping at Capri, where Frieda met the Brewsters for the first time, they did not get back to the Fontana Vecchia until late September, when the worst of the heat had passed. Lawrence had become almost as afraid of the Sicilian summer as of the English winter.

The first order of business was to revise *Women in Love* to stave off Heseltine's libel action. This he did by switching the hair colors of the characters in question, making Pussum fair and Halliday dark, instead of vice versa as they were in real life and his original text. In the end, however, Secker had to agree to pay Heseltine fifty pounds and withdraw all outstanding copies of the first English edition from circulation.

Lawrence was furious about the settlement and called it "hush-money." He sounded off to Kot: "Well, they are both such abject shits it is a pity they cant be flushed down a sewer." But from then on he was more guarded about boasting that he had captured people "to the life." He wondered uneasily if Norman Douglas might identify himself as James Argyle in the as yet unpublished *Aaron's Rod.*

Well he might have worried. Lawrence's Argyle was Douglas to the life, instantly and gleefully recognized by all who knew him, with his "wicked whimsicality that was very attractive, when levelled against someone else" and "his face all red and softened and inflamed, his eyes gone small and wicked under his bushy grey brows."

On November 5, 1921, there came a letter which, like the invitation to Germany in 1912, changed Lawrence's life. It was sent from Taos, New Mexico, by Mabel Dodge Sterne, a wealthy patron of the arts. Most un-English in style, it was rolled up like a papyrus and covered with handwriting—the black bold penmanship of an American heiress—so large that the words looked magnified. Mrs. Sterne introduced herself as an admirer of *Sea and Sardinia* and invited him to come and apply his genius for description to a magical place of mountain desert at an altitude of seven thousand feet, inhabited by Indians who lived in pyramid houses and worshipped the sun. As a lure, she enclosed leaves of a pungent Indian herb and a bit of a medicinal root. She also offered him house and subsistence and a chance to join her crusade, which was to "bring together the two ends of humanity—our own thin end, and the last dark strand from the previous, pre-white era."

Lawrence liked the sound of Taos; it began with the same letters as Taormina. He nibbled the root, which tasted of licorice, sniffed the leaves, and wrote back that same afternoon saying, "Truly, the q-b and I would like to come to Taos—there are no little bees."

Scrupulously self-reliant as ever, he told Mrs. Sterne that he had about two thousand dollars in his American bank and would look after the costs of the voyage himself, as well as their living expenses in Taos. If she would cable and tell him precisely what it would cost to live, he would pay for the cost of the cable. He and his wife needed no servants; they did all their own work, even washing the floors, themselves. He had several other questions: Were the Indians sad and dying out? What did the prosperous Americans in the area do? And what was the nearest port? He did have one fear: "Is there a colony of rather dreadful sub-arty people?" But he dismissed it: "Even if there is, it couldn't be worse than Florence." (He was soon to learn how very wrong he was.)

To go to America made sound financial sense. The United States clearly was going to continue to provide him with the best part of his income, and he calculated that novels with American settings would probably sell better. His only real concern in making this lightning decision was that he must avoid "that awful New York altogether."

Frieda wrote separately to thank Mrs. Sterne for giving them the push they needed to get them out of the stultifying colony of Italianate Englishmen. She saw that the expatriate hothouse of Taormina was no good for Lawrence, "a man who wants something genuine."

But Lawrence's readiness to go had as much to do with his physical as his financial state. Having taken ill in Capri, once back in Sicily he found that Italy had "gone a little rancid in my mouth"; he couldn't get the taste out and was, he said, in a hell of a temper. He was in bed much of the following two months, and fought back thoughts of death. Yet, writing to Catherine Carswell, he spoke of making a will and, in the same breath, of his fascination with the Etruscans, worshippers of the afterlife, whose cities of the dead were scattered around Sicily and central Italy. To Kot, he disclaimed any suspicion that the sudden determination to go to America was linked with his health. "You will say it is just my winter influenza," he said defensively. "But finally I shall go."

A month in bed hardly stemmed a flow of work that would have put a healthy writer to shame. By early December he was sending off to his New York and London agents a load of finished manuscripts, including six unpublished short stories, among them "The Captain's Doll," "The Ladybird," and "The Horse-Dealer's Daughter," as well as a new version of "The Fox," to which he had "put a long tail." He did not know if he would ever finish *Mr. Noon*.

He was determined to leave Europe with a clean slate—all his stories finished, typed, proofs corrected; all his accounts settled—and with as much money as possible in the pipeline. But he would have worked hard anyway. When he wrote to Earl Brewster, "If I hadn't my own stories to amuse myself with I should die, chiefly of spleen," it was as clear an admission as he ever made that he worked to keep alive. Mrs. Sterne knew about his poor health. She had heard from Leo Stein (Gertrude Stein's brother, who had met Lawrence in Florence), "I wonder which will give out first: his lungs or his wits."

Sick in bed as usual at Christmas—it saved him from going out to a horrible Christmas dinner, he wrote cheerily to Kot—he pored over steamship and cargo boat schedules, trying to find a way to sail to the warm part of America without passing through New York. He wrote letter after letter, hunting out exotic routes: Naples to Galveston, Bordeaux to New Orleans. He even wondered about sailing direct to Los Angeles or San Francisco.

His enthusiasm for the unseen Taos mounted as 1922 began. Nothing in the East, he assured Mabel, could offer him the Indians and "the old sun magic." On January 2 he turned down Brewster's invitation to Ceylon. He told Mabel that he would be in New Mexico by March at the latest, and that he and Frieda would sail from Bordeaux on January 15. But as the "flu" held on and he had severe headaches, the prospect of reaching the French port in time receded and he reluctantly booked passage on the only alternative: Palermo to New York on February 6. Yet letter after letter shows him "chasing ships to get to New Orleans, so as to avoid New York."

In the end, he could not face New York. The fear of its atmosphere—

especially in winter—that had paralyzed him late in 1915 had now grown to the force of superstition. Sick, exhausted, terrified, he received a letter from Brewster in Ceylon on January 18 like a message from destiny. In a flash, he changed all his plans. Just as he had accepted the summons to New Mexico the day it came, he replied to Brewster the same day: "Suddenly, for the first time, I suddenly feel you may be right and I wrong: that I am kicking against the pricks." The East, he now saw, was the source of life and truth; America was only the extreme periphery. "Oh God, must one go to the extreme limit, then to come back?" All became clear. The road to Taos lay through Ceylon. He cancelled the Palermo–New York booking and began investigating ships to Colombo.

BEFORE he could leave, there was some unfinished business: the manuscript of Maurice Magnus. On December 21, 1921, from his sickbed, Lawrence wrote to Norman Douglas:

> Dear Douglas,
>
> Apparently the shades of Magnus are going to give us no peace. Michael Borg [one of Magnus's creditors in Malta] & Don Mauro both wrote and asked me if I would help to get the "Legion" ms published. I said I would try in America,—thought I could do nothing in Europe. —I don't know who really is responsible for the MS. But I set to write an introduction giving all I knew about M.—not unkindly, I hope.* I wanted also portraits of him and of his mother—photographs. Do you agree to my doing this? I wish you ["you" is underlined three times] would do it really, and let me stand clear. If you will do it, I will write to an American publisher for you. —If you don't want, then I'll go ahead, rather unwillingly. Can you tell me about the Hohenzollern myth?—who was the mother, and who the grandfather. If I went ahead, I should propose to an American publisher to buy the thing outright—for whatever he'd give: 400 dollars, or more if possible. Then if you could agree with Michael Borg to let the Malta debts be paid first—about £60, I believe—then out of what remained I could have a bit for my introduction & the money he owes me—some £23 you know—or even if I had just £20 to clear the debt—and you the rest. I've got an agent in New York—he might manage something. I should like Michael Borg to be paid: he is poor enough, and Magnus should never have let him in. And even if you only got about £20 it is better than a slap in the eye.
>   But to tell the truth I'd like best to be out of it altogether. If you'll

---

* Someone, probably Douglas, underlined "not unkindly, I hope" in green and put a large "!" in the margin.

Lawrence as a child in a group family portrait: left to right, front row, Ada, Lydia, Bert (David Herbert), Arthur; back row, Emily, George, Ernest.

Nottingham Road in Eastwood in 1911.

Lawrence's birthplace: 8a
Victoria Street, Eastwood, where
his mother turned the front room
into a shop to supplement her
husband's wages as a miner.

4

5

From 1908 to the end of 1911, Lawrence taught at the Davidson Road School, Croydon—one of the new turn-of-the-century state schools described by Sherlock Holmes to Watson as "light-houses, my boy, beacons of the future, capsules with hundreds of bright little seeds in each, out of which will spring the wiser, better England of the future."

The young schoolmaster in 1908.

The women in Lawrence's bachelor life

Louie Burrows, Lawrence's fiancée from 1910 to early 1912.

Jessie Chambers, the closest friend of his youth, who launched his literary career, he said, "like a princess cutting a thread."

Alice Dax and her daughter Phyllis, born in October 1912, the child who Alice said "would never have been conceived but for an unendurable passion which only *he* [Lawrence] had roused and my husband had slaked."

Helen Corke, the Croydon schoolteacher who inspired *The Trespasser*.

Marie Jones with her
husband, John,
Lawrence's landlords
on Colworth Road,
Croydon.

11

10

Ada, Lawrence's younger sister, who
nursed him back to health in
Croydon in 1911 and to whom he
said, "No one understands but you."

Edward Garnett, Duckworth's reader and Lawrence's early mentor, who cut *Sons and Lovers* drastically.

Lydia Lawrence during her last illness in 1910.

The rising young author, whose new novel, *Sons and Lovers*, was widely reviewed in 1913.

THE LADIES' FIELD   JULY 26, 1913

BOOKS OF   THE DAY.

By E. M. Alpe.

MR. D. H. LAWRENCE.
Whose new novel, "Sons and Lovers," is reviewed on this page.

15

Frieda von Richthofen as a young girl, ready and eager for what the future might bring.

(opposite) An intimate moment between Frieda and Ernest Weekley in Germany around the time of their engagement.

16

The von Richthofen sisters of Metz, c. 1895: Frieda (center), flanked by the brains of the family, Else (left), and the beauty, Nusch (right).

18 Agnes and Charles Weekley, with their son Ernest and his young German bride.

Frieda's bohemian circle
before she met Lawrence. Her
lovers: (top) the Austrian psychoanalyst Dr. Otto Gross of
Graz (also the lover of her sister Else Jaffe and many others) and (bottom) the Swiss
anarchist and artist Ernst
Frick of Ascona.

21

The Jaffes: Edgar and
Else, with their children,
Friedel, Marianne, and
the baby, Peter—Otto
Gross's son—born
December 24, 1907 (the
year in which Frieda
Weekley had her affair
with Gross).

22

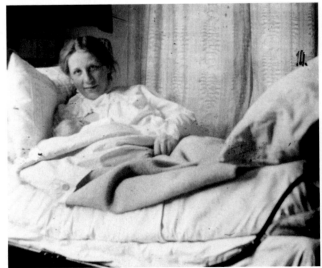

The Magna Mater: Frieda
Schloffer Gross, Otto Gross's
wife and Else Jaffe's best friend,
who bore children both to her
husband and to Ernst Frick, her
subsequent lover.

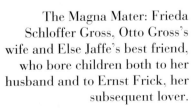

Elsa (left), Barby, and Monty: the children left behind, longing for the mother they were not allowed to mention. Lawrence would not let the grieving Frieda mention them either.

Lawrence's cherished *Schwiegermutter*, the Baroness Anna von Richthofen.

The wedding party, Kensington, July 13, 1914: Katherine Mansfield, second from left, and John Middleton Murry, right, were witnesses for Lawrence and Frieda.

Katherine Mansfield and John
Middleton Murry, who
joined the Lawrences in
Berkshire and in Cornwall.

Part of the cluster of cottages at Higher Tregerthen,
Zennor, Cornwall. Had Lawrence and Frieda not been
evicted as possible German spies in 1917, they might
have lived there forever—burrowed, Lawrence thought,
like a fox under the hill.

William Henry Hocking, the handsome farmer
from Lower Tregerthen Farm, to whom
Lawrence was strongly attracted during his
Cornish years.

Lawrence's Ladies, the two titled Englishwomen who helped him through his difficulties during the First World War: (left) Lady Ottoline Morrell with her lover, the Hon. Bertrand Russell, and (below) Lady Cynthia Asquith and her middle son, Michael.

31

Maurice Magnus (left) and
Norman Douglas (below), the
Florentine expatriates whom
Lawrence captured brilliantly
in his introduction to Magnus's
Memoir of the Foreign Legion.
The introduction, written after
Magnus's suicide, led to a
celebrated literary row,
launched by Douglas.

32

33

"A ruddy, country-looking girl with soft brown hair and sturdy body, and slow movements, full of unusual energy. She has big, wondering eyes...." Lawrence's description of Constance Chatterley in *Lady Chatterley's Lover* serves equally well for Rosalind Thornycroft Baynes.

34

Rosalind Thornycroft
Baynes, with her
daughter Bridget.

35

Lawrence and Frieda with friends on an outing to the
Disappearing River near Thirroul, Australia, the country of
which Lawrence said: "in truth I sit easier in my skin here
than anywhere."

Which was the real Kangaroo? Australian Major-General Charles Rosenthal (right), S. S. Koteliansky, "Kot" (bottom left), and Dr. David M. Eder (top left) have been suggested as models for Ben Cooley, "Kangaroo," the Diggers' leader in Lawrence's Australian novel.

The first couple of Taos, New Mexico: Mabel Dodge Stern, c. 1917; Tony Luhan, 1920.

The Hon. Dorothy Brett in Taos,
c. 1923, posing in her new
Western hat.

Kiowa Ranch on Lobo Mountain north
of Taos. Lawrence was so averse to the
possession of property that he insisted
that Frieda be its legal owner.

43

Lawrence and Frieda baking
bread at Kiowa Ranch.

44

Frieda with Witter Bynner
(left) and Willard "Spud"
Johnson in 1923 on the eve
of their trip to Mexico.

Frieda and Lawrence at their house
in Chapala, Mexico, where he began
The Plumed Serpent in 1923.

Lawrence and Frieda, leaving
the United States in September
1925, after his tuberculosis had
been diagnosed.

47

The new protectors: (top) Aldous and Maria Huxley with their Bugatti in the south of France in the 1930s; (bottom) Richard Aldington displaying the confidence that so annoyed Lawrence during their disastrous holiday at Port-Cros in 1928. Brigit Patmore, Aldington's lover, hovers decorously submerged.

48

On the beach: Lawrence, with his sister Ada Clarke, probably taken in 1927 in Lincolnshire during his last visit to England.

Villa Mirenda, the spacious villa on a hilltop outside of Florence where the Lawrences had the whole top floor and where he wrote *Lady Chatterley's Lover* in 1926–27.

51

Norman Douglas on holiday in the Italian Tyrol with Pino Orioli, whose bookshop in Florence published *Lady Chatterley's Lover* in 1928.

Fight with an Amazon, painted by Lawrence at the Villa Mirenda, leaves little doubt about the models for the struggling couple.

52

Paris. March. 26. 1929.

Total money received in English cheques. to date. £1224 - 5 - 3

" " " in cash " " £ 136 - 17 - 0

" " " in dollar cheques " " £ 268 - 4 - 0

gross receipts . Mar. 26. 1929 £ 1629 .. 6 .. 3

total cost to date £ . 364 . 10 .. 0

gross profits to date = £1264 . 16 .. 3

total profit to date £ 1264 . 16 .. 3

10% of gross profits = 126 .. 9 .. 0
already paid to Pino = 102 .. 10 .. 0
due to Pino 23 .. 19 - 0

Paid to Pino Orioli as 10% discount. £24. March 26. 1929
to Carletto £ 1

To Pino & Carletto £ 25 March 26./ 29

final gross profit £ 1239 .. 16 .. 3 . March 26 . 1929

Paid in all to Orioli for percentage £126. – to Carletto £8. – March 26 1929

to Pino to date. £10 .. 10 - 0 . Florence. 10 July 1929

" Carletto " " £1.. 0 - 0 " .. - - -

53

A page from the neat account book in which Lawrence kept track of sales of his privately printed *Lady Chatterley's Lover*.

54

Lawrence's passport photograph, taken in February 1929, the year before his death.

Capitano Angelo Ravagli with the family he left for Frieda. His younger son, Federico, born in 1927, was named in her honor.

56

The grave at Vence where Lawrence was buried on March 4, 1930.

The Lawrence chapel at Kiowa Ranch, containing Ravagli's home-made rose window and what may or may not be Lawrence's ashes.

All friends now: Mabel, Frieda, and Brett on the steps of Kiowa Ranch, 1935.

The survivors: (top) Mabel and Tony Luhan at the Big House, Los Gallos, 1949, the twenty-fifth year of their marriage; (bottom) Mr. and Mrs. Angelo Ravagli, at their home in Taos in 1954, two years before Frieda's death.

"Lawrence never knew who he was working for." Four years after Frieda's death, the legalization of the unexpurgated *Lady Chatterley's Lover* sent sales soaring to the benefit of her children and those of Angelo Ravagli.

do an introduction to catch the public eye—American—why, you might effect a sale.

I am so very sick of Taormina, that I hope to sail away to New Mexico in January or February, with Frieda. Oh I am so sick & surfeited of Europe, so tired, so tired.

I hope you are well, and cheerful, and working. I won't mention Christmas.

D. H. Lawrence

In my introduction I give a sketch of Magnus as I knew him in Florence, Montecassino, here, & Malta. In the first of course you figure, under a disguised name: along with me. The only vice I give you is that of drinking the best part of the bottle of whisky, instead of the worst part, like me. Do you mind at all?

The reference to "the only vice I give you" should have alerted Douglas that, far from being reluctant, Lawrence had the introduction nearly written. He had, in fact, told Mountsier a month before that the completed "Magnus MS" would soon be on its way to New York. Neither did he indicate to Douglas that he was assassinating Magnus's character for all time, portraying him unforgettably as a scamp, a treacherous little scoundrel, and a little mincing pigeon.

Douglas did own the rights. However, he understood perfectly well that a book with Lawrence's name on it was salable whereas one by Magnus alone was not. He replied by return of post and disclaimed any copyright interest: "Whoever wants it may ram it up his exhaust pipe. . . . By all means do what you like with the MS. . . . Pocket all the cash yourself." (Douglas wrote in a friendly spirit; he had not then read the parody of himself as James Argyle in *Aaron's Rod*.)

With Douglas's consent, Lawrence then got down to work in earnest. He let himself go. The result, he felt, as he often did, was one of the best things he had ever done. It was literal truth, he said, posting the finished essay to Mountsier on January 26, 1922. Magnus's actual manuscript would be sent directly to New York from Malta, Lawrence explained, and asked Mountsier to send any money it earned back to Malta to clear Magnus's debts there. He wanted to be paid separately, and only for his introduction.

The "Introduction" to the *Memoirs of the Foreign Legion* contains Lawrence's clearest statements on the subject of homosexuality—too clear for Martin Secker's taste. Secker cut three pages before the book was published in 1924 and the deleted passages were not revealed until Keith Cushman's scholarly edition in 1987. They show Lawrence exposing Magnus as a homosexual who, in his memoir, pretended that he was not. To Lawrence, the sodomistic legionnaires were guilty only of the sin of wasting their sacred blood passions:

But Magnus? —Nay, he is a liar, he is a hypocrite. To start with, the "vice" which he holds his hands up so horrified at . . . he had it himself. . . . him to talk about *girants** and sodomy. When he himself just paid money for his share of love . . . or else he begged the love and then borrowed money . . . But both love and money he got from uneducated men with warm blood: his inferiors!

"It doesn't matter *what* you do, it's the *way you do it*!" —That was one of his favorite clap-traps. I quite agree, my dear. It *is* the way you do it. You spy out a comely looking individual, of the "lower classes," you invite him to smokes and drinks—and afterwards you *pay* him. . . .

The little Judas, he betrayed everybody with a kiss: coming up with a kiss of love, and then afterwards cleaning out triumphant, having got all he wanted, thank you.

Lawrence was not a hypocrite. He was deploring not homosexual acts but dishonesty and the prostitution of love. Nonetheless, there is a fascinated revulsion, throughout the introduction, with the practice of a sexual act performed by male with male, described in veiled but richly admiring terms, in so many of his works.

Yet the main theme of his introduction is not sex but money, and Lawrence's guilt over his own reluctance to part with it. Now that Lawrence's private letters covering the same period in his life are available, it is clear that his introduction to Magnus's memoir opens with an exaggeration of his own poverty in 1919—the foundation upon which the whole sorry tale against Magnus is built.

"I landed in Italy," Lawrence wrote, "with nine pounds in my pocket and about twelve pounds lying in the bank in London. Nothing more. My wife, I hoped, would arrive in Florence with two or three pounds remaining." This was not true. Lawrence came to Florence in 1919 with forty pounds in sterling, which he cashed into lire as soon as he arrived; he explained all this in a letter to Kot on November 29, 1919. He undoubtedly had more in his London and American banks. Another fifty pounds reached him in Florence in a matter of days—money that he was expecting from Seltzer. As for Frieda, she arrived from Germany with at very least the ten pounds given her by Lawrence's sister Ada. She probably had money from Else as well.

In the same way, the introduction exaggerates Magnus's actual debts. In it Lawrence says, with heavy disapproval, that these amounted to one hundred pounds. Yet in the letter to Douglas asking for permission to publish the memoir, he said that these debts came to sixty-three pounds. Further to show Magnus in his essay as a wastrel and a spendthrift, in

---

* In French slang, according to Keith Cushman's *Memoir of Maurice Magnus,* a "girond" is a young passive male homosexual.

his introduction Lawrence inflates the price of the expensive San Domenico Hotel in Taormina where Magnus stayed: fifty lire a day in the introduction, but forty lire a day in the letters to friends in 1920 warning them to stay clear of the San Domenico.

The disparity helps to explain Lawrence's guilty conscience. He had to exaggerate the distance between himself and Magnus because they had so much in common. Magnus indulged in the very pleasures that Lawrence most fiercely denied himself: homosexuality and extravagance. In Magnus, Lawrence had met an unlikely blood brother, poured out his innermost secrets to him, and then left him to his fate.

There is no more telling passage in the cruel, brilliant, and defensive introduction than Lawrence's statement that when he heard the full account of Magnus's death, "I *realized* what it must have meant to be the hunted, desperate man: everything seemed to stand still. I could, by giving half my money, have saved his life. I had chosen not to save his life."

The introduction to *Memoirs of the Foreign Legion by M.M.*, posted off to Mountsier on January 26, 1922, was Lawrence's attempt to wash his hands of this lingering, haunting guilt.

12

CALLING IT AUSTRALIA

January–September 1922

> Poor Richard Lovat wearied himself to death
> struggling with the problem of himself, and calling
> it Australia.
>
> *Kangaroo*

The first Mabel Sterne heard about the Lawrences' change of plan was a letter from Frieda on January 27, 1922:

> We were coming *straight* to you at Taos but now we are not—L says he cant face America *yet*—He does'nt feel strong enough! So we are first going to the East to Ceylon—We have got friends there, two Americans, "Mayflowerers," and Buddhists. Strengthened with Buddha, noisy, rampagious America might be easier to tackle.

Lawrence could not complain of his wife's lack of submissiveness when it came to decisions about where to live. When "Lawrence sprang Ceylon onto me," as Frieda told Mabel, she accepted the change of plan as force majeure. She accepted also his view that Europe was sick. With her children embarked on their adult lives—Monty, twenty-one, was at Oxford; Elsa, twenty, in Switzerland; and Barbara, eighteen, at art school—she was ready to see the wider world.

Tidying up at the Fontana Vecchia, Lawrence communicated directly with his stepson, perhaps for the first time, sending him a copy of *Sea and Sardinia*. Monty loved it. It was the first book by Lawrence he had dared look at. He found the "q.b." "Mamma to the -nth," and passed it on to his sisters.

The Lawrences' finances were in good shape. *The Lost Girl* had just won the James Tait Black Prize in Edinburgh, and the hundred pounds reached them in Sicily. (It was the only work of Lawrence's ever to win an award.) In the American bank account kept for him in the small town of Charleroi, Pennsylvania, by Mountsier as his agent, he had $1,729.54 (about £350), and more in his London and Italian banks. A measure of the real value of that sum is Ezra Pound's campaign in London in 1922 for a fund to provide T. S. Eliot with an income of £250 a year in order that Eliot might leave his job at Lloyds Bank and devote himself to poetry. Lawrence was a £400-a-year man, going around the world, paying his way.

They took four trunks, organized meticulously by Lawrence: one with household goods, one with books, one each for clothes; also, two small suitcases, a hatbox (essential in those days), and two small hand satchels. This feat of efficient packing was hopelessly spoiled by a Sicilian friend, who at the last minute sentimentally presented them with a large painted wooden panel, the side of a peasant cart. They were glad to have it, and added it to the luggage. With him, Lawrence also took another Sicilian memento—a novel, *Maestro Don Gesualdo* by the Sicilian writer Giovanni Verga, who had just died. Lawrence had met Verga in Catania, admired his strength and reserve, and relished the challenge of translating Verga's artfully crafted Sicilian peasant speech into English.

Lawrence and Frieda embarked at Naples on February 26, on the S.S. *Osterley*. Leaving the Mediterranean, Lawrence was able to exercise his powers of description on natural phenomena the likes of which had never passed before his eyes. There was the desert ("little sharp sand hills so red and pink-gold"); the Suez Canal ("the horizon sharp like a knife edge"); and Mount Sinai (now no dream of a Congregational chapel imagination but "real, like a dagger" and "red like old dried blood"). As the ship left the Red Sea, Lawrence saw himself escaping the ideological world of Zeus, Jehovah, and Christ and joyfully facing the Indian Ocean, with its "little flying fish" and "little black dolphins that run about like pigs."

The Lawrences were good shipboard companions. They were interested in everybody and had a lot to say, Frieda particularly, sitting in a deck chair embroidering a rug while Lawrence made the rounds. He even turned up on deck for a religious service. Before disembarking they had the address of Mrs. Anna Jenkins, a lively Australian musician and patron of the arts from Perth, whose outspoken and intelligent friendliness put them in mind to call in at Western Australia on the way to America.

*   *   *

ON March 13, 1922, the *Osterley* docked at Colombo, Ceylon's chief port and its capital. Lawrence looked around him and told Achsah Brewster, "I shall never leave it." Six weeks later he left. He had had enough—of the heat, of the heavy sweet smell of fruit, coconut, and coconut oil. He had never felt so sick in his life. He found the little temples vulgar, the faces of the yellow-robed, shaved monks nasty. As for the birds and beasts, of which he was usually so fond, they "hammer and clang and rattle and cackle and explode all the livelong day, and run little machines all the livelong night." In sum, the East: "too boneless and negative . . . I don't like it one bit."

A racial theory followed: the East was no environment for the white man, but rather for the dark-skinned, whose blood-consciousness was tuned to the sun and the heat. Lawrence did not like the races to mix. News from Germany that the French had stationed black troops in the Rhineland sickened him; he declared it should be stopped. The prospect of democratic America depressed him as well. Once again he formulated his idea of natural aristocracy: "the right, the sacred duty to wield undisputed authority."

He was determined to push on for Australia—although, now worldly-wiser, he feared he might not like that either. His dissatisfaction did not extend to the Brewsters. He was very fond of them and their young daughter, Harwood, so much so that he declared, "I consider you truly my friends, therefore I shall tell you your faults." He told them the faults of their beloved Buddha, too: passive, always seated, expressionless "like a mud pool that has no bottom to it."

His short stay in Ceylon was not wasted. In his copious correspondence, he rendered impressions of the visiting Prince of Wales which as good as forecast trouble for the future Edward VIII. To his sister Emily: "Poor devil . . . all twitchy: and seems worn out and disheartened. No wonder, badgered about like a doll among a mob of children. A woman threw a bouquet, and he nearly jumped out of his skin." And to an English friend in Sicily: "They all secretly hate him for being a Prince, and make a Princely butt of him—and he knows it."

This blend of disdain and identification yielded a fine poem, "Elephant," which captures the absurdity of the spectacular elephant procession put on for the "pale little wisp of a Prince of Wales, diffident, up in a small pagoda" while the mountainous beasts bow down to him. It catches, too, the irony of the Walesian motto, "Ich Dien" ("I serve"), which sentences a man in the name of royalty to be "drudge to the public."

"I wish they had given the three feathers to me," says the poet, referring to the emblem of the Prince of Wales.

Serve me, I am meet to be served.
Being royal to the gods.

From the distance of Ceylon Lawrence saw his father in new perspective: "a true pagan." He had not done justice to his father in *Sons and Lovers,* Lawrence told Brewster, and wished he could rewrite it. In keeping with his inner shift from the female to the male, Lawrence now saw his mother as righteous and cruel, a woman who had portrayed her husband as a good-for-nothing drunkard, when the man had an unquenchable relish for living and a deep love for his family. Thinking aloud to Brewster, Lawrence recalled how his father would look at his row of frightened children and say, "Never mind, my duckies, you needna be afraid of me. I'll do ye na harm."

Then it was back to sea, but not straight to Taos.

ON May 4, 1922, the writer with perhaps the most highly developed sense of place in English literature reached Australia, a vast landmass nearly the size of the United States, with then a mere seven million people dotted along its edges. The day he arrived he pronounced judgment to Robert Mountsier: "a queer godforsaken place: not so much new as non-existent, in the real sense: though they call themselves very 'alive.' Air beautiful and pure and sky fresh, high—that part really good." He did not expect to stay long.

A few days later, up in the inland hills, he got his first look at what Australians call the bush and was hit by such a blast of nothingness that he was frightened half to death. He felt, he declared, groping for words for distant friends, as if he had seen a pre-primeval ghost.

His dear *Schwiegermutter* inspired the finest of the geographical word-portraits polished over succeeding days. He wrote her:

The land is here: sky high and blue and new, as if no one had ever taken a breath from it; and the air is new, strong, fresh as silver, and the land is terribly big and empty, still uninhabited. The "bush" is hoary and unending, no noise, still, and the white trunks of the gum trees all a bit burnt; a forest, a preforest: not a primeval forest: somewhat like a dream. . . . It is *too* new, you see: too vast. It needs hundreds of years yet before it can live. This is the land where the unborn souls, strange and not to be known, which shall be born in 500 years, live. A grey, foreign spirit.

He said much the same to Albert Curtis Brown, who had become his English literary agent in April 1921. "I suppose it will have its day, this place," he said. "But its day won't be our day."

The spirit of place descended upon Lawrence instantly—not so much like the Holy Ghost, more like a physical allergy. One whiff and he had it. His swift reactions to a change of environment sound physiological. For a few magic hours or even days, he felt better: his most magnificent visual descriptions were, as Paul Delany has noted, first impressions. Then he felt worse. Euphoria gave way to disillusion and he reacted characteristically, not with disappointment but with anger.

A few days after their arrival, their shipboard acquaintance Mrs. Jenkins bore them like a trophy up into the hills to Darlington, the Ascona of Western Australia. One of the proprietors of the boarding house where they stayed was Mollie Skinner, an unmarried nurse and budding writer, who had published one book and was working on another. A member of a Perth military family, she could hardly believe her good fortune when the author of *Sons and Lovers* fell into her charge, and with a titled German wife for good measure. Miss Skinner showed Lawrence her own work. Always attentive to new writers, he read it, and gave her his recipe to splash down reality. "Write bit by bit the scenes you have witnessed round the people you know."

During the next fortnight, shuttled back and forth to bookshops in Perth and barbecues in the bush, the Lawrences were lionized. At first Frieda was the more impressive: aristocratic, beautiful and friendly, utterly devoted to the frail man, who, by rugged Australian standards, was unprepossessing until he started to speak. Frieda seemed to think the earth revolved around him and told all who would listen how her husband was such a fiendish worker that he would leave the breakfast table in the middle of a mouthful when an idea struck him.

In Perth Mrs. Jenkins introduced him to other local intellectuals, including a radical and poet, William Siebenhaar, who also gave him work to read. Lawrence was pleased to find his own books there, even *The Rainbow,* of which he did not possess a copy. *The Rainbow* was prominent at Perth Literary Institute, where no one knew that it was a banned book in London. He told everybody that he was only passing through and had no intention of writing anything about Australia.

In his global wanderings after the war, Lawrence made an enormous impact. While his literary reputation, based chiefly on *Sons and Lovers,* preceded him, his admirers were unprepared for his charm and directness. His three weeks in Western Australia left a rich literary legacy and one local author, Katherine Susannah Prichard, failed to meet him because the prospect so unnerved her that she went into premature labor. Mollie Skinner was almost as shaken. She was so moved when he left Perth that she blurted out, to her embarrassssment, "You have hit me in the solar plexus!"

*   *   *

ON May 18, having posted the Verga translation (finished) to New York for Mountsier to sell, Lawrence and Frieda left for Sydney aboard the M.S. *Malwa,* a small one-class ship with only forty passengers. He did not think he would stay long in Sydney; he wanted to see the South Sea islands; he had no idea where he would be a month hence. "I love trying things and discovering how I hate them," he wrote engagingly to Brewster. With a brief call at Adelaide and an overnight stop at Melbourne, which was celebrating Empire Day, their journey around the south coast of Australia ("on a sea swelling from the Antarctic") took nine days; they reached Sydney on the east coast before dawn on Saturday, May 27. Two days out he had no thought of work. Yet he disembarked at Sydney with a book in his head. Something clearly had entered his mind.

The resulting novel, *Kangaroo,* fixes like a camera on a Lawrence-like couple almost from the first minute they set foot in Sydney. Its opening scene is a long shot. Workmen on their lunch break lounging in the park on Macquarie Street near the quay "with that air of owning a city which belongs to a good Australian" observe with some amusement a foreign-looking pair with a gladstone bag and a hatbox leaving a boarding house. The woman is "mature, handsome, fresh-faced . . . might have been a Russian" and the man "smallish . . . pale-faced, with a dark beard." The men pronounce the couple "Bolshy," or "Fritzies, most likely."

By Monday, the Lawrences, like the foreign-looking couple in the book, after exploring Sydney, admiring the magnificent vista of harbor, peninsulas, bays, and islands, and loathing what man had done to it ("loused over with thousands of small promiscuous bungalows," says *Kangaroo*), traveled on the train forty miles to the south, to Thirroul, a small beach resort. They were in search of rented accommodation of the kind advertised in the *Sydney Morning Herald.* (The seaside was cheaper than Sydney in June, the start of the Australian winter.) Leaving the train, they crossed the road to the office of a real estate agent named Alfred Callcott and by six o'clock that evening were installed in a new and spacious holiday bungalow at 3 Craig Street, on the edge of a sand cliff overlooking the crashing Pacific breakers.

The name of the brick house, Wyewurk, was a bit of Australian whimsy suggesting relaxation. (Nearby, not surprisingly, was a house called Wyewurrie.) Wyewurk, built in 1910, was rather grand for down-at-heels Thirroul, which was part mining town as well as resort. With its single story enclosed by wide, open verandas, the house was one of the first examples in Australia of the California-Edwardian bungalow. And Lawrence, wanting somewhere to settle while waiting for the money being sent by Mountsier from New York, was pleased with the low rent: thirty shillings a week, furnished.

With a bedroom each and one to spare, Frieda was reminded to write ahead to warn Mabel Dodge Sterne in Taos that she and Lawrence needed plenty of room: "By the way *dont give* us too little a place to live in, we are much too quarrelsome—it's quite fatal." They could afford to pay for space, she said, now that they were no longer as poor as they had been. Lawrence added his own reminder that he insisted on paying his rent, whatever house was given them, but "No, not too small, if it can be avoided." They both needed to keep clear of each other.

Thirroul was a raw town of unpaved streets and corrugated iron roofs set between the sea and a long, low, black rock pocked with coal mines and topped with bush. Its municipal services included electric lighting but not sewers. Earth closets were emptied weekly by a public servant popularly known as the shit-carter, a man who embodied the attitude Lawrence described to Catherine Carswell as "Happy-go-lucky don't-you-bother we're-in-Austrylia." Though "shit" was not a word Lawrence shied away from in conversation, when he came to describe this official in *Kangaroo* he used the politer local term "sanitary man," but caught the cheekiness that amused him. In *Kangaroo,* when the new arrivals ask the sanitary man whether he will take the ashes and rubbish away too, the reply is a nasal "Neow." So what was the householder supposed to do with them? " 'Do what you like with 'em.' And he marched off with the can. It was not rudeness. It was a kind of colonial humour."

Yet Lawrence had decided within a day that he did not really like the egalitarian Australian personality: "The hateful newness, the democratic conceit, every man a little pope of perfection . . ." he wrote to Mountsier. "Is America awful like this?" To his mother-in-law, he allowed himself a more pointedly political comment: "The working people are very discontented—always threaten more strikes—always more socialism." He wished he had stayed in more ordered, more English Western Australia.

But Frieda was overjoyed to have her own place again; she loved the broad verandas of Wyewurk, the red walls, the dark jarrah-wood furniture, the fireplace of arched brick, and the constant roar of the sea. She did not even finish her embroidery because, Lawrence wrote Brewster, "she housewifes." They both threw themselves into the ritual washing and scrubbing, which Wyewurk needed as much as any Italian farmhouse, and Frieda scattered around the interior the familiar table cloths and cushions salvaged from their Cornish cottage, the household Penates carried wherever they went.

They fell into their established routine, doing their own work. Frieda did the shopping, marking herself out as foreign (according to *Kangaroo*) by carrying a basket when the local custom was to carry everything, from eggs and cabbages to bottles of beer, in a suitcase. Every morning Lawrence made breakfast, chopped wood, lit the stove, and settled down to write. At noon they swam in the breakers—perhaps nude; they had the beach to themselves—and washed off the salt under a little outdoor shower next to the house.

They took the place initially for a month. On June 3, four days after they arrived, Lawrence began his new novel. He went, as usual, at a fast clip, writing about three thousand words a day in neat handwriting, in a series of lined exercise books, and hoped that he and Frieda could catch the earliest possible ship to San Francisco, which left Sydney on July 6.

The feat of fast composition was accomplished with his magpie technique: ingredients taken from everywhere. Lawrence liked reading the weekly *Sydney Bulletin,* and a passage in his book describing a kangaroo being savaged by a wild cat can be dated from the issue of the *"Bully"* from which it was lifted. The virile Australian character Jack Callcott (with a name appropriated from the real estate agent who had rented them the house) says that one day in the North "I saw a full-grown male kangaroo backed up against a tree, with the flesh of one leg torn clean from the bone." And a columnist in the *Bulletin* of June 8 wrote: "I saw a full-grown kangaroo backed up against a tree, the flesh of one leg torn clean from the bone."

Everything Lawrence saw and did went into the book. Wyewurk, the jarrah wood, the verandas, the outdoor shower; the modest sights of Thirroul, such as the statue of a World War I soldier, the library, the football field; the tin cans and other detritus of hasty civilization scattered everywhere; the day trip south to Wollongong when his hat blew into the sea and Frieda collapsed laughing: he found a place for them all. He brazenly called one chapter of odds and ends "Bits," and drew again on the lazy technique of addressing the reader, although none too respectfully: "If you don't like the novel, don't read it."

At the heart of the book he put a chapter that was not about Australia at all: "The Nightmare," the history of his bitter experiences in England during the war. He threw everything into that too, from the friendship with the handsome Cornish farmer and the expulsion from Cornwall to the medical examination in Derby, including the inspection for hemorrhoids. The book was an odd construct, he wrote to friends abroad. "Even the Ulysseans will spit at it." Although Joyce's *Ulysses* had been published in Paris only three months earlier and Lawrence had not yet seen a copy, it was common literary knowledge, from the extracts that had appeared in English and American literary reviews, that *Ulysses* was a collage of different writing styles, newspaper headlines, snatches of music, dreams, and flashbacks.

Eight days into its composition, Lawrence's book had a title; hoping to finish it as fast as he could, he did little else. By June 21, more than halfway through, he got stuck. The book was about "no love at all, and attempt at revolution," he told his New York publisher, with "not so much as the letter S of sex." He feared he might be up against a serious writing block of the kind that had held up *Aaron's Rod* for two years and had left *Mr. Noon* permanently unfinished. Indecision and changes of mind forced him to take a razor or scissors and cut whole pages clean out of his text.

But he got himself restarted. By July 15, the book was done: forty-two days from start to finish. The following weekend, he invited two English couples from the *Malwa*—the Marchbanks and the Forresters, handsome couples of stalwart men and winsome wives—to Wyewurk for the weekend and, in a burst of extravagance, hired a car with driver to take them all on a day's excursion to the Loddon River.

The photographs taken that day, of the picnic on the rocks in the river, show a rarely seen Lawrence: smiling, relaxed, happy, at his most unselfconscious—a perfect illustration of his assertion in a letter to Brewster about Australia: "In truth, I sit easier in my skin here than anywhere." The visitors enjoyed themselves too, even though they wondered at the expense. However, Lawrence, so frugal with his money, could be generous when he had it. With the security of another novel behind him, he was happy to splash money on a spree with some friends.

Hardly had the guests departed when there came a great tropical storm that for more than a day buried Wyewurk under great sheets of water. The most dramatic manifestation of nature's force they had ever seen, it arrived too late for the Australian novel, which was already on its way to New York. But it was too good to waste. Lawrence wrote it into the manuscript later, as he also inserted the havoc that the storm had wreaked on the beach, washing away all the sand and leaving nothing but sharp, exposed rocks.

When the sky was clear once more, it was time to go. On August 9 the Lawrences moved out of Wyewurk, left for Sydney, and two days later set sail for San Francisco.

HE left behind him a mystery. How could an author who borrowed so literally from life produce at such speed a political thriller about a secret fascist army, full of the kind of atmosphere that would take other writers months to absorb? How could the climactic chapter be a vivid dramatization of riots that had taken place in 1920 and 1921 between the "Diggers" (returned servicemen who had fought for Britain against Germany) and socialists in Sydney? And how could Lawrence have known that the Diggers' leader, who precipitated both riots, looked as much like a kangaroo as any human being dressed in an officer's uniform possibly could? At very least, this feat of reconstruction, along with a brilliant exposure of the psychological conflict of his marriage and the clearest account of his own experience in England during the First World

War, makes *Kangaroo* the most underappreciated and biographically provocative of any of his novels.

Kangaroo is the story of preparations for a right-wing coup in New South Wales. The background is historically accurate. Australian cities after the war were seething with sectarian and political strife. There was widespread unemployment; the urban slums were foul. The several hundred thousand Diggers returned from France to a country fearful of following Russia into Red Revolution.

The state of New South Wales was particularly tense. The Australian Labor party, which had opposed Australian participation in the war, unexpectedly won power in 1920. It seemed highly possible to the Protestant establishment—commercial, masonic, and military—that armed insurrection was on its way at last; they believed that Labor had fallen into the hands of even more radical elements, the International Workers of the World—the Wobblies—and Communists. Adding to loyalist fears were the Irish. One third of Sydney's population was Irish, mostly immigrant, anti-Protestant and anti-Crown, fiercely resentful of England's refusal to grant Ireland Home Rule and its savage treatment of the leaders of the 1916 Easter Rising in Dublin.

To counteract these dissident elements, at the end of World War I clandestine, right-wing paramilitary groups had begun to form, with the unofficial endorsement of Australian state and federal authorities, who wanted a force to call on "if the balloon goes up." In 1920 this secret movement surfaced in the form of the King and Empire Alliance. Like the American Protective League in the United States, the alliance saw itself as a band of patriots ready to defend their country against the subversive alien tide. Exactly how much of an underground movement continued to run beneath the alliance in the 1920s is unclear. However, enough remained to emerge in the depression years of the 1930s, when the socialists were back in power in New South Wales, as a network of secret right-wing armies known as the New Guard.

In May 1920, two years before Lawrence's arrival in Australia, the conflict between right and left boiled over at a riot at Moore Park in Sydney. More than 150,000 people—one sixth of the population of Sydney—turned up to protest against the deportation of a German Catholic priest who had been interned for opposing the war. This crowd, an array of Irish, socialists, and Communists, had just been addressed by an Irish priest, Father Maurice O'Reilly, when twenty thousand Diggers, exhorted by the head of the alliance, Major General Sir Charles Rosenthal, one of Australia's World War generals, arrived. At a counted signal, the Diggers attacked the crowd and, waving the Union Jack, stormed the platform. According to the Sydney *Catholic Press*, Father O'Reilly was besieged, but he caught up a chair, held it aloft, and invited the howling mob to come and get him.

The following year there was a smaller but more violent riot with the same elements. On May Day the Diggers broke up a union celebration as it was being addressed by a Communist union leader. Again Major General Rosenthal was in the background.

For many years after the publication of *Kangaroo* it was assumed that Lawrence had brought the novel's politics with him in his luggage from Italy. In an introduction to the novel in 1950, Richard Aldington declared that the vivid scenes of political conflict could only be transpositions of the fascist-socialist struggles Lawrence had witnessed in Italy. Aldington took literally Lawrence's assertion that he had met nobody in Australia and assumed, wrongly, that no such political violence as described in the novel took place in Australia. Thus, Aldington concluded, misleading a generation or more of readers, "some of these Australian characters and the scenes between people are wholly imagined."

In 1981, the Australian journalist Robert Darroch demolished this assumption forever. In a deft piece of literary detective work, *D. H. Lawrence in Australia,* Darroch called attention to the existence of the ex-servicemen's clubs that had preceded the quasi-fascist New Guard of the 1930s. He pointed out the similarities of the riot in *Kangaroo*—in the chapter "A Row in Town," the Diggers attack the socialists—to Sydney's actual Red Flag riots. In the novel, at the cry of *"Eight!"*

> the hall was like a bomb that has exploded. . . . There was a most fearful roar, and a mad whirl of men, broken chairs, pieces of chairs brandished, men fighting madly with fists, claws, pieces of wood—any weapon they could lay hold of. The red flag suddenly flashing like blood, and bellowing rage at the sight of it. A Union Jack torn to fragments, stamped upon. A mob with many different centres, some fighting frenziedly round a red flag, some clutching fragments of a Union Jack, as if it were God incarnate.

Darroch went much further, however. He claimed that, far from inventing the charismatic Jewish leader Ben Cooley, whose nickname is Kangaroo, Lawrence, on his trips to Sydney to arrange American visas for himself and Frieda, actually met him, in the person of Major General Rosenthal. Part of Darroch's evidence is a photograph of Rosenthal in full uniform; the photo is a credible illustration of Lawrence's description of Kangaroo, whose "pendulous" (Lawrence's adjective) jowls, ample paunch, and broad hips answer the question posed in the novel:

" 'Why call him "Kangaroo"?'

" 'Looks like one,' was the answer."

Moreover, having correlated street names and scenic descriptions in the book with the fragmentary details of Lawrence's known movements, Darroch maintained that in Sydney Lawrence also met Colonel W.J.R. Scott, another high officer in the secret army. It was Scott, argued Darroch, who was the model for the Diggers' organizer, Jack Callcott, in *Kangaroo,* and it was Scott, with Rosenthal, who told Lawrence all the details of their secret movement at a meeting at Rosenthal's club. This meeting corresponds to a scene in the book. Darroch contended that the two men wanted to enlist Lawrence as a writer for their movement. Then, when he refused, they feared that he might be a spy who had just elicited all the details of their organization. Therefore, they forced him to swear to secrecy.

Darroch thus alleged that there was a sinister reality behind the scene in *Kangaroo* where Callcott demands of Richard Somers, the English writer he has taken into his trust: "We want some sort of security that you'll keep quiet, before we let you leave Australia."

According to Darroch, Somers's reply—"You can be quite assured nothing will come out through me"—may be, in the light of *Kangaroo,* published in England and America the following year, "one of the most spectacularly broken promises in literary history." Moreover, in Darroch's view, fear of retribution from the Diggers explains the emphatic insistence of both Lawrences that, despite evidence to the contrary, they had met no one in Australia, and also helps to account for Lawrence's terror of assassination later in Mexico.

DARROCH's book has been much criticized for going beyond the evidence and resting its case on an unproven allegation of an actual meeting of Rosenthal, Scott, and Lawrence. There are clearly other models for the character of Kangaroo—Lawrence's good friend Koteliansky and, even more clearly, Dr. David Eder, who answers the character's physical description as well as sharing some of the leader's maternal qualities and leadership aspirations. Both Kot and Eder, like the fictional Kangaroo, were Jewish. The actual Major General Rosenthal was not Jewish, but Lawrence also had available to him the very model of an Australian Jewish general in the form of Sir John Monash. Monash was Australia's outstanding First World War general and, as Bruce Steele has pointed out, bore many of the characteristics of Lawrence's Kangaroo. Monash had a brilliant mind and was a natural leader, with an enormous following among ex-servicemen. Yet he was also a disappointed man who had not been given a position in the Australian postwar defense establishment.

A search for exact models for Lawrence's characters is, in any event, both dangerous and unnecessary. No artist captures "reality." The James Argyle of *Aaron's Rod* is not Norman Douglas any more than Magritte's painting of a pipe is a real pipe. While Lawrence demonstrably, even shamelessly, helped himself to what he saw, he shaped his material for his own ends. His genius was imaginative, not reportorial. He disdained research and was careless with details, not minding much if, as in *Kangaroo,* he called a jellyfish an octopus.

None of these objections, however, invalidates the questions Darroch posed. He showed, as one of Lawrence's Cambridge biographers, David Ellis, has acknowledged, that *Kangaroo* "gives a much truer picture of the state of the Australian nation than was previously thought." Darroch also strengthened the legitimacy of the question raised by so much of Lawrence's fiction: "Did he make anything up?"

Lawrence, of course, could have patched together his paramilitary tale simply from hearsay and old newspapers stored under Wyewurk's verandas for hygienic purposes. And he was no stranger to thoughts of secret armies. The year before he came to Australia, under the influence of his reading of Walt Whitman, he had incorporated a sketch of a secret League of Comrades in a passage in *Fantasia of the Unconscious* that was deleted before it reached print.

Since Darroch launched the hunt, the most plausible theory of the factual origin of the plot of *Kangaroo* came in 1990, from two Australian sleuths—a journalist and a postman—who found that sailing with Lawrence and Frieda from Perth to Sydney on the S.S. *Malwa* was the very Father O'Reilly who had brandished a chair at Rosenthal at the Moore Park riot in 1920. It requires little imagination to envisage that the political priest, returning to Sydney after seven months in Europe, and the loquacious, eternally curious English author spent some of the long journey talking to each other. Lawrence was a good listener, especially when he glimpsed a book in what he was being told.

Darroch's thesis is as impossible to disprove as to prove. The gaps in Lawrence's recorded movements do leave room for secret meetings in Sydney and, in retrospect, his and Frieda's protests that they knew not a soul in the region do seem excessive. The absence of written evidence is open to interpretation, for Lawrence omitted from his vast correspondence whole areas of his experience, such as his tuberculosis, Frieda's love affair with Ernst Frick, and the financial dependence of the von Richthofen family on Edgar Jaffe.

What Lawrence's letters written from Australia do reveal clearly, however, is his own right-wing sympathies. Although Somers in *Kangaroo* leans slightly more to the side of the socialists than to the Diggers, Lawrence himself, in 1922, leaned the other way. He was unhappy about the dark anarchic races waiting to pour into Australia and sensed behind them the yellow Japanese waiting to descend on Australia "like a ripe pear." He also continued hostile toward organized labor, as when he asked Mountsier whether an American rail strike presaged "bad Labour troubles" for the United States, amounting to a virtual revolution:

There must come a break somewhere. —And when there has come a break, then I shall come into my own. As things are, however . . . I hate it—the public—the monster with a million worm-like heads. No, gradually I shall call together a choice minority, more fierce and aristocratic in spirit.

He wrote those impassioned words the day he packed off *Kangaroo* to New York.

THE themes of politics and marriage are entwined in *Kangaroo* like the strands of the double helix. There is no doubt where Lawrence got the facts for the novel's portrait of a troubled but inseparable couple. The wife bears three of Frieda's baptismal names: Mrs. Lawrence's "Emma Maria Frieda Johanna" has become "Harriet Emma Marianna Johanna," and Harriet's nationality is given as "not English."*

More revealing was Lawrence's choice of name for the husband, Richard Lovat Somers. For "RLS," read "DHL." Lawrence had long identified with Robert Louis Stevenson, another childhood invalid whose vivid imagination turned him into a world traveler in search of stories (and of health). Lawrence knew that Stevenson had visited Australia (he was there at least four times, and had even passed through Thirroul) and he knew, too, what for the tubercular Stevenson lay at journey's end: death in Samoa. Contemplating his own circumnavigation, Lawrence scoffed at Stevenson: "Idiot to go to Samoa just to dream and get thrilled about Scotch bogs and mosses. No wonder he died. If I go to Samoa, it will be to forget, not to remember."

In *Kangaroo* Lawrence has Somers, bearded, married, childless, arrive in Australia as a writer of poems and essays, with an income of four hundred a year, who has decided that in Europe "everything was done for, played out, finished, and he must go to a new country." Somers is torn between a life of solitude as a writer or as a leader in the world of men. His dead mother still haunts him in his dreams, her face blending with that of his wife—and he has problems with his wife. She is incensed that he has begun to take pride in his ability to live in isolation from society but fails to notice that it is she who makes it possible. Also, she is enraged by his meaningless demands for submission.

Harriet Somers, like Frieda Lawrence, is something of a sexual expert

* In his original manuscript, Lawrence spelled both "Harriett" and "Lovatt" with two "t"s, a style adopted by the Cambridge University Press in its revised edition of the novel in 1994. But Lawrence was probably just misspelling the common name, for he wrote the name of Harriet Monroe, editor of *Poetry*, as "Harriett." Quotations in this book, however, use the more conventional spelling as easier on the eye and in accordance to the standard Penguin edition of *Kangaroo*.

as well. She compliments her husband, in the novel's only consummated sexual encounter, when he grows aroused as she rubs him dry in the little outdoor shower and then takes her on the spot. "That was done with style," she declares heartily. "That was *chic*. Straight from the sea, like another creature." But chic sex does not solve their marital difficulties. Harriet is fed up with his conspiratorial meetings with Kangaroo and Jack Callcott, "revolution rubbish and a stunt of male activity." She senses, too, that he has still not solved the problem of the homosexual attraction.

Somers falls in love with the pendulous Kangaroo—not only with his politics but also with his soft, motherly, Jewish body. Indeed, in a facetious chapter on the state of the Somerses' marriage, "Harriet and Lovat at Sea," Somers decides that Harriet will only accept him as a lord and master when he accepts a lord and master for himself. Or, in the narrator's words, full of homoerotic import: "Let him [Somers] once truly submit to the dark majesty, break open his doors to the fearful god who is master, and enters us from below, the lower doors; let himself once admit a Master, the unspeakable god: and the rest would happen."

But Somers retreats in fear from the menace of the clandestine organization and of the man. When Kangaroo is mortally injured during the "row in town," Somers grudgingly visits him twice. The encounters are powerful scenes of homosexual temptation in which, once more, Lawrence does not seem to be in control of his meaning. On the first visit, Somers senses, in words that recall the odor of "marsh gas" that Lawrence detected around Keynes and his circle, that the room is filled with "an unpleasant, discernible stench": " 'My sewers leak,' said Kangaroo bitterly, as if divining the other's thought." He then begs for Somers's love, and when Somers hesitates, accuses him of fear. The accusation strikes home. Somers asks himself, "Was it just fear that made him hold back from admitting his love for the other man?"

Summoned for a final visit to the deathbed, Somers again hears Kangaroo plead, "Say you love me." Somers refuses. "No . . . I can't say it." Kangaroo then whispers, "You've killed me. You've killed me, Lovat!"

How? By withholding what it would have cost him nothing to give. Jack Callcott spells it out for Somers in a caustic colloquial statement of anal retention: "Some folks is stingy about sixpence, and others is stingy about saying two words that would give another poor devil his peace of mind."

Stinginess. "I could, by giving half my money, have saved his life. I had chosen not to save his life." It is the charge that Lawrence leveled against himself for the death of Maurice Magnus.

Lawrence called *Kangaroo* a "thought adventure." Others have called all of his work a life adventure. Some critics argue that, taken together, all of Lawrence's writing—novels, poems, letters, essays, and journalism—constitutes one continuous autobiography. If so, the turning point of his life and work came in July 1922, when in *Kangaroo* he recreated his war years, the darkest hours of his life, culminating with the humiliation of the examination in Derby, when the jeering doctors commanded him to "Bend forward—further—further" and "Somers bent forward, lower, and realized that the puppy was standing aloof behind him to look into his anus."

It is as if Lawrence had to travel halfway around the world to expose to his readers the dark door where he craved to be entered. That done, he could reject the temptations offered by Kangaroo and return to his wife. She has fought against the homosexual element in him, and won. The conclusion of *Kangaroo* is Somers's recognition, much like Gilbert's in *Mr. Noon* and Lawrence's own when he said good-bye to William Henry Hocking, that "she was all he had in the world." There was no living without her.

AT the end of the century in which it was written, *Kangaroo* has a meaning larger than politics or marriage: the power of an environment over the people who live in it. Fifty years before the popular Australian soap opera of the same name, Lawrence summed up the Australian collective personality in chapter two of *Kangaroo,* which he titled "Neighbours." He saw Australians, huddled in their suburbs, just a footstep away from each other, "alert with question and with offering, and very ready to be huffy, or even nasty, if the offering were refused." Aggressive friendliness was their defense against the terrifying emptiness of their continent, which glowered over them with "a terrible ageless watchfulness, waiting for a far-off end, watching the myriad intruding white men."

In Australia debate has raged as to whether *Kangaroo* is the best novel ever written about Australia or the worst, a condescending slap at national pride, drawing on every colonial prejudice about Australia as a godforsaken land of swaggerers and cultureless louts. There has even been fierce controversy over whether Wyewurk is worth preserving. Is it one of Australia's few literary monuments, or simply an undistinguished seaside bungalow where D. H. Lawrence once spent a few weeks writing a second-rate novel?

The new interest in the environment and Aboriginal culture has worked in *Kangaroo*'s favor. "It is time to move beyond automatic defensiveness and hurt national pride," an Australian literary scholar, David Tacey, has claimed, "and to realise that the alienation Lawrence felt is part of the tradition in Australian writing which views the landscape as hostile to European consciousness." Australia's is a white society transplanted onto black soil, Tacey declared: "It would be naive and irresponsible of us to pretend that the gap between us and the land does not exist."

To those who now try to explain Lawrence's curious psychology as a struggle to define the borders of his own existence and to separate from an overpowering mother, *Kangaroo* offers incomparable evidence. His fear of the impersonal Australian wilderness seems to be the starkest expression of his dread of being drawn back into nonexistence, into the Mother, into the pouch. The spirit of the place scared him off. Somers says, "It's too strong. It would lure me quite away from myself." And the unseen narrator, speaking over Somers's head, asks: "What was the good of trying to be an alert conscious man here? You couldn't. Drift, drift into a sort of obscurity, backwards into a nameless past."

Lawrence said as much to a friend in Western Australia, almost apologizing for leaving:

> For some things too I love Australia: its weird, far-away natural beauty and its remote, almost coal-age pristine quality. Only it's too far for me. I can't reach so awfully far. Further than Egypt. I feel I slither on the edge of a gulf, reaching to grasp its atmosphere and spirit. It eludes me, and always would.

At the novel's end, Somers makes his peace with the bush, which, when spring arrives, is covered with yellow wattle flowers. Harriet says that if "I had *three* lives, I'd wish to stay. It's the loveliest thing I've *ever* known." But Lawrence had only one life, and every breath he took told him that it would be short.

In the event, Lawrence bequeathed Australia enough flattering slogans to last it until the unborn souls of the bush come to life. The Australian tourist industry's boast—"The friendliest country in the world"—comes from *Kangaroo*. A phrase from one of Lawrence's letters to a friend in Sicily is set in bronze on Writers' Walk in Sydney: "Australia has a marvellous sky and air and blue clarity and a hoary sort of land beneath it, like a Sleeping Princess on whom the dust of ages has settled. Wonder if she'll ever get up."

ON September 4, 1922, Lawrence and Frieda landed at San Francisco, achieving his seven-year dream of entering America without passing through New York. But had Lawrence actually stumbled into a secret nest of gun-carrying veterans in New South Wales? It is one of the unanswerable questions about his life. The possibility cannot be dismissed on the grounds that he did not mention it in his letters. Something about his stay troubled him after he left. When in America and arranging the publication of *Kangaroo*, he requested that it not appear in Australia for the time being, and he asked his New York publisher, Thomas Seltzer, "Do you think the Australian Govt. or the Diggers might resent anything?"

If Frieda knew the answer, she did not give it away. Years later, questioned by the Cambridge scholar F. R. Leavis, she replied as if she did not make any great distinction between her husband and Richard Lovat Somers. "In *Kangaroo*," she said, "I think that Harriet was right in fighting his idea to lead a revolution. His task, God given, was to *write;* what would a silly little revolution in Australia have amounted to? 'Not a hill of beans.' " One thing seems certain: the heavy yellow antipodal animal upon which Lawrence based his great poem "Kangaroo" was one he saw in the Sydney zoo.

13

THE SEARCH FOR HEALTH
IN THE SOUTHWEST

September 1922–December 1923

*I feel from my experience at Santa Fe, that the
chances of life are considerably more in our favour
there than in the most healthy part of the continent
east of the Rocky Mountains.*
—from the diary of an eighteenth-century tubercular from Virginia

*I*n the late nineteenth and early twentieth centuries the American
Southwest was a dumping ground for the nation's tuberculars. The in-
flux began in the 1880s once the Indian menace ended and railways
arrived. Frustrated doctors in the East urged their otherwise incurable
patients to "go West and rough it." With between one million and two
million people afflicted, popular magazines and medical journals alike
extolled the healing powers of getting out into the pure fresh air and
meeting nature on its own terms. This led to an arduous pilgrimage;
some invalids spent three months on stretchers just to get there. Yet for
many the "ranch cure" worked, including John B. Stetson, a consumptive from Philadelphia who designed the Western riding hat to which he
gave his name.

Along with the invasion came the stigma. Signs warning "Consumptives Not Accepted" appeared in hotels and restaurants; Texas and California tried to ban the afflicted altogether; and in 1914 the Southwestern
states lobbied to get Congress to create federal tent cities and turn old
army forts into sanatoriums to contain the coughing, spitting immigra-

tion. The main result, not surprisingly, was to encourage consumptives to disguise their condition.

New Mexico alone was welcoming. A territory, not a state until 1912, it was eager for new population. Proud of the healing properties of the area's hot springs, high altitude, and dry climate, the Territory of New Mexico's Bureau of Immigration in 1906 appealed to tuberculars unreservedly: "Health seekers are invited. New Mexico does not intend to shut the door upon them." Splendid sanatoriums were built at Silver City, Socorro, Santa Fe, and, most spectacularly, at Las Vegas (New Mexico), where the Atchison, Topeka and Santa Fe Railway set a magnificent hotel beside the hot springs that had soothed the Spanish, the Indians, and travelers along the Santa Fe Trail for centuries.

At the turn of the century, the area of northern New Mexico around Santa Fe and Taos became an art colony; writers and painters from the East were drawn by its spectacular natural beauty and rich layers of civilization stretching from the Spanish to the pre-Columbian. Throwing away their neckties and pulling on silver-and-turquoise jewelry and Navajo shirts, they felt miraculously liberated from the raw commercialism of the rest of the United States.

For one who had long dreamed of going to America, Lawrence thus arrived in September 1922 at not only the newest (with Arizona) but the least American of the states. Santa Fe, with its governor's palace built for the viceroy of New Spain in 1609, proclaimed itself the oldest capital city in North America. The lack of a direct railway connection had helped to preserve its unique Spanish atmosphere.

Waiting for Lawrence on the platform at the station at Lamy, twenty miles from Santa Fe, was the woman he knew only from letters: Mabel Dodge Sterne. Short and square, with a flat calm voice and an income of fourteen thousand dollars a year, she was now devoting her life to building a bridge between what she saw as Indian and American cultures. Her hair had even been cut into a Dutch bob with straight bangs to make her look more Indian. Mabel had summoned Lawrence to write a novel about the place where she felt closest to what she called "at-one-ment" with the universe.

He was neither the first nor the last of the artists she drew to New Mexico, writing on her rough-textured desert-colored stationery emblazoned with cactus and moon. Thomas Wolfe, in 1935, received the full treatment after the publication of *Of Time and the River:* "You brush up one's *awareness* terribly. Experience of environment one is so used to that one doesn't notice any more awakens again so *vividly* through reading this book." Wolfe came, but, unlike Lawrence, stayed only one day—and complained loudly around Santa Fe about the way Mabel had pursued him with telegrams.

But it was Lawrence who most captured the spirit of the place, although not in the way she had wanted. His three visits, between 1922 and 1925, during the last of which they did not meet at all, immortalized Mabel as the woman who brought Lawrence to Taos.

Mabel is easy to caricature: the Ottoline of the Golden West, a self-important grande dame using her money to pose as a patron of the arts, writing much nonsense and setting herself against a theatrical backdrop of her own creation. Also, the American dowager with cultural pretensions has long been a stock comic figure, epitomized by the stately Mrs. Rittenhouse, played by Margaret Dumont in the Marx Brothers' *A Night at the Opera,* whose lorgnette and pearls ill-conceal a menopausal lust.

Yet, like Ottoline Morrell, Mabel looks less ridiculous today: at worst, a thwarted and undereducated but intelligent woman; at best, someone who did a great deal to improve the living conditions of the Native Americans in northern New Mexico and to make Taos an artistic center. Moreover, Mabel was a good writer. She had an ear for dialogue, a reporter's sharp eye, and a great hostess's instinct for bringing people together.

Born to a wealthy family in Buffalo, New York, in 1879, Mabel had a succession of husbands and lovers (including the young American revolutionary John Reed, who wrote *Ten Days That Shook the World* and became the only Harvard graduate to be buried in the Kremlin). She had lived much abroad. During her New York years, around the First World War, she was psychoanalyzed by A. A. Brill, an Austrian Jew and disciple of Freud's, one of Manhattan's first analysts. Brill encouraged Mabel to write, and she became a syndicated columnist for the Hearst chain. Her biweekly advice, for which she was paid ten dollars a column, appeared on the editorial pages of Hearst's largest-circulation papers, dispensing theories of human development based on Nietzsche and Freud under headlines like "Supernormal, Normal and Misfit: Which Are You?"

Like Lawrence's, Mabel's life had broken in two halves. Rebirth began the day in 1917 she arrived in New Mexico with her third husband, the painter Maurice Sterne. Within hours she had recognized her Shangri-la, and within months published her last Hearst column, announcing her departure for her earthly paradise and inviting artists to join her and "start over." Shortly after that, she began an affair with the spectacularly handsome Tony Luhan, head of the Taos Tribal Council. Their love was consummated in a tepee, and Maurice Sterne sent packing with an allowance of $100 a month.

AT his first sight of Mabel, waiting with her Cadillac at Lamy station, Lawrence must have been distracted by the man at her side. He knew that Mabel had an Indian lover (he told Catherine Carswell that Mabel had had "two white husbands and one Jew: now this") and he was looking forward to a "redskin welcome." But he was not prepared for Tony's physical presence, nor for the ambiguities of class that mixed race presented. Should they all eat together?

Lawrence's idea of a mixed marriage was himself and Frieda, his fantasies of "Red Indians" expressed in the group of strolling players who dress up as the "Natcha-Kee-Tawara Troupe" in *The Lost Girl*. But Antonio Luhan (accented on the second syllable; Mabel had changed the spelling from the original "Lujan" because so many pronounced the "j") was the platonic ideal of the Noble Savage, a tall, magisterial man from the Taos Pueblo, who wore his hair in long braids interwoven with purple-and-white ribbons. Mabel said that Tony had taught her to despise possessions; if he did despise them, he, in his quiet way, nevertheless enjoyed quite a few of them, such as good riding boots, expensive tailored pants, and big cars. Lawrence did not know how to react to him, and behaved awkwardly, scurrying around to the far side of Frieda when they all perched on stools at the station's lunch counter.

The two women sat in the back for the drive into Santa Fe, and Frieda cast unsubtly admiring glances at Tony's broad back. "Do you feel him like a rock to lean on?" she asked loudly, and was suddenly scornful about Lawrence's hopelessness with a motorcar.

In Santa Fe as in Florence, Lawrence faced unperturbed the phenomenon of male homosexuality openly manifested. His host for his first night in New Mexico was Harold Witter Bynner, a poet, playwright, and lecturer. Alerted by Mabel that Lawrence was on his way and needed accommodation for the night, Bynner eagerly offered his only bedroom, with adjoining bath, to the Lawrences, and shifted himself and his young lover, Willard Johnson, to studio couches for the night. Johnson, nicknamed Spud, had been Bynner's student at the University of California. He was out at a Tom Mix movie when the visitors drove in, but came home in time for dinner. "Un ménage, hein," said Frieda knowingly to Mabel, one woman of the world to another.

Bynner, known to his friends as Hal, was an urbane, balding Bostonian of leftish politics who had moved to Santa Fe only seven months before. He had arrived to lecture, collapsed (from influenza and nerves) and stayed. Perhaps Santa Fe allowed him for the first time to be open about his homosexuality; in 1919 he had proposed marriage to the poet Edna St. Vincent Millay and was relieved to be able to extricate himself gracefully. Santa Fe also allowed him to indulge his taste for fancy dress—he had a wardrobe of silk kimonos and caftans from his travels in the Far East—and for many years he led the annual parade in Santa Fe in deerstalker costume. While living in New York Bynner had been literary editor of *McClure's Magazine,* and in 1910, he arranged for the first book publication of Ezra Pound. His work, particularly his translations of Chinese poetry, was widely admired. Such was Bynner's reputation in the early 1920s that friends later said that "no one would have guessed that in the long run it would be Ezra and not Hal."

Silk neckerchiefs and silver jewelry notwithstanding, Bynner was first and foremost a Harvard man. His alma mater was the real love of his life. Class of 1902, two years ahead of Franklin D. Roosevelt, he called his first book of poetry *An Ode to Harvard* and in his will (he died in 1968) left all his papers to Harvard, including a clipping from the *Harvard Library Bulletin* announcing that he was leaving them.

Bynner, friend of Amy Lowell and Harriet Monroe, and past president of the American Poetry Society, had read a great deal of Lawrence's work. He loved *Sons and Lovers* and *Sea and Sardinia,* but found *Psychoanalysis and the Unconscious* absurd rubbish. Curious to meet the famous author, he invited to supper that evening, also to have a look, Alice Corbin Henderson, poet and former assistant editor of *Poetry,* who had herself moved to Santa Fe in 1916 because of tuberculosis. Thus the pillars of the Santa Fe literary establishment were waiting to see what manner of celebrity Mabel's Cadillac would bring.

THE D. H. Lawrence of 1922 was famous. That year the British adventurer T. E. Lawrence chose to write under the name Ross rather than his own. "Lawrence was impossible," he said, "since there is a very great but very strange man writing book after book as D.H.L." In postwar America, moreover, following the success of *The Rainbow* and *Women in Love,* Lawrence's name was even then synonymous with sex and passion, and, in popular culture, good for a laugh. "Don't interrupt me," said the heroine to her sweetheart in a popular show of the time, in a line that brought down the house, "I am in the midst of one of the most passionate passages of D. H. Lawrence." And Lawrence received much fan mail along the lines of a letter from a reader in New York City: "Would the recounting of a personal recollection, which has haunted me from infancy and which has only this year been plain to me through reading two of your books, be of interest to you?"

Arriving at Bynner's, Lawrence lived up to his reputation. The first sight Bynner had was of a thin agile figure getting out of the car, holding one end of a painted-wood Sicilian panel. Suddenly Tony put the car in reverse, the panel cracked in two, and Lawrence got a tremendous thwack. He exploded. "It's your fault, Frieda!" he shouted. "You've made me carry that vile thing round the world, but I'm done with it. Take it Mr Bynner, keep it, it's yours! Put it out of my sight! Tony, you're a fool!"

Frieda utterly ignored the explosion. Bynner was charmed. He instantly took sides, and never swerved. For him Frieda was "a solid, hearty, wise, and delightful woman," and her genuine love for Lawrence probably her worst fault. Frieda responded in kind. She had found a friend in whom she could confide about her troubles with Lawrence. Besides, Bynner was gregarious, fun, and mixed a good cocktail.

That first evening Lawrence demonstrated that an arduous journey had not upset his self-sufficiency. He startled his host by going into the kitchen and helping the maid chop the vegetables for dinner. Next morning when Bynner rose early to prepare breakfast, he found that Lawrence had already laid the table, prepared the food, swept the floor, and made the bed.

Then Mabel and Tony bore the Lawrences off for the rough seventy-mile drive north to Taos. The last few miles were breathtaking, as the road—the old route from Santa Fe to Colorado Springs—opened suddenly after a long climb to reveal a vast lunar landscape in smoldering Technicolor.

Lawrence did not arrive on a stretcher or admit that he was a "health seeker." Yet his swift acceptance of Mabel's invitation to New Mexico was part of a consistent, if unspoken, program of self-cure. His statement on his first sight of the Taos valley—

> I think New Mexico was the greatest experience from the outside world that I have ever had. . . . The moment I saw the brilliant, proud morning shine high up over the deserts of Santa Fé, something stood still in my soul, and I started to attend.

is justly celebrated, but it was also a beautiful way of saying that New Mexico was the greatest hope of drawing a clear breath he ever had.

Yet the spectacular landscape revealed a savage, impersonal beauty indifferent to man. The seven-thousand-foot-high desert of the Colorado plateau, bordered by the mountains named Sangre de Cristo (Blood of Christ) because they turn from green to red at sunset and slashed deep into the earth's crust by the gorge of the Rio Grande, was and remains a fitting amphitheater for the apocalypse.

By a quirk of history, that same summer another painfully thin semi-invalid man considered a genius saw for the first time the New Mexican desert. In 1922 J. Robert Oppenheimer, then a young physicist who had never weighed more than 125 pounds in his life, came west on a pack trip for his health. Oppenheimer fell in love with the brown hills, mesas, and dry canyons shaded by cottonwood trees *(los alamos)*, and formed in the back of his mind the clandestine possibilities of its desolate isolation.

The region still carries an air of magic and menace. Its sands, waters, air, and prehistoric emanations attract healers of every persuasion, while the lonely black crosses of a flagellant sect, the Penitentes, are a reminder that this is a place where no one is watching, where the bizarre can go undetected and anything is possible, from human sacrifice to the construction of a bomb that can destroy the world.

For all Frieda's insistence that Lawrence needed "genuine" places, they usually ended up in resorts and artists' colonies. Of all they sampled in their wanderings, Taos was far and away the most claustrophobic and self-dramatizing. In 1922 it was a small Western town of two thousand inhabitants clustered around a dusty plaza full of shops, hitching posts, and covered wagons. At one end, surrounded by fields, lay Mabel's estate, the Big House, with its corrals, five guest houses, and servants' quarters, and at the other end was the Taos Pueblo, where six hundred Indians lived in an adobe honeycomb. Lawrence wrote his sister-in-law Else that the pueblo resembled "a pile of earth-coloured cube-boxes in a heap."

Tony deposited Lawrence and Frieda at a new five-room adobe named the Pink House, which he had built especially for them on Indian land adjoining Mabel's property. Everything about it was to the Lawrences' taste—the Navajo rugs, Southwestern pottery, and adobe fireplaces, the fresh whitewash on the walls (for once Lawrence would not have to do it himself), and the stripped pine beams. The irregular lines and uneven surfaces everywhere proclaimed that no machine tool had ever been near the house.

Like a good hostess, Mabel had their visit well organized. No sooner had Lawrence arrived than she packed him off with Tony and a friend of hers from Buffalo for a three-day trip to an Apache gathering—"120 miles away across desert and through cañons," Lawrence wrote to Kot back in London. That left Mabel and Frieda to discover how much they had in common. They were the same age, forty-three, had rich and checkered pasts, and shared the same psychoanalytic worldview and fondness for quotations from *Thus Spake Zarathustra.* Mabel's Brill, like Frieda's Otto Gross, believed that sexual repression was harmful and that women especially suffered from it. "If you find a woman depressed and out of sorts with herself and weeping," Brill wrote in his *Basic Principles of Psychoanalysis,* "you may safely conclude that something is wrong with her love life."

Mabel, too, just like Frieda and like Frieda's German contemporary Alma Mahler, expressed herself through living with and through famous men. Mabel saw her destiny as enabling male genius to flower and regenerate society. At the same time, she understood Frieda's wish to be appreciated in her own right, not to be seen as a mere appendage to Lawrence.

In those early days Frieda talked freely to Mabel. She told her about Lawrence's entanglements in Cornwall with Esther Andrews and William Henry Hocking. She talked about the love affairs she had had when she returned to Germany to see her mother, and she told Mabel how she had gotten Lawrence into bed within the first twenty minutes of their first meeting. She also confided in Mabel that when she had informed Lawrence she was starting the menopause, he wept.

Mabel could easily match Frieda's memories. She, too, was a sexual outlaw. As a young wife, she had had to leave Buffalo in a hurry when her husband's sudden death brought to light the scandal of her love affair with her obstetrician (who may also have been the father of her child). She was also a *Kulturträger*. In Florence before the war, with her second husband, Edwin Dodge, a wealthy young Bostonian student of architecture, she had held court at her Renaissance Villa Curonia. During the war she moved to Greenwich Village, where she conducted a memorable salon whose guests included Lincoln Steffens and Walter Lippmann.

That she had no more children by her subsequent husbands or by Tony was probably the result of her long battle with venereal disease, although she is unlikely to have discussed that subject with Frieda. Mabel had first contracted gonorrhea from her Buffalo lover, then syphilis from later partners, including Tony. Syphilis was as rampant among the Taos Indians as among other American males, and Mabel's efforts to help the local pueblos included a strong campaign to curb venereal disease. During Lawrence's stay in Taos, she was receiving painful weekly injections of an arsenic compound, which may have contributed to the wild mood swings and fits of weeping that soon were to infuriate Lawrence.

Mabel, perhaps even more than Frieda, was highly conscious of her approaching menopause, and, according to Lois Rudnick, her biographer, saw colonizing Taos as a way of extending her fertility.

THE two women's friendship stopped when Lawrence returned. He cooperated enthusiastically with Mabel's determination that he write a book about her place and about her. The idea appealed to him, for he equated Mabel with America itself. Accordingly, he read her poems. He listened eagerly to her life story and to her clumsily stated convictions, one of which was that "the deepest kind of living is in the trying and doing of it." As if she were another of his pupils, he set her an assignment. She was to write down the significant events of her personal life in Taos: how she met Tony, how she got rid of Tony's Indian wife (in fact, by buying her off for thirty-five dollars a month), and how she had parted from her third husband, Maurice Sterne. She must, Lawrence insisted like an analyst, remember even the things she did not want to remember. Painfully Mabel obliged, and trusted Lawrence to put it all in a book with her beloved New Mexico as the glorious setting. In those early weeks, he managed to begin, and penciled six pages of a novel about "Sybil Monde," a willful American woman who abandons industrialized society to seek a mythic role.

Lawrence overwhelmed Mabel with the force of his personality. While she was devoted to Tony, as a partner and as a lover, he drove her to tears with his silence, and silence was not one of Lawrence's failings. In the long hours Lawrence spent with her, at her house or riding through the desert, Mabel absorbed his brilliant talk and ideas. She tried to remake herself to his fierce standards for women's behavior. She scrubbed her own floor (but only once). She knitted him a scarf with her own hands. Just like Frieda, she abandoned fashionable clothes and started to wear homely pink-checked gingham pinafores, with a ribbon tied around the waist. The Alice in Wonderland look hardly suited her solid shape, but Mabel consoled herself that the costume looked even worse on Frieda, who was fatter. Frieda didn't worry about how she looked. "Lawrence likes fat," she told Mabel. "He says my stomach is like a big loaf of bread."

Still, Lawrence reproached Mabel for lack of modesty. He disapproved of her sunbathing on her sundeck clad only in a burnoose and moccasins, and when he was shocked by her uncurtained bathroom windows he allowed him to paint over the glass with brightly colored phoenixes and geometric designs.

Lawrence met Mabel halfway. He and Frieda dined often at the Big House and participated in Mabel's "Indian evenings." At these, Tony led a line of Indians from the Taos Pueblo into the dining room after dinner; dressed in feathers and war paint, they would dance to the drum. Then Mabel would invite the entire company to "dance like the Indians," and all together would hop and rattle in a circle around the room, Lawrence yelling and waving his arms with the rest. But perhaps the best part of Lawrence's Western orientation course was riding lessons with Tony. Not holding back the laughter, Tony taught Lawrence and Frieda both how to mount and control a horse; Lawrence was soon adept enough to ride for hours.

THAT autumn Mabel was by no means as solely preoccupied with Lawrence as their fevered letters to each other might indicate. She and Tony were deeply involved in the first national battle to secure Indian rights.

Her most notable recruit before Lawrence had been John Collier, a socialist and social reformer. When Collier moved from New York to New Mexico at her invitation, he felt that he had discovered among the Pueblo Indians "a red Atlantis," a model for all Americans in communal spirit and lack of envy. In September 1922 Collier was just launching a national campaign against the Bursum Bill, introduced in Congress to hand over ancient Indian land and water rights, without compensation, to commercial developers.

The Bursum Bill reflected the postwar isolationism and conservatism of the United States. Not only was the national mood in favour of restricting foreign immigration in order to preserve the existing white-Protestant balance (part of President Warren Harding's promised "return to normalcy"), but at the same time it had no respect for indigenous cultures. White Americans considered the Indians lucky to have been colonized by Europeans and even more so to have been made dependents of the federal government, looked after on reservations.

By the time of the Bursum Bill, Collier, Mabel, and other "friends of the Indians" were already angry about the neglect of Indian welfare; there were only two doctors for ten pueblos around Santa Fe, and little education beyond the eighth grade. The Bursum Bill was the last straw. The anti-Bursum campaign attracted progressive American artists and writers, many of whom, like Bynner, had been part of a prewar alliance of artists and socialists in New York.

Lawrence pleased Mabel by swiftly catching the sense of the campaign. Good journalist that he was, within nine days of arrival he had written an article on the Indian question for *The New York Times*. He also signed the national petition, "Protests of Artists and Writers Against the Bursum Bill," along with, among others, Carl Sandburg, Zane Grey, Vachel Lindsay, and Edgar Lee Masters.*

THERE was no reason for Mabel to sense the growing hostility of both Lawrences. On the contrary, she seemed to be the refuge for each from the other. Frieda, weeping one day, told Mabel she could take it no longer; the previous evening Lawrence had been tender and loving, but in the morning he hit her and said he would not be a woman's servant. "Sometimes I believe he is mad," Frieda said. She further confided in Mabel that Lawrence sometimes beat her after sex because he was angry with himself for "sinking" into the flesh. Mabel believed these reports, for she herself had seen the bruises on Frieda's body when they all went swimming at hot-spring pools. She also knew that Lawrence still so hated any mention of Frieda's children that when Frieda wanted to know about the health of her daughter Elsa, who had been ill, she had to get Mabel to cable surreptitiously for news.

Lawrence, for his part, had complained loudly to Mabel about Frieda.

* The Bursum Bill was killed in January 1923, but a replacement soon appeared. John Collier and the Taos–Santa Fe crusaders fought on until they had secured for the Indians a measure of control over their water and land rights.

She was insensitive to his work and aspirations; she was hopeless as a nurse; he loathed those heavy German hands upon him when he was ill.

Mabel, moreover, had witnessed their appalling public fights with each other, and like Katherine Mansfield in Cornwall, she wickedly recorded the exchanges. Lawrence, detesting the way Frieda would sit with her cigarette drooping in the corner of her mouth, with one eye closed against the smoke, snarled, "Take that dirty cigarette out of your mouth! And stop sticking out that fat belly of yours!"

To which Frieda replied, "You better stop that talk or I'll tell about *your* things." (Frieda's repartee lacked subtlety, but it could silence her husband.)

But Mabel had underestimated the bond between husband and wife, and also Frieda's power. Once Frieda became jealous of Mabel, Mabel's relationship with Lawrence was doomed—and jealousy did not take long to appear. For Frieda, the idea of Lawrence closeted for hours with Mabel talking about "the womb behind the womb" was as unacceptable as that of Lawrence strolling arm in arm with Ottoline around the gardens of Garsington. She soon put her foot down and insisted that the sessions on Lawrence's book on Mabel continue at their own house. Mabel hated this, of course, for with Frieda present, the "flow" between herself and Lawrence stopped.

It was only a short time too before Mabel found herself among Lawrence's devouring women. Within the first fortnight he grew fed up with "living under the wing of the padrona" and began to think of escaping from Taos back to Santa Fe. Not long after, even though the Big House and the Pink House were only two hundred yards apart, their inhabitants were communicating by note.

Lawrence now saw Mabel as willful, and willfulness he now ranked as the most American of sins. Mabel certainly was what would today be called manipulative. She organized too much for him, while his nature demanded him to be independent, even of kindness. Moreover, he felt that her aggressive advances were sexual; that while talking her high-flown theories, she was making her square body indelicately available. (Later Mabel conceded that, although her passion for Lawrence had not been physical, she had behaved as if it were.)

To Frieda, Mabel tried to defend herself. She insisted that she wanted to seduce Lawrence's spirit, not his body. Frieda told her that was just as well. Lawrence, she said, was dry and brittle, a nightmare to live with. She said she ought to leave him and make a life for herself before it was too late. Mabel said (or later said she had said) that she told Frieda not even to think of abandoning him—that she was the only possible wife for Lawrence.

The very next day, according to Mabel, Lawrence came to see her to say that he and Frieda wanted to move out of Taos. Mabel had an old ranch, which she had given her son, John, in the foothills of the mountains seventeen miles north of Taos. He and Frieda had seen it, liked it, and would rent it from her. They wanted to be alone.

Lawrence then sent Mabel a manifesto. In it he scolded her for abusing the power of her money, for bullying Tony and all the men in her life, and for totally misunderstanding his marriage: "The central relation between Frieda and me," he said, "is the best thing in my life, and, as far as I go, the best thing in life."

Mabel was terribly distressed. She had willed Lawrence to come to Taos, even practiced witchcraft to get him there, but having got him she could not hold him. Bynner laughed at her. She was well clear of Lawrence, he said, and mocked Alice Corbin for her own case of "Lawrengitis." Bynner told Mabel, "My own only shudder was over what you had let him do to your house. Anglican influence is bad enough at best, but why should you, of all people, defer to Lawrence, of all people, in any question of taste?"

ONE of Lawrence's lifelong problems was that he could bear neither to live alone nor to be contradicted. This required an unusual combination of qualities from his companions, as Frieda's bruises showed. As soon as he had determined on moving up to the ranch to be alone, he began to invite people to come there with him.

First, he tried to enlist Mabel's Buffalo friend Bessie Freeman; then he lobbied Mountsier. Unexpectedly perhaps, among the Taos artists Lawrence found two recruits, who turned out to be the best disciples he was ever to have. They were Danish painters traveling the United States in a Model T Ford, good-tempered, short of cash, and uninterested in philosophical argument. Introduced by Walter Ufer, a Danish artist who had been one of the founders of the Taos art colony, Lawrence swiftly saw the young Danes' potential as handymen, protectors, and chauffeurs, and offered to pay all their expenses if they would move with him and Frieda up to the ranch for the winter.

The Danes, as everybody called them—Knud Merrild, twenty-eight, and Kai Götzsche, thirty-four—knew perfectly well that Lawrence wanted them because they had a car, could do heavy work, and could even amuse him with their flute and fiddle, but they fell under the spell of the blazing blue eyes. The philosophy Lawrence preached made sense to them—that civilization was corrupt, that self-sufficiency in isolation was the answer. And they had been snubbed by Mabel. On bad terms with Ufer at the time, she had turned her back on them at first introduction; two unknown Scandinavians added no jewels to her crown. In response, the pair sneered at Mabel's "Indian evenings" and were glad to hear Lawrence say that he was going to deny Mabel her dearest wish: "Never, never, in my life shall I write that book," he told them.

Complex and dark as Lawrence's motives were for breaking with

Mabel, it is plain that once again he was following the tubercular's handbook. He had not, despite his hopes, felt well in Taos; in moving up to a mountain ranch he was seeking fresher air, higher altitude, and a more primitive environment. Since he avoided doctors, the actual condition of his chest at the end of 1922 is not known. But he told Mountsier simply that on Mabel's estate, and under her protection, "I don't breathe free."

AT the beginning of December, Lawrence, Frieda, and the Danes made the move—not, in the event, to Mabel's high ranch, which turned out to be too primitive for speedy renovation, but to two cabins lower down the mountain, nearer the main road and near the Del Monte Ranch, which was run by a family named Hawk. Lawrence liked these neighbors, five minutes away: twenty-five-year-old Bill Hawk; his new wife, Rachel; and his younger sister, Elizabeth. The elder Hawk, Alfred, then in California, had come to New Mexico from the East as yet another of its consumptive pilgrims.

In preparation for wilderness life, Lawrence outfitted himself with Western gear. His first pair of cowboy boots cost the not inconsiderable sum of twenty dollars (his rent for the ranch was a hundred dollars for six months) but he was inordinately pleased with them. He wrote Mountsier, "You should see me—cowboy hat, good one, $5: sheepskin coat— $12.50—corduroy riding-breeches, very nice, $5." And his boots were the best: "You know Justins Cowboy boots are 'world famous'? I didnt. There are others much cheaper."

In many ways, it was Higher Tregerthen all over again, if not Rananim. There was a pair of cabins, with the happy difference that Merrild and Götzsche, unlike the Murrys in Cornwall, were neither literary nor resentful. The Danes admired Lawrence tremendously. He was extremely generous. He bought their food, gave them lessons in Spanish, and paid them to design covers for his books. He offered to help them organize exhibitions in Taos, where his influence was vastly greater than theirs. "If you ever in any way can profit by my name," he told them, "you are welcome to do so."

And the Danes liked Frieda. When one day Lawrence stormed against their Model T and the evils of the motorcar in general, Frieda simply got into the backseat, saying, "We will just imagine it's a Rolls Royce."

Lawrence threw himself into the outdoor work of the ranch, such as chopping down trees for firewood for both cabins, but as usual he kept up his intensive literary production. That winter he continued to revise his *Studies in Classic American Literature,* making them, after his experience of Mabel, more misogynistic and, now that he had seen American culture, more critical of that as well. He corrected the proofs of

Kangaroo, keeping in, against Mountsier's and Frieda's advice, the flash-back war episode, "Nightmare." He also wrote a new ending for the American edition. Moreover, he persisted in efforts to help William Siebenhaar, the Dutch emigrant writer he had met in Perth, and helped him get a publisher for his translation of the Dutch classic *Max Have-laar.*

Lawrence needed no persuading that the business of America was business. He wrote frankly to his German mother-in-law, telling her that America was far more of a bully than Germany; in fact, America was the greatest bully in history, because its money, which the rest of the world wanted, made it proud and overpowerful: "You know, these people have *only* money. . . . One could only say: 'America, your money is shit; go and shit more'—then America would be a little nothing." Unfortunately, he needed the American money. *Women in Love* had sold more than ten thousand copies. "Why do they read me? But anyhow, they *do* read me—which is more than England does."

For once, therefore, he had plenty of money. He asked Seltzer to be sure he always had two thousand dollars in his account at the Chase National Bank. He earned half as much from his journalism and essays as from his books, and in the United States alone made well over five thousand dollars that year, two thirds the annual salary of a U.S. senator.

Now that he had money, he paid his old debts to Ottoline Morrell and Eddie Marsh, sending them the fifteen and twenty pounds, respectively, that they had lent him during the first year of the war. He also sent Else Jaffe ten pounds for the children. At last, he wrote Mary Cannan in Sicily, he could lend and not borrow.

There was a long, cold winter ahead, albeit with warm rooms. Even so he returned to a well-wisher in New York a gift copy of *Ulysses.* He had tried to read it, he said, as in Europe his name was usually mentioned with James Joyce's and he felt he ought "to know in what company I creep to immortality." All the same, he conceded, with apologies: "I am one of the people who can't read *Ulysses.* Only bits." He was anyway so busy chopping and caulking seams and cooking that he had no time even to write letters—or so he reported to Mary Cannan on a day in which he wrote six.

SUCH was his importance as an author that both his agent, Robert Mountsier, his publisher, Thomas Seltzer ("a tiny Jew, but trustworthy"), and Seltzer's wife, Adele, made the long train journey west to taste life on Lawrence's mountain. Diehard city dwellers all three, they submitted to log cabin life for the privilege of being near him.

The Seltzers were particularly smitten. Lawrence was their principal author. Russian-born Thomas Seltzer had been an independent publisher only since 1919 and was struggling to establish his small firm at a time when business was bad. He had taken a chance on *Women in Love,* printing a private edition in 1920 when no one else would touch the book, and had published a stream of Lawrence's works ever since, including, novels and short stories apart, the play *Touch and Go,* the psychology books, and *Sea and Sardinia.* Meeting Lawrence in the flesh was, for both of them, in Adele's words, a "stupendous experience." She described it to a skeptical friend:

> He loses nothing by being seen at close range. As for his wife, she's a Norse goddess. . . . Lawrence is a captivating personality, always flashing sparks. When he's in the mood to sing and make fun, he is utterly charming, with an elfish grace. My wholly masculine man, Thomas, has succumbed to him as completely as I. You should hear him imitate various American accents. It makes you roll with laughter.

And why did she love Lawrence so much? Adele Seltzer, like so many of Lawrence's smitten women, fell into Lawrencian prose:

> I cannot tell you why anymore than I can tell you why I love the glow of a sunset, the opal of dawn, the murmur of running waters. In the field of human emotions, in the eternal passional struggle, that is what Lawrence is to me. Like the elements, he can be fierce and wild, tigerish, bearish (but *not* brutish). . . . His Q.B. knows he is not brutish.

Lawrence, said Adele, was in no way affected; his ranch was no "show ranch" but "really roughing it." The Seltzers pitched in with all the chores, for Frieda had made it clear to them that, being a baroness born, she was no good at housekeeping and that what cooking she knew, Lawrence had taught her. It was bliss. For a whole week they spoke to nobody but the Lawrences and the two picturesque young Danes—themselves, said Adele, "Norse gods."

The Seltzers saw in the New Year of 1923 with the Lawrences, the Danes, and the Lawrences' small black French bull terrier in the Lawrences' log cabin. Adele concluded:

> Lawrence is a Titan, and I go about with an ever-present sense of wonder that we, Thomas & I, little, little Jews, should be the publishers of the great English giant of this age . . . not because with Jewish shrewdness we outwitted some other publisher . . . but because Lawrence's "Women in Love" went begging for a publisher, and we were the only people who understood its greatness & had faith in him as a writer.

This reverence survived an unpleasant scene. Lawrence had declared to Seltzer, in front of Adele and Frieda, that "the core of himself" was "domination of the male. That's something you two females couldn't understand, and you can put your two heads together until they crack like nuts." When Adele objected, Lawrence turned pale and stalked off into the snow for four hours.

THE coming of Christmas revived the tensions with the Taos crowd. There was a big Indian ceremony the Lawrences wanted to see, with their guests. They had hoped that Mabel would invite them all to the Big House. But Mabel felt that she was being exploited; the Lawrences, having rejected her, now wanted to make use of her. She told them that she had her hands full with her son's wedding.

As she did. Her twenty-year-old son, John, had decided to marry the Corbins' daughter, "Little Alice," so called to distinguish her from her mother, "Big Alice." Little Alice was indeed little, at least in age—only fifteen. That her parents and Mabel blessed the marriage is a mark of the unorthodoxy of the Taos colony.

The Lawrences were not invited to the wedding on December 20. However, Lawrence, as an acknowledged expert on the human heart, was invited to give the young bridegroom a talk on married life. He obliged. He told John that he must keep the center of himself always alone and that if his young bride crossed him in anything, he should beat her.

Lawrence did manage to see the dance at the Taos Pueblo, but he was not much moved by it. He had begun to sense the difficulty in carrying out his intention to write a novel about America. The United States he found to be soulless, new, and commercial; even the Indians were "very American—no inside life."

In Taos the Lawrences stayed with Nina Witt, another Buffalo heiress gone native (to the extent of having married the elderly, one-armed local sheriff and sawmill operator, Lee Witt). At the Witts', the Danes noticed Lawrence's compulsive habit, wherever he was staying, of going into the kitchen to do the dishes and, while spouting his views on the evils of mechanization and the bloodless American spirit, rearranging all the china and glass on the shelves, scrubbing the drainboard, and washing the dishpan and hanging it on its nail.

That was the genial side of Lawrence. Frieda had a bad time with the other side that winter. The Danes also came to have doubts about his sanity. They felt they were invited over to the Lawrences' cabin too often—as if the couple could not bear to be alone together. Lawrence in a rage was a terrifying sight: the blue eyes blazed and narrowed, the skin went pale, his voice rose to a high pitch, and his movements became quicker than ever.

Even the bull terrier, Bibbles, felt his wrath. Lawrence loved the dog, one of Mabel's pups, and had written a poem to her. When he caught her tearing at the meat of a killed steer, however, he beat her so savagely that the animal went to live with the Danes. "There let her stay," said Lawrence defiantly. Eventually Bibbles returned to the Lawrences' cabin for a reconciliation, but made the mistake of going into heat.

Lawrence lost control of himself and attacked the dog again. She retreated to the Danes' cabin and hid under the couch, but Lawrence came after her, white-faced and trembling, muttering in words too applicable to his wife about "the love-bitch" and her lack of loyalty. "Love," he raged, "seems usually to be just a dirty excuse for disloyalties." He dragged the cowering animal out into the open, kicked her, then hurled her out into the snow. The Danes watched this insane performance in stunned horror. Merrild said later that he nearly hit Lawrence but, as a champion swimmer, much the stronger of the two, feared he would have gone berserk himself.

The exhibition was so out of keeping with Lawrence's usual reverence for birds and beasts that Merrild had to ask himself how he reconciled the two faces of the man:

> There is, of course, no denial that Lawrence was at that moment cruel to the dog, grossly so. But he was so to us, to his wife, and to everybody for that matter, at times, and mostly so to himself. He could be the very devil. Nevertheless, in spite of this, or because of it, we liked him just the same—the dog episode included. Lawrence loved animals and humanity more passionately than most of us do, and he who loves much shall be forgiven much. . . . Honestly, I don't think there is any reason to try to defend him.

Seltzer, too, later strove to balance Lawrence the devil with Lawrence the man. He chose to remember the man, "natural, without pose and, at bottom, sane":

> Follow him in the kitchen when he cooks, when he washes and irons his own underwear, when he does chores for Frieda . . . when he walks with you in the country . . . in his conversation he is almost always inspiring and interesting because of his extraordinary ability to create a flow, a current between himself and the other person. . . . So many people dwell only on his fierce outbreaks. But to me his outbreaks, even if they belonged to the man, were not of the essence of him.

Frieda, however, had to live with the devil as well as the man. One day, in front of the Danes, he knocked the eternal cigarette out of her mouth and then ground the rest of the packet into the table with the heel of his hand and threw it into the fire. Later Frieda sneaked down to the Danes' cabin with a carton for safekeeping. Almost as furtively, she would speak to the Danes about her children. Once when she dared to show their photographs around, Lawrence snatched them from her hand and ripped them to pieces.

The Danes were not homosexual, as they had to insist many times in later years when asked about their winter with the notorious Lawrence. Nor, they added, responding to the inevitable next question, was he. As painters, however, they observed him closely. When they all swam naked in the hot springs, they saw that he was not self-conscious about his body although it was much thinner and whiter than theirs. It did not, to them, look sickly. The oddity about his naked appearance was the profusion of red hair all over his face and head, which overbalanced the rest of him.

Young Robert Mountsier, like the dog, ended up with the worst of Lawrence. His visit was not a success. He had never been west before and, after offering to pay his expenses roundtrip, Lawrence put him up in an unheated room in the Danes' cabin, with only porridge for breakfast. Then Mountsier was persuaded onto a horse, only to have the horse fall, breaking Mountsier's wrist.

More was broken than a bone. Lawrence grew angry with Mountsier, who, he decided, was anti-Seltzer and, like Mabel, a secret destroyer. He would act for himself, he said, take charge of all his business affairs, and save the ten percent commission. Later he was annoyed and surly when Mountsier sent the bill for his trip; the rail fare had come to three hundred dollars.

Lawrence's desire to be his own business manager came into conflict with his urge to keep constantly on the move. It was difficult for all the necessary correspondence, contracts, and bank statements to keep up with him. He made matters worse by playing off publisher against agent—Curtis Brown against Secker in London, Seltzer against Mountsier in New York—and the two publishers against each other. He also had complicated problems arising from former books. He had to bring a lawsuit in New York to retrieve publishing rights from two previous publishers, Benjamin Huebsch and Mitchell Kennerley, from whom he had received nothing for the American publication of *Sons and Lovers*.

HARDLY had 1923 dawned when Lawrence began to talk of moving on. The desire has been widely, and not inaccurately, attributed to his incurable restlessness. Yet he would have had to leave in any event, because he and Frieda had entered San Francisco in September as visitors, declaring that they intended to stay no longer than six months, that they planned to return to England, and that they intended neither to settle nor to work in the United States. The only question facing them in early 1923 was whether to return to England or not. Frieda had no doubt. After so long away, she was determined, whatever Lawrence said, to see her children again and to visit her aging mother.

Once again he decided, she followed. England was out. It had rejected him and "I stomach that feeling badly." While he knew how English he was at heart and recognized openly that his incessant travel was "a form of running away from oneself," their next destination would be Mexico.

But eager as ever for companions (or chaperones), he persuaded Bynner and Willard Johnson to go with them. For Mabel, this was the unkindest cut. She had longed to escort him to Old Mexico herself. But Bynner was the chosen guide, and Lawrence treated him almost as a scoutmaster. He wrote humbly to Santa Fe to ask, "I would awfully like to take the little black dog with us? Could we do it, do you think?"

All that remained before he could go was to pay his income tax, which was due on March 15. Mountsier sent him the figures but Lawrence recalculated the deductions, adding on the heavy cost of Mountsier's train fare. He chose to pay in New Mexico rather than in New York because New Mexico had no state income tax. After deductions and the allowed exemption of $2,500, his taxable income for 1922 was only $1,740.40, on which he paid tax of $70.

The Lawrences' departure (without dog) for Mexico on March 20, 1923, marked the end of his first short stay at the place with which, next to Nottingham, he is most associated. He left no healthier than when he arrived. As he wrote Seltzer,

> I've still got a bit of my cold. Want very much to go south. . . . Feel the U.S.A. so terribly sterile, even *negative*. I tell you what, there is no life of the blood here. The blood can't flow properly. Only nerves, nerve-vibration, nerve-irritation. It wearies the inside of my bones. I want to go. Voglio andarmene.

IN Mexico City, installed at the Monte Carlo, a small Italian-run hotel on the Avenida Uruguay near the cathedral and the main plaza, and glad to be back in a Latin culture where he could drink wine, Lawrence decided that he preferred Old Mexico to New, but not by very much. Within five days he was dreaming of England and wrote Murry to look for a decent cottage for him for the summer; in the autumn he would go back to Sicily, the place he had liked best. For Murry he described Mexico's "gruesome Aztec carvings"—"sub-cruel, a bit ghastly." Mexico City was too American, he said, while the countryside was too scarred by battle.

The revolution Australia feared during Lawrence's stay never took place, but Mexico, between 1910 and 1920, had had the real thing, a combination of bolshevism, nationalism, and peasant revolt against foreign investors and American domination. A strongly socialist coalition had won control of the federal government in 1920 and encouraged the redistribution of land. However, the rich and powerful interests of the revolution's opponents were combining against the new leftist president, Alvaro Obregón, and the gunfire lingered on.

Obregón's most notable appointment was his minister of public education, José Vasconcelos, a well-traveled and cultured intellectual who swiftly secured an international reputation for his radical program to cure mass illiteracy. It was Vasconcelos who commissioned politically committed artists such as Diego Rivera and José Clemente Orozco to create the brilliantly colored primitivist murals (at the University of Mexico, the Palacio Nacional, and other public buildings) that constitute a visual manifesto of the revolution. And it was Vasconcelos who caused a memorable tantrum.

Vasconcelos invited the group of literary visitors, of whom Lawrence was the centerpiece, to lunch on April 27. They arrived to find that at the last minute President Obregón had summoned his minister to an emergency cabinet meeting—not surprising, as an emissary of President Warren G. Harding was on his way to Mexico City. The United States had withheld recognition of Obregón's government because of a number of matters outstanding: Mexico's huge debt to the United States, American claims for reimbursement of holdings nationalized during the revolution, and a dispute about American interests in Mexican oil.

Vasconcelos sent apologies and asked his guests to return next day. The others agreed, but not Lawrence, who flew into a paroxysm of anger. His convulsive losses of control were becoming a social embarrassment. This storm took ten minutes to quell and those who did not know him were dumbfounded as he ranted about being pushed around by an insignificant minister from a backward country. Carleton Beals, an American newspaperman in the party, finding the outburst most un-English, put it down to what he believed to be Lawrence's consumption. Beals, another of those Americans who preferred Frieda, admired her "great poise, calm and breeding."

Perhaps it was just as well that Lawrence stayed away the next day, when the others returned for lunch, for he believed that the revolutionary government's efforts to raise the peons to modern standards of literacy (even to the point of giving them cheap editions of the classics) were criminal, and he probably would have told Vasconcelos so in no uncertain terms.

MEXICO can make harsh demands on the traveler even today. In 1922 the quartet from New Mexico all fell victim to various ailments. Bynner and Johnson separately had to enter the hospital for treatment. It may have been the heat and discomfort, along with his own deteriorating health, that brought Lawrence's public battles with Frieda to a new intensity. Frederic Leighton, an American importer who showed them around Mexico City, said he had never seen anyone issue such a stream of vile abuse upon his wife, or upon anyone else. Bynner recorded for posterity a scene of nauseating awfulness at their hotel where Lawrence, flushed with wine, became infuriated once more by the sight of Frieda's cigarette:

> "Take it out, I say, you sniffing bitch!" And then, though she was seated behind a corner table, half hidden from everyone by the cloth, "There you sit with that thing in your mouth and your legs open to every man in the room! And you wonder why no decent woman in England would have anything to do with you!" Flinging the remaining drops of his Chianti at her, he darted past the other tables into the lobby and then out into the street.

When Bynner, as did all onlookers, wondered why Frieda so passively put up with this abuse, she answered that she had no alternative. With no way of earning her living, she did not want to be a burden on her family in Germany. She had learned that the best response to his tirades was silence, even though saying nothing made people think she was stupid. His anger came from realizing that she liked people more than he did. "He does things for people, Hal, because he's soft in some ways," she said. "He writes interesting letters all the time to people he doesn't really like, which is not what I would do."

While they were in Mexico City, word reached them that Mabel had married Tony. Lawrence was deeply shocked. He felt that people should know their place and had complained loudly about Tony's constant intrusive presence. "Why does Mabel keep dragging that fat Indian around?" he would say.

The American press, however, was fascinated with the news. "Why Bohemia's Queen Married an Indian Chief," the *Pittsburgh Post* headlined its story. The answer was that John Collier and other friends of the Indians had warned Mabel that her affair with Tony—outrageous behavior by the mores of the times—had come to the attention of the Justice Department and was strengthening the hand of the anti-Indian lobby in Washington and New York. As an Indian, Tony was, after all, a ward of the federal government.

(The marriage was more than a political gesture. It was a good, if turbulent, one and lasted until Mabel's death in 1962. Although Tony occasionally returned to his first wife in the pueblo and had casual affairs, including one with the artist Georgia O'Keeffe, he was indeed the rock of strength that Frieda recognized him to be. One later guest of the Luhans remembered Tony shooing them all away one night when Mabel was unwell and commanding her, "You sick woman. You go to bed.")

In Mexico City, Lawrence's outbursts notwithstanding, the four of them were not short of invitations or guides. They went to the well-known tourist spots—for example, the bullring just outside the city, where they saw a bullfight which Lawrence fled after half an hour. At Teotihuacán they climbed the Pyramids of the Sun and Moon, studded with stone images of the feathered serpent, Quetzalcoatl. They saw the floating gardens of Xochimilco and took short trips to Cuernavaca, to Puebla (where Frieda and Lawrence had a loud fight in the dining room of the Hotel del Jardín) and also to Tehuacán and Orizaba. Lawrence soon had the feeling he had seen it all and wanted to return to England.

The speed with which he changed destination was as irrational as his tantrums. A chance remark was sufficient to catapult him in imagination to another part of the globe. "Had enough of the New World," he wrote Murry a month after arriving in Mexico. He sent a dozen letters or cards in one day announcing that he and Frieda would sail for England the following week. All of a sudden, Lawrence changed tack. Perhaps he would stay a while in Mexico and take a house, or a *hacienda,* as he now began to call it.

The sight of the Aztec ruins and the lush countryside outside Mexico City had given him the idea for a book. Perhaps that is how Lawrence preserved his sanity. Just when nowhere seemed home and his temper was blazing out of control, a novel took root, steadying and defining him. Having decided to stay on in Mexico, he declared that England was a bog. As for the scenic spot he had just left, he wrote Merrild, "Spit on Taos for me." Full of a sense of adventure, he then went northwest by himself to Lake Chapala, Mexico's largest, near the city of Guadalajara, to find a place for them to live.

As usual, he did not go into the unknown but rather to places where he had contacts. In Guadalajara, he looked up Idella Purnell, a former poetry student of Bynner's at Berkeley, and then went on to the nearby town of Chapala. One look and he telegraphed Frieda: "Chapala paradise. Take evening train." Frieda knew her man. Waiting in Mexico City with Bynner and Johnson, she said, "When he finds a place by himself he always likes it."

Once again a tourist resort seemed a safe haven. Chapala, he wrote Bynner, was "just enough of a watering place to be *easy.*" Again he used his chest as a metaphor; to Seltzer he wrote, "I shall begin a novel now, as soon as I can take breath," and to Catherine Carswell that he would be back in England by August "but wanted to get this novel off my chest." He could not understand himself why he went out to buy a ticket for New York or Europe, then drew back: "Wonder what ails me," he wrote to Murry. "You'll think I do nothing but change my plans."

But a letter to Merrild and Götzsche summed it up: "When I feel sick I want to go back. When I feel well I want to stay." He promised his mother-in-law, who was yearning to see them, that they would be in Baden-Baden by September.

IN Guadalajara as elsewhere, when he was in a good mood, meeting people for the first time and having had a little but not too much to drink, Lawrence was entrancing company. Idella Purnell was dazzled by his mimicry. He did not act just with his voice, but with his whole body, collapsing into a chair laughing until he recovered himself. He would ride an imaginary bicycle around the room, crying "Ting-a-ling-a-ling!"; he would do the Indian Sun Dance with a slow tread and constant hum. For the young American woman and her father, he imitated Ezra Pound introducing his homespun parents from the Midwest to London literary society. Suddenly, she said in her memoir of Lawrence, "Ezra Pound—was standing before you. He made us see the parents and feel sorry for them . . . and see the son, and even feel a little sorry for him."

In Chapala Lawrence sat under a tree, and on or about May 10, after two false starts, began a novel about Mexico—the wrong Mexico, not Mabel's but Obregón's. Keeping to his ambition to write a novel in every continent, he planned another rush job, as in Australia. He would finish by the end of June.

He opened his story with a vividly observed report of the visit to the bullfight with Bynner and Johnson, and of a tea party with the expatriates they had met around Mexico City. He had done massive reading on Mexican history in preparation for the trip and could well have stopped there, having achieved a travel book on a par with *Sea and Sardinia* and *Twilight in Italy,* but he did not want to stop.

At Chapala he and Frieda had a house of their own, with Bynner and Johnson nearby in a hotel. He settled into an agreeable routine. He lived barefoot in trousers and shirts. In the mornings, with his back against a tree overlooking the lake, he sat and wrote, and watched the women washing their clothes in the lake. In the evening, wearing white bathing trunks, he swam. Then the two Americans would wander over and they would all sit and talk on the veranda, Bynner and Lawrence arguing hotly with each other.

Bynner's rancor against Lawrence has subsequently been ascribed to his satirization as Owen Rhys in the opening chapters of *The Plumed Serpent,* but the antagonism was well developed before Bynner read the literary use Lawrence had made of him. Lawrence, Bynner wrote a friend from Chapala that summer, was scarcely human. Lawrence hated humanity, Bynner said, and was only at ease with animals because they could not talk back to him. And he knew that Lawrence hated him: "He is having his revenge on me in a novel—which Spud is copying and I am not allowed to read. . . . He has been defeated by people all through his life and has consequently lashed their paper images with his poor fury."

The novel taking shape was to be Lawrence's revenge on far more than Witter Bynner: on Mabel, on Christianity, on European culture, and on the whole female sex. *The Plumed Serpent* may be his greatest failure, but it was also to be his most intellectually adventurous work. In a desperate emotional and physical state, he sought to create a vision of an alternative Mexico, a whole new religious and political system, with laws, rituals, hymns, and mythology.

As *Kangaroo*'s had the year before, the title emerged as he wrote. He chose the name of the god, which combined the name of a mountain bird with beautiful tail feathers (Quetzal) and that of a serpent (Coatl). "Shall I call it 'Quetzalcoatl'?" he asked poor Seltzer, who winced. "Or will people be afraid to ask for a book with that name?" In the book, Lawrence maintained, there was no sex.

Frieda also saw the new book as their triumph over all their enemies, the most splendid thing Lawrence had ever done. A letter to Adele Seltzer shows how much in harmony she and Lawrence were about their life adventure. Frieda did not complain of having been dragged to Mexico; it had enlarged her view of the world. As she told Adele, "It's given us a lot, the country so hard and wild and unsentimental."

However, it has not escaped the notice of later feminist critics that Lawrence began the novel in the company of a homosexual couple and that its two male characters represent ideals of the male body: the imposing Don Ramón Carrasco, "a tall, big, handsome man who gave the effect of bigness," and the small but sensual Don Cipriano, with "full, yet beautiful buttocks."

In Chapala there was no pretense that Bynner, forty-two and wealthy, was not keeping Spud Johnson, penniless and twenty-six. They laughingly teased Johnson as being like the local "fifi boys," who strolled along the lakefront in the evening. Frieda wrote the Danes that both men were nice "but Bynner is an old lady and Johnson a young one." Lawrence, in his letters, gives no hint of the disturbing effect on a man with his anxieties of traveling with homosexual lovers. But his novel does. The description of the bullfight scene that opens *The Plumed Serpent* is a grotesque fantasy of homosexual intercourse:

> The bull once more lowered his head and pushed his sharp, flourishing horns in the horse's belly, working them up and down inside there with a sort of vague satisfaction. . . .
> This she had paid to see. Human cowardice and beastliness, a smell of blood, a nauseous whiff of bursten bowels! She turned her face away.

"She" is the heroine, an Irishwoman, called Kate Burns in the first version, Kate Leslie subsequently. The sight sickens Kate, but Owen (Bynner) has a "sharp look, like a little boy who may make himself sick, but who is watching at the shambles with all his eyes, knowing it is forbidden." His young companion Villiers (Johnson) just "looked intense and abstract, getting the sensation." Then the bull attacks again.

> . . . the horse was up-ended absurdly, one of the bull's horns between his hind legs and deep in his inside. . . . his rear was still heaved up, with the bull's horn working vigorously up and down inside him . . . And a huge heap of bowels coming out. And a nauseous stench.

As in *Kangaroo*, the novel's most powerful sensory image is one of excremental smell. (To the Kleinian critic Margaret Storch, the "bursten bowels" of the opening chapter of *The Plumed Serpent* represent a release of anal aggression against the controlling mother.) Whatever Lawrence's private views on the relationship between Bynner and Johnson, he seems to have tried to pry them apart. Not long after, he recommended to Seltzer that he hire the able Johnson as an editorial assistant: "I think he ought to have a proper job, not be just Bynner's amanuensis."

By June 8 the novel was half done: 450 pages of manuscript with an inconclusive ending. Lawrence then put it aside. The "enemy" was getting him down, he told Adele Seltzer; "doesn't want me to write my novel either." He did not name the enemy.

For a hypersensitive man Lawrence was curiously tolerant of civil unrest. He and Frieda accompanied Bynner, Johnson, and other friends on a three-day lake trip even though there was talk of new revolution. Although Lawrence did not enjoy riding in trains with armed soldiers lying on the top, nor living in a village guarded by twenty soldiers, nor having a servant with a revolver sleeping outside his window, he felt none of the terror roused in him by the mere thought of going back to England. He merely shrugged and put up with the reverberations of revolution. "The country is a sort of no-man's-land as far as security goes," he told Adele Seltzer. The tension brought out a certain bravado. "If I can't stand Europe we'll come back to Mexico and spit on our hands and stick knives and revolvers in our belts," he told Merrild.

By the end of June, Lawrence had worked out their plans: New York, then on to England. A strike at Veracruz preventing them from going by boat, on July 9 he and Frieda left by train for New York via Laredo, and were vaccinated at the border—free of charge, Lawrence was pleased to note. Hardly had they turned their backs on Mexico when Pancho Villa, the colorful revolutionary hero, who had stirred Lawrence's imagination, was assassinated.

Lawrence marked his trip up the eastern coast of the United States with the verbal snapshots he usually accorded more exotic places. Texas: "fierce hot—queer show"; New Orleans: "steamy decayed town, feel sick all the time"; the Mississippi: "a vast and weary river that looks as if it had never wanted to start flowing," and finally New York: "a great stupid city, without background or atmosphere." An hour out of town on the Lackawanna Railway, he came to rest in Morris Plains, New Jersey: "pretty, rural, remote, nice . . . Desolate inside."

The Seltzers had taken a cottage in Morris Plains for the whole season just in order to house their beloved Lawrence, who hated cities, for a few weeks. The Seltzers, at the Lawrences' invitation, even moved in with them. Of Frieda Adele observed, "He complicates things *for* her. I believe, without him she would be grandly simple."

High summer passed as Lawrence read proofs for three books—*Kangaroo; Birds, Beasts and Flowers* (poems of nature, which are some of his most appealing work), and his translation of the Verga novel—and agonized over the impending trip to England. "God knows," he wrote Kot, "if I shall be able to bring myself across the Atlantic." He bought tickets for them both and waited to see what he would do. By now, their deepest instincts were pulling Lawrence and Frieda apart. She desperately wanted to see her children and her mother. He was driven by the desire to see more of Mexico to enrich his political-religious novel, and by his dread of England.

Lawrence was fond of a biblical image from his chapel childhood to express his sudden stubborn halts: Balaam's ass, which understood the will of God better than his master and refused, in spite of beatings, to carry Balaam where God did not wish him to go. In 1922 he had used the mythical beast to explain his reluctance to go straight from Sicily to New Mexico and in 1923 he drew on it again to cover his otherwise inexplicable resistance to returning home. To his mother-in-law, he said his soul "is like Balaam's ass, and *can't* travel any farther." Yet what he was groping to name was a physical feeling. The stubborn force was in his belly. He told Murry, "I can't stomach the chasing of those Weekley children." To Amy Lowell he wrote: "I ought to have gone to England. I wanted to go. But my inside self wouldn't let me."

By the first of August, he had pretty well decided not to go, but they fought about it all week, little deterred by the news that shook America—President Harding's sudden death on August 2 from apoplexy, and his replacement by Calvin Coolidge—right until the moment on August 18 when Lawrence escorted Frieda to the ship and came on board to say good-bye. She begged him to come, even without luggage. But Balaam's ass won out and Frieda sailed alone. Lawrence wrote and asked Jack Murry to look after her.

It was not so much a trial separation as a de facto one, brought about by irreconcilable needs to be in different places. Frieda was so much on his mind that while giving an interview to the New York *Evening Post* about the death of mechanized civilization, he said that it was only women's inertia that had saved the world. "If it had been left to the men," he said, flapping his hand out the window at New York, "it would have been destroyed long ago." He would continue his search for the thread of belief that would carry civilization on after world destruction. He would look west, he said, but his wife would not. "I guess she's going back to England in half an hour," he said, looking at his watch. Yet they did not know when they would see each other again.

Lawrence knew he did not fully understand himself: "my Self is a mystery that impinges on the infinite." He tried to clarify his quest in an essay for Murry's new literary review, *Adelphi:* "We write a novel or two, we are called erotic or depraved or idiotic or boring. What does it matter, we go the road just the same. If you see the point of the great old commandment, *Know thyself,* then you see the point of all art."

But his letters show that, without acknowledging it, he had already decided what he would do next. He would clutch once more at the reassuring Danes. The two painters had made their way in their Model T to Los Angeles. Even before Frieda left, Lawrence wrote to them that he thought he would join them, or, as he put it, forsake the "white civilisation," which made him "sicker than ever," and return to the West. Then they could all go off together, perhaps on a donkey to explore the Mexican mountains, perhaps on a sailing ship to the South Sea islands. He was glad he had enough money to go where he wished. Hardly was Frieda out of sight of land when Lawrence wrote the Danes that he was California bound.

But it was not so much the call of the West as a recoil from England that determined his actions. "England," he said in his condolence letter to Willie Hopkin in Eastwood upon the death of Sallie Hopkin, "seems full of graves to me." One grave in particular. The tragedy of the Lawrences' marriage was their incomprehension of each other's greatest sadness—his loss of his mother, hers of her children.

THERE followed a curious period of Lawrence's frenetic crammed life which seemed to change scene, characters, and even language every few months. It began with one of his rare journeys on his own. Going west by train, he stopped off for four days to visit Mabel's mother in Buffalo. There he put on his best behavior with the "blue bloods" and profited from it; after the visit, a new character, Mabel's mother, the Buffalo dowager Sara Cook Ganson, was added to his repertoire of impersonations. Changing trains at Chicago, he took the measure of the city— "floods of muddy-flowing people oozed thick in the canyon-beds of the streets"—before heading on the Union Pacific to Los Angeles. Merrild and Götzsche, only mildly glad to see him, installed him at the Hotel Miramar in Santa Monica where he sat on the lawn under the palm trees and watched old men play miniature golf.

He then moved to a rooming house on West Twenty-seventh Street in Los Angeles. While the Danes painted murals for a Brentwood geologist, he rewrote the first half of Mollie Skinner's Western Australian novel, went through ship schedules to find a boat that would take the three of them to the South Seas, then decided that they should all go to Mexico.

At that point even the stolid Merrild dug in his heels. He felt that he was too much in Lawrence's sway. Refusing to come to Mexico, he left Götzsche to act as chauffeur and nurse to Lawrence for three months. The odd couple set out on September 25, Götzsche doing all the driving, to travel down the length of California, to Palm Springs ("pale whitish desert—a bit deathly"), through the "broken, lost, hopeless little towns" of lower California and the western coast of Mexico, through which the Chinese "run about like vermin," and where the cockroaches too ran at full speed.

They reached Guadalajara by mid-October, and Lawrence settled in for some serious work. By mid-November he had turned Mollie Skinner's "House of Ellis" into *The Boy in the Bush,* with a twist added in the form of two final chapters completely his own. These present the solution for a man in conflict between wife and mistress: to have, in all but the legal sense, two wives.

But Lawrence had, instead of a second wife, a Danish driver. Their relationship seems to have been, uncharacteristically for Lawrence, untroubled and trusting, but even the mild-mannered Götzsche began to avoid Lawrence at times and to entertain doubts about his sanity. It was a grueling trip—by car, by train, and, over washed-out roads, by muleback—and dangerous. Mexico was in new turmoil. The myriad opponents of the revolution were organizing against Obregón, who was prepared brutally to crush them. Assassinations were commonplace.

Götzsche could see how Lawrence was missing Frieda and wondering why she did not write. In fact, Lawrence, seriously wifeless for the first time in a decade, was swirling with thoughts of how he would bring Frieda back. He kept planning her return trip to the United States and sent trunk keys to Seltzer in New York to hold for her arrival. He also sent Frieda books to read.

WHEN Lawrence wrote to Murry in August, "I wish you'd look after her a bit: would it be a nuisance?," he as good as passed Frieda over to him. Katherine Mansfield had died of tuberculosis in Paris in January 1923 at the age of thirty-four; Lawrence then healed the breach with Murry with a moving letter about the living presence of the dead, ending with a genuine note of apology. "I wish it needn't all have been as it has been," he wrote. "I do wish it." Yet he knew that Murry, who had hardly been a faithful husband, was on the loose.

Murry indeed was a widower with a roving eye. In April he had persuaded the shy deaf painter Dorothy Brett to surrender, at thirty-nine, her long-preserved virginity. Vulnerable Brett fell in love with him and soon, in her diary, was writing eerie letters to her dead friend Katherine about the strange beauty of physical love.

Brett knew that Murry would not marry her. Humbly she offered him her body and soul—"take just that much that you have the need of & the courage to take no more." Her fear (half a hope) that she was pregnant by Murry ended just as Frieda arrived.

Frieda took a bed-sitter at the top of the rooming house on Pond Street, Hampstead, where Lawrence's old friend Mark Gertler lived. She was back in the country where among their mutual friends she was by no means the favorite spouse. Gertler was soon reporting to Frieda's old enemy Kot that Murry was a constant visitor to her room and "god knows what else."

Her apparent intimacy with Murry revived Kot's belief that Frieda was a disaster for Lawrence. Gertler found her just a bore. "She is worse than she might be because she apes Lawrence and his ideas coming out of her large German body sound silly and vulgar," he said. But he loved impersonating her guttural gush: "The country is so Real, the landscape is so *Real* and the people are so REAL!"

Gertler and Kot were worried about the sound of the symptoms Lawrence described in his letters. Gertler himself had tuberculosis. Recently emerged from a long spell in a sanatorium in Scotland, he dreaded a recurrence of blood-spitting, the signal that would send him back in. He looked after himself very carefully, avoiding overexcitement and fatigue, and felt that Lawrence should do the same. To their dismay, Frieda appeared to be quite as bad as her husband at denying the very existence of the disease. When Lawrence informed Seltzer of Katherine Mansfield's death, he did not mention the cause, saying only that she had "died suddenly," while Frieda flatly declared to Adele that Katherine's death had been inevitable because "she chose a death road and *dare* not face reality!"

Kot suggested to Frieda that she go to Germany and wait for Lawrence there. But, to Kot's disgust, when she left for the Continent she took Murry with her. In Mexico, Lawrence suspected what Frieda was up to. He knew that Murry, who was on his way to Switzerland, had accompanied Frieda at least as far as Paris. A month passed before Lawrence heard from Murry that he had finally arrived in Switzerland. Lawrence could only reply: "From Frieda not a word—suppose Germany has swallowed her." Brett's letters to Murry's intended destination in Switzerland failed to reach him.

Murry later left contradictory testimony about what had actually passed between them. In one letter to Frieda late in their lives, he regretted having turned her down in 1923. However, as Murry was fairly promiscuous and they had already spent considerable time alone together in London, it seems possible that what Murry refused was cohabitation. Frieda, as she told Mabel and others, would have liked to make a fresh start. A new protector would have been welcome, especially one who would keep her in Europe. But none was in the offing.

Frieda nurtured no hard feelings. It was not her way. Back in London, she kept booming at Murry and Brett, to Brett's mortification, that the two of them ought to marry. She did little to communicate with Lawrence. For weeks he was totally out of touch. However, when he did hear, the message was clear. If he wanted to see her, he had to return to England.

There was no choice. As he wrote to Mabel (making peace in a civilized exchange of letters in which he thanked her for bringing him to Taos), "I shall give in once more in the long fight." The decision halted progress on the Mexican novel.

LAWRENCE liked to think of himself as obeying Frieda's summons, even though she had cabled the one word "Come" (which reached Lawrence as "cone") only because Murry and Kot pushed her into it. He tried to sound distant and collected, and told her that he would stay only long enough to make a financial arrangement so that she could live independently if she wished. But to his mother-in-law, he poured out his heart: "Oh Schwiegermutter Schwiegermutter, you understand, as my mother finally understood, that the man does not need, does not ask for love from his wife, but strength, strength, strength.... And the stupid woman always sings love! love! love!"

Love was exactly what Frieda felt she gave. In answer to Kot's open criticism, she rounded on him in another of the angry, defensive letters that marked their long acquaintance. "When you say Lawrence has loved me I have loved him a thousand times more!" she wrote. "And to really love includes everything, intelligence and faith and sacrifice—and passion!" If she ever came to think of Lawrence as a great man, he would be a lifeless thing to her, and a bore. Besides, while she might rank poorly, compared to her husband, in Kot's mind and "in the world of men," there was another world: "a deeper one, where life itself flows, there I am at home!"

*   *   *

BEFORE leaving Mexico, Lawrence packed off Mollie Skinner's transformed novel, *The Boy in the Bush* (she burst into tears when she saw the changes). The book was set for publication under both their names the following April. He bought a serape ("Shades of Hal," he joked to Spud Johnson), and, with Götzsche, embarked on the S.S. *Toledo* at Veracruz on November 22, just ahead of the De la Huerta Rebellion, which launched an open campaign against President Obregón for selling out to American interests. Lawrence paid all Götzsche's expenses for the journey.

He arrived at Plymouth on December 7, 1923. He took the long boat-train ride to London, stepped out at Waterloo Station, where Frieda, Murry, and Kot were lined up to greet him, inhaled one whiff of the acrid fog, and said, "I can't bear it."

And he could not. Almost immediately he was bedridden. The circumnavigator who had begun his world journey with excited descriptions of the Red Sea now lobbed his spirit-of-place miniatures back in the direction from which he had come. For Bynner back in Santa Fe, he summed up London: "gloom—yellow air—bad cold—bed—old house—Morris wall-paper—visitors—English voices—tea in old cups—poor D.H.L. perfectly miserable, as if he was in his tomb."

He also wrote to Mabel, now Luhan, and asked if they might come back to Taos.

14

BLOOD

January 1924–February 14, 1925

*I*n what was to be a year of murderous fantasies, Lawrence began 1924 by polishing off Murry. In "Jimmy and the Desperate Woman," the first of three quick short stories, a man who looks like Murry ("the strong chin . . . the beautiful dark-grey eyes with long lashes, and the thick black brows") and who works like Murry ("editor of a high-class, rather high-brow, rather successful magazine") steals the wife of a Midlands miner only to realize that his life will be haunted by the man he has wronged. In "The Border-Line," a ghost hounds to death the English journalist who has married his widow. In "The Last Laugh," a sexual adventurer in Hampstead is struck stone dead by a laughing apparition he has seen in the bushes.

With his compulsion to use and reuse the fabric of his own life, Lawrence made the remarried widow of "The Border-Line"

a handsome woman of forty, no longer slim, but attractive in her soft, full feminine way. . . . Fifteen years of marriage to an Englishman—or rather to two Englishmen—had not altered her racially. Daughter of a German baron she was.

At this point in his life, according to Richard Aldington, he was gripped by such a paroxysm of hate that the anti-Murry stories approach the borderline of sanity. To Aldington, they proved that Lawrence's work barely makes sense without a knowledge of their author's biography.

The appearance of the supernatural in "The Border-Line" and "The Last Laugh" suggests that Lawrence's faith in the nearness of the dead verged on a belief in ghosts. They reveal a man tortured by barely controllable visions of himself as a dead man, trapped on the far side of the border, watching the living make love. Finishing the trio of stories, Lawrence told his agent Curtis Brown, "Don't send any of these to the *Adelphi*, in any case." Yet beyond his resentment against Murry the stories reveal his own lingering guilt toward Ernest Weekley. It is not only Murry whom they punish.

New Mexico was once again the promised land. Lawrence took friends to a movie house in the Strand to see a western called *The Covered Wagon* and hummed "Oh! Susanna" as the lights went down. He advised Curtis Brown, whose son had lung trouble, to take the boy to New Mexico. He planned his own return. It had been a mistake, he wrote Mabel, to take Taos too seriously; next time he would have an honest laugh at it.

But he still hoped to take a band of followers with him. At a small (and subsequently overpublicized) dinner at the Café Royal he summoned his closest London friends and invited them, one by one, to come to New Mexico. Three accepted on the spot: Brett, Murry, and Catherine Carswell. Murry capped the evening with an ambiguous toast in which (accounts vary) he swore either never to betray him or never to betray him again. The party came to a dismal end when Lawrence, drunk on port and far more ill than his friends realized, vomited onto the table and passed out.

In a professional author, the compulsion to write and the compulsion to earn are not easily distinguished. Lawrence marked his return to the Old World with an outpouring of journalism—that is, of his own special brand, which offered as social analysis his own, intensely personal, response to what he saw. One of his articles, about the nature of the Englishman, was so scathing that Murry refused to publish it in *Adelphi*. (Frieda later blamed its tone on the tension of his reunion with her.) "Coming Home" can be read as an attack either on the duplicity of all Englishmen or on one in particular, a man with beautiful dark-gray eyes and long dark lashes:

> Look into his nice, bright, apparently-smiling English eyes. They are not smiling. . . . The eyes are not really at ease, and the nice, fresh face is not at ease either. . . . There strays out of him, in spite of all his

self-containing, the faint effluence of fear, and the sense of impotence, and a quiver of spite, of subdued malice.

A short visit to Baden-Baden to see his agreeable *Schwiegermutter* (to whom he was "Fritzl") inspired "A Letter from Germany," for *The Laughing Horse.* In the event, the article did not appear in print until after Lawrence's death and after Hitler's ascent to power, but then was greeted as an uncanny premonition of things to come. Lawrence's lightning impression of the Weimar Republic in 1924 shows how sensitive to external reality his inward-tuned antennae actually were.

But at night you feel strange things stirring in the darkness, strange feelings stirring out of this still-unconquered Black Forest. You stiffen your backbone and you listen to the night. There is a sense of danger . . . a queer *bristling* feeling of uncanny danger. . . .
Something about the Germanic races is unalterable.
White-skinned, elemental, and dangerous. . . .
It is a fate; nobody now can alter it. . . .

LESS than three months from the day they arrived in London, Lawrence and Frieda were back on a ship heading for New York. They had patched up their differences. Frieda had seen her mother and her children, and, at Catherine Carswell's home, reintroduced Lawrence to the two girls. Uxoriously, Lawrence now included in his letters profuse greetings from his wife and himself.

For an unfaithful wife of a relatively monogamous husband, Frieda had a good deal to be jealous about. As they headed west on the *Aquitania,* she, who so liked to have a spare man around, found that Lawrence, just like his *Boy in the Bush,* had a spare wife. Dorothy Brett was the lone survivor of the New Mexico volunteers. Murry had dropped out once he found that Brett was going along (he probably had never really intended to abandon the *Adelphi*). Catherine Carswell had also sent regrets. That left Frieda to share Lawrence with an unmarried woman whose only lover she had just stolen.

Lawrence had acquired, in effect, a new Magnus: a hanger-on whom Frieda fiercely resented and for whom he felt an ill-defined responsibility. Brett, to be sure, was no financial burden. As Lawrence relayed to the Brewsters, she was "a painter, very deaf, about as old as I am, has a modest but sufficient income, and is daughter of Viscount Esher." However, she was an emotional sponge: rootless at forty, only recently sexually awakened, then dropped. Lawrence was acutely aware of her predicament and knew something of its origins.

Her mother had died when she was very young, leaving Brett with a homosexual father who had married only for appearances' sake. Unloved by him, sexually molested by one of his friends, and bullied by her brothers, she grew up afraid of men and refused her family's attempts to marry her off. Instead, she trained at the Slade School of Fine Art with Mark Gertler, Stanley Spencer, and Dora Carrington (with whom she had developed a predilection for being called by her surname). Sure of her modest abilities as an artist, Brett was totally unconfident of herself as a woman and, with her drooping cheeks, receding chin, prominent upper teeth, and eager eyes, retained the look of a gawky, apologetic girl—or, as Lawrence captured it in one of his cruelly apt animal comparisons, "sometimes like a bird, sometimes a squirrel, sometimes a rabbit: never quite like a woman."

Brett was further handicapped by deafness. She carried everywhere her flat metal ear trumpet, which she anthropomorphized pathetically as "Toby." Vulnerable as she entered middle age, there was little she could do to protect herself from falling in love. Effortlessly, as they sailed, she transferred her hopeless attachment from Murry to Lawrence.

Like Mabel, Brett saw nothing sexual in her devotion and attributed it to Lawrence's enhanced vision of life. As she explained to Witter Bynner some years later, "He was extremely human, but his idea of a human was different. I think one might say, that he kept the rigid code of a child, do you remember your codes as a child, how unrelenting and rigid and violent they were?"

They arrived at New York in a blizzard on March 11, 1924. Lawrence began to see that passing through the portals of the United States was no simple matter. Even as he had ended his first trip to New York, the Statue of Liberty had become one of his threatening women, "clenching her fist in the harbour." All visitors upon entering had to swear that they were neither anarchists, nor polygamists, nor immigrants. Even so, they were assessed for "deformities" and "condition of health, mental and physical." Brett's deafness caused some delay with the federal medical inspectors; then the customs authorities wanted to charge duty on her painting supplies. In the end, the three were admitted for six months— all that Lawrence wanted, for the main purpose of the journey was to return to Mexico. He felt he could not finish "Quetzalcoatl" without the living reality of Mexico around him.

Thomas Seltzer was at the pier to greet them. Lawrence, unhappy with him, had tried to keep the details of his arrival quiet but Seltzer found them out and presented himself anyway. He really needed Lawrence's support, for he was facing trial for publishing the allegedly obscene *Casanova's Homecoming* by Arthur Schnitzler, and with legal costs mounting, his small firm was in the red. Greeting Lawrence, Seltzer had to break the news that the expected royalties had not been paid into Lawrence's Chase National Bank account.

Lawrence blamed the ambitious Adele Seltzer as a pernicious influence on her husband. The truth, however, was that the kind of avant-garde publisher who, like Seltzer, was willing to take a risk on a Lawrence tended to be a poor businessman. Lawrence's own blend of artistic audacity and fiscal conservatism was, and remains, rare.

Lawrence scolded Seltzer, but not without sympathy. His mistake, Lawrence said, was to strive to be a big publisher as well as a creative one: "You're not born for success in the Knopf sense, any more than I am." Nonetheless, Lawrence shrewdly wrung enough money out of Seltzer before he left New York to buy his and Frieda's tickets west and pay the second half of his 1923 federal income tax by March 15 as well. The first tax installment was $43.74; his American earnings for 1923 were $5,681, slightly higher than for 1922—a good income at a time when a woman's topcoat cost $25 and Mabel Dodge Luhan was independently wealthy on an annual $14,000.

THE return to what Lawrence called "Mabeltown" was a triumph of hope over experience, but it began well. Harold Witter Bynner gave them a welcoming dinner in Santa Fe, where they arrived on March 24. He was delighted to see "the great-hearted Frieda" again, he wrote his mother back East, and even glad to see Lawrence. Bynner was much amused at the project of returning to Taos without quarreling with Mabel.

At Taos everyone, even the Indians, seemed glad to see them. Mabel, just returning with Tony from wintering in New York (where she had an apartment at 1 Fifth Avenue) and California, assured Lawrence on long rides and in quiet asides that she had changed. She was now submissive, less willful. She assigned the Lawrences to what she called the Two-story House and Brett to a studio in her compound and introduced them to her assembled coterie. Ida Rauh, an actress from New York, had founded the Provincetown Players. Spud Johnson had been lured away from Santa Fe (and from Bynner) to become Mabel's secretary. Jaime de Angulo was an anthropologist from Mexico. Lawrence did not much like the volatile Mexican but could see that de Angulo, with his connection with the distinguished Mexican archaeologist Manuel Gamio, the excavator of the pyramids at Teotihuacán, would be useful for his new book.

There was no problem in acclimatizing Brett to a natural habitat for painters. She was swiftly entranced by the desert and the Indians; she loved the way Tony, with his handsome head, plucked eyebrows, and long braids, would make an exit, flinging his blanket over his shoulder and announcing, "I go to pueblo now." Brett soon adopted her own Western costume of culottes, boots, sombrero, and belt with dagger.

Within days of their arrival, Mabel made an astonishing gesture, from either goodwill or manipulative instinct. Noticing that Lawrence was restless and speaking wistfully of her run-down ranch on Lobo Mountain, she took the ranch away from her son, on whom she had previously bestowed it, and gave it to the Lawrences, along with 160 acres of land. Strictly speaking, the gift was made to Frieda, not because Mabel had any special love for Frieda—she did not—but because Lawrence would not have accepted it otherwise. Some stern internal god still forbade him to own property. The man who a dozen years earlier had told his fiancée, Louie Burrows, that any house they owned would have to be hers still observed this self-restricting ordinance. Nothing in it, however, stopped him from rejoicing in his wife's ownership.

To Frieda's mother, Lawrence wrote gleefully that her daughter was now a "Guts-Besitzer"—a lady of the manor. He sent a flurry of letters to England, to everybody from Lady Cynthia Asquith and E. M. Forster (who had just sent him a copy of his new novel, *A Passage to India*) to his adolescent niece, Peggy, announcing that Frieda had become the proud owner of a little ranch of her own.

Lawrence was unhappy about the gift all the same. He did not want to be beholden to Mabel. But Frieda found her own solution; learning that Else was sending the original manuscript of *Sons and Lovers*, which had been found in Bavaria, she gave it to Mabel in exchange for the ranch. The gesture was not well received. The psychoanalytically attuned Mabel interpreted it as a slap at her own wish to be the overflowing, all-giving mother who expects nothing in return.

What Mabel did want from Lawrence, he withheld: time alone together to discuss the "flow" of the universe. Instead she now had to compete for him not only with Frieda but with Brett. Mabel hated the ear trumpet, which Brett positioned as if to snatch every word passing between Mabel and Lawrence. Mabel, in poor health that spring, was also irritated beyond endurance by Brett's English accent and mannerisms. (Because of her deafness, Brett never lost or modified the upper-class tones of her Victorian childhood. Well into her nineties, after she had lived half a century in New Mexico, Brett was still exclaiming, "Oh dyeah, oh dyeah, oh *dyeah*," or "D'y blame meh? D'y blame *meh*?")

Brett as good as ignored Frieda, who she had decided bored Lawrence. She was in awe of Mabel, however. She admired her physical presence, her gaiety, and her ability to organize lavish hospitality and entertainment, which, when it was good, was very good indeed.

Charades at the Big House, with Lawrence in charge, were to a high standard. One night he had them act out the scene of Tony being introduced to Mabel's mother. Lawrence, who had met the formidable Sara Cook Ganson the year before, played the wealthy dowager, with big hat, lorgnette, and shawl while Tony, wrapped in his blanket, played himself. Another diversion for the house party was a trip to San Domingo outside

Santa Fe to see the Indian spring crop dances. It yielded Lawrence two more articles, "Indians and Entertainment" for *The New York Times Magazine* and "The Dance of the Sprouting Corn" for the *Theatre Arts Monthly* and Murry's *Adelphi.*

The expressionlessness of the Indians made a deep impression on him: "Mindless, without effort . . . they dance on and on." Their ritual stirred ideas latent since his college botany days: that man was just part of the great pageant of nature, in which the inanimate held equal place with the animate. He postulated (much in the spirit of Yeats, who asked in a poem written about the same time, "How can we know the dancer from the dance?") that there was little distinction to be made between human beings and their environment.

> They were simply parts of the pageant—not to be judged: violence, war, atrocity were part of the changeless unjudgeable mystery.

The Indian rite took place in a universe where, unlike Greek tragedy or Christianity, there was no struggle between good and evil:

> There is no Onlooker. There is no Mind. There is no dominant idea. And finally, there is no judgement: absolutely no judgement.

Against this unjudging backdrop, Lawrence wrote the most violent work of his life.

His mood was benign at first when they moved up to the ranch early in May, leaving their trunks and good clothes back at the Two-story House, which was to remain their base. With a view over the desert, the distant mountains, and the Rio Grande canyon, he wrote "Pan in America." It is a warm statement of that part of his philosophy which has aged far better than his views on the redemptive power of sex. He believed in the unity of all creation, that "life consists in a live relatedness between man and his universe" and not in a "conquest of anything by anything." He felt at one with the pine tree outside his ranch against which he crouched every morning to write, his notebook on his knees:

> Here, on this little ranch under the Rocky mountains, a big pine tree rises like a guardian spirit in front of the cabin where we live. . . .
> The tree's life penetrates my life, and my life the tree's. We cannot live near another, as we do, without affecting one another.

In harmony with nature he may have been, but not with the people around him. Brett had moved with them up to Lobo (soon renamed

Kiowa) Ranch because, Lawrence told Mabel, he needed her as a buffer between him and Frieda. "Typist" might be a better word. The Lawrences took the main, three-room log cabin (which allowed them the requisite separate bedrooms); they kept another, with two rooms, for guests, and left Brett to squeeze into a one-room cabin so small that the bed took one half and a stove and table the other. Her lot was not brightened by the news from London that Murry had married a secretary in the *Adelphi* office. Lawrence, however, glad to see Murry tethered once again, sent him warm good wishes for a peaceful life, "with a wife, a home, and probably children."

Brett accepted humiliation with exhilaration. She worked hard alongside her idol, shoveling goat dung and gathering rocks, while Frieda, irritated by Brett's soulful sighing at Lawrence, lay on her bed smoking, occasionally coming out to see how they were getting on and to snap at Brett.

Lawrence himself kept needling Brett. Why couldn't she spell, or sew? He knew the answer: "You children brought up by nurses and in nurseries, what do you know of life? . . . Nothing—nothing! You take no part in the actual work of every day living. I hate your class—I hate it!"

Brett, like the Danes of the previous season, watched in silence his outbursts of cruelty to animals. He smacked the puppies because they sucked at each other all day and he could not bear it. He chopped off the head of a hen that had become broody even though he had hung the bird upside down for days "to cool her underneath." Brett also saw him smash a wooden chair he had just made when a letter from Mabel enraged him. For Brett, however, overreaction was part and parcel with oversensitivity; she was simply glad when the storms subsided.

Lawrence threw himself into ranching. He spent $457 on supplies to repair the place. He hired three Indians and a Mexican carpenter to help (and subsequently sacked the Mexican for calling Frieda "Chiquita"). He built an adobe oven in which he baked the bread himself. He showed Brett how to make dandelion wine from his recipe:

Saucepan of water
halftinful of dandelions
boil briskly for an hour or 1½ hours
—
strain, and put in 1 heaped cupful of sugar
—
when just pleasantly warm, crumble in a yeast cake—stir up—and leave in a warm place for 3 or 4 hours
—
strain bottle. Cork *tight*.
—
keep warmish.

With Frieda, too, entering the frontier spirit, cooking enormous meals for the whole crew, churning butter, scrubbing floors, and making her own clothes, Lawrence was happy. He rode twenty miles a day. He cleaned the well and bought a cow. "I don't write—don't want to—don't care," he said.

Trouble began at the end of May. Mabel, with Tony and her latest protégé, Clarence Thompson, a young writer from New York, drove up for a few days' visit. There was a pleasant excursion to the Red River, then a scene. Tony had gone off into the woods and shot a porcupine that was eating the trees. Lawrence was furious; Tony could not see why. It was a classic conflict of cultures. "I *like* the porcupines," said Lawrence. "They going to kill all the trees if you don't keep 'em down," said Tony. An ugly mood settled over the group, which was already split literally into two camps, with Tony and the Indians staying on higher ground where they cooked their meals at an open fire.

The morning after the porcupine incident, Mabel dispatched Clarence to summon Lawrence to talk to her. Lawrence refused. If she wanted to talk to him, she would have to come to his place. Mabel lost control. Unwell, always in a high state of nerves in Lawrence's presence (for she still believed, as she said in her poem "Plum," that no one knew as well as "Lorenzo" how to reach a woman's "available, invisible Being"), she flew into his kitchen, where he was washing dishes with Frieda and Brett, and demanded that he come to her cabin to talk alone. This time he obeyed. The door slammed, and Mabel collapsed in uncontrollable weeping out of which one coherent cry emerged: "How can you treat me like this?"

A good question. Ranching was on his mind, but matricide was in his heart. In between caulking, shingling, and riding two miles in each direction each day to get the milk and the mail, Lawrence was nurturing three long tales that are masterworks of misogyny. The first to be written, "The Woman Who Rode Away," ends with the moment of the ritual killing of a woman; it stands high among the works for which feminists hate Lawrence and that caused Kate Millett to rank him with Henry Miller and Norman Mailer for pornographic sadism.

A more dispassionate critic, Charles Rossman, also identifies the story as the culmination of a long trail of mayhem against Lawrence's female characters. Rossman argues that Lawrence, having murdered one woman in "The Fox" and taught others docilely to submit in "The Captain's Doll," "The Ladybird," and *The Lost Girl*, produced in "The Woman Who Rode Away" a woman who is duped and drugged into acquiescing in her own death: "No expert on the psychology of brainwashing could write a better scenario than this."

"It is a testimonial to the power of Lawrence's art," Rossman says, "that so many readers can vicariously participate, in the name of myth or religion, in her murder." Rossman believes that when writing "The Woman Who Rode Away," Lawrence persuaded himself that he was constructing a regenerative myth, in the manner of Frazer's *The Golden Bough,* as he had done with "England, My England."

The subterranean elements of the story had been smoldering for a long time, as their presence in his early works such as *The White Peacock* and *Sons and Lovers* shows. For twelve years, moreover, Lawrence had lived with Frieda's overweening sexual superiority. Upon returning to New Mexico in 1924, he also faced once more the spectacle of Mabel, keeping an ostentatiously virile Indian as her sexual partner while surrounding herself with effeminate white men. (Both Spud Johnson and the disturbingly attractive new arrival, Clarence Thompson, were homosexual.) Over all, as Lawrence struggled within himself, he recognized the utter indifference of the vast landscape to all forms of human suffering. What is astonishing is the speed with which these dark thoughts were fused by casual events.

On May 17, Lawrence, riding in the high mountains, first saw the high, shallow Indian ceremonial cave at Arroyo Seco, curtained by a waterfall, which he would use as the backdrop for the execution in "The Woman Who Rode Away." A week later, on May 24, he met the flamboyant Clarence Thompson. On or about May 27 Mabel threw her hysterics. On June 12 he began the tale of the willful white woman who gives her heart to the Indians—literally. On June 18 he went down to Taos for a party at Mabel's house, and presented the story, finished and typed, to his hostess.

THE story is told in flat, slow dream language. A beautiful blond woman was a "rather dazzling girl from Berkeley" when she married a Dutch-American mine owner in Mexico. Now, at thirty-three, with two children, she is bored and beginning to grow stout. She decides that it is her destiny "to wander into the secret haunts of these timeless, mysterious, marvellous Indians of the mountains," even though her husband has warned her that all Indians are savages and that one sacred tribe still practices human sacrifice. When he leaves home on a business trip, she leaves, too, riding off into the mountains, dressed (carefully, like all Lawrence's women) in linen breeches, riding skirt, scarlet neck scarf, white blouse, and black felt hat. She is neither afraid nor lonely.

On the third day the Woman—the story gives her no name—is captured by the wild Indians she has come to see. They force her to climb high above the timberline to a hidden village. There the old chief asks if she has come to give her heart to the Indians. Politely, she says yes. When she refuses to take off her clothes, they strip her naked, slashing off even her boots with sharp knives. To cover herself, they offer a white cotton shift and blue woolen tunic. There is no suggestion of sexual intent in their actions. She is still unafraid.

Fed a sweetened herb drink that leaves her in a "relaxed, confused, victimised state," she extracts from the young Indian who guards her a hazy explanation for her capture. It is that the Indians have lost their power over the sun to the white men, who have stolen it to replace their own potency, which they have surrendered to their strident, independent white women. This theft has disrupted the order of nature; to restore it and return to the Indians their rightful power, a white woman must be sacrificed.

"But," she faltered, "why do you hate us so? Why do you hate me?"

"No, we don't hate," he said softly, looking with a curious glitter into her face.

"You do," she said, forlorn and hopeless.

Time passes in a drugged haze. When the shortest day of the year approaches the Woman is borne on a litter, to the accompaniment of drums, dancers, and a cheering throng, to a high cave. There she is stripped once more; naked priests in barbaric ecstasy fumigate her, anoint her with oils, and, turning her to the crowd, display the back of her white body with its long blond hair streaming down. By now the Woman understands her crime and punishment: "Her kind of woman-hood, intensely personal and individual . . . the quivering nervous consciousness of the highly-bred white woman was to be destroyed again, womanhood was to be cast once more into the great stream of impersonal sex and impersonal passion."

The Woman is then laid "on a large flat stone, the four powerful men holding her by the outstretched arms and legs." All wait for the moment when the sun's rays will penetrate the column of ice and the old priest will plunge home his dagger to "accomplish the sacrifice and achieve the power."

Power? Lawrence concludes his tale, just before the blood begins to spurt, with a single phrase: "The mastery that man must hold, and that passes from race to race."

WHATEVER chord there is in human nature that makes men hate women and women feel that they deserve it, Lawrence struck with this story. Its philosophy and psychology can be argued with. Its sensual force cannot. To read it is to feel it. "The Woman Who Rode Away" is an atavistic analogue to Oppenheimer's bomb, a high-density package of vengeance of the primitive against the civilized, of the male against the female.

That it is a projection of Lawrence's own inner conflict is part of its grotesque beauty. It fixes Mabel, like a voodoo doll, to be stuck with a knife. It fixes Frieda too. The Woman's wish to give her heart to the Indians may have been Mabel's, but the body too freely given—white, plump, golden-haired—is Frieda's.

And Lawrence's own. The story is an exquisite, excruciating expression of the wish to be penetrated, heightened by the erotic touch of ice.

FOR Kate Millett's polemic, *Sexual Politics,* published in 1970, this story was a trophy of sadistic triumphalism: "human sacrifice performed upon the woman to the greater glory and potency of the male." Millett even detects a suggestion of ritual buggery in the way the woman's back is exposed to the crowd. "The conversion of human genitals into weapons," said Millett, "has led him [Lawrence] from sex to war. Probably it is the perversion of sexuality into slaughter, indeed the story's very travesty and denial of sexuality, which accounts for its monstrous, even demented air."

"The Woman Who Rode Away" *is* monstrous, even demented—if Lawrence is thought of as a triumphant macho swaggerer. If, however, the Woman is seen to be Lawrence himself, the tale is a powerful expression of inner torment, and not without wider meaning. That a man must kill the woman in himself before he can become a man is indeed a belief that passes from race to race.

Lawrence wrote the story just as the June 1924 issue of *Vanity Fair* appeared, carrying his short essay "On Being a Man." In that swift bit of journalism he concludes that the white man has become too afraid of blood to achieve the noble goal of true virility.

IN the close acquaintance Lawrence formed with Clarence Thompson during those turbulent months, he was continuing his association with those he had once so passionately warned the young David Garnett against: "male lovers of men." Thompson was a tall, fair, and haughty twenty-two-year-old who had dropped out of Harvard in order to go West to write. He had been sent to Mabel by her New York friend Alice Sprague. Even more than Bynner, Clarence affected theatrical dress; for desert riding he chose grandee costume, with Spanish billowing sleeves, and lots of Indian silver jewelry. He lived, according to a local witness, with a Chinese houseboy, and "longed for Lawrence in his strange effeminate way." The two of them spent long hours alone together, riding in the desert or sitting talking in the car. The pair were so close that summer that Mabel believed they had a sexual relationship. Brett was highly curious about their intense conversations and rows.

In his letters to the East Coast and to England, Lawrence said merely that the young New Yorker was "a nice boy" and "not weak really, at all." He was franker in a play he was writing about Taos, in which the petulant character called Clarence enters, "in rose-coloured trousers and much jewellery." When the others laugh at his pink pants, he announces, "Then I shall take them *right* off." The stage direction is "Flounces out."

Mabel's suspicions were alerted when Clarence confided that June: "Lawrence is planning that pretty soon he and I are going to ride off into the desert on horseback and never be seen again!" Yet something must have soured between the two men for Thompson to have betrayed the secret. Perhaps Clarence had realized that even were Lawrence looking (as Maurice Magnus told Norman Douglas) for "bisexual types" for himself, he was not going to go much further than flirtation.

Mabel felt it her duty to tell Frieda about the proposed flight into the desert. "Just let them try it!" Frieda snorted. "The idea! Lawrence would be back inside a week with his head hanging."

Frieda took matters into her own hands. At Mabel's party she watched Lawrence and Clarence disapppear into Taos and return with a bottle of moonshine. (Prohibition, the constitutional ban on the sale of liquors containing over half of one percent of alcohol, was in force all during the decade that encompassed Lawrence's three stays in America.) When the men returned, Frieda began dancing with Clarence. Both were good dancers, and they circled on and on while Lawrence glowered. He himself was a poor dancer and disapproved of social dancing as "indecent tail-wagging." Nonetheless, he grabbed Mabel and began to bob awkwardly about, only to see Frieda and Clarence melt out of the door and into the night.

Mabel was shocked: the morality of her desert Bohemia did not include casual pairing-off.

There followed a night of farce with a cast of self-dramatizing people chasing each other over the dirt roads of Taos. Lawrence affected to be unperturbed by Frieda's absence, and went home to bed. The party broke up, but the errant couple did not reappear. Tony and Mabel retired to their bedroom on the upper porch of the Big House, but she (according to the richly comic account in her memoirs) could not sleep for curiosity. With eyes and ears straining at the window, she waited until at last she heard the voices of Frieda and Clarence returning. She threw on a wrapper and was heading out the door when Tony bellowed, "Come back here!"

She kept going. At Clarence's cottage she found him alone. "I have been learning the truth!" he announced in affected tones, and conveyed it: Lawrence was trying to kill Mabel. Every time he came to Taos he deliberately left her a little weaker and sicker. "He *wants* you *dead*," Clarence told her. "He wants to *know* you are in the ground." All this had come from Frieda, who had told Clarence she was scared.

"You have all believed Frieda was the strong one," Clarence went on. "You don't *know* that man's power. None of you know what he has done to her." He wanted to save Mabel, Clarence said, before it was too late; it was too late to save Frieda. This dramatic recitative was spoiled by the sound of a car starting. Tony was leaving home.

Mabel panicked. She could not live without Tony. On the condition that she promise never to see Lawrence again, Clarence agreed to go in his car and try to fetch Tony back. Mabel then ran barefoot to the Lawrences'.

Only Frieda was awake. She shrugged off her disappearance with Clarence. They had just gone to the plaza. She was more interested in Tony's storming out but assured Mabel that he would come back. So Mabel thought that *she* had an angry husband? Lawrence was angry even in his sleep, Frieda declared, and proved it by taking Mabel in to witness the spectacle of Lawrence mumbling and groaning in his bed.

Next morning Lawrence, not knowing of all that had passed behind his back, announced that he and Frieda would return to the ranch immediately if Clarence would drive them (a three-hour journey, such was the condition of the road). But he soon saw that Clarence was more likely to hit him than chauffeur him. Tony—who, as Frieda had predicted, had returned—offered to drive them instead. Mabel was left with Lawrence's new short story to read.

Back at the ranch, with twelve bottles of smuggled whisky and two of Bibbles's puppies, Lawrence saw himself as the innocent above the battle. The Taos scene, he told Bynner, was "a lot of ravelled knitting, and oneself the kitten trying to pick one's way out of it."

Tony, however, had had enough. He had not liked Lawrence since the day Lawrence painted a green snake on an outhouse. He had been further angered when Mabel gave Lawrence the ranch, for he had been accustomed to let his Indian friends camp, hunt, and graze horses there. He had probably heard, too, the kind of joke that Lawrence was making around Taos: how he would like to see Mabel tarred and feathered and run out of town on a rail. Therefore, when he told Mabel, "I think we done enough for those Lawrences," he meant it. Next day he sent his nephew up to take back the horse he had lent Lawrence.

Lawrence was furious. As if he had been accused of stealing them, he sent a second horse back too.

LAWRENCE responded to Tony's repossession by creating a horse that nobody could take away from him. The principal character in the second great story of that summer is a gigantic stallion so transfiguringly male that he humbles a wealthy American mother and daughter into changing their lives and forswearing the company of mere men.

"St. Mawr," some sixty thousand words long, is really a short novel with another of Lawrence's bifurcated plots; it begins in England and ends on a ranch in the Rockies. The heroine is Lou Witt (her name drawn from Lee and Nina Witt of Taos, who had entertained him the previous year). But Lou's willful use of her American wealth is Mabel's. "I think, if I can, I will buy him," she says of the stallion, which she sees in England and brings to America.

The horse's human counterpart can be guessed from his coloring— reddish-gold; his air "of tense, alert quietness which betrays an animal that can be dangerous"; and his name. "Mawr," the Welsh word for "large" or "great," is not very far from "Lawr," as Frieda called Lawrence. With Brett typing in her cabin and Frieda smoking over at their own, it is little wonder Lawrence briefly thought of calling this story "Two Ladies and a Horse."

In "St. Mawr" Lawrence once again does not seem in control of his meaning. His famed dictum "Never trust the artist. Trust the tale" reflects the bewilderment of a writer at the powerful phrases that surge out of his pen.

"St. Mawr" purports to show a woman's redemption by a divine male force. Awakened to her true being by the violent majesty of the horse, Lou Witt rejects men and goes to live with her mother in the ascetic wilderness of the Rocky Mountains. The critic David Cavitch has called the story inadequate intellectually to its complex materials. The heroine is not redeemed, but terrified by the destructive force revealed in the horse. And St. Mawr himself is hardly the epitome of maleness, for he recoils from the sexual act: "Don't seem to fancy the mares, for some reason," says his groom.

Perhaps the most vivid scene shows St. Mawr rearing in fright at a dead snake and being reined in so tightly by Lou's husband, Rico, that he topples over, crushing the man's ribs and ankle and unable to get himself upright. (The scene obviously derives from Robert Mountsier's unhappy visit to Del Monte Ranch at the end of 1922, when his horse fell on him and broke his wrist.) In the story the horse's fall reveals

a pale gold belly, and hoofs that worked and flashed in the air, and St Mawr writhing, straining his head terrifically upwards, his great eyes starting from the naked lines of his nose. With a great neck arching cruelly from the ground, he was pulling frantically at the reins, which Rico still held tight.

The horror, Cavitch believes, lies not in the accident but in the symbolic spectacle of phallic thrashing and plunging, an outburst of emotion that suggests a male fear of coitus that could only be Lawrence's own.

In "St. Mawr" Lawrence dashes through a forest of abstractions, repeating words carelessly, casually endorsing fascism over bolshevism (for at least keeping the lid on things), hunting for the boundaries between male and female, animal and man, good and evil, and in the end failing to find what he set out for. Is nature—vast, wild, vicious, indifferent to man—evil? Can humans help being anything except frightened by the meaninglessness of it all? Lawrence seems to despair of comprehending man's place in nature. He sees "mankind, like a horse, ridden by a stranger, smooth-faced, evil rider. Evil himself, smooth-faced and pseudo-handsome, riding mankind past the dead snake, to the last break."

The only possible human response, Lawrence appears to say, is to refuse to surrender. When Lou Witt first sees St. Mawr, the sight of the animal's power and unyielding ferocity make her want to cry. But she prevents herself. Tears are useless. "You had to keep holding on, in this life, never give way, and never give in. Tears only left one weakened and ragged."

This great theme—the awe and despair of the human in the face of the nonhuman—presented with dazzling descriptions of landscape, shows Lawrence at his dangerous best. "St. Mawr" was written by a man tormented by sexual panic and by lacerated lungs whose true state he could not much longer conceal from himself.

In each of the great stories of the Southwest he wrote that summer, the main characters are women of wealth. Rarely in his fiction did Lawrence convey the helplessness of the woman without money—Frieda's position in their own marriage. But a new ingredient had been added to the marriage: Frieda was now a woman of property. Does the anger of the stories of the summer of 1924 convey Lawrence's premonition that one day Frieda would occupy her ranch without him—and not alone?

"St. Mawr" was not quite finished when he began to spit blood.

THERE was a temporary truce in relations with Taos. Mabel had made the first move, sending Lawrence and Frieda separate friendly postcards while on a trip down to Santa Fe. Lawrence countered with "Come and see us up here—if you can get anyone to drive you to this lion's den." Frieda, even more adept at following darkness with light, gushed to Mabel that they had all calmed down and she was full of joy, living on her ranch alone with Lawrence, sleeping under the stars, and helping to build a new porch for their cabin. Even Clarence relented, sending up to Kiowa a conciliatory gift; Lawrence was too powerful an influence over them all not to be forgiven.

When Clarence returned to New York, Lawrence wrote to him at the Harvard Club, asking him to look after Frieda's nephew, who was coming to America to study for a year. He reassured Clarence cheerily that the trauma of the summer (whatever it was) was "like having one's appendix out: not possible twice."

Both Lawrence and Mabel believed that her excesses of emotion were caused by the menopause. He supported her theory that the loss of fertility would be compensated by a resurgence of creative powers, for, as he told her, "The burden of consciousness is too great for a woman to carry. She has enough to bear with her ever-recurring menstruation."

Mabel had published her own thoughts on the subject in a poem, "Change," which she gave him to read.

> Scarlet days fading out to white,
> What shall I do in white days, God?
> All my years have been
> Crimson, scarlet, and orange;
> How shall heart beat on in this dawn pallor? . . .
>
> (Ah! God! Can't You stop
> This change?
> Can't I stay in my body?)

Lawrence tinkered with the poem, and in one of his flirtations with plagiarism incorporated it into the longer poem "Change of Life":

> Warm of me fading to white!
> God, what shall I do in the white days?
> My years have been
> Ruddy, rosy, and orange.
> How can my heart keep beating in this pallor of whitish
>   brine!
> . . . .
> God! Oh make it stop,
> This change!
> Don't take the blood of my body!

THE sight of his own blood came on August 3. Lawrence, who coughed all the time and had been complaining of a sore throat, suddenly brought up bright red blotches. Brett saw it; so did Spud Johnson, who was staying with them. Frieda, frightened, sent a message down to the Hawks, asking them to drive to telephone the doctor. When Lawrence heard, he hurled an egg cup at her. "I'll go out and hide in the sage brush until he goes," he threatened. "I'll teach you." But Frieda also wrote Mabel and asked for help.

L gave me a shock—spitting blood yesterday! You know how frightening blood is but I think it is only bronchial and the altitude. Anyhow he is rather better than worse and in bed and I want him to stay till it's quite healed—Spud helps and is not in the way—Do fetch him Thurs-

day and stay I think that will give Lawr time to recover . . . I wish you
could send some camphorated oil or bring it—and aspirin . . . I hope
you will get a rest—I shant feel all right till L is better . . .

But when Dr. T. P. Martin came, driven up by Clarence, he agreed with
Lawrence that it was only a touch of bronchial trouble—sore tubes, not
lungs. Frieda prepared a mustard plaster and Lawrence sat up and
grinned. He was soon shouting instructions at them all from his bed on
how to make the bread.

The cure for the crisis was one from which healthier and happier
couples would shrink: a two-week camping trip together, the Luhans
and the Lawrences, with Tony driving the Cadillac a thousand miles
over bumpy dirt roads. The sore throat continued—"It hurts like
billy-o," Lawrence told Mabel, asking her to bring a good gargle—and
soon spread to include a nagging earache as well. But the goal was
enticing: a drive through the red rocks of Navajo country, and at the end
the annual Hopi snake dances in Arizona.

Brett stayed behind to look after the ranch and to send Lawrence
letters which, she adoringly pointed out, were written on only one side
of "soft paper like a hanky . . . so that you can blow your nose in it
without getting inky & bury it in the sand."

The trip was a disaster. In Albuquerque Lawrence embarrassed Mabel
in the dining room of the Harvey House by reading out the items on the
menu in a loud mocking voice. Mabel felt he was embarrassed to be seen
sharing a table with a man of a different race. He then antagonized both
women by telling Mabel, "Frieda is the freest woman I have ever
known." Frieda slashed back, "And do you think I care for your compliments when you only say them to annoy Mabel?"

Tony had not forgiven Lawrence. The antagonism was mutual, the
price predictable. Fortunately, as an illiterate, Tony probably never knew
of the portrait in "St. Mawr" of the impassive self-important Indian who

was ready to trade his sex, which, in his opinion, every white woman
was secretly pining for, for the white woman's money and social priv-
ileges. In the daytime all the thrill and excitement of the white man's
motor-cars and moving pictures and ice-cream sodas . . . In the night,
the soft, watery-soft warmth of an Indian or half-Indian woman.

Were that not sufficient, "St. Mawr" goes on to describe this Indian as
"not a very good driver, not quick and marvellous as some white men
are."

When they returned, before finishing "St. Mawr," Lawrence dashed
off for *The Laughing Horse* an article whose title accurately describes his
condition: "Back from the Snake Dance—Tired Out." Mabel was so

disappointed with its flat, listless tone that she stopped speaking to him; she declared that it might have been written by an exhausted business-man. As in a sense it was. Lawrence had found the dances "interesting but not beautiful" and disliked being part of the crowds of tourists who had made their way across the desert in long black cars to see the all-too-American Indians hold live rattlesnakes in their mouths. The spectacle reaffirmed his determination to return to the real Mexico.

Unsettlingly, he and Frieda began to hear from the Taos grapevine what a bad bargain they had made in giving Mabel the manuscript of *Sons and Lovers*. The run-down ranch was worth only about a thousand dollars, local opinion guessed, but the manuscript of Lawrence's best-known work must have a value of up to fifty thousand dollars. Lawrence was shaken. He had never thought of his manuscripts as capital assets. He wrote Seltzer and asked him to put the rest into a safe deposit box.

Kiowa Ranch was, in truth, a bit of a gift horse: its water supply was only one small spring, which trickled so slowly that it took three minutes to fill a bucket. Also, it stood at such high altitude—8,500 feet, 2,500 feet higher than Taos—that very little could grow there and it was uninhabitable in winter.

Height above sea level was assuming a great significance in Lawrence's life. Conventional wisdom held that high altitudes were good for bad chests—up to the undetermined point where they became harmful. Law-rence was beginning to blame the height of the ranch for his sore bron-chials. He also gave the name *Altitude* to the little Taos play he never finished.

Back from the snake dance, tired out, he turned his hand to his third story of the summer, which did for Brett what "The Woman Who Rode Away" had done for Mabel. "The Princess" tells of an aristocratic thirty-eight-year-old English virgin, fearful of men thanks to an eccentric fa-ther, who leaves England for the American Southwest. There, riding along a high trail above the timberline, she rashly gives herself to her swarthy black-eyed Mexican guide who pants like an animal with desire. She does not enjoy the experiment and refuses to repeat it. The Mexican, angry, says, "I make you," and repeatedly rapes her until they are both senseless.

Did Lawrence know what he was doing? Was his mind as tired as his body? A joking note to Clarence suggests that it was: "I burned that hideous Indian doll—seriously set fire to her. She was too ugly." The ritual execution he describes is an enactment of the scene in *Sons and Lovers* where young Paul gleefully throws his sister's wax doll onto the fire.

The three Southwest stories, he observed to Curtis Brown, might make a book. At least two of the three—"The Woman Who Rode Away" and "St. Mawr"—rank with his finest work. In 1956 the critic F. R.

Leavis called "St. Mawr" a prose poem equal in achievement to "The Waste Land." More recent scholars, conscious of the feminist challenge, have tried to determine what led Lawrence, at the age of thirty-nine, to write such attacks on the female.

Charles Rossman has argued that the persistent punishment of women in Lawrence's work of the postwar period amounts to an obsession. From his earlier view that men and women were equally to blame for the failure of their relationship, Lawrence had come to see men being destroyed by women's new independence. In the three Southwestern stories of 1924, white women are punished for the crime of refusing to bow to masculine dominance. Lawrence, says Rossman, "decided, as it were, to get his own back."

David Cavitch has suggested that the three stories—"a unified but sadly disturbing group"—show the severity of Lawrence's psychological plight. The guilt over his murderous resentment toward a maternal figure, present from his earliest work, had collided with his terror of the destructive brutality and remoteness of masculinity. In the summer of 1924, says Cavitch, "by confronting the irreducible dilemma in his soul, he imperiled his very sanity."

FROM Eastwood in September Lawrence received news of two deaths. Frances ("Frankie") Cooper, his old friend and neighbor from Walker Street, had died of tuberculosis, the disease that had claimed most of the family. Frankie's sister—his college friend Gertie, who had been confined to a sanatorium when Lawrence was in Croydon—was now seemingly cured and, as one of the two survivors among the five Cooper sisters, had made her home with Lawrence's sister Ada and her husband, Eddie Clarke, since 1919. Of the Coopers, Lawrence wrote Ada, "Curious how often one thinks of them. I only hope Gertie keeps well." Then, on September 10, 1924, just after Lawrence had sent him ten pounds, his father died of bronchopneumonia and heart failure.

Arthur Lawrence's death at seventy-seven was hardly premature. Even so, Lawrence, oversensitive to almost everything else, showed relatively little reaction to what Freud called the most important event in a man's life. To Ada, he said, "It does upset one"; to Emily, he wrote to ask anxiously about the grave. "Didn't you bury father with mother? Wasn't there room?" He sent twenty pounds to Ada and ten to Emily, to help with the funeral expenses, and promised to pay the school fees for his niece, Peggy. "Send a little plan of the future . . ." he wrote Peggy, "and we'll fix it up."

It was a generous commitment, as there was now a real chance that Seltzer might go bankrupt. With uncharacteristic contrition, Lawrence wrote to Mountsier, whom he had sacked as his New York agent for warning him against Seltzer, saying, "You were right and I was wrong."

For the moment, however, Lawrence's finances were in good shape. His agents had extracted enough from Seltzer to put $2,285.21 into his Chase National Bank account. There was over three hundred pounds in banks in London. Money was rolling in, and so much new work was awaiting publication that his publishers had to worry about a logjam. The Magnus book was out at last in London and would appear in New York the following January. *The Boy in the Bush* was out too (Mollie Skinner was stung to find it being reviewed as if it were all Lawrence's own work).

In early autumn he was gripped by his usual compulsion to go south, its force revealed by repetition in the personal correspondence so voluminous it is a wonder that he found time to write anything else. To Murry, "The birds are all coming down from the mountains—I feel like going south too—always want to go south." To Secker, "I feel like going south soon. I always want to go south." To his mother-in-law, "Ich möchte wieder südwärts gehen." He even wrote into "St. Mawr": "To go South! Always to go South, away from the arctic horror as far as possible! This was Lou's instinct."

It was hardly a spiritual longing. He felt dreadful. "The high altitude and the thin cold air changing now to autumn have given me a sore chest and throat which doesn't get better quickly," he told his sister Emily, while to Murry—about to become a father for the first time—he wrote a warm forgiving letter, letting his deepest feelings run together: "Perhaps you will find fulfillment in a baby. . . . The high thin air gets my chest, bronchially. . . . Did I tell you my father died on Sept. 10th, the day before my birthday."

Frieda did not want to go south. Even more than Lawrence she loved the ranch, the first thing she could call her own since the children had been taken from her. She was less terrified of winter, mainly fearing, as she told her mother, "fatness is going to overtake me again, when I'm no longer riding." She had, she said, grown to be part of the country there, and had enjoyed entertaining her nephew, who had come west to see them. They both worried about leaving all their hard work to the risk of the elements or marauders.

Failing to find an Indian couple to live at the ranch as caretakers, they packed all their valuables, even the beds, and deposited them at the Hawk ranch. They found a man to shutter the windows and arranged for the horses to be taken down when the snow came. Then they left for Mexico, with Brett in tow. The ranch cure had not worked.

ARRIVING in Mexico City on October 20, Lawrence found everybody coughing and sneezing. He blamed his new cold on the "genius loci."

They were much welcomed at their old hotel, which cost only two dollars a day with food—and without private bathrooms, though these, after the ranch, were hardly essential.

He lunched with Somerset Maugham ("a narrow-gutted artist with a stutter"), sat for his photograph, and was more flattered than he cared to admit to be invited to dinner by the local branch of P.E.N., the international writers' organization. Frieda and Brett helped him struggle into a boiled shirt and dinner jacket, but when he arrived he found that the meal was at a Chinese restaurant and the others were in business suits.

Shortly they moved southeast, to Oaxaca, arriving on November 9 after a two-day journey on a tiny train on a single-track line with two coaches and twenty soldiers to fight off attackers. Oaxaca was the seat of counterrevolution. The anti-socialist coalition of Catholic and land-owners' interests was fighting on, even though the national government had successfully suppressed the main rebellion with the help of arms and ammunition from the United States, now Mexico's ally.

The state of Oaxaca itself was full of tension. Its governor, García Vigil, had been taken off a train and assassinated only seven months before Lawrence's arrival. Foreigners were being fired on. An American woman had been murdered—literally scalped when her hair caught in the wheels of her wagon as she toppled after being shot by the land redistributors trying to take over her hacienda.

Lawrence and Frieda despised the disorder of it all. "They say the next revolution begins on Monday," Lawrence wrote Spud Johnson. "It's a mess." He was contemptuous of the national government's giddy mood of expansion, building everything from roads and railways to a new national stadium. So much did Frieda hate the lawlessness that she wrote to Clarence Thompson that she had almost come to believe in morals— "life becomes such an untidy show without."

Both Lawrences blamed bolshevism. To Murry, Lawrence declared, "Socialism is a dud. . . . The Spanish-American population just rots on top of the black savage mass." Calling on the new governor at the state palace, Lawrence was dismayed to find him to be an Indian from the hills. He enjoyed a private laugh when the governor invited him to go with him the next day to the opening of a new road which had not even been begun.

Lawrence poured his scorn into a series of essays on Mexico. In "See Mexico After," he sneered: "Of course, Mexico went in for civilisation long, long, long ago. But it got left." If one considered civilization as a snake stretching around the globe, the Mexico of 1924 was the tail. His skepticism was shared by his own government. Britain was by no means as enthusiastic about the new Mexico as the United States was, and had withheld diplomatic recognition.

But for Lawrence the anarchy was a price worth paying. The climate of beautiful Oaxaca was what he had come for, changelessly warm and sunny, and they found a wonderful place to live when an English Catholic priest, brother of the English vice consul in Mexico City, offered them half of his long low white house fronting the Avenida Pino Suarez. There they enjoyed big rooms, servants, a wide veranda with orange and lemon trees at the back, and a view of dark blue mountains in the distance. Brett and her typewriter (but not her ear trumpet, which had been lost and was being replaced by one improvised by a local tinsmith) were installed at the one-story Hotel Francia near the lively central *zocalo* and much favored by European tourists.

In the soft air, Lawrence's throat and chest at last relented. Immersed in the Mexican street scene—full of blanket weavers, pottery sellers, peasant women with black eyes and blue rebozos, open-air butcher shops with ribbons of fly-covered meat—he resumed the project he had come for.

Into his writing he slipped casual bits of information he had picked up from his reading: for example, that the strong odor of the Mexican leather sandals, huaraches, resulted from tanning with human excrement. He laughed to see Brett's face when he told her. But he appears to have acquired this exotic fact from Bernal Díaz's *The Discovery and Conquest of Mexico* and transposed it from the sixteenth century to the twentieth. Similar gaffes had the expatriate community in Mexico City convulsed with laughter when eventually they read *The Plumed Serpent*. But the pungent, if inaccurate, detail also reveals Lawrence the travel writer at his overconfident best. As he blithely admitted in his *Fantasia of the Unconscious*, "I only remember hints—and I proceed by intuition."

Smelly or not, huaraches are comfortable (when broken in), and Lawrence wore them, with socks, as he shopped and saw the sights of Oaxaca in his checked tweed suit and Panama hat.

Back in Taos, Mabel, still reeling, was alarmed to receive a letter saying that he might "toddle back" to Taos if he didn't like Oaxaca. Bynner scolded her. She should take what Lawrence had to offer and not expect friendship on any normal terms, Bynner said. "Your perturbation over D.H. continues to strike me as funny. I suppose it is because you persist with the herd in taking him as an important mind. He always seems to me a strange, sick, precocious child, to be considered accordingly. Somebody else's child, thank God!"

LAWRENCE's greatest act of spite against Mabel was to set his Taos experience in the wrong Mexico. In his work, all the color and culture of her beloved American Southwest appeared transposed to the foreign country south of the border where she could claim no credit. "Even 'The Woman Who Rode Away,' about the sacrificial cave, he gave to Mexico!" she complained later in her book about Lawrence. "He did not do what I called him to do. He did another thing."

That thing was *The Plumed Serpent*. Dismissing what he had written the year before at Chapala as too tame and touristy, he began again. He kept the spirit of the first chapters but sharpened the satire of foreigners in Mexico City, especially the American leftists who had come down to enjoy the revolt of the masses. The caricature of Bynner became less sociological (in the first version Owen Rhys is "Bolshevist by conviction but a capitalist by practice") and more psychological. The suggestions of homosexual voyeurism in the bullfight scene became more pronounced and Lawrence added the old-womanish way that Bynner, taking his seat at the arena, spread out his raincoat to protect his bottom.

Then, changing key, he began lavishly to adorn and enrich the religion he was creating for the book. Even in the first version, this new faith, based on the revival of ancient gods, was a complete structure, with its own creation myth, code of commandments, and symbolism. But as he reworked the book, Lawrence made it far more elaborate, most conspicuously by the addition of long poems as hymns. (Striking insertions into the text, hard on the modern reader's eye, these hymns, such as "Jesus' Farewell" and "The Song of the Great Dog," owe their rhythm and inspiration to the Sankey and Moody hymns of Lawrence's chapel-going boyhood.)

Fortunately for an author with a penchant for writing from life, the state of Mexico was trying to do for itself just what Lawrence was trying to do in his book: depose the twin gods of capitalism and Catholicism and establish a national ethos based on the peasantry and ancient heritage. *The Plumed Serpent* is not just Lawrence's florid private vision of a new society, a projection of his savage internal conflicts. There is much of the modern Mexico in it.

Three weeks after Lawrence's arrival in Oaxaca, General Plutarco Elías Calles, the Partida Laborista's hand-picked successor to President Obregón, was installed as Mexico's new president. Not long after, General Socrates Tomás Montes entered Lawrence's pages. Lawrence's president, who must be overthrown before the new religious state can come into being, is a "sincere and passionate" man, with all his ideas "American and European," a lonely atheist who somehow wants to rescue his country from poverty and ignorance but is bewildered by its Aztec reverence for blood and death. "In this [assessment of the character and aims of the actual President Calles]," says the historian Peter Calvert, "as in so many other things, Lawrence is at once wholly wrong and at the same time not too wide of the mark."

Lawrence believed that the masses needed a priest as leader. As his own candidate, he created the character of Don Ramón Carrasco, a Mexican intellectual, who would replace the discredited Jesus and dislodge the bolshevists by appearing as the Living Quetzalcoatl, the ancient god returned to his people. Ramón has a partner, General Cipriano Viedma, an Oxford-trained Indian who becomes (Lawrence giving no quarter to his readers) the Living Huitzilopochtli.

Their new religion is to form a state within a state, based on the sacredness of masculinity and the comradeship of men, banded together as the Men of Quetzalcoatl. The novel shows a rally of these brothers, in which, to thudding drums and flashing torches, Ramón, tall and beautiful, appears before the crowd in a ceremony of dedication, with his bare gleaming torso and his blue and white serape folded on his arm:

> Everybody looked up. Ramón had flung his right arm tense into the air, and was looking up at the black dark sky. The men of the ring did the same, and the naked arms were thrust aloft like so many rockets.
> "Up! up! up!" said a wild voice.
> "Up! up!" cried the men of the ring, in a wild chorus.
> And involuntarily the men in the crowd twitched, then shot their arms upwards, turning their faces to the dark heavens.

To Lawrence's later readers, this passage strongly evokes the Third Reich and has contributed to the charge that Lawrence was a fascist. But in 1924 Hitler was in jail for the Munich Beer Hall Putsch—he was not to reach power for another nine years—and Lawrence was less under the influence of European events than of Mexican archaeology. While in Oaxaca, he visited the dramatic pre-Columbian ruins at Mitla, where the carved pyramids and ceremonial pavings invite visions of the ancient chants and rituals once performed there.

AND where in this crowd of shouting, saluting males was D. H. Lawrence—the figure so recognizable in all his other novels? He is there, in the body of Frieda and the character of Kate Leslie, a twice-married European woman: beautiful if stout, a steady smoker, and the mother of grown children who live happily without her in England while she explores Mexico and tries to bring blue-eyed common sense to a world of black-eyed instinct.

If the body is Frieda's, Kate's views are Lawrence's. When starting the novel a second time, he raised her age by two years to forty (the age he would reach on his next birthday). Not that author and wife were far apart on politics and religion. Both Lawrence and Frieda believed in the message of *The Plumed Serpent:* that Christianity was outmoded and destructive and that the white races must find new modes of leadership to prevent the dark races from dragging them into anarchy. And both believed that Lawrence's new novel was the best of them all.

One reason the book had remained unfinished when Lawrence left Mexico the previous winter was that he had not known what to do with the character of Kate. In his first draft (in which her surname is Burns) she meets at a lakeside village the European Ramón and the Indian Cipriano, who tell her their plans to lead Mexico to a new theocracy based on the ancient Mexican gods reincarnated as themselves. They invite her to join their religion as a goddess. Kate declines and returns to England. It was a most inconclusive ending. Lawrence clearly did not know what to do with the New Woman encountering primitive culture.

His savage summer stories of 1924 can be read as experiments in radical solutions—trying out first death, then exile, and finally rape as fates for independent white women who consort with the untamed. But *The Plumed Serpent* as it now exists shows how he found his answer: to have Kate marry the little general Cipriano and become the green-robed goddess Malintzi in the new religion.

This transformation from tourist to goddess requires Kate to surrender all her old values. The sensitive European woman who, at the start of the novel, cannot bear to watch a bullfight, must learn to accept blood sacrifice, which she does by watching the execution of men who have tried to assassinate Ramón. For the scene, Lawrence created a boy's comic-strip orgy of gore. Cipriano dips his fist into the wounds of the victims, then raises it dripping in exultation while Ramón, also covered with blood, which runs down his arm and his back, moves in for the kill,

> holding down the head of the bandit by the hair and stabbing him with short stabs in the throat, one, two, while blood shot out like a red projectile, there was a strange sound like a soda-syphon, a ghastly bubbling, one final terrible convulsion from the loins of the stricken men.

BUT neither the flashes of fascism nor the blood lust was responsible for making *The Plumed Serpent* a target for feminist literary critics, starting with Simone de Beauvoir in *The Second Sex*. The provocation was rather the book's next-to-last chapter, called "Kate Is a Wife," in which she surrenders to Cipriano not only her will and independence of thought but her right to orgasm.

Every one of Lawrence's books, according to Kate Millett's case for the prosecution, instructs a woman in how to be a wife. In *The Plumed Serpent,* it is Ramón's young bride, Teresa, totally submerging her self in her husband, who explains to the twice-married Kate what the duties of a true wife are: "He is a man, and a column of blood. I am a woman, and a valley of blood. I shall not contradict him. How can I? My soul is inside him, and I am far from contradicting him when he is trying with all his might to do something that *he* knows about." The doctrine comes straight from Frieda's idol Nietzsche and had been preached at her by Lawrence for a dozen years. Nietzsche's Zarathustra says, "The man's happiness is: I will. The woman's happiness is: He will."

But Kate has more to learn as a new kind of wife, a new mode of sexual intercourse. When she approaches orgasm with Cipriano,

> by a dark and powerful instinct he drew away from her as soon as this desire rose again in her, for the white ecstasy of frictional satisfaction, the throes of Aphrodite of the foam. She could see that to him, it was repulsive. He just removed himself, dark and unchangeable, away from her.

To his feminist critics, this may be the single most offensive passage in all of Lawrence.

There is, however, a different interpretation of Cipriano's behavior, one less hostile to Lawrence: it is that what the little Indian general is teaching Kate is *coitus reservatus,* an oriental sexual technique of prolonged pleasure without climax. For Lawrence, in his lush descriptions of the joy of frictionless sex, does not say that Cipriano allows himself the satisfaction he denies his wife. Rather, once Kate has learned to hold herself back,

> he, in his dark, hot silence would bring her back to the new, soft, heavy, hot flow, when she was like a fountain gushing noiseless and with urgent softness from the volcanic deeps. . . . And there was no such thing as conscious 'satisfaction.' What happened was dark and untellable.

Either way—male domination or tantric sex—the dark untellable act shows Lawrence working out a solution for the sexual problem he most openly acknowledged in his own marriage, Frieda's insistence on multiple and protracted orgasm.

The fictional Kate had insisted on multiple orgasm too, in her marriage to her second husband, Joachim, an Irish revolutionary:

> the seething electric female ecstasy, which knows such spasms of delirium . . . what she used to call her "satisfaction." She had loved Joachim for this, that again and again, and again he could give her this orgiastic "satisfaction," in spasms that made her cry aloud.

This last sentence, as explicit as anything in Lawrence's long repertory of renditions of the sexual act, offers evidence—or is it a plea?—that he, at least at times, had been able sexually to satisfy Frieda.

It is a testimony to Lawrence's belief in the importance of marriage that he ends *The Plumed Serpent,* the most political of his leadership novels, with a quiet accommodation between a husband and his wife. Cipriano and Kate marry because they love and need each other. Kate thinks, as she surrenders much of what she has held dear: "The individual, like the perfect being, does not and cannot exist, in the vivid world. We are all fragments. And at the best, halves." And in the ambiguous final exchange between the new husband and wife as the book ends—"You won't let me go!" Kate says to Cipriano—it is by no means clear that the husband holds the upper hand.

THE break with Brett came in January 1925. It is a wonder that it took so long. They were a crowd of three much of the time, or a couple consisting of Brett and Lawrence, as they left Frieda behind and went off to visit English friends in Oaxaca, to paint or to discuss the typing of his work. Finally Frieda told Lawrence to get rid of her. Dutifully, quite unlike Don Ramón or Don Cipriano, he obeyed. He wrote and sent to Brett's hotel the kind of letter required to make a formal declaration to someone who is seen every day:

> You, Frieda and I don't make a happy combination now. The best is that we should prepare to separate: that you should go your own way. I am not angry; except that I hate "situations" and feel humiliated by them. . . . I am grateful for the things you have done for me. But we must stand apart.

The letter was not really polite; it was an order to get out of town. Were it not clear enough, Frieda burst in on Brett to deliver her own letter, and a speech as well. She accused Brett of *not* having an affair with Lawrence. Sex she could understand. But the curate-spinster relationship between the two of them made her sick. There was no such thing as friendship without sex. (She was delivering another Nietzschean potted truth much in vogue at the time. Mr. Duffy, the repressed Irish bachelor bank clerk in "A Painful Case" in Joyce's *Dubliners,* who, like Frieda, translates Nietzsche for pleasure, pens the aphorism, "Love between man and man is impossible because there must not be sexual intercourse and friendship between man and woman is impossible because there must be sexual intercourse.")

Possibly also borrowing from Nietzsche, Lawrence used essentially the same words in a long letter to Brett, sent to her in Mexico City where she stopped on her way back to Taos (having dutifully accepted his command to leave): "Friendship between a man and a woman, as a thing of first importance to either, is impossible: and I know it." The two of them could not be friends, he said, until Brett had a husband or a lover.

That done, Lawrence sent William Hawk at the Hawk Ranch twenty-five dollars for the keep of his own horses and told him to get the money for Brett's two horses from her.

HE was a married man. His wife wanted to return to Europe to see her mother; he would go too. Also, he needed to see his sisters. As he prepared to book passage for two on a cargo boat, he fell violently ill; he went down, in his own words, as if he had been shot in the intestines.

The local doctor blamed malaria, plus grippe. But it struck the very day he finished his book and was more than an illness. It was a surrender. The search for Rananim was over. *The Plumed Serpent* was the last stop on the quest he had begun with Bertrand Russell and David Eder: the creation of an ideal state that would reorder every aspect of life, including the relations between men and women. The book, so exhausting to write, with its cinematographic spectacle, long hymns, and complete philosophic, economic, and ethical system, nearly killed him.

Trembling, racked with stomach cramps and a high fever, Lawrence did not expect to survive. Frieda also believed he was dying. One long night when he thought he would not see morning, he told her, "But if I die, nothing has mattered but you, nothing at all." It was the tribute Frieda had craved all her life—"that with all his genius, I should have mattered so much. It seemed incredible."

But Lawrence had already delivered an even more heartrending farewell from husband to wife. There is a scene in *The Plumed Serpent* where Kate recalls the dying words of her second husband, the passionate revolutionary Joachim, whose children she wanted but never had, whose health was ruined by his struggle to change the world, and whose death left her with half of her life to fill:

> Kate, perhaps I've let you down. . . . But I couldn't help myself. I feel as if I'd brought you to the doors of life and was leaving you there. Kate, don't be disappointed in life because of me. I didn't really get anywhere. I haven't really got anywhere. I feel as if I'd made a mistake. But perhaps when I'm dead I shall be able to do more for you than I have done while I was alive. Say you'll never feel disappointed!

Lawrence's words were prophetic but premature. The book that would care for Frieda after his death was still to be written.

15

THE BORDER-LINE

February–September 1925

*H*e recovered. *Too weak to stand, Lawrence was so determined to* get out of Oaxaca and back to Mexico City as the first stage of returning to England that he allowed himself to be carried by stretcher to the train. He and Frieda had fixed upon sea air as the cure for the diseases they had decided were ailing him: influenza, inflammation of the bowels, and his old malaria from Ceylon, reactivated by aerial transmission from the military hospital in Oaxaca.

Then Frieda fell ill as well. In Mexico City they indulged in the unaccustomed luxury of two sunny rooms, with a drawing room and an electric fire, on the top floor of the Imperial Hotel on the fashionable Paseo de la Reforma. They counted the days until they could get a ship to England, where, they agreed, they would live at sea level, perhaps in Devon. "Altitude," declared Frieda, "is poison for malaria."

When Lawrence was well enough to go out, he looked so cadaverous that people stared. Frieda bought him some rouge and, like Aschenbach in *Death in Venice,* he colored his cheeks. He joked that he had given himself "such a lovely, healthy complexion that no one ever turned to stare at me again."

To Brett, with whom she was on good terms now that distance separated them, Frieda reported, "L has *Malaria* really and I have a scrap too, my nose is *too* thin, I dont like it—I had better stay fat!" To her mother, Frieda wrote nearer the truth:

> Oh, Anna, a time of purgatory lies behind me, but *behind* me—Now *forwards* once again—L is asleep—the worst was the emotional depression and the *nerves,* it drove one to despair—It was as if he couldn't or wouldn't live on.
> . . . Think, if I'd lost Lorenzo, in spite of all the difficulties, it would be unthinkable for me.

Lawrence woke up in time to read the letter and add cheerfully, "Yes, Schwiegermutter, one doesn't die so easily."

They were not out of purgatory. At the hotel Lawrence suffered a pulmonary hemorrhage—not just spitting blood, as at the ranch, but a continuous flow from the mouth, like a nosebleed that would not stop. For once a good doctor was available: Sydney Ulfelder, head of surgery at the American Hospital, was said to be one of the best in Mexico City. Ulfelder insisted on an X ray; following it, either he or a man whom Frieda called "the analyst doctor" did not mince words: Lawrence had tuberculosis. They were both told. To Frieda privately it was further explained that Lawrence's tuberculosis was in the third stage and that he had only two years to live.

Then they received an extra blow. A sea voyage was out of the question. And to choose England over New Mexico, with lungs like that? The medical orders were either to stay in Mexico in the sun or return to the ranch. They decided on the ranch.

How long had Lawrence had tuberculosis? David Garnett, a trained scientist, had observed Lawrence spitting blood at the Cearne in 1913. Various London friends during the war, including Dr. Ernest Jones, believed Lawrence consumptive. One of Lawrence's later biographers, Harry T. Moore, developed the theory that Lawrence's celebrated anger may have released adrenocorticoid hormones that prolonged his life. Another, Dr. William Ober, a medical literary historian who studied the evidence of Lawrence's case, has argued that the same rushes of rage could equally have curtailed it. Ober's guess was that Lawrence's tuberculosis began in Croydon, when his double pneumonia reawakened an arrested juvenile infection.

In any event, in February 1924 the word was out, the diagnosis inescapable. But they escaped it. The mutual power of denial was one of the forces that held their marriage together. From now on, it would ally them in an unspoken conspiracy against seeking proper treatment. Frieda's "great religion," like Lawrence's own, was a faith in the body's wisdom to know what was best for itself. All the same, that bitter day in Mexico City, Frieda did accept that Lawrence would never be fully well again, and she cried all night.

Soon, however, Lawrence had recovered enough to go to lunch with some Mexican nationalist writers and to insult them by saying, "What genius has Mexico ever produced?" The writers walked out.

LAWRENCE must have known that an ordeal awaited them at the border. The journey in itself was a nightmare: four days on a Pullman train, sharing the drawing room with a Mexican family of nine. Lawrence all the same began a new novel. As he was not strong enough to hold a pen, he dictated to Frieda, who wrote it all down in the kind of ruled school notebook he used for composition.

The surviving fragment of "The Flying Fish" shows that Lawrence had put the oiled torsos and flaming torches of *The Plumed Serpent* well behind him and was yearning for England and things English. His new fictional mask was Gethin Day, a soldier nearing forty who, lying fevered with malaria in an abysmal town in southern Mexico, disgusted with the nauseous tropics and perpetual revolution, is summoned home because his sister is dying. Home is "Daybrook," a sixteenth-century stone house "among the hills in the middle of England" on a knoll, above a river, with the woods rising steep behind. Lawrence never finished "The Flying Fish" because he wrote it, he said later, "so near the borderline of death" that he could not carry it through.

It was the American borderline, however, that, as he told Amy Lowell, "nearly killed me a second time." "The Emigration Dept is Dept of Labour," he explained, "and you taste the Bolshevist method in its conduct." He had other words too, to describe the service, which has never been celebrated for the warmth of its welcome to the United States: "insulting, hateful, filthy with insolence and of the bottom-doggy order."

But his reception was far more awful than he had ever feared. Even though friends at the American Embassy in Mexico City had tried to ease his passage, when the train came to El Paso (one of the rail crossing points between the United States and Mexico) he came up against the kind of doctor he most dreaded—an inspector, not a healer. He and Frieda were asked to leave the train. He was stripped and detained while officials deliberated whether to admit a man in his condition. It was more than a day before they learned that he would be granted a visitor's visa, but, as before, only for six months. From that moment on, he knew that he was unlikely to be able to enter the United States another time.

*   *   *

At Santa Fe they saw Bynner, who was shocked by the deterioration in Lawrence's condition; then, not stopping in Taos, they went straight up to Lobo Mountain. They stayed for a week at the Hawks' Del Monte Ranch before moving up to Kiowa early in April. He was happy to be back. It was sunny and most of the snow was gone. They made log fires, an Indian couple helped out, and Frieda did all the cooking and boasted that she was developing into a chef.

Brett remained two miles below them, in the Danes' old cabin at Del Monte, a curious transplant, even for those parts: a shy, deaf, upper-class Englishwoman of middle years living alone on a New Mexican mountain. She wanted to come up and live nearer the Lawrences in the tiny cabin she had had the previous year, but Frieda vetoed it. She restricted Brett's visits to Kiowa to pre-arranged times on Monday, Wednesday, and Saturday.

Lawrence was sharing his life with an elemental woman. Frieda was a good intellectual companion, who read his work as he wrote it and kept up with much of his vast reading of other books in several languages. But in her personal relationships she was incapable of subtlety or of holding anything back. She wrote Brett blunt letters: "No, dont come this afternoon . . . you bully me here on my own ground . . . I wish you no ill, but dont want you in my life."

Brett was not as timid as she looked. As she was still doing Lawrence's typing, she ventured up to Kiowa on her own initiative, only to have Frieda slam the door in her face. There was a screaming, shouting scene; Brett told Frieda to go to hell. Lawrence once more caved in to his wife. Having assured Brett in February, when he and Frieda unexpectedly decided to return to the ranch, that the three of them could coexist happily if they tried, he now declared the exact opposite: "You are a born separator. . . . It is no good our trying to get along together."

Brett was not naïve. From living close to the two of them, she knew the dark truth. She had heard Lawrence coarsely accuse Frieda of pulling up her skirts at every man, and she had heard Frieda's complaints about their unsatisfactory sex life. As Brett later told a friend, "Whenever she forced him to it, he beat her up afterwards." By the time the Lawrences returned to the ranch that spring, it is unlikely that Lawrence could have performed his marital duties even if forced. Very soon he came down with another "chill" and went to bed.

Children were still on his mind. He had a recurring dream of his nephew William as a boy who came running to meet him with out-stretched arms, only to be halted by a deep chasm between them. He was fascinated with William Hawk's little son and would draw the boy toward him, holding him between his knees and gazing at him intently. When he heard that Nina Witt, having divorced her husband, the Taos sheriff and sawmill owner, was back in New York, intending to marry a younger man and hoping to have a baby, he snapped, "Children no longer come from 47 year olds." Frieda was then forty-five.

The fight had gone out of him. On one of the days when Brett's presence was tolerated, he was reading out his new biblical play, *David,* for her, Frieda, and Ida Rauh—singing the songs, doing the voices for all the parts—when suddenly Frieda roughly told him to go away; he got on her nerves; she didn't want to hear any more. "Don't be so impertinent," he said mildly.

His new moderation showed also in a dispute with his neighbor Alfred Hawk, the owner of Del Monte Ranch, who charged him more for some irrigation pipes than Lawrence thought they were worth. Lawrence offered to pay the difference, even though he did not agree about it. "I am much too like you in temperament not to know what it means, suddenly to feel blazing mad," he wrote his neighbor. "I'm awfully sorry, and would rather have paid for the pipes twice over." All the same he asked Hawk to wait for the balance until Seltzer paid him. He was still being very careful with his money, even though he was not short (Knopf had just given him an unexpected advance on royalties for *The Plumed Serpent*). He refused to pay two dollars for two chickens, saying it would have to be two for $1.50 or no deal.

They kept four horses, plus chickens and a cow. The cow, which he named Susan, got the benefit of the ambivalence he accorded anything female. He loved her, milked her (believing milk essential for his "chest going wrong") but flew into a rage when, as he looked for the black animal, she would hide in the trees and stand stock-still while he walked straight past. With echoes of his character George Saxton in *The White Peacock,* who says of his cow, "I would like to squeeze her until she screams," Lawrence said of Susan, "I felt more like killing her than milking her." The importance of the cow, however, lay in his self-treatment program.

He had turned Kiowa Ranch into a sanatorium for one. He lay out on the small porch in the clear, cold, dry air, drinking milk, eating eggs, taking, when his strength permitted, light exercise and even riding a horse. He dosed himself with bottles of Pantanberge Solution, which were brought up from the drugstore in Taos along with the fresh meat, vegetables, and typing paper that were in short supply. He stayed clear of Taos. The estrangement from the Luhans was complete. Although Mabel and Tony were in Taos the whole summer of 1925, they avoided the Lawrences. So did Clarence Thompson, back in Taos for the summer.

Lawrence's hate was now directed not at Frieda but at Mexico, "especially Oaxaca for having done me in." Frieda's nephew Friedel Jaffe came for a long visit—welcome enough, but Lawrence was glad when the young man's visa expired and he had to leave the United States.

"One would think the place was Paradise, the way it's hedged in," Lawrence wrote Ada. He told her he was happiest when he and Frieda were alone. They took no daily newspaper.

The world had not forgotten him. He received sacks of mail—from critics, from fans, from students requesting his autograph or guidance on life; most of it he threw into the fire (keeping the envelopes, however, for spitting in).

He ignored the fundamental prescription for curing tuberculosis: absolute rest. Protesting as usual, "I don't do any work since we are here . . . I never felt less literary," he finished his play *David*, revised *The Plumed Serpent*, and wrote a number of essays that are among his best. The resulting book *Reflections on the Death of a Porcupine* (about a porcupine he killed himself, he maintained, not the one that Tony Luhan had shot) wonderfully ponders the morality of humans exploiting the animal kingdom. He turned out four essays on the philosophy of the novel. With his flair for titling his shorter work, he used "Why the Novel Matters" to say just that: "The novel is the book of life"—prescriptive, not in delivering theories of right and wrong, but rather in stimulating the instinct for life. "Morality and the Novel" maintains that the novel reveals "the relation between man and his circumambient universe" and is, therefore, "the highest example of subtle inter-relatedness that man has discovered."

As usual making no great distinction between his literary work and his private correspondence, he poured out the same heartfelt theory to his Australian coauthor Mollie Skinner: "And that again is what I think about writing a novel: one can live so intensely with one's characters and the experience one creates or records, it is a life in itself, far better than the vulgar thing that people *call* life."

The occasion for the letter was the death of Mollie's brother Jack. Jack, Lawrence said consolingly to Mollie, had lived a full life, and "Death's not sad, when one has lived." But if the novel was his own anchor to that vulgar thing called life, Lawrence in mid-1925 had to confront the fact that he had no novel in progress.

WAITING for them in the stillness of what appears in "St. Mawr" as a little tumbledown ranch amid the tall blue balsam pines above the motionless desert was the scandal caused by *Memoirs of the Foreign Legion by M.M. with an Introduction by D. H. Lawrence*. The short book had been published in London the previous September, with one cut, Martin Secker informed him: "at the end, where you let yourself go on the subject of M.'s attitude toward certain things." The New York edition had appeared in January while Lawrence was still in Oaxaca.

Reviewers pounced on the book for its blatant violation of the ancient convention against speaking ill of the dead. "There are a number of bad smells recorded in this book," said Ben Ray Redman of the New York *Herald Tribune* in a review titled "But Why, Mr. Lawrence?" "But the worst smell of all emanates from the Introduction, the rottenness of which is as blatant as its reason for existence is obscure." The New York *World*'s "First Reader" doubted whether "a posthumous book ever carried a more savage sketch of a dead writer." Nothing that Lawrence had ever written, said the New York *Sun,* threw so much light on his own enigmatic character: "He detested the author in life; he befriended him in life while detesting him. Now, hating him still, he befriends him by publishing his book through Alfred A. Knopf, Inc."

The introduction's brilliance, its wit, and its grasp of character were acknowledged. One critic agreed with Lawrence's own judgment that it was the best thing he had ever written. But it made him look a cad. A member of the public touched a nerve with a letter asking how Lawrence dared to make a lot of money out of another man's work.

In London, a short article in *The Owlglass* sprang to the defense of the late "M.M." Lawrence's portrait, it said, quoting someone who had known the late unidentified legionnaire, was terribly unjust to a man who was not only brave but witty and amusing and most likable. *The Owlglass* ventured a guess that the "N.D." to whom Lawrence referred in his introduction might just be the expatriate writer Norman Douglas.

"Is it?" came a loud bellow from Florence.

In "D. H. Lawrence and Maurice Magnus: A Plea for Better Manners," an essay privately printed in Florence late in January 1925, and almost as brilliant as Lawrence's own, Norman Douglas counterattacked.

> Why, of course it is. There is no mistaking that "wicked red face," those shabby clothes coupled with the bluff, grandiose manner of what may once have been a gentleman. I should recognize myself at a mile's distance, especially knowing, as I do, friend Lawrence's idiosyncracies [*sic*] in the matter of portraiture . . . what he makes a point of seeing, and what he makes a point of not seeing. For he is not congenitally blind; he is only blind when it suits his convenience.

Douglas made three main accusations against Lawrence: that he had helped himself to Magnus's manuscripts knowing that they belonged to Douglas as literary executor; that he had shown bad manners in ridiculing a man unable to defend himself and in exploiting the details of another's life for his own literary ends; and—worst—that Lawrence had suggested that Douglas had despised Maurice Magnus (whom Douglas named openly). "One does not consort with people whom one despises," wrote Douglas; "one does not despise people who show one a thousand kindnesses."

Acidly, Douglas complimented Lawrence on his writing style. He cited as an example the introduction's description of Magnus sitting down to work in the morning dressed "like a little pontiff" in his blue silk dressing gown: "I commend this short paragraph to those simpletons who say that friend Lawrence cannot write; it is a perfect etching—not a stroke too much or too little; there he is, 'M.M.' in matutinal garb, once and for ever."

Douglas, of course, did not mention homosexuality. He homed in instead on Lawrence's preoccupation with money. The fact that Magnus had "most unfortunately" borrowed money from Lawrence was, said Douglas, "the key to this whole feline Introduction." He dismissed Lawrence's claim to have written it in order to help repay Magnus's debts to a Maltese businessman. Not only had Lawrence exaggerated Magnus's debts, Douglas said, but the Maltese creditor (Michael Borg), far from trying to recover his money, had Magnus's remains exhumed from the public grave and buried in his own family plot. This was proof, concluded Douglas, "that some people can still be trusted to behave like gentlemen."

No gentleman. Douglas could have chosen no better stick with which to beat the collier's son before the London literary establishment. Douglas himself, of course, was no gentleman in omitting from his case the relevant fact that he had as good as given the manuscript to Lawrence in 1921. Lawrence's friend Aldington also thought it a bit rich for an open and public pedophile to proclaim himself a gentleman. Douglas publicly mauled and fondled the Italian street urchins whose favors he bought.

Lawrence was angry at the injustice of Douglas's accusation about the rights; he sent Curtis Brown a copy of the dismissive letter about the manuscript in which Douglas wrote, "Whosoever wants it may ram it up his exhaust pipe." What is more, he was disgusted because the outrageous behavior of both Magnus and Douglas was so much more sordid than he had printed, and Douglas also had refused to give Magnus a penny in his hour of need. Lawrence associated Douglas's attack with the circle around Murry and told his agent not to give Murry first look at his stories.

But Douglas was also partly right. Lawrence *was* selectively blind. Once he had arranged to go ahead with actual publication of the manuscript, he had not asked the formal permission customarily sought from a literary executor, nor had he given Douglas any inkling that his introduction would disparage the work it introduced. Above all—what Douglas could not say in print—Lawrence blithely ignored his own fascination with homosexuals, about which he had confided in Magnus and which had drawn him to Magnus in the first place, making him prey to Magnus's wheedling. Also, as a point of fact, Lawrence in his introduction had indeed made Magnus's debts out to be larger than they were.

In the London literary arena, Douglas had won the round. Although Lawrence defended himself well in the *New Statesman* the following January, the scandal rumbled on and further blackened his reputation as an uncouth ingrate who liked to kick people in the shins.

That was certainly how Thomas Seltzer felt. Even before Lawrence left Mexico City, Seltzer cabled him desperately: "Is it true you are giving books to Knopf I cannot believe it I will pay your royalties don't fear but your [*sic*] hurt my chances you endanger all if you leave me."

Lawrence was indeed giving his new work to Knopf—*St. Mawr,* to be published as a book, and the new novel of Mexico as well. Knopf, however, disliked Lawrence's choice of title for the novel, "Quetzal-coatl," quite as much as Seltzer had, and insisted on *The Plumed Serpent.* Lawrence was not happy about the change. He still associated viperous female qualities with snakes. He complained to Knopf's wife that "it sounds like a certain sort of 'lady in a hat.' "

THE July 20, 1925, issue of *Time,* America's glossy new weekly magazine, reviewed *St. Mawr,* giving it the attention appropriate to a new novel by a major writer. *Time,* to help its readers understand the tale of a red-gold stallion who changes the life of two idle rich American women, expounded on "The Significance,"

> Author Lawrence looks into life as a mystical physiologist. He would lead men back through the wombs of the ages to the birthday of the species, lest they forget the elements of their nature. For him, good and evil lie far underneath manners and exist only where the primal passions are pure or emasculate. St. Mawr, the burning bay stallion, incarnates the Lawrentian purity as has no other creature.

Then *Time* dignified Author Lawrence with a biographical passage called "The Author":

> Born to coal-mining in Nottingham, 40 years ago, David Herbert Lawrence scavenged crumbs of scholarship as he could. An unusual mother aided in this. He taught, wrote verse, published *Sons and Lovers* in 1913, his first important novel. He has wandered the earth as few men do—especially Australia, Mexico and the southwest U.S. In England, lately, he has been closely associated with John Middleton Murry, the late Katherine Mansfield's husband, in the publication of Murry's review, the *Adelphi.*

The review caused one of *Time*'s readers to explode in disgust.

> We have some good breeding stock in Montana and once in another state I knew a farmer who owned a red-gold stallion, but never in all my experience have I seen one that spouted a "dark invisible flame."
> Let us hope Lou found the place where she could "be very still" so still that David Lawrence will not find it necessary to write a sequel to this horse book.

Lawrence hated *Time*'s know-it-all, overfamiliar tone. He had not even known that the magazine (founded in 1923) existed, he told a writer who asked to interview him. He agreed to the interview all the same, on condition that the article not appear until he had gone back to England.

IN August Kyle Crichton, a journalist who had moved to New Mexico for his tuberculosis, drove up to Kiowa Ranch with his wife, dreading the glowering solemn figure he expected to find. Instead he found himself greeted by an unassuming, lively, friendly man, who was wearing a blue denim shirt buttoned at the neck, without a tie, with brown striped pants that obviously belonged to an old suit, and black woolen socks with sandals, and who was very pleased with the cow shed he had just built. Lawrence, Crichton observed, looked at him steadily as he talked, with small bright blue eyes, mimicking as he went the various animals and people he was talking about.

(As David Garnett had earlier noticed, Lawrence was a brilliant satirist in conversation, although a comparatively poor one in writing. The reason, Garnett thought, was that "in talk his satire was mostly laughter, whereas in print he scolded.")

Lawrence soon had Crichton and his wife rocking with laughter. He screwed an imaginary monocle into his eye and enacted his first meeting with Ford Madox Ford (whom he still called Hueffer, although Ford had changed his name), talking, as Crichton recounted, "in the humph-humph almost unintelligible way that Ford's friends remember so well." Lawrence was telling how Ford, who knew nothing about agriculture, claimed to a Russian who had asked whether the English grew rye, "Yaws, yaws . . . rye . . . rye is one of our-ah lawgest crops."

"And rye," Lawrence shouted in merriment, "there isn't half an acre of rye in all England." Ford was a bit of a fool, he said, recovering himself, "but he gave me the first push and he was a kind man."

To Crichton, Lawrence and Frieda seemed much in accord. They read the same things. They particularly liked the magazines *American* and *Adventure;* other than that they read what people sent them. They had only ten books in the house. They didn't take any when they traveled. Frieda praised his skill: "He is the most practical of men. He can cook, he can mend, he can turn his hand to anything," she told their visitor, and quietly advised praise of the cow shed. "He did it all himself."

Husband and wife disagreed only when Crichton asked what made a man a writer. Frieda answered first. "Egotism. A writer thinks he knows something nobody else knows and he wants to tell it; he wants to show the world what a great fellow he is."

Without anger, Lawrence contradicted. "It isn't that. You don't write for anybody in particular; you don't really mind what individuals think or say about what you write. A man writes rather from a deep moral sense—for the race, as it were. That sounds highfalutin, but that's really what it amounts to. You want to see it published well enough, but you don't care what's said about it."

As the Lawrences bantered, laughing, and Lawrence set the table for tea and deftly cut thin slices of bread from a loaf he had made himself, Crichton marveled at the gulf between the man and his reputation:

> It is hard to believe that the lively, lovable man who stood on the hill-side, by his tiny ranch house and pointed out to you the dim peak of the Sandias at Albuquerque, 150 miles away, can be the same person who is used as the modern straw man to bear the brunt of the attacks of the purists. . . . You will begin to realize how a genuine artist functions, and how impossible it is for him to be anything but an artist.

Lawrence liked the Crichtons. As they said good-bye, he gave them precise instructions for a shortcut: through a canyon, across a river high from the rains. "You'll have trouble," he said as he waved them off, "but you can make it."

The shortcut worked. Crichton ended the article he subsequently wrote with the highest compliment of the American West: "a real guy— that red-headed fellow up there."

LAWRENCE left Kiowa Ranch for the last time on September 10, 1925. He wrote to Anne Conway, a kindly Scottish friend from Mexico City, "It grieves me to leave my horses, and my cow Susan, and the cat Timsy Wemyss, and the white cock Moses—and the place."

In New York, after visiting the rejected Seltzers, who put on a brave and hopeful face (in vain; Lawrence never gave Seltzer any more of his books, and Seltzer's firm ceased publishing in 1927) they boarded the S.S. *Resolute.* As celebrities they were photographed on deck by International Newsreel Photos—he gaunt and wrung out, with the dazed staring eyes of one come out of the tomb; Frieda fashionable for once, beautiful, defiant, and sad.

The press agency reported them as en route to Egypt after five years in Mexico and Australia. A better caption would have been Lawrence's words written to thank Mrs. Conway, who had sent Frieda a sprig of white heather: "Whatever else married people share and don't share, their luck is one."

Lawrence was never to go beyond Europe again. His refusal to admit the seriousness of his illness was turning from the stubborn to the heroic as he went home to face the final years of his life, in which nothing would become him like the leaving of it.

Part Four

16

MRS. LAWRENCE'S LOVER

1926–1927

*B*ack *at his sister Emily's house in Nottingham, Lawrence dosed* himself with Regesan Catarrh Jelly but could not stop his cough. "Of course I'm in bed with a cold, the moment I come here," he wrote Martin Secker.

The proofs of *The Plumed Serpent* had arrived, with the word "se-rape" spelled "sarape" as often as not. Lawrence conceded that it was advisable to stick to one form or the other. "God knows why I changed. . . . Bore!" For him, as for many great writers, to the annoy-ance of the scholars who follow in their wake, consistency was no great concern. As for punctuation, when an eagle-eyed American librarian from Brooklyn sent him a list of all the errors in his books, he replied, "hyphen or no hyphen is the same to me." Lawrence knew his failings in this regard. When the Italian critic Carlo Linati called his work breath-less and undisciplined, Lawrence wrote back amiably to ask if Linati thought that books should be "sort of toys, nicely built up." His own were not. He could "not bear art that you can walk round and admire."

"Whoever reads me," he declared, "will be in the thick of the scrimmage, and if he doesn't like it—if he wants a safe seat in the audience—let him read somebody else."

In London, before and after the Midlands visit, staying first at Garland's Hotel (it no longer exists) on Suffolk Street off Pall Mall, then in a borrowed flat on Gower Street, the Lawrences saw Frieda's daughters and talked Barby out of an engagement with an Irishman Lawrence thought unsuitable. In a letter to Brett, Lawrence confided: "Privately, I can't stand Frieda's children. They have a sort of suburban bounce and *suffisance* which puts me off." Frieda's son, her cherished Monty, now working at the Victoria and Albert Museum, stayed away. "The boy," Lawrence told Brett, "kept his loftiness to the Vic and Albert Museum, and soon, very probably, will sit in one of the glass cases, as a specimen of the perfect young Englishman."

They whirled through a list of friends and literati: the Eders, the Carswells, John Middleton Murry, Rose Macaulay, Richard Aldington. The partner of the handsome Aldington was not his legal wife, Hilda Doolittle, but his wartime mistress, the beautiful Arabella (Dorothy Yorke). Lawrence noted wryly that Hilda was refusing Aldington a divorce even though she had gone off to Cornwall with their old friend Cecil Gray, and had borne Gray a child.

Lawrence reunited also with old friends from his Capri days: Compton and Faith Mackenzie. Mackenzie, now editor of *Gramophone*, divided his time between London and his two Scottish islands, while Faith spent much of her time in their house on Capri. The two men enjoyed an abrasive camaraderie. (In later years Mackenzie would recall how Lawrence came to his house one morning on Capri and, chiding him for not being dressed, added, "I hate those damned silk pyjamas." "Not as much," Mackenzie replied cheerfully, "as I hate that godawful grey flannel shirt you wear every other day.")

The young novelist William Gerhardie met the Lawrences for the first time that autumn. He was captivated. Invited to tea next day, he stayed eight hours. He was intrigued by Lawrence's curious combination of passion and gaucheness, and also by his attempts to tone down his German wife. When Gerhardie was introduced to Frieda, she had said by way of greeting, "What do you make of life?"

"Come, come," murmured Lawrence.

He tried to mute her again when she heard him criticizing a man whom Gerhardie greatly admired, Lord Beaverbrook, proprietor of the fiercely anti-German *Daily Express* and *Sunday Express,* and jumped in to join the attack. "Not so much intensity, Frieda," Lawrence ventured.

"If I want to be intense," she shot back, "I'll be intense, and you can go to hell!"

As "The Flying Fish" indicates, Lawrence was ready to become re-Englished. England was beautiful, safe and kindly; it was home. Preparing to depart for Italy, he thought he was an exile simply because of the weather. "If only this climate were not so accursed, with a pall of smoke hanging over the perpetual funeral of the sun," he told his sister, "we could have a house in Derbyshire and be jolly. But I always cough—so what's the good."

Two old friends whom he failed to see were Mark Gertler and Samuel Koteliansky. Earlier that autumn Gertler had begun once more to spit up blood and, following the more usual course for people diagnosed consumptive, had checked himself back in to the Mundesley Sanatorium in Norfolk, where specialists could examine his lungs. Gertler accepted— and informed his friends—that he would have to be "a beastly invalid" for several months. Almost as part of his treatment, he determined to avoid Lawrence, for, as he wrote Kot, "I think the kind of disturbance he creates is the wrong sort, and does one only harm."

To Kot, who had not heard from Lawrence since March, apparently because Lawrence was angry at Kot's collaboration with Murry, Gertler maintained that Lawrence was not at all trying to get away from Brett: "I should not be a bit surprised if he were *still* intrigued. . . . If he wanted to get rid of a person I think he could be pretty direct, and if he couldn't, Frieda could. No, I think he and Brett will drag on for ages yet, probably even conspiring against us."

Gertler was right. Instead of using distance to detach Brett's grip, Lawrence kept on manipulating her life from afar. Much as he had once instructed Rosalind Baynes how to travel from England to Italy, he now advised Brett. He told her how to secure her visa, even how to go to the bank. Having recommended Capri as her next destination, where she could be looked after by his friends (Faith Mackenzie and Earl and Achsah Brewster, now returned from Ceylon) until he and Frieda joined her there, he suggested that she choose between the Consulich Line, which charged $209 for first-class passage from New York to Naples, or the Navigazione Italiana, on which she might risk second class, for a mere $135.

Brett, however, still infatuated, fabricated an excuse about her passport and returned to England in the hope of seeing him. Her maneuver failed: the Lawrences had just left for Baden-Baden. But the flow of advice continued. Lawrence wrote and told her she ought to see Dr. David Eder, now practicing at 2 Harley Place, to try hypnosis for her deafness. "He knows all about those things," he said, "and is a friend of mine, a *nice* man, not a liar. . . . He'll do you for nothing if you tell him it's from me."

At Baden-Baden, Frieda had her hair cut ("bobbed, permanently waved, fluffed," Lawrence wrote Brett disapprovingly). Frieda, however, loved her new style and said it made her look like Jane Austen. As before, Lawrence enjoyed playing the son-in-law among ancient aristo-

crats and émigrés at the elegant German spa. He could hardly believe his
ears, he said, when he heard himself saying (in German, of course)—
"But Excellence, those are trumps!"

Then they reached Italy, the land of sun, which they had left three
years and three novels before. Frieda, however, refused to go anywhere
as far south as Capri or Sicily; she insisted on remaining in the north,
where her children could visit easily. At Secker's suggestion, they settled
for the wintry sun of the Italian Riviera at Spotorno, between Nice and
Genoa, in a three-story stucco villa called Bernarda on a steep hillside
overlooking the Mediterranean.

"I'm not crazy about the Riviera, as the Americans say," Lawrence
wrote Nancy Pearn, the agent at Curtis Brown for his magazine articles.
But it was Europe all the same. In an essay, "Europe v. America," he
expressed his relief at being back:

> The Europeans still have a vague idea that the universe is greater than
> they are, and isn't going to change very radically. . . . But the Ameri-
> cans are tense . . . as if they felt that once they slackened, the world
> would really collapse. It wouldn't.

Swiftly he began the familiar chant for visitors. He invited Murry and
his wife, promising them a bedroom and kitchen for themselves, and
sent Blanche Knopf (the wife of Alfred Knopf) a powerful evocation of
Italy: "we eat fried chicken and pasta and smell rosemary and basilica in
the cooking once more—and somebody's always roasting coffee—and
the oranges are already yellow."

The two men were doomed to misalliance. Murry, who had wanted to
come, sadly declined the invitation because his wife was pregnant again.
Lawrence, disappointed, let fly with one of the free-association letters he
often sent in Murry's direction. He scolded Murry first for complaining
about the unwanted pregnancy ("call the baby Benvenuto"), then for
taking himself and his magazine, *Adelphi,* too seriously, and then for
getting religion. Boisterously, Lawrence told him to forget publishing, to
start writing for money, and to get on with living his life. "Bah, that one
should be a mountain of mere words! Heave-O! my boy! get out of it!"

To Kot (their warm correspondence resuming once a safe distance
separated them), Lawrence wrote tartly, "If our little friend had stuck to
me or my way a bit, he wouldn't be where he is."

Frieda, who, as Lawrence knew, still regarded Kot as her prime enemy, added a postscript to ask Kot sweetly if they could not now be
friends. She appended some comments, too, to the end of one of
Lawrence's long letters to Brett, announcing, among other things, that
suddenly she felt happy, for no reason at all: "just feel like it and basta."

A few weeks later, another postscript suggested that perhaps there was a reason: "We have a nice little Bersaglieri officer to whom the villa belongs I am thrilled by his cockfeathers he is almost as nice as the feathers!"

Did Brett get the unsubtle message? A plumed serpent had glided into their lives; Lawrence's replacement had arrived.

EARLY in the new year *The Plumed Serpent*, with a jacket design by Brett for which she was paid fifty dollars, appeared in London and New York, to mixed but respectful reviews: "He tears the heart out of Mexico as he tore it out of Australia," said L. P. Hartley in the *Saturday Review*. Hartley deplored the wooden characterizations, as did Charles Marriott in the *Manchester Guardian*. Marriott all the same found it "an intensely religious book" that pursued with the richness of Lawrence's imagination "the desired connection with the mystery of the cosmos [which] is the most interesting theme in the world." For Katherine Anne Porter, writing in *New York Herald Tribune Books*, the novel was a complete failure. "All Mexico is here," she said. Unfortunately, so was all of D. H. Lawrence himself: every character down to the last dancing Indian was a mouthpiece for the author. "When you have read this book read *Sons and Lovers* again," Porter concluded. "You will realize the catastrophe that has overtaken Lawrence."

Lawrence, at forty, was conscious of what this ambitious book had cost him. As he had told Murry, he now wanted to enjoy his life, not to pour his vitality into books telling other people how to enjoy theirs. He was well aware of how much of the world he had not yet tasted: Russia, for example. He asked Kot for a Russian grammar book and thought he would start at least learning the language. He mused (prescient once again) on the eventual outcome of the Soviet Communist experiment: "I wonder if Russia has had all her troubles and her revolutions, just to bring about a state of complete materialism and cheapness. . . . But I suppose it's on the cards."

He told Adele Seltzer, too, that he thought he might try Russia, for he felt like staying "outside that clenched grip of America for a bit." This was the start of a long series of veiled acknowledgments that the real deterrent to a return to New Mexico was the clenched fist of U.S. Immigration.

In December Frieda's daughter Barby came to visit. At Ernest Weekley's unforgiving insistence, she was staying at a pensione nearby in Alassio, with an English chaperone, rather than at the notorious Lawrences'. Yet she spent much of her time at the Villa Bernarda and was with them for Christmas. It was a heady atmosphere for someone brought up in a London suburb. Lawrence did like Barby, but was jealous. Seeing the closeness between mother and daughter, hearing

Barby call Frieda "Ma," he saw that the bond he had spent thirteen years trying to obliterate was unbroken.

His sisters' children still served as his own. For Christmas he sent an avuncular letter to Ada's son, John Clarke, giving him ten shillings and enclosing another ten for a present for "Auntie Gertie" (Ada's lodger Gertie Cooper). Young John was to put "From Bert and Frieda" on the label, "and do it respectably, so as not to shame us, and don't be wessel-brained, or there'll be death in the pot." Lawrence signed, "Love from your Auntie Frieda and your ever estimable Uncle Bert."

But stepfatherhood had its compensations. Some people thought Barby was Lawrence's own daughter; also, she was someone new to advise. He told her to forget what she had learned at the Royal Academy's art school and simply to play with her paints. He scolded her for letting herself be taken to tea by a stranger—even though the stranger was an English admiral who had introduced himself while watching her at her easel. As for the attraction that sprang up between himself and Barby, he characteristically projected it and told a neighbor that Barby had tried to flirt with him.

Lawrence was learning that his tall, beautiful stepdaughter had a sharp tongue in a league with his own. "I wouldn't marry you, Barby, if you had a million pounds," he told her admiringly, and the two of them spent long hours in happy venomous conversation. Avidly he listened to her withering descriptions of Grandma Weekley, who had brought up the three Weekley children determined to eradicate any trace of their unmentionable mother. By the third week of January 1926, Lawrence had enshrined Barby's rebelliousness (and killed off Grandma) in *The Virgin and the Gipsy,* a novella written at the rate of two thousand words a day and sent straight off to Secker for typing. The work bears the signs of haste, as well it might: in the weeks before Christmas Lawrence had produced three new short stories, "Smile," "Sun," and "Glad Ghosts," some twenty-five thousand words in all. *The Virgin and the Gipsy* is nonetheless a rollicking tale on a familiar theme: well-born girl breaches class barriers and finds sensual truth in arms of swarthy primitive.

BUT there was a better example, much closer to home. Lieutenant (later Captain) Angelo Ravagli certainly did exist; he was a thirty-four-year-old officer in the Italian infantry. But Lawrence had already invented him. General Cipriano, who marries and masters Kate in *The Plumed Serpent,* is almost a premonition of Ravagli: a cocky, alert little man with dark eyes, a knowing way with women, and a devotion to a charismatic national savior—in Ravagli's case, Mussolini.

Every weekend Ravagli, whose wife and children lived in Savona, farther along the coast and closer to Genoa, would come to visit Spotorno. He impressed both Lawrences with his handiness around the house. When the stove smoked and Lawrence cursed, Ravagli took off his uniform, put on overalls, took apart the stovepipe, cleaned it, and climbed onto the roof to inspect the chimney. Lawrence was outclassed at his own game. In return, he tried teaching Ravagli English, but did not get very far.

The affair between Ravagli and Frieda probably started early in 1926 if not sooner. Neither was one for long courtships. Barby, who herself flirted with Ravagli, saw the signs. One night Lawrence threw a glass of wine at Frieda and snarled at Barby, "Don't imagine your mother loves you; she doesn't love anybody, look at her false face." Barby furiously told Lawrence that her mother was too good for him. She wondered if he really loved her. "It is indecent to ask," Lawrence retorted coldly. "Haven't I just helped her with her rotten painting?"

This new rival caught Lawrence at a vulnerable time, for early in the new year his other stepdaughter, Elsa Weekley, arrived. The constant presence of two tall, self-possessed young women talking rapidly in a clear, confident King's English that carried from room to room left him feeling an outsider in his own home: "absolutely swamped out," he wrote to William Hawk at Del Monte Ranch.

The tension between husband and wife was undisguised. Barby saw her mother in tears after a row, with her neck scratched and Lawrence exhausted. He pretended not to understand Frieda at all. "Why does your mother want to be so *important?*" he asked Barby.

Frieda did want to be important, or at least recognized for competence. With wild enthusiasm, demanding dictionaries, she threw herself into translating *David* into German. She was undoubtedly rankled to hear Lawrence's high praise of her clever sister Else's translation of *The Boy in the Bush;* he had liked it so much that he was eager for Else to do *The Plumed Serpent* as well. He told his German publisher that he preferred his sister-in-law's work to that of his previous translator because "she gets my rhythm so well: perhaps a little lighter, quicker than Herr Franzius." Toward Frieda's efforts, Lawrence was condescending. "She loves it," he told Secker, "and has become the authoress, I . . . the housemaid of the Villa B." He assured Secker that he corrected Frieda's work before sending it on.

Lawrence decided (perhaps at Frieda's urging) that Elsa could now do his typing. He wrote to Brett on Capri (where, as in North America, she slaved away, turning his manuscripts into clean copies) and asked her to send back his typewriter. His stepdaughter, he explained, was a trained typist and knew enough German to decipher Frieda's muddled notes. For Brett, waiting patiently for Lawrence to turn up, this was a further blow. Lawrence had already conveyed to her that Frieda, friendly letters notwithstanding, had declared "an implacable intention of never seeing you again and never speaking to you if she does see you—and I say nothing."

As if to counterbalance Frieda's reinforcement with "daughters who are by no means mine," Lawrence's sister Ada arrived from the Midlands with a woman friend in tow. Thus Lawrence found himself at the center of a household, surrounded by five women from three different backgrounds. The weather did not help by turning unusually cold. Like many Italian houses, the Villa Bernarda had no fireplace; in the worst of the winter, inhabitants were expected to shiver and wait for the return of the sun. Not surprisingly, just as Ada arrived, Lawrence went down with what he called his annual flu—much coughing, but this year accompanied by hemorrhages, "like at the ranch, only worse," he told Brett.

Ada and Frieda had not been under the same roof since Derbyshire in 1919, when they had fought over caring for the flu-stricken Lawrence. Now Ada found herself in an alien environment, confronted with one familiar sight: bedridden Bert. She reverted to type, and he responded. Frieda could hear him complaining about her to his sister. Ada felt so much in command that she elbowed Frieda aside in the kitchen, and once, after settling her Bert for the night, she locked the door to his room and pocketed the key.

This blatant outrage—shutting a wife out of her husband's bedroom—may have been a response to the Ravagli affair. Lawrence probably told Ada about it directly. If so, she would not have been surprised. Like the rest of Lawrence's family, she had long believed that Frieda was immoral.

There was a colossal scene. Ada told Frieda, "I hate you from the bottom of my heart." Frieda replied in kind, then took her daughters and moved out, leaving Lawrence and the two Midlands matrons in possession of the Villa Bernarda. As soon as he was better, however, Lawrence, taking Ada and her friend with him, left for Monte Carlo without leaving an address. Frieda and the girls then moved back in, and when Angelo Ravagli next visited Spotorno, he found the three of them alone.

Lawrence had gotten himself out on a limb. Once his two visitors had to return to England, he was on his own, with no one to look after him. Sitting on the beach at Monte Carlo he felt sad and lonely, and contemplated the wreck of his family life. To Ada, who was scarcely out of sight, he wrote a longing letter, "I was awfully sorry we had all this upset. I was so looking forward to your coming." Then he sent a telegram to Brett on Capri telling her he was on his way.

OUT of this debacle emerged a mesmeric short story. "The Rocking-Horse Winner," written very quickly in February 1926, is another example of Lawrence's mastery of the tale and his sureness with their titles.

The story, which, like *The Virgin and the Gipsy,* has an English set-ting, is almost a child's parody of "St. Mawr." The powerful stallion has become a wooden horse; the setting has shrunk from the wild Rockies to an English nursery; and the awesome power of the natural world has given way to the supernatural. The leading character is a young boy. Frenzied by his mother's craving for wealth and his father's inability to satisfy it, he finds that his toy horse, ridden wildly, reveals to him the names of the winners in forthcoming races. He passes the tips on to the family gardener, who uses them to place bets at the racetrack, and before long five shillings has turned into ten thousand pounds. One night, just before the boy is about to be expelled from the nest (his father is sending him off to Eton), his mother finds him in the dark nursery "plunging to and fro" on the wooden steed. Collapsing from the strain, he is carried off to die—but not before shrieking triumphantly to his mother that his horse has won the Derby and she now has eighty thousand pounds.

"The Rocking-Horse Winner" is widely considered to be Lawrence's attack on materialism. But a deeper theme, well brought out in John Mills's 1949 film, with himself as the father and Valerie Hobson as the mother, is the maddening impotence of the child: a boy's desperate wish to be the man his father is not and to compensate his mother for her frustrations. But with only childish equipment, rocked frantically in the rhythm of masturbation, he rewards his mother with an orgasm of riches and his death.

"The Rocking-Horse Winner" displays the familiar Lawrence pattern of contrasting couples, good and bad. The boy has, in effect, two sets of parents: brittle upper-class Mummy and Daddy who are always dressing for dinner and going out to smart parties; and their hired substitutes, who look after him better—the comforting nanny and the rough-spoken, virile, but gentle gardener. It is noteworthy that the little boy who kills himself trying to make his mother happy is called Paul, the name that Lawrence gave his self-portrait in *Sons and Lovers.*

The story was one of several written as a favor for Cynthia Asquith, who was preparing a collection of ghost stories. Like most of Lawrence's favors, it was double-edged. The story conspicuously drew on painful elements in Cynthia's own life: her autistic son, John, a deranged boy in a world of his own; her unsatisfactory marriage; and her gravest char-acter defect (as Lawrence saw it), greed.

However, Lawrence once again betrayed himself far more than he did his friends. The story is a male nightmare of being drawn back into infantilism by the malignancy of a mother's desires. It also betrays a desperation for money: the winning sums mount up like a cash register until the climactic jackpot is achieved.

Yet if the story is so personal a testament, how to account for its

strange power? Because Lawrence's vivid images and psychological perceptions reach into the reader's own unconscious. Writing "The
Rocking-Horse Winner" in February 1926, he plunged, with the preci-
sion and pain of a spinal tap, into the dark current that flows between
mother and son.

THAT money had to be gathered in, Lawrence needed no persuading.
Never had he related his earnings so clearly to their emotional and
physical cost. He knew that, in every sense, he wrote to stay alive.
Writing drained off his spleen, he told Earl Brewster. Yet writing with
too much intensity threatened his life. He could see the dismal down-
ward spiral. The weaker he got, the more money he would need. Yet for
the first time in a long while he had no major book either awaiting
publication or in progress. Meanwhile, Seltzer, who owed him five thousand dollars, was going bankrupt.

Lawrence calculated that he needed three hundred pounds a year.
Fine. He would write to earn that and no more. He warmed to the
possibilities of more journalism. He told Nancy Pearn that from now on
he would just do short stories and smaller things, like book reviews:
"They could choose the book. But they'd have to make it clear, whether
I could say what I wanted or not." Both Secker and Knopf wanted him
to do another novel, but *The Plumed Serpent* had taken too much out of
him. When Alfred Knopf complained to him that it was becoming harder
and harder to sell good books, Lawrence commented to Brett, "Then let
him sell bad ones."

Was that the genesis of one of the most notorious novels of the twentieth century? In a matter of months Lawrence would begin the book
that was to become his own lucky winner, bringing in more money than
all the rest.

FROM a nightmare of impotence to the reality seems to have been a
matter of weeks. Lawrence's arrival on Capri on February 27, 1926, was
Brett's dream come true. He joined her as a guest of the Brewsters and,
from what he said, she believed that he had left Frieda. As they walked
and talked by the hour, he described the latest scenes in a drama she
knew all too well. "You have no idea, Brett," he said, "how humiliating
it is to beat a woman; afterwards one feels simply humiliated." But
Frieda was impossible.

Giddy in each other's company, they clowned for their hosts and one
evening shocked the ascetic Brewsters by coming in to dinner dressed in
costume. Lawrence was a schoolmaster with his hair parted in the middle, collar turned up, face powdered, and eyes blackened, while on his

arm Brett was a surrealistic flapper, with dead-white face, slicked-back hair, bright scarlet lips, and blue eye shadow. The Brewsters were gratifyingly scandalized. They did not react, however, to what now seems more shocking: Lawrence's persistent attempts to kiss "the child," as they called their thirteen-year-old daughter. Harwood kept refusing but Lawrence went on loudly insisting.

In a bachelor mood, Lawrence twice saw Faith Mackenzie and took her out to dinner where, warmed by the wine and the attentive blue gaze, she unwisely poured out the secrets of her open marriage. She was to regret her loosened tongue when some months later she read Lawrence's short story "Two Blue Birds," about a woman who lives apart from her husband and takes lovers; and when Compton Mackenzie read "The Man Who Loved Islands," another story Lawrence wrote that spring, he called in his lawyers. But the Mackenzies' marriage obviously intrigued Lawrence for its parallel with his own, and he told Ada that Faith was "another who loves her husband but can't live with him."

But the Brewsters were leaving for India. Following his policy of seeking protectors, he crossed to Ravello on the mainland to visit Millicent Beveridge and Mabel Harrison, two painters he had known in Sicily. Brett came, too. She was trying to persuade him to return to the United States but he replied that he did not have the strength "to cope with Consuls." Not that there was much of an obstacle for any British subject who was healthy. Brett was returning as an immigrant under the newly established quota system, which heavily favored Northern Europeans, the English above all.

At Ravello Brett achieved her long wish to have Lawrence make love to her. Or at least to try. They had separate rooms at the same *pensione,* where one night, repeating his dictum that friendship was impossible without sex, he got into her bed. In Brett's words, "nothing happened." She did not know what to do. Next night Lawrence said, "Let's try again." The result was the same.

Lawrence got out of bed crossly and, dipping into his boyhood or his botanical vocabulary, said, "Your pubes are wrong." ("Pubes" is a term for pubic hair, two syllables in Latin, but pronounced in the Midlands, and perhaps elsewhere, as "pyoobz.") Poor Brett did not consider the possibility that it was his anatomy, not hers, that was at fault—even though he had told her earlier that his illness had left him as weak as "a white geranium in a pot." He could have spared himself some anguish by recognizing his complete lack of physical desire for his gawky, sisterly friend. But he did not; to him the failed performance was a devastating failure, a symptom of the male menopause. Next morning Brett found him furiously packing his bags to leave. She argued that he could not walk out on his artist friends, who were counting on him for a trip through Italy. Sacrificially, she offered to leave herself, hoping that he would try to persuade her to stay. But he did not. Instead, he helped her pack and got her onto the steamer to Capri so fast that she left her laundry behind.

Brett did not realize, any more than Mabel had in Taos in September 1924, that she was seeing Lawrence for the last time. His intimate letters to her in the years that were left to him testify to their closeness; there were certain things each could say only to the other.

LAWRENCE may have intended to repay adultery with adultery, but his resolve was weakened by the conciliatory letters now arriving from Spotorno. By early March Frieda was back in a wife-of-the-artist mood. She made light of the temporary separation in a letter to Mabel, another old adversary to whom distance lent enchantment: "I have the children here and something in me came to life again in them too—I hope L is taking a new lease of life, that Plumed Serpent took it out of him (out of me too) it went almost too far." Frieda assured Mabel that they would see her again at the ranch if Lawrence's health held up. She expected him back soon from Capri.

And back he came. After a touristic swing from Rome to Ravenna, he was greeted, so he told Ada triumphantly, by "three females very glad to see me . . . but there's a bit of anger still working in my inside." More humbly, he explained to his mother-in-law (whom Frieda obviously had kept fully informed of the row) that he had recovered from the bad temper in which he had stormed off: "But really one has to forget a lot, and to live on." He did have a touch of bronchitis, he told the baroness, but so did most Englishmen of forty.

For a month the Lawrences lived happily as a family of four. The girls told their mother to fix herself up and be nicer to Lawrence. He told them that Ada depressed him. He loved the way Elsa and Barby flew at Frieda, giving her a dose of her own medicine. "It makes me die with laughing," he wrote to Brett. And he wrote to their aunt Else Jaffe—with colossal cheek, as if he had had no influence on their development— "They are nice girls really, it is Frieda who, in a sense, has made a bad use of them."

Near the end of April the lease on the Villa Bernarda was up and they left *en famille* to reestablish themselves near Florence. Ravagli turned up to say good-bye.

THE road to the tiny hilltop village of San Paolo (sometimes spelled San Polo) Mosciano, seven miles southwest of Florence, rises from the flat plain of the Arno through a cinquecento scene of terraced fields, cypresses, red-tiled villas, and the occasional campanile. In early May 1926, for twenty-five pounds, the Lawrences took a year's lease on the *piano nobile* of the Villa Mirenda, a large stately square villa on the crest of a hill. From the back they looked out on a pleasant garden with pines and an old pump and down a slope to the tiny church, with its priest's house and peasant cottage, and farther on to a tiny cluster of pretty houses around a piazza no bigger than an opera set. From the garden in front of the Mirenda they could see the red-roofed sprawl of Florence and rising through the haze, the Duomo.

Lawrence had chosen to settle in the region in order to write a travel book about the Etruscans, the ancient inhabitants of Tuscany and Umbria. His interest had been awakened in 1921 by Etruscan ruins in Sicily, and now back in Italy, he began intensive reading about Etruscan remains. He identified intensely with what he saw as a proud, spontaneous, and happy race that had fallen victim to the Romans.

After the girls left, Lawrence and Frieda enjoyed another period of solitude. In the cool evenings, they embroidered together. They made expeditions into Florence, taking a horse cart down the dusty road (now paved and bypassed by a modern motorway) to the tram terminus at Vingone, from which it was a half hour's ride into the center of the city. For the festival of San Giovanni on June 24, they stayed the night and saw the fireworks. Lawrence was inspired to several articles, including "Fireworks in Florence," in which he marveled at the ignorance of the Florentines, in spite of their most famous statue, of the name David: "Tell them your name is David, and they remain utterly impervious and blank. You cannot bring them to utter it."

The pleasure of the Mirenda was enhanced by agreeable neighbors. An English artist, Arthur Wilkinson, and his Scottish wife, Lilian, had come to the Tuscan hills with their children in search of the simple life devoted to nature, art, health, and culture. The two families liked the same kind of thing: visiting for tea, playing charades, singing around the piano, and making fun of one another once they got home. Privately, the Wilkinsons referred to the Lawrences as "The Author" and "Mrs. Author"; Frieda was sometimes "Mrs. Lorenzo." But Lawrence also had his fun with "the Wilks." He was scornful of their left-wing vegetarian lifestyle and sent Secker a pen portrait of the head of the family: "artist, red beard, Rucksack, violin case—you can see him— but seems nice."

Florence, of course, was Norman Douglas territory. For a time Lawrence avoided his literary adversary, but he resumed his friendship with the rest of the expatriate coterie. Early lunch guests at the Mirenda were the witty writer and journalist Reggie Turner and a jocular rotund antiquarian bookseller, Giuseppe (Pino) Orioli, whom they had first met in Cornwall. Orioli had helped them find the Mirenda and was soon to play a leading role in Lawrence's campaign to make himself some real money.

Of all their temporary homes in their wandering life, the spacious and serene Mirenda was probably the most beautiful; it shared the distinction, with their Cornwall cottage and the Villa Fontana Vecchia in Sicily, of holding them for two years. Frieda, settled in to what she described as a Medici villa, was increasingly reluctant to budge, even for Germany. But for Lawrence the summer trip north was becoming almost as imperative as the autumn migration south. He worked out their itinerary for the hottest months: first, Baden-Baden; then England, where, he suggested to Kot, the two of them might go to Dorset to have a look at Murry's second baby, "son and heir, another John Middleton, ye Gods!"; then, on the return journey, Austria, to visit Frieda's younger sister, Nusch. The Etruscans could wait.

IN the Tuscan summer, with its early harvest and golden heat, they flopped about in the rope-soled sandals Lawrence had ordered from Capri—Frieda's just one size smaller than his own. One June day they went to lunch with Sir George and Lady Ida Sitwell at the rambling hilltop Castello di Montegufoni, from which Sir George reigned as king of Chiantishire: he was the highest-ranking man in the English colony scattered in the region around Florence. In England, the Sitwells' Derbyshire family seat, Renishaw, was just a short drive from Lawrence's native Eastwood.

Informing Ada of their aristocratic invitation, Lawrence nonchalantly described the Sitwells as local Derbyshire folk: "They have a castle about 14 miles out. But their home place is near Chesterfield: I guess you've heard of them, one way or another. It's their boys who write." Lawrence did not burden his unliterary sister with the names of the Sitwells' boys, Osbert or Sacheverell, nor of their girl, Edith, who also wrote.

In the end, the visit exhausted him. Sir George insisted on showing the Lawrences his collection of antique beds—"those four-poster golden venetian monsters that look like Mexican high-altars," Lawrence wrote a friend: "Room after room, and nothing but bed after bed." To his politely sarcastic "Do you put your guests into them?" Sir George had answered haughtily that the beds were not to sleep in: they were museum pieces. And when the tired Lawrence made the mistake of sitting down on one of the carved gilt chairs, his host had snapped, "Oh! Those chairs are not to sit in!" "Queer couple," was Lawrence's conclusion.

The Sitwells' also. Lady Ida's account, written to Osbert, shows how the Lawrences looked through the upper-class end of the English telescope:

A Mr D. H. Lawrence came over the other day, a funny little petit-maître of a man with flat features and a beard. He says he is a writer, and seems to know all of you. His wife is a large German. She went round the house with your father, and when he showed her anything, would look at him, lean against one of the gilded beds, and breathe heavily.

They headed north in July, at Frieda's insistence. Lawrence was reluctant to move, as he felt well. Yet he enjoyed their fortnight in Baden-Baden, where he resumed playing whist with his mother-in-law, sipped the hot waters, listened to music in the Kurhaus, and promised to return in the autumn for an inhalation cure.

From Germany he resumed a correspondence that was greatly to trouble his later followers. Rolf Gardiner in 1926 was a young Cambridge graduate for whom Lawrence was a prophet. Gardiner, who was founding youth forest camps in England and in Germany, had read *The Plumed Serpent* in just the way that Lawrence had intended—as a blueprint for national rebirth through the creation of a state within a state— and had begun to dream of a Celto-Germanic version. He treasured the words of encouragement Lawrence had written him, that "one must look for real guts and self-responsibility to the Northern peoples."

Undeniably racist as this and similar utterances are, Lawrence set them in a context in which he stopped well short of fanaticism and even of advocating political action. To his young disciple, Lawrence urged (with an endearing confusion about the spelling of the name of his wife's first husband): "Don't be too ernest—earnest—how does one spell it?— nor overburdened by a mission." He was far from enamored of the pettifogging fascism he saw at close range in Italy. "Italy is in such a state of nervous tension, with her fascism," he wrote his sister Emily, "it reacts on everything," and he told their friend Ravagli that somebody ought to put a ring through Mussolini's nose. He thought Germany less politically charged, and preferred it.

In London in August 1926, coming up the stairs at their rented flat at 25 Rossetti Garden Mansions, Lawrence encountered his stepson. Montague Weekley, unlike his sisters, had never accepted his mother's remarriage; but at twenty-six, with an Oxford degree and his promising museum career well begun, he was ready to relent. (Frieda's wish to be near the Victoria and Albert Museum was one reason why they had taken a place in Chelsea, rather than the usual Hampstead, which Lawrence—and not he alone—believed to be a healthier part of London.)

"It is a safe job," Monty said, proudly telling his stepfather of his museum work. "Remember," Lawrence replied, fastening on the young man his bluest gaze, "only the dead are safe."

Lawrence then proceeded to talk, and talk brilliantly. Monty felt that for the first time in his life he was in the presence of a genius; he understood at last why his mother had done what she had done.

Stepfather and stepson were acutely sensitive to the difference in their accents. Monty, who had a polished Standard English accent and also a good ear (he could mimic their Mamma's guttural English in a way that convulsed his sisters), noticed with surprise that Lawrence's voice retained strong Nottinghamshire vowels. Discussing painters, Lawrence dismissed Sargent as "sooch a bahd peeynter."

"Odd for a man who has known Asquith and Morrell," Monty thought to himself. But stepsons do not have the most sympathetic of ears.

Anecdotal impressions such as these are the only evidence of the sound of Lawrence's voice. Famous as he was, Lawrence never took the opportunity to record his voice as Yeats, Shaw, and Joyce had done, and even, a generation or two earlier, Tennyson, Tolstoy, and Browning. The omission may have been deliberate on Lawrence's part; he also shied away from speaking on the radio. The many attempts to capture in words the peculiar timbre of his voice—Rebecca West called it "curious, hollow, like the soft hoot of an owl"—suggest that it was high and reedy, and might have been recognized at the time as a consumptive's voice.

As soon as he could, Lawrence cleared out of London. Continuing the ambitious traveling of a man who had nearly died the year before, he went to the north of Scotland to visit Millicent Beveridge, then to Sutton on Sea in Lincolnshire for a holiday with both sisters. The day that Frieda arrived, Emily and Ada departed.

For Frieda and Lawrence both, the flat bleak North Sea coast brought vivid memories. From a rented bungalow named Duneville, Frieda splashed in the surf, while Lawrence, not daring to risk his bronchials, contented himself with writing to friends many descriptions of the sweep of sand, sea, and sky.

He had something more urgent to convey to Ada. Their good friend, her lodger, Gertie Cooper, was displaying renewed symptoms of the Cooper family curse. Lawrence told Ada exactly what she must do: find the best chest specialist in Nottingham and demand "an X-ray photograph." "When we see how the thing is, if it has started, and how far it's gone, we shall know much better where we are. Ask him too if he would suggest an analysis of the sputum." He enlisted Kot as well, to get Gertler's doctor to examine Gertie and also to find out how much Mundesley, Gertler's sanatorium, cost. (Mundesley, in north Norfolk, was used by wealthy people who did not want to travel abroad. Its fees were at least five guineas a week.)

It was advice he would have done better to apply to himself, but, turning forty-one, he felt remarkably well. He sent Kot a comic seaside postcard of a woman in striped bathing drawers cavorting on the sands. He apologized for its vulgarity—it was the only thing he could find to write on—but the card's jaunty printed message—"This Is How I Feel"— expressed his own thoughts exactly.

He was beginning to think that perhaps England—London apart— might actually be good for his health and that he might make it his home for at least the warmer months of the year. With that optimism he went to revisit the place of his birth.

LIKE so many of the experiences which triggered one of his major novels, the return to Eastwood was brief. Lawrence sailed into Willie Hopkin's house one day in mid-September as if he had never been away and said, "Come along, Willie. I want you to go for a walk with me."

The walk took them on a circuit of his past; his former homes on Walker Street and The Breech; Beauvale School, with its belfry and playground where he had suffered such agonies as a child; past the Ram Inn and the mines, and out into the countryside past the landmarks of *The White Peacock*. As they passed the cottage where Jessie Chambers's sister, May, and her husband used to live, Hopkin, as an older man and longtime friend, boldly dared to ask why Lawrence had never married Jessie. Lawrence snapped: "I should have had too easy a life, nearly everything my own way, and my genius would have been destroyed." (His answer, however irritable, supports Frieda's own theory that he demanded a state of constant combat from a wife.)

Other sights triggered other memories: the old cottage of a forest ranger reminded Lawrence that the man who had lived there used to beat his wife. They saw Robin Hood's Well, avoided Haggs Farm, passed the seat of the mine-owning Barber family, Lamb Close House, and returned via Moorgreen Colliery—ugly in its modernization, and ominously silent.

Lawrence was shaken by what he saw. In his mood of reconciliation with the place of his birth, he found it at war with itself, torn over the very industry that had sustained the warm life of his family and his community: coal. British miners had not worked since late April, when the National Association of Mine Owners tore up their contracts and invited the men to return for lower wages. The owners were trying to reduce costs because the decision of Stanley Baldwin's Conservative government to return to the gold standard had pushed up the price of British coal in overseas markets—a price already high because of over-manning and overproduction. The miners, however, considered themselves locked out. In May a national general strike, called by the trade-union movement in sympathy, collapsed after nine days, leaving the miners stranded.

They refused to return to work, but strike pay was patchy at best. When Lawrence returned to the Midlands, he witnessed hunger and bitterness, violence and arrests. He saw the disorderly rush back to work as crowds jeered those men who accepted the offer made by the pit owners in an attempt to break the five-month-old stoppage.

Lawrence, now older, wiser, and more compassionate, sympathized with the miners. Yet he saw the unrest as the beginning of a slow revolution—"the spear through the side of *my* England"—all the more alarming after what he had observed in Mexico.

He was equally shocked at the change in the landscape. Conservative policies had encouraged private speculative housing development, and there were no planning restrictions. Outward from Eastwood spread rows and rows of semi-detached villas in harsh geometric lines (or as he later described them, "great plasterings of brick dwellings on the hopeless countryside"). He was further saddened by the mechanization of the mines. He had always thought of the mines as organic outgrowths of their pastoral surroundings but now their black charm had disappeared under electric lights, generating plants, and chemical vats.

Not everyone thought the new suburbia ugly. Ada and Eddie Clarke, with whom Lawrence was staying in nearby Ripley, were proud of their neat, modern house, whose light-hearted name, "Torestin," was taken from Lawrence's *Kangaroo*. Lawrence wondered, seeing his sister's villa with its tiled hall, foreign knickknacks, and glass doors opening onto lawn and flower garden, what their mother would say. Would she think this evidence of affluence reward for all her efforts to push her children higher in the world?

The Clarkes' prosperity extended to a motorcar. Next day Ada and Eddie drove Lawrence through the Derbyshire countryside on a circular tour through Bolsover, through Chesterfield, past (and possibly into the grounds of) Renishaw, the Sitwells' great brownstone pile, and back through Chesterfield. Everywhere his eyes were pained by the sight of sullen colliers, silent mines, blighted countryside. Depressed, he dashed off an essay, "Return to Bestwood," very shortly after and sent it for German publication. It blamed the whole sorry spectacle on the mortal struggle for property.

Lawrence's political philosophy, always hazy, now lurched back toward socialism. His essay called for state ownership, plus what was fondly known to the British left by Keir Hardie's phrase "a change of heart":

> I know that we could, if we could, establish little by little a true democracy in England: we could nationalise the land and industries

and means of transport, and make the whole thing work infinitely better than at present, *if we would*. It all depends on the spirit in which the thing is done.

Of what he had seen, he wrote to Else Jaffe, with her doctorate in industrial sociology, that class hatred was "the quiet volcano over which English life is built." To Secker, as he prepared to return to Italy, he ventured that were he ever to do an English novel he would have to come to England to do it. These were the first hints of a tenth novel, which would be as much about class as about sex.

There was also the first hint that he would never go back to the ranch. "In my opinion, it would be better to sell it," he wrote Rachel Hawk at Del Monte. To Mrs. Hawk, he blamed Frieda's hostility to Brett. To his sister Emily, he said that he wanted a permanent place in England; the ranch was too far.

BACK at the Mirenda in late October—having vetoed a visit to Germany because of the expense—he made some household improvements. He had the walls whitewashed, bought a warm stove and new rush matting for the floor, and entertained the Aldingtons for an enjoyable five days. For Compton Mackenzie's *Gramophone,* which was preparing a series on the musical favorites of celebrities, he sent a list of his own choices: favorite composer, Mozart; favorite song, a Hebridean folk song, "Kishmul's Gallery"; favorite singer, an Indian singing to a drum. He then sat down and wrote *Lady Chatterley's Lover.*

The first draft as usual went quickly: a tale of the fall of the England of landed gentry and great houses. By November 15 he could report to Secker that it was "a novel in the Derbyshire coal-mining districts— already rather improper." By the last week in November it was finished.

When the book was published two years later, the search was swiftly on for the real-life model for the crippled and impotent Sir Clifford Chatterley of Wragby Hall whose wife runs off with his gamekeeper. There was none to guess that the true model for the aristocratic husband, "with bright, haunted blue eyes," who can no longer make love to his wife, was the author himself.

Of the three complete versions of *Lady Chatterley* Lawrence wrote, the first was the most tender and least angry. There were comparatively few rude words in it, and no sodomy. But it was a clear and bold step into language he had not dared before. The gamekeeper (named Parkin in the first and second versions) calls himself "my lady's fucker" and invites Constance Chatterley to appreciate "manly fucking." With its simple and straightforward plot, the story reads like an adult version of *The Secret Garden.* Frances Hodgson Burnett's classic, published in

1911, is a child-scale tale of a discontented upper-class female, shut up in a great house with an aristocratic invalid, who escapes to nature and, under the tutelage of one of the workers on the estate, awakens to the pleasures of the earth and vernacular English.

Frieda wholeheartedly encouraged *Lady Chatterley*. Every afternoon Lawrence read aloud to her what he had written out under the pine trees that morning. In the evening they sat at the table in the Mirenda's kitchen writing their letters. One night as they sat there, she eating a persimmon with a spoon and he wearing the spectacles he needed for close work, she tried to convey in a letter to Monty what the new book was about—the war between the classes and between soul and body—then halted: "No I don't explain it well, the *animal* part." At this rare expression of humility, Lawrence scrawled, "Ooray!!! Eureka!" and added an invitation to Monty and Barby to join them for Christmas.

To Mabel, Frieda wrote scolding her for thinking that her life was one long struggle to hold on to Lawrence: "I am jolly glad to be alone sometimes, so is he, but we are both glad to come together again, very glad!"

It was true. They were the picture of domesticity—throwing themselves into making the Mirenda comfortable, doing their various projects, chatting in their fluent if ungrammatical Italian to the Mirenda peasants who worked the fields—except that Frieda was having an affair with Angelo Ravagli.

Did Lawrence know? Frieda later claimed to Mabel that he had got the plot of *Lady Chatterley* from her and her lover. As Mabel, with her penchant for dialogue, reconstructed their conversation:

"From you and Angellino!!!??"

"Yes!"

"Had it been going on long & Lorenzo got it intuitively?"

"*Yes!!* He just got it out of the air!"

The truth was less ethereal. Lawrence kept a close eye on Frieda. He suspected (and Frieda later confirmed to Mabel) that she would use the excuse of visiting her mother to make a detour to Ravagli's garrison. Certainly Ravagli (now promoted to *capitano*) was not welcome when, just as the first draft of *Lady Chatterley* was being completed, he came to visit. He descended, joked Lawrence to Secker, "with such a dense fog of that peculiar inert Italian misery, dreariness, that I am only just re-covering."

That was not the impression that Ravagli made on women. With his warm dark eyes and easy grace, he was a skilled womanizer, the kind of man who automatically slides his hand under the table to grasp the hand of the woman he has just met. When Mabel met him five years later, she found him—although a complete provincial who had never been outside Italy, and a believer in Mussolini as the flower of the world—"a candid happy creature, [in] whose wide brow and wide apart brown eyes lies no slightest consciousness of anything but amiable and affectionate delight. There is something of the noble child about him and a beauty of cheerful health. We all like him."

WHY does an artist in words pick up a brush? "Things happen," Lawrence said, trying to explain his plunge into paint at the age of forty-one, "and we have no choice." He attributed his sudden compulsion to paint to the arrival of Maria Huxley, the young Belgian wife of Aldous Huxley, bearing canvases. She brought them along on a whim after finding them abandoned at her rented house. Lawrence accepted the gift, took some paint, turpentine, and powdered colors left over from redecorating the Mirenda, distributed the mixture among some kitchen casseroles, picked up a housepainter's brush and lo: pictures emerged. They surprised him, much as his first poems had done, by seeming to come out of nowhere.

They did not come from nowhere. His slumbering sensual self was exploding onto canvas. Paint had been his first medium; many of his best friends were painters; his most direct self-portrait, Paul Morel in *Sons and Lovers,* was a painter. However, while as a young man he had been an avid copyist, now, restoring his lost potency in paint, he found the courage to draw on his imagination, and picture-making became an orgy.

As a painter Lawrence was not, like Winston Churchill, good by amateur standards. His Danish painter friends in New Mexico in 1922 had thought his copies poor, conscientious at best, and in 1991, at an exhibition of full-scale color reproductions of the Mirenda paintings in London, nobody was very enthusiastic. He was simply Lawrence: the same artist in paint as on paper, with the same strengths and weaknesses, but without the genius, and working from the same inner compulsion to organize his experience on paper.

An appreciative introduction to a book of reproductions of his paintings, published in 1964, made the most of their good points, particularly the strong sense of color and the physical world, but it also acknowledged that Lawrence clearly had not been trained in anatomy. "His paintings of the nude are always a struggle," said Mervyn Levy, "and in this respect profoundly revealing."

Lawrence clearly did not know what connected the knee bone to the thigh bone—or, as the Wilkinsons, trying to be tactful, pointed out to him, the hand to the wrist. He thanked them and said he always appreciated informed criticism. At a later stage he asked Earl Brewster to send him some French photographs of nudes so that he could better draw the unclothed body. But he hardly needed a model. Most of the women look like Frieda—breasts like Gloire de Dijon roses, pale blond hair from head to pubes; the men tend to look like himself, dark, gaunt, bearded, with narrow shoulders. He was inordinately proud of his paintings, Harold Acton, the young English author and aesthete who visited him at Scandicci remembered. He was quite pleased too that they were shocking.

First to be shocked were the Wilkinsons, who came over from their Villa Poggi to see, they thought, a newly decorated room at the Mirenda. He proudly displayed "The Holy Family," which showed a child watching a young man kiss a semi-nude young woman. Privately, as they later said, they found it "a revolting blot on the wall" which looked like "Uncle Roger and an imbecile fat woman with most of her clothes missing, and a pert child, bunched together in a most unpleasant group." Politely, however, they listened to Lawrence's explanation that it was a modern painting, after which he served them tea. But he had noticed their reaction. "Why do vegetarians always behave as if the world was vegetably propagated, even?" he asked Secker.

Two other pictures followed fast, and he marveled to Brett that he had become quite a serious painter. "It's rather fun, discovering one can paint one's own ideas and one's own feelings—and a change from writing."

He worked hard at everything else, too. He revised his *Movements in European History* to suit the censors of the Irish Free State. He wrote the music for his biblical play, which was to be performed in London, scoring *David* for pipe, tambourines, and a tom-tom. He did a review for *T.P.'s Weekly* and said, with his usual thick skin about his journalism, that if the magazine didn't want it, it needn't pay, and if it wanted to make cuts, it could. He also kept up, with some anxiety, a steady barrage of encouragement to Gertie Cooper.

Gertie was now at Mundesley. The X ray upon which Lawrence had insisted showed a hole at the top of the left lung. His advice, in long letters, was unsparingly detailed. She must eat as much as she could and swallow Pantanberge Solution with a raw egg, but complain if they forced too much milk on her. Above all, she must not protest against the sanatorium regime. She was going away only for a short time. The alternative, he said, was "the danger of going away forever, from everybody."

Not long after, he was able to congratulate Gertie for having gained two and a half pounds, and when her weight rose even more, Frieda added her compliments: "How splendid gaining 5 lbs! I feel quite envious (not for myself Lord preserve me) but for L."

What Lawrence said to Gertie and what he said to Ada, however, were quite different. Gertie's left lung was in a bad state. "I suspected it all the time—," Lawrence told his sister, "and the fact that they can't get the temperature down means that they can't stop the germ's activity." At least the gain in weight meant that the germ was not winning. Gertie would be in the sanatorium for Christmas, "but better there, than in the cemetery." He wrote to her doctor for more information.

He would not come to England for Christmas after all, even to see the production of *The Widowing of Mrs. Holroyd:* "I've journeyed enough," he told Rolf Gardiner. "Then my health is always risky." With this decision, England took on a luminous paradisiacal air—a place where a kind of Rananim might yet be established, in a house in the country, perhaps, with a big barn and some land, where young people could hike, dance, work the farm, and learn "wordless music like the Indians have."

In December, he began the second version of *Lady Chatterley.* At the same time, to Rolf Gardiner, he wrote his most eloquent tribute to the place where he had been born. He recommended that his young disciple go to Eastwood, stand in front of the third house on Walker Street, and look out ("I know that view better than any in the world"), then, beyond the town, go through the fields and woods, glimpse a small red farm ("Miriam's farm—where I got my first incentive to write"), and from the hills, regard the scene: "That's the country of my heart."

"I'll go with you there some day," he promised Gardiner. But his elegiac tone suggests that he knew he never would.

His painting and his new book were inextricably entwined: "Am working at another novel—scene Derbyshire coal area!!—Also I am painting quite a big (dimensionally) picture." The new painting illustrated Boccaccio's story of nuns discovering a naked sleeping gardener: "penis and all—rather fun."

The word "penis" was making an entrance into his novel as well. The gamekeeper says to Constance Chatterley, after she has been well initiated into manly fucking: " 'I'm not ashamed of what I've got atween my legs.' He meant his penis. She thought of the naked man, the passion and the mystery of him: the mystery of the penis! And she knew, as every woman knows, that the penis is the column of blood, the living fountain of fulness in life."

Lawrence boasted of having placed a phallus (or a lingam, as Brewster called it) in each painting, and argued that he had done so deliberately, reverentially: "It represents a deep, deep life which has been denied in us, and still is denied."

However, it is not the male organ that most strikes the viewer's eye, but rather the human backside. Of one painting, *The Rape of the Sabine Women,* he said it might be called *Study in Arses.* So could many of the others. His poor sense of anatomy, and probably Frieda's own rotund shape, resulted in an exaggerated proportion of rump to limb.

*   *   *

AT Christmas, he played the squire. He and Frieda invited the *contadini* from the farm in for a party. Their fir tree with its candles and ornaments was a northern novelty in those parts. Afterward he described the peasants' childlike pleasure to Gertie as if she, too, were like a child: "You too have pine woods round the Mundesley, don't you?"

As 1926 became 1927, he painted on. "Painting is a much more amusing art than writing, and much less to it. . . ." he wrote Martin Secker. "Think I shall try to sell pictures, and make a living that way."

Frieda showered on his paintings the same uncritical praise she gave to his writing and to her own handiwork. In a burst of zeal, she made herself some dresses, jackets, a coat, and some tall hats, and pronounced herself better than Paquin. Intimately involved in all his work, and to an unknowable extent directing it, she gushed of the first pictures, "*So fine.*"

Lawrence, too, was characteristically immodest; he was pleased with all his efforts—the latest canvas, *Fight with an Amazon,* most of all. That picture, signed like the others "Lorenzo," shows a fierce and bearded dark thin man grappling with a large blond nude, who digs her fingernails desperately into his thigh.

But the painting was also a sign that he was losing his will to write. He claimed to dislike even writing letters, although he told Kot that he was pushing on with the second draft of the novel "in sudden intense whacks." Bad news from Mundesley further upset his equilibrium. The weight gain had been deceptive. Gertie's left lung had to be removed. He said he refused to think about it but seemed to think of little else. He wrote Gertie complimenting her on her one sound lung. In the same letter he sent a picture from their past, of Sunday evenings in Eastwood and her dead sister Frances, that Gertie must have found painfully poignant:

> Do you remember, how we all used to feel so sugary about the vesper verse: Lord keep us safe this night, secure from all our fears—? Then off out into the dark, with Dicky Pogmore and the Chambers and all the rest. And how Alan used to love the lumps of mince-pie from the pantry? And Frances did her hair up in brussel-sprouts, and made herself a cup of ovaltine or something of that sort! Sometimes it seems so far off. And sometimes it is like yesterday.

The past haunted him. Out of the blue he heard from his old friend Arthur McLeod, with whom he had taught at the Davidson Road School. He was glad, for he had been dreaming lately that he was back in Croydon and the class had gone home before he marked the register. "Why should I feel so worried about not having marked the register?" he asked McLeod. "But I do." He inquired after all the old Croydon crowd—Jones the landlord and Hilda Mary Jones ("that baby I used to nurse," who must now be nineteen)—and he sent two pounds toward the retirement present of his old headmaster, Philip Smith, who, he said, had always treated him decently. The thought of Gertie's impending operation was always on his mind. It gave him, he said, the "jim-jams."

Even New Mexico was receding behind a cloud of nostalgia. He savored news from Taos, how Brett was ditching and haying at the ranch and getting along at last with Mabel. The two women were "thick as two peas," Lawrence commented to Spud Johnson, "being the only ones left in the pod." He promised to send Spud an article for *The Laughing Horse*—"something to keep his pecker up," he joked. (Lawrence increasingly used this earthy slang for penis, insisting that "pecker" had a sexual connotation only in American slang.)

He continued to refer to his painting and his new book in the same breath, using the same adjectives for both—"scandalous," "naughty," "improper"—and he delighted in imagining how the world would react. He gaily assured Secker that the novel was unprintable and, with a kind of flasher's swagger, said of his pictures, "When I've done enough—all with their shirt off—I'll have an exhibition of 'em in London."

But more than to shock, their intention was to attack; book and paintings were weapons to force the world to accept his unacceptable self. He could not have made it clearer than in a letter to Brett:

> I've done my novel—I like it—but it's so improper, according to the poor conventional fools, that it'll never be printed. And I will *not* cut it. Even my pictures, which seem to me absolutely innocent, I find people *can't even look* at them. . . . I wish I could paint a picture that would just *kill* every cowardly and ill-minded person that looked at it. My word, what a slaughter!

He finished the second version of his novel in February 1927. For once he selected at the start the title that would stick. "I shall call it *Lady Chatterley's Lover:* nice and old-fashioned sounding." He asked Secker to look in *Debrett's* or *Who's Who* to see if there were any real Chatterleys to worry about.

Another painting, *Flight Back into Paradise* (two male figures struggling over a female), emerged against the background of news of an impending visit from Ravagli and Frieda's announcement that in March she would go away for a month or so—to Germany, she said.

Lawrence did not want to go north—"too much flu." He chose the other direction. To the always obliging Brewsters, he suggested that he visit them in Ravello and that afterward he and Earl walk north of Rome to look at the Etruscan tombs. They were both at the dangerous age for men, Lawrence told Earl (who was also in his forties)—a time of life when the psyche changed, and the body with it: "It is as well to know the thing is physiological: though that doesn't nullify the psychological reality."

He and Brewster were both victims of a swindle, he declared, "a sex swindle." Amplifying his theme, he went on, "One is swindled out of one's proper sex life, a great deal. But it is nobody's individual fault: fault of the age: our own fault as well."

The statement was absurd. Just like his new novel, it was a desperate attempt to rationalize his lonely shame. But it was also a declaration of the necessary arrogance of the artist: the right to find the universal in the individual, to take himself, an impotent cuckold, as a mirror of the world.

17

FIGHTING BACK

1927

---

*T*he same instinct that took him to Australia and New Mexico now decreed a descent into the underworld. Lawrence had done his homework. He knew that the pre-Christian Etruscans believed in a life after death not very different from the one they knew, and had equipped their dead with essentials for starting again. He and Brewster began their tour with a visit to the museum of the Villa Giulia in Rome to see the collection of cooking pots, tools, weapons, jewels, small statues, and other objects excavated from Etruscan tombs. They then went northwest over the Campagna to their first site: Cerveteri, a necropolis of giant molehills laid out in avenues lined with dark aromatic pines and funerary architecture. It was at Cerveteri, on a warm, still April afternoon, that Lawrence, descending into the spacious burial chambers with their stone slabs carved like beds to hold the dead, got his first taste of the tomb as "a house, a home."

Next they moved on to Tarquinia, where a vast city of the dead lies beneath a hilltop overlooking the rolling fields of Latium. More than a thousand tombs were built belowground between the sixth and first centuries B.C., with only small protuberances marking their entrances, and then sealed up, as if the Etruscans anticipated, as Lawrence later wrote, that their neighbors, the Romans, would wipe them out entirely "in order to make room for Rome with a very big R." When they were first excavated, starting in the nineteenth century, they were revealed to contain bright, beautifully preserved wall paintings illustrating the Etruscan ways of life and love. At the time of the visit by Lawrence and Brewster, the celebrated painted tombs of Tarquinia had been open to the public for only about ten years. The two men eagerly followed guides holding torches and stepped down into the darkness.

After three days, they traveled north across the Maremma, the desolate salt marshes that defeated every ruler of the region until Mussolini. At Vulci the tombs were only ruins, damp chambers cut into the face of the rock, and they had to wriggle in on their bellies to see them. Finally, they moved on to Volterra, the most northerly of the Etruscan cities, near Florence. There, where most of the tombs had been filled in, Lawrence had to be content with ruined city walls and, with an icy rain falling, the museum. Even so he was moved. In the sepulchral urns and sculptures he saw all around him the signs of preparation for the journey of the soul: scene after scene of farewell, and with a rich variety of beast—horses, centaurs, dolphins, sea horses—waiting as transport to the other world.

It was a grueling trip for a man who, before he left, had hardly been able to walk around the Mirenda without gasping for breath. Lawrence thought of Gertie Cooper all the way, and, as it was Easter, of Jesus Christ as well. He wrote Mabel, "Those three days in the tomb begin to have a terrible significance, and reality, for me." Yet he was pleased at having discovered a race uncontaminated by Christianity: handsome forgotten people, whose careless sensuality, in dancing, fighting, racing, and dying, corresponded with his own vision of a society at peace with the body.

He returned to the Mirenda on April 11 after being shaken for five hours in a bus. Frieda had been back for nearly a week, reading, like an editor, the proofs of *Mornings in Mexico*, Lawrence's essays about to be brought out by both Secker and Knopf. While waiting, she also wrote to Mabel in her gushing style:

> Today came your letter. I have just come back from Germany into the most bursting Tuscan spring, it almost rattles with eagerness—Am sitting alone (which does'nt often happen) reading the Hopi snake dance proofs, it is good to have one's past so safe in these writings—Yes, I am sure we would'nt quarrel anymore; all this winter we lived so peacefully Lawrence and I and with one's usual forgetfulness I cant believe that we ever quarrelled so dreadfully!

Frieda gushed too about Lawrence's painting, in scarcely veiled sexual terms which Lawrence would use almost verbatim two years later in an essay, "Introduction to These Paintings."

> —And the first conception of one is very thrilling where Lawrence gets his paints and his glass bits puts his overall on, takes a bit of charcoal from the kitchen is quite still and suddenly darts at the canvas, goes on for a few hours; I sit and watch and then its there and we both feel dead tired.

Her letter ended with another revealing image: "With my usual immorality of loving so many places I like it here too, but sometimes *long* for the ranch."

When Lawrence returned, he collapsed, his head full of the necropolis: "the near-at-hand city of their dear dead." He resumed his own spring song, "Flowery Tuscany"; the beauty of the sculpted Italian hillsides proved to him that, contrary to what he had seen in England, "it *can* be done. Man *can* live on earth and by the earth without disfiguring the landscape."

But he could not recapture the mood in which he had begun. He fought against depression. With nature renewing itself all around him, April was indeed the cruellest month, and he lamely finished the Tuscan essay, which was published in *New Criterion* in October, arguing that the transitoriness of human life does not matter: "Man is only tragical because he is afraid of death. For my part, if the sun always shines, and always will shine, in spite of millions of clouds of words, then death, somehow, does not have many terrors."

Struggling for composure, he had to contend with the reality of Angelo Ravagli. Now stationed at Gradisca northwest of Trieste, Ravagli had sent some piano music for Frieda. Lawrence politely wrote and thanked him: "My wife plays it with joy." Ravagli promised a visit, and duly turned up, not once but twice. The first time he announced his visit by telegram; the second he simply appeared. Lawrence was suspicious to the point of asking to examine Ravagli's military travel documents. But the orders were genuine; Ravagli had been ordered to make a further visit to Florence on the same court-martial case that had required his first trip, and had not invented a pretext for seeing Frieda. Lawrence, mollified, showed him around the Mirenda (cordially, Ravagli thought) and gave him tea.

There were other visitors—Barbara Weekley, Aldous and Maria Huxley, and Edith and Osbert Sitwell, who motored over from their parents' castle at Montegufoni. The Sitwell visit passed far more pleasantly than any of them had expected; Edith and Osbert, unlike their parents, whom they ridiculed in conversation as "the Gingers," knew and admired

Lawrence's work. Osbert considered Lawrence a true genius. The two-hour tea party, however, left them all disturbed. Lawrence and Frieda took a long walk in the woods to discuss it, and Lawrence then unburdened himself with a long letter to Kot about the strange pair of siblings, totally absorbed in themselves and their parents.

The Sitwells too were left uneasy. Osbert was in a state of some crisis at the time; he was struggling against his own homosexuality and was shaken by the marriage of their younger brother, Sacheverell; although he enjoyed meeting Lawrence, he had found the paintings "crudely hideous." Edith bristled at Lawrence's snide remarks about their origins. She and her brothers had had what she considered a hellish childhood and refused to be made to feel guilty about its imagined advantages.

The ground was laid that day at the Mirenda for an animosity that would flare up when *Lady Chatterley's Lover* appeared and the Sitwells read of the emasculated and nervous Clifford Chatterley and his unmarried older sister with her long, thin face—a curious pair who mocked their parents and who had grown up, with a younger brother, isolated and literary, shut away in a crenellated Derbyshire stately home within sight of the fires of the coal pits. Later, when Osbert developed Parkinson's disease and was confined, like Clifford Chatterley, to a wheelchair, Edith's grudge against Lawrence was set for life.

LAWRENCE had not lost his sense of fun. He would sing the Salvation Army hymn "Throw Out the Lifeline," standing up and tossing out an imaginary rope and reeling it in. He reviewed Ernest Hemingway's *In Our Time* and obviously enjoyed himself parodying Hemingway's *faux naïf* style:

> Nothing matters. Everything happens. One wants to keep oneself loose. Avoid one thing only: getting connected up. Don't get connected up. If you get held by anything, break it. Don't be held. Break it, and get away.

One night at the arty Wilkinsons', when everybody was asked to perform, he did his "Celtic Twilight" set piece with imaginary harp, quavering Yeats's "I will arise and go now" in earnest falsetto. Unfortunately, the nonliterary company did not get the joke, and on the way home to the Mirenda he scolded Frieda for letting him do it.

Tired out, Lawrence did not enjoy Barby's company as much as he had the previous year. He now found his stepdaughter querulous, complaining, and less beautiful; he said she had become "tall as a telegraph pole."

Lady Chatterley's Lover lay in a drawer. Nancy Pearn, who at Curtis Brown was selling his articles as fast as he could write them, thought his decision not to try to publish it sound. If the book was, as he claimed, the furthest he had ever gone in describing the sex relation, she feared it might damage his magazine market. For the past two years, "little things," as he called them, had brought in most of his income and he maintained that it was a waste of time to write novels.

Distressing details of Gertie Cooper's operation reached an exhausted man. To gloomy Kot, he confided:

> Gertie has been a horrible business—in a hospital in London these last two months—left lung removed, six ribs removed, glands in the neck—too horrible—better die. . . . Why not chloroform & the long sleep! . . . Why aren't we better at dying, straight dying? . . . Why save life in this ghastly way?

But Gertie's treatment worked. Born the same year, 1885, as Lawrence, she lived on until 1942. His own life had not much longer to run.

Morbidity was alien to his temperament and thoughts of death merely speeded up the never sluggish wheels of production. In what he described to Secker as "not a working season," he (among other things) corrected the proofs of *Mornings in Mexico* in half a day, finished "Flowery Tuscany," sent off to his agents several other essays, book reviews, and an important short story, "None of That," began a large canvas called *Resurrection,* and wrote, in a week, the first version of his short novel on the resurrection—all peripheral to his main project, the Etruscan essays, for which, while writing, he embarked on a correspondence to locate photographs.

THE resurrection story intruded itself into his imagination just as he began his Etruscan articles. However much he had admired the liveliness of the Etruscan tombs, he had not been cured of his dread of the loneliness of death—of going away, as he had warned Gertie, from everybody, for ever.

The story, told in his most unashamed pseudo-biblical language, tells of Christ waking inside a carved hole in a rock: "He was alone; and having died, was even beyond loneliness." Painfully fighting off the wish to remain dead, Christ—called only "the man who died"—chooses to try life a second time. Helpless and afraid, he seeks the protection of a peasant who allows him to lie in the sun in his yard (much like Lawrence at Kiowa Ranch). Looking up at the trees and the sky, conscious of his thin legs, colorless arms, and waxy hands, he watches the flamboyant farmyard rooster trying to break free from its tether.

> And the cock, with the flat, brilliant glance, glanced back at him, with a bird's half-seeing look. And always the man who had died saw not

the bird alone, but the short, sharp wave of life of which the bird was the crest.

It is hard not to see Ravagli as the saucy cock flaunting himself in front of the "utterly inert" man with his dead-white face and black beard. Nor the tethered male creature as Lawrence himself. The story ends equating resurrection with erection. The Christ figure is sexually awakened, for the first time in his life, by a priestess of the goddess Isis, who chafes his lower body with oil. In her hands he becomes a new man—and more than a man: an expectant father.

Lawrence thanked Earl Brewster for having given him the idea for the story. When they were in Volterra Brewster had seen an Italian Easter toy of a rooster climbing out of a shell and quipped: "The Escaped Cock, a story of the Resurrection."

As ever, Lawrence emphatically denied the vernacular meaning of a plain English word. He refused to acknowledge that "cock" connoted anything but a rooster, just as he denied the blasphemous pun contained in the story's climactic line, uttered as the man observes the miracle between his legs: "I am risen!" Lawrence's English publisher Martin Secker was not so pure-minded. When the short novel was published in book form in London, Secker made him change the title from "The Escaped Cock" to *The Man Who Died*.

In recent years *The Man Who Died* has been interpreted as an antidote to "The Woman Who Rode Away," with Christianity replacing Woman in Lawrence's imagination as the despised emasculating force. But the story "None of That," written in the same weeks, perhaps in revenge for Ravagli's visits to the Mirenda, shows that Lawrence's misogyny was not dead. "None of That" is a savage and gleeful fable of an American woman (blond, willful, rich, and plump) gang-raped to death by a group of Mexican toreadors; she, who insists that she will have "none of that," ends up getting a great deal of it, including "a few deep, strange bruises." This sinister coda to the stories of the summer of 1924 shows that the old rage against the female still burned.

DID Lawrence write too much? In "An Indiscretion," an eloquent little pamphlet published that year, his friend Richard Aldington tackled the charge that Lawrence wrote too carelessly and too often. "One of the elementary requisites of a great writer is a ceaseless industry," Aldington said. "All this regrettable splurging is a condition of Lawrence's genius." He called Lawrence a great living example of an English heretic—exiled to a foreign land in the tradition of Swift and Byron, hated like Pope, and mocked like Blake, who frolicked in the nude with his wife. But the English love their heretics, said Aldington, for they know they are the salt of the earth. "I think," he concluded, "England owes Lawrence an apology"; and he quoted *Kangaroo*'s description of the writer Richard Lovat Somers: "One of the most intensely English Englishmen England ever produced, with a passion for his country, even if it were often a passion of hatred."

IN May 1927, illness and work notwithstanding, Lawrence tried to fit in a quick trip back to England. His biblical play, *David,* was to be performed on May 22 and 23 by The Incorporated Stage Society, a group dedicated to original new drama. The two performances were to be followed by a debate for Stage Society members and friends at Central Hall, Westminster; the society took its work seriously, having brought the works of Lady Gregory, George Farquhar, George Bernard Shaw, and Eugene O'Neill to London audiences.

David was to receive a modestly lavish production, with a budget of three hundred pounds and a cast of thirty-five, not counting numerous supporting players and musicians, even though the society's production of Lawrence's *The Widowing of Mrs. Holroyd* had received caustic reviews the previous winter.

Lawrence wanted to be there, to see that it was done his way. At the end of April, even as his strength flagged, he assured the play's director, Phyllis Whitworth, that he would be in London by May 8. On May 13, when his "infernal cold mixed with malaria" recurred and sent him back to bed, he had not given up hope of making the trip. Nothing daunted, he sent Mrs. Whitworth meticulous instructions. Accepting the truth of what friends had told him—that *Mrs. Holroyd* had been spoiled by a long-drawn-out last act—he conceded reluctantly that although *David* was supposed to be slow, archaic, and religious, it might need speeding up.

The costumes preoccupied him, as they did in all his books. He knew precisely what he wanted the cast to wear.

For the men, a short sleeveless shirt, to the knee: over that, on occasion, a longish loose-sleeved coat of cotton or wool, may be coloured, tied in at the waist: then, on occasion, a burnous mantle. For the women, a long sleeveless shirt, loose or tied, & sometimes a shorter, wide-sleeved coloured coat.

Opening night at the Regent Theatre on Sunday evening, May 22, however, found him still bedridden at the Villa Mirenda, with what he was now calling "malaria again."

Unfortunately, *David* drew, if anything, worse notices than had *Mrs. Holroyd,* and the news swiftly reached Florence. Lawrence let fly to Mrs. Whitworth; the reviewers "hadn't enough spunk to hear a cow bellow."

Frieda too wrote to console Mrs. Whitworth, drawing on her favorite insult, "canaille" (which Lawrence often used after he met her). The critical attack on *David* wounded her personally, as she had had high hopes of a German production of her translation. To Mrs. Whitworth she wrote, "I am so cross on your account, you must feel very sore after all your work—Is almost everybody so 'canaille'? We had such enthusiastic letters about the production of 'David' and then the press! It seems a real cabal. . . . But *do* go on fighting, *don't* give in, one has got to win!"

His variously described illnesses stopped thoughts of travel. Mabel and Brett had pleaded by cable for Lawrence and Frieda to come back to Taos and to bring the Brewsters with them; there would be houses for both families. But Lawrence rejoined that, while a change of continent would do him good, his medical advice was that New Mexico's was "a bleeding altitude": "good for lungs, bad for bronchials." Perhaps next year, he said.

In the heavy heat of the Tuscan summer he wrote in the morning and refreshed himself in the afternoon by painting, sometimes putting the thick oils onto the canvas with his thumb. To escape the heat and try to recover his strength, he and Frieda went in early June with Aldous and Maria Huxley to Forte dei Marmi on the Mediterranean coast between La Spezia and Viareggio.

The Huxleys were a glamorous couple: young, cosmopolitan, artistic, elegant, seductive. They talked freely about sex; Aldous had had many affairs and liked to boast of sketching Maria in the nude. Her only complaint was that lying on the bed made her cold. They had a grand new Italian car in which to drive the Lawrences about. (They offered Lawrence their old car, but he refused to learn to drive.)

At thirty-three Aldous was as dazzled by Lawrence as he had been at twenty-one, when he had agreed at first sight to go with Lawrence to Rananim in Florida. In the intervening years, he had become a highly successful novelist—one who also had a habit of putting his friends into his books. In the dozen or so years since they had all met, Garsington had served as a marriage bureau for both Aldous and his older brother, Julian. Aldous married Maria Nys, who had been Ottoline Morrell's ward during the war, and Julian married Juliette Baillot, the Swiss governess to Ottoline's daughter. Out of awe of Lawrence and also from a desire to use him for literary purposes, Aldous fastened onto him in 1927, and from then on he and Maria jostled the Brewsters for the role of chief protectors of Lawrence's last years.

Two days were enough to change Forte dei Marmi in Lawrence's eyes from a calm and refreshing seaside resort to a place littered with villas and jellyfish. He allowed himself to venture into the water nonetheless, then returned to the Mirenda to finish his Etruscan essays. He resumed his regular and pleasant routine—up at seven; breakfast; into the woods (with a pillow) to write; lunch; siesta; then painting or gathering fruit—until one hot afternoon he shouted out for Frieda. She ran into his room and found him lying on the bed with blood slowly streaming from his mouth.

The doctor who came, a Professor Giglioli, was, Lawrence believed, the best doctor in Florence. Giglioli certainly was the best from Lawrence's point of view. He did not use the word they did not wish to hear; he treated the symptoms, not the disease. He gave what Lawrence called Coagulin to stop the bleeding and prescribed altitude to counteract the effects of the sea: nothing lower than two thousand feet would do. And he said there was no point going to a sanatorium; Lawrence could lie down at home.

To Mark Gertler, a veteran of the sanatoriums, Lawrence sent a euphemistic description of his symptoms: a series of bronchial hemorrhages brought on by chronic bronchial congestion aggravated by sea bathing. He had had "little ones" before. But Professor Giglioli had told him that hemorrhages took the bad blood out of the system and that the time to worry was when they did not stop, "but they do stop: so it's nothing to worry about—only one must lie in bed when they come on."

(Gertler did not like the sound of it. He passed the letter on to Kot, saying he did not know what "bronchial congestion" meant but that obviously Lawrence had lung trouble and that he must write and instruct him on a good daily routine.)

Altitude was no problem; Nusch and her new husband lived in the Austrian Tyrol. There, in the pine woods, Lawrence wrote his sister Ada cheerfully, "I ought to get this chronic bronchial congestion cleared up a lot. I hope so, for I'm tired of it."

Aldous Huxley (perhaps after private words with Giglioli) was less cheerful. He wrote to his father about "our poor friend, DHL, the novelist":

down with a nasty attack of haemorrhage from the lungs—longstanding tb, which has suddenly taken a turn for the worse. This is decidedly not a temperature to be ill in, and the poor wretch is not strong enough, nor secure enough from fresh bleedings, to move away from Florence into the cool of the mountains.

But Aldous noticed that illness was making Lawrence nicer. As he described Lawrence to his father:

an extraordinary man, for whom I have a great admiration and liking—but difficult to get on with, passionate, queer, violent. However, age is improving him and now his illness has cured him of his violences and left him touchingly gentle. The doctor seemed to think he'd be all right; but with these haemorrhages one can never be quite certain. A particularly violent bout of bleeding can happen, even when the patient seems to be getting much better, and the end can be quite sudden and unexpected.

Lawrence spent most of July in bed, during heat so intense that the Arno shrank to a bed of cracked earth and the very touch of the bedclothes scorched him. Just as he thought he was well enough to withstand the night-train journey to Austria, a walk in the woods started the bleeding all over again. Frieda wept, and Lawrence joked to Pino Orioli that he felt like "all the martyrs in the world." He still talked of visiting more Etruscan sites, to make a second book to accompany the first, which he had finished and hoped would be popular and make him some money. (A legitimate hope. *Etruscan Places,* published posthumously in 1932, is perhaps the pinnacle of Lawrence's travel writing: brilliantly casual, personal, informative, evocative, and philosophical, all at the same time.)

He continued to see himself as two people, one ill, one well. Confident that the healthy man would return, he wrote his old acquaintance Bessie Freeman from Taos that in eight days he planned a journey, first to Austria, then to Munich and Baden-Baden, although for the moment he was in bed. Almost naïvely, he added, "Nice people die. It's what scares me more and more." But the hemorrhages returned and he could scarcely creep about.

Bleeding, he worked on. He wrote much advice to his two sisters about their family businesses and their gardens. He reread the works of Norman Douglas. To Martin Secker: "They are good, you know. They haven't gone thin."

As quick to forget as to anger, he had ended his feud with Douglas (or, more likely, Orioli and Douglas had engineered its ending). One day when Lawrence was in Orioli's bookshop, Douglas sauntered in, probably on cue, and said, "Have a pinch of snuff, dearie." Lawrence replied that his father was the only other man who had ever given him snuff, and took it.

It was to Douglas as a friend, therefore, that Lawrence announced the last day in July that he was well enough to escape from the "frictional, irritant kind of heat": "But we're getting out Thursday night—D.V.—going to Villach—to the Wörthersee or Ossiachersee—meet F's younger sister there—*und Mann.* I hope it'll be nice, & we'll soon forget tutti questi guai!" The *guai*—troubles—were his hemorrhaging lungs. He longed, he told his old enemy, to feel chirpy again.

*   *   *

GERMANIC surroundings were always a relief to him after Italy. At Villach, an Austrian resort, he was glad to escape the bossiness of fascist Italy; glad, too, to be back where he could be cool again and smell rain, and where the river (the Drau) was fast and ice-green, not sluggish and brown. His German persona fitted him as comfortably as the woolen Tyrolean jacket he immediately bought himself. With his German relatives and friends there was less of the violent irritability that dogged his English and American relationships. He was delighted to see his sister-in-law Nusch again, and she him. Beautiful and suntanned, flopping about in summer pajamas, she was happy to have an appreciative listener for her confidences about her second unhappy marriage. "Aber was ist es mit der Ehe, Lorenzo," she asked flirtatiously, "dass man es so hassen muss?" ("But what is it about marriage, Lorenzo, that makes us hate it so?") He privately thought that Nusch was wasted on Emil Krug, the bank manager she had chosen—and also that she was much better than her sister Frieda at making a man feel that he was a man.

Nusch came along when they moved on to Bavaria. There at the Villa Jaffe in Irschenhausen, the von Richthofen sisters were reunited. To Emil Krug, as one brother-in-law to another, he described the scene: "You can imagine the three sisters here together, how they talk! They sit in the sun or in the shade, and schwätzen, schwätzen all day long. Impossible that any three people should have so much to say to one another."

At Else's little pine house in the forest, with the blue outline of the Alps in the distance and with poignant memories of how Edgar Jaffe had loved the place so, Lawrence felt slightly better. The old servant, who remembered him well, force-fed him venison, partridge, and trout, saying "Der Mister muss futtern" (The mister must tuck in). He bought some watercolors, translated *Cavalleria Rusticana,* played solitaire, gathered mushrooms, and met the intellectuals from Munich who came out for a look at him. Lawrence was surprised to find out how well-known he was in Germany.

A dramatist who was also a doctor, Max Mohr, wanted to meet him and sent one of his plays for Lawrence's opinion. True to form, Lawrence read it attentively, discussed it with Frieda, and wrote back (in cheerful if clumsy German) exactly what he thought. The play had failed to understand man as a self-centered animal.

You know, of course you know, every animal has its own intelligence, its own clever mind. Likewise the man-animal must have his own; he's an ice-creature, so he has to be sharp and quiet and sly and cruel and horrible and dangerous as a polar bear; and jolly as a whale or a walrus or a *seal* (what is *seal* in German?). . . . No, but apologies if I'm a bit satirical: I should myself like to be a thoroughly poisonous animal.

Another literary medical man was summoned out to Irschenhausen by a friend of Else's who was shocked when he saw Lawrence's physical state. Lawrence was happy to meet the new doctor, Hans Carossa, because he was a poet, even though his specialty was tuberculosis.

Carossa examined Lawrence, who then triumphantly reported to Else that he "could hear nothing in the lungs, says that must be healed—only the bronchials—and doctors aren't a bit interested in bronchials. —But he says I shouldn't do any hot-air inhalations: that will start the bleeding again."

What Carossa told Else's friend Franz Schoenberner was rather different: "An average man with those lungs would have died long ago." An artist, however, said Carossa, was driven by inner forces and was unpredictable. He gave Lawrence two or three years at most.

With the weather rainy and Frieda yearning for the Mirenda, Lawrence was content at Irschenhausen, sleeping and drinking beer. There he turned forty-two, showered with gifts by his German family—socks, ties, handkerchiefs, a barometer, and (from his brother-in-law) thirty bottles of malt beer. From England Ada sent, at his request, a shirt: cotton, neck size 15½, sleeve length short.

Then it was on to Baden-Baden where his *Schwiegermutter* was, as ever, a delight to him. She could not do enough for him; she seemed younger and loved going out to tea and the theater. Against Carossa's advice he did an *Inhalationkur*—he told Else to tell Carossa that the steam was cold, not hot—and sat obediently every morning at the Kurhaus Eden with a blanket over his head, inhaling air from the radium springs. He prided himself on the return of his appetite, although it flagged at the sight of the elderly gentlefolk at his mother-in-law's residence tucking into big German helpings: "wagonloads of potatoes, and cutlets big as carpets," topped off with a little cognac and a few snails at bedtime. He admired the old baroness's robust health but half wondered why she should have it, and not he.

From the Midlands his sisters were urging him to go to a sanatorium. He refused. He told Emily it would only depress him.

BACK at the Villa Mirenda in mid-October, writing, painting, listening to Frieda pounding out the *Messiah* on the piano, he missed his mother-in-law. He wanted to clear out of Italy for good. He invited the Brewsters to join them at the ranch the following spring, to help chop down trees. Perhaps he would even go farther—circle the world in the other direction, going from San Francisco to Sarawak. Irritably, he toyed with the possibilities of Egypt, then Ireland. However, when his friends in both places began to drop hints that they might not welcome a visit from the Lawrences, he felt rejected. The titles of two new stories reflect his state of mind: "The Undying Man" and "A Dream of Life."

"I'm better when I grumble," he said, and hoped he was like his old grandmother, who had pronounced herself getting worse every year for forty years. But he wanted to be anywhere but Italy, and in Italy, anywhere but Florence. He was bored by Italy and "When a place goes against my grain, I am never well in it."

The reverse was true. Once he was ill in a place, he never liked it again. The hemorrhages of the summer of 1927 put paid to any thoughts of the Villa Mirenda as a permanent home, and offered good rail connections to all the places they liked to travel. Frieda would have settled there forever. But he pressed on in his search for the place where he could draw a clear breath.

The old drowning fantasies and dreams came back; he said he felt beneath a very black flood. Like Edgar Allan Poe (who had had a tubercular wife), Lawrence vividly externalized the sensations of walls closing in and of fighting for breath in a maelstrom of fluid. He went in to Florence far less often, and walked only with difficulty.

He was invaded, too, by animal fantasies, with himself as both predator and victim. He painted a picture of a jaguar leaping on a man. He wrote Aldington that "most people look on me as if I was a queer sort of animal in a cage—or should be in a cage—sort of wart-hog": the perfect metaphor for the self-loathing of a man whose body is betraying him with a socially repellent disease.

Guiltily, he reproached himself for laziness. Part of his prodigious capacity for denial went into ignoring how much he got done. He tried to assist Kot with a publishing venture in London by writing an autobiographical dream-sketch of himself waking after a thousand-year sleep. The surviving fragment of the unfinished piece ends with the frankest admission thus far of his impending death: "I am like a butterfly, and I shall only live a little while. That is why I don't want to eat."

But Lawrence had so distanced himself from the idea of tuberculosis that in late November he pitied and patronized a fellow sufferer who came to see him, another young friend from Rananim days. Lawrence had known him in Cornwall as Dikran Kouyoumdjian, but when he appeared in Florence in 1927 the world knew him as Michael Arlen, the author of the best-selling novel *The Green Hat*. Arlen was ill and Lawrence confided the details to his diary: "had a tubercular testicle removed—so it only means more tuberculosis."

Arlen had earned so much—nearly a million dollars—from his novel that he had had to turn himself into a trust. To himself Lawrence speculated wickedly that Arlen, still only thirty-one, might not even live until the age of thirty-five, when the trust would allow him to draw on the capital.

Lawrence pitied Arlen his lack of a wife, of "somebody to comfort him a bit, his fortune isn't enough." Even so, he succumbed to the temptation of talking to Arlen about his own poverty, and the next day felt ashamed. He knew he was torn; he despised people who made money the center of their lives. But he also despised paupers. "Definitely I hate the whole money-making world, Tom & Dick as well as en gros," he confided to his diary. "But I won't be done by either."

Arlen only deepened the association of tuberculosis with money in Lawrence's mind. He worried obsessively as much about Gertie Cooper's finances as about her health. To Ada, he offered to pay Gertie fifty pounds a year by automatic transfer from his bank. "I'd never know," he said, "when it goes out that way. . . . And don't tell anybody. I hate these money things talked about."

Yet he complained so loudly to other friends about his poverty that Aldington offered to send him some money. Lawrence refused it; he had enough to live on, it was true, but only because he lived like a road-sweeper. His letters of this time are conspicuously free of the precise details of prices and bank balances that had accompanied any discussion of his financial affairs earlier in his life. It seems as if he was not really poor but was terribly frightened by the prospect of diminishing earning power. He was, above all, a man who paid his bills, and these now included the taxes on the New Mexican ranch and food for the horses that Brett was looking after.

Suddenly the answer appeared. Norman Douglas had made a great deal of money for himself by letting Pino Orioli publish his latest novel in Florence, rather than putting it in the hands of a commercial publisher in London or New York. Orioli had printed seven hundred copies of *In the Beginning* and sold them by private subscription for two guineas each, netting fourteen hundred pounds, most of which went straight to Douglas.

Self-publication would rescue Lawrence from Secker and Knopf, from whom he had earned little and who were reluctant to touch his new book. It would also circumvent the new tax of twenty percent that His Majesty's Government had introduced in July on any royalties paid to people living abroad.

The logic was inescapable. He wrote Mabel that he would publish his "last winter's novel" in Florence, privately, "and rake in the badly-needed shekels and avoid all the publicity." He took the set-aside novel out of the cupboard and began it a third time.

"SEXUAL intercourse began in 1963," says the famous line of Philip Larkin, ". . . between the end of the Chatterley ban and the Beatles' first LP." A more accurate date might be December 1927, when Lawrence wrote the final version of *Lady Chatterley's Lover*. And the book's publication the following year, so the editors of the Cambridge edition of Lawrence's letters for 1927–1928 claim, was comparable in its long-term significance to the appearance of Joyce's *Ulysses* six years earlier.

So it was, but not artistically. *Ulysses* not only put onto the page words and acts hitherto unprintable; with its stream-of-consciousness technique for conveying the half-formed thoughts of the human mind, it changed the direction of the modern novel. *Lady Chatterley's Lover*, in contrast, is one of Lawrence's inferior works, with neither the structural grandeur and psychological subtlety of *The Rainbow* and *Women in Love*, nor the warmth and realism of *Sons and Lovers*. It is also a work that now seems false to its own intention.

But in its impact on society—Lawrence's intention, after all—*Lady Chatterley* is in a league with the female contraceptive pill, not with a modernist novel. Two legal decisions—the jury verdict in the celebrated trial in London in 1960, *Regina v. Penguin Books*, and the federal court order in New York a year earlier which allowed it to be sent through the mails—virtually abolished literary censorship in Britain and the United States, with repercussions that are still being felt. There are those who consider that the circulation of a low-priced edition of Constance Chatterley's discovery of the joys of warm-hearted fucking, to the accompaniment of her gamekeeper's lavish praise for her cunt and arse, launched the permissive 1960s all by itself.

"God forbid," Lawrence said late in 1928 in a letter to Ottoline Morrell, "that I should be taken as urging loose sex activity." But that is how the world took his novel. It was a bomb, not a book.

IN rewriting *Lady Chatterley* for the third time, it is argued, Lawrence ruined a good book. The second version (longer by twenty thousand words than its successor, and now known as *John Thomas and Lady Jane*) was far subtler and more beautifully written, perhaps on a par with *The Rainbow*. If Lawrence did ruin it, however, he did so with bold, sure strokes. It was his habit to write every novel three times. As he had explained in a letter seven years earlier, "I don't mean copying and revising as I go along, but literally. After I finish the first draft I put it aside and write another. Then I put the second aside and write a third."

In December 1927 he changed the name of the gamekeeper from Parkin to Mellors, and raised the man's social status from a rough, likable agricultural worker and minor Communist party official to an ex-army man, with better education (and better teeth), who talks sententiously about little except sex. He gave Constance Chatterley a previous adultery, introducing a new character, Michaelis (transparently based on Michael Arlen), for the purpose. He coarsened the characters of Mrs. Bolton, the impotent Sir Clifford's nurse, and of Constance Chatterley's sister, Hilda.

He thought the result should be called "Tenderness" but it was the least tender of the three. It was the work of an angry, bitter man, who was describing in detail acts he would not perform again, who scarcely drew a breath without pain, and who needed to earn a lot of money fast.

The third *Lady Chatterley* is unquestionably the most pornographic of the three, its plot punctuated and propelled by seven scenes of sexual intercourse of increasing intensity, and variety, with much graphic undressing: the classic formula for writing intended to arouse. The celebrated dirty words, used sparingly in the previous versions, now appeared in profusion. He dared the word "cunt" for the first time.

The story, as the world now knows it, is set in the 1920s. It opens with Constance Chatterley, "a ruddy, country-looking girl with soft brown hair and sturdy body, and slow movements, full of unusual energy," living at Wragby Hall in the Midlands with her husband, Sir Clifford, who is paralyzed from the waist down from an injury suffered in the war. She nurses him and listens to him read boring texts aloud; mutilation has made him not only impotent but cerebral. With cold rationality, Clifford suggests that Connie might have a baby by another man—to give Wragby an heir and also to have a child running about the place. She goes so far as to have an affair with the "sad dog" Michaelis (not much fun, as he suffers from premature ejaculation) but refuses his suggestion that she divorce Clifford and marry him.

Walking in the park around the great house, Connie meets Mellors the gamekeeper; her dormant female instincts are aroused, first by the sight of some baby chicks, then by the man himself. In a series of encounters in and around his idyllic woodland hut, Mellors instructs her in the joys of sex. He himself has foregone them for some time out of disgust for his wife, a vulgar, aggressive, and promiscuous woman with the castrating name of Bertha Coutts.

Connie becomes obsessed with the idea of having a child, and soon becomes pregnant. Could she—should she—pass it off as her husband's? After several pastoral interludes with Mellors—running nude through the woods in the rain, decorating each other's private parts with wildflowers—she decides to acknowledge him as the father and to break free from her sterile upper-class life, mechanized in every aspect from her husband's mines to his wheelchair.

The story ends with the lovers separated, but planning to marry. In a long letter Mellors outlines his beatific vision: he and Connie will make a new life together, built on "the peace that comes with fucking," on their coming child, and on the small farm they will run, capitalized (as he acknowledges) by Connie's private income of several hundred pounds a year.

*   *   *

THE charge of misogyny hits home once again. Just like *The Plumed Serpent, Lady Chatterley's Lover* is a book in which a man condescendingly instructs a woman in how to be a woman. Mellors, ruddy man of the forest, knows what is good for Connie; she, overcivilized, unawakened, does not know what she needs; her "big, wondering eyes" make her seem passive and naïve as well as slow. He laughingly and aggressively teaches her, with rough dialect and rude words.

After their fifth rendezvous, for example, Mellors addresses Connie in coarse terms of endearment she professes not to have heard before.

"What is cunt?" she said.
   "An doesn't ter know? Cunt! It's thee down theer; an' what I get when I'm i'side thee, and what tha gets when I'm i'side thee; it's a'as it is, all on't."
   "All on't," she teased. "Cunt! It's like fuck then."
   "Nay, nay! Fuck's only what you do. Animals fuck. But cunt's a lot more than that. It's thee, dost see: an' tha'rt a lot besides an animal, aren't ter?"

Mellors also introduces her to vaginal orgasm ("new strange thrills rippling inside her . . . like bells . . . up and up to a culmination"), then to simultaneous orgasm, a topic of much discussion among men in the early pages of the book. " 'We came off together that time,' he said." Again, she needs a lesson:
   " 'Don't people often come off together?' she asked with naive curiosity."
He answers: " 'A good many of them never. You can see by the raw look of them.' "
Connie even has to have "balls" defined. Mellors tells her that her husband, Sir Clifford, is the "sort of youngish gentleman a bit like a lady, and no balls."
   " 'What balls?'
   " 'Balls! A man's balls!' "
Just as Mellors thrusts obscene language into Connie, he forces her to take his penis in her rectum. That the lovers' sixth sexual encounter, on their "night of sensual passion," is an act of anal intercourse went unrecognized during the 1960 *Chatterley* trial. The defense for Penguin Books was well aware of the meaning of Connie's "phallic hunting out" in "the last and deepest recess of organic shame," but held its breath while the prosecution sailed past it.
The prosecution's lawyers in fact did suspect that the passage in question referred to buggery but thought that unless they could prove it from

an earlier reference in the book—where Mellors and Connie's father speak of sex "in the Benvenuto Cellini way"—there was not enough in the later lines about "burning out shames" to establish this interpretation. They therefore shrank from suggesting buggery in their cross-examination. The chief counsel for the prosecution, Mervyn Griffith-Jones, read out the passage in full in his final speech, saying that it was difficult to know what Lawrence was "driving at."

In the famous scene, Connie is "startled" by Mellors's new approach to her body, but "almost unwilling" she lets him have his way and is "pierced again with piercing thrills of sensuality, different, sharper, more terrible than the thrills of tenderness":

> Burning out the shames, the deepest, oldest shames, in the most secret places. It cost her an effort to let him have his way and his will of her. She had to be a passive, consenting thing, like a slave, a physical slave. Yet the passion licked round her, consuming, and when the sensual flame of it pressed through her bowels and her breast, she really thought she was dying: yet a poignant, marvellous death.
>
> She had often wondered what Abélard meant, when he said that in their year of love he and Héloise had passed through all the stages and refinements of passion. . . . The refinements of passion, the extravagances of sensuality! And necessary, forever necessary, to burn out false shames and smelt out the heaviest ore of the body into purity.

Once the obvious meaning was pointed out—notably by John Sparrow, the warden of All Souls, Oxford, in an article in *Encounter* ("*Lady Chatterley's Lover:* An Undisclosed Element in the Case") in January 1962—it was impossible to miss. It becomes all the more blatant after a reading of *Mr. Noon,* in which similar hostile sodomy occurs, and it adds a new dimension to the horror of the story "None of That" (written seven months earlier), in which the raped body of the American matron in Mexico displays "strange deep bruises."

Sparrow argued—undoubtedly correctly—that if the prosecution, judge, or jury had realized that this passage referred to "a certain 'unnatural' sexual practice," the trial verdict, which cleared the book of violating the Obscene Publications Act of 1959, would almost certainly have gone the other way. Buggery—or, to give it, as Sparrow did, its Latin name, *penetratio per anum*—was at that time a felony in English law, punishable by life imprisonment for both parties, even if husband and wife.

The defense's case, supported by eminent academic and professional witnesses, was based on Lawrence's own insistence that the book was a proclamation of the beauty of sex. It called the bishop of Woolwich to the witness stand to pronounce *Lady Chatterley* a book in which Christians could find elucidation on the holy communion of sexual love, giving London newspapers license for such headlines as "A BOOK ALL CHRISTIANS SHOULD READ."

By the time the sodomitic truth was unearthed, it was too late. *Lady Chatterley* and the permissive age were well launched.

A more important question remains. Was Lawrence in *Lady Chatterley*, as Diana Trilling later charged after reading *Mr. Noon*, being dishonest with his readers? Did the campaigner for truth and openness have a secret agenda?

Sparrow accused Lawrence of deception and losing his nerve. He argued that in the very book in which he made his most violent protest about censorship, Lawrence became his own censor; that in the very passage where he said he was being most honest he was in fact coded, evasive, and deceptive. Lawrence's subliminal message, Sparrow declared, was the antithesis of what the book was supposed to be about—not love at all but, in Lawrence's own description of the night of sensual passion, "sensuality . . . reckless, shameless sensuality." "This failure of integrity, this fundamental dishonesty" on Lawrence's part, Sparrow concluded, "may account for the failure of *Lady Chatterley's Lover* as a work of art."

Once launched, this line of attack was easily carried far. *Lady Chatterley*, far from being an ecstatic proclamation of the redemptive power of sex, can be read as a coded advocacy of male domination of the female, the old Nietzschean party line. It was as if, said one scholar, "the only way the male could reach fulfillment was to assert himself utterly, wilfully, perversely, *using* the female 'like a slave' in sex."

Lady Chatterley's Lover has also been found guilty on two other counts. One is arrogance. Lawrence persuaded himself that he could reclaim four-letter words from obscenity by associating them with the sacred act of love. But while his book was instrumental in making certain four-letter words printable, it did not remove their obscene force. The currency of language cannot be changed by one writer, acting alone. (Lawrence, it can be argued, even deceived himself about his boldness in breaking the taboos of language. In his own vocabulary, there was a forbidden word—not "fuck" or "cunt," but "tuberculosis.")

The most lasting charge is ludicrousness. Katherine Anne Porter had good fun in "A Wreath for the Gamekeeper" in 1961, just as the book went into mass circulation. She picked out the scene where

> the impulsive woman takes off to the woods stark naked except for a pair of rubbers, lifting her heavy breasts to the rain (she is constitutionally overweight) and doing eurhythmic movements she had learned long ago in Dresden

and where the gamekeeper takes after her, tripping her up and splashing with her in the water. It "could," said Porter, "I suppose, be funnier, but

I cannot think how." The frolicking pair, she added wickedly, are fairly apt representations of the author and his wife, "as one would need only to have seen photographs to recognise."

Attempts to film the book run up against the same difficulty. Ken Russell's four-part series for the BBC in 1993 had the critics vying to outdo each other at its expense. "Aye, well, 'appen I did tune in to *Lady Chatterley* again . . ." said Garry Bushell in the London tabloid *The Sun*, "and what a shock!":

> For starters there was the tender moment when Mellors and her Ladyship got on first name terms, just three leg-overs into their relationship. . . . And wasn't it romantic of him to say it with flowers? He did things with bluebells that they never tell you about on Gardeners' Question Time.

But upon whom is the joke? The sexual act is, as Constance Chatterley thinks to herself, ludicrous to all but the participants. *Lady Chatterley* achieves seven times a feat that *Ulysses* does not attempt even once: a description of the full sexual act. It describes in informative detail the phenomenon of male detumescence and retumescence within a short space of time, and it conveys the sensations of the female orgasm in a way that even feminist critics must recognize as accurate. Bernard Shaw was being only slightly ironic when he said that *Lady Chatterley* was a book that every schoolgirl of sixteen should read.

It is a mark of Lawrence's power that *Lady Chatterley's Lover* can contain all of these interpretations at once.

Even the charge of misogyny is reversible. The novel can equally be read as the triumph of the female over the male. It is, as the Lawrence scholar Lydia Blanchard has pointed out, the woman who conquers. The title is possessive: Mellors is Lady Chatterley's lover, not vice versa. It is Connie who makes the first move by demanding a key to Mellors's hut, and she gets what she wants out of him in the end: escape from a hopeless marriage, sexual fulfillment, a new life, and above all, a baby. When Mellors accuses her, "That was why you wanted me, then, to get a child?" she acknowledges to herself that it is true.

Lawrence, in sum, poses a terrible problem for women. It was well put by the author of a critical study of his poetry, Susan Gilbert, who asked herself how Lawrence could speak to her so directly when his work is full of hideous phrases like "the living male power" and polemics urging women to submit their minds and bodies to men.

Gilbert's answer—and the reason, she decided, why Lawrence appealed to so many women writers of his time—Hilda Doolittle, Katherine Mansfield, Amy Lowell, Catherine Carswell, and Mabel Dodge Luhan—was that he understood women's feelings; he had absorbed from his mother what a woman thinks and feels and suffers. Distant from his father, he did not learn what it is like inside a man's head, and his male characters are in consequence strutting puppets. In Lawrence, man is always the second sex. His leading characters are women; their consciousness is central. It was this vision of female primacy, Gilbert said, that left him shaken and angry: "the theology of the phallus was . . . only one strategy in an ongoing sexual battle that worsened as he aged."

The phallic hunting-out of Constance Chatterley was part of this battle.

Like everything in Lawrence's contradictory life, therefore, *Lady Chatterley's Lover* can be read two ways. If it is the worst of his novels, it may also be the best; certainly it is the most accessible. It is beautifully plotted and tells a clear story. If it is sensational, it is also instructional; generations of young people have claimed to have been freed by it from shame about the body—and not only in the past. The book is being avidly read in Asian societies just emerging from sexual repression and the tyranny of the family.

Even the supposed biographical portraits are double-sided. The character of Sir Clifford Chatterley emerged from the mind of a man stuck under his pine tree at the Mirenda while the feathered Ravagli poached his wife. But the sickly aristocrat has the nicer characteristics of Lawrence too: he is a man who writes lively and amusing letters and who has the gift of mimicking his friends. He is above all a man back from the grave: "He had so very nearly lost life that what remained was wonderfully precious to him."

The conventional view of Lawrence-as-gamekeeper leaves him open to the charge of cruelty. When Mellors taunts the man in the wheelchair with his impotence ("It's not for a man i' the shape you're in, Sir Clifford, to twit me for havin' a cod between my legs"), it goes, says the medical-literary historian Dr. William Ober, "beyond the bounds of what one man may decently say to another." But it does not go beyond the bounds of what a man may say to himself. With his adeptness at splitting parts of himself, Lawrence displaced his sexual frustration onto the impotent Lord Chatterley, and his longed-for virility onto Mellors.

In the same way he split Frieda. He assigned the sexual dormancy he wished for her to Connie, and her clitoridal urgencies to the promiscuous Bertha Coutts. Mellors even accuses his first wife of giving herself to a woodcutter (much as David Garnett had reported Frieda doing in Bavaria) and blames her insatiability for causing his long lack of interest in sex. Few readers, of course, were equipped to spot the traces of Else Jaffe in Connie's handsome sister, whose husband had been in Parliament and who is now a freethinking widow who takes lovers and does not want to remarry. Also unnoticed were the echoes of Frieda's girlhood. Connie's nude run through the woods is pure German expression, much like the naked Hedy Lamarr's similar sprint in *Ecstasy*.

The multiple sources that fertilized each character—something that Edith Sitwell refused to recognize in her anger at seeing her family in the Chatterleys of Wragby Hall—are a useful reminder that fiction is always fiction and the literal equation of characters with real people is always wrong.

Lawrence tried to explain the phenomenon in a letter to Ottoline Morrell. As if asking her forgiveness (now that they were both older and unwell) for the supposed portrait of her in *Women in Love,* he explained that, while it was she who had moved his imagination, what appeared in that book was not her: "Any more than a photograph of me is me, or even 'like' me. The so-called portraits of Ottoline can't possibly *be* Ottoline—no one knows that better than an artist. But Ottoline has moved men's imagination, deeply, and that's perhaps the most a woman can do."

Lawrence was aware, however, that there were laws of libel. In the third writing of the book, he was clearly worried that too much of Constance Chatterley resembled Rosalind Baynes, his lover of 1920. He toned down the description of her flowerlike russet beauty and removed other identifying marks, such as her work as an illustrator of children's books. The major similarities remain. The third Lady Chatterley is, as Rosalind was, the daughter of a well-known member of the Royal Academy, the wife of a Cambridge man, and an adulteress. But unlike some of Lawrence's other friends, Rosalind Baynes was unlikely to sue. In 1926 she had married Arthur Popham—as Lawrence noted with quiet pleasure, "a widower, in the British Museum, and they live in London. I'm glad she's settled down again."

As *Lady Chatterley* changes over time, it is easy to ignore the historical context in which the book was written. Lawrence's use of an impotent central character has been criticized as a lazy literary device. But he was writing for an audience that had just come through the First World War; his stories of sex beyond the grave, whatever they meant privately to him, mirrored the fantasies of millions of war widows. Similarly, to a generation surrounded by amputees—the *mutilés de guerre* for whom seats are still reserved on French public transport—Sir Clifford Chatterley's plight did not seem contrived. Hemingway used the same device, an impotent central character, in *The Sun Also Rises,* published in 1926. As his Jake Barnes says, "It was a rotten way to be wounded."

Now that the era of sexual permissiveness has become almost as dated as Lawrence's book, the sexual content of *Lady Chatterley's Lover* is less startling than its social comment. Beneath the filter of sex lies a lament for a disintegrating England, its lovely landscape disappearing under urban sprawl, its great parks littered with newspapers, its traditional communities collapsing, a mining industry in death throes, the sexes at war with each other: the whole presided over by an inept monarchy embarrassed by the disparity between its own wealth and the poverty and squalor around it.

Even the biographical significance of *Lady Chatterley's Lover* has changed over time, with the emergence of so many more of Lawrence's letters. What stands out now is not impotence but child-hunger. This novel, so widely considered to have advocated sexual license, has no reference to contraception; all three versions end with Connie expecting a child. It can be read as one long dream of pregnancy: the anxious waiting for confirmation, the soft first flush of the early weeks, the pride of the swelling belly. "Kiss my womb and say you're glad it's there," Connie tells Mellors. And, in his own way, Clifford Chatterley longs for a child almost as much as his wife does. Their most direct conversations with each other concern the possibility that Connie might use another man as a breeding substitute.

Did the Lawrences have such conversations? Did their hope of becoming parents ever die? Four years after *Lady Chatterley* was written, the fifty-two-year-old Frieda arrived in Taos as a widow with Angelo Ravagli in tow. There she asked an astonished Mabel Luhan if she thought it was too late to have a baby.

18

THE BOOKSELLER

1928

Why does anybody look to me for a best-seller? I'm the wrong bird.
—D. H. Lawrence to Thomas Seltzer, November 13, 1926

*S*elling Lady Chatterley's Lover *brought into play Lawrence's strong-*est instincts. It allowed him to push his message out upon an unwilling world, outwit his enemies, and cut out middlemen while accumulating the first real nest egg he had ever had. While Pino Orioli was nominally the publisher, Lawrence was in charge. He provided the capital—about three hundred pounds; he designed the cover, chose the paper, and kept the accounts. His books interested him as much as his book. Orioli, who was to receive ten percent of the profits, was not an entirely trusted partner. Lawrence would come into the dark little shop at 6 Lungarno Corsini to oversee in person the details of postage and packing. As only a thousand copies were printed, because the type for the first half had to be broken up in order to set the second half, each copy was precious. He knew where almost every one was and whether it had been paid for. He demanded payment in advance: two guineas or ten dollars.

While the book was being typed (partly by Maria Huxley and partly by Catherine Carswell) and readied for the printers, he and Frieda in early 1928 went with the Huxleys to the village of Les Diablerets in Switzerland. Their two-month stay marked a new travel pattern of accelerated restlessness within a narrow radius. Over the next two years the Lawrences would shuttle between an array of Alpine and western Mediterranean resorts in a desperate search for relief from the cough that Lawrence said (in bed again, with his annual turn-of-the-year "flu") "goes raking on." He had new explanations for the state of his chest: "change of life" and "chagrin. Then the microbes pounce."

At Diablerets they were surrounded by a pride of Huxleys: Aldous, Maria, and their eight-year-old son, Matthew; Julian, the biologist, his wife, Juliette, and their two sons, eight and five; and Juliette's mother. Lawrence and Frieda had their own separate chalet two minutes away. Cozily warmed by three stoves, Lawrence felt as safe there as if on a ship. He did not dream of skiing but allowed himself to venture occasionally, wearing dark glasses against the glare, with Frieda on a little toboggan. Mountain snow retained the deathly connotations of *Women in Love*. He found it "very white and still, and a bit frightening."

He felt well enough at the altitude of 3,500 feet to begin to think that he might brave their ranch in New Mexico, twice as high. He spoke of the place often and invited Aldous and Maria (just as he had invited the Brewsters) to come there with them for six months the following year.

He enjoyed accompanying the Huxley wives on long walks with their small boys. It is a mystery why Aldous and Julian Huxley, scientific rationalists well aware that Lawrence had tuberculosis, should have allowed him in such proximity to their children, yet they did. Julian was more alarmed about Lawrence's utter unreasonableness on the subject of science. The two had many furious arguments in which Lawrence dismissed any claim of so-called scientific evidence and said that he only trusted ideas he could feel in his solar plexus. Aldous had reasons of his own for wanting Lawrence close at hand; he was using him and Frieda as models for Mark and Mary Rampion in his new novel, *Point Counter Point*, overdue at his publisher's.

Juliette Huxley, even prettier than when Lawrence had met her at Garsington, had no inkling that Lawrence was consumptive. "We thought it was a bad cold," she said later. During that long holiday she got to know him quite well and found him as lovable as Frieda was tiresome. When she read bits of the new novel, however, she was deeply shocked.

Lawrence was irritated at her reaction, but expected no less from Martin Secker or Alfred Knopf. They had been pestering him for another novel and were unhappy at one that sounded unpublishable. Lawrence offered to prepare them an expurgated version, if only to protect his copyright. Curtis Brown had warned him that obscene and blasphemous works were unprotected and thus easy prey for pirates, but he needed no reminding, having signed an international petition of writers on behalf of James Joyce, protesting the pirate edition of *Ulysses* being sold in the United States with not a penny going to Joyce.

But cleaning up *Lady Chatterley* was no easy task, for he had no desire to give either Secker or Knopf another book, considering the poor income he had made from them. Doggedly, he went through with the exercise, but confessed to Blanche Knopf, "I somehow didn't get on very well with the expurgation: I somehow went quite colourblind, and couldn't tell *purple* from pink." He told her to brace for a shock even from the doctored version. Three women had read the manuscript apart from Frieda; two had gone into a rage (Nellie Morrison, who had refused to continue typing it, and Juliette Huxley) and the third (Maria Huxley) "into a queer delight."

At the end of February Frieda left Lawrence on his own at Diablerets when she went off to visit her mother. Juliette Huxley looked after him, even accompanying him part of the way on his return journey to Milan. There, to his delight, Frieda's train from Baden-Baden arrived at exactly the same moment as his own and porters brought them instantly together (a scene that would be worth recovering from the celestial video-tape).

BACK at the Villa Mirenda Lawrence and Orioli took the *Chatterley* manuscript to the printer's, the Tipografia Giuntina, and Lawrence then threw himself into bookselling in earnest. The sale was to be conducted entirely by private subscription. He would not advertise the book or even send out review copies, in order to prevent news of its indecent content alerting public authorities in the United States and Britain. Zealously he wrote to his friends asking them to subscribe and enclosed order forms. The richer the friend, the more forms he enclosed; Mabel got fifty. He let them all know that he had to live on the proceeds and that they were buying a scandalous book. To those bookshops he thought would be interested in selling it, he wrote to say that he regretted he could offer only a fifteen percent trade discount.

The campaign brought gratifyingly swift results, and he and Orioli soon had enough orders to allow the printing to begin. Part of the pleasure, as the checks poured in, was to see old enemies turned into friends: John Maynard Keynes, Ottoline Morrell, Somerset Maugham—even (he ordered three copies) Lord Beaverbrook.

That spring visitors to the Mirenda included Else Jaffe and Alfred Weber ("They've been as good as married, and as bad, for many years," Lawrence wrote to Earl Brewster) and Barbara Weekley. Then Frieda, with her sister, escorted Barby back to Alassio on the northern Italian coast and went on by herself to Spotorno, where, Lawrence knew, she would see Angelo Ravagli.

Lawrence seems by then to have accepted Frieda's affair. He told Barby, "Every heart has a right to its own secrets." He had plenty to keep him occupied. He painted more canvases and put on a lucrative spurt of popular journalism. Urged by Nancy Pearn at Curtis Brown, he found that he was good at writing for the "GBP," the Great British Public. He had great success with a half dozen or more articles for the London *Evening News* on subjects close to his heart: "Master in His Own House," "When She Asks Why," and "Over-Earnest Ladies." He welcomed the ideas the editors threw at him, such as "Why I Don't Like London," although, as he told Nancy Pearn, "Why London Doesn't Like Me" might be more to the point.

Why Tuscany did not like him was even more to the point. The gains of Diablerets faded with the spring rains, and his chest was sore again. He had many days in bed, which did not deter him from correcting the proofs of the first half of *Lady Chatterley*—a nightmarish task, as the Italian printers had even less idea than Frieda had of where to place the apostrophe in English contractions. The corrections had to be completed before the printers could set the second half. He also managed to organize the binding and the distribution of two thousand leaflets for the book, and to have two hundred copies run off on cheaper paper for his friends. When he was well enough, he visited Florence to nudge the operation along. He guessed (with fair accuracy) that he would clear something like six thousand dollars after his and Orioli's expenses were paid.

When the money rolled in, he dreamed he would sail around the world on a seven-hundred-dollar ticket, and then turn up in New Mexico for a good long stay at the ranch. Or perhaps they would stay instead in Santa Fe where, he wrote Witter Bynner, "one could have friends among men, instead of *ces femmes.*"

In any case, he was convinced that the beautiful Mirenda was bad for his health and that anywhere on the face of the earth would be preferable. But Frieda emphatically disagreed, and under her influence, but also to avoid packing up, he reluctantly signed the lease for another six months. Nonetheless, he arranged for his paintings to be taken down from the walls and sent to London.

He had four offers for a gallery exhibition, including one from Alfred Stieglitz in New York. His choice was the Warren Gallery in Mayfair, run by Dorothy Warren, who was a friend of Barby's and Ottoline Morrell's niece. He asked Mark Gertler for advice on how to pack pictures: "God knows when we'll come back, and it's no good just abandoning them. Would you take the big pictures off their stretchers and roll them?—paint is a bit thick in places, it might crack off."

With all missions accomplished—book in press, pictures off to London, sales campaign organized—on June 10 he shut the door of the Mirenda behind him and, with Frieda, embarked with the Brewsters on a trip through southeastern France and Switzerland. The party stopped the first night at Turin, then headed into the French Alps. He promised his numerous correspondents that he would send them his address when he had one.

Three days later they checked into the Hotel des Touristes at St. Nizier de Pariset in Savoie. The village had all the requisites: lovely air, elevation of 3,500 feet, view of Mont Blanc. Lawrence instantly dashed off more than half a dozen postcards telling family, friends, and business associates where they could find him.

He wrote too soon. Next morning they were all asked to leave. The coughing that had shattered the small hours forced the manager to tell them that it was against hotel policy to have consumptives as guests. As if Lawrence were a child, Frieda and the Brewsters conspired to hide the truth. They loudly exclaimed to each other how disappointing it was that the hotel they had liked so much the night before had turned out to be dreadful, not to be borne for another minute.

Lawrence knew the truth all too well: the warthog was repellent to society. But he went along with the game. He pretended in all his letters, to his mother-in-law, to Ada, to Kot, to Secker, to his agents, all of whom had to be sent his new address—the Grand Hotel at Chexbres-sur-Vevey in Switzerland—that he now realized that he preferred Switzerland to France, that the French hotel was too high, too raw, too bleak, too comfortless, and so badly managed that the staff could not even be trusted to forward his mail.

To Orioli at least he was frank: "The insolent French people actually asked us to go away because I coughed. They said they didn't have anybody who coughed. I felt very mad."

He was now controlling his altitude like a pilot. Having climbed to 3,500 at Diablerets in February and felt well, he would hold at Chexbres, but only for a fortnight; in spite of its beautiful view of Lake Geneva, it was only 1,800 feet above sea level and he wanted to get back to at least three thousand feet by July. His doctors, he said, had advised him to try to stay at that height for three months without coming down. His engineer's image of what was wrong with him ("really my bronchials, not my lungs," he reminded Ada) pictured his bronchial passages as tubes that needed hardening, to which end he swallowed a potion of creosote mixed with chalk.

The doggedly loyal Brewsters ("very nice, the Brewsters, look after me so well") stayed with him, but Frieda was less solicitous. As soon as they were installed at Chexbres, she took off for another week with her mother. Perhaps she really did visit her mother. However, she did not return on the appointed day. Lawrence was beside himself. With the Brewsters watching helplessly—there was something childlike, they felt, in the way he looked forward so eagerly to her return—he met every possible train. He ran back to the hotel to bolt his lunch, saying that

Frieda was probably late because she had lost her passport, then returned to his vigil; but even the ten o'clock train did not disgorge her. In the morning, however, there she was, saying she had missed connections and had to come by motorcar from Vevey at midnight. Lawrence hoped they had settled down for a bit, especially as Frieda was suddenly reluctant to go to New Mexico and he did not know why.

The Huxleys arrived shortly after, en route from Paris to Italy, jostling the Brewsters for the role of most attentive courtiers. Altogether, "we're quite a party," Lawrence wrote Mabel. In fact, the Huxleys looked depressed, which made him depressed.

At Chexbres the first copy of *Lady Chatterley* was put into his hands. He was delighted with its appearance, the terra-cotta cover just as he had designed, emblazoned with his personal emblem, a phoenix. Just as he had his first novel, when it was still called "Laetitia," he treated it like a female: "Everybody thinks she looks most beautiful, outwardly."

Early copies went out to subscribers, including Alfred Stieglitz and Witter Bynner. He was very sparing with free copies: one went to his old mentor, Edward Garnett, who had once told him that he would like to see a book describing "the whole act." Another went to his doctor, Giglioli, in Florence, who in return sent a bill for 1,345 lire. "Not cheap!" exclaimed Lawrence, but he settled it immediately: "One doesn't want to have those things unpaid."

Determined to move higher up, he and Frieda crossed over into German-speaking Switzerland and found themselves a primitive chalet at four thousand feet, a mile above Gsteig-bei-Gstaad. They booked the Brewsters into the Hotel Viktoria down in the village. Their own little house, just below the snow line, was eerily high and remote; if good for his bronchials, it was a risk to his psyche. To Orioli, he joked: "Rather lonely . . . I hope we shan't want to die, if bad weather comes"; and to Nancy Pearn: "If it pours with rain, which God forbid, I hope we shan't die of gloom."

The Brewsters followed as if pulled on a string. On their very first day in Gsteig, they puffed up the hill to the Lawrences' for tea and found him in bed suffering from a slight hemorrhage. This he explained as a cold in his bronchials that had brought on asthma.

Frieda placidly tolerated the unworldliness of the "Mayflowerers"— "Achsah always in white and her soul is so white too, like white of egg, and they call Lawr 'David,' and she paints him as a blue eyed *Eunuch!*"

Frieda was not usually tolerant. One of Lawrence's new admirers was Maria Cristina Chambers, a Mexican writer married to an American editor and living on Long Island. She was so smitten with Lawrence from his works that she sent him her photograph, her life story, and a suggestion that she come over to meet him. He sent a warning:

But now listen—what do you expect to find? Here am I, forty-two, with rather bad health: and a wife who is by no means the soul of patience. . . . If you come to have a pleasant trip, well and good. But if you come for the thrill of meeting me, you'll only be disappointed. . . . My wife doesn't look on me as a shrine, and objects to that attitude in other people: at which one can't wonder.

If he had his ideal community, or if Mrs. Chambers were to come to the ranch, the prospect would be different. But in Europe, he said, she would be cooped up in a hotel and conversation would be difficult.

Relatives, however, were a different matter. Conscious that his elder sister Emily had never been to visit him, he dutifully invited her and his niece Peggy to Gsteig, as the chalet had plenty of spare room. He told Emily that he thought the place would do him good once he had got used to the altitude. The peasants had made him a bench and table under the trees where he could sit in the mornings and try to paint. "But," he said, "I am too hazy yet to get anything done."

He got things done, all the same. Seated at his small table under the trees, he turned out watercolors, a short story ("Blue Moccasins"), a clutch of articles, including "Over-Earnest Ladies," for the London *Evening News,* and four book reviews for *Vogue. England and the Octopus* by the architect Clough Williams-Ellis gave him another chance to air his views on English housing blight; the "octopus" of the title, Lawrence explained,

> being the millions of little streets of mean little houses that are getting England in her grip and devouring her. It is a depressing theme, and the author rubs it in. We see them all, those millions of beastly little red houses spreading like an eruption over the face of rural England.

He worked because he could not walk without gasping. He wrote Gertie Cooper, "Everywhere is steep, steep—and I just can't climb." His jokes about resurrection became more literal: "I wish the Lord would make a new man of me," he told Kot, "for I'm not much to boast of now."

He enjoyed being on his magic mountain while his book rocked the world below, and dealing smoothly with his customers by long distance. His meticulous attention to their orders is a credit to his clerical training at J. H. Haywood and Sons, the Nottingham surgical appliance factory where he had worked at sixteen. He kept Orioli on a tight leash:

> Will you please send at once *three copies* to Miss Allanah Harper, 101 *bis* rue de la Tombe, *Issoire, Paris* (*paid*—I have her cheque)
> Whenever you suggest we collect on delivery, send me the invoice at the same time as the order. Archie Douglas—has he paid?

He scolded Orioli for sending copies out to booksellers without pre-payment; if the book were suppressed, the shops might use it as an excuse not to pay. *"Send all orders to me, here,"* he commanded his partner. And he was stony about refunds. When an American subscriber complained that he had not received his copy of *Lady Chatterley* even though his international money order had been cashed, Lawrence told Orioli, "It's his funeral." The pounds sterling raised were paid either into his account at the Aldwych branch of Westminster Bank or into Haskard & Casardi Ltd., a bank in Florence, where he held sterling and lire accounts.

The excitement invigorated him. Frieda saw it as a tonic to his system, and herself enjoyed the drama of secret shipments, plain wrappers, false titles. At the end of Lawrence's excited letter of instruction to Enid Hilton, Willie Hopkin's daughter, who was helping with distribution in London, Frieda added a warning not to get into trouble: "You seem such a small thing for a conspirator." Enid had a bulk supply of sixty copies from which she was, by train or taxi, to shift forty to Richard Aldington in Berkshire. She was also to relieve Kot of the cache of three dozen in his house on Acacia Avenue in St. John's Wood. Lawrence knew that Kot would be too scared to hold them for long.

Lawrence liked those who liked his book all the more, such as the photographer Stieglitz and his wife, Georgia O'Keeffe. (Both were effusive in its praise.) He wondered how they would receive his paintings. He feared that hostility to his book would spread to his paintings, and hostility there was. By the end of July three London book exporters had canceled their orders and 114 copies were being returned to Florence.

THREE great streams of self-deception were coming together: the unacceptability of his book, his painting, and his health. All had been declared unwelcome; he would force the world to take them all. He was furious when Martin Secker rejected the expurgated typescript of *Lady Chatterley* as "quite unpublishable." (Secker added that Knopf in New York would undoubtedly share his views, but Knopf, in fact, was less disapproving.) Lawrence insisted, even though he had taken precautions to prevent his sisters or his mother-in-law from reading the book and to keep its content secret until publication, that there was nothing indecent about it. He told Laurence Pollinger, who handled his books at Curtis Brown's agency, that people took the Marquis de Sade much more calmly. He defied anybody to find his book anything "but wholesome and natural": "Bah, bogeys! People should have the phallic symbol branded on their foreheads, to cure them of their hypocrisy."

He blamed society for refusing to accept in print words that were spoken every day. The hypocrisy was real, but so was the law. Blind, as

Norman Douglas had charged, when it suited him, Lawrence shut his
eyes to the power of his prose to stimulate sexual excitement—what his
prologue to *Women in Love* calls "that hot, flushing, roused" feeling. He
also refused to believe that his language crossed the recognized boundaries of printable English. Aldous Huxley had felt obliged to tell him that
even his proposed subtitle for *Lady Chatterley*—"John Thomas and
Lady Jane," English slang for the primary male and female sexual or-
gans—would prevent the book's legal importation into Britain.

By now *Lady Chatterley* was, like his own body, a contagious object
to be turned back at borders. Foyle's, the London bookseller, returned
six copies of "a book we could not handle in any way." An American
reviewer who had rashly praised it in the New York *Sun* was banned
from ever reviewing for the newspaper again (even though the review
had been pulled after only one edition and the page replated). When a
New York bookseller refused to touch it, saying that he had no doubt
whatever that U.S. Customs would prohibit its entry, Lawrence began to
realize that he was in serious difficulties on the other side of the Atlantic.
Reports were reaching him that most of his American subscribers—Spud
Johnson in Taos, for one—had not received their ordered copies. "What
a blow," he wrote Ottoline Morrell, "if they are lost and we have to
refund the money."

The blow was not long in coming. On August 11 the postal authorities
in San Francisco seized and confiscated five copies of *Lady Chatterley's
Lover* destined for Fresno. He was glad he had not risked sending his
paintings to America, and began to wonder anew how he might ever get
himself back to the United States. Brett advised him to try to creep in,
but he knew that he could not. To his fan Maria Chambers, now a
regular correspondent, he spoke first of spies—he warned her not to talk
to booksellers who might be agents for the police—and in the next
breath said, "I should like to come to America this autumn—but this
infernal cough—which is not a death cough at all, but an unspeakable
nuisance—is for the time master of my movements."

But would London reject his pictures? So many had been offended by
his book that an exhibition might only make things worse. (The Sitwells
were already claiming that Wragby Hall was modeled on their Renishaw.) He worried angrily that he had not heard from Dorothy Warren,
but soon she wrote at length that the pictures were framed and looking
wonderful and that she was quite prepared to shock the bourgeoisie. She
enclosed six guineas for three copies of *Lady Chatterley*.

Nancy Pearn was pleased to hear that Lawrence might come to England for the gallery opening. He might use the opportunity, she suggested, to do an interview with the BBC. His newspaper articles had
made him well-known among a wider audience, and the new medium of
radio, people at Curtis Brown had discovered, offered "quite a useful

and dignified bit of publicity." Lawrence recoiled: "The thought of broadcasting makes my blood run cold anyhow." Thus died posterity's best chance of knowing the sound of his voice.

HE still regretted his childlessness, in tones that make *Lady Chatterley* seem a defiant blow against a world in which he would leave no heir. To a young painter friend of Barby's he wrote, "Perhaps if I'd have had children, I'd have been a comfortable body with all my novels circulating like steam among all the safe people, and everybody pleased." He also congratulated Laurence Pollinger on another child. "I think children are a great help, they give an immediate importance to life, and block out a lot of depressing vistas. I say so, having none—only 'vistas democratic'!"

He threw a good party at the Hotel Viktoria for Frieda's forty-ninth birthday on August 11 but was very conscious of the menopause. Tactlessly, he complained in a letter to Ada (who had just passed forty) about Catherine Carswell's "horrid nervous and irritable state—woman of fifty! My heaven when a woman's over forty, she needs to watch herself nervously as well as physically. So many go to pieces then."

Frieda was slimming, on what Lawrence described as a "grape diet," but with little effect. He asked his sister Emily to bring from England for Frieda two undershirts (large), plus two pairs of underpants, three pairs of silk and wool stockings, and a green cotton eiderdown "for a *single bed,* for me." He sent seven pounds to help with the costs and their travel.

The thought of being confined in a chalet with his older sister and his niece with nothing to do but sit and stare at the rocks and pine trees began to depress him. With reason. When they came, he found he had little to say to them and they got on his nerves. He had to hide *Lady Chatterley* like a skeleton in his cupboard. He was relieved when he could get them out of the house to go sightseeing.

He sent the second half of "The Escaped Cock" to Nancy Pearn for typing, saying that it was "rather lovely—but I feel tender about giving it out for publication—as I felt tender about Lady C." As with *Lady C.,* he ignored its outrageousness even though, when a short form had appeared in the American review *Forum* (which paid him $150) in February, readers angered at the fable of a sexualized Christ wrote to the editor to call Lawrence a menace to society, an enemy of mankind, and a traitor. "And I thought it a perfectly harmless story," he wrote Maria Chambers, "merely an attempt to show the resurrection *in the flesh,* instead of in vacuo and in abstraction. . . . But there you are. The letters lament that there is no Inquisition."

Still collecting remedies, he wrote to the Brewsters for a clay pack to put on his chest and hoped, after his visit to England, to take up the

Huxleys' offer to chauffeur him to more Etruscan places: Arezzo, Cortona, Chiusi, Orvieto, and Rome.

The book was selling well—he had sold about six hundred in Europe and already cleared more than seven hundred pounds' profit—but the limited stock was dwindling and there were only about two hundred copies left. With the type broken up, there was no chance of reprinting. His distrust of America and Americans intensified as he realized that as many as 140 copies posted there had gone missing; perhaps the American booksellers had really received them and were lying in order to avoid paying for them. He began to feel sorry for his old publisher Thomas Seltzer.

He needed entertaining, and the Brewsters did their duty. One day they brought four visiting Americans to tea. They also had staying with them a Hindu friend, Boshi Sen, a scientist and masseur, who trooped up the mountain with them for the daily obeisance. Boshi Sen gave Lawrence a Hindu massage and joined in the charades the Lawrences so enjoyed. Lawrence was still an incorrigible performer. He baptized the Hindu with wine, singing and ending with war whoops of the Navajo Indians, while the others cowered, terrified that his antics would set off another hemorrhage.

The following day, Lawrence wrote the wonderful essay "Hymns in a Man's Life," in which he confessed that of all the great poems that had meant most to him—from Keats's odes to Goethe's lyrics—none was as much part of him as were the banal Nonconformist hymns of his childhood. These were the battle cries of stout souls, he said. Hymns like "Hold the Fort, for I Am Coming" were sung by men who "still believed in the fight for life and the fun of it." They were, he said (the article was written for German publication), the clue to the ordinary Englishman.

THE first of September brought new snow to the mountaintops and sent the cows down to lower pasture. Lawrence's terror of approaching winter set in, with its associated recoil from England. To Kot he wrote, "Autumn here now, chilly, cloudy—time to go. I doubt I shan't come to England—damn England." Frieda would go to London for the exhibition; he would go south.

He was homeless, the Mirenda given up. He wished over and over that they were at the ranch in New Mexico. They certainly did not want to sell it—it was Frieda's, he reminded the Taos bank manager who wrote to inquire if they would accept an offer of two thousand dollars for it—but, he said, they could discuss it when they came over "before long." He meant to go if he could, firmly convinced of the principle that it was good to alternate altitude with sea.

In the meantime, he and Frieda retained a vision of the ranch unchanged. Frieda grew uneasy when she heard from Brett that the floor was bare; she distinctly remembered a Navajo rug and would not like to find it gone when they returned.

The plan for the winter was to join Richard Aldington and some friends on the Ile de Port-Cros, off Hyères, where Aldington had rented a converted fortress. First, with the Brewsters still in tow, he accompanied Frieda on his annual trip to Baden-Baden. It was as pleasant as ever. Frieda read Goethe while Lawrence played patience with his mother-in-law, both cheating to win. He sat with the old lady through open-air concerts in the garden of their hotel and drove with her through the woods in a two-horse coach. He even visited a fish farm at her insistence, although her old legs ached with the walking. The closer he drew to his *Schwiegermutter,* the more detached he was from the memory of his own mother. He used his mother as his prime example of righteousness in an article aptly titled "Women Are So Cocksure": "She was convinced about some things: one of them being that a man ought not to drink beer. . . . When my father came in tipsy, she saw scarlet."

In the same mood, he had taken to idealizing his late father. He painted a watercolor, *Accident in a Mine*—a group of naked men carrying the body of a wounded miner—and he told Earl Brewster that his father and Norman Douglas were the only people he had known who always followed joy. (This is the second recorded instance of Lawrence's curious comparison of his father with the bluff old pedophile.)

The Brewsters drove him to Nice where, like a parcel, on October 2, he was passed over to the care of Else Jaffe and Alfred Weber; they took him west along the coast to Le Lavandou, where the Huxleys were installed. Frieda set off to Italy to pack up the Mirenda. He wrote and asked Orioli to put her up in Florence so that she would not have to stay the night alone at the villa, then settled to wait for her return.

When Aldington and his party reached Le Lavandou, they found that the others had left but Frieda had not returned. Why didn't Lawrence come with them to the island and let Frieda join them there? He refused. He hung about Le Lavandou alone, walking along the beach, watching the men play *boules,* and sending off wistful picture postcards on a familiar theme: "no word from Frieda—but I hope she'll come soon"; "thought I'd have heard from her today, but not a sign"; "höre noch nichts von der Frieda."

He got very cross with the little railway on which Frieda was supposed to arrive for having a strike. He was cross, too, with the French for ruining their coast with bungalows: "Man is everywhere vile." For ten days he waited. On October 12—at last—she joined him, having been forced by the strike, she said, to take a three-hour taxi ride from St. Raphaël. They turned up on Port-Cros on October 15, two weeks later than expected. Aldington noted wryly that packing up the Mirenda had somehow required a detour through Trieste. (Ravagli was stationed north of Trieste.)

LaVigie—"The Lookout"—was the holiday retreat of the editor of the *Nouvelle Revue Française* and offered the prospect of the kind of colony Lawrence had once craved: private rooms around an inner courtyard, a communal great room with a big log fire, and the air full of the scent of pine trees, wild lavender, and rosemary. At the pinnacle of the small craggy island, the walled Vigie offered dazzling views of the blue Mediterranean—but at the price of a three-quarter-hour walk uphill from the port.

It was a ludicrous site for a man in Lawrence's condition. He staggered up to the fort, then was stuck, while the others descended daily to swim or to eat at the hotel, the only place of entertainment on the island. His coughing echoed around the compound. While Lawrence emphasized in his letters that there was no shop on the island, what was on the others' minds was that there was no doctor. The two-hour motorboat journey was impossible in bad weather and he was hemorrhaging again. The group resolved never to leave him alone.

Five wretched weeks began with a week in bed "with that flu cold." He blamed Frieda for bringing Italian germs from Italy. Everybody knew that Frieda had been off with Ravagli. Aldington, moreover, an old friend, had heard Frieda moaning since 1925 that Lawrence was impotent. Brigit Patmore, another old friend who was one of the party, felt that Lawrence actually encouraged Frieda's interest in the Italian officer, knowing that she was a healthy sensual woman who needed male attention.

Matters were not helped by the fact that Aldington (still legally married to Hilda Doolittle) was in transition between mistresses and had arrived with them both—the American model Arabella, with whom he had lived for the past decade, and the equally beautiful Patmore, an Irish writer with whom he would spend the next. Patmore, who had known Aldington and the Lawrences from their Mecklenburgh Square days in London during the war, now found Aldington handsomer than ever: tall, broad-shouldered, exultantly healthy, with blue eyes full of light.

It was a steamy scene, as Aldington later chortled, "full of jape and jest and adultery." At one point, he, Arabella, and Brigit were all in bed together. Arabella also had an affair with their Sicilian manservant. It was the kind of lust-in-action that Lawrence detested, made worse by torrential rain and his confinement to his solitary bed.

Bruised as he was by the critics, he could not say that *Lady Chatterley* had entirely ruined his literary reputation. One of its first reviews, in

T.P.'s Weekly, was all he could have desired: "a fine novel, bold and—stark is the only word to describe it. And it is so amazingly uncynical. . . . The prose is really beautiful . . . there is none like him."

Then his *Collected Poems,* published in October, had an excellent notice in *The Observer.* The reviewer had listed the poems' irritating flaws—crude generalizations about life, embarrassing personal revelations, inelegance of expression—and forgave them: "The fact remains that Mr. Lawrence, passionate, brooding, glowering, worshipping man, is undoubtedly a man of genius and big and fiery enough to eat a dozen of his merely clever contemporaries."

At La Vigie, Lawrence spoke constantly of New Mexico and his longing for its high, dry climate. When Brett wrote to inquire about buying the ranch herself, he replied that Frieda would do nothing about it without coming over herself. But by November of 1928, there was less chance of that than ever. As he explained to Brett, he dreamed often of the ranch.

> But at present I feel America is rather hostile to me, and they might do something mean to one, if one came over. Then again there is the question of passports and visas. It isn't much good coming with the ordinary six-months visa. I would like to be able to stay, if we come, for at least a year. . . . If they *wanted* to be spiteful, they'd hold me up about my health.

Staying indoors, Lawrence read Aldous Huxley's new novel, *Point Counter Point.* He said it made him ill—not for the caricature of himself and Frieda as Mark and Mary Rampion, but for its brittle sex, rape, and murder. He was envious when he heard how well it was selling (ten thousand copies and reprinted within the month). But he laughed off the recognizable portrait of himself and accepted that, as he wrote William Gerhardie, "Aldous' admiration is only skin deep."

Aldous did genuinely admire Lawrence. Much like Lawrence, he was airily contemptuous when people insisted on taking his characters as mirrors of reality. "Rampion is just some of Lawrence's notions on legs," he insisted. "The actual character of the man was incomparably queerer and more complex than that."

Yet if he did not catch the whole man, Aldous caught a fair fragment. His Rampion was an English working-class writer and painter who did his own housework and was married to an aristocratic wife who had "never so much as fried an egg when she married him" but who enjoyed their tramp-style of life.

> For Rampion, there was a kind of moral compulsion to live the life of the poor. Even when he was making quite a reasonable income,

they kept only one maid and continued to do a great part of the housework themselves. It was a case, with him, of *noblesse oblige*—or rather *roture oblige*. To live like the rich, in a comfortable abstraction from material cares would be, he felt, a kind of betrayal of his class, his own people. If he sat still and paid servants to work for him, he would somehow be insulting his mother's memory, he would be posthumously telling her that he was too good to lead the life she had led.

Aldous gave a fair rendition of Frieda, too. *Point Counter Point* relates how Rampion's wife shocked her puritanical husband with her matter-of-fact talk of fornication and adultery, but how impressed he was at the same time with her unaffected sensuality. It "took him a long time to unlearn the puritanism of his childhood."

The novel also catches the flavor of the Lawrences' constant bickering about their marriage, the way her "I'd like to know what you'd be doing if you'd never met me" was countered by his "I'd be where I am and be doing exactly what I'm doing now." The narrator comments: "He didn't mean it, of course; for he knew, better than anyone, how much he owed to her, how much he had learnt from her example and precept. But it amused him to annoy her."

The brunt of Lawrence's anger fell on Aldington. While Lawrence stayed behind with a sheepskin rug over his knees, Frieda would descend, laughing, with the handsome Aldington and the other women for the beach. A photograph taken during their stay shows a nude Aldington displaying his phallic reality on the rocks while Patmore, wearing only a bathing cap, crouches up to her shoulders in the shallow water. Of Aldington, Lawrence snarled, "He can't live on his charm for ever." Patmore felt that Aldington might have restrained his high spirits at least until he was out of Lawrence's hearing. But Aldington was soon fed up to the teeth with Lawrence. Having read part of the manuscript of Aldington's new war novel, *Death of a Hero,* Lawrence told him he was on the way to an insane asylum.

Neither tension nor illness kept Lawrence from lots more journalism, having fun while putting his message—the threat of the independent modern woman—before the Great British Public. If the newspapers rejected or cut his pieces he did not mind, because he could sell them elsewhere. He sold "The Real Trouble About Women" to the *Daily Express* and "Sex Locked Out" and "Do Women Change?" to the *Sunday Dispatch*. He was delighted when the *Dispatch* enthusiastically gave him twenty-five guineas for "Sex Locked Out"—only two thousand words, he marveled, and written in an hour and a half! That was a far better length for him than a thousand words, he told Nancy Pearn: "Gives me more swing."

Bad-tempered as he could be, Lawrence was equable about being interrupted. One day Patmore shouted through his window that there were three rainbows in the valley, then guiltily saw that he was working. But he merely looked up, said, "There, there," and carried on.

The British popular press was sending him fat checks but it was also savaging his book. At La Vigie they all sat in front of the fire and read aloud the attacks on *Lady Chatterley* as one of the filthiest books ever written. The *Sunday Chronicle* ran on its front page, "Lewd Book Banned," and wondered whether Mr. D. H. Lawrence, "the famous novelist and poet," could possibly have written it.

John Bull reached for superlatives. "Famous Novelist's Shameful Book: A Landmark in Evil" carried a pen sketch of the bearded Lawrence, captioned "the world-famous novelist, who has prostituted art to pornography." The commentary described "the fetid masterpiece of this sex-sodden genius—produced furtively abroad and changing hands at from five to twenty guineas" as "a cesspool, the most obscene book in the English language." Lawrence hoped that the attack had "not cut much ice." He was wrong.

In retrospect, the celebrated *John Bull* attack is remarkable for the tribute it pays to his gifts: "Mr. Lawrence is a man of genius. As a psychologist he is in the front rank of living writers; as a stylist he stands supreme." Only because of his greatness, said *John Bull,* had Lawrence succeeded in producing "the foulest book in English literature" and probably, even taking into consideration the excursions into the lascivious by Oriental writers, in world literature. A more limited talent could not have written it.

The anonymous critic noted that sex had dogged all Lawrence's previous books: "Mr. Lawrence has a diseased mind. . . . Now, since he has failed to conquer his obsession, the obsession has conquered him. He can write about nothing else, apparently."

In a sense, *John Bull's* psychological assessment was true. But Lawrence's response was truer. His letter to Morris Ernst, the renowned New York expert on press freedom, is a classic denunciation of the evil of censorship:

> Myself, I believe that censorship helps nobody, and hurts many. . . .
> Our civilisation cannot afford to let the censor-moron loose. The
> censor-moron does not really hate anything but the living and growing
> human consciousness. . . .
>   Print this letter, if you like—or any bit of it. I believe in the living
> extending consciousness of man. I believe the consciousness of man
> has now to embrace the emotions and passions of sex, and the deep
> effects of human physical contact. This is the glimmering edge of our
> awareness and our field of understanding, in the endless business of
> knowing ourselves. And no censor must or shall or even can really
> interfere.

The idyll at La Vigie ended abruptly as the accumulated tensions boiled over. Aldington described the horror of it all to Hilda Doolittle (whom he addressed fondly as "Astraea"):

> My dear, you can imagine it. Lawrence, acrid, violent, bitterly resentful of my health, creating a monstrous atmosphere of emotional hatred which was utterly unnecessary. Up in that lonely Vigie, a mile from the nearest house, it was like a series of demented scenes from some southern Wuthering Heights. Most fortunately, I kept my head and my temper and a certain aloofness but I emerged with the conviction that Lawrence is really malevolent and evil.

Aldington did not mention to Hilda his own contribution to the poisonous atmosphere. Instead, even though he had, that very year, publicly declared Lawrence to be one of England's great heretics, he summed up his private views on Lawrence the man with the fervent prayer: "I hope I never see him again."

The wish was mutual.

THE next stop was another resort. With his London exhibition postponed until June of the next year, Lawrence selected Bandol, a pretty port on a pleasant little bay between Marseilles and Toulon. Katherine Mansfield had sheltered there during her illness, staying, although Lawrence claimed not to have known this, at the same hotel. Lawrence was no francophile. The French language bored him, and so did the French, "rather self-centred smallish people"; he never wanted to speak to them, but with so many places ruled out—England, Germany, Italy, mountains, and (after Port-Cros) islands—there was little left to choose.

With all their household goods in store, they were now true itinerants. Home for Frieda was Room 12 at the Hôtel Beau Rivage, and for Lawrence 12B. Frieda complained that without a house to look after she had nothing to do, but Lawrence liked the warmth and effortlessness of hotel life (at only two dollars a day), and he laughed at Frieda for yearning for a place of her own. Women were like devils, he said—and off to the London popular press flew another rash of articles, including "Is England Still a Man's Country?" for the *Daily Express.*

As if to replace the friend lost in Aldington, Lawrence bought himself another. He invited, sight unseen, at his own expense, a young Welsh writer, Rhys Davies, to come as his guest to the Beau Rivage. That Davies was staying in Nice, Lawrence had learned from Charles Lahr, owner of the Progressive Bookshop on Red Lion Street in London's

Holborn. Lawrence thought he might get on well with Davies because he too had emerged from a British mining community (the Rhondda Valley in southern Wales).

Davies, a tall, sharp-nosed young man with soulful eyes, came with mixed feelings. At twenty-five, just starting his career, he could hardly turn down an invitation from the great author but, like Kyle Crichton in New Mexico, he dreaded the remote figure he expected to find: "a kind of John the Baptist in the wilderness." He was quite taken aback by the relaxed and smiling figure in a faded blue blazer, wispy cotton trousers, and floppy black hat who met him with a hired car at the train. Davies found Frieda even more comfortable, and when he confided to her how much young people in London looked up to Lawrence, she begged him to tell Lawrence because "he feels *everybody* hates him in England."

When Davies obliged, however, he saw the other side of Lawrence: the instant rage, the violent denunciation of the imagined enemy. Lawrence harangued Davies about the current breed of young writers; they had *him* to thank for what freedom they enjoyed and they were too cowardly to use it. As for people in England, they treated him as if he were in a cage. "I know I'm like a monkey in a cage," he snapped to Davies. "But if someone puts a finger in my cage, I bite—and I bite hard."

There was another display of the famous wrath at dinner when Frieda enthused so vigorously about a book she was reading on Rasputin that Lawrence threatened to slap her across the face. In the dining room at the Beau Rivage Davies heard, for the first time in his life, a husband publicly use the word "fuck" to his wife. Davies looked around nervously—there were English people at other tables—but Lawrence was oblivious.

Davies himself felt the storm another day when he and Frieda stayed too long at a café and were late getting back for lunch. Lawrence, pacing up and down outside the hotel, flew into a jig of rage when he saw them. Frieda said nothing and swept regally past into the dining room, whereupon Lawrence, quieted down, offered lobster as an act of contrition. Davies declined the luxury (a supplementary charge on the fixed menu), but Frieda took it with pleasure. Davies reported back to Charles Lahr: "He's queer, with extremely fixed views and passions, but I like him. . . . He wants me to start a rebel paper—a cheap rag, not 'arty' and 'singe people's bottoms' in it. Says he'll help. I like Mrs. Lawrence too. They have queer little bursts of fury with each other."

Davies was an active, if closeted, homosexual. Had Lawrence divined Davies's homosexuality when he invited him to be his guest at the Beau Rivage? He had used words suggesting effeminacy when he had read Davies's novel, *The Withered Root,* and criticized it for lack of "spunk" and the author's inability to let a character "get his pecker up." He also observed to Charles Lahr about a character in a Davies story that "he's no more aware of the two young women than if they were two chamber-pots—and uses them more or less as such."

But Lawrence liked Davies so much that the visit was just the start of a close association over the next few months. Lawrence may simply have wanted a young protégé and a new buffer against Frieda. Or he may have been indulging in a homosexual flirtation such as he had had with the pink-trousered Clarence Thompson in Taos. Either way, thanks to the healthy state of his bank balance, he could now summon people when he wanted them. And he liked looking after the young. One day when Davies was ill, Lawrence appeared at his door with his personal traveling medical kit, an aged gladstone bag full of tiny bottles and boxes, from which he produced a dark syrup for Davies to swallow.

In Davies's judgment, as indeed in the view of Bynner in Santa Fe, Lawrence was not homosexual. Unlike both Orioli and Aldington, each of whom later declared the belief that Lawrence's rage stemmed from a refusal to admit his homosexuality, Davies considered that Lawrence's mining background, with its strong emphasis on virility and comradeship, had forced him to mask the deeply feminine side of his nature with a false masculinity.

A measure of Lawrence's obtuseness on the subject, however, is the title he gave to the new collection of light verse on which he was working: *Pansies*. Davies pointed out to him that the word in Britain had a double meaning. Lawrence claimed not to know it (a claim hard to believe from anyone who had spent long in Richard Aldington's robust company, for Aldington's speech was full of "pansies," "fairies," and "sods"). *His* "Pansies," Lawrence insisted, were a pun on the French *pensées*.

THE "pansies" blossomed in profusion. Having hardly written a poem for three years, now Lawrence could not stop. He liked to think of them as light verse and Frieda delightedly called them "real doggerel." Some, like "The English Are So Nice!", fit the bill. So does "My Naughty Book," which appears in his *Collected Poems* with expletives like "fuck" and "shit" deleted.

But no amount of jauntiness can conceal the cries of impotence in the short verses. "Basta!" begins, "When a man can love no more . . . and desire has failed . . ." "Nullus" says, "Life has gone away, below my low-water mark." "Dies Irae" declares that "desire is dead. / And the end of all things is inside us." And in just four lines, "Man Reaches a Point" describes a man alone because he has nothing left with which "to draw / other flesh" to his own.

Some of the longer, powerful poems in the collection that eventually emerged, such as "The Elephant Is Slow to Mate," rank with Lawrence's best and do not deserve flippant dismissal as *pensées*. "The Risen Lord" expresses all that he was trying to say in his resurrection novel: "I have conquered the fear of death, / but the fear of life is still here . . ."

He sent the poems to Nancy Pearn on December 9: another manuscript done in a hurry. She was to sell them as she could, in bits and pieces, deleting any lines she thought unacceptable; he would do a complete book later.

THIS time the change of place worked. At Bandol he felt better than he had in months. For once it was Frieda who was ill, with an eye infection. He wrote to Rhys Davies, who had returned to Nice, that "she never has anything wrong, so when she *does,* she minds." He postponed his planned trip to see Orioli in Florence when he heard that the city was drenched with rain. Expecting Barby for Christmas, they stayed put.

The season was brightened when Rhys Davies reappeared on December 23, with a rich and strapping young Australian in tow. P. R. Stephensen greeted Lawrence with the news that he would like to bring out a book of reproductions of his paintings. Lawrence was delighted and agreed to write a long introduction explaining how and why he painted. The two did not stay for Christmas, but Davies sent Lawrence a silk dressing gown, shocking him with the extravagance. Sternly, he thanked and scolded Davies: "*Knowing* your finances and having lived for years with similar ones," he said, he always forbade any present dearer than two and sixpence.

At Christmas Lawrence and Frieda were alone. Barby had not turned up, nor had Frieda's elder daughter, Elsa, whom they had hoped would join them with her fiancé. Frieda was in tears because she did not have a single present but Lawrence claimed bravely to Ada that he himself was not bothered. "I say if the sun shines and one feels well that's feast enough—I don't like festivating anyhow." For their presents he sent his sisters copies of *Lady Chatterley.* He advised Emily not to read it, nor to let his niece Peggy read it either; if they left the pages uncut, he said, the book would be worth more.

Frieda was still restless; Lawrence told everybody she didn't know what she wanted, but she did. She wanted to go back to Italy. He refused; perhaps Spain would be their next place in the sun. He had a thousand pounds to spend and wanted to move on.

It had been a good year. In the same twelve months when his English royalties from Martin Secker amounted to a paltry £165, *Lady Chatterley* had brought him gross profits of £1,024, of which ninety percent was his to keep. He could honestly boast that he had put himself on his feet "by publishing Lady C. for myself." The only sensible thing, against all his puritanical inclination, was to invest it. He sought the advice of Curtis Brown's New York office, which put him in touch with a stockbroker. Thus, the writer who had a moral compulsion to live the life of the poor, and whose first idea of a windfall had been his mother's dividend from the Eastwood Cooperative Society, found himself at the end of 1928 a Wall Street stockholder, with six thousand dollars' worth of American utilities and rails.

19

A DYING ANIMAL

1929

*M*iraculously, 1928 turned into 1929 without Lawrence spending a single day in bed. His appetite returned. "It's *so* important," he wrote Gertie Cooper, now convalescing as he once had in Bournemouth, "it makes all life different."

He wrote his satiric little poems in his room in the morning; he and Frieda had an aperitif at a café on the front at lunch. A satisfying sequence of visitors appeared; first, the Julian Huxleys, then, a clean-cut American academic, Brewster Ghiselin, whom Lawrence described to Juliette Huxley as "a very good-looking young man—Californian—studying at Oxford—and come to admire me," and, he wrote her brother-in-law, Aldous, "you know what a depressing effect admirers have on me." Yet he invited Ghiselin to spend his whole vacation in Bandol and to become a member of their household.

Their family group was expanded by the arrival of Barby. At twenty-five Barby was a tall and elegant figure, with the best features of both her parents. Ghiselin thought she was handsome and took her out to tea but Lawrence could see that his stepdaughter was depressed and self-preoccupied. He blamed "a messy second-rate Studio crowd" and hoped she could snap out of it.

Aldous and Maria stopped by on the way to Florence to see them. Even Lawrence's sister Ada Clarke turned up. Somehow she had made her peace with Frieda, and the two women swept off to Toulon to go shopping. Frieda now congratulated herself that she had turned an enemy into a friend.

Ada was none too happy, however, about *Lady Chatterley*. She had read her Christmas present and told her brother that she had never realized how much of himself he had withheld from her. Their old closeness was still there. Lawrence listened sympathetically to the effect of the continuing Midlands coal strike on the Clarkes' tailoring business. When she went home, once again he was mournful and felt like a rag. As in 1926, he wrote her the same day: "My dear Sister . . . I felt awfully unhappy after you had left this afternoon—chiefly because you seem miserable, and I don't know what to say or do." He promised her that they would "come through" and that someday before too long they would make a life together, in the sun, away from the cares of business. Did he sense that they would never see each other again?

As if as a valedictory, he sent Ada and her husband fifty pounds to repay them for the rent on Mountain Cottage at Middleton-by-Wirksworth in Derbyshire in 1918–1919. "I feel it's the right time to pay it back," Lawrence explained to his brother-in-law, whose father had just died. "If you want any ready money, do let me lend it you."

So where next? Bandol, he told Ghiselin, was not far enough south. Corsica? Spain? *Not* Russia. Bad for his health. Liberia? "Tropical and dangerous." He even toyed with the idea of South Africa, or Natal. He didn't know. Frieda wanted Lake Garda (convenient to Ravagli); above all, she wanted a house, where she could hang curtains and pictures. Lawrence granted that they might return to Italy later, but he abandoned his plan to go to Tuscany to finish the Etruscan essays because he was scared of "tombs in winter."

The ranch beckoned and he looked into traveling by Dollar (Shipping) Line from Marseilles the last week in March or first week in April, but he was now fixed on going as an immigrant in order to stay for a year and had to face his double undesirability. He insisted, as he wrote Maria Cristina Chambers, that he did not seriously expect trouble,

> yet once before, at El Paso we were held up by U.S. authorities and detained till next day—I was called a liar to my face, when I was speaking plain truth—and kept stripped, being examined by a down-at-heel fellow who was supposed to be a doctor but was much more likely to be a liquor runner—all of which I have not forgotten and shall never forget.

P. R. Stephensen's plans for a book of Lawrence's paintings were progressing rapidly, and proofs of the photographic reproductions reached Bandol from London. He was disappointed in the way colors came out but nonetheless delighted at the prospect of a big expensive book. Seeing that he might clear as much as five hundred pounds from it, he briskly finished a ten-thousand-word foreword, "Introduction to These Paintings."

Now he had to worry about getting another book past the eagle eye of Uncle Sam. This one would be perfectly proper, even if half the pictures did contain nudes, he wrote Mrs. Chambers, and were it anybody else's book, it would pass Customs without comment. "As it is mine, they are almost sure to fuss, just out of spite."

Since the previous summer, he had been resigned to the fact that *Lady Chatterley* was contraband in the United States. But before the month was out, the news he had been dreading arrived. On January 18 Scotland Yard had come unannounced to Laurence Pollinger's office to say that they had seized six copies of *Lady Chatterley* as an indecent publication and that these—and any other copies they could find—would be destroyed. They swiftly found more: the six copies posted to Brigit Patmore's London home on Bedford Row. Her son, who was at home, was questioned by a detective from the Yard. Worse was to follow.

One week later, three of Lawrence's manuscripts failed to arrive at the Curtis Brown office on Henrietta Street in Covent Garden even though he had sent them, sealed and by registered post, from Bandol. The missing papers included two copies of the manuscripts of *Pansies* and the long foreword for the book of paintings. He had no copy of the foreword.

A published book was one thing, private correspondence another. What rights of seizure could the police have over unpublished manuscripts?

The question was important enough to be raised in the House of Commons. The home secretary was asked whether he had instructed that manuscripts sent by the author D. H. Lawrence from Bandol in France to his London literary agent should be intercepted. Sir William Joynson-Hicks (still remembered for his nickname, Jix) replied in the best traditions of the Home Office. There was no such thing as literary censorship in Britain. The packet in which the poems were found was opened purely as part of routine random postal searches to see if any material being sent through the mails violated either the Post Office Act of 1908 or the Postal Union Convention of Stockholm of 1924. Once opened, however, the seized materials of Lawrence were seen to be indecent beyond a doubt and would be held for two months to give the author a chance to prove to the contrary.

The poems contained the words "shit" and "piss." Lawrence was furious and frightened; he realized that he might risk arrest if he ever returned to England. Now he was a pariah in the two countries where his main readership lay.

Lawrence knew, in spite of his many tirades against his lily-livered countrymen, that he could count on support at home. There was a strong undercurrent of dissent in British life, of which he and his work were a part and which was finally to succeed with the *Lady Chatterley* trial of 1960. In the parliamentary debate on February 28, 1929, among those who rose to defend Lawrence in the House and deride Jix for hypocrisy was the leader of the Labour party, James Ramsay MacDonald.

Persecution bred paranoia. Spurred by Norman Douglas, Lawrence began to believe that a loyal supporter, Harold Mason of the Centaur Bookshop in Philadelphia, was cheating him on copies of *Lady Chatterley*. He suspected too that the admirable Gotham Book Mart in Manhattan was pirating the book. "What is one to do, nowadays, between policemen and prudes and swindlers," he stated rhetorically to the poet Marianne Moore, editor of *The Dial,* in which some of his *Pansies* were printed.

More upsetting was the hint from Mabel that Brett was selling Lawrence manuscripts that had been left behind at the ranch. It was a seed of suspicion that fell on fertile ground.

WHEN they left Kiowa Ranch for Europe in the autumn of 1925, expecting to be back before long, the Lawrences had casually left behind some manuscripts and papers in a little wooden cupboard that Lawrence had made. There was no lock on the cupboard, which, like the ranch itself, was at the mercy of rodents, the elements, and marauders.

When as things turned out they had not returned, Brett, who was living in and around Taos and looking after the ranch, began to dream of buying it for herself. She hoped to raise money for the purchase by selling some of her paintings, and to that end, in the winter of 1928–1929, she went to Manhattan to see Alfred Stieglitz and other figures in the art world. At first she stayed in Mabel's Fifth Avenue apartment; but Mabel asked her to leave, for Brett was an untidy lodger, in New York as in Taos. She then moved into the Shelton Hotel but, having failed to sell her pictures, was short of cash. Accordingly, she sold one of six copies of a story she had typed for Lawrence and which he had (so she claimed) given her in payment.

When Mabel mischievously bruited something of this transaction to the Lawrences, it required only a short leap of their frustrated imaginations to envision Brett, by then back at the now almost mythical ranch, as pillaging their entire stock. Their anxiety coincided with Lawrence's realization that his health would not permit him even to contemplate a return to New Mexico that year. He reported to Mabel with his usual optimism: "I *am* better—I am really quite well and quite myself so long as I stay fairly quiet. . . . But the minute I start walking at all far, especially uphill, and running round, especially in a town, I go all queer."

Perhaps, he said to Mabel, someone ought to go to the ranch to gather up all the manuscripts left behind; then, the suspicion gaining strength in his mind, he wrote the same day to Brett: "I worry sometimes a bit about the ranch. Do you think we ought to deposit the MSS. in some safe place? They are getting valuable now, they may come in so handy some rainy day. And so many have already been stolen from me. All the early ones are gone for good." He asked Brett outright if she seriously wanted to buy the place. If so, could she raise more than the two thousand dollars the Taos bank manager had offered them for it? He said they did not want to sell it but if they could never (he underlined the word "never") get back, there seemed no point in keeping it.

Lawrence was being overbold. He wanted to sell the ranch, but Frieda did not. The disagreement between them, like the anxiety over the manuscripts, ran deep, as it touched the unspoken question of her future after his death. He might despair of ever getting back, but she certainly did not, and she wanted to keep her toehold in the United States. She wanted to know (perhaps prompted by the sensible Else) what and where her assets were. Prime among these were the manuscripts.

The tension between them led to a period of crazy vacillation. The decision that Lawrence would go to Paris to arrange a new private edition of *Lady Chatterley* seems to have been made in a rush. There is no mention of it in his correspondence until five days before he left.

In mid-February both Lawrences had been excited about the prospect of going to Corsica. But Corsica was ruled out when some people returned from there, looking, Lawrence told the Brewsters, "still frozen." Instead they decided to move to Spain. On March 2 he wrote three letters announcing that they were leaving for Spain in a few days to take a house for six months. Abruptly, on or about March 7, Lawrence announced to the Huxleys that he was coming to Paris and that Frieda would go to Baden-Baden to see her mother and would join him later.

Two things helped to change his mind. One was that Frieda dug in her heels and absolutely refused to go to Spain. At the same time he realized that Rhys Davies was going to Paris for a month on the way back to England. The pieces fell into place.

Worried about the dwindling supplies of *Lady Chatterley* and alarmed to hear from the Huxleys that a pirated edition was being sold in Paris for an exorbitant sum, he had been hoping to arrange a Paris edition to fight the pirates. He had been corresponding with Parisian booksellers and half hoped that Sylvia Beach might issue his book from her famous

Shakespeare and Co. bookshop, as she had done with Joyce's *Ulysses* (even though he knew, he told Rhys Davies, that she was all wrapped up in Joyce "and considers me a rival show"). But he had little wish to go to Paris himself, and in January had asked Kot to go for him.

In March the failure of the plan to go to Spain and the availability of Davies as escort to Paris gave him courage. Davies would accompany him and stay in the same hotel, "so I shan't be alone," he wrote Emily, and added that as the Huxleys were living outside Paris, "I shall have them too." At this stage in his life his dependence was reasonable: a semi-invalid, he needed people to look after him.

For the trip, with his new wealth, he bought a gray suit for 750 francs, some ties and French gloves and shoes, although what he really wanted, he joked to Aldous, was "a reincarnation into a dashing body that doesn't cough." Davies got a look at the unreincarnated body when they stopped for the night on the way north. Lawrence had booked them into the same hotel room, where he took himself for a bath in the curtained-off space in the corner without drawing the curtains. Davies, glimpsing Lawrence drying himself, thought he had never seen such a frail, wasted frame; Lawrence, he thought, should not be going to Paris.

Davies was right. As a business decision the trip to Paris was sound. For a man in Lawrence's condition, it was foolhardy. It took him to the kind of place he usually avoided literally like the plague: a polluted northern metropolis at a cold and raw time of the year. He began his journey on March 11 with a sore throat and went to bed with "the grippe" when he arrived. He never regained his health.

WITH his horror of cities and his ties with Germany, Lawrence had spent very little time in Paris for an English writer of his stature. Paris was the center for avant-garde writers and publishers fleeing Anglo-American censorship; Ford Madox Ford was there with a new young wife and a new young review, *Transatlantic*. Many literary people wanted to meet the famous Lawrence; P.E.N. asked to give him a dinner; he refused, but took tea with some French writers, including François Mauriac. With Aldous, to whom he apologized for Davies's lack of polish, he went to visit Harry Crosby and his wife, Caresse, whose Black Sun Press had published a deluxe edition of Lawrence's short story "Sun" with water-color illustrations by Lawrence himself, and who were interested in doing the same with "The Escaped Cock."

The Crosbys were a Fitzgerald kind of couple: young, glamorous, and extravagant Americans in Paris. Crosby was a lanky Boston blueblood and the nephew of J. P. Morgan. His seductive, darkly pretty wife was a good poet. He called her Caresse, but when he fell in love with her, she was "Polly" Peabody, the wife of a fellow Bostonian, Richard Rogers Peabody. They had lived in Paris since 1921, spent money wildly on race horses, on entertaining, and on their Black Sun Press, which had made a name for itself by publishing new work by Lawrence, Kay Boyle, Hart Crane, and Joyce.

The Crosbys revered Joyce, the reclusive star of the Parisian literary world, and offered to bring him home to meet Lawrence. Joyce declined; he said his eye hurt him.

That was the closest the two banned novelists came to meeting each other. They had no wish to do so. Lawrence had found *Ulysses* cerebral and obscene and he hated the excerpts from "Work in Progress" (later *Finnegans Wake*) that Black Sun was publishing; he called them "stewed-up fragments of quotation in the sauce of a would-be dirty mind." When the Crosbys insisted on playing for him the recording of Joyce reading from *Ulysses*, Lawrence scoffed: "a Jesuit preacher who believes in the cross upside down."

Joyce did not think much of Lawrence either. When his friend the Italian writer Nino Frank remarked that Lawrence was in Paris and might be included in a new literary review, the fastidious Joyce retorted, "That man really writes very badly. You might ask instead for something from his friend Aldous Huxley, who at least dresses decently."

Joyce had read what he called, with his compulsion to pun, *Lady Chatterbox's Lover*. He had found it full of "the usual sloppy English"; allowed that there was "a lyrical bit about nudism in a wood," and concluded, with the disdain of a Continental Irishman, that the book was "a piece of propaganda in favour of something which, outside of D.H.L.'s country at any rate, makes all the propaganda for itself."

(The two authors undoubtedly knew their novels were rivals not only in notoriety but in sales. Joyce, on a visit to Copenhagen in 1936, was displeased to find *Lady Chatterley* outselling *Ulysses*.)

Feeling shaky, Lawrence nonetheless set out the first morning to meet Sylvia Beach. Davies, shepherding him to her shop at 12 Rue de l'Odéon, saw him fly into one of his apoplectic fits when the taxi driver could not find the address. Davies, like so many before him, forgave these outbursts because he felt that Lawrence was so perceptive and gave so much more than he took that his irritability, so clearly caused by his health, was a minor blemish.

Sylvia Beach and Lawrence swiftly fell into animated conversation. She had already informed Aldous Huxley that while she would happily sell unexpurgated copies of *Lady Chatterley* in her shop, she would not bring it out under her own imprint. She did not want to get the reputation of being an "erotic" publisher. Besides (Lawrence had been right) she was so proud of *Ulysses*—the only book she ever published—and so devoted to Joyce, the only man in her life, that she did not want to sully her record with a lesser, and preachy, work, which she called "a sermon-on-the-mount of Venus."

But Sylvia felt the force of Lawrence's charm. She liked his poems better than his prose, and said later if he had suggested that she publish those, she probably could not have resisted him. In the event, she did him a great favor. She directed him to another American expatriate publisher, Edward Titus, and within days Titus had agreed to bring out a Paris Popular Edition of *Lady Chatterley*, which was to prove highly profitable to them both.

While Lawrence was engrossed with Sylvia Beach, he was spotted by the young American novelist Edward Dahlberg, who frequented the little bookstore that was home away from home for generations of American writers abroad. Dahlberg was eager to meet Lawrence, who had done him the astonishing favor, without ever having met him and simply on request, of agreeing to write an introduction to Dahlberg's first novel, *Bottom Dogs* (something that Joyce, indifferent to other writers, would never do). Just as generously, when Lawrence learned that Dahlberg was living in digs on one meal a day, he sent him five pounds plus the advice always to write with great bitterness.

Dahlberg, gazing at his benefactor, saw "a goatish jaw with beard, russet, earthed hair, and a potato nose . . . and squash seeds for teeth." When he bumped into Lawrence later on the Boulevard Raspail, he was shocked to realize, as he later recalled, "that the man was dying in his clothes," and helped him back to his hotel.

Davies, who had an adjoining room at the Hôtel Grand Versailles, was kept awake by the coughing all during the night. Once when it was particularly severe, he got up and went in to find Lawrence writhing on the bed. He suggested calling a doctor, but Lawrence grew furious and asked Davies instead simply to sit by his bed. Davies obliged and remained there until Lawrence had calmed down.

Paris being a medical as well as a literary center, the Huxleys managed to get Lawrence to a specialist in bronchial diseases, who examined him and made an appointment for an X ray. But half an hour before the time, Lawrence, all dressed, refused to leave the hotel, and made Davies cancel. The X ray was hardly necessary, for the French specialist had told Aldous that he could tell just by listening that one lung was practically gone. Lawrence, however, blamed the filthy Paris air for the way he felt; it "simply stinks of petrol"; all cities were death traps.

Lawrence's friends knew how ill he was. But how much was Frieda to blame? Almost entirely, according to Aldous and Maria Huxley. Idealizers of the genius, they blamed the wife. They poured out their feelings to Mark Gertler and his fiancée, who were visiting Paris, and Gertler swiftly passed the word to Kot: "It really seems almost as if it is she who is slowly killing him. Can she be so bad? They say it is sheer stupidity, and that her influence is so great that nothing can be done."

Rhys Davies held the opposite view. He liked Frieda and saw her exuberant insouciance as Lawrence's lifeline. While she was in Baden-

Baden he sent her written reports on Lawrence's health; the day she arrived in Paris, he turned the job of nursing back over to her, moved to a room across the hall, and went out for the afternoon. When he got back to the hotel, he knocked on their door. He was told to come in and was treated to a rare sight: the Lawrences in bed together.

They had crawled under the velvet spread for a few hours of what Davies assumed was "connubial reunion." As Davies entered, he saw Lawrence's bearded head nestling contentedly on Frieda's ample bosom. Frieda laughed at Davies's embarrassment and invited him to sit down. She then sat up and devoured the bar of nougat Davies had brought her as a treat. Whatever restorative remedy she administered, it worked. Even the Huxleys had to admit that Frieda's entrance into the sickroom had the effect of "the raising of Lazarus."

It was as good a demonstration as any of what bound them together. Lawrence and Frieda held absolutely the same philosophy of life—few Roman Catholics shared dogma to the same degree—that the body knew what was best for itself. This was also Else Jaffe's view. Else thought that her sister and Lawrence had a perfectly rational philosophy toward dealing with his illness: "that everyone must live and die according to his own precept." Else believed that were it not for trusting his own instinct Lawrence would have died years before.

Frieda seemed to have had no fear of catching his infection. Yet their habit of sleeping separately was obviously a preventative, and so was Lawrence's aversion to kissing on the mouth. They each also seemed to consider her weight some kind of insulation against disease; her Ruben-esque shape reassured them both.

Fortified by Frieda, Lawrence attended a buffet supper party given by Titus's wife, the cosmetologist Helena Rubinstein. Madame Rubinstein scolded Lawrence for his short story "Sun," which she said was sending women off to the rocks and beaches in the South of France to burn their bodies in a new cult of sun-worship. "In that case," he replied amiably, "I should have scrapped the story." She found him a nice little man who sat silently staring into space while his "pushy" wife held the stage.

The old polarity affected the Crosbys too. They found Lawrence full of wisdom and they disliked Frieda. But their sympathies were with her the day that the Lawrences came out to visit them at their mill outside Paris. Frieda loved their gramophone and insisted on playing over and over again their record of Bessie Smith singing "Empty Bed Blues" until Lawrence (perhaps after hearing the lyrics) could take it no longer and broke the record over her head.

Frieda put up with such abuse as part of their marital quid pro quo. For all its drawbacks, her life with Lawrence gave her freedom, purpose, and security. She mocked Mabel for still thinking that she hung on to Lawrence like grim death and explained in a letter that "it's the other

way about. He hates to be without me nowadays, even for a few hours."
The two of them were just off to Spain, she said:

> Lawr has much too much to do & is beastly famous, it's humiliat-
> ing—I wish we were nobody & nothing as when we first were to-
> gether—It's not good enough being "prominent." Hope you
> flourish—We *will* come to Taos, when L is stronger & the signs are
> favourable—Love F.

HIS purpose achieved at the price of Paris doing its malignant worst, and
determined never to go north of Lyon again, Lawrence departed for
Barcelona, then Majorca, from which he hoped great benefits. He knew
that Chopin had been happy there (an unfortunate association with
another short-lived consumptive genius), and at the Hotel Royal in
Palma de Mallorca, he found that he could sleep. His nerves relented at
last. But within a week the Spanish joined the many other nationalities
upon which he inflicted a class libel. He filled his letters with scathing
comments about the natives: "Dead-bodied people with rather ugly
faces and a certain staleness." He disliked their "Spanishy faces, dead
unpleasant masks, a bit like city English"; he liked the Italians—even the
French—better.

Changing hotels, he dashed off more articles. *Lady C.* had not spoiled
his newspaper market. For the *Sunday Dispatch* he wrote "Women
Don't Change," and "The Real Trouble About Women" for the *Daily
Express*. His belief that in writing for the English popular press he was
writing for his own kind was reinforced by the letters he was receiving
(not all complimentary) from men he had known as boys at school in
Eastwood.

An important essay, "Pornography and Obscenity," was completed in
ten days from inception to final typing. In it, he put the case for the
defense of *Lady Chatterley*—that is, he differentiated between a work
like his own, created to remove "the dirty little secret from sex," and
pornography, designed to stimulate masturbation, which he described
extravagantly as "the deepest and most dangerous cancer of our civilisation."

Like so many of his essays, "Pornography and Obscenity" is intensely
readable and wildly illogical. While Lawrence put superbly his analysis
of the use of censorship as an instrument of repression, he got into
dangerous territory from which he could not extricate himself:

> The sex functions and the excrementory functions in the human body
> work so close together, yet they are, so to speak, utterly different in
> direction. Sex is a creative flow, the excrementory flow is towards
> dissolution. . . . In the really healthy human being the distinction be-
> tween the two is instant. . . .

But in the degraded human being the deep instincts have gone dead, and then the two flows become identical. *This* is the secret of really vulgar and of pornographical people: the sex flow and the excrement flow is the same to them. . . . Then sex is dirty and dirt is sex, and sexual excitement becomes a playing with dirt, and any sign of sex in a woman becomes a show of her dirt.

Read in the light of the later revelations about Lady Chatterley's phallic rooting-out, Lawrence's tortuous distinction between anal and genital eroticism disappears. He never assimilated the paradox captured in two lines of Yeats: "Love has pitched his mansion in / The place of excrement." But the audience of 1929 took Lawrence at his plainest meaning and by December was buying "Pornography and Obscenity," reprinted as a pamphlet, at a rate of twelve hundred copies a week.

He struggled with Secker to clean up *Pansies* for England—substituting "my-eye" for "cat-piss," for example—but Secker, worried about the formidable Jix, nonetheless insisted on removing some of the poems before publication. The book of his paintings appeared; he wished it had been done in Germany, where the color reproduction would have been better.

Majorca was satisfyingly clear and sunny, although not as beautiful as Sicily. He was not well. He blamed "a little whack of malaria." He wrote endless letters—literary letters to literary friends, and homier ones to his family; for his sister Emily, his teeth chattered "like a sewing machine," but for Rhys Davies they were "like castanets."

In spite of his linguistic cleansing efforts in *Lady Chatterley,* he still used the familiar Anglo-Saxon words as expletives. The language of his correspondence, as if emboldened by *Lady Chatterley,* was more casually foul; there are more shits, bitches, and pisses. To Stephensen he wrote snidely (and with obvious memories of Mabel and Tony) about the persistence of the class system: "Many ladies, very many, have love affairs with their chauffeurs—the chauffeur is the favorite fucker." And he referred to a London book exporter as a "methodising shit-bag." (This phrase was censored from Aldous Huxley's 1932 collection of Lawrence's letters even though "shit-bag" was, as Aldington had observed, a term that Lawrence often called Frieda in public.)

Frieda was still moaning for a house, "so I suppose we'd better go and look for one," he told Caresse Crosby. Frieda's priorities were clear. She would prefer to return to the ranch; failing that, to Italy, preferably near Lake Garda; but she insisted on a house. Lawrence played one wish against the other. He wrote and asked Brett if she thought she could raise five thousand dollars, to top a new offer they had received for the ranch, so that with the proceeds, he could then reconcile Frieda to the loss of the ranch by promising that she could do up a house in Italy. It seemed like parting with youth and freedom to give up the ranch, but he could not see his way past the immigration barrier.

To his fury, he heard that in England word was spreading that he was dying. Ada even read it in the newspapers. He blamed the Huxleys; it was a mistake to stay with people, he fumed. He wrote to all and sundry that he was not about to die just yet. He had had flu in Paris, he acknowledged, but Majorca was agreeing with him. As he summed up for Catherine Carswell, "cough rather a nuisance, so don't walk much, but eat well and sleep well and feel alright in myself. I think I'm a tough and stringy bird." He would not risk England, however. Detectives had told Curtis Brown that he could be arrested if he tried to reenter.

Just as he saw all his problems as external to himself—cities, censors, treacherous friends—so he saw the demon in his lungs. "I feel so strongly as if my illness weren't really me," he wrote Mabel. "I feel perfectly well and even perfectly healthy—till the devil starts scratching and squeezing, and I feel perfectly awful." To John Middleton Murry, he graphically pictured himself as an animal in a hostile environment. The two were in correspondence again and Murry had sent photographs of his children, as well as the bitter news that his wife had consumption. But there was to be no reconciliation, for Murry had criticized Lawrence's *Collected Poems* in a review, calling them untrue to life. Lawrence retorted: "I am tired of being told there is no such animal by animals who are merely different. If I am a giraffe, and the ordinary Englishmen who write about me . . . are nice well-behaved dogs, there it is, the animals are different."

Nonetheless, Murry, sensing that time was running out, offered to come to Majorca to see him. Lawrence told him to stay home. He and Murry did not know each other, he said, and should not pretend to do so. There was no point in their meeting—"We are a dissonance"—but, in any event, there was no need; he was not dying.

To those from whom he was more emotionally detached, his generosity and kindness survived. He urged Harwood Brewster to get away from her parents and to study medicine if she chose; he scolded the Brewsters (much as he had the Meynells about Mary Saleeby in Hampshire fourteen years earlier) for letting a girl go unschooled. Harwood needed proper teaching. The Brewsters took the point and arranged to send Harwood to boarding school in England, choosing one that suited their own alternative lifestyle; Harwood became one of the first pupils at the new progressive and coeducational Dartington Hall in Devon.

And to the Australian Stephensen, the publisher of his art book, who had complained about *Kangaroo*, Lawrence said, with genuine modesty: "You may indeed know something much deeper and more vital about Australia and the Australian future. . . . I should hate to think I ever said the last word about anything."

He also clarified and modified his politics. He told his sister Emily that, were he to be in England for the forthcoming general election, he would vote Labour without hesitation. Stanley Baldwin, the Conservative prime minister, was a "mealy-mouthed nonentity," and Lloyd George, the Liberal leader, whom during the war he had called a clever little Welsh rat, was now a "treacherous bug." But above all: "My sympathies are with Labour," but then, he added teasingly to his sister, he did not live at such a genteel address as she had achieved in Nottingham.

By mutual agreement, he and Frieda left Majorca for separate destinations. She, even though she had badly sprained her ankle on the rocks while bathing, went to London for the exhibition of his paintings and he went back to the shelter of the Huxleys at Forte dei Marmi.

IT was Frieda's first taste of the honor without the fight of being Mrs. D. H. Lawrence. Just short of her fiftieth birthday, she had a wonderful time as the star of the opening party for the exhibition, limping in a bright-colored evening dress she had made herself and carrying a bunch of lilies. (She thought she was better-looking now that she was older, although, as she wrote to her confidant, Witter Bynner, her hair was no longer "an unmixed colour" and she would have to dye it.)

When the reviews came out, however, it was clear that the London art world was even more appalled than Osbert Sitwell and the Wilkinsons had been at the Villa Mirenda. Critics condemned the paintings on artistic grounds (but in words different only in degree from those used more recently to describe them, like "daft" and "curious." Despite the lifting of the ban on April 13, 1989, and much publicity, in the form of exhibitions of full-scale color reproductions, magazine articles, and television documentaries, there has been little demand to bring them back to England.)

Those who did praise the paintings in 1929 valued them for the insight they gave into the cross-fertilization of images between pen and brush. The painter Gwen John admired their "stupendous gift of self-expression." The *Nottingham Evening Post* loyally applauded their qualities of composition, harmony of color, and delicacy of touch. But the special correspondent of the *Daily Express* spoke for the majority. He could not decide whether the composition or the subject matter were the uglier:

> "Spring," a study of six nude boys, is revolting. "Fight with an Amazon," representing a hideous, bearded man holding a fair-haired woman in his lascivious grip, while wolves with dripping jaws look on expectantly, is frankly indecent. "Boccaccio Story," another of these works of art, is better not described.

Crowds jammed the gallery. It was a matter of time—three weeks, to be precise—before the Metropolitan Police obeyed the clamor in the press and burst in on the exhibition. They did not, as many public voices urged, close it altogether, but rather took away thirteen of the twenty-five canvases—anything with a penis or pubic hair. They left the other nudes.

Monty Weekley, now curator of the Bethnal Green Museum of Childhood, a branch of the Victoria and Albert, relished the fight with the police. Frieda did not mind it at all either; she saw it as a good advertisement for *Lady Chatterley's Lover*.

WHILE Frieda was in London, Lawrence was in a *pensione* near the Huxleys at Forte dei Marmi. He visited their wealthy friends Count Luigi Franchetti and his American wife, Yvonne (later Mrs. Hamish Hamilton); she found him very impressive and retained a lasting memory of piercing blue eyes. The resort was too hot but of course he could not go in the water, and the company irritated him. Maria Cristina Chambers had arrived from New York to meet her idol, and the meeting (as Lawrence had warned her) had not gone well. He found her, like Ivy Low at Fiascherino years before, self-preoccupied, cringing yet impudent. He was distressed too by Maria's involvement with a woman called Costanza: "tangled up," he said, "in a way I dislike extremely." (He perhaps sensed the bisexuality in Maria, who had tried to commit suicide in 1915 on account of a thwarted crush on Ottoline Morrell and later, when the Huxleys were in Hollywood, became actively lesbian.)

Fed up with "an atmosphere of women, women, women," Lawrence decided to flee to Florence. Mrs. Chambers, seeing how wrung out he was, did his packing for him, and Maria Huxley drove him to Pisa to catch the train. But in Florence he came down with stomach pains which he attributed to drinking ice water, and put himself in the care of the motherly Orioli. Racked with cramps, he lay in Orioli's flat, listening to the blaring horns of the Florentine traffic. There the news reached him that the paintings which he loved, the physical products of his body, the adornment of his home, were in police custody. But the news did not reach him from Frieda.

"She never writes," he moaned to Ada. She had not even written about the exhibition, let alone the police raid. All he got was a telegram to say that she was staying on in London.

Frieda did write a letter to Mabel, however. She seemed more worried about the fate of the manuscripts at the ranch than about the paintings: "She [Brett] *must* give them to you to put in the bank & tell us what there is, she had no right to break into that little wooden cupboard." At that point, briefly, Frieda was willing to have the ranch sold, if only to be done with Brett.

But Lawrence's letters to her were grumpy and matter-of-fact, with scarcely a word of love, just the urgent instructions that pass between two people who know each other too well to put their feelings on paper; he signed himself "L" or even "DHL." He asked her to buy him some Carter's Little Liver Pills and implored her to stop bothering his agents about his business affairs. But he did tell her, almost childishly, about his latest illness; "My lower man hurts and it makes my chest sore."

Ill and deeply distressed about the loss of his pictures, he then learned that Orioli, who had nursed him, made him cups of tea, and taken him for a carriage drive into the hills, had plans to leave Florence. He felt utterly woebegone. He did not want to stay alone in the oven-hot flat with just a servant to look after him. Suddenly, like a *dea ex machina* (but actually in response to a telegram from Orioli) Frieda swooped down to take him off to Baden-Baden. He was much relieved and sent fifteen pounds to England for his nieces' and nephew's summer holidays.

FROM Forte, Aldous Huxley watched the spectacle with dismay. He wrote their mutual friend, the poet Robert Nichols: "How horrible this gradually approaching dissolution is—and in this case specially horrible, because so unnecessary, the result simply of the man's strange obstinacy against professional medicine."

And to his brother Julian, in despair:

So that's that. It's no good. He doesn't *want* to know how ill he is; that, I believe, is the fundamental reason why he won't go to doctors and homes. . . . He rationalises the fear in all kinds of ways . . . he just wanders about, very tired and at bottom wretched, from one place to another, imagining that the next place will make him feel better and, when he gets [to] the next place, regretting the one before and looking back on it as a paradise. But of course no place will make him feel any better than any other now that he's as ill as he is.

He's a great deal worse than he was when you saw him at Diablerets—coughs more, breathes very quickly and shallowly, has no energy. (It's pathetic to see the way he just sits and does nothing. He hasn't written a line or painted a stroke for the last 3 months. Just lack of vital strength.) He still talks a good deal and can get amused and excited into the semblance of health for an hour or two at a time. But it is only a semblance, I'm afraid. I think he's even worse than he was in Paris in March (when he had a touch of flu to complicate matters). The Doctor told M [Maria] that he might drag on for quite a little time like this, unless he got a cold which turned into bronchitis or pneumonia, when he'd simply be asphyxiated. He has gone to Germany now—or is just going: for he has been in Florence these last days—of all places in this weather! We have given up trying to persuade him to be reasonable. He doesn't want to be and no one can persuade him to be—except possibly Frieda. But Frieda is worse than he is. We've told her that she's a fool and a criminal; but it has no more effect than telling an elephant. So it's hopeless. Short of handcuffing him and taking him to a sanatorium by force, there's nothing to be done.

Frieda was as indifferent as Lawrence to professional medicine, but she was no fool. Still an active partner in "the firm," she agreed with her husband that Dorothy Warren must not put his paintings at risk by using them as a test case in a court challenge against artistic censorship; an unfavorable verdict might end with the paintings being burned.* The exhibition, Frieda lectured Dorothy from Florence, had been a victory in itself. Together, she (Frieda) and Lawrence had got "a new way of looking at things started"; they must work steadily toward "a far vision . . . I am glad to be with Lawrence. We are so *sure* of ourselves in the long run."

THERE could have been no greater sign of his weakened condition than his new resentment of his mother-in-law. Arriving in Baden-Baden in July 1929 in time for her seventy-eighth birthday, he was conscious that the old lady was going to outlive him. For the first time in his many visits to the Black Forest, he found the quiet procession of spa days—the open-air concerts, the beer-drinking in rose-filled gardens, the effusive German manners—irritating. He even found the pine trees monotonous: "Why can't they have leaves!"

His bad temper grew worse when the old baroness first moved in with them at their *Gasthaus* on the outskirts of town, then insisted on taking them to a barnlike health hotel on top of a mountain to escape the heat. Anna von Richthofen had become one of his devouring women. He complained to Ada: "That old woman would see me die by inches and yards rather than relinquish her 'mountain air.' She stands in the road and gulps the air in greedy gulps—and says—it does me so much good! it gives me strength, strength!"

Just as greedy was his mother-in-law's insistence that one of her family always be with her; she was insanely selfish because of her disgusting fear of dying. He hoped he would never sink so low.

Considering his own deterioration—he was too ill to walk or read and was in his room most of the time—his anger is understandable. More remarkable is that he had not let himself feel it before. A stronger man would not have put up with such a demanding mother-in-law without protest. The old lady obviously had long been possessive, and now, with her sentimentality and demand for endless card games, he found her

---

* A hearing in Magistrate's Court on August 8 ruled that the pictures were not to be burned but returned to Lawrence on the condition that they never be shown in Britain. The authorities, perhaps out of frustration, burned four copies of the book of reproductions instead.

tedious. But he so craved a mother, so liked aristocratic company, and so little wished to antagonize Frieda that the traditional son-in-law reactions did not surface until he was desperately ill. Even so, he remained for five weeks, one of his longest visits ever to his *Schwiegermutter*. While they were there, Frieda turned fifty—an event celebrated by a dinner of champagne and trout, which was followed next day, Lawrence observed, by one of the worst moods he had ever seen her in.

Temperamentally, Lawrence and Frieda were more alike than his friends realized. They had the same capacity for changing from light to dark in a flash, and the same blindness to their motives. Each professed a love of solitude but actually needed to be surrounded by people. Each easily felt victimized.

Frieda, always inclined to paranoia, that summer fell into a paroxysm of suspicion about Brett. She was now sure that Brett had sold a major manuscript (*The Plumed Serpent* was one of those unaccounted for); otherwise, how could she have got the money to stay so long at the Shelton Hotel that winter? Lawrence, in his weakened condition, could not calm her down, and her ranting vituperative letters to Brett give some idea of the verbal battering he had to live with day by day.

> I never thought much of you or your "love," for anybody, but to do that [sell the MSS] is more than I expected you to do—you are a poor failure of a thing and try to highfalute, one feels sorry for you, not very, because you look after yourself hard enough & that's all the pretence of caring for others is to serve the hon. Dorothy.

When, the same day, another letter from Brett arrived offering to buy the ranch, Frieda let loose again: "Is your soul so split that somewhere you serenely float in a beatic [*sic*] vision of a beautifully solid Brett & underneath you are so horrid & diabolical! You cost Lawr a lot of his faith & it can never be restored."

If the manuscripts were a coded way of discussing Frieda's financial provision after Lawrence's death, so was her new preoccupation with his agents and publishers: "Fancies herself quite a business-woman," said Lawrence to Titus, sarcastically. Frieda snarled at Brett that she had enough money—and that she would be coming back to Taos. "*I don't want to sell the ranch*," she underlined in several of these letters.

Was Frieda waiting for Lawrence to die so that she could go back to the ranch? The possibility cannot be ruled out. The ingredients of her future were in place: Ravagli, the ranch, the continuing friendships with Witter Bynner and Mabel, the growing income from *Lady Chatterley*. It must have crossed her mind.

The barrage against Brett continued into August. She demanded that Brett send a list of all the manuscripts and deliver them all to a safe deposit box at the Taos bank. She told Brett to stop her monkey tricks; the Lawrences could turn her out of the ranch "lock stock & barrel quite ignominously [*sic*]"; and, Frieda swore, "as far as I can help it, you shall not swindle us, I will go to any length." She kept repeating, with underlining, "I don't want to sell the ranch."

Two weeks later Lawrence apologized, but not very warmly, to Brett for falsely accusing her. Most of the manuscripts that Lawrence thought were at the ranch had turned up in Curtis Brown's New York office.

Frieda instantly wrote a friendly letter, telling Brett that she bore her no ill will for being called a hyena and the cause of Lawrence's illness. She explained again that it was Lawrence's own bad health that made him vicious and that she herself was neither possessive nor jealous. It was he who was clinging on to her, she said, in a letter in which she as good as acknowledged their respective adulteries: "But no, he hates me to be away, his life is *too* much based on me—I feel—So you have it *all* wrong—What's between him & me is *there,* if he & I have other relationships, it's all to the good—but your affection for him seemed to be mostly hatred for me."

Frieda did have, in her mixture of paranoia and good nature, her own clear sense of mission; she felt that she was carrying a burden for world literature. Without her, she considered that Lawrence would have died in Mexico; indeed, she felt that she had kept him alive virtually from the day she had met him, so ill and depressed had he been after his mother's death. And she had done more, rescuing him from provincialism and broadening his horizons. Someday she would be recognized, she told Brett, as if gathering her credentials as keeper of the flame:

> I think I have in my patience and belief conquered his disgust with life & the deathloving side of him—It *was* hardwork & you did not help & you remember all those nasty letters you wrote about saying: he was sacrificed to the children & all the horrid things about me? like hymns of hate & I was a hyena? Was'nt it really you who hated? *It all bores me stiff!!*

Lawrence ascribed Frieda's mood swings to her being German. From Baden-Baden he explained to Orioli, "They love things just because they think they have a sentimental reason for loving them—das Heimatland, der Tannenbaum . . ." They then "come out with such startling and really, silly bursts of hatred. . . . that's why, as a bourgeois crowd, they are so monstrously ugly. My God, how ugly they can be!"

WHY Lawrence did not see to his will is a mystery. He told Ada, who had just found the manuscript of *The Rainbow* in her attic, that if he died, his manuscripts and paintings would have to be sold to secure something of an income for Frieda. He made a wry joke that suggests that the wish to be a father would be the last thing to die: "And finally, if it comes to heirlooms, I've got no children of my own—at least at present." As it was, he had no use for heirlooms, and his brother George's elder son, Ernest, was the family heir.

Income from *Lady Chatterley* continued to pour in. The Titus edition of three thousand, at sixty francs a copy, was sold out by August and matched the profits of Orioli's edition. It was unabridged and contained an introduction by Lawrence, "My Skirmish With Jolly Roger," describing the tribulations of the Florence edition. Lawrence and Titus shared an extra three hundred dollars when Random House published the introduction as a single pamphlet. He also had the satisfaction of the publication of an unexpurgated edition of *Pansies* by Charles Lahr, the left-wing eccentric London bookseller who was now a regular correspondent. Davies had smuggled the manuscript back to London when he returned from Paris, and Lahr's edition of five hundred copies at two guineas swiftly sold out. Even the ill-fated exhibition at the Warren Gallery yielded him a bit of money from picture sales.

Another book was lost to the law, nonetheless, when Heinemann withdrew its planned publication of a collection of Lawrence short stories, *The Man Who Loved Islands,* because Compton Mackenzie threatened to sue for libel over the title story. Lawrence accepted the decision because he did not want any more fuss, but he was furious. The character was not Monty [Mackenzie], he insisted: "He may have loved islands, but where the libel or the further likeness comes in, I dont see." The man was no more Mackenzie than he was himself.

"Of course, it isn't," Mackenzie agreed later in an interview with the BBC. "But people will say that it is. Against that background is this preposterous character." Lawrence had a bad habit, he said, of staying with people and then going home to reproduce with uncanny accuracy their surroundings, against which he put characters from the wilds of his imagination. Lawrence, to Mackenzie, was as "incapable of a portrait on paper as he was on canvas."

LEAVING Baden-Baden at the end of August, Lawrence and Frieda moved to Rottach in Bavaria. Frieda's ankle was still paining her and she had visited doctors in London and Baden, to no avail. At Rottach, Dr. Max Mohr, now a good friend, recommended a local bone-setter, a farmer. Within a minute, the man snapped the bone back into its proper socket, and Frieda was cured.

The incident looked like a miracle designed to confirm Lawrence's mistrust of doctors. He wrote ten or more letters, in almost the same words, telling the tale of the rustic healer who succeeded where the avaricious medical profession had failed. To Earl Brewster, he exclaimed, "And I paid 12 guineas to a Park Lane specialist, and the long-bearded Medizinalrat in Baden-Baden is still to pay. Doctors should all be put at once in prison." To his sister Emily: "Imagine those beastly doctors 12 guineas I paid the one in London, and the one in Baden not yet paid. It makes one mad."

Returning to the Bavarian foothills, where they had spent their honeymoon—"and how lovely it was! oh God," he wrote Mohr—he was still stuck in bed most of the time. He did a "cure" and subjected himself to new diagnoses: the "animal man" in him was in a state of change and needed a change of diet. On advice, he took arsenic and phosphorus twice a day, gave up salt and bread, and ate only raw fruit, raw vegetables, and porridge. "They say I can get well in quite a short time," he wrote Enid Hilton in London. "I hope it's true—it may be, really."

Within a week, however, he felt poisoned, and gave up the arsenic and phosphorus but stuck to the diet. He promised Orioli that he would live for a hundred years and would put wreaths on the graves of all those who had determined that he was dying.

LAWRENCE was still an object of awe and reverence in Else's circle. Mohr was so impressed with Lawrence's magical powers that he allowed his three-year-old daughter to hold Lawrence's hand and play constantly with him. He no more feared contagion from Lorenzo's body than from his books. "Behind everything," Mohr wrote later, "there stood and stands forever the power and saving magic of his life." But Frieda thought Lawrence was going to die. More than once she went into his bedroom to see him lying so still she thought he was dead already.

HE no longer hid the truth from himself. He knew he was dying; death was no longer a borderline, it was a descent. If in all his work he had used sex as a metaphor for health, he had now written his final plea— *Lady Chatterley*—and it had not been granted. Now he stared into the blackness. A vase of blue flowers by his bed inspired "Bavarian Gentians," one of his greatest and loneliest poems:

Reach me a gentian, give me a torch!
let me guide myself with the blue, forked torch of this flower
down the darker and darker stairs, where blue is darkened on blueness
even where Persephone goes . . .

That same bitter month inspired his magnificent "The Ship of Death," the culmination of all he had learned from his Etruscan friends:

> Now it is autumn and the falling fruit
> and the long journey towards oblivion. . . .
> And it is time to go, to bid farewell
> to one's own self, and find an exit
> from the fallen self. . . .
> . . . .
> Oh build your ship of death, your little ark
> and furnish it with food, with little cakes, and wine
> for the dark flight down oblivion.

If confronting the extinction of self is the ultimate duty of the artist, Lawrence showed unparalleled courage. He did it again and again. Yet he could not name the disease that was killing him.

THE annual move south produced the annual brief optimism. Lawrence chose to return to Bandol because he had felt well there the previous winter; he still expected the Spirit of Place to cure him. Germany was now the villain: its psyche nearly killed him. He hoped, he wrote Nancy Pearn, that it had been "the low-water mark, for I don't want to go any lower."

For Frieda's sake, he rented a house for six months—a concrete imitation of a Roman villa, with central heating, a garden, a marble bathroom, and gilt chandeliers. Aptly named Beau Soleil, it had French windows through which he could see the sea as he lay on a bed. Frieda could swim every day. His only complaint was that the house did not have an open fire. He summoned the Brewsters from Capri, apologizing for the ugliness of the French coast but saying they could arrange a nice neighborly winter.

The wandering Brewsters obliged. They were more restless than ever now that Harwood was at Dartington Hall. Lawrence sent the girl a friendly letter to ease the homesickness she might feel as an American in an English school: "It will seem strange at first, but I'm sure after a while you'll love it. And I do hope you get a footing in the world among other people, and independent of your father and mother. Thank goodness it is not too late."

The acolytes gathered. Max Mohr came and remained for a whole month. Norman Douglas turned up with Orioli and did not think much of the Beau Soleil: "one of those dreadful little bungalows built of gaudy cardboard—there may have been one or two bricks in it as well—which grow up overnight." Lawrence was glad to see the pair, even though he disapproved of the way they were "on the razzle" (pursuing a good time), and produced a bottle of cognac.

Having the house, with peasants hoeing the slopes of the fields above, soothed both Lawrences. Their goods had arrived from the Mirenda, although he was cross about the shipping cost of 1,148 francs. As he wrote Brewster Ghiselin, Frieda was happy: "hangs up curtains and buys chairs—and I lie in bed and look at the islands out to sea, and think of the Greeks, and cough, and wish either that I was different or the world was different." Domesticity was helped by the adoption of a stray marmalade cat who, Lawrence told the Huxleys, had "howled like a lion on the terrace till I let him live here." He said he liked the cat but did not love him.

Frieda hoped the sun would drive the crossness out of Lawrence. It succeeded to the extent of allowing her a gramophone—a gift from the Crosbys after the record-smashing incident—but he would only let her play it in the kitchen. He was still cross with the way she kept on interfering in his business affairs and he advised Laurence Pollinger to ignore her; he had told her to stop it "but she feels the usual 'call.' "

Whatever the Huxleys may have thought about her qualities as a nurse, Frieda did try to look after her husband. She saw to a special breakfast recommended by Max Mohr as the newest German idea: an apple, prunes, and almonds put through the mincing machine. More to her taste, she made jokes and played Schubert loudly on the piano; the last thing Lawrence wanted, she knew, was to be treated like an invalid. She allowed herself to hope. To Kot, after scolding him as usual, she wrote, "Christ rose only once but Lawr. has done the trick many times, it seems to me." Wickedly and wistfully, she added, "I wish I could drop into your drawing-room and smoke 7 of your cigarettes! and hear you tell me *what* bores we are!!"

The Brewsters took them out on long drives; Earl massaged Lawrence daily with coconut oil. The Huxleys, from Madrid, promised to arrive in February. Lawrence rather hoped, he wrote Else, they would not. They were having marital difficulties, and he felt that Aldous intruded in his own affairs. However, he wrote and asked Maria Huxley to send him a tin of "that new food Bemax, English—the vitamin B food."

He was now racing against time. He turned his "Skirmish with Jolly Roger" into a brilliant essay, "À Propos of Lady Chatterley's Lover," wrote more than fifty poems (which would appear as *Last Poems*), and assorted articles including three for *Vanity Fair*, with sad titles: "Nobody Loves Me," "The Real Thing," and "We Need One Another." He also applied himself to writing an introduction to a book on the Revelation of St. John the Divine by an English friend, Frederick Carter.

His critical eye was as sharp as ever. Reading some work sent him by the German translator who was about to do *Lady Chatterley,* he re-marked how poorly Yeats survived the transition to another language. He liked Yeats: "But there is a certain shoddy quality in nearly all the Irish, which they cover with an 'Irish' style." He was no happier with a translation of Thornton Wilder, but then he did not like Wilder's "high-school American" anyway. He kept up his heavy correspondence but his letters show only flashes of his old wish to convey the physical world around him—"Such dark paw marks of the wind on the sea," he wrote Maria Huxley. Mainly, he was too tired to bother; at times he did not even feel like reading.

He could still talk. Frederick Carter, invited down from Paris for the week to be Lawrence's guest at the Beau Rivage and to discuss a new manuscript, *Apocalypse,* marveled at his malicious and satirical bril-liance as a storyteller. Carter observed to himself that Lawrence was more masculine in his conversation than in his writing. He noticed also Lawrence's habit of spitting carefully into an envelope.

He was not always in bed. He offended their good local French cook by making his own bread, and under her hostile eyes he sat in the kitchen and made sure it baked safely. He leaped up, too, when he saw the cat attack the goldfish he had been sent as a gift, and a few days later, when the cat managed to kill one of the fish, he spanked it. This led to a dispute with Frieda. She argued that it was a cat's instinct to kill fish. Not so to Lawrence. The cat knew they wanted him to leave the goldfish bowl alone, and owed them loyalty because they fed him. "It's your fault, you spoil him," he snapped at Frieda. "If he wanted to eat *me,* you would let him."

Now more than ever his books and his health converged; when his lungs ached, he blamed the hatred against his work for coming to at-tack him in the chest. The unreachable New Mexico became like Vi-oletta's vision of Paris in the last act of *La Traviata;* if only he could return. He thumbed over his mental snapshots of America: Central Park, with its "horrid brown rocks," and Salt Lake City, "such a clean respectable place with a glorified chapel. But the country round was weird." He wrote to Bynner, "I believe I'd get better in no time in New Mexico. . . . I wish there weren't all these passport difficulties." He had the practical details worked out in his mind; they would rent a fur-nished place in Santa Fe at the start, to acclimatize themselves to the altitude, and then return to Santa Fe for the winters, spending only summers at the ranch. He confessed that after *Lady Chatterley* he did not know whether he was acceptable to immigration, yet "I do really and firmly believe, though, that it's Europe that has made me so ill. . . . Anyhow in New Mexico the sun and the air are alive, let man be what he may."

The Wall Street crash of late October 1929 had added to his miseries.

476 *A Dying Animal*

He was torn between guilt at having succumbed to the lure of speculative investment, and anxiety about losing his hard-earned money. He forbade Frieda even to look in the newspapers to see how their shares had fallen. Fortunately, his losses were small, but the collapse worried him also for its effect on the sale of *Pansies*.

His London friends were more concerned to get him proper treatment. Kot and Gertler persuaded the English chest specialist Dr. Andrew Morland of the Mundesley Sanatorium to go to Bandol to examine him. Morland, who was to be traveling in the south of France anyway, agreed. Lawrence resisted. It might be a waste of time "to talk with a doctor who will want to talk about lungs when the trouble is bronchials. If I knew a doctor who understood bronchials!" But Frieda told Kot that she would be glad if "that doctor" would come.

Growing weaker—by December he could scarcely walk—he was shattered by the news that golden Harry Crosby, who had returned to New England for the Harvard-Yale game, had killed himself and someone else's wife in a suicide pact in a New York hotel. Lawrence could hardly believe it. Only weeks before, when the Crosbys had published *The Escaped Cock,* he had had a charming letter from Caresse telling how Harry had just shot a pheasant cock, the first game of the season, in the garden of their mill. Harry was only thirty-two. Lawrence sat in bed, swathed in a scarf of Frieda's to protect his aching ears, and repeated over and over, "That's all he could do with life, throw it away." The only possible cause he could see for Crosby's suicide (although he knew of Crosby's anarchic promiscuity and troubled marriage) was wealth. Shattered as he was, he allowed himself a black (and eerily prophetic) joke: "The wife is on her way back to Paris already with the ashes (his only) in a silver jar."

THE faithful gathered around the dying man: the Brewsters, Ida Rauh (his acquaintance from Taos and the wife of the socialist Max Eastman), her son, Daniel, and the di Chiaras, old friends from Capri. It was his last colony. He took great comfort in the numbers around him for Christmas, and boasted to Ada, "We are by no means lonely." Harwood Brewster joined them from her English boarding school, bringing hampers of English festive food from Lawrence's sisters. He wrote and told Brett that they would be back at the ranch in March or April.

He faced Christmas in bed, with his sisters' plum pudding and a cake, and a linseed poultice on his "bronchs." He selected gifts for everyone, and for the Brewsters painted a clock face with a rising sun. On December 23 he wrote humbly to Kot and said that yes, after all, he would be so pleased to see Dr. Morland if he were to be kind enough to stop off at Bandol. But, he insisted to Gertler: "It's not the lungs."

On Christmas Eve he rose from his sickbed to make lemon tarts. On Christmas Day his seven friends all trooped over for tea. On January 1 he got up again and managed to walk to the village to a lunch given by the di Chiaras. It was a noble effort, made to celebrate what would be his last, and short, New Year.

20

UNFINISHED

1930

I respect him for dying when he was cornered.
—D. H. Lawrence, Introduction to
Memoirs of the Foreign Legion by M.M.

"*I* have decided to go to the sanatorium. . . ." These words, uttered a few years earlier, might have saved his life. Written to Ada on February 3, 1930, they were not so much a surrender as Lawrence's acceptance that there was nothing left to try.

In mid-January Dr. Morland arrived from England and after a thorough examination concluded that Lawrence had been suffering from tuberculosis for from ten to fifteen years, and that all that he seemed to know about treatment had been gleaned from Mark Gertler: to walk three or four miles every morning and drink lots of milk. An X ray, the first taken since Mexico City in 1925, confirmed the disease's long duration. It showed too, however, that Lawrence's constant insistence that he was getting better was not without foundation. The plates revealed many scars and healed cavities; there was only one new, open lesion and that was small.

Dr. Morland, prompted by Gertler and Kot, gave Lawrence simple, unambiguous instructions. He was to go to a higher altitude, away from the seaside, and enter a sanatorium. Lawrence told the doctor that he wanted to go to New Mexico but Morland dismissed the idea out of hand; he could not survive a six-thousand-mile journey. Morland himself would have preferred to get Lawrence to Mundesley back in Norfolk; but for Lawrence, England, with its hovering detectives, was out of the question. They agreed on a sanatorium above Vence which was not too far away and met (more or less) Morland's standards.

To Edward Titus, who sent him nearly eight thousand francs from the Paris edition of *Lady Chatterley,* Lawrence relayed Morland's advice: absolute rest, *no* work, no people, not even thinking. "Well," he added cheerfully, "it's a hard world—I must not ever go to the hotel for lunch again—such a nice lunch."

He still had not relaxed his taboo on the name of his disease. Nor had he accepted that he would never return to New Mexico. He wrote to Mabel, explaining that he was going to a sanatorium for "acute bronchitis . . . aggravated by the lung." He pretended that he would come as soon as he could get a place in the U.S. immigration quota; a six-month visa was no good. He even returned to his old love, studying ship timetables, and—reviving his determination to avoid New York—thought he and Frieda would sail from Marseilles to San Francisco. Once again he used his unacceptable novel as a shield for his unacceptable body: "The real trouble is my health—and I feel the Americans don't like me. They are afraid of *Lady C.*" But when they arrived, he said he and Frieda would start a school, dedicated to giving the young a new concept of life. Perhaps, he thought with some poignance, his true calling was to be a teacher and he should not have fought so long against it.

The cloud over this dream was Frieda's aversion to Brett. He worried that if he came to New Mexico he would spend his energy, as before, mediating between the two of them and, he told Mabel, "I can't stand rows: I can't." But: "It is useless to lie here and die."

Else Jaffe was with them, then Barby came, still depressed; "Oh dear O!" was all he could say. His stepdaughter became more than ever a part of their little family and he liked to have her looking after him and making him porridge. When Frieda suggested that Barby could go on ahead to the ranch and stay with Mabel, he rounded on her furiously. "You might just as well throw Barby into the sea!" he said. But he did suggest—shades of "St. Mawr"—that if mother and daughter could really love each other, they might make a life together. He did not need to utter the implicit "after I'm gone."

Ada and Emily wanted to come down together from Nottingham but he put them off; they should wait until he came out of the sanatorium, he advised, and was walking about; then perhaps they could take over the housekeeping and allow Frieda to go away for a rest after the strain of nursing him. He was glad of visitors, he said, because Frieda needed someone to keep her balanced.

Frieda was not very balanced. While Lawrence was in the sanatorium, she contemplated a trip to her mother, which would have allowed her to detour past Ravagli's garrison, but Ravagli himself scolded her and told her that, if Lawrence was that ill, her duty was to remain near him. At the same time she kept up her barrage against Brett for misunderstanding the Lawrence marriage: "Are you really so unutterably *dense* that you can't see L's & my relationship or is it evil & you don't want to?" Could Brett not see that "if he grumbles, he is *sick* & grumbles at me"? Three days later, in one of her magnificent unapologetic reversals (after she learned of Brett's father's death), she wrote and asked Brett to come over to Vence: "He suffers much—I feel that the few who are fond of him should be with him to buck him up—*now!*"

In her frenzy Frieda complained intemperately to Titus in Paris, too, about how little Lawrence had earned from the American publication of his books: "Lawr having sweatted his guts out for this filthy humanity, that does'nt even pay him back in money *not* to *speak* of *life*." She was glad to hear that Titus was reprinting another ten thousand copies of his *Chatterley* edition.

As Lawrence lay in bed at Bandol, waiting to be transferred to Vence, Else visited and he told her, "Else, I would do anything to get well." Anything, that is, except stop working. He produced a four-thousand-word introduction to Kot's translation of "The Grand Inquisitor" by Dostoevsky and turned what had been his introduction to Frederick Carter's book on St. John the Divine into a short book of his own, *Apocalypse.* Work was the way to recover from sadness, he told Caresse Crosby, still shattered by Harry's suicide, but she should not try to rush herself. "It was too dreadful a blow—and," he said, letting slip his own thoughts on self-destruction, "it was wrong."

His weight continued to drop. He was in constant pain and could not sleep. He wished he could go up to the Brewsters' farmhouse to see the countryside in springtime but could not leave the Villa Beau Soleil. The weather was sunny and the almond trees were all in blossom—"beautiful," he wrote Max Mohr, "but I am not allowed any more to go out and see them."

He convinced all around him that he was just going through one of his bad patches. Earl Brewster left on another visit to India. Lawrence told him he must go; they would see each other in May. Ada and Emily remained in England, as instructed; Lawrence wrote his sisters not to worry: he was in slow danger, but nothing immediate; he was "about the same—anyhow no worse."

To Frieda fell the task of breaking the news to their friends. To Kot she wrote: "I have pulled L. through many times; he'll get better." To Mabel she was more distressed:

Lawr is very ill & I cant think of anything but the *present* & the next few days—But I feel he'll get better again—Dr Moreland said he would be dead in 3 months if he did'nt go into a sanatorium—But they know so much & he *does'nt want to go* —That doctor in Mexico told me L would'nt live longer than 2 years—It's 6 years ago!

When the time came to transfer to Vence, Earl Brewster accompanied them on the journey in a private railway car along the French coast from Toulon to Antibes. There a friend of Barby's, Blair Hughes-Stanton, a book illustrator, met them and drove Lawrence up to the sanatorium, a large multistory chalet with the unfortunate name of Ad Astra, perched on a hilltop a thousand feet above the Mediterranean. On the way they passed the cemetery; Lawrence said to Frieda, "You will bury me here," and she replied that she would not; the place was too ugly. Frieda moved into the Hôtel Nouvel in Vence, where Barby joined her. She wrote again to Mabel that she was troubled about Lawrence. He could not eat or write; "this winter he wrote something on the Apocalypse, or rather before that time, so good, but now he can't write and is so unhappy." She wished they could come to the ranch: "Today I am quite despairing. . . . I wish L could have all the people that are fond of him round him it would help him to live—Love Frieda."

Meanwhile, efforts were intensifying on the other side of the Atlantic to mount a rescue. Mabel, with her money and influence, was seen as the best hope. Maria Cristina Chambers wrote to her from Great Neck, Long Island, and pleaded:

> February 10, 1930
> . . . I *know* you are the one to help Lawrence. And what he needs is *someone* to go over and get everything in proper shape for his coming to America. Then to bring him and Frieda over. Oh my dear friend! . . . I'm convinced that Brett won't do a thing to harm either Frieda or that beloved Lawrence. Convinced that if you can get them to your heavenly casa, all the gods will descend to put a wreath of flowers on your kind, lovely head. . . . I don't think there is any difficulty about his getting in the country. And once here, why, after his six months are up he doesn't go to Canada and then come in again. You should keep him in Taos for the rest of his life. Or, my dear. Why not take him to Mexico. He can get in Mexico any day, I know. And there are very fine, warm desert places there until he would be better. It's in your kind and very able hands to get Lawrence somewhere where he can get better.

SANATORIUM life surprised Lawrence by its ordinariness. It was just like a hotel except that there were doctors around. There seemed to be little rhyme or reason to the regulations. The doctors took him off milk—it was bad for his liver—and made him walk down two flights of stairs for his meals. But it was dull, with everybody chattering in French, and depressing, with children crying. After eight days, with no perceptible improvement, he allowed himself—perhaps for the first time—to refer to his disease by name, but only adjectivally: "There is a very slight tubercular trouble," he wrote Titus, but really the "bronchial-asthmatic condition" was responsible for sapping his appetite and weight.

To the depths of his Protestant being, he felt, as he had told his young American friend Grace Crawford in 1911 when he nearly died from double pneumonia, "It is very stupid to be ill." He could not sleep, coughed constantly, and ached all over. But he did not complain. He wanted to be cheered up and scolded himself for being "very egoistic . . . that's the worst of being sick."

He missed Frieda, who was spending the nights at her hotel, and asked her to stay with him. Flippantly, he told Barby, "It isn't often I want your mother, but I do want her tonight to stay." For much of their marriage his illness had deprived him of the comfort he had described so wonderfully in *Sons and Lovers:* "Paul loved to sleep with his mother. Sleep is still the most perfect, in spite of hygienists, when it is shared with a beloved." A bed was moved into his room for Frieda but then he sent her away, making her cry. Later he apologized. According to her, his words were "You know I want nothing but you, but sometimes something is stronger in me."

As he lay dying, he worked. He began reviewing a new book, *Art Nonsense and Other Essays,* by the English designer and medievalist Eric Gill. He opened with an attack: "Mr Gill is not a born writer: he is crude and crass. Still less is he a born thinker, in the reasoning and argumentative sense of the word. He is again a crude and crass amateur . . . like a tiresome uneducated workman arguing in a pub."

He kept up his letter-writing but the letters grew shorter and shorter, as if he were running out of breath. He told Ada about the sanatorium, "Shan't stay long" and "Does me no good." He lit into Caresse Crosby for accepting too low a price for *The Escaped Cock:* "Did you sell the whole edition, *including the vellums,* for $2,250?" If she had, she was not the businesswoman he had expected her to be and had made him vulnerable once more to the predations of "those little Jew booksellers." He had a number of visitors, more distinguished than at Bandol, as news of his condition circulated (and as he was now in a more fashionable part of the Côte d'Azur). H. G. Wells came. So did the Aga Khan, who had seen and admired his paintings in London. The sculptor Jo Davidson appeared and made, with Lawrence asking many practical questions about method, a clay bust of his head; it was nearly a death mask, a cadaverous triangle of bone and hair, with deep sunken eyes. Ida Rauh reappeared, and Laurence Pollinger from Curtis Brown in London.

Two weeks was all Lawrence could take. He wanted to get out of the institution and move into a house. Frieda and Barby scoured Vence, trying to find a landlord willing to accept a consumptive. Finally, with the sanatorium's consent, they rented the Villa Robermond and engaged a local doctor, a Corsican, to attend Lawrence, as well as an English nurse from Nice to live in.

At this point the Huxleys arrived from London, where the play of *Point Counter Point* had just opened. With the Brewsters absent, they took charge. They helped Frieda through the necessary arrangements while at the same time disapproving of everything she did and said. They despaired of teaching her the rudiments of sickroom hygiene, such as giving Lawrence his own cup. Maria, inspecting the Villa Robermond, felt that Frieda had made a mess of the kitchen in only one day, so she scrubbed it until it met her own high standard.

On Saturday, March 1, Lawrence was ready to leave Ad Astra. For the first time in his life, he let Frieda help him put on his shoes. She guided him into a taxi and sent Ada a telegram saying that newspaper reports of Lawrence's condition were exaggerated. At the new villa, he settled into bed and asked once more for hers to be brought into his room so that he could see her from where he lay.

The next morning he read a book about Christopher Columbus. Barby brought him in his lunch and he ate it. After lunch he felt hot and asked for a thermometer. Frieda began to cry. "Don't cry," he said. By the afternoon when the Huxleys arrived, he was delirious and having hallucinations that he was out of his body. "Look at *him* there in the bed!" he commanded Maria. Then, conscious again, he grabbed her wrists and said, "Maria, don't let me die."

By evening his head hurt and he asked for morphine. At nine o'clock, while Aldous and Barby were out fetching the Corsican doctor, the superintendent from the sanatorium came and gave him an injection. Maria and Frieda stayed at the bedside. Beginning to breathe more regularly, he said, "Now I feel better." At ten o'clock he died. It was a Sunday—eighteen years, perhaps to the day, since he had walked into Frieda Weekley's parlor. He was forty-four years old and weighed about eighty-five pounds. His review of the Gill book lay unfinished.

But enough had been written to make the review publishable. In it he had gone beyond his initial attack to say why the book had moved him. Far from being religious, certainly far from being a Roman Catholic like Gill, he nonetheless wholeheartedly agreed with Gill's statement that a man was free when what he "likes to do is to please God." Lawrence gave his own interpretation:

> "To please God" in this sense only means happily doing one's best at the job in hand, and being livingly absorbed in an activity which makes one in touch with—with the heart of all things; call it God. It is a state which any man or woman achieves when busy and concentrated on a job which calls forth real skill and attention, or devotion.

The last thing he wrote, it would do for an epitaph.

21

IN HER OWN RIGHT

—————

"*If England ever produced a perfect rose he was it.*" Frieda swung into high gear as widow, sending fulsome letters in all directions. To E. M. Forster, recipient of the foregoing, she continued:

> He has left me his love without a grudge . . . and that from that other side, that I did not know before his death, he gives me his strength and his love for life—Don't feel sorry for me, it would be wrong—I am so rich. What woman has had what I have had? now I have my grief—It's other people I pity, I can tell you, who never knew the glamour and wonder of things.

To Mabel in Taos she wrote:

> I think he stands firm on his feet; on his beautiful light feet for all eternity. I have got him so forever, I *don't* grieve; I do think how he managed his own body & soul, that frail body so marvelously how he never swelled any bigger than from his toes to his head; nor his soul

swelled, it was just himself; a new thing on the earth forever. How generous he was really & how patient with us all & specially with me.

To Witter Bynner, her dear friend Hal, she wrote of Lawrence in the present tense, with an apparent reference to her long sexual deprivation: "And now his bones are in the earth and he has become of the elements again. . . . And my pride is that I saw him right through, and you know it was diabolically hard at times. In every way you know!"

The young American Brewster Ghiselin was one of those to receive, in addition to the effusion ("You do understand, he gave me most of my *life* and now he gave me death—that great other I knew nothing about—now I know"), some hint of her plans: "I want to bring him to the ranch, with a red Indian funeral and make it a lovely place for him."

THE news of Lawrence's death, carried around the world on March 4 by American and British wire services, came as a shock to friends who had grown accustomed to reports of him nearly dying. Even Kot, the most attentive of Lawrence's correspondents, had written to him only the previous week asking why he never mentioned his health. Monty Weekley spoke for many when he said in a loving letter of sympathy to his mother that Lawrence had pulled through so often that no one had been in serious doubt that he would do so again.

Ada was stunned. On the morning of Monday, March 3, a postcard had arrived in Derbyshire from Lawrence saying he was about the same, "anyhow no worse"; then at noon a telegram came informing her that her brother was dead and would be buried the following day. There was no chance that she and Emily could even get to the funeral. Bitterly, Ada poured her heart out to Kot: "To think that I, who meant so much to him [in] years gone by was not there at the end. . . . My brother to me was never the famous author & artist but just the kind, gentle brother who looked after & cared for me right from the time he took me by the hand to school. And he never let me down." Ada felt that she had been duped into postponing her visit until it was too late.

In Taos the news was greeted with mixed feelings. "It is hard to realize we shall never see him again," Rachel Hawk of Del Monte Ranch wrote Mabel, "but it is comforting to know that our nerves shall not be put on the ragged edge as we all more or less expected."

Only ten people attended the funeral, including the Huxleys, Barby, and Achsah Brewster. Frieda wore the scarlet and gold dress of which, when she bought it, Lawrence had said, "If you were a year or two younger, it would suit you better." There were no prayers. For the grave in the cemetery at Vence, Frieda commissioned a pillar studded with red, black, and white pebbles in the shape of a phoenix.

The tone of the English obituaries hurt Lawrence's staunch admirers. Catherine Carswell was offended at the portrait of a morose and thwarted man; the Lawrence she had known was intensely amusing, never sentimental, and clever at everything. Rhys Davies was angry that the critics who had hounded Lawrence in life were virtually dancing on his grave. Forster, his old animosity long faded, was now a great admirer of Lawrence's work, particularly of *The Plumed Serpent;* he wrote to *The Nation and Athenaeum* to declare sorrowfully that "no one who alienates both Mrs. Grundy and Aspatia can hope for a good obituary Press."

To a later age, accustomed to the antagonism that Lawrence's name arouses, the death notices, taken overall, do not seem disparaging or hostile. While the conservative London *Daily Telegraph* used the occasion for a leading article condemning Lawrence's influence, the equally conservative *Daily Mail* said merely that his work had lacked reticence but that it had intense virility and gusto. In Boston, where the notorious Watch and Ward Society held sway, the respected *Evening Transcript* praised Lawrence's "introspective wisdom" and "vivid pictorial appeal."

The consensus was one of flawed greatness and an early promise less than fulfilled. *The Times* of London, under the headline "D. H. Lawrence, A Writer of Genius," commented that some of his writings were among the best in English literature but regretted that "fascinated and horrified by physical passion, he paraded his disgust and fear in the trappings of a showy masculinity." The *Manchester Guardian* was generous: "Gifted with extraordinary powers of sensuous divination, few writers have so intimately realized in words the electric force in the form and movements of animal life or the burning beauty of nature's colours." The *Glasgow Herald* recognized Lawrence as one of the half-dozen greatest novelists of the age, and declared his tragedy to have been shrinking from "contact with different sides of himself."

Some of the critical assessments offered in the spring of 1930 anticipated the view of Lawrence that would emerge at the end of his century. In *Life and Letters* Dilys Powell predicted that Lawrence's importance as a writer of narrative and descriptive prose would outstrip his value as a moralist, while Harriet Monroe in *Poetry* judged Lawrence "a poet of uncertain inspiration, and a careless and casual technician," but an unparalleled letter-writer: "Of all our numerous correspondents, famous and obscure, none has ever sent us letters more interesting, more revealing, than his."

English obituaries emphasized Lawrence's humble origins as a Nottinghamshire miner's son and scholarship boy, and several remarked that he owed his career to a certain woman. But the woman was not Frieda.

In an autobiographical sketch published in the *Sunday Dispatch* as

"Myself Revealed" in 1928, Lawrence had paid a graceful and quiet tribute, without naming her, to Jessie Chambers, whom he described as the "chief friend" of his youth. Drawing on this essay, the *Daily Mail,* under "Early Fame Owed to a Girl," retold the story of the girl who had copied out his poems and sent them to the *English Review*—launching him, as Lawrence had written, "like a princess cutting a thread." The *Mail*'s obituary concluded curtly that he had a German wife.

The short shrift given Frieda raises the question: Was his marriage to a von Richthofen, spanning the bitter years from 1914 to 1930, Lawrence's greatest offense against English society?

FRIEDA was stranded in Vence with more worries than she could handle. Her daughter Barby was distraught to the point of hysteria over Lawrence's death, and physically ill as well, with what doctors diagnosed as possible tuberculosis of the bone. And Lawrence had left no will. Simply to begin to deal with his affairs, Frieda had to join with the relative Lawrence liked least—his brother, George, to whom he had not spoken for years after a row about Frieda—in an application to the probate court in London for letters of administration. Her own legal position was all too clear. As the widow of an intestate, all she could claim was a payment of a thousand pounds, his furniture and personal belongings, and the interest from his estate for the rest of her life. After her death everything would pass to Lawrence's next of kin: his brother and two sisters.

At first Frieda thought she would have enough to live on from the sale of manuscripts and paintings, plus the royalties from *Lady Chatterley.* As the book was beyond the pale of English law, she thought its earnings could come direct to her. But very soon she was informed that her rights over any of these assets were uncertain, and that the checks arriving from Edward Titus in Paris from *Chatterley* sales had to be paid into the estate's account. She began to think that she might have to rely on friends in Taos to donate enough money to bring her and the body back to the ranch.

Not surprisingly, she began looking for protectors. When from Florence Pino Orioli cabled, "Coraggio," saying that "Norman and I want you to come here," she hesitated, but when a telegram arrived from Capitano Angelo Ravagli, sending condolences on the loss of "carissimo Lawrence" and inviting her to accept his family's hospitality, she went, within the month.

By now she and her lover knew each other very well. True to her matriarchal principles, she was on good terms with his wife, Ina-Serafina, as well, and was godmother to their youngest son, born the previous September and named Federico in her honor.

At the end of March, back at the Villa Bernarda in Spotorno where she and Lawrence had lived in the months between November 1925 and April 1926, she shared the house with her godchild and an old nurse, wrote her tear-stained replies to the letters of condolence, and enjoyed the consolation of Ravagli, home on a month's furlough. (Ravagli's wife was as usual conveniently in Savona, where she taught in a secondary school.) As Frieda wrote a woman friend in Vence, the *capitano* was so—her favorite adjective—"*real*," so lacking in any "high falute," and so genuinely concerned for her welfare that she could see that she was going to be all right.

Indeed she was. In March 1930, then and there, they made their plans: Ravagli would take a six-month leave from the army and they would go to the ranch together. She returned to Vence; then, leaving the distressed Barby alone in the Villa Robermond, went off to London to try to clarify her situation.

WITHOUT Lawrence to control her, Frieda flailed about wildly in all directions. She fell into a terrible row with Caresse Crosby in Paris over the manuscript and watercolor illustrations of Lawrence's story "Sun." When she wrote to Caresse asking for their return, Caresse sent back the watercolors with a warm, friendly note explaining that she did not have the manuscript because Lawrence had given it to Harry, who had taken it with him to New York on his fatal journey in November; it had not been seen since his suicide. All the same, she would be happy for the Black Sun to bring out any of Lawrence's unpublished work that Frieda chose to send her.

Back came one of Frieda's hymns of hate. She denied that Lawrence had ever given the manuscript to Harry and suggested that Caresse was just a hard-faced businesswoman up to "the usual tricks." Caresse could forget about printing another word of Lawrence's unless the missing manuscript were returned immediately. She signed herself "Yours in disgust."

Clearly Frieda needed literary as well as financial guidance. Lawrence's many publishers—Orioli, Titus, Secker—were vying for the many manuscripts, such as *Apocalypse* and *The Virgin and the Gipsy*, ready to be turned into print. Then there were Lawrence's letters.

But even with these there was rivalry. At Frieda's urging, Aldous Huxley, still reeling from the impact of the death of the man who, he wrote to a friend, was "the most extraordinary and impressive human being I have ever known," immediately began to prepare a collection. He rejected the suggestion of "Tom" Eliot of Faber and Faber that he write a book on Lawrence the poet. Declining any payment for himself, he spent the next months shuttling between the south of France, Paris, and

London, gathering letters from Lawrence's correspondents as far back as Helen Corke and Arthur McLeod in Croydon. Kot helped by gathering together Lawrence's Hampstead circle—Catherine Carswell, Barbara Low, David Garnett, Mark Gertler, and the Eders—to discuss the project. Edward Garnett sent a request, readily granted, that the more personal passages in the letters be suppressed in the interests of Lawrence's own scruples and the protection of privacy of persons still living.

An initial obstacle immediately appeared. With Lawrence's death, many of his friends realized they were biographers. Mabel above all saw that her hoard of letters from Lawrence was the nucleus of a book; her *Lorenzo in Taos* was already well under way, and she refused to cooperate with Aldous. Ada withheld her letters, too, for her memoir, *Young Lorenzo,* to be published by Orioli in 1931. Surprisingly, even Kot was among the holdouts; he kept back his more than three hundred letters although, almost unique among Lawrence's circle, he had no biographical ambitions. (Antagonism to Frieda seems to have been behind his noncooperation.) The collection was thus weakened at the start, for Lawrence had written more letters to this loyal, reclusive Russian bachelor than to anyone else—a measure of the strength of their curious friendship.

Another difficulty was that Aldous could scarcely begin to tap the vast range of Lawrence's correspondents. In consequence, in spite of a splendid and enduring portrait of Lawrence by Aldous as its introduction, *The Letters of D. H. Lawrence,* published in 1932, was hardly representative. With the foreign and familial sides of Lawrence's life underrepresented, and with his rude language decorously deleted, the book was tilted heavily in an impersonal and literary direction.

While Aldous was at work, Murry thought he might be of assistance to the widow. He traveled to Vence at the end of April, and in no time at all found himself in her bed. Frieda later claimed that what happened was a seduction (although such an experienced woman could not lightly claim to have been taken unawares). As she described the event for Mabel: "In his so beautiful voice he read me that 'Rainbow' and then the worst happened! There really is something *perverse* in him!"

Murry's perversity, other commentators have since observed, lay in leaving a mortally ill wife and two small children in England in order to attend to Frieda's needs in France. His second wife, Violet, died of consumption the following March. But for Murry the trip to the South of France had been worth it. Whatever had passed between him and Frieda in 1923 and so infuriated Lawrence, it was nothing to the consummation in Vence in 1930. "With her, and with her for the first time in my life," Murry confided to his journal many years later, "I knew what fulfilment in love really meant." Much nearer the event, just after his wife's death and also after the publication of his own biography of Lawrence, *Son of Woman*, Murry thanked Frieda:

> You see, Frieda, you were to me a way of love about which I knew nothing. . . . I don't loathe the religious in sex. And why I don't loathe it really is *because of you*. You don't know what you did for me in Vence a year ago: in a very certain sense you recreated me, and I became a new man. I revere you for it. You gave me back myself.

Murry was fumbling for the accolade Otto Gross gave Frieda during their affair in 1907: "all my powers have been revitalized through you." One can only imagine, if the embraces of Frieda, stout and fifty, had so impressed the twice-married and sexually sophisticated Murry, what effect she must have had in her prime on the inexperienced and frustrated young Lawrence.

But Murry gave Frieda something in return: the key to securing Lawrence's estate for herself. He reminded her that Lawrence had made a will during the war, when they had all lived near each other in Buckinghamshire. "If this will turned up, all would be mine," she explained to Titus and began sending frantic telegrams to Brett to see if by any chance a will might have been among the papers left in Taos.

News of the sexual congress in Vence swiftly traveled along the Lawrence circuit, from Hampstead to Taos. It made Kot dislike Frieda all the more, while Aldous feared that Murry was using the affair as a means of insinuating himself as Frieda's literary adviser. Even the Lawrence relatives in the Midlands heard about it (probably through Kot, who was close to Ada). They were dour people but not naïve, and George Lawrence, who felt that Frieda had turned his brother into a pornographer, commented sourly that she was "knocking around with half a dozen."

FRIEDA'S more immediate problem was Barby. The young woman had been (so Frieda believed) half in love with Lawrence herself. In the late summer of 1930 she suffered a complete mental breakdown. Frieda has often been blamed; the apparent ease with which she forgot Lawrence, it has been suggested, reawakened the anguish of abandonment Barby suffered as a child when her mother one day disappeared.

Undoubtedly, the spectacle of Frieda's assignation with Ravagli, followed by a fling with Murry so soon after Lawrence's death, was shattering. Of the three Weekley children, Barby had been the most resistant to Weekley family propaganda against Frieda and the most diligent in restoring ties with her mother once she was an independent adult. In contrast, her sister, Elsa (now Mrs. Bernal Seaman), was exceedingly pro-Weekley and intolerant of what their brother Monty called "the whole business"—the Lawrence connection. Yet suddenly Barby was confronted by evidence that the Weekley charge of Frieda's sexual irresponsibility might be true. What is more, like many children of broken homes, she cherished the wild idea that her parents might someday get back together again, and urged her mother to go back to Ernest.

Nonetheless, Barby's breakdown at Vence in 1930 was so complete and her symptoms so grave, that the causes cannot lightly be ascribed to immediate events. She had been severely depressed well before Lawrence's death, as he had noted with alarm. Her symptoms were uncontrollable; she tore off her clothes, threw objects at Frieda and her nurse, crawled about on the floor like an infant, and made advances to visitors. Frieda told Mabel that she even attacked her brother when, with Elsa, he came out to Vence to see what could be done.

Frieda thought she could bear no more that year. She was proud of Barby's beauty, wit, and talent, grateful for the repayment of years of maternal grief and longing. She had intended Barby to come with her to the ranch that autumn. Yet the breakdown, whatever its origins, revealed the extent to which Frieda was prepared to put her erotic faith into practice. Confronted with Barby's apparent libidinous frenzy, an old local doctor prescribed an ingenious remedy—sexual relations—and Frieda readily agreed. (His words, as Frieda relayed them to Mabel, were "Il lui faut un mâle, madame.") Frieda therefore hired a young Italian workman, Nicola, a servant in the employ of the Villa Robermond's caretaker, to share Barby's bed.

Decades later, Barby insisted that the unorthodox therapy had done her no harm. Nicola, as she understood it, had been engaged as a kind of male nurse, to feed her, wash her, dress her; sex was simply part of the total care administered. Frieda's sisters, however, thought otherwise. When they learned what had happened—in November at Baden-Baden, at their mother's funeral (the old *Baronin* having managed to outlive Lawrence, as he knew she would)—they were horrified that Frieda could have allowed such an experiment on her own daughter. By winter, however, Barby had been escorted by Monty and Elsa back to England where, looked after by an uncle and aunt in Kent, she fully recovered.

LAWRENCE'S first biographers were professional writers, and they worked fast. First off the mark was Mabel, who in the spring of 1930 sent Frieda a rough draft of *Lorenzo in Taos*. Frieda was appalled. Mabel had emphasized the comic elements of their life in Taos at the expense of the spiritual, and made it seem as if they all had been playing a giant game of charades. Angrily Frieda wrote back: "No Mabel, we were all *more* than that! I know we were! It is unfair to any of us to put only our sicknesses down & meannessess & not much else—It all had more meaning & affection & tenderness—" She begged Mabel to write it all again, telling how the Indians had changed them all into a deeper awareness of their connection with the earth and to show that without Mabel's invitation to Taos, Lawrence could never have written *Lady Chatterley* or *Apocalypse,* nor could he have died so bravely. She wished Mabel had portrayed their marital quarrels as caused by something other than her own jealousy. She had not been jealous. She had allowed, even begged him, "to choose any other woman he liked better than me."

Before Mabel's book was published, Murry got his own biography out. Published, by Cape, on April 15, 1931, *Son of Woman* infuriated many of Lawrence's friends, particularly Aldous, Kot, and Catherine Carswell. It called attention, albeit in polite and guarded terms, to Lawrence's impotence and anal proclivities. Huxley called the book "vindictive hagiography," "slimy," and "the slug's-eye view of poor L," without acknowledging that he knew that Murry had been to bed with Frieda and undoubtedly had precise details of Lawrence's deficiencies as a lover. Frieda, too, wrote angrily to Murry, and she ceremonially burned the book—even though she intended to rely on him to pursue her court claim on Lawrence's estate.

Ada, assisted by a collaborator, brought out *Young Lorenzo* in 1931, only to be greeted by Lawrence's old fiancée Louie Burrows emerging from the shadows of the past, threatening to sue for what she considered an unflattering portrait of herself. Catherine Carswell's *The Savage Pilgrimage,* far more flattering to Lawrence, appeared in June 1932, in spite of a threatened injunction from Murry, who did not like the way he was portrayed. Earl and Achsah Brewster offended no one with their informative and friendly *D. H. Lawrence: Reminiscences and Correspondence* in 1934. But Mabel's book, which emerged from Knopf in 1932, also gave offense to the inner circle, by enforcing the reputation of Lawrence the wife-beater.

A copy of *Lorenzo in Taos* reached Lawrence's former worshipper Ivy Low, the Eders' niece, now married to the Soviet diplomat Max Litvinov and living in Moscow. Mabel's tortured fascination with Lawrence made Ivy rethink her own painful virginal passion in Fiascherino in 1914. The London friend (apparently the writer Naomi Mitchison) who had sent her the book maintained that it showed Mabel to be a cold-blooded voluptuary who was trying to take Lawrence away from Frieda. Ivy disagreed: from her own experience, she declared, any sort of voluptuary would have had a lean time with Lawrence:

> I never really wanted him. . . . Not that I EVER believed in Lawrence as a fucker. If he made Frieda black and blue, as Mabel says in her book, I'm convinced it was the only violence he ever committed against any woman. . . . I dare say Frieda was the only woman with whom he

could be potent and that was probably the true inwardness of his life-long tie with that utterly unbearable, false, honey-sweet woman.

But Frieda got her own back. She had always taken herself seriously as a writer and her moving autobiography, *Not I, but the Wind . . . ,* published in 1934, if cavalier with hard fact, is strong on emotional truth; it gives a vivid, well-written, and romantic account of her life with Lawrence as she—and perhaps occasionally he—saw it. Because she liked to write, she understood, and performed well, the role for which she had been preparing since she first saw Lawrence: explaining his work. Introducing the authorized abridged edition of *Lady Chatterley's Lover,* for example, she declared extravagantly, "I feel that even in this revised form it has all the beauty of the original edition." (Secker published the expurgated novel in 1932, and soon orders were pouring in by the thousands.)

In June 1931, Frieda, accompanied by Ravagli, made her long-awaited reentry into New Mexico. Mabel, needless to say, was riveted by the spectacle. There were melodramatic quarrels, as with Lawrence. Frieda still threw plates and forks, especially when Ravagli insisted on proclaiming Mussolini the greatest man who ever lived. But he, sensible and engaging, with an officer's bearing, bossed Frieda about with a success that Lawrence would have envied.

Mabel avidly relayed all the details to her friend Una Jeffers in Carmel, California. "She talks of him [Lawrence] all the time & weeps & then laughs, & is all rosy & wrinkled & fuzzy haired & moist—with bright green pinpoints of light in her mad little eyes with their chiffoné eyelids."

Frieda, as portrayed by Mabel, was totally unapologetic about having arrived with someone else's husband in tow: "It's such a *vonerful* country—where you arrive with a man & nobody says a *vord* (!!!) but I couldn't come *alone! I* am the kind of *voman* who must *have* a man!"

Mabel had met Una's husband, Robinson Jeffers, a messianic poet and an admirer of Lawrence's, in 1930, and taken him up as Lawrence's heir; *Lorenzo in Taos* was dedicated to him. The Jefferses lived in a stone tower in Carmel, an artists' colony on the Monterey coast south of San Francisco. Una, according to Lois Rudnick's biography, *Mabel Dodge Luhan: New Woman, New Worlds,* saw herself, like Frieda, holding her marriage as a sacred trust, a work of art continually in the making. Thus she relished all the information (including even copies of Frieda's letters) that Mabel passed on to her.

For Ravagli, there was the shock of seeing the famous ranch for the first time. A shack with no electricity or running water was not an Italian's view of America, and for Ravagli isolation held no virtue. How-

ever, the breathtaking view over the desert, distant gorge, and mountains soon worked its magic and within a few days he had the place
swept up and repairs begun.

Then and for the years to come, Frieda was in constant danger of
losing her Angie to his family, to Italy, and to his beloved Duce. On that
first visit, even though she was short of funds, she immediately bought
Ravagli a car—Tony Luhan's La Salle—and she reported to Martha
Crotch, a good friend in Vence, how happy they were together. "We
have been fond of each other for years," she wrote Mrs. Crotch (known
as Auntie) in July 1931, "and that an old bird like me, is still capable of
real passion and can inspire it too, seems a miracle." They were getting
too fond of each other, she said; there were the wife and children to
consider. But in the meantime they were in paradise.

One evening the Taos crowd was summoned up to Kiowa, where a
transformation awaited them: long tables with wonderful food under
the trees, a dance floor cleared on the hard earth, a gramophone to
provide the music, Frieda looking like a Valkyrie squaw with blond hair
flying and a white buckskin dress, and over all a huge illuminated sign
proclaiming "Una Noce in Venezia." Ravagli, with his practical Italian
approach to the supernatural, had hung a pickle jar with a candle in it
over the symbol of a phoenix carved in Lawrence's big pine tree, and in
his white flannel trousers he gravely and tenderly guided the women, one
by one, through the latest dance steps. Mabel had to admit that her host
was an excellent dancer, and laughed to see Brett succumbing to the
Latin charm: "circling slowly in his arms with an intent look upon her
face."

But Brett was shocked. Even though she understood that Frieda was
at heart a timid woman, afraid of being alone, and that Ravagli was the
kind of man she should have had all along, Brett wrote in disgust, also
to Una Jeffers:

> That Lawrence got caught by her, was his great trajedy [*sic*] that he
> died rather than be disloyal to his early young passion was his ultimate
> folly, but from what she has told me, I just thank God he is out of pain
> and out of her clutches, the old strumpet. She has made these detours
> all her life, with her first husband and probably with Lawrence when
> she went to Germany or anywhere without him. So what is love? when
> a woman stands over a man with a club, and clubs everyone male or
> female, that comes within striking distance, and now weeps copiously,
> so she says, in the bushes for the same man dead, and sleeps joyously
> with the el Capitano at night, I keep on asking myself that question,
> what the hell is love?

The idyll could not continue unless the new couple resolved their
problems in Europe. Ravagli returned to his family and his regiment

while Frieda went back to London to battle for the estate. She needed it in full if she was to buy Ravagli out of the army. No money, no new life in New Mexico.

FOR a long while Ada sympathized with Frieda's claim. She wanted no money for herself and went out to Vence hoping that her sister-in-law would replace the lost Bert in her life. But Frieda dissipated this goodwill by sending Ada letter after letter insulting the Lawrence family and protesting that it was she who had made their brother a genius. As the case progressed, Ada changed sides, supported by Kot, who was disgusted at the spectacle of Lawrence's hard-earned money being spent on what he called Frieda's "future husbands." Aldous scoffed to a friend that "the stupid woman" was embarking on unnecessary and expensive legal proceedings. He said that he liked Frieda but she was in many ways impossible: "Her diplomatic methods consist in calling everyone a liar, a swine and a lousy swindler, and then in the next letter being charming—and then she's surprised that people don't succumb to the charm."

Distrustful and primitive Frieda undoubtedly was. Émile Delavenay, a distinguished French scholar and an early biographer of Lawrence who met her in London in the summer of 1932, judged that everything she said "required careful scrutiny" and that she would brazenly lie when her interest was at stake—denying her affair with Murry, for example, when she needed his testimony on Lawrence's will. E. M. Forster, who saw her soon after Lawrence's death, recoiled:

> She would rebuke me for disobeying the Message and then stop and watch me with a shy smile. Very proud of having no friends, equally so of her apparatus for collecting and compelling them. —And the tripe without the poetry was not attractive, and I retired unashamed into my academic tower. He and she haven't had a bad life, but it seems vulgar when they proclaim it as Ensample and a Mystery.

None of the English circle, Murry apart, seemed to believe that a widow deserved solid financial support. Aldous at least might have considered that Lawrence's legacy might more appropriately be lodged with Frieda, who had shared his life and traveled the world with him for eighteen years, than with his disliked brother George.

By the time the case came to court on November 3, 1932, Frieda had assumed fiendish proportions to the Lawrence family. They saw her as she sat there, in the words of George Lawrence's son William, "dressed up like a Guy Fawkes effigy—thick woollen stockings, heavy old boots, thick woollen skirts, smoking Woodbines." They construed her appearance as an act to convince the judge of her poverty if she did not get the entire estate and considered that her counteroffer to them—five hundred pounds each in exchange for surrender of the copyrights—was a derisory gift of their brother's money.

The legal action was a terrible experience for them. Emily would have accepted Frieda's offer merely to avoid the publicity. She was stung by the deposition made by Pino Orioli and Norman Douglas that Lawrence hated his family; did she not have her brother's loving letters and many gifts to prove to the contrary? However, the three Lawrence siblings went into court united, believing that they were being generous in promising Frieda a lifetime income from the estate, with all copyrights reverting to them after her death.

Frieda's position was outlined to her chief witness, Murry, by her solicitors, Field Roscoe & Co. of Lincoln's Inn. They appreciated that the existing arrangement—the entire estate passing to Lawrence's next of kin—was undoubtedly bitter for Mrs. Lawrence and that it was undoubtedly contrary to her late husband's intention. However, if no will could be found, the law assumed that the testator had destroyed it with the intention of revoking it and the court was obliged to proceed upon the basis of intestacy. The only hope was either to find the will or to produce independent evidence of its existence and its contents.

The independent witness duly appeared, although his independence might have been questioned had the court known that he had been the widow's lover. Murry duly swore in court that he and Lawrence together had made identical wills on November 9, 1914, leaving everything to their respective partners. Murry produced his own will in evidence. Frieda's evidence was submitted in a written statement which said that she had last seen the will in New Mexico; that he had raised the question of a new one just before she died and that, when she dissuaded him because he was so ill, he said that in any case all would go to her.

Frieda won, with the judgment delivered in words to warm her heart. The judge referred to Lawrence as a distinguished man and to the Lawrences as a devoted couple, *citoyens du monde*, who carried their papers around the globe. He accepted that the will had been lost in New Mexico and that Lawrence had intended his entire estate to go to his wife. He declared also that Frieda's offer of a gift of five hundred pounds to Lawrence's brother and sister was generous.

Ada refused to accept her share of the settlement. She wanted nothing.

In retrospect, Lawrence's failure to leave behind an up-to-date and accessible will shows an uncharacteristic carelessness with finances. In his failing last years, he may, like many people, have seen writing a will as a virtual invitation to death. Or he may have found it too painful, as one of his letters to Ada suggests, to be reminded once again of his lack of a child to be his heir. His thoughts, whatever they were, cannot have included a vision of what actually happened—that all of his money, including the eventual rich earnings of a legalized *Lady Chatterley*, would pass (minus agent's fees to Laurence Pollinger and the agency he founded) to the children of Frieda's first and third husbands.

YET Frieda was secure at last, and about to enter the happiest part of her life, a return to normalcy after the psychological turbulence of her relationship with Lawrence. She and Ravagli returned to the ranch in 1933 and he began building them a modern log house, with electricity and running water, lower down on Lobo Mountain. (The original Kiowa cabins were thereafter referred to as the upper ranch.) She agreed to pay him $120 a month (not a small sum, in the depths of the Great Depression), the payments to continue even when he was visiting his wife in Italy, and to leave him half her estate when she died.

But Ravagli worked hard for Frieda. He managed her business and tax affairs, as Lawrence had done, and capably adapted to the requirements of the Western outdoor life. Driving his La Salle, he was often in Taos, where he soon made friends. Aldous Huxley, when he and Maria came for the summer in 1937 on their way to Hollywood, found Ravagli to be an amiable, intelligent middle-class Italian. He looked carefully for signs that Ravagli was exploiting Frieda and found none.

That was not entirely true. Ravagli got a great deal of money out of Frieda. Their first winter he persuaded her to pay for a trip for them both to Buenos Aires to visit his brother and sister—a long and uninteresting journey for Frieda. While he danced with the girls on the boat, she sat in her cabin and wrote memoirs of her girlhood in Metz and Berlin, and upon arrival found his Argentinian relatives depressing.

Their departure from Taos had been traumatic. That summer Ravagli had persuaded her to lend an Italian friend from Taos, Nick Luciani, a thousand dollars to go to California and buy grapes, the loan to be repaid when the grapes were sold to Luciani's Italian customers. Ravagli went along to California to supervise the project, but disaster struck on the way back, when a truckload of the grapes overturned. When the expected profits from the venture did not materialize, Frieda sued Luciani to get her money back.

Luciani counterattacked with two lawsuits—one against Ravagli for false representation, and a second against Frieda for not returning the thousand dollars his wife had left in a purse at Frieda's house. The outcome, as reported in the Taos newspaper just before Christmas, 1933, was an "Italian Opera-Bouffe," with "Mrs D. H. Lawrence and Capitano Angelo Ravagli Arrested on Eve of Departure for South America." Frieda was exonerated when Mrs. Luciani, who had been working for her as a cook, agreed that she had left the purse with Frieda for safekeeping. Ravagli was released on bond, only to be faced with a fresh warrant for his arrest. He had to escape across the border to Colorado, and Frieda had to make her way there separately in order to join him for the drive to New Orleans to catch the boat.

FROM England, the Lawrence family noted bitterly that Frieda was getting a much bigger kick out of life than ever she got while Lawrence lived. It was true. In spite of Ravagli's escapades, Frieda was indeed enjoying her new life, getting up with the sun, making bread, feeding the horses, and growing vegetables. She cheerfully wore the dreadful clothes—the dirndls, checks, pinafores, and ankle socks—that pleased her. She and Ravagli wintered in California, where the Huxleys were now in permanent residence, Aldous having tapped riches as a screenwriter for Metro-Goldwyn-Mayer (and learning, over time, the joys of mescaline, which led to his book *The Doors of Perception*, forerunner of the drug culture of the sixties). Through the Huxleys, Frieda and Ravagli met the film world, notably Charlie Chaplin.

With their charm and the Lawrence connection, they made friends easily—the writer Dudley Nichols, author of many distinguished screenplays including *The Informer* and *Sister Kenny*, became a particularly good friend of Frieda's—and Ravagli used some of his time to study English at a high school at night. One winter was spent in Carmel, where their friends included Robinson and Una Jeffers, and Henry Miller. Una Jeffers was a close friend of Mabel's and Brett's as well, and acquired a remarkable collection of contradictory versions of certain events in Taos.

Toward Ravagli, as long as he did not desert her for Italy, Frieda was tolerance itself. She allowed him a very free rein in Taos. When he was on one of his visits to his family, she corresponded happily with his wife, Ina-Serafina, as if they were co-wives, with a mutual interest in their Angie's health, and in 1936 Ina-Serafina obligingly helped with the shipping of Lawrence's paintings from Vence to Taos. Ravagli often complained that Frieda was not giving him enough money, but she kept him in line, much as Lawrence had done to her, telling him that the life he demanded was costlier than he recognized. She tried hard to find him projects to compensate for the military career he had given up for her sake. Once she entertained the hope that they had found gold on the ranch (Frieda would need gold, Brett observed sourly, to hold Ravagli). While she wished he were a more assiduous farmer, she indulged his interest in pottery.

The material benefits to Ravagli notwithstanding, they were a highly compatible couple and remained together for a quarter of a century, during the last years of which they were husband and wife. It was certainly the happiest of Frieda's three marriages. Ravagli continued to flirt, but so did she. Mabel was astonished at Frieda's enduring ability to get a crush on any handsome male.

*   *   *

In March 1935, five years after his death, a small group gathered at the grave of D. H. Lawrence in Vence. One of them was the special corre-spondent of the London *Daily Express,* turned Lawrencian for the day: "The sun shone on the walled-in space where the body lay. The phoenix, made of pebbles, by the peasants, who were his friends, gleamed yel-low."

The occasion was the first step in removing Lawrence's body to New Mexico. It was, said the *Express*'s headline, "The Last Wish of D. H. Lawrence" to be buried on Kiowa Ranch in San Cristobal. "An Italian friend was sent here by Mrs. Lawrence to exhume the body." The ashes would be placed "in a little temple which has been built by Mrs. Law-rence, Indians, and others who loved her husband."

Ravagli was something more than an Italian friend; he had not loved D. H. Lawrence and there is no hint that Lawrence ever expressed any wish about his final resting place. That apart, it was true that Ravagli with his own hands had built a little concrete chapel on a slope above the ranch and, a nice touch, had stuck an agricultural wheel over the door to form a rustic rose window. Frieda loved it; it reminded her, she said, of the temple of Isis in *The Escaped Cock.* All that was missing was Lawrence's body, to enshrine in the tomb. She asked their good friend Earl Brewster, who was in France, to help organize the transport.

However, when Brewster, after consulting Thomas Cook's, told Frieda the cost of shipping a body across the Atlantic, she decided that ashes would do just as well. Brewster agreed to supervise the exhumation and cremation. Yet when she did not send the correct papers in time, Brew-ster had to inform Ravagli, who was on one of his periodic visits back to Italy, that he would have to go to Vence and handle it himself.

Ravagli did not enjoy his assignment. There was a morass of French and American bureaucracy to wade through for the necessary docu-ments. He wrote agonized letters to Auntie Crotch, Frieda's friend (who had held an exhibition of Lawrence's paintings in Vence and was keep-ing them in storage), complaining, in his broken English, that "the consulate generale don't want give me a answer" and had told him to wait a few days "when can bak from vacation the vice consulate."

Frieda was not having an easy time either. Ravagli had left her with Mabel in Taos, but when she contracted double pneumonia, she had to go to the hospital in Albuquerque for six weeks. She was convalescing with friends in Santa Fe, however, by the time Ravagli and the ashes were on the *Conte de Savoia,* sailing from Marseilles to New York.

Nothing more marks Lawrence as a latter-day Jesus than the uncertain fate of his ashes, carried across an ocean and a continent, and fought over as if they were relics of the True Cross. Trouble began in New York when U.S. Customs hesitated to admit a funerary urn containing human remains as part of the baggage of a tourist. (Ravagli, like Lawrence, kept reentering the United States on a short-term visitor's visa.) Alfred Stieglitz had to intercede with the customs authorities before Ravagli, with his precious burden, finally boarded the train for the Southwest.

When the train arrived at Lamy, New Mexico (still the nearest rail stop to Santa Fe), Frieda and friends were waiting on the platform to greet Ravagli after his six-month absence. Not until they were all nearly back at Santa Fe did they realize (so the farcical Taos legend goes) that the urn had been left behind at the station; they had to turn around and drive back to retrieve it. (A variant of the tale had Bynner accidentally overturning the urn at a dinner in Santa Fe and refilling it with ash from the fireplace.) The next festive stop was in Taos, where they enjoyed an alcoholic tea party at the studio of Nicolai Fechin, a Russian émigré portraitist and landscape artist. Once again (according to Ravagli) the ashes got left behind and had to be retrieved a day or so later.

The plot thickened with the arrival of Frieda's daughter Barby, with her new husband, Stuart Barr, a journalist with Reuters. Barby had recovered from her breakdown but she was still a highly excitable woman, and prone to suspicion, for which there was ample ground in Ravagli's relationship to her mother. The rumor in Taos, Brett reported to Una Jeffers on September 14, 1935, was that Barby and Stuart had come expressly to break up "the Angelino ménage." In any event, it seems to have been Barby who picked up, and conveyed to Frieda, the terrible news that Brett and Mabel were planning to steal the ashes and scatter them over the desert.

Some such plan seems to have existed. While Brett always insisted that she was not a party to it, Mabel never denied it. Certainly Mabel never denied her belief that Lawrence's ashes would have been more appropriately scattered to the desert winds than enshrined in a gimcrack chapel which she dubbed "the Angelino temple." The fear in the Taos colony was that Ravagli wanted to turn "the shrine" into a tourist attraction and charge admission; alarm intensified when the local paper carried a public invitation from Frieda for everybody to come to the dedication ceremony, at which a Mexican mariachi band would play.

Mabel and Tony (still solidly married, as they would remain for the rest of their days) talked a local judge out of presiding over the ceremony. They tried to get the Indians to boycott it as well, but a few turned up regardless and performed a ritual dance around a bonfire in front of the chapel at sunset. Frieda was satisfied.

She had settled any possibility of theft. As Ravagli was mixing the concrete for the slab that would become the altar of the chapel, she emptied the ashes into the mix, congratulating herself on victory over Mabel at last. Also using Una Jeffers in Carmel as a confidante, she declared:

When I remember how I had stood in front of Lawrence's narrow grave and thought Here lies the only thing that really ever was mine, he gave himself body & soul—And this "my friends" wanted to steal from me. . . . Now I get over it . . . I wish you had been at the ceremony, it was simple & beautiful.

The unforgiving Brett sent quite a different version of the whole affair to Una:

Has Mabel told you the story of the ashes? Lord how ironical Lawrence must feel . . . you know I have always the feeling that the dead are not not nearly so dead as we think. . . . To be the adoring widow of a great man . . . how easy that is . . . to be the wife of a great man . . . how difficult . . . and there you have the whole problem . . . but even then an adoring widow might at least realize that ashes need respect . . . remembrance . . . tenderness . . . that a tea-table and a tea-party is hardly respectful and forgetting them altogether in a house of a friend . . . in fact "leaving them behind" is hardly tender . . . bunk . . . Una . . . just the bunk . . . and is a Mausoleum looking like a station toilet a fitting resting place for a man so Pan-like as Lawrence . . . [?]

The ashes, in any event, were at rest—if they *were* Lawrence's ashes. Something had gone very wrong in New York, according to Stieglitz. He wrote to Brett that, after having helped Ravagli with the customs red tape, he found the ashes in their urn standing outside the door of his art gallery in the Shelton Hotel. "I left [*sic*] them go their natural way," he said delphically. "Someday I'll tell you the story. Nothing like it has ever happened. Angelo really has no idea of what did happen."

Or perhaps Ravagli did. In 1956, after Frieda's death, drinking bourbon in Taos with a Belgian relative of Maria Huxley's and about to return to Italy, Ravagli confessed that Lawrence's ashes had never left France. Fearing that very large customs duties would be levied on the import of human remains, he said he had scattered the ashes in Vence and crossed the Atlantic with an empty urn, which was then refilled with a convenient substitute in New York.

If true, it would explain the irreverence with which Frieda and Ravagli kept giggling over, and losing, the sacred dust.

This ambiguity of resting place gave rise to the sense that Lawrence was nowhere and everywhere. Fifteen years later even Penguin Books did not seem to know where he was buried. In March 1950, bringing out ten of Lawrence's less well-known books (including *Kangaroo, The Lost Girl,* and *Etruscan Places*) to mark the twentieth anniversary of his death, Penguin described him as resting in "the little cemetery of Vence, perched above the Mediterranean, his grave . . . marked by a phoenix carved upon a simple stone."

IN time the row about the ashes was just a minor tremor in the long friendship of Frieda, Brett, and Mabel. A classic photograph on the steps of Kiowa Ranch shows them beaming happily: Mabel in her headband, Brett in cowboy dress, and Frieda in a gaudy, floppy housedress, managing to laugh and smoke a cigarette at the same time. They were to grow old as friends and neighbors, three of the mega-women of northern New Mexico, a formidable group that included the painter Georgia O'Keeffe, Stieglitz's wife and Brett's friend, who had moved to Taos for the desert colors and the big sky, and Millicent Rodgers, the collector of Indian art. The Millicent Rodgers Museum is now, like the Lawrence ranch (the property of the University of New Mexico), one of the tourist attractions of the area, a welcome human haven in an overpowering landscape.

DURING the first half of their life in New Mexico, Frieda and Ravagli had far more serious brushes with the law. At the end of 1935, Bynner pleaded with Mabel to stop being silly and—for the sake of all who loved Frieda and the ranch—to use her influence in Washington to get Ravagli a place in the Italian immigration quota so that he would not have to keep traveling in and out of the country. (Mabel did have friends in high places; as a supporter of the New Deal, she was an active member of Writers and Artists of Taos for Roosevelt.)

In 1939, however, the FBI came to call. Ravagli was threatened with deportation, accused of being a kept man in an illicit relationship as well as of another offense of unspecified moral turpitude. Frieda was indignant. It was obvious, she said, that their own relationship was intimate and by conventional standards immoral, but suggestions that Ravagli had done anything else wrong were ridiculous; he just liked to have a good time. The threat blew over, thanks to the intervention of Roosevelt's secretary of labor, Frances Perkins.

The couple suffered fresh anxiety when the United States entered World War II and they became enemy aliens. Earlier in the decade, Frieda had been an admirer of Hitler; among her papers is an untitled statement in defense of *Mein Kampf,* which says in part:

> People are slow in coming along—A few year's ago a man called Hitler wrote a book—People said it was badly written, said it was boring. Others said it was crazy and insignificant.
>
> But for all that it has been effective in its ideology. It gave masses of people a new impetus. The book was not badly written—It said what it wanted to say quite clearly.

She also had kept among her mementos a postcard sent by her sister Else in 1934 showing a smiling picture of "Our Beloved Führer." But by 1939 Frieda was utterly appalled by Hitler, and was so upset by stories of storm troopers and the concentration camps that she wrote Monty that she felt "like turning into one of those awful propaganda women to help save what can be saved of decency in the world." Frieda and Ravagli's apprehension ended not long after Pearl Harbor when they received a reassuring letter—Mabel's political influence once again?—from another member of the Roosevelt cabinet, Attorney General Francis Biddle.

But their names remained in federal files. In July 1944 an inspector from the FBI's El Paso office came to question Frieda about a possible violation of the White Slave Traffic Act, also known as the Mann Act. An anonymous woman informant in New York had complained to the New York Society for the Suppression of Vice that her daughter had engaged in "debaucheries of sex while visiting with Frieda Lawrence and others in New Mexico." The society had passed the information on to the FBI.

The El Paso FBI office already had the artists' colony at Taos in its black books for having a bad reputation "for immorals." Its agents would not have had to look far for evidence of Frieda's indifference to standards that J. Edgar Hoover's America held dear. She often had Bynner and his lover, Robert Curtis, to stay at the ranch, and she was forever receiving odd Lawrence disciples who wandered in. One young man insisted—as Brett relayed to Una Jeffers—on coming to the table wearing not so much as a fig leaf. Nothing bothered Frieda.

The FBI's dossier on Frieda was reminiscent of that in England in the First World War. It contained allegations that she might be a German spy and listed her name as "Frieda Lawrence, with alias Freiin Von Richthofen." The files further suggested that a book called *"The Letters of D. H. Lawrence, 1909–1915* by Robert Graves" might possibly be a code book. Also, that Frieda had been interned during World War I; also, that she was a sister of the famous flying ace. Moreover, that her late husband, D. H. Lawrence, had made considerable trouble for the El Paso immigration authorities after they had tried to keep him from crossing from Mexico into the United States at El Paso in 1925. To its credit, the FBI discarded all the errors, rumor, and misinformation. The result of its investigation was that "the subject" had a good reputation in Taos, that she had not violated federal law, and that the case should be closed.

The following year, however, when Frieda got around to applying for naturalization as an American citizen, her petition dragged on for two years, at the end of which she was told that she would have to appear at a public hearing at the Taos courthouse to be questioned "as to your past and present behavior." "Certain witnesses," the Justice Department wrote her ominously, would be introduced; she would have the right to be represented by an attorney. On January 14, 1947, her lawyer informed the U.S. Immigration Service that his client was withdrawing her petition for citizenship.

The hide-and-seek with puritanical American officialdom ended in 1950. Upon the presentation of a certificate swearing to Ina-Serafina Ravagli's consent to a formal dissolution of her marriage, the Taos County Court granted Ravagli a divorce in August; in the same courthouse two months later, he and Frieda were married. (Neither the divorce nor the remarriage was recognized under Italian law.) Frieda had anyway been using the name Ravagli on her renewed British passport. She never applied for American citizenship again, saying she was too old to bother.

FRIEDA had done the right thing in recognizing Taos as her natural habitat. She became one of its great sights, with her clear, laughing eyes, wide smile, and saffron-rinsed hair. As Georgia O'Keeffe described her for Stieglitz, who never came out to New Mexico:

> I can remember very clearly the first time I saw her, standing in a doorway there, with her hair all frizzy, wearing a cheap red calico dress that looked as if she'd wiped the frying pan with it. She was not thin and not young, but there was something wonderful about her. . . . She was very beautiful. Oh, Frieda would come into this house with that huge voice of hers. "Georgia!" Her voice would fill the house. She stayed top of the heap. I really liked her.

She became an object of pilgrimage for the faithful and the famous. Leopold Stokowski, Leonard Bernstein, and Tennessee Williams were among those who found her on her mountain. People must really want to see her, she joked to her son, to come up that rotten road. Williams first sought her out in 1938, describing himself as a young writer who had a profound admiration for her late husband and whose life had been very much like his: "nomadic, restless, uncertain." On a later visit to Taos, the playwright had suddenly been taken to the Taos hospital (Mabel's gift to the community) for abdominal surgery; when he was recovered, Frieda picked him up, determined that he should see the ranch. Driving the car (he said) "like a firetruck," she sped him up into the mountains, where he collapsed from the altitude, and she had to drive him straight back to the hospital.

Over the years she became a perceptive commentator on Lawrence's work. In *Not I, but the Wind . . .*, she saw that, like many preachers, he had been blind to the force that was driving him—not the joy of sex but man's fear of woman. "In his heart of hearts I think he always dreaded women, felt that they were in the end more powerful than men."

She wrote many illuminating letters. Lawrence and Murry, she said, had had no sexual affair, but neither did Lawrence "disbelieve in homosexuality." She worked on a number of essays and fragments of a fictionalized autobiography, which were eventually compiled and edited by her good friend E. W. Tedlock of the University of New Mexico.

Frieda willingly shared the biographical facts of her life with academics, as long as they were Lawrence enthusiasts:

Dear Professor Fay,
Your facts are mostly right. . . . Many young people have come and told me how reading Lawrence has completely changed their lives. They would not say that when reading Somerset Maugham. . . . Lawrence was trying to find a new way of life. . . .
   In our old age Mabel Brett & I are friends. Our fights are over. I always liked Mabel better than Lawrence did. I was never jealous of either of them but they thought I was. I had no reason to be. Brett came too close to Lawrence's and my life together But I was jealous of Lawrence's sister Ada and Lady Ottoline. Of course I cannot be as detached from all this as an outsider can be, this was and is my life.
Good wishes, Frieda Lawrence.

With gusto, she fought the good fight. Any detractor of Lawrence's had to duck for cover. In 1939, when William Y. Tindall, a Columbia University professor and a Joycean, wrote a witty, scholarly book, *D. H. Lawrence and Susan His Cow,* accusing Lawrence of animism, fascism, and sloppy thinking, she sent him a personal letter: "Was not the purpose of your book to show that Lawrence was a fool and you much too smart to swallow him. . . . I am old and alone now but the glow of his world makes one feel rich, richer than ever your wife will be with all your cleverness."

She tangled too with Bennett Cerf, the humorist and president of Random House, who had written a comic piece about visiting the Villa Mirenda in 1929 and finding it full of rotting food and flies. Frieda retorted that she understood that Mr. Cerf was a collector and writer of jokes. However, his article was bad and inaccurate. In 1929 she and Lawrence were living in Bandol, not Florence, and she could not recall their ever meeting him. She concluded with a "Pah!" and one of her uncomplimentary closings:

Please take my sincere *contempt.*
To my friends I am "Frieda" but to your kind
   I am
                                                    Mrs D H Lawrence

She scolded the eminent Cambridge University scholar F. R. Leavis for over-Englishing Lawrence. From *The Rainbow* on, she explained to Leavis (who had made a personal crusade of championing Lawrence's greatness), "Lawrence is no longer a British writer, but a universal one." Ursula Brangwen's childhood was her own, she explained, and the relationship of Ursula to Tom Brangwen hers with her father.

Frieda was probably unaware that Leavis, who identified with Lawrence as a fellow victim of the English literary establishment as represented by T. S. Eliot and the *Times Literary Supplement,* called his wife Queenie because Lawrence had referred to Frieda as the Queen Bee, or that the Leavises felt it proper to indulge in spectacular public arguments with each other because the battling Lawrences had done the same. (The Leavises called their fights "creative quarreling.") She died too soon to know that the poets Sylvia Plath and Ted Hughes, who met at Cambridge in the early 1950s, named their first child Frieda in her honor. She died too soon, also, to know that the young English writer Alfred Alvarez, who had spent a summer at the ranch and was much under the influence of Lawrence and Leavis, was later to marry her beautiful granddaughter, Ursula Barr, because he saw her as the reincarnation of "her marvellous, scandalous grandmother." (In his book *Life After Marriage*, Alvarez recounts how he even prepared the breakfast the first morning of his marriage and tidied the house because he wanted to be just like Lawrence.)

AFTER the war Frieda and Ravagli bought a house near Galveston, at Port Isabel, Texas, the most southerly point in the United States. There they lived peacefully during the winters, watching wrestling on television, receiving European visitors such as Frieda's sister Nusch and Ida Wilhelmly, her children's old German nurse, exploring southern Texas, and enjoying the fish the fishermen brought them straight out of the water. Back in New Mexico they spent less time at the ranch and more at their new house, a more modern one, at El Prado on flat land much nearer Taos. There Frieda got up early and watered the flowers, then, with her pack of Lucky Strikes, went back to bed to read Dickens and George Eliot, emerging to condemn them as Lawrence would have done: "I *loathe* that Little Dorrit!" She exchanged frequent visits with her chosen neighbor—none other than Brett. By 1945 Frieda and Brett were such friends that when Frieda bought the El Prado property, she had more land than she needed and gave some to Brett so that she could build her own house and studio and live an independent life.

*   *   *

AFTER the war more relatives came out to New Mexico to visit Frieda: Else's son, Friedel (who had immigrated to the United States); and Monty Weekley and Barby, who came several times. Monty and Barby were much amused by the way their mother used their father's expressions; she would dismiss something she did not like as "a lot of my-eye," or complain of people who gave her "nothing but lip." Frieda had come to England as a bride, and it was Ernest Weekley, not Lawrence, who shaped her idiom.

Much in demand among American Lawrence-lovers, she said she did not want to spread herself around as "Mrs. D. H. Lawrence" and refused to preside over a tea. Yet she enjoyed speaking out. At a panel discussion on Lawrence at the University of California at Los Angeles in 1952, she listened while Aldous Huxley tried to explain Lawrence's brutal jibe to Katherine Mansfield about stewing in her consumption. Lawrence, Huxley said, was really speaking about himself, and complaining that Katherine was complaining. Lawrence, Aldous said, didn't complain, "but he did react—."

Frieda broke in: "Ja, he did react, worse than complaining."

NOT until June 1952—that is, after she was legally Mrs. Angelo Ravagli—did Frieda dare to leave the United States and travel to England. Her good friends the Igor Stravinskys saw her off in New York. In England she met Murry, happy at last, with the woman who was to become his fourth wife; she had lunch with the Bernard Shaws. Quizzed by Shaw about the truth of the story that she had broken a plate over Lawrence's head, she replied that it was true: "Lawrence had said to me women had no souls and couldn't love. So I broke a plate over his head."

The visit gave her the opportunity to see her five grandchildren, one of whom, a pupil at St. Paul's, told her, "Oh, they know all about Lawrence and you at the school!" Elsa's husband, Teddy Seaman, drove Frieda slowly past their house in Putney in South London but did not invite her inside. Ernest Weekley, then eighty-seven, was living there and the family felt that he could not have stood the shock of seeing his ex-wife.*

Weekley had retired from the University of Nottingham in 1938, having commuted there from London for more than two decades to escape the scandal, which rumbled on. Such was the respect for him at the university that until he left there was hardly a work by Lawrence in the library, and Lawrence's name was spoken only sotto voce. The obituaries upon Weekley's death in 1954 mentioned his distinguished

---

* An unsubstantiated statement in Harry T. Moore's biographies of Lawrence, *The Priest of Love* and *The Intelligent Heart,* says that upon Lawrence's death Weekley had asked Frieda if she would marry him again.

record as an etymologist and his many publications but tactfully omitted any reference to his marriage. However, his family, clearing out his desk drawer, found a photograph of a straw-hatted Weekley gazing tenderly at a demure Frieda in her bonnet, seated under a tree in the Black Forest in the summer of their courtship.

In her last years Frieda enjoyed a long and sentimental correspondence with Murry in which they went over and over their love affair and what it would have meant to Lawrence if they had gone off together in 1923. "It drove me crazy—really crazy, I think—wanting you so badly," Murry wrote her. Had she loved him as much as he had loved her?

She dodged, but asked "Do you remember the sweet names he called me? '——— ———' was the one I hated most." (She did not specify the words; however, Aldington's comment that Lawrence frequently called her a shit-bag suggests what they may have been.)

It had been her destiny, she believed, to see Lawrence through to the bitter end. She told her old lover candidly, "I believe my deepest feeling for L. was a profound compassion. He wanted so much that he could never have with his intensity. I felt so terribly sorry for him or I could never have stood it all."

Frieda suffered a stroke at her home outside Taos on August 8, 1956, thereby missing Bynner's seventy-fifth birthday party the following day. She had already inscribed his present, a copy of *Bay*, Lawrence's book of pems, thanking Hal for being a good friend even though she often had given him cause to scold her. She died three days later, on her own (seventy-seventh) birthday. Ravagli wrote his stepchildren a moving account of the last hours of "my beloved Frieda."

Ravagli swiftly prepared his return to Italy. He left behind the large collection of Lawrence's paintings which had been shipped from Vence to Taos, lodging them with Saki Karavas, the proprietor of the Fonda del Taos Hotel, where they remain. He resumed life with his Italian wife, his American divorce and remarriage not having been recognized in Italy, and lived to see the value of his half of Frieda's estate soar after the *Lady Chatterley* trial released the book into mass circulation. As Ravagli and Saki Karavas joked to each other, Lawrence never knew whom he was working for.

Ravagli organized a fine funeral. Frieda lay in state at the Hanlon Funeral Home in Taos, wearing a new dress she had made out of gray and pink silk Ravagli had brought her from Italy, and her favorite little yellow velvet shoes; she held, at his suggestion, a straw hat trimmed with the same material. The funeral cortège then wound and bumped up the long dirt road to Kiowa Ranch. Fifteen honorary pallbearers followed as the casket was carried up the steep hillside to Angelino's memorial temple. They included three men who had welcomed Frieda on the day she first arrived with Lawrence in Santa Fe in September 1923: Witter Bynner, Spud Johnson, and Tony Luhan.

The service consisted of two readings. A young writer, another to whom Frieda had given a piece of land, read the Lawrence poem "Song of a Man Who Has Come Through," from which she had taken the title of her autobiography, which expresses her belief in the impersonality of the self: "Not I, not I, but the wind that blows through me." Then, thanks probably to Ravagli's flair with gadgetry, Frieda's own deep voice boomed out, reciting Psalm 121, "I will lift up mine eyes unto the hills . . ." She was buried in a grave just in front of the temple with its relics—Lawrence's old hat, jacket, and typewriter—and the visitors' book with names from all over the world.

But she had not uttered her last word. In her will, Frieda had requested that after her death an advertisement be placed in the Taos newspaper *El Crepuscolo,* thanking all her friends for their friendship. She signed it with the full name by which she wished to be remembered: Frieda Emma Johanna Maria Lawrence Ravagli. In an editorial entitled "Frieda," Spud Johnson, the paper's editor, praised the joy and vitality she had brought to Taos.

It was a bravura farewell, her own answer to Lawrence's veiled plea in *The Plumed Serpent,* "Say you'll never feel disappointed!"

As the widow of D. H. Lawrence—his widow for longer than she was his wife—Frieda was never disappointed. As full of contradictions as he ever was, in their life together she had been able to enlarge and enrich his vision of female sexuality even though her own pattern of erotic expression was anarchic, devilish, and very far from the norm. Settled down after his death into a shallower, but more comfortable relationship with a man as easygoing as herself, she was able to devote a quarter of a century to preaching Lawrence's message and building his legend. If someone had told her that she was one of the shapers of the twentieth century—the transmitter of the erotic philosophy of Otto Gross, through the agency of Lawrence and *Lady Chatterley,* to a generation ready to believe that all you need is love—she would have thought it no more than she deserved.

She had already said as much herself—and given credit to the never-forgotten lover of her Munich years. Shortly before her death she wrote that the fundamental influence in her life had been "a great friend, a young Austrian doctor who had been a pupil of Freud's." "Lawrence," she claimed proudly, "through this friend and through me had almost direct contact with these then new ideas."

She never tired of defending herself. Declarations had issued from her for years—from those hurled at Forster and Russell, to those aimed at the writers and critics who pursued her after Lawrence's death. "You belittle *him* if you think I was just a passionate female to him and rather dumb," she told Edward Gilbert, an English critic and friend of Murry's who tried to interpret Lawrence's philosophy to her. She sneered to Una Jeffers, after the American publication of Jessie Chambers's anonymous autobiography (*D. H. Lawrence: A Personal Record*), that if Lawrence had married Jessie, he would have never amounted to more than "a little local poet, a watered down Thomas Hardy." And Brett, of course, had been receiving Frieda's rabbit punches for years: "Lawrence would have been & written differently if he had lived with another woman . . . why *should'nt* we have quarrelled? We were'nt Buddhas with crossed legs"; "I kept him alive—I am not ashamed of how I was—not I! . . . I shall come into my own too along with him, nothing will stop it, Brett."

Frieda's most impassioned self-defense was reserved for Kot, her greatest detractor. When, in 1932, he once again reminded her that she was self-important and unworthy of Lawrence, she retorted with an address to posterity:

> His life and his writing was one—and I say to everybody who wants to have *anything* to do with him or me: hats off to our relationship! Bring off the same if you can!

A BIBLIOGRAPHICAL NOTE

ON JOYCE'S "THE DEAD" AND
LAWRENCE'S "THE SHADOW IN THE ROSE GARDEN"

THE MANUSCRIPT of "The Vicar's Garden," from which Lawrence later wrote "The Shadow in the Rose Garden," is now at the Humanities Research Center of the University of Texas at Austin; the typescript is at the Bancroft Library of the University of California, Berkeley. It was probably written in 1908, and was based, Jessie Chambers believed, on a visit to a garden when they were on holiday at Robin Hood's Bay in August 1907. Professor Keith Cushman of the University of North Carolina, Greensboro, has called "The Vicar's Garden" a much slighter piece than its successor, with a plot that barely seems to exist.

There is no evidence of exactly when Lawrence transformed the sketch into the story. The most likely time, as volume ii of the Cambridge University Press edition of Lawrence's letters acknowledges, was the summer of 1913, when Lawrence was in England, writing in great haste so as to leave a collection of stories behind before he returned to the Continent. (John Worthen, in his introduction to the Cambridge University Press edition of *The Prussian Officer and Other Stories,* allows the possibility that Lawrence made the revisions in August 1911, when he is known to have reworked some unidentified stories and sent them to Austin Harrison of the *English Review.*) However, "The Shadow in the Rose Garden" was definitely typed for the first time in the summer of 1913, and not until December 21, 1913, did Lawrence first mention it by name. He wrote Edward Garnett from Italy in December to say that he had received a check for ten pounds "for a very short story called 'Shadow in a Rose Garden,' which I think you never saw." A week later he asked Garnett to send Ezra Pound a sovereign as commission for selling this story and "The Christening" to *Smart Set. Smart Set* published the story in March 1914.

If the unpublished "The Dead" was a source that influenced Lawrence in his remaking of "The Shadow in the Rose Garden," he would most likely have read it while he was in England in the summer of 1913, between June 19 and August 7. If the revising occurred at the earlier date, in August 1911, Lawrence would have to have come across "The Dead" between the autumn of 1909 (when, still teaching in Croydon, he first entered the London literary world) and August 1911. Although the later period is more probable, both are possible, for the Joyce text was in London for many years and seen by many people.

The manuscript of *Dubliners* reached London long before Lawrence did. Joyce, teaching in Trieste, first sent his collection of short stories to Grant Richards in London in October 1905. Richards did not reply until Joyce had written again but in February 1906 enthusiastically accepted it for publication. However, his printers balked, out of fear of the laws holding them responsible for any obscene material set in type. Richards accordingly began demanding the omission of certain phrases and of one story entirely. By October 1906 the contract was abandoned by mutual consent and the manuscript returned to Trieste. In the meantime, in 1907 Joyce wrote "The Dead" and added it to the collection, which he then sent to several other London publishers, including Elkin Mathews, John Long, and Hutchinson.

In January 1908 Mathews's reader, Major Dermot Freyer, rejected *Dubliners*. Two of the stories, Freyer said, were almost obscene; for the rest, most of the characters were overfond of drink and physically repulsive. But he conceded that "the last 20 pages of 'The Dead' finds the author at his best."

By late 1909, desperate for a publisher, Joyce went to Dublin and persuaded the Irish firm of Maunsel & Company to take it over. Maunsel agreed, and went so far as to have *Dubliners* set in type and printed in galley and page proofs. But more delays ensued, for similar reasons. Maunsel and its printers feared the book's insults to royalty, offenses to "public decency," and libels of the Dublin public houses and business establishments whose real names Joyce had used. In the summer of 1912, after Joyce traveled again to Dublin to try to get the book out, Maunsel took fright, with a vengeance. It destroyed the whole edition of one thousand copies of *Dubliners* and broke up the type. Joyce, embittered and enraged, left Ireland for good, taking his own author's proof copy with him back to Trieste.

It was with these salvaged proof sheets that Joyce, by post from Trieste, renewed his assault on the London publishing world. In December 1912, he sent the Maunsel sheets to Martin Secker, the publisher who since June 2, 1911, had been pressing Lawrence for a book of stories. At the same time, Joyce wrote and asked Yeats to intervene, but to no avail. Secker rejected the book.

Joyce kept up his campaign. In March 1913 he tried Elkin Mathews once again, this time sending the printed pages and offering to defray any expense himself. He further said that if Mathews definitely declined his offer, the company should hand the book on to another publisher (John Long again) who might be interested.

It is not clear, because so few of Joyce's letters of this period have survived, where these printed sheets (and possibly also the original manuscript of *Dubliners*) were in London between Easter and November 1913—the period encompassing Lawrence's return visit to England and his intensive reworking of "The Shadow in the Rose Garden." The conjunction of Lawrence's eye and Joyce's pages must remain speculative. However, in a letter written to England on October 6, 1913, Joyce describes himself as still waiting for news of his book; this suggests that it was still in London. Michael Howard, historian of the London publishing firm of Jonathan Cape, estimates that some twenty-two publishers in all had seen and rejected *Dubliners* before, in late November 1913, Grant Richards, responding to another plea from Joyce, offered to look at the book again, and then agreed to bring it out the following year.

There is a reasonable possibility that the well-connected Edward Garnett was one of those who had a look at the Maunsel sheets in 1913, and that Lawrence, accordingly, had the opportunity to read them. The possibility lies in an unpublished reader's report that Garnett wrote for Duckworth in the autumn of 1914, rejecting *A Portrait of the Artist as a Young Man*. This report, which can be seen in the Berg Collection at the New York Public Library, reveals that Garnett had read *Dubliners*. That in itself would not be surprising, as by then the book had been out for a few months, under Grant Richards's imprint. Yet Garnett curiously refers to Joyce's publisher as Maunsel. This error indicates that he saw Joyce's pages the previous year. His letter says:

> Joyce published some very clever stories, (with Maunsel) in the summer, but the book was probably not successful, as the stories were rather "realistic" studies of unprepossessing types. . . . In the MS. now submitted, he gives us reminiscences of his schooldays, of his family life in Dublin and of his adolescence. . . . But the style is too discursive and his point of view will be called "a little sordid." . . . Decline with thanks.

Garnett did not like complex or intellectual writers. He wrote a more formal (and now famous) letter of rejection, which Duckworth sent to J. B. Pinker, who by late 1914 was the London literary agent for both Joyce and Lawrence. *A Portrait of the Artist as a Young Man*, he declared,

> wants going through carefully from start to finish. . . . Unless the author will use restraint and proportion he will not gain readers. His pen and his thoughts seem to have run away with him sometimes. . . .
> And at the end of the book there is a complete falling to bits. . . . This MS. wants time and trouble spent on it, to make it a more finished piece of work, to shape it more carefully as the product of the craftsmanship, mind and imagination of an artist.

It is worth recording also that there exists a letter, written to Garnett by his wife, Constance, which reads: "Herewith I post the Joyce book—which I found at once this morning on looking for it." Unfortunately, her letter, at Eton College Library, is undated. Her grandson and biographer, Richard Garnett, estimates the date as 1910 and points out that the letter could refer to a different Joyce. Yet it could also mean that Garnett saw *Dubliners* at an earlier stage of his acquaintance with Lawrence.

Postulating that Lawrence saw "The Dead" in published form the following year before he made his further revisions to "The Shadow in the Rose Garden" is easier. *Dubliners* was published in London on June 15, 1914, to good reviews—rave reviews, in the case of the *New Statesman* and *Everyman*. That summer saw Lawrence back in England once again, and again under great pressure of time. He and Frieda then expected to leave England soon and return to Italy in September. Duckworth was eager to publish a book of his short stories. On July 2, Lawrence accordingly requested his typist, Douglas Clayton, to send him some of his old manuscripts "as soon as you can: I must get this stuff ready for a volume." And while visiting the Cearne from July 4 to July 7, 1914, he decided to make the book mainly a collection of previously published work. He then set to work in a great hurry, sending the first batch of rewritten stories to Duckworth on Thursday, July 9, and the remainder by the following Tuesday.

There is little question that his quick work in 1914 deepened the story's tragic value. However, as is noted in chapter 7, page 171, one effect of the alterations was to remove some of the similarities to "The Dead."

To be sure, Joyce was not shy of borrowing either. According to his biographer Richard Ellmann, he had taken the ending of "The Dead" from George Moore's novel *Vain Fortune*, published in 1895. That story, too, captures the moment of alienation of a husband and wife in a hotel bedroom. There is an inquisition about the past and the shock of learning of the death of a past lover.

The Moore novel's concluding scene takes place in a hotel room on the wedding night of a writer and a young widow. She interrogates him about his past, and together they discuss whether or not the young actress (Emily) whom he has jilted might commit suicide. Suddenly they discover a letter lying on the mantelpiece; it informs them that Emily has killed herself. The rest of the wedding night is thereupon spent in a discussion of their mutual grief and guilt. The wife (Julia) then falls asleep in an armchair, and the husband's interior monologue takes over. His wife seems to him

very beautiful as she slept, her face turned a little on one side, and again he asked himself if he loved her. Then, going to the window, he drew the curtains softly, so as not to awaken her; and as he stood watching a thin discoloured day breaking over the roofs, it again seemed to him that Emily's suicide was the better part. "Those who do not perform their task in life are never happy." The words drilled themselves into his brain with relentless insistency. He felt a terrible emptiness within him which he could not fill. He looked at his wife and quailed a little at the thought that had suddenly come upon him. She was something like himself—that was why he had married her. We are attracted by what is like ourselves. Emily's passion might have stirred him. Now he would have to settle down to live with Julia, and their similar natures would grow more and more like one another. Then, turning on his thoughts, he dismissed them. They were the morbid feverish fancies of an exceptional, of a terrible night. He opened the window quietly so as not to awaken his wife. And in the melancholy greyness of the dawn he looked down into the street and wondered what the end would be. He did not think he would live long. . . . He would hang on for another few years, no doubt; during that time he must try to make his wife happy.

Moore's plot is far less intense and more conventional. It concerns a man's guilt, not a woman's, and there is none of the anger and jealousy between husband and wife that fuel both the Lawrence and the Joyce stories. Moore's story also lacks the powerful sensory trigger which, in both later works, releases the wife's memories of her buried past. In Joyce it is music; in Lawrence it is the scent of flowers. In any event, if George Moore recognized any trace of his novel in "The Dead," he did not say so when in 1915 he wrote Edward Marsh that while some of the stories in Joyce's *Dubliners* were trivial and disagreeable, "the book contains one story, the longest in the book and the last story, which seemed to me perfection whilst I read it."

NOTES AND SOURCES

---

*R*eferences to the text are indicated by the last words in the relevant text or by key words preceding.

I have made certain abbreviations in referring to frequently cited books, publications, libraries, and people. University libraries and special collections are denoted by the name of the university unless otherwise abbreviated. Further information on the location of specific collections appears in the acknowledgments. Unverified or speculative information is contained in brackets; uncertain dates are indicated by [?]. "No date" is indicated by [n.d.]. I have indicated the location of cited unpublished work.

Most works are cited by their author's surname; if necessary, a shortened form of the title follows. The volumes in Cambridge University Press's edition of *The Letters of D. H. Lawrence* are indicated by a roman numeral followed by the page number: thus "iv. 237" is page 237 of the fourth volume. The three volumes of Edward Nehls's *D. H. Lawrence: A Composite Biography* are cited as "N" plus roman numeral followed by page number and preceded by the name of the contributor. Thus, "Neville N i. 153" indicates George Neville's comments on page 153 of the first volume of the Nehls series.

Full references to books and major academic papers will be found in the bibliography.

Biographies and collections of letters, apart from Frieda Lawrence's letters and memoirs, are referred to by author or editor, not by subject. Thus, "Furbank" refers to P. N. Furbank's *Selected Letters of E. M. Forster.*

I have not put in page references to Lawrence's novels or poems identified by title, or to short stories appearing in *The Collected Tales of D. H. Lawrence.*

ABBREVIATIONS:

Ada: Ada Lawrence Clarke
AH: Aldous Huxley
Berkeley: Bancroft Library, University of California at Berkeley
BL: British Library
Brett: *Lawrence and Brett* by Dorothy Brett.
Cincinnati: University of Cincinnati Library
CP: Collected Poems
DB: Dorothy Brett; initials are used when she is a correspondent. References to her book, *Lawrence and Brett,* are listed as Brett.
DHLR: D. H. Lawrence Review
EG: Edward Garnett
EJ: Else Jaffe
ET: *D. H. Lawrence: A Personal Record,* by "E.T." (Jessie Chambers)
EW: Ernest Weekley
FG: Frieda Gross
FL: Frieda Lawrence. Her autobiography, *Not I, but the Wind . . . ,* is cited as *Not I.*
FLC: First Lady Chatterley
Harvard: Houghton Library, Harvard
IH: The Intelligent Heart, by Harry T. Moore
JC: Jessie Chambers
JMM: John Middleton Murry
KM: Katherine Mansfield
Kraft: *Selected Letters of Witter Bynner,* ed. Joseph Kraft
Kot: S. S. Koteliansky
LCL: Lady Chatterley's Lover
Luhan: *Lorenzo in Taos,* by Mabel Dodge Luhan. Page references are to the 1932 Knopf edition.
MDL: Mabel Dodge Luhan
Memoirs: Frieda Lawrence: The Memoirs and the Correspondence, ed. E. W. Tedlock. Page references are to the second (New York) edition, published by Knopf in 1964.
MG: Mark Gertler
MM: Maurice Magnus
MM: Memoir of Maurice Magnus, by D. H. Lawrence, ed. K. Cushman. Incorporates MM's *Memoirs of the Foreign Legion,* including the passages excised before publication by Martin Secker.
Moore and Montague: *Frieda Lawrence and Her Circle: Letters from, to and about Frieda Lawrence,* ed. Harry T. Moore and Dale B. Montague
N: Edward Nehls, *A Composite Biography of D. H. Lawrence.* This work's three volumes are cited as N i., N ii., and N iii.

NCL: Nottingham County Library
ND: Norman Douglas
Not I: Not I, but the Wind . . . , by Frieda Lawrence.
NW: Northwestern University
NYPL: Berg Collection, New York Public Library
RA: Richard Aldington
P: D. H. Lawrence Phoenix: The Posthumous Papers
PII: Phoenix II: Uncollected, Unpublished, and Other Prose Works
P/U: Psychology and the Unconscious
SL: Selected Letters
SIU: Southern Illinois University
Texas: Harry C. Ransom Humanities Research Center, University of Texas at
   Austin
TLS: Times Literary Supplement
Turner: "The Otto Gross–Frieda Weekley Correspondence," *DHLR* 22:2 (Sum-
   mer 1990)
UJ: Una Jeffers
UNM: University of New Mexico
W: John Worthen, *D. H. Lawrence: The Early Years*
WB: Harold Witter Bynner
Yale: Beinecke Library, Yale

NOTES

INTRODUCTION

9   "But Why": Ben Ray Redman, "But Why, Mr. Lawrence?" *New York Herald Tribune Books,* March 8, 1925
9   loathsome rascal: ibid.
10   "written worse": Noel Annan, "Mission Impossible!" *New York Review of Books,* January 17, 1991, 15
10   "as I've got any": ii. 191
12   "monogamous marriage": "Lawrence in Love," Diana Trilling, *New York Times Book Review,* December 16, 1984, 24–25
12   more on *Kangaroo:* "The Sanity of Lawrence," Philip Larkin, *TLS,* June 13, 1960, 671
14   "scrupulous meanness": Joyce, *Letters* ii., 134; Hulme, "Romanticism and Classicism," *Speculations* 126
15   terror that she would leave him: W, chapter 15, "1912 Abroad"

PROLOGUE: BORN AGAIN AGAIN

For a detailed account of Lawrence's childhood, see W.

21   "Sunnybrae": Croydon directory, 1911; i. 115
21   South Croydon line: letter from Croydon Local Studies Library, July 18, 1991; also visits to 12 and 16 Colworth Road
22   "not for any money": i. 268
22   pneumonia and feverish inflammation: County of London death certif-icate 280, Lewisham sub-district, for William Ernest Lawrence, October 11, 1901, gives causes of death as erysipelas, pneumonia, and pleuritis.
22   by his bed: Neville 63

22   Jehovah Junior: Hopkin N i. 76
22   "colours always three shades brighter": Neville 77
23   disoriented: "Foreword to Collected Poems," in *D. H. Lawrence: The Complete Poems,* 851
23   "No one understands but you": i. 243
23   led her to school: Ada to Kot, March 5, 1930 (BL)
23   "Xmas here with us": Ada to Louie Burrows, Tuesday, November 28, 1911, quoted in part in W 322 and i. 328–29, n. 1 (NCL)
24   "venturesome": i. 329
24   "be all right": i. 328
24   six feet away: visit to 16 Colworth Road
24   pack up and go: Delavenay ii. 656

CHAPTER 1: NEW AGE, OLD ADAM

25   three hundred trains: M. W. G. Skinner, *Croydon's Railways.* Southhampton, England: Kingfisher Railway Productions, 1985
25   "can I want?": i. 86
26   nearly tenfold: Census figures show Croydon's population rising from 16,712 in 1841 to 153,885 in 1901.
26   "a smart, quiet quarter": i. 82
26   at home: i. 78
26   "folks here": i. 83
26   "it is wonderful": i. 90
26   "England of the future": A. Conan Doyle, "The Naval Treaty," in *Memoirs of Sherlock Holmes*
26   "solid and good": i. 83
27   "some admiration": M. D. Eder, "Good Breeding or Eugenics—XII," *New Age,* July 18, 1908, 227
27   "missis best": i. 83
27   helpless with laughter: Among the many accounts of Lawrence as mimic are Patmore 80, Tomlinson 28–29, and Purnell Stone N ii. 267.
28   "*faithfully* from life": i. 68 (re Alice Hall)
28   "laugh at me so brightly": i. 97
28   homesickness: i. 82
28   letters of application: i. 54
29   London polish: May Chambers Holbrook N iii. 611
29   colored pencil: Charles Leeming, David Gerard taped interviews (hereinafter "Gerard interview," NCL)
29   "herd of pigs": i. 85
29   punishment book: i. 84
29   "fury against me" . . . "discipline weaves": "Discipline," CP 929 (an early draft). These lines do not appear in the revised version of "Discipline," CP 92–93.
29   "true-born poet": *Schoolteacher,* Draper 32–33
30   "incalculable and uncontrollable": Dr. J. D. Chambers N i. 48–49
30   social superior: i. 43; W 191
30   "as I am here": i. 88
30   on the mouth: i. 99
30   Alice Dax: For her background, see i. 43 n. 2 and Hilton.
30   guidance in growing up: i. 54; i. 45
30   enslaved to a woman: i. 56
31   "after I saw her": i. 59
31   "soon be better": i. 62

31   woodshed: "Vivid Reflection of the Young DHL," *Daily Telegraph,* September 20, 1960. The letters must have disturbed Blanche Jennings's peace of mind. She was never to marry, and remained with the post office until she retired in 1941 with the rank of assistant supervisor. She not only treasured Lawrence's letters but kept his photograph on her mantelpiece all her life.

31   "like this to you": i. 65

31   "my buttocks prance": "Virgin Youth," CP 40

31   "lusty souls of my boys": "Discipline," CP 928

32   "blow the whistle": i. 385

32   a can of the polish: i. 332

32   "From me to the boys": from "The Best of School," CP 51

32   "not a joke": i. 78

32   undistinguished record: W 86

32   the uniforms: W 83

33   high in the profession: W 115–17; Neville N i. 45

33   did know botany: W 186–87

33   long walks together: George Lawrence, Gerard interview (NCL)

34   "life we call God": i. 256

34   on the move: i. 57–58

34   slid from him: i. 78

35   their human masters . . . struggle for food: See Milton.

35   traps for their natures . . . "animal instinct": Milton 72, 94

36   "and I need": Howe 7

36   "inexpressible": i. 127

36   "end of the volume": i. 103

36   "consumptive. Bah": ibid.

36   "result of the change": i. 106

37   "because we are children": i. 107

37   loved literature: Corke, *Infancy* 122, 188

37   "original of my George": i. 65, n. 2

37   "defer to me also": i. 65

37   notorious: Carey, "Revolted by the Masses," *TLS,* January 12–18, 1990; also Carey, *The Intellectuals and the Masses*

37   "halt and the maimed" . . . " 'Hallelujah Chorus' ": i. 81

38   runt of the litter: See Carey, *Intellectuals,* and M. D. Eder, *New Age* thirteen-part series on eugenics, May 9–July 25, 1908

38   unwanted child: Neville 65

38   shop failed: W 33

38   two maids W 17 and 39

38   machine-made lace: W 14

39   touchstone of truth: See Price, 242–52; 322–33

39   "be near": ibid.

39   "on up to bed": Alice Hall Holditch, Gerard interview (NCL)

40   in jail: W 45–46

40   sharp drop: W 45–47

40   chances of survival: "Birth Spacing and Child Survival" by D. Maine and R. McNamara (Center for Population and Family Health, New York: Columbia University Center for Population and Family Health, 1985), drawing on the World Fertility Survey, says that children born either at the start or the end of a birth interval of less than two years are about 50 percent more likely than other children to die at ages one through four.

40   hit their mother again: "Discord in Childhood," CP 36

41   "sick monkey": George Lawrence, Gerard interview (NCL)

41   "I don't know": Ada N i. 17
41   bootlaces: ibid.
41   "instruction in art": *Kipps* (Harmondsworth, England: Penguin, 1946), 54.
42   "rather not have said": "Foreword to Collected Poems," CP 849
42   "hesitate to say so": i. 38, n. 2; 40
42   "We'll collaborate, shall we?": i. 130
42   "most folks can stand": i. 79
42   "what does it matter?": i. 142
43   "en famille": i. 253
43   "faintly horrifying": i. 298
43   "a bag of mud": Neville, 51
43   "better at it": Delavenay ii. 656
43   "crumbs off the doorstep": i. 207
43   "Miserere Domine": i. 300
44   "No one else seemed to": Delavenay ii. 656
44   "sinner that she is": i. 253
44   "larking about": i. 257; also i. 138, i. 248
44   "body of my Hilda Mary": i. 99
44   wasted with the children: i. 248
44   sexual drive in childhood: Gay 147
44   walked out without a word: Hobman 8
44   "graceful in his energy": This and subsequent quotes are from "The Old Adam," in *The Mortal Coil and Other Stories*. First published in *A Modern Lover* (London: Secker, 1934).

CHAPTER 2: IN WANT OF A WIFE

46   "repent at leisure": Congreve, *The Old Bachelor,* act 5, scene 8.
46   births out of wedlock: In 1910 there were 36,675 illegitimate births in England and Wales, 5 percent of the total births (Office of Population Census and Surveys, *Birth Statistics 1837–1983, Historical Series,* London: Her Majesty's Stationery Office, 1987). See also Lawrence's story "The Christening."
46   at the age of twelve: W 53
46   sitting on his mother's lap: memo of conversation with Professor M. M. Lewis of the University of Nottingham, April 17, 1963 (Texas)
47   "mard-arse": W 78 and N i. 33
47   try to straighten it up: William Lawrence, Gerard interview (NCL)
47   to get the insects: Neville 40
47   casually discussed at Haggs Farm: ibid. 72–73
47   "not true!": Neville 82
47   fought them off: ibid. 90
48   young male passenger: See Ruderman 116
48   "not wool": Mabel Thurley Collishaw, N i. 29
48   considered them engaged: W 159
48   possessive about their Bert: ET 51
48   heavy, clumsy gait: Ada N i. 51
48   not the right wife: Ada to Louie Burrows, February 22, 1913 (University of Nottingham)
48   "his wife": ET 66
48   "none whatever": ET 133, W 162
48   "bonds of my chastity": "Restlessness": CP 180; W 249
48   "not things passive": i. 103

48   thrown out by her father: Neville 15
48   "so far": ET 126
· 48   few thoughtless minutes: ibid.
49   "afraid—and passion!" WP 44
49   "in anything but 'Son' ": i. 69
49   his moral responsibilities: W 263
49   "so easily peg out": ET 167
49   "you wouldn't like": ibid.
49   "duffer she is": i. 153
50   "uncorsetted in doorways": Ackroyd, *Eliot* 44
50   "he would not act": ibid. 43
50   "ejaculation of words": Holroyd i. 108
50   "momentary complete concentration": Corke, Gerard interview (NCL)
50   "in love with beauty": Corke, "The Writing of *The Trespasser*" 228
51   hook on the bedroom door: "Violinist's Tragic End," *The Surrey Comet*,
       August 14, 1909
51   "assigned for his act": ibid.
51   probably lesbian: W 213
51   where the Corkes lived: Corke, *Infancy* 177
51   "troublous thing before": Corke, "The Writing of *The Trespasser*" 230
51   "the economic whip": Corke, *Infancy* 157
51   under Macartney's tutelage: Corke, "The Writing of *The Trespasser*" 23
51   guilty lovers: W 255
51   Siegmund and Sieglinde: Corke, "The Writing of *The Trespasser*"
       231–33
52   "Coldness in Love": *CP* 98
52   "rather daft": i. 139
52   "It's IT this year!": Hunt 19
52   friends to buy it: i. 11
52   working class: See Belford.
53   "hitherto had gone quite unvoiced": Ford N i. 109
53   "gentry of Virginia": ibid.
53   kiss the visitors good night: i. 144
53   "an editor's office": Ford N i. 112
53   "approach him in conversation?": Ford N i. 110
53   "bring it off": ibid.
53   "A collier's son a poet!": ET 57
53   "odious class snobbery": Richard Aldington, "D. H. Lawrence: Ten
       Years After," *Saturday Review of Literature*, June 24, 1939
53   in a London suburb: ibid.
53   as a London schoolmaster: For a description of Lawrence's "countrified"
       manner, see Rhys N i. 129.
54   his father's dialect: Hopkin N i. 25.
54   walrus-mustached mouth: Kyle S. Crichton, "D. H. Lawrence Lives at
       the Top of the World," *New York World*, October 11, 1925
54   champagne served as an accompaniment: ET 176
54   Pound had a growing reputation: i. 145; Tytell 70
54   to tell her friends: Hunt N i. 127
54   all he could for Lawrence: ET 174–76.
54   combined: W 217
55   "W B Yeats & all the Swells": i. 145
55   "awful slum courtyard": RA to Peter Russell, February 17, 1952
       (State University of New York at Buffalo)
55   "pronounce 'Chianti' ": i. 175

55   "yellow machine round and round": i. 168
55   "nobody on earth wants them": i. 171
55   "Was that criminal?": i. 171
56   five shillings a packet: Holroyd i. 161
56   "Scent of Irises": *CP* 90
56   "Lilies in the Fire": CP 86–87
56   "great good": i. 157
57   "finished now with her": i. 157
57   "property of humanity": Corke, "The Writing of *The Trespasser*" 232
57   for five years: ibid. 233
57   "my problem": Corke, *Infancy* 210
58   "the best Russian school": Draper 44–45.
58   "my thumbs on your throat": i. 160
58   or to give her up: Corke, *Infancy* 180
58   dark red dress . . . "smiles, are sorrowful": ibid. 187
58   irreplaceable: Corke, *Infancy* 188, 190–91
59   "except for the feasting": Corke, *Croydon* 23
59   "to reply on the instant": ibid. 30
59   of Jessie and Lawrence: W 259
59   "if I have the heart to tell her": i. 173
59   if she could return: ibid.
59   "must be nothing": ET 182
60   "let them go to blazes": i. 172
60   "my little girl": i. 61
60   "Lapwings". . . . "Beggar and the Box": i. 163
60   "Tendrils": i. 167
60   fill a curio shop: ibid.
60   " 'Crab-apples' seems": i. 169
60   "a sickening business": i. 162
60   hated literary world: i. 162
61   "homes in England": i. 174
61   "rotten work of genius": i. 178
61   "which this is not": i. 339
61   withdrew the book: ibid.
61   "section of our subscribers": *The Times*, December 2, 1909
61   "possibly be any question": ibid.
62   "suspect to be essentially insipid": ibid.
62   "But what about the free libraries?": H. D. Rawnsley, letter to *The Times*, December 10, 1909
62   looked like a fish: i. 192, 195; Holditch, Gerard interview (NCL)
63   they fight nature: Milton 72, 94
63   enfeeble their sons and husbands: See Milton, 72; Storch, 57.
63   "squeeze her until she screamed": Brenda Maddox, "Damagers of the Breast," *TLS*, June 7, 1991; Storch 50
63   struggle to escape: P. T. Whelan, "Review of Sheila Macleod's *Lawrence's Men and Women*," *DHLR*, vol. 19, no. 1 (summer 1987), 40
63   "To possess property worries me": i. 196–97
64   "happy with her—yes": i. 197
64   "I was very glad": i. 193
64   "generous as the sun": i. 195
64   prevent him marrying her: i. 197
65   slept on the floor: i. 198
65   "something to end it?": George Lawrence, Gerard interview (NCL)
65   overdose in her milk: ibid. and Holditch, Gerard interview (NCL)

65 "Present-at-the-Death": Lydia Lawrence Certificate of Death, Registered, December 9, 1910
65 betrothed to Louie: i. 191
65 "I could never love you": ET 184
65 "nothing to do": ibid.
65 "I'm made this way": i. 191; ET 183
65 "daft as Dostoieffsky": i. 199
65 "I'm incorrigibly ill-bred": i. 200

CHAPTER 3: WAITING, PUZZLED

66 "is very damnable": i. 322
66 "physical, I suppose": i. 201
66 luxuriate in her sympathy: i. 206
66 "sane and strong and healthy": i. 202
66 "have to burn this": i. 206
66 Cornwall, perhaps?: i. 207
66 "you see": i. 214
66 father of a large brood: i. 209.
67 "tearful girl": i. 212
67 the lightning attack: Smith N i. 141
67 most arid of his life: ET 191
67 "sleep-heavy, unwell": i. 260
67 "stupid, and very helpless": i. 120
67 "transit doesn't matter so much": i. 220
68 "living by sheer effort": i. 234
68 "its presence: with father": i. 230
68 Louie, who did not understand one bit: i. 243
68 "is it not so?": i. 230–31
68 "substitute for a wife": i. 235
68 "alter me what I am": i. 237
68 "run away": i. 235–36, 236–38
68 related to Jessie Chambers: i. 238
68 be a good husband: i. 250–51
69 "rather superficial man of me": i. 240
69 "deep-seeing man of me": ibid.
69 "soul-intimate": i. 239
69 "I shall thank you": i. 238
69 threats to break her windows: W 360; Hilton
69 only chance she would get: Hilton
69 "finished the poem": W 364
70 "a croaking crow": i. 233
70 "shifting it this week": i. 243
70 curse the English climate: i. 245, 247
70 in a scarlet bandana: i. 252
70 "how many volts a second?": i. 268
70 took to his bed: ibid.
70 "nor drink, nor smoke": i. 272
70 "anywhere else": i. 245
70 "decent and amiable as boys": i. 246
70 could hardly eat: i. 243
70 "some departed traveller": "In Trouble and Shame," CP 134
70 "Troth with the Dead": W 488–89 gives a table showing the conjectured dates of composition of these poems.

70   "generous adventure left": i. 245
70   "an awfully big adventure": *Peter Pan,* act III. Barrie's play, written in 1905, was an enormous popular success.
71   "can't paint, and vice versa": i. 245
71   tore it into thirty pieces: i. 282
71   "but it is impossible": i. 274
71   "Addi-i-i-o": i. 253
71   "like my houri plump": i. 281
71   consumptives were more passionate than other mortals: Hermione De Almeida, *Romantic Medicine and John Keats,* 118–19; René J. Dubos, "Consumption and the Romantic Age," in *The White Plague*
72   "accumulation of dissatisfied love": i. 321
72   "one's feeling and instinct": i. 259
72   "bubbling red into fire": i. 263
72   "cold as the icy tomb": i. 276
72   coronation of George V: i. 276
72   when they were married?: i. 218
72   "blundering forwardness": ibid.
72   looking after children instead: Patmore 52
73   "you could be all the rest": i. 293
73   the size of the stipulated sum: ibid.
73   a gynecological operation: i. 225
73   "a hundred sheets in half an hour?": i. 266
73   "articles of temptation that Jones gave me": i. 286
73   "save where I am not held": i. 185
73   "because I'm sorry for her": i. 286
73   "that settles you": George Lawrence, Gerard interview (NCL)
74   "flung yourself a bit farther": i. 292
74   anger at Louie's tenacious virginity: i. 403n
74   "the man is always the younger": i. 197
75   "soul sympathy": i. 67
75   "It makes a man much more satisfactory": i. 66
75   "one better than your two": i. 257
75   "prettiest youngster in all England": i. 254
75   "my own and thine": ibid.
75   his own insides dissolving: i. 272n
75   "my supremest wish": i. 255
75   "will have to be yours"; i. 302
75   "meine lieben Schatz. (Brahms)": i. 277
76   "with elements of greatness": i. 225 n. 2
76   "the work of a woman": Draper 36; i. 229 n. 1
76   "the farmhouses of the Trent Valley?": Draper 37
76   "returning to Nature": ibid.
76   "the day be spring and the clouds high": Draper 40
76   "making it 'like' something else": ibid.
76   "how vivid the impression it leaves!": Furbank, *SL* 250
77   "vanity, screech and defilement": Draper 40
77   except with a young miner: Mackenzie, *My Life and Times: Octave Five, 1915–1923* 167–88.
77   talked of suing: Holditch, Gerard interview (NCL)
77   Alice "Gall" Hall: i. 280
77   persistent demands of Louie's family: i. 290
78   bicycle: i. 296
78   the Daxes "very well": i. 296

78   "Mrs Jones has gone out": i. 315
78   "too poor to have it done": i. 311
78   make a fortune in literature: i. 312
78   "slit in a tight skin": i. 263
78   *"Mein Gott!"*: i. 302–303
78   "a stove chimney got red hot": i. 306
78   "I am so tired": i. 311
78   "I shall work it off": i. 312
79   "a grain of meaning out": i. 318
79   the death of him: i. 319
79   "gone away into Death": i. 313
79   "wicked" but "clever": i. 348
79   "for which she yearned": from "Second Best," *English Review,* February 1912, 461–69. A revised version appears in *The Tales of D. H. Lawrence.*
79   "very tenderly": ibid.
79   good short stories for the Century Company: Jefferson 143
80   "oh American!": i. 307
80   back to his classroom on time: ibid.
80   not infallible eye: Garnett's distinguished service to English literature was blighted by his rejection for Duckworth of Joyce's *A Portrait of the Artist as a Young Man* and Lawrence's *The Rainbow.*
80   "cheekiness, intensity and pride": R. Garnett 269.
80   Lawrence accepted: i. 311
80   Garnett's house: R. Garnett 151
80   enchanted: ibid.; author's visit to the Cearne; i. 314
81   Keeper of the Printed Books: R. Garnett 268
81   earnings as a clerk: W 111
81   "feeling in my writing": i. 315
81   "I must leave school, really": i. 323
81   "lead in my veins": i. 321
81   "loathe to plead my cause": i. 320
81   Rolfe Scott-James: i. 318 and n. 4; i. 324
81   "reality of creative art": Scott-James, R. A., "Edward Garnett," *The Spectator,* February 27, 1937, 362
82   "big wigs of the literary world": Jones, Delaveny ii. 656
82   "very ill": *CP* 851
82   "waiting, puzzled": i. 328

CHAPTER 4: NOT YET CONSUMPTION

83   "fear now is a relapse": Ada to EG, n.d. (1911) (NYPL)
83   short story: i. 343
83   "Saga": i. 330
83   so that he could shave: i. 333
84   "hanging onto my shoulder": Ada to Louie Burrows, December 20, 1911 (NYPL); W 323
84   "Walküre, on nimble air": i. 341
84   would be too exciting: i. 331
84   even the children: i. 332
84   "vampire type of female": Ada to Kot, October 21, 1920 (BL)
84   to see Jessie Chambers: W 330
84   from the shoulders up: Ada N i. 51
84   with his mother: ET 200

84   poor health had been noticed: Philip Smith, N i. 89

84   superintendent of school attendance officers: Archives Development Office, Croydon Local Studies Library, to BM, July 28, 1992

84   classic picture of the consumptive: F. B. Smith 19ff

85   compulsory treatment of prostitutes: Davenport-Hines 166–67, 184

85   for the sake of the family: ibid. 167–68, 184

85   "the product of carelessness": John Burns 85–87

85   dying of the disease, one by one: W 6

86   "everyone is crying": Hilda Shaw to LB, April 6, 1911 (NCL)

86   "almost unpardonable": i. 334

86   "die of mortification": i. 343

86   "if I'm high": i. 341

86   "too much for me, damn it": ibid.

86   "almost completely cleared up": Ada to EG, December 17, 1911; W 337 n. 2; full text, NYPL

86   "He has to give up school too": ibid.

87   Stevenson, seriously ill: *Oxford Companion to English Literature* 783

87   tested negative: Harley Williams

87   an X ray of the chest: Richard M. Burke

88   how to behave: Noel Dean Bordswell, *Advice to Consumptives* (London: A. & C. Black, 1910); F. W. Burton-Fanning, *The Open-Air Treatment of Pulmonary Tuberculosis: Modern Methods of Treatment* (London: Cassell, 1909)

88   "than the inhabitants of London": R. G. Latham, M.D., *The Complete Works of Thomas Sydenham, M.D., translated from the Latin Edition of Dr. Greenhill with a Life of the Author* (London: Sydenham Society, 1848–50), vol. 2, Appendix C

88   to the south coast direct: i. 335

88   "like a bird": i. 349

88   Bournemouth as an invalid: i. 361

88   "glad when I get away": i. 360

89   "complicating": i. 354

89   "like a good 'un": i. 351

89   "ham and eggs": i. 347

89   vicious cold: i. 352

89   "a rotten one": ibid.

89   "which lingers": i. 354

89   "to the midlands": i. 345

89   "Help me out": i. 343

90   "I want to go over sea": i. 354

90   "work of art": i. 359

90   Images of blood: To Helen Corke, DHL wrote that he saw "withered beech as red as blood, sprinkling its spray" on the snow (i. 362); to Garnet he referred to "scarlet sweets we used to suck, and get bloody mouths" (i. 365).

90   "and the fault is all mine": i. 361

91   "house of the unconventional Garnett": Corke, *Infancy* 214–15

91   "the only one on the earth": James Boulton, *Lawrence in Love:* Letters from D. H. Lawrence to Louie Burrows, University of Nottingham, 1968, xxvi

91   "kissing like nuts": i. 359

92   "*call her* a girl": W 338

92   "cup of tea": i. 366

92   "such good spirit": i. 367

92   "and people he knew best": Claire Tomalin, "A Son, His Lovers and Paradise Lost," *Independent on Sunday,* September 1, 1991

93   she was pregnant: Enid Hilton claims that Dax was pregnant when Lawrence asked her to run away with him. If he asked her on the occasion of their meeting in February 1912, she was barely a month pregnant. Hilton 279

93   "roused and my husband had slaked": *Memoirs* 248

93   "committed to paper.": i. 366

93   Alice free to dream: Meyers 46; W 366; Hilton 279

94   "whose baby was it going to be?": *Noon* 122

94   "not going to be a cart-horse": ET 208

94   morning early in March: W 367, 562–63, discusses the possible dates of the meeting.

94   "in all England": i. 376

CHAPTER 5: THE GIANTESS

95   bombing the barracks: Ernst Frick was arrested in the spring of 1912. Cantonal records do not show the date but the arrest was long imminent and he was definitely in prison by May 6, as Letter 56 from Frieda Schloffer Gross (FG) to Else Jaffe (EJ) indicates.

        The Gross-Jaffe letters are in the possession of Professor Martin Green of Tufts University, and the numbering hereinafter is his.

95   sending money for his assistance: JC, "The Letters of Jessie Chambers," *DHLR,* vol. 12, nos. 1 and 2 (1979), 101

95   abetting a suicide: Green, *Mountain of Truth* 37

95   young girl from the Rhine Valley: *Memoirs* 394; Ian Weekley to BM, July 17, 1991

95   tyrannous cook: *Memoirs* 88; Lucas 28

95   first adultery: "Fullness," *Memoirs* 93; i. 409, n. 1; Lucas 33

96   giving her mind: See Green, *von Richthofen Sisters* 1–196, on the background to the affair and the sexual and intellectual atmosphere of Heidelberg and Munich at the turn of the century.

96   Else had sent a hundred marks: EJ to FG, August 6, 1911, Letter 49

96   Cambridge every Saturday: R. Lucas 29

96   "nothing to do": see ET 184

96   Alone much of the time: *Memoirs* 145

96   draping herself with a shawl: W 376

97   "I despise Nottingham": *Memoirs* 157

97   "consider myself a happy man": *Memoirs* 157

97   Bohemian barony from Frederick the Great: Dr. Patrick Freiherr von Richthofen to BM, October 10, 1992; Ian Weekley to BM, July 21, 1992

97   in 1862: ibid.; also Green, *von Richthofen Sisters* 11, and *Memoirs* 42; translation of *Freiin,* John Worthen to BM, June 4, 1994.

97   second-biggest garrison town: W 373; *Memoirs* 42, 79; Green, *von Richthofen Sisters* 12

97   unhappily ever after: *Memoirs* 470

97   "ein Atavismus": *Memoirs* 28

97   maimed hand and nervous disposition: Green, *von Richthofen Sisters* 12–13

97   Oswald von Richthofen: interview with Baron Hermann von Richthofen, July 12, 1992

98   credentials: *Memoirs* 42; R. Lucas 20

98   "a nice entertainment": *Memoirs* 143

98	lack of a fortune . . . the only men they met: *Memoirs* 79 (quoting Else Jaffe)
98	spent on his mistress: W 374
98	sorely tried: Letter from Barbara Barr to BM, June 30, 1989
98	proposed marriage: W 373; *Memoirs* 79
98	an appointment waiting: W 372
98	grieved at the thought of being parted: *Memoirs* 79
98	"she ought to be an empress": EW to Else von Richthofen, August 18, 1989 (Tedlock papers, UNM)
98	"separated for a little while": ibid.
99	"washed-out looking thing": Barbara Barr to BM, June 30, 1989
99	"put on my nightdress at once": D. Garnett, *Great Friends*. A censored account appears in *Memoirs* 84.
99	"horror": *Memoirs* 84
99	to judge from . . . *Mr. Noon*: "Johanna had had far more sensual satisfaction out of her husband, Everard, than out of her other lovers" (*Noon* 242).
99	happier every day: *Memoirs* 146
99	affectionately called Fritz: EW to EJ, August 5, 1900 (UNM)
99	jealous if the baby was a boy: *Memoirs* 145
100	"some great work on political economy": Green, *von Richthofen Sisters* 16
100	"easily use a few hundred": *Memoirs* 150
100	"for all of us": ibid.
100	"when one is married!": ibid. 151
100	"no small thing": ibid. 149
100	"above his 'Momamo' ": ibid. 150
100	her copy of *Thus Spake Zarathustra*: ibid. 152
100	"my old friend": FL to UJ, July 15, 1935 (Berkeley)
100	"but the Wind": "Song of a Man Who Has Come Through," *CP* 250
100	"A thing is the sum of its effects": See Orage.
100	direct expression of Nietzsche's ideas: Nehamas 47
101	*The G.B.S. Perpetual Calendar,* price one shilling, was advertised in *The New Age,* May 23, 1908, 80.
101	They did not quarrel: *Memoirs* 146–47
101	"the source of nourishment": ibid. 158
101	"we are arrogant": ibid. 156–57
101	a brusque army officer: i. 391, 395, 575; *Memoirs* 91
101	"an Iphegenie sacrifice": Green, *von Richthofen Sisters* 18
101	Hamburg textile manufacturers: This and other details of Edgar Jaffe's background are from Green, *von Richthofen Sisters* 24
101	Elsa had hopes: ibid. 23
101	*Archiv für Sozialwissenschaft*: ibid. 24.
102	feeling should win: Albrow 46–47
102	"nodes of the anti-Bismarck movement": Green, *von Richthofen Sisters* 24
102	summoned him to be her lover: Turner 188
102	history of the erotic movement: Green, *von Richthofen Sisters* 44; Turner 140
102	"romantic idea of a genius": Jones, *Free Associations* 173–74
103	during sexual intercourse: *Noon,* 161
103	changed his clothes or went home: Green, *Mountain of Truth* 28
103	"decadence": Turner 188; *Memoirs* 99
103.	the punishing patriarch: Green, *von Richthofen Sisters* 37

103	complete sexual freedom: Green, *Mountain of Truth* 28
104	"street-corner": Turner 197
104	"golden child": ibid. 165; also *Memoirs* 95
104	"my Turkish horse": Turner 169, 194
104	Fliess: letter of October 1897. Jones, *Freud* i. 356, n. 1
104	appear in English: Gay 465 n.
104	thanked her: Green, *von Richthofen Sisters* 46; Turner 193
105	their children: Turner 190
105	euphemisms for orgasm: *Not I* 1; Green, *von Richthofen Sisters* 33
105	erotic emancipation: Green, *von Richthofen Sisters* 55
105	week in Holland: Turner 196
105	living death in Nottingham: ibid.
105	"like Brünnhilde and Krimhilde": ibid.
105	"I go away only to return": ibid. 187
106	"Teutonic woman?": ibid. 195
106	"not *only* for your sake": ibid. 174
106	"signs of the future": ibid. 191
106	her course: ibid. 189
106	"a greeting from the future": ibid. 165
106	"aristocratic way": ibid. 188
106	"from the people": ibid. 174
106	"I cannot understand it": ibid. 166
106	his affair with her sister: ibid. 176
107	"I myself have felt": Green, *von Richthofen Sisters* 53
107	"the existence of a good fellow": Turner 192
107	she had a new lover: ibid.
107	"rage of 'giving' ": ibid. 196
107	"For ever, Beloved, Otto": ibid. 193
107	*very* careful": *Memoirs* 161
107	registered the boy as his own: Heidelberg birth certificate lists the child's name as Edgar Peter Behrend Jaffe.
107	Frieda Gross's new son: Information from Harald Szeemann, October 9, 1992
108	"anything but a civilising factor": C. G. Jung to S. Freud, Turner 142
108	"doctors we will remain": ibid. 143
108	Freud was steering: Gay 409
108	Jones was most reluctant: Ernest Jones to Freud, May 13, 1908 (Archives of the Institute of Psycho-Analysis)
109	"to send me": ibid.
109	taking cocaine: Ernest Jones to Sigmund Freud, June 26, 1908 (Archives of the Institute of Psycho-Analysis)
109	learned more from Gross: Ernest Jones to Sigmund Freud, May 18, 1914 (Archives of the Institute of Psycho-Analysis)
109	liaison with Alfred Weber: Green, *Mountain of Truth* 31. By 1911 the relationship was well established, according to FG to EJ, October 9, [1911?], Letter 52.
110	brother and sister through their mothers' mother: ibid.
110	derailment of a tram in November 1908: details from Harald Szeemann and Swiss police and cantonal archives
110	he drew strength from her: FG to EJ, Letter 45 [dated only as 2 1911]
110	"Unfortunately they were never days": FG to EJ, April 10, 1911, Letter 48
110	"that's all right with me": ibid.
110	"as little inclination towards that as possible": ibid.

111   intended to move abroad: Harald Szeemann to BM, October 9, 1992, based on Frick's letter to the Zurich police, in Staatsarchiv, Zurich-Irschel

111   "can't love at all any more, and not just only me": FG to EJ, August 6, 1911, Letter 49

111   "complete instability": FG to EJ, February 16, 1911, Letter 46

111   three thousand marks duly arrived: FG to EJ, August 11, 1911, Letter 50

111   "weaker than if I had a child": FG to EJ, September 2, 1911, Letter 51

111   "when they had only rows together": ibid.

112   "just got to be a great enemy of the English": Ernst Frick to EJ, October 9, 1911, Letter 53

112   "How he must have suffered!": *Memoirs* 102

112   autobiography: *Not I,* 1

112   "may have to be modified": S. J. Hills, "Frieda Lawrence," *TLS,* September 6, 1985

CHAPTER 6: UNENGLISHED

117   Within twenty minutes: W 382, 566 n. 40; "Notes on D. H. Lawrence," Lewis Richmond, Nottingham County Record Office, based on information from William Hopkin. Also Luhan 103.

117   he tells how: W 382 says the instant seduction "could not have happened" yet maintains at the same time that *Mr. Noon* is "a remarkable guide" to the events of May–September 1912, containing "a great deal of direct recreation of the events" and that a biography of DHL which did not draw from it would be absurd. Worthen's biographical principles—followed in the present biography—are to make clear when *Mr. Noon* is being used as a source and also when *Mr. Noon* is used to supply something not confirmed by other sources. I have taken Lewis Richmond and Mabel Dodge Luhan as corroborating sources for the seduction at first sight and have taken the fictional creation of such a scene, transposed to Germany in *Mr. Noon,* as evidence that, contrary to Worthen's assertion, such fast work was possible.

117   "so powerfully communicated": David Lodge, "Comedy of Eros," *The New Republic,* December 10, 1984, 99

118   heard the same story from Frieda: Luhan 103

118   "into a paradise": *Not I* 1

118   a half-hour before lunch: ibid. 2

118   had him in class: Lucas 40

119   did not say "v" for "w": Frieda's voice, reading "Bavarian Gentians," can be heard on tape at the BL's National Sound Archive.

119   "leaped through our words": *Not I* 2

119   *Oedipus* and other Greek plays: i. 525 n. 1; ii. 137

119   "in incest with his mother": *English Review,* February 1912, 461–69; also W 443, 448

120   love *is* sex: *Noon* 161

120   Everard: When Lawrence wrote *Mr. Noon,* the name Everard also carried an association with Everard Meynell, a son of the family who lent him a cottage in Sussex in 1915.

121   an excellent and witty teacher: Ian Weekley, in "Myths of Time," a letter to the *London Sunday Times,* September 23, 1990, deplores the use of "dreary" to describe his grandfather, whom he remembered as witty, a lovely storyteller, and a superb raconteur.

121   "gentlemen": W 187
121   returning one day as a professor: BM interview with Julia Weekley, January 14, 1991
121   German university: W 380
121   Fritz Krenkow: i. 77 n. 1
121   invited Lawrence to lunch: i. 374
121   refuse a lady: Delavenay ii. 707
121   stayed too long at his office: the late Dr. Peter Boulden of Deal, Kent, to Thérèse Wright; Lewis Richmond memoir, Nottingham County Record Office
121   ridiculed her . . . "You take no notice": *Not I* 2
121   dishonor her husband's house: ibid. 3
121   Weekley reproved her: "A Distant Friend," Nottingham *Daily Guardian*, October 20, 1913
122   "torture to him": JC in Delavenay ii. 671. The character of Clara, Mrs. Baxter Dawes, is a composite; there is much of the freethinking Alice Dax in her, but clearly not the clothes.
122   "don't know what that was": W 38
122   abandoned by his old friends: Neville 100–108
122   "try to make happiness": "The Married Man," in *Collected Plays* 198–99
123   "will never marry": i. 377
123   "war on my adjectives": i. 381
123   a week together: i. 382
123   "the boys happy": i. 386
123   "home I've got": i. 384
124   "woman of a lifetime": ibid.
124   what his housekeeper might say: R. Garnett 174, 346
124   "At the Cearne": *CP* 891–92
124   "tell him today": i. 388
124   fierce temper: ibid.
124   socialists in Switzerland: Green, *Mountain of Truth*, 34
124   "to monopolise her": i. 388
124   "say good-bye to me, Monty": C. Montague Weekley interview, National Sound Archive (BL)
124   "we're in England": i. 389
125   "anything like it": i. 395
126   "barracks, cathedral": i. 393
126   "only my Englishness": i. 391
127   "sisters—no!": i. 393
127   "but I think there is not": *News of the World*, October 20, 1913, 1
127   "cake-haver": C. M. Weekley, Gerard interview (NCL)
128   but angrily: i. 394–95
128   "on Saturday": i. 395
129   "always help": i. 397
129   suspicions were correct: i. 409
129   any deliberate ambiguity . . . was a lie: i. 393
129   "The truth is never true": *Noon* 188
129   "loving man": *Memoirs* 162
129   family home: ibid.
129   in England and Wales: Office of Population Census and Surveys, *Marriage and Divorce Statistics: England and Wales, 1837–1983, Statistical Series* (London: Her Majesty's Stationery Office).
129   "happy with him": *Memoirs* 162

130   "cry out hysterically": ibid. 163–65
130   "worse than death": ibid. 164
130   "nice chin": i. 396
130   "nothing at all": i. 398
130   "hot as H": i. 398
130   "mother to protect him": *Memoirs* 166
131   "his to smash": Maude Weekley to FL, *Memoirs* 166
131   "put it down": *TLS,* May 30, 1912, 1
131   "very strange": i. 400
131   into marrying Lawrence: i. 409
131   "opposition to you": i. 402
131   "married respectable people": i. 406
131   "clumsily handed": i. 401
131   "have that definite desire": i. 402–403
131   "it is *my life*": i. 402–403
132   "I believe it": i. 403
132   "natures aren't alike": i. 404
132   "well and sane": ibid.
133   the Eastwood nurse: i. 496 n. 5; i. 520
133   by his writing: i. 526
133   "arranging *affairs*": i. 401
133   "let the common-sense match it": i. 402
133   "with each other": i. 400
134   "I'm glad they are like that": "She Said as Well to Me," *CP* 254
135   "it is a thrill": i. 410
135   "savagely religious": i. 418
135   "profusion of them, everywhere": i. 413
136   "during the period of her divorce": EJ to FG, June 17, 1912, Letter 58
136   "children to make visits": ibid.
136   "erotic happiness": ibid.
136   Peeping Tom: W. H. Auden, "D. H. Lawrence," *The Dyer's Hand,* New York, 1968, 288; Mackenzie 167–68
137   rent-free: Weber N i. 166
137   put on a dressing gown: i. 415
137   "conversation as in England?": Ernst Frick to FL; June 1912, Letter 57
137   "prisoner about your freedom": ibid.
137   to stay away: FG to EJ, June 17, 1912, Letter 58
137   bare in the sun: i. 441
138   "shall be sorry": i. 402
138   "because she must have some": FG to EJ, June 17, 1912, Letter 58
138   as have many since: Meyers, *D. H. Lawrence; A Life* 331
138   Syphilis . . . Hunt and Mansfield: Belford 120, Tomalin 78
138   "under the bed and miow": i. 438
138   "put up with me": i. 439
139   "people who love each other": i. 419
139   "mother of my children," i. 43
139   "every Sunday": Corke N i. 96
139   say it all again: i. 429
140   escorted her to the station: i. 430
140   "other people's affairs": i. 530
140   staring blankly out: *Memoirs* 109

140   "six months hence": i. 421
140   "very very alive": David Garnett to Constance Garnett, [n.d.] 1912, dated "Thursday" and beginning "I came down here yesterday" (Texas)
140   "mongrel and underbred": D. Garnett N i. 174
141   "upper classes for the lower": ibid. i. 173
141   lioness: ibid. i. 174
141   "the only great mimic I have known": ibid. i. 177
141   "for that young man": i. 429
141   unpublishable: i. 421 n. 4
141   "flaming sods": i. 422
141   "can breed": ibid.
141   "stick by him": i. 423
141   reshaping it: W 420
142   refusing divorce: i. 424
142   "nose to my wagon": i. 430
142   "great thighs": *Noon* 319–20
142   eleven days out of thirty-one: W 425
143   "and dripped": "A Chapel Among the Mountains," *PII* 29
143   While they waited for him: i. 433
143   thoughts of home: D. Garnett N i. 176
143   "she is so ill": i. 440
143   "I believe in marriage": i. 440–41
144   not surprised: David learned it from Lawrence himself the following year at the Cearne. D. Garnett, *Golden Echo* 246–47.
144   to a woodcutter: Worthen (W 428) dismisses this anecdote as implausible. It appears, however, not only in D. Garnett's memoirs but referred to in *LCL*, where Mellors accuses his first wife of giving herself to a woodcutter.
144   no hard feelings: D. Garnett, *Great Friends* 81
144   missed the path: W 430; i. 450
144   "the night before last": *Noon* 344; D. Garnett, *Great Friends* 81
144   "what does it matter?": *Noon* 351
144   staggered Diana Trilling: See introduction, note for p. 5.
145   "secret of English greatness": *Noon* 241
145   "the catastrophe that overtook Lawrence": Holbrook, "Sons and Mothers" 52
145   answer favored: See W 428.
145   "have a drink": *Noon* 255
145   "before you've done": *P*, "Christs in the Tirol" 84
145   projection of the hate: W 417
145   "consummate hate and misery": "The Crucifix Among the Mountains," *Twilight in Italy* 12
145   "never spends a penny": David Garnett to Constance Garnett, [n.d.] 1912 (Texas)
146   coarse plain cambric: Cecily Lambert N i. 465
146   "why should I look?": Seymour 254
146   never pressed on toward its publication: Melvyn Bragg, introduction to *Mr. Noon* (London: Grafton, 1985); Dennis Jackson and Lydia Blanchard, "*Mr. Noon's* Critical Reception," *DHLR*, vol. 20, no. 2 (summer 1988), 147; Lindeth Vasey, introduction to *Mr. Noon* xxxiii
147   "sodomitic solution": Holbrook, "Sons and Mothers" 48
147   "at the wonder": "Song of a Man Who Has Come Through," *CP* 250.

147   "of my subjection": "Elysium," *CP* 262
147   "strange lust": "Rabbit Snared in the Night," *CP* 242
148   "quick of my darkness": "Manifesto," *CP* 266.
148   "Lovelier than Paradise": "Elysium," 261
148   "life trails on": *Noon* 359
148   overlooking the lake: i. 509; *Not I* 49
148   "not to seem swank": i. 456
148   "being the best": quoted in Moore, *PL* 155
149   wash sheets: *Not I* 51
149   cook macaroni: i. 475
149   "as a jewel": i. 456
149   "only inferior": i. 412
149   spittoon: i. 463; *Not I* 49
149   would sleep: *Not I* 53
149   "three is sufficient": i. 486
149   "have to pay back": ibid.
150   "call it *Sons and Lovers*": i. 462
150   threw herself into the rewriting: i. 479, W 442
150   starker oedipal opposition: W 438–39; W's chapter 16 deals with the extent of the revisions to *SL*.
150   an English fault: i. 449, 479
150   "that I know": i. 479
150   the finest thing a mother could do: W 415
150   draft of morphia: Storch 106–107
150   her Metz lover, von Henning: i. 404
151   "one sheds ones sicknesses in books": ii. 90
151   saw her face in crowds: W 453
151   "smothered": Adamowski 201
151   was to remain with him: i. 452
151   "written a great book": i. 476–77
151   "quite gorgeous": i. 482
151   knew the book was too long: i. 481–82
151   "filthy hound": i. 484
152   dead to the children: i. 489
152   only through lawyers: i. 496
152   "come and see me?": i. 468
152   "daren't allow it": ibid.
152   "at Christmas": i. 460
152   "love it so": i. 464
152   even one card: R. Lucas 96
152   "my friend now": i. 488
152   "venomous cold": i. 490
152   "preach my heart out": i. 493
152   "your awareness of me": "Both Sides of the Medal," *CP* 235
152   "balls-aching rot": i. 495
153   "Balls!": i. 494
153   "Shit!": ibid.
153   "Bitch!": i. 495
153   "Arse-licking": ibid.
153   two-fingered salute: i. 497
153   "Fancy me": i. 498
153   "Stinker!": ibid.
153   "trust in the Lord": i. 497
153   "Some new bloke?": i. 497–98; *Memoirs* 176

CHAPTER 7: THE WEDDING RING

154	"don't mix": R. Garnet 274
155	chopping and changing: i. 542
155	"seedy": i. 549
155	"outcasts we feel": *Memoirs* 181
155	"left your father, not you": ibid. 178
155	"domestic": i. 543
155	"badly to removal": ii. 32
155	"unwieldy mass": ii. 19
156	"*Why* was I born?": ii. 63
156	father's mistress: Green, *von Richthofen Sisters* 14, 25
156	five thousand marks: FG to EJ, ca. 1913, Letter 64
157	"Put it all in": i. 514
157	"Essere—o non essere": i. 505
157	"hot spiced darkness": "The Spinner and the Monks," *Twilight in Italy* 21
157	"drawn sword between us": i. 551
157	"two tails left": i. 521
157	"carousing": i. 513
157	"squeeze myself small": i. 547
157	unfit to be a human being: i. 538
158	sent it anyway: i. 530
158	"on to the couch": "The Fight for Barbara," act 4
158	"3 uncles from one aunt": ii. 23
158	"seems generous": i. 502
158	"woman at the back of me": i. 503
158	"is always true": ibid.
158	"your best wisdom?": *Zarathustra* 62
158	"insult that man": i. 504
159	"What 'Prussian Officer'?": ii. 241
159	"with my sabre": Cushman, *Lawrence at Work* 209
159	"men without women": i. 469
159	"autobiographical": ii. 21
159	"too hot": ii. 67
159	"at the same time, tender!": from "Once," which appears in *Mortal Coil* 162–63
159	"between men and women": ii. 546
160	"to be a pest": ibid.
160	"got to live": i. 526
160	"whatever it is": i. 517
160	"I hope to God it will sell": ii. 20
160	"that style any more": ii. 551
160	"re-write the book": ii. 550–51
160	"arrogant females!": i. 549
160	"over the children": ibid.
160	"civilized forms it takes!": *Memoirs* 183
160	"writing machine": i. 549
161	"God Almightiness" onto the page: i. 550
161	"L's health now" . . . "Not true": i. 549
161	"of rare excellence": Draper 75
161	"share lives": E. M. Alpe, "Books of the Day," *The Ladies Field*, July 26, 1913, 424
162	"to illuminate both sides simultaneously": Draper 68

162   "which his art has transfigured": Alfred B. Kuttner, *"Sons and Lovers: A Freudian Appreciation," Psychoanalytic Review,* vol. 3 (1916), 295–317

162   "have more sense": i. 544

162   "You" . . . "your aunt": *Memoirs* 111

163   "coming home?": *Not I* 57

163   wear them to bed: Julia Weekley interview, Burford, January 1991

163   Ida, also left: Ian Weekley to BM, July 17, 1991

163   chamber pot: Barbara Barr to BM, January n.d., 1991

163   after she went away: In a letter to UJ, July 16 [1935?], Frieda described the children as forming "a little unit, just like *The Virgin and The Gypsy.*" Berkeley

163   "those Lawrences!": R. Garnett 274

164   "forgetting the past": ibid. 346

164   netted the raspberries: The description of DHL at the Garnetts' is from ibid. 275–76.

165   clowning in the water: ii. 46

165   "bathing tents": ii. 37

165   deeper-seated: BM, conversations with Barbara Barr and Sybille Bedford. Also, a concluding note in Moore and Montague, 137, says, "The present editors deplore Frieda's occasional outbursts of anti-Semitism in these letters, which were uncharacteristic of her conversation."

165   "circumstances all round": ii. 29

165   "be going out": ii. 30

165   "round at the Cearne": ii. 33

165   "Frieda's underclothing": ii. 36

165   "another story": ii. 37

166   "keep a list": ii. 39

166   "get them done": ii. 41

166   "type-written": ibid.

166   "when it is done": ii. 48

166   "come filtering in": ii. 52

166   a German poem: "Previously unknown mss. by Lawrence acquired by Nottingham Univ.," *Times Higher Educational Supplement,* November 9, 1990

166   hasty revision: Delavenay, *D. H. Lawrence: The Man and His Work* 192

167   original core: "The Vicar's Garden," MS 72/231 Bancroft Library, Berkeley

167   T.S. Eliot, among others: Eliot, "After Strange Gods"

167   similarity of the theme of the Lawrence short story to . . . "The Dead": Keith Cushman, *DHLR* 8:1 (spring 1975), 44

172   "Frieda doesn't care": ii. 46

172   refusing divorce: Alpers 145

172   "lad of 23": ii. 32

173   "of another man": ii. 35

173   "30/ clerk": ibid.

173   "finish one's job first": ii. 28

173   "personal contact!": Savage 41

173   "cul de sac": ii. 43

174   "upper classes": i. 501

174   Moore and Bertrand Russell: Woodeson 108–109

174   interested in poetry: Lucas 104

174   terribly ill: Marsh N i. 199

174	upper-class vowels: Cynthia Asquith interview, National Sound Archive
174	"a Pentecost to one": Asquith, *Diaries* 18–19
174	"ears plugged": BBC Third Programme, September 7, 1949
175	"gibing": ibid
175	"in the world": Asquith, *Diaries* 18–19
175	"awfully good to us!": ii. 51
175	"cold-blooded sister from Ceylon": ii. 54
175	"thankful": i. 518
175	"a man and his wife": ii. 71
176	"to mention her": ii. 70
176	"to let go a bit": ii. 73
176	"quick of cold death": "The Return Journey," *Twilight in Italy,* 153
176	"to these two old ladies": ibid. 147
176	not to cross the Swiss border: FG to EJ, September 15, 1912, Letter 63
177	"over the ear": ii. 88; Arnold Armin, "In the Footsteps of D. H. Lawrence in Switzerland: Some New Biographical Material," *Texas Studies in Literature & Language* (summer 1961), 184–88
177	took Ernst Frick to La Spezia: from Harald Szeemann; also, entry for *Abmeldung nach Zurich,* Bundesarchiv, Bern (Szeemann)
177	"rain and dark": i. 88
177	"Italy can stink": ii. 89
178	"won't have": ii. 95
178	"Despisers of the Body": *Zarasthustra* 63
178	"that killed him": ii. 96
178	"It's sickening": ii. 108
178	"Keats, Shelley, Burns": ii. 101
178	"amid the waves": ii. 85
178	asylum in Austria: Green, *Mountain of Truth* 141
179	"dominated by women": *The Standard,* October 20, 1913, 8
179	"too much with the co-respondent": "A Distant Friend: Nottingham Divorce Suit, Author as Co-Respondent," Nottingham *Daily Guardian,* October 20, 1913
179	"much her responsibility": R. Garnett 277
179	subversive force: Haste 21, 28
180	"really was upset": ii. 107
180	abuse her hospitality any longer: Dawn MacLeod Wilson to BM, re Lawrence's comments to Helen Cochrane, May 29, 1989
180	the Burrowses of Leicestershire: For the history of the writing of "The Sisters" see Sagar *Calendar,* 43–51; for the use of the von Richthofen, plus Burrows, background, see Green, *von Richthofen Sisters* 342–43.
180	"outbursts of work": ii. 143
181	had been crying: Constance Garnett to EG, February 5 [1914], R. Garnett 281
181	"you men can't do things alone": *Memoirs* 190
181	"getting it out clean": ii. 146
181	"of both of us": ii. 164
181	"a Cockney": ii. 165
181	"deeply happy": ii. 161
181	"will or no": ii. 120
181	"cold and dark": ii. 128
182	"half-educated": Barnes 137–38
182	"the girl's a swell!": Low, N i. 217

182 "Joseph Conrad": ibid. 215
183 man came into the room: ibid. 220
183 retitled by Frieda: ii. 173
184 "radically-unchanged element": ii. 183
184 "falling to bits": Ellmann 404
185 access to her children: ii. 169
185 make progress on solving the problem: ii. 162, 195
186 "very interesting": ii. 186
186 "to espouse": John Carswell 74
187 "I am one": ii. 196
187 "trouble about the children": ii. 197
187 and they ran: ii. 199
187 "maggoty Weekley house": ii. 199

CHAPTER 8: THE WIDER WAR

188 "scoundrel": W. Jackson Bate, *Life of Johnson* (London: Chatto and Windus, 1978), 9
188 took her breath away: Hassall 387 n. 3
188 "war with Germany": ibid.
189 following day: ii. 205 n. 6; ii. 268
189 "machinery piercing and tearing?": Baron 5
190 Savage left, convinced: Savage N i. 211
190 "Get it *done!*": Tomalin 130
191 "if you ever have time": ii. 211–12
191 "Frieda has always . . . with themselves": ii. 213–14
191 to understand anything outside themselves: ii. 215
192 ten pounds a month: Carrington 35; Woodeson 77
192 "Lippo Lippi cherub": Hassall 241
192 fled to Buckinghamshire: Woodeson 148
192 "a *Baroness,* you know": ibid. 159
192 for Sunday lunch: ii. 213
192 Marsh's suggestion: Hassall 289
193 "who shall work it": ii. 222–23
193 "thin-gutted charity": ii. 223
193 "shall keep it": ii. 226
193 Hilda Shaw: i. 480
194 writing farewells: Tomalin 132
194 "utterly repulsive to me": Alpers 170
194 "hard enough to bear": ibid.
194 "a wide smile": Mackenzie, N i. 248. Mackenzie's account is fictionalized in his novel, *The Four Winds of Love, The South Wind,* but he assured Nehls (N i. 570 n. 41) that it was "factually and conversationally exact."
195 "about the English": ibid. 252
195 made her stop: ibid.
195 much to confide: "Katherine Mansfield Day by Day,'" *Memoirs* 425
195 gonorrhea: Tomalin 78
196 "banks of the Susquehannah": Holmes 62, 66
196 Hebrew songs: ii. 252 n. 3
196 "talked the Island": Murry, *Journal* 65 of Katherine Mansfield
196 through their connections: Hobman 118
196 living in her house: ii. 492
197 on festival occasions: Hobman 58–60

197   "extraordinarily nice": Furbank ii. 5
197   "real decency": ii. 259
197   "shop together": ii. 272
198   "I can't find anybody": ii. 266
198   "to protect me": ii. 262
198   Catholic journalists: Meynell 281
198   pretentious in her life: Asquith, *Diaries* 37–78
198   smell of damp: visit to Greatham, October 10, 1991
198   fire was immoral: Aldington N i. 507
199   "address you as one": Lago and Furbank 219
199   consummated sexual encounter: Furbank ii. 35
199   "said '——— ———' ": Lago and Furbank 220
199   "primal being?": ii. 282–83
199   "he's up to": Lago and Furbank 222
200   "others to take": ibid. 219
200   "inarticulate and *unformed*": Furbank ii. 11
200   "have improved!": ibid.
200   "cannot know him": Forster papers, King's College Library
200   "marriage bell": Russell N i. 282
200   pearls and purple velvet: vii. 235
200   hiring a "fly": ii. 278
201   "asking a question": ii. 304
201   slave to reason: Russell to Ernest Jones, January 25, 1957 (Archives of the Institute for Psycho-Analysis)
201   put the world right: ibid.
201   "whole of mankind": ii. 294
201   "rather afraid": ii. 300
202   talked at and around him: ibid.
202   nightclothes: ii. 321
202   his work at the Treasury: Skidelsky 302
202   "marsh-stagnancy": ii. 309
202   "sewer": ii. 320
203   "love a woman": ii. 321
203   "assembly of an unreal world": ii. 307
203   different world: ii. 238
204   a series of public lectures: ii. 359
204   "one's belly": ii. 315
204   "women saints": ii. 297
204   "their prices!": ii. 324
205   divorce costs: ii. 327 n. 2
205   wept bitterly: FL, foreword to *LCL*; *Memoirs* 454
205   "*never* meet again": Hunt N i. 289
205   "to Authority": Ford, N i. 288; Moore, *Intelligent Heart* 194
205   cousin of the Kaiser: Martin Pawly, "On the Contrary," London *Sunday Telegraph*, March 28, 1993
205   "alien enemies!": Carrington 92
206   "cut out for": ii. 351
206   the same joke: ibid.
206   "two million": ii. 340
206   "as he does his": *Memoirs* 195
206   "being the adventure": ii. 636
206   "impersonal thing is in everybody": *Memoirs* 193
206   "*Wille zur Macht*": ibid.
206   "who move upon it": DHL, "Study of Thomas Hardy," *P* 419

206 fear of the female: ibid. 490
206 "nations crave": ibid. 491
207 "the blue distance": ii. 431
207 building the summerhouse: Seymour 225
208 "Of course he didn't": Seymour 240
208 "Do come": Ottoline Morrell to Lytton Strachey, [n.d.] (BL)
208 "dreams of avarice": G. Smith, 86
208 "a good turn": Farjeon 100
208 "to anybody": ibid. 118–19
209 "comin' back no more": ii. 332; Eleanor Farjeon N i. 299 and i. 575 n. 120
209 "for nothing else": ii. 430
209 "children now": ii. 343
209 "made himself": Fisher N i. 304
210 "nearly two years ago": ibid.
210 on Lawrence's typewriter: Asquith, *Diaries* 37
210 rusty sickle: B. Lucas 288–93
210 "terror, and pain": Meynell 288
210 "Mrs. Badleg": ibid. 288–89
210 a visitor who had left the sickle: B. Lucas 289
212 "fighting line": ii. 221; CUP *PO*, xxxi
212 "bottom of the sea": ii. 635
212 "long run": ibid. 635–36
213 told Cynthia what was wrong: Asquith, *Diaries* 19
213 until 1943: "autism" entry, *Oxford Companion of the Mind,* Richard Gregory, ed. (Oxford: Oxford University Press, 1987)
213 Will to Destroy: Cynthia Asquith, "D. H. Lawrence—As I Knew Him," BBC Radio 3, September 7, 1949
213 "ought to die": ii. 360
214 "the Eternal": ii. 363
214 "Caesar": ii. 371
214 letter to Cynthia Asquith: ii. 368
214 "It isn't bosh": ii. 371
214 "worst of all": ii. 370–71
214 "course of years": Moore, *Bertrand Russell* 70–96
214 "State-marriage is a lie": Harry T. Moore, ed., "D. H. Lawrence's Letters to Betrand Russell" contains Lawrence's penciled comments on Russell's manuscripts.
214 "impersonal freedom": ii. 389
214 obliged with an article: ii. 387
214 "I hate it": ii. 392
215 "mental blood-lust": ii. 392
215 morbid rubbish: Russell, *Portraits* 104; also, N i. 284
215 cordial terms: iii. 71
215 Auschwitz: Russell N i. 284–85
216 "so long ago": Brome 103
216 "tempestuous situations": Jones, *Free Associations* 251–52
216 love for long: ibid.
216 "social and personal freedom": Lea 45
216 "after so long a silence": ii. 391
216 bits and pieces: ii. 377
216 blue Persian rug: Hassall 369
216 consulting his children: Barbara Barr to BM, June 30, 1989
217 "in *bliss*": ii. 377

217   would sink: Murry, *Two Worlds* 351
217   "eternal, beyond anxiety": ii. 415–16
217   to surrender: ii. 428 n. 3
217   two weeks later: ii. 440 n. 3
217   advance on royalties: ii. 457 n. 2
218   "the book is so dull": G. Smith 85
218   "to protect it": Lago and Furbank 321
218   ate his lungs: ii. 465
218   survive until spring: Seymour 246
218   "her regard": G. B. Shaw, letter to *Time and Tide*, August 6, 1931,
        863
218   "extinguishes on paper": Asquith, *Diaries* 98
219   "medicinal to my soul": G. Smith 88
219   " 'sisters' of this life": ii. 474
219   "for supposed immorality": Copley 5
219   planting potatoes and tobacco: Heseltine N i. 347
219   need to fight: ii. 444
220   "climate perfect": ii. 452
220   "cursed New York": ii. 450
220   Russian toque: ii. 454
220   bad for his chest: Carswell, 37
220   passing through: ii. 419
220   necessary doctor's letter: ii. 623 and n. 3
220   "almost to *madness*": ii. 474
220   in the pouring rain: HD to Amy Lowell, November [n.d.] 1915 (Har-
        vard)
220   "across the sea": ii. 474
220   "slumbering strength": ibid.
220   "spectral submission": ibid.
220   fear of the medical profession: G. Smith, 315
220   he obliged: ii. 482
220   westward: ii. 491
220   first step to Florida: ii. 489–90

CHAPTER 9: THE YEARS THE DAMAGE WAS DONE

221   "Dear Mr. Russell": *Memoirs* 198
221   "on the brink" . . . "further": ii. 500
222   already dead: ii. 532
222   "sight of": *Memoirs* 198
222   forbidden to travel: Moorehead 254–56
222   "mustn't think about anything": ii. 530
222   a great writer: 474n
222   "in several quarters": Copley 16
222   "terrible artists' wives": Delany 200
222   must be mad: ibid.
223   "untrammelled life is very splendid": Copley 10
223   "I thank heaven": ii. 539
223   "almost impossible": Copley 17
223   very poor: ii. 566
223   six feet four inches high: visit to Higher Tregerthen, October 13,
        1990
223   live there forever: ii. 583
224   insult: ibid.

224   could not afford: ii. 579
224   bohemians and dubious couples: Stevens 11
224   "nuts go to the toe": Lea Cammack to BM, October 13, 1990
224   take a better look at them: *Memoirs* 202
224   made a dresser: ii. 582
224   royal blue: ii. 585
224   Coconut matting: ii. 585–86
225   "Blutbruderschaft": ii. 571
225   might find Lawrence changed: ibid.
225   seething with hate: ii. 558 n. 4
225   "enjoy playing with": Sullivan-Scott 261
225   thing about Shelley: Murry, *Two Worlds,* 411
225   "had enough of you": Sullivan-Scott 263
226   Katherine particularly: See also Murry, *Two Worlds,* 403–406.
226   " 'near this table' ": Sullivan-Scott 267
226   "big soft woman": ibid. 263
226   "sat down too": ibid. 267
226   "macaroni cheese": ibid. 268
226   "anyone but you": ibid.
226   tuberculosis from Lawrence: Tomalin, 163
227   simultaneous orgasm: Birkin suffers from this frustration, and Comp-
        ton Mackenzie reported Lawrence having complained of the problem
        to him, *My Life and Times: Octave Five,* 167–88
227   "for the other sex": *PII* 92
227   "kindling" . . . "nearness": ibid. 92
227   "possess the bodies of such men": ibid. 106
227   "move him instead": ibid.
228   after his death: Bennett Cerf published the foreword in the Modern
        Library edition in 1936, but the prologue did not appear until *PII* in
        1968 with the considerable understatement that "serious readers will
        be interested to see what Lawrence finally omitted" (*PII* xi).
228   "killing me" . . . "obscene bug": Murry, *Two Worlds* 408–417
228   "windbags and nothings": ii. 611
229   "complete identity": ii. 667
229   "end-of-the-world": iii. 25
230   "pulsing frictional to-and-fro": *PII* xiii, 276
230   murderous aggression: G. Ford 182; Cox 181
230   "shake it over them": ii. 650
231   "the novel I write": ii. 610
231   "pig-sty": O. Sitwell 21
231   no pacifist: iii. 84
231   "impossible feet": ii. 618
232   he had consumption: ii. 623
232   even his house: iii. 627
232   he asked Catherine Carswell: ibid.
232   total of fifty-two: "German Estimate of British Losses," *The Times*
        (London), May 1, 1916, 1
232   "did she find him?": Stevens 82
232   "do with him": ibid.
233   come home: ibid. 49
233   "take an interest": ii. 642
233   a luxury: See iii. 89–90.
233   "irreverent and destructive": ii. 659
233   without terror: ii. 641

234 "tears one's lungs": ii. 650
234 "without anxiety": ii. 641 and n. 1. A word is missing in the text of the letter.
234 a day with them: ii. 664
234 delicate coloring: FL to Catherine Carswell, [n.d.] 1916 (John Carswell)
234 "What do you want us to wear?": ibid.
234 anything from their mother: ibid.
234 "real book": ii. 659
234 "The Latter Days": ibid.
234 "nothing to do with her": iii. 44
235 "into a novel": ibid.
235 "anyhow I *think* so": *Memoirs* 210
235 "kick them downstairs": ibid.
235 sue for libel: iii. 109
236 "the secret purpose of *Women in Love*": Murry, *Son of Woman* 118
236 "mechanical movements": iii. 48
236 scorning American democracy: iii. 4
236 "die outright": iii. 88
236 "cannot breathe": iii. 78
236 "than the physical": iii. 75
237 main source of income: iii. 75–76
237 "more innocent than children": iii. 24
237 "American trousseau": FL (signed "Columbina") to Mountsier [n.d.], Higher Tregerthen (Texas)
237 not clearing out in 1915: iii. 367
237 "National Service": iii. 92
237 he told Catherine Carswell: iii. 93
237 list for Rananim: iii. 8
237 "une passade": Delavenay 284 says that Frieda told Mabel in 1922 that Lawrence had had "une passade" with Esther Andrews in 1917 in Cornwall. See also Luhan 51.
237 a relief to her: FL to MDL. Lucas dates letter April 28, 1930. Berkeley
237 "Poems of a Married Man": iii. 86
238 "the future for me": iii. 124
238 "unreal plane": Asquith, *Diaries* 294
238 pushing the pram: ibid. 296
238 "diarrhoea": iii. 119
238 "aggregate London": iii. 117
238 *Small Gardens:* iii. 103, 108
238 "vivid one": Draper 111
238 "insurpassable vividness": ibid.
238 mass democracy: iii. 4 and *PI* 669–718
238 "imaginary portrait again": iii. 104
239 "standeth complete": Meyers 210
239 "ever get it?": ii. 643
239 consummated their love: Delany, "Men in Love," *London Review of Books,* July 25, 1991, 21; Meyers 214. However, Hocking's brother William strongly denied that the relationship was homosexual: *DHLR,* vol. 6, no. 3 (fall 1973), 250
239 "fought him and won": *Memoirs* 360
239 dreadfully unhappy: Luhan 51
239 bad heart: Stevens 111
239 Bosigran Castle: Lea Cammack to BM, November 5, 1990
240 apart from the Lawrences: Gray 115

240 "self-abasement": ibid. 126
240 "immune to none": ibid. New afterword by Pauline Gray.
240 "no place": ibid. 115
240 as they slept: Stevens 109
241 forced to leave his seaside home: FitzGerald 6
241 monks in monasteries: "Monks and Military Service," *The Times* (London), October 15, 1917
241 advice to amputees: "The Wounds of War," ibid.
241 did not go to church: Stevens 108
241 *Berliner Tageblatt*: ii. 609
242 clearly had been searched: *Not I* 77
242 "better than I do": ibid. 78
242 "the field outside": iii. 168; also, Stevens 110
242 paid until the following year: *Memoirs* 213
243 "To St. Ives—Lawrence": Stevens 113
243 to "spend the raid": Fraser 239
243 sardines and pears: Asquith, *Diaries,* October 28, 1917
243 "bellies and breasts": Asquith, ibid.
243 "pretty ill": H.D. to AL, November 14, 1917 (Yale)
243 "I am not": iii. 178
244 "You want": iii. 180
244 *"no idea of what he is like"*: Norman Holmes Pearson's preface to *H.D.'s Tribute to Freud* (Boston: David R. Godine, 1974), xii
245 black-and-gold brocade: Patmore 83; N iii. 99
245 Eder's relatives: iii. 174
245 a complication: iii. 173
245 "a little girl": iii. 161
245 "Paraguay, Colombia": iii. 174
245 "Frieda and me together": iii. 201
246 reported to Benjamin Huebsch: iii. 400
246 another two hundred: iii. 207n
246 "prostitutey": Lambert, N i. 465
246 "too much married": ibid. 503
246 "with other folk": iii. 223
246 twenty pounds to spend: iii. 240
247 "navel of England": Moore, *Intelligent Heart* 242
247 "point of the intellectual": Healey and Cushman 132
247 "nobody can deny": ibid.
247 "jaguars of wrath": iii. 247
247 "glad of their presence": iii. 289
247 "meals are islands" . . . "it saves one": iii. 245
247 "a damn girt cart-oss": William Lawrence, Gerard interview (NCL)
248 "one *is* the present": iii. 278
248 set up to investigate: *The Times* (London), September 3, 1917
249 "find a substitute": iii. 358
250 sleeping apart: Tomalin 490–91
250 "Jamais": iii. 307
250 "stewing": Murry, *Journal of Katherine Mansfield* 146
250 "in one's soul": iii. 291
250 "on my mind": iii. 302
250 "kind of incest": ibid.
250 "Hence our fight": ibid.
251 "who created it": Greiff 81
251 anesthetize his bride: Millett 265

251	"man and a male": Millett on this passage from "The Fox," ibid.
251	"all of them": iii. 306
252	"out of Europe this year": iii. 316
252	"midst of things": iii. 320
252	anguished: EJ to FG, September [?] 1919, Letter 74
252	"gem of life": iii. 333
252	producing two articles: See Sagar *Calendar* 93.
252	"very nice indeed": iii. 340
253	"it has to me": iii. 337
253	to each other: Margaret Needham to BM, February 14, 1990
253	"sick monkey": iii. 340
253	"end of the world": iii. 351
253	"do the writing up?": iii. 353
253	"our State begins": ibid.
253	"to clear out": iii. 367
254	"to be pregnant": iii. 213
254	"steady her": iii. 314
254	"younger generation": iii. 275
254	"it is a girl": iii. 366
254	"pull you in half!": Hilda Brown Cottrell, N i. 496
254	humiliating Frieda: Cecily Lambert Minchin, N i. 504–505
255	"not having any one stay": Amy Lowell to DHL, August 13, 1919, Healey and Cushman 80–82. This was the second, and stronger, of two discouraging letters.
255	Rosalind was a freethinker: Thornycroft 30
255	medical career from scandal: Thornycroft 88; BM interview with Chloë Baynes Green, August 15, 1991
255	Godwin's own father blamed: Thornycroft 61n
256	pacifists: ibid. 56
256	"must be deeper": iii. 478
256	"my own sister-in-law!": Herbert Farjeon, N i. 460; BM interview with Annabel Farjeon Anrep, May 24, 1990
256	wash up: BM interview with Bridget Baynes Coffey, September 20, 1990
256	assured Else: iii. 346
256	*English Review*: iii. 565
257	fifty-five pounds: ibid.
257	twenty pounds for translations: iii. 402

CHAPTER 10: *LEGIONNAIRE'S DISEASE*

261	"nothing yet": iii. 419
261	"your Auntie Frieda": iii. 418
261	"waiting for Frieda": iii. 419
261	"wire from her": iii. 420
261	"wait for Mrs Lawrence": ibid.
261	"be long": ibid.
261	"here quickly": ibid.
261	"this day week": iii. 422
261	"on Dec 2nd": iii. 423
261	"next Wednesday": ibid.
261	"is coming": iii. 426
261	"is here": iii. 428
261	thinner: iii. 427

262   the unfinished manuscript: iii. xxii; iii. 544
262   "stay here a while": iii. 438
262   before dawn . . . argued: *MM* 40
262   *amico:* iii. 594
262   Crimea: MM to ND, July 18, 1920 (Yale), gives background of his
        Russian memoirs.
262   "masculine pederast": Benkovitz, *A Passionate Prodigality* 126
263   "for one minute": D. Garnett, "The Bolter," review of Mark Hollo-
        way's *Norman Douglas, New Statesman,* December 10, 1976, 841.
        Also see Holloway 229–32.
263   Natural History Museum: Holloway 229–32
263   open his mouth: "He more than once told me he had a syphilitic throat
        and invited me to inspect it, opening his mouth wide." Benkovitz, 125
263   pregnant mistress's husband: Holloway 101
263   "*deserved* it, my dear": ibid. 172
263   met in Capri: *MM* 109
263   best imitations: Tomlinson 29
263   "half an hour": *MM* 29
263   "dye it that": ibid. 38
264   "fetch me": ibid. 33
264   "I had never met": ibid. 30
264   "mistrust the world too much": ibid. 35
264   "stroke for the public": iii. 311
265   " 'passeth understanding' ": MM to ND, October 5, 1917 (Yale)
265   "heavenly unbroken sleep": Holloway 249
265   helped him write it: ibid. 248
265   peddling the manuscript: MM to ND, January 29, 1920 (Yale)
265   three hundred pounds: MM to ND, May 12, 1918 (Yale)
265   serialization: MM to ND, January 29, 1920 (Yale)
265   tragedy of his life: Holloway 246
265   "in one's body": *MM* 143
266   "in the face": ibid.
266   "that sort of thing": *MM* 144–45
266   "unbearable burden": ibid. 147
266   offer it to a publisher: MM to ND, May 9, 1920 (Yale)
266   straightforward story all the same: DHL to Stanley Unwin, April 2,
        1920 (University of Reading)
267   "ends: finally": iii. 488
267   "erupts again": iii. 485
267   linen and a toothbrush: MM to ND, May 9, 1920 (Yale)
267   ninety thousand words: ibid.
267   reached Taormina on April 26: ibid.
267   Both agree: ibid.; *MM* 68
267   was frosty, scolding Magnus: *MM* 66
267   Magnus wrote Douglas: MM to ND, May 9, 1920 (Yale)
268   Magnus's hotel bill: See iii. 648 for Taormina hotel prices.
268   "most commodious house": ibid.
268   papers, and their proceeds: ibid.
268   he told Unwin: DHL to Stanley Unwin, May 4, 1920 (University of
        Reading)
268   writing again to Unwin: DHL to Stanley Unwin, May 15, 1920 (Uni-
        versity of Reading)
268   On or about May 5: iii. 512; iii. 513–15
268   "thrilling": iii. 527

269	ninety lire: *MM* 79
269	"Knock-out!": iii. 530
269	"Mrs Gilbert Cannan & his wife": MM to ND, October 28, 1920 (Yale)
270	"No, I don't": iii. 535
270	"beastly island": *MM* 87
270	to see a friend: iii. 540
270	"do anything you want": *MM* 87
270	begun *Mr. Noon*: iii. 522 and n. 3; CUP *Noon* xxiii
270	Unwin had rejected: Stanley Unwin to DHL rejected the manuscript on May 31, 1920, as unlikely to find sufficient sale, and on June 25, 1930, wrote DHL that they had written to MM at Valletta saying they feared they could not make a success of his book (University of Reading).
270	*"awfully good"*: iii. 564
270	"going to Germany": MM to ND, July 18, 1920 (Yale)
270	"come & see you": iii. 575

CHAPTER 11: WHERE THE CLIMATE'S SULTRY

271	kept private: See Thornycroft; BM interview with Chloe Baynes Green, August 15, 1991
271	not coming as well: iii. 601
271	fond he was: iii. 346
271	instantly seize: iii. 415–16
271	night at the Savoy: Thornycroft 60
272	wartime detention: See "Army Officer's Suit for Divorce. Baynes v. Baynes and Hooper," *The Times* (London), April 27, 1921; also see Thornycroft 60.
272	headlines: ibid.; also Thornycroft 61–62
272	any money for support: Thornycroft 68
272	misgivings: iii. 463
272	castor oil: Thornycroft 73
272	glared at by English females: iii. 591
272	eleven: iii. 592
273	model for his Tess: Thornycroft 15
273	"sex in your life?": The scene and quotations are taken from Thornycroft 78–79.
274	"And so to bed": ibid. 79
274	Sir George Clausen: Clausen's color portrait, painted in 1907, appears as the frontispiece in Thornycroft.
275	"Divine Providence": iii. 594
275	"because of the way he took her": Its restoration to the text of *AR* is described in Sagar, *Calendar* 120.
275	"would be sad": iii. 601
276	Friedele's behavior: FG to EJ, [n.d. but evidently later than March 1921], Letter 78
276	Peppino D'Allura: conversation with Mark Kinkead-Weekes, August 16, 1992. Also, "*I peccati e gli amori di Taormina* by Gaetano Saglimbeni (Sins and Loves of Taormina) and Lady Chatterley's Mule Driver," *The European*, August 31–September 2, 1990, 13
277	misogynistic as it is brilliant: Nixon 167
279	"David Herbert Lawrence": Aldington, preface to *Aaron's Rod* (Penguin, 1950)
279	suitcase containing manuscripts: Inventory of effects of the Late Maurice Magnus. Malta. November 23, 1920 (ND Collection, Yale)

279 "sick of it": DHL to ND, November 16, 1920 (Yale)
280 "give them tuberculosis": See, for example, *Fantasia of the Unconscious* (New York: Viking, 1960), 97 and 159.
280 "in the air now": iv. 27
280 "own bastard spawn": from "Psychoanalysis vs. Morality" in *Psychoanalysis and the Unconscious* (Penguin) 207
280 "real motivity": ibid.
280 "Freudian unconscious": iii. 466
280 "will seem to you": iii. 735
280 "To hell with them": iii. 656
281 more stupid than the Italians: iii. 645
281 Connecticut farmhouse: iii. 659–78
281 "without touching the American": iii. 714
281 "no one smash" . . . "Ghibelline business": iii. 676–77
281 "Zion stunt": iii. 690
282 *"wary* of them": iii. 678
282 "rising high in key": Earl Brewster N ii. 59
282 "era of war ahead": iii. 732
282 "never beg": iv. 51
282 "first strawberries": iii. 721
282 raincoat: iii. 723
283 "for Bavaria": iii. 728
283 "after the war": iii. 717
283 "moneyhogs in motorcars": iv. 33
283 at her disposal: Will of Doctor of Philosophy Edgar Jaffe, March 10, 1920 (Staatsarchiv, Munich)
283 the support of Peter: FG to EJ, May 27, 1911, Letter 80
283 Gross had died: FG to EJ [spring, n.d.] 1920, Letter 75
283 "done with the money?": BM interview with Barbara Barr, August 22, 1992
283 "below the knee": iii. 723
283 shopping list: iv. 39
283 "or anybody else's": iv. 49
283 "to this hotel": iv. 44
283 "speaks good English": iv. 38
284 "mere exposition": Draper 162
284 "sub-human and bestial": Draper 172
284 to Frieda Gross: iv. 39
284 "mankind is craving": *Fantasia* 88
284 *"read and write—never"*: *Fantasia* 87
284 "when they come": iv. 30
284 " 'rewrite the stories' ": Zytaruk 222
284 "not to put my name": iv. 165
284 paid for it: iv. 151
285 unable to breathe: iv. 64
285 withhold the second part: iii. 630
285 suit for libel: iv. 87
285 withdraw all outstanding copies: ibid.
285 "hush-money": iv. 130
285 "flushed down a sewer": iv. 114
285 wondered uneasily: iv. 129
286 like a papyrus: Luhan 5
286 bold penmanship: Mabel Luhan's handwriting can be seen in her letters at Yale, Berkeley, and Texas.

286   worshipped the sun: iv. 123
286   medicinal root: Luhan 5
286   "pre-white era": ibid.
286   same letters: iv. 111
286   "no little bees": iv. 111–12
286   "Is there a colony": iv. 111
286   "New York altogether": iv. 123
286   "genuine": Luhan 7
287   "rancid in my mouth": iv. 105
287   making a will: ibid.
287   "I shall go": iv. 114
287   "a long tail": iv. 126
287   "chiefly of spleen": iv. 109
287   horrible Christmas dinner: iv. 151
287   "sun magic": iv. 154
287   Palermo to New York: iv. 166
287   "avoid New York": iv. 162, 165
288   "against the pricks": iv. 170
288   "to come back?": ibid.
288   to Colombo: iv. 175
289   portraying him unforgettably: *MM* 108
289   "all the cash yourself": Sagar 120
289   only for his introduction: iv. 178
290   "But Magnus?": *MM* 93–94
290   forty pounds in sterling: iii. 425
290   Another fifty pounds: iii. 428
290   ten pounds: *MM* 29
290   sixty-three pounds: DHL to ND, December 21, 1920 (Yale)
291   stay clear of the San Domenico: iii. 517, 648
291   "save his life": *MM* 92
291   lingering, haunting guilt: See Lawrence's Letter to the *New Statesman*
        (v. 395): "To discharge an obligation I do not admit, I wrote the
        Introduction."

CHAPTER 12: *CALLING IT AUSTRALIA*

292   "easier to tackle": Luhan 15
292   "Ceylon onto me": ibid.
293   "Mamma to the -nth": BM interview with Barbara Barr, October 14,
        1989
293     $1,729.54: Lawrence's account book, Charleroi National Bank (North-
        western)
293   fund to provide T. S. Eliot: Ackroyd 101
293   They took: iv. 108–9
293   painted wooden panel: Brewster N ii. 123
293   peasant speech into English: G. M. Hyde 38; Davis 84
293   exercise his powers of description: iv. 211–12
293   embroidering a rug: Mrs. A. L. Jenkins N ii. 116
293   in mind to call: ibid.
294   "never leave it": Achsah Brewster N ii. 123
294   heat . . . so sick: iv. 239, 224; N ii. 119
294   nasty: iv. 225
294   "livelong night": iv. 225
294   "negative": iv. 231

294   "one bit": iv. 221
294   dark-skinned: Earl Brewster N ii. 118
294   should be stopped: iv. 182–83 and n. 3
294   "undisputed authority": iv. 226; N ii. 122
294   might not like that either: iv. 228
294   "your faults": Earl Brewster N ii. 118
294   "no bottom to it": Achsah Brewster N ii. 130
294   "out of his skin": iv. 215
294   "he knows it": iv. 218
295   "a true pagan": Achsah Brewster N ii. 130
295   "harm": ibid.
295   "that part really good": iv. 235
295   blast of nothingness: Skinner N ii. 137; iv. 238
295   ghost: iv. 239
295   "foreign spirit": iv. 238
295   "won't be our day": iv. 240
296   "people you know": R. Darroch 13
296   an idea struck him: Jenkins N ii. 116
296   radical and poet: Naomi Segal, *Who and What Was Siebenhaar: A Note on the Life and Persecution of a Western Australian Anarchist.* Perth: Centre for Western Australian History, U. of Western Australia, 1988.
296   "solar plexus!": Skinner N ii. 139
297   "how I hate them": iv. 239
297   "Antarctic": iv. 242
297   no thought of work: iv. 244
297   *Morning Herald:* Davis 31
297   Alfred Callcott: ibid. 75
298   "quite fatal": iv. 269
298   "be avoided": ibid.
298   shit-carter: Davis 65ff.
298   "we're-in-Austrylia": iv. 271
298   "awful like this?": iv. 247
298   "more socialism": iv. 249
298   "housewifes": iv. 266
299   began his new novel: See iv. 251 n. 4.
299   "from the bone": Darroch 68–69
299   scattered everywhere: iv. 268
299   hat blew into the sea: iv. 272
299   "spit at it": iv. 275
300   "attempt at revolution": iv. 267
300   clean out of his text: Steele, "*Kangaroo*: Fiction and Fact" 28
300   "here than anywhere": iv. 266
300   wondered at the expense: Forrester ii. 158
301   network of secret right-wing armies: R. Darroch 26–27. See also Andrew Morton's *The Secret Army and the Premier.* Sydney: University of New South Wales Press, 1989.
301   riot at Moore Park: Hall and Ruffels 12; R. Darroch 86
302   "wholly imagined": Aldington, introduction to Penguin *Kangaroo* 8
303   a sinister reality: R. Darroch 105
303   Sir John Monash: Bruce Steele, introduction to CUP *Kangaroo* xxviii
304   "than was previously thought": David Ellis, "Lawrence in Australia: The Darroch Controversy," *DHLR*, vol. 21, no. 2 (summer 1989), 167–74

304   *Fantasia of the Unconscious:* Steele, introduction to CUP *Kangaroo* and letter to BM, February 4, 1993

304   pour into Australia: iv. 246

305   "aristocratic in spirit": iv. 277

305   "not to remember": iii. 549

306   "thought adventure": iv. 353

307   one continuous autobiography: Gerald Doherty, "One Vast Herme-neutic Sentence: The Total Lawrentian Text," *PMLA*, October 1991, 1124–45

307   cultureless louts: BM interview with Robert Darroch, November 13, 1989; see also Barlett and "D. H. Lawrence met none of us, yet he found us hollow and shallow," by "I.M.," *The Age*, September 1948.

308   "does not exist": David J. Tacey, "On Not Crossing the Gap: Lawrence and our Genius Loci," *Quadrant*, November 1990, 69–73

308   "eludes me, and always would": iv. 272

308   "ever get up": iv. 244

309   "Diggers might resent anything?": iv. 320

309   " 'hill of beans' ": *Memoirs* 413

CHAPTER 13: THE SEARCH FOR HEALTH IN THE SOUTHWEST

310   "east of the Rocky Mountains": Billy Jones, *Health-Seekers* 56

310   nation's tuberculars: Billy Jones 182–83

310   "go West and rough it": Burke 93

311   disguise their condition: Billy Jones 191

311   "shut the door upon them": ibid. 189

311   look more Indian: Rudnick 153

311   "at-one-ment": Rudnick 133

311   "reading this book": MDL to Thomas Wolfe, August 25, 1939 (Harvard)

312   "Which Are You?": Rudnick 140

312   "last Hearst column": It appeared on February 8, 1918. See Rudnick 166.

312   in a tepee: Rudnick 155

312   "now this": iv. 313

313   "redskin welcome": iv. 277

313   lunch counter: Luhan 36

313   "rock to lean on?": Luhan 38

313   poet, playwright, and lecturer: "Poet, Dramatist, Lecturer": agent's leaflet advertising Bynner's services as lecturer and dramatic reader, ca. 1915 (Harvard)

313   at a Tom Mix movie: Johnson N ii. 234

313   "Un ménage, hein": Luhan 40; for Bynner's background, see Kraft.

314   "Ezra and not Hal": BM interview with Tom Meyer, May 30, 1990

314   absurd rubbish: Kraft 96

314   meet the famous author: Bynner N ii. 170; Bynner's account differs from Mabel Luhan's own, which was that the decision to lodge the Lawrences at Bynner's was taken at the last minute. See Luhan 39.

314   "book after book as D.H.L.": Benkovitz (19 n. 11) quotes T. E. Lawrence's letter to Charlotte F. Shaw, August 22, 1926.

314   "passionate passages of D. H. Lawrence": Lacy 228

314   "be of interest to you?": Letter from Mrs. Tarkington Baker to DHL, March 20, 1922 (NW)

314   "you're a fool!": Bynner, *Journey* 2
315   worst fault: Kraft 102–3
315   cocktail: *Memoirs* 221
315   "started to attend": "New Mexico," *P* 142
315   thin semi-invalid: Rhodes 676
316   "genuine": Luhan 71
316   self-dramatizing: Watson 33
316   "cube-boxes in a heap": iv. 310
316   "through cañons": iv. 296
316   "her love life": Rudnick 138
317   William Henry Hocking: Luhan 51
317   first twenty minutes: Luhan 103
317   memorable salon: Rudnick 36, 76
317   venereal disease, injections: Rudnick 176
317   "doing of it": MDL to Thomas Wolfe, [n.d.] 1935 (Harvard)
317   thirty-five dollars: Rudnick 155
318   "loaf of bread": Luhan 79
318   "dance like the Indians": ibid. 193–94
318   Not holding back: ibid. 46
318   to ride for hours: iv. 312
319   *The New York Times:* "Certain Americans and an Englishman," *The New York Times Sunday Magazine,* December 24, 1922, 3, 9
319   "he is mad": Luhan 89
319   "sinking" into the flesh: Rudnick 216
320   "that fat belly of yours!": MDL to WB, January 20, 1950 (Harvard)
320   "womb behind the womb": Rudnick 196
320   "padrona": iv. 305
320   most American of sins: iv. 351
320   too late: Luhan 90
321   rent it from her: iv. 335
321   wanted to be alone: Luhan 90
321   "best thing in life": iv. 337
321   witchcraft: Rudnick 195
321   "Lawrengitis" . . . "question of taste?": WB to MDL, February 12, 1923 (Yale)
321   turned her back: Merrild 29
321   "write that book": ibid. 30
322   "don't breathe free": iv. 324
322   too primitive: iv. 343; Merrild (64–66) blames Mabel for the change of plan.
322   Western gear: iv. 336
322   "welcome to do so": Merrild xi
322   "Rolls Royce": Merrild 31
323   against Mountsier's: iv. 319–20
323   "little nothing": iv. 352
323   "more than England does": iv. 363
323   U.S. senator: Senators and Representatives alike earned $7,500 a year in 1922.
323   "creep to immortality": iv. 340
323   no time even to write: iv. 352, 350
323   "but trustworthy": iv. 367
324   "roll with laughter": Adele Seltzer to Dorothy Hoskins, January 7, 1923 (Lacy 251)
324   "brutish": ibid.

324 "faith in him as a writer": Adele Seltzer to Dorothy Hoskins, January 15, 1923 (Lacy 252)
324 an unpleasant scene: Lacy 188
325 beat her: Luhan 78
325 "no inside life": iv. 362
325 on its nail: Merrild 185–87
326 live with the Danes: iv. 367; Merrild 168
326 "excuse for disloyalties": iv. 368
326 "to try to defend him": Merrild 177
326 "the essence of him": Thomas Seltzer to Knud Merrild, November 5, 1934, Lacy 276
327 ripped them to pieces: Merrild 139
327 not homosexual: Merrild 297
327 anti-Seltzer: iv. 384
327 neither to settle nor to work: U.S. Department of Labor, List of Alien Passengers Arriving at San Francisco on S.S. *Tahiti*, September 4, 1922, entries 5 and 6
328 "that feeling badly": iv. 314
328 "running away from oneself": iv. 313
328 "do you think?": iv. 408
328 recalculated the deductions: iv. 392
328 taxable income: iv. 400
328 "andarmene": iv. 406–407
328 had liked best: iv. 416
328 "a bit ghastly": ibid.
329 consumption: Carleton Beals N ii. 226–30; N ii. 497 n. 11
329 "breeding": ibid.
329 were criminal: iv. 419
329 vile abuse: Frederic Leighton N ii. 229
330 "out into the street": Bynner, *Journey* 31
330 "not what I would do": ibid. 62
330 "that fat Indian around?": Rudnick 202
330 good, if turbulent: ibid. 155; see also 228 for Mabel's affair with the spiritual healer Jean Toomer.
331 fight in the dining room: Kraft 100
331 "New World": iv. 425
331 "Spit on Taos": iv. 422
331 "Chapala paradise": iv. 435
331 "always likes it": Kraft 102
331 "to be *easy*": iv. 436
331 "take breath": iv. 437
331 "off my chest": iv. 454
331 "change my plans": iv. 437
331 "want to stay": iv. 439
332 "sorry for him": Purnell Stone N ii. 268
332 could not talk back: Kraft 104–5
332 "his poor fury": ibid.
333 "with that name?": iv. 457
333 "wild and unsentimental": iv. 455
333 feminist critics: Storch 157–59
333 "a young one": iv. 434
334 controlling mother: Storch 168
334 "amanuensis": iv. 457
334 "my novel either": iv. 444–45

334   "as far as security goes": iv. 445
334   "in our belts": iv. 463
334   pleased to note: iv. 468
335   "queer show": ibid.
335   "sick all the time": iv. 470
335   "to start flowing": ibid.
335   "without background or atmosphere": iv. 479
335   "Desolate inside": iv. 473
335   "grandly simple": Lacy 267
335   "across the Atlantic": iv. 462
335   to see her children: iv. 458
335   Balaam's ass: iv. 177, 180–81, 479
335   "any farther": iv. 479
335   "those Weekley children": iv. 480
335   "wouldn't let me": iv. 487
335   look after her: iv. 480
336   giving an interview: *New York Evening Post,* August 20, 1923
336   "the infinite": "The Proper Study," P 720
336   "of all art": ibid. 719
336   "sicker than ever": iv. 481
336   "full of graves": iv. 327
336   "blue bloods": iv. 492
336   "canyon-beds of the streets": iv. 494
337   miniature golf: DHL to Dr. Canby, September 1, 1923 (Yale)
337   "a bit deathly": iv. 505
337   "hopeless little towns": iv. 507
337   "vermin": iv. 506
337   doubts about his sanity: Götzsche ii. 266
337   "nuisance?": iv. 480
338   "I do wish it": iv. 375
338   beauty of physical love: Hignett 136
338   "to take no more": DB to JMM, May 28, 1923 (Cincinnati)
338   "god knows what else": Hignett 138
338   "so REAL!": Woodeson 296
338   "face reality!": iv. 385
339   "swallowed her": iv. 520
339   "long fight": iv. 526
339   "cone": iv. 526
339   "love! love!": iv. 532
339   "When you say": *Memoirs* 223
340   "Shades of Hal": iv. 536
340   "can't bear it": Hignett 142
340   "in his tomb": iv. 546
340   back to Taos: iv. 545

CHAPTER 14: BLOOD

342   borderline of sanity: Benkovitz 140–41; see also Rossman, "D. H.
       Lawrence and Mexico," 181, for the statement that Lawrence's art is
       incomplete in itself.
342   "in any case": v. 26
342   "Oh! Susanna": DB N ii. 308; Brett 26
342   honest laugh: iv. 555
342   betray him again: Catherine Carswell 222; Lea 120; Murry, *Reminis-
       cences* 175; John Carswell 202–203; Brett N ii. 302–304

343 "subdued malice": "Coming Home," *PII* 254
343 "Fritzl": *Not I* 153
343 things to come: Clark 300
343 "nobody now can alter it": "Letter from Germany," *P* 109–10
343 "daughter of Viscount Esher": iv. 550
343 Her mother had died: For Brett's early life, see Hignett 30.
344 "like a woman": description of Brett (as "James") in "The Last Laugh" 834
344 "violent they were?": DB to WB, February 9, 1951 (Harvard)
344 "in the harbour": iv. 481
344 polygamists, nor immigrants: U.S. Immigration List of Alien Passengers entering the U.S. at New York on S.S. *Aquitania,* March 5, 1924
345 "the Knopf sense": v. 79
345 $43.74: v. 39
345 $5,681: tax return, March 14, 1924 (Texas)
345 quarreling with Mabel: Kraft 111
345 "to pueblo now": Brett 53–54
346 "Guts-Besitzer": v. 29
346 little ranch of her own: v. 30
346 original manuscript of *Sons and Lovers: Memoirs* 335; Luhan 192
346 "D'y blame *meh*?": John Ciardi, taped interview with DB for CBS, 1961 (UNM)
347 "Indians and Entertainment": v. 36; the article appears in *Mornings in Mexico.*
347 "dance on and on": "Dance of the Sprouting Corn," *Mornings in Mexico* 110
347 "without affecting one another": "Pan in America," *P* 24–25
348 "probably children": v. 43
348 "I hate it!": Brett 148
348 "to cool her underneath": Brett 153
348 "Chiquita": Luhan 196
348 dandelion wine: FL papers (Texas)
349 making her own clothes: Bynner later defended Frieda against charges made by Diana Trilling in her "Letter of Introduction" to *The Selected Letters of D. H. Lawrence* that Frieda was mindless and "had no way of dealing with the ordinary, whether it was eating a meal or making a dress." Unpublished paper, Bynner collection, Harvard.
349 "don't care": v. 46
349 "*like* the porcupines": Luhan 204
349 "available, invisible Being": "Plum," Luhan 244
349 "treat me like this?": Luhan 206
349 acquiescing: Rossman, "Myth and Misunderstanding" 92ff.
352 sadistic triumphalism: Millett 293
352 true virility: "On Being a Man," *P* 620–22
352 to go West to write: Meyers 310–11
352 "strange effeminate way": Foster, *Lawrence in Taos* 156, 160
352 sexual relationship: Rudnick 216
352 conversations and rows: Brett 110
353 "nice boy": v. 48
353 "not weak really, at all": v. 59
353 "much jewellery": "Altitude," *Collected Plays* 535
353 "never be seen again!": Luhan 222
353 "head hanging": ibid. 222–23

353   "tail-wagging": ibid. 189
353   a night of farce: ibid. 226–33
354   whisky and . . . puppies: v. 60
354   "pick one's way out of it": v. 65
354   out of town on a rail: Andrew Dasbury to Edward Nehls, May 6, 1956
        (Texas)
354   "those Lawrences": Luhan 241
355   "Lawr," as Frieda called Lawrence: FL to MDL, August 3, 1924. Also
        v. 349; v. 569; vi. 375
355   "Two Ladies and a Horse": v. 173
355   recoils from the sexual act: Cavitch 154
355   fear of coitus: ibid. 156–58
356   "lion's den": v. 64
356   "not possible twice": v. 107
357   "menstruation": Luhan 61
357   "Change": Luhan 157
357   "teach you": Brett 140, DB N ii. 357
358   "till L is better": FL to MDL, August 3, 1924 (Yale)
358   how to make the bread: Brett 141–42
358   "billy-o": v. 90
358   "in the sand": v. 101–2 n. 1
358   antagonized both women: Luhan 265
359   businessman: v. 103 n. 1
359   "interesting but not beautiful": v. 101
359   rattlesnakes in their mouths: "Hopi Snake Dance," *Mornings* 149
359   fifty thousand dollars: Luhan 265
359   "too ugly": v. 106
360   "The Waste Land": F. R. Leavis, *D. H. Lawrence: Novelist* 5, 279
360   "get his own back": Rossman, "Myth" 91
360   Cavitch has suggested: Cavitch 169
360   "Gertie keeps well": v. 115
360   bronchopneumonia and heart failure: Death Certificate of John Arthur
        Lawrence, 77, Retired Coal Miner Stallman of 17 Bailey Street, East-
        wood
360   in a man's life: Freud, introduction to second edition of *Interpretation
        of Dreams,* 1908. See also E. Jones, *Freud* i. 324.
360   "upset one": v. 142
360   "Wasn't there room?": v. 139
360   "fix it up": v. 140
361   "I was wrong": v. 127
361   "to go south": v. 121
361   "always want to go south": v. 122
361   "südwärts gehen": v. 138
361   "doesn't get better quickly": v. 125
361   a warm forgiving letter: v. 143
361   "no longer riding": v. 135
361   "genius loci": v. 160
362   "with a stutter": v. 157
362   "begins on Monday": v. 156
362   "untidy show": v. 172
362   To Murry, Lawrence declared: v. 168
362   "got left": "See Mexico After," *P* 115
363   convulsed with laughter: Parmenter 56
363   "toddle back": v. 158

363 "Somebody else's child, thank God!": WB to MDL, November 24, 1924 (Harvard)

364 "Even 'The Woman' . . . did another thing": Luhan 280

364 "capitalist by practice": from the original manuscript of *Plumed Serpent,* at Harvard

364 savage internal conflicts: See Worthen, *Novel* 158–59.

364 "wide of the mark": Calvert 219

366 best of them all: v. 190

366 Simone de Beauvoir: "D. H. Lawrence and Phallic Pride," *The Second Sex* 245–53

367 "He will": Nietzsche, *Zarathustra* 92

367 pleasure without climax: Parmenter 313

368 "stand apart": v. 192

368 friendship without sex: Brett 108

368 aphorism: Joyce's brother Stanislaus claimed that Joyce had lifted this aphorism from his own diaries (Stanislaus Joyce, "The Background to *Dubliners,*" *The Listener,* March 25, 1954).

368 "and I know it": v. 204

369 cargo boat: v. 211

369 intestines: Parmenter 317

369 "nothing at all": *Not I* 132

369 "seemed incredible": ibid.

CHAPTER 15: THE BORDER-LINE

370 diseases: v. 212 and n. 4; FL to DB, February 25, 1925 (Cincinnati)

370 "poison for malaria": v. 218

370 "stare at me again": Brett, N ii. 398–99

371 "stay fat!": v. 215

371 "die so easily": v. 216

371 two years to live: *Not I* 133; FL N ii. 394–95. Dr. Luis Quintanilla (N ii. 396) claims that Lawrence was not told the diagnosis. Parmenter (354) discusses whether Ulfelder himself or "the analyst doctor" broke the news.

371 How long: Moore, *Intelligent Heart* 386; Ober 90–97; Corke, in Hahn, *Lorenzo* 55; Templeton

372 "ever produced?": Parmenter 149

372 "in the middle of England": "The Flying Fish," *P* 780

372 "borderline of death": Brewster 288

372 told Amy Lowell: v. 230

372 stripped and detained: vii. 144

373 "in my life": v. 234–35 n. 2

373 "get along together": v. 234

373 "beat her up afterwards": Hignett 218

373 gazing at him intently: Brett 229

374 "from 47 year olds": v. 40

374 "impertinent": Brett 220

374 "pipes twice over": v. 249

374 "chest going wrong": v. 244

374 "milking her": v. 263

374 "done me in": v. 263

375 "hedged in": v. 278

375 "less literary": v. 263

375 "people *call* life": v. 293

375 "one has lived": ibid.
375 "certain things": *MM* 13. See also Secker.
376 "existence is obscure": Redman
376 "of a dead writer": "Portrait of a Rat (Gold Medal)," *New York World,* June 23, 1925
376 "through Alfred A. Knopf, Inc.": "The Foreign Legion," *The Sun,* 1925[?]
376 most likable: *The Owlglass,* November 1, 1924
376 "suits his convenience": Douglas, *MM* 105ff.
377 mauled: Benkovitz 55
377 sordid than he had printed: v. 231
377 hour of need: ibid.
377 literary executor: Although Lawrence had been told by Douglas on December 26, 1921 (v. 396), that he could go ahead and publish Magnus's book—"Pocket all the cash yourself"—the status of Magnus's copyrights was by no means clear. Not only did Douglas cool toward Lawrence after reading the unflattering portrait of himself in *Aaron's Rod,* published in 1922, but also Lawrence had a later warning against the project. On March 5, 1923, Borg's Maltese lawyer wrote to Thomas Seltzer formally forbidding Lawrence to publish "Dregs" without Borg's agreement, on the grounds that Borg was the "legal referee of all the personal effects, inc. mss. of the late Magnus" (Avvocato William Harding to Thomas Seltzer, ND papers [Yale]).
377 confided in Magnus: See Chapter 10.
377 larger than they were: Aldington (*Pinorman* 179) criticizes Douglas for not helping out Magnus but says that while Lawrence said he possessed only £60, his diary shows that he had £171 at the time.
377 defended himself: "The Late Mr. Maurice Magnus: A Letter," *P* 806–807
378 "Is it true": telegram from Seltzer to DHL, c/o British Consulate, Mexico City, February 7, 1925 (Yale)
378 " 'lady in a hat' ": v. 256
379 Kyle Crichton: The following description is taken from Kyle S. Crichton, "D. H. Lawrence Lives at the Top of the World," Sunday book section, *New York World,* October 11, 1925.
380 "and the place": v. 291
380 "their luck is one": v. 290

CHAPTER 16: MRS. LAWRENCE'S LOVER

383 Regesan Catarrh Jelly: v. 350
383 "I come here": v. 315
383 "Bore!": v. 318
383 "hyphen or no hyphen": iv. 443
383 "toys": v. 200–201
384 "puts me off": v. 332–33
384 "young Englishman": ibid.
384 Mackenzie would recall: interview, National Sound Archive
384 "What do you": Gerhardie N iii. 13
384 "go to hell!": ibid.
385 "what's the good": v. 324
385 "beastly invalid": Carrington 216
385 "does one only harm": ibid. 218
385 "conspiring against us": ibid. 219

385	now advised Brett: v. 299–300
385	fabricated an excuse: Hignett 180
385	"it's from me": v. 333
385	"fluffed": v. 335
385	Austen: v. 344
386	"trumps!": v. 329
386	insisted: v. 326
386	"Americans say": v. 341
386	"It wouldn't": "Europe v. America," *P* 117
386	"already yellow": v. 342
386	scolded Murry: v. 367–68
386	"out of it!": ibid.
386	"where he is": v. 374
386	be friends: ibid.
386	"and basta": v. 344
387	"as the feathers!": v. 350
387	"out of Australia": Draper 266
387	"most interesting theme in the world": ibid. 263
387	"overtaken Lawrence": ibid. 271
387	to enjoy theirs: v. 490
387	"on the cards": v. 367
387	"for a bit": v. 364
387	Barby came to visit: Barr, "I Look Back" 256
388	"Uncle Bert": v. 359–60
388	flirt with him: Barr N iii. 24–26
388	sharp tongue: interviews with Mrs. Barbara Barr, October 1989 and August 1992
388	"million pounds": Barr N iii. 26
388	venomous conversation: Barbara Barr, Gerard interview (NCL)
388	infantry: Ravagli N iii. 18
389	teaching Ravagli English: ibid.
389	early in 1926: see Britton 15; Meyers 341
389	saw the signs: Barr, "I Look Back" 256
389	"false face": *Not I* 158
389	"rotten painting?": ibid. 159
389	outsider: v. 405
389	"swamped out": v. 394
389	"so *important?*": *Not I* 159
389	"Herr Franzius": v. 332
389	"housemaid of the Villa B.": v. 388
389	muddled notes: v. 389
390	"I say nothing": v. 390
390	"by no means mine": v. 394
390	"only worse": v. 390
390	"bottom of my heart": *Not I* 159
390	three of them alone: Ravagli N iii. 27
390	"your coming": v. 399
392	he told Earl Brewster: iv. 109
392	"what I wanted or not": v. 551
392	"bad ones": v. 492
392	all the rest: vii. 3
392	"humiliated": Brett N iii. 31
393	insisting: ibid. 40
393	"can't live with him": v. 403

393 "with Consuls": Brett N iii. 32
393 "nothing happened": This account is from Hignett 191–92, based on Brett's unpublished manuscripts.
393 "pyoobz": Derek Britton to BM, May 13, 1994
393 "in a pot": Brett N iii. 38
394 say only to the other: Hignett 192; v. 404
394 conciliatory: v. 406; Brett N iii. 42, 51
394 "almost too far": Luhan 291. The phrase "out of me too" is deleted from original manuscript at Yale.
394 "in my inside": v. 413
394 "to live on": v. 411
394 "die with laughing": v. 420
394 "bad use of them": v. 416
395 "to utter it": "Fireworks in Florence," *P* 124
395 "Mrs Lorenzo": Sagar, "Lawrence and the Wilkinsons" 73
395 "seems nice": v. 443
396 "ye Gods!": v. 483
396 one size smaller: vi. 42
396 "boys who write": iv. 468
396 "nothing but bed after bed": v. 474
396 "sit in!": v. 474
396 "Queer couple": v. 483
397 "breathe heavily": O. Sitwell 278
397 inhalation cure: v. 502
397 graduate: Gardiner N iii. 76
397 "Northern peoples": v. 497
397 "overburdened by a mission": v. 497
397 "reacts on everything": v. 499
397 Chelsea: v. 498
397 "It is a safe job": The account of this conversation is from C. Montague Weekley, Gerard interview (NCL).
398 "sooch": ibid.
398 "hoot of an owl": West N ii. 62
398 Emily and Ada departed: v. 516–17
398 Lawrence told Ada: v. 526
398 how much Mundesley: v. 516
399 postcard: v. 527, 529
399 warmer months of the year: v. 534
399 "walk with me": The description of the walk is taken from Britton (401ff.).
400 miners stranded: Britton 66–69
400 disorderly rush: ibid. 134
400 revolution: v. 533
400 "spear": v. 592
400 "hopeless countryside": *LCL*; Britton 120
400 higher in the world: "Return to Bestwood," *PII* 261
401 "thing is done": ibid. 265
401 "English life is built": v. 515
401 "sell it": v. 537
401 to a drum: v. 570
401 sat down and wrote: Britton 3; vi. 563
401 "rather improper": v. 576
401 author himself: For a summary of the evidence that Lawrence was indeed impotent by 1926, see Britton 273.

401	no sodomy: Britton (50) says the anal act was introduced in the second version, *John Thomas and Lady Jane.*
402	"the *animal* part": v. 570
402	"very glad!": v. 568
402	fluent if ungrammatical: Aldington, *An Indiscretion*
402	"out of the air!": Rudnick 295, based on letter from MDL to UJ, June 3 [1931] (Berkeley)
402	"just recovering": v. 576
402	hand under the table: MDL to UJ, July 2 [1931] (Berkeley)
402	believer in Mussolini: MDL to UJ, June 3 [1931] (Berkeley)
403	"We all like him": ibid.
403	"Things happen": "Making Pictures" from *Assorted Articles PII* 602
403	copies poor, conscientious at best: Merrild 209
403	"profoundly revealing": Levy 13
403	unclothed body: vi. 506
404	Harold Acton: interview with Sir Harold Acton, October 13, 1989
404	"most unpleasant group": Sagar, "Lawrence and the Wilkinsons" 67
404	"vegetably propagated, even?": v. 576; Sagar, "Lawrence and the Wilkinsons" 67
404	"change from writing": v. 585
404	make cuts: v. 573
404	left lung: v. 538
404	too much milk: v. 545
404	"forever, from everybody": v. 541
404	"but for L.": v. 567
404	Lawrence told his sister: v. 578
405	"cemetery": v. 579
405	"always risky": v. 591
405	"country of my heart": v. 592
405	"big (dimensionally)": v. 596
405	"rather fun": v. 59
405	"still is denied": v. 648
405	rump to limb: See Nixon 227.
406	"Mundesley, don't you?": v. 609
406	"a living that way": v. 619
406	better than Paquin: v. 622
406	"*So* fine": v. 605
406	even writing letters: v. 626, 646
406	"intense whacks": v. 628
406	refused to think: v. 630
406	"sometimes it is like yesterday": v. 634
406	"the register?": v. 640
407	"jim-jams": v. 645
407	"in the pod": v. 601
407	"pecker up": ibid.
407	American slang: v. 176
407	"an exhibition of 'em": v. 600
407	"what a slaughter!": v. 651
407	Chatterleys to worry about: v. 638
407	away for a month: v. 656
407	"too much flu": v. 653
408	"the psychological reality": v. 648
408	"sex swindle": ibid.

CHAPTER 17: FIGHTING BACK

409   "a house, a home": "Cerveteri," *Etruscan Places* 10
410   "very big R": ibid.
410   "terrible significance, and reality, for me": vi. 37
410   wrote to Mabel: Luhan 324
411   "dear dead": "Cerveteri," *Etruscan Places* 6
411   "disfiguring the landscape": "Flowery Tuscany," *P* 48
411   "with joy": v. 646
411   gave him tea: Ravagli N iii. 144
412   disturbed: v. 65; O. Sitwell N iii. 142–43
412   strange pair of siblings: vi. 67; *Not I* 183; Britton 217–18; E. Sitwell 108
412   Sacheverell: Britton 217–18
412   "crudely hideous": O. Sitwell N iii. 142
412   imagined advantages: E. Sitwell 108
412   reeling it in: A. Brewster 282
412   "and get away": *P* 366
412   letting him do it: Barr N iii. 138
412   "telegraph pole": vi. 40–42
413   sex relation: vi. 29
413   "little things": vi. 29 n. 5
413   "ghastly way?": vi. 42
413   "not a working season": vi. 68
414   "The Escaped Cock": Earl Brewster N iii. 136
414   made him change the title: vi. 40 n. 1
414   despised emasculating force: Rossman, "You Are the Call" 320
414   "Lawrence's genius": Aldington, *Indiscretion*
415   "passion of hatred": ibid.
415   in London by May 8: DHL to Phyllis Whitworth, April 30, 1927 (R. Whitworth)
415   "malaria again": vi. 62
415   "coloured coat": DHL to Phyllis Whitworth, May 13, 1927 (R. Whitworth)
415   "cow bellow": DHL to Phyllis Whitworth, May 28, 1927 (R. Whitworth)
416   "got to win!": FL to Phyllis Whitworth, [n.d.] (R. Whitworth)
416   "bleeding altitude": vi. 136
417   from his mouth: *Not I* 173; Frieda N iii. 146
417   Coagulin: vi. 98
417   To Mark Gertler: vii. 109
417   routine: Carrington 224 (August 9, 1927)
417   "tired of it": v. 98
418   "sudden and unexpected": G. Smith 288–89
418   "martyrs in the world": vi. 104
418   "scares me more and more": ibid.
418   "gone thin": vi. 45
418   "questi guai": vi. 111
419   "hate it so?": vi. 226
419   "say to one another": vi. 141
419   "muss futtern": vi. 158
419   "poisonous animal": vi. 161–62
420   "bleeding again": vi. 172
420   three years at most: Franz Schoenberner N iii. 160

420   shirt: vi. 142
420   "big as carpets": vi. 172–73
420   to a sanatorium: vi. 191
420   missed his mother-in-law: vi. 194, 218
421   "well in it": vi. 208
421   "sort of wart-hog": vi. 221
421   "don't want to eat": from "Autobiographical Fragment," *P* 836
421   "more tuberculosis": vi. 225 and n. 2
422   "done by either": ibid.
422   "money things talked about": vi. 137
422   "all the publicity": vi. 223
422   "Beatles' first LP": Larkin, "Annus Mirabilis." *In High Windows.* London: Faber and Faber, 1974. The full quote includes the phrase "(Which was a bit late for me—)."
423   wrote the final version of *LCL*: Sagar, *Calendar* 167–68
423   *Ulysses* six years earlier: vi. 7
423   launched the permissive 1960s: See Mary Kenny, "The Not-So-Lovable Legacy of Lady Chatterley," *London Sunday Telegraph,* January 8, 1989; also "Chatterley Objection" [by Mrs. Mary Whitehouse], *The Times* (London), September 11, 1989.
423   "loose sex activity": vii. 106
423   ruined a good book: introduction to *FLC*
423   "write a third": DHL to Henry James Forman, N ii. 106
426   "driving at": This and other comments on the trial are from Richard DuCann, Q.C. to BM, March 27, 1994.
426   " 'unnatural' sexual practice": Sparrow 35
427   headlines: Montgomery Hyde 31
427   "work of art": Sparrow 41
427   " 'like a slave' ": Knight 406
427   Porter had good fun: Porter
428   "Gardeners' Question Time": Garry Bushell, *The Sun,* June 23, 1993
428   schoolgirl of sixteen should read: Holroyd iii. 274
428   The title is possessive: Lydia Blanchard, "Women Look at Lady Chatterley"
428   it is true: ibid.
429   "as he aged": Gilbert, "Some Notes" 98
429   Asian societies: See Xianzhi Liu, "D. H. Lawrence in China," *DHLR,* vol. 23, no. 1 (spring 1991), 37–42.
429   "wonderfully precious to him": *FLC* 19
429   "decently say to another": Ober 104
430   "most a woman can do": vi. 409
430   Constance Chatterley resembled Rosalind Baynes: Britton's *Lady Chatterley: The Making of the Novel* (1988) illuminated the biographical parallels between Rosalind Baynes and Constance Chatterley before the publication of Rosalind's memoir, *Time Which Spaces Us Apart* (1991), confirmed the affair. Britton also discussed Lawrence's efforts to diminish the resemblance to Rosalind.
430   "settled down again": v. 475
430   "rotten way to be wounded": Hemingway, *The Sun Also Rises,* chapter 1
431   too late to have a baby: MDL to UJ, July 15 [1931] (Berkeley)

Chapter 18: The Bookseller

432   "wrong bird": v. 574

433   "raking on": vi. 255
433   "microbes pounce": vi. 409
433   "a bit frightening": vi. 276
433   solar plexus: Bedford 92
433   "a bad cold": BM interview with Lady Juliette Huxley, July 3, 1989
434   "*purple* from pink": vi. 309
434   "queer delight": ibid.
434   trade discount: vi. 362–63
434   "as good as married": vi. 317
435   "its own secrets": Barr N iii. 189
435   more to the point: vi. 438
435   seven-hundred-dollar ticket: vi. 367
435   "*ces femmes*": vi. 365
435   "crack off": vi. 405–406
436   for another minute: Achsah Brewster N iii. 218
436   "very mad": vi. 428
436   "not my lungs": vi. 439
436   "look after me so well": vi. 433
437   Vevey at midnight: Achsah Brewster N iii. 219
437   reluctant to go: vi. 437
437   "quite a party": vi. 436
437   "beautiful, outwardly": vi. 440
437   "Not cheap!": vi. 480
437   "unpaid": vi. 483
437   "if bad weather comes": vi. 453
437   "die of gloom": ibid.
437   "blue eyed *Eunuch*!": vi. 487
438   "one can't wonder": vi. 419
438   "get anything done": vi. 456
438   "rural England": review of *England and the Octopus*, P 385
438   "can't climb": vi. 481
438   "boast of now": vi. 530
438   "Douglas—has he paid?": vi. 515–16
439   "*orders to me, here*": vi. 400
439   "funeral": vii. 137
439   "conspirator": vi. 490
439   "quite unpublishable": vi. 333
439   "cure them of their hypocrisy": ibid.
440   "a book we could not handle": vi. 479–80 n. 3
440   "refund the money": vi. 490
440   "master of my movements": vi. 521–22
440   modeled on their Renishaw: vi. 579 n. 2
441   "bit of publicity": vi. 552
441   "blood run cold anyhow": ibid.
441   "and everybody pleased": vi. 412
441   " 'vistas democratic'!": vi. 552
441   "go to pieces then": vi. 439
441   "*single bed,* for me": vi. 509
441   "tender about Lady C.": vi. 526
441   "no Inquisition": vi. 378
442   "the ordinary Englishman": from "Hymns in a Man's Life," *PII* 601
442   alternate altitude with sea: vi. 551
443   when they returned: FL to DB, August 12, 1928 (Cincinnati)
443   "saw scarlet": from "Women Are So Cocksure," P 167

443	followed joy: Brewster 289
443	"come soon": vi. 587
443	"not a sign": ibid.
443	"von der Frieda": ibid.
443	"vile": vi. 588
444	detour through Trieste: Aldington N iii. 253
444	never to leave him alone: Patmore N iii. 257
444	"with that flu cold": vi. 598
444	full of light: Doyle 121
444	"jest and adultery": ibid. 120
445	"none like him": vi. 576–77 n. 2
445	"clever contemporaries": *Observer,* vi. 617 n. 3
445	"hold me up about my health": vii. 25
445	"skin deep": vi. 617
445	"more complex than that": G. Smith 339–40
445	His Rampion: Huxley, *Point Counter Point* 154–55
446	"amused him to annoy her": ibid. 158
446	"charm for ever": Patmore N iii. 257
446	insane asylum: RA wrote to H.D. ("Astraea"): "I feel his trying to prove to me at Port-Cros that I was going mad is a rather serious symptom!" [n.d.] (Yale)
446	hour and a half: vii. 26; vi. 28 n. 5
446	"more swing": vii. 29
447	"There, there": Patmore N iii. 256
447	"can really interfere": vi. 613
448	"malevolent and evil": RA to H.D., March 20, 1929 (Yale)
448	"see him again": ibid.
448	"smallish people": vii. 53
448	nothing to do: vii. 52
449	"in the wilderness": Davies, *Print* 138
449	"*everybody* hates him in England": ibid.
449	slap her across the face: ibid. 145
449	"little bursts of fury": Rhys Davies to Charles Lahr, [n.d. 1928?] (David Callard)
449	"get his pecker up": vi. 533
450	"uses them more or less as such": vii. 162
450	view of Bynner: Kraft 200
450	"real doggerel": vii. 64
451	"when she *does,* she minds": vii. 50
451	"years with similar ones": vii. 720
451	"festivating anyhow": vii. 107
451	worth more: vii. 69, 76
451	He had a thousand pounds . . . move on: vii. 85–86
451	"publishing Lady C. for myself": vi. 547
452	stockbroker: vii. 565 n. 5
452	utilities and rails: ibid.; Worthen, *Literary Life* xx. 162 n. 1

CHAPTER 19: A DYING ANIMAL

453	"life different": vii. 210
453	"to admire me": vii. 120
453	"admirers have on me": vii. 118
454	"Studio crowd": vii. 125
454	enemy into a friend: *Memoirs* 232

454 "what to say or do": vii. 186
454 "lend it you": vii. 194
454 "tombs in winter": vii. 40
454 stay for a year: vii. 290
454 "shall never forget": vii. 144
455 "out of spite": ibid.
455 raised in the House of Commons: vii. 5–6; Parliamentary Debates on the Seizure of *Pansies* mss, N iii. 311–12
456 "swindlers": vii. 174
456 given her in payment: Hignett 202–204
457 "go all queer": vii. 203
457 "gone for good": vii. 205
457 "still frozen": vii. 213
458 "rival show": vii. 67
458 "shan't be alone": vii. 210
458 French gloves and shoes: vii. 207
458 "body that doesn't cough": ibid.
458 should not be going to Paris: Davies, *Print* 155
458 the same with "The Escaped Cock": vii. 404, vii. 4
459 eye hurt him: vii. 233 n. 3
459 cerebral and obscene: Delany, "A Would-Be Dirty Mind"
459 "dirty mind": vi. 507
459 "cross upside down": Hugh Ford 197
459 "dresses decently": Ellmann 612
459 Joyce had read: ibid. 615 and 615n.
459 outselling *Ulysses*: ibid. 692
459 find the address: Rhys Davies N iii. 14
459 animated conversation: Dahlberg, *Samuel Beckett's Wake and Other Uncollected Prose.* Dublin: Dalkey Archive Press, 1989
459 "erotic" . . . "sermon-on-the-mount": Fitch 280
460 could not have resisted him: Hugh Ford 30
460 Dahlberg was eager: Dahlberg, "D. H. Lawrence," *The Freeman*, 1952, 281–82; also N iii. 710 n. 85
460 calmed down: Rhys Davies N iii. 315
460 practically gone: G. Smith 313
460 "stinks of petrol": vii. 234
460 "nothing can be done": Carrington 228
461 the Lawrences in bed together: Davies, *Print* 157–60
461 "raising of Lazarus": AH to WB, January 9, 1959 (Harvard)
461 "his own precept": Jaffe N iii. 426
461 "scrapped the story": Helena Rubinstein, *Just for Luck,* serialized by London International Press, 1962
461 "pushy" wife: Hugh Ford 119
461 "Empty Bed Blues": vii. 291 n. 4
462 "signs are favourable": FL to MDL, April 6, 1929 (Yale)
462 "certain staleness": vii. 275
462 "city English": vii. 283
462 school in Eastwood: vii. 189
462 "cancer of our civilisation": "Pornography and Obscenity," *P* 179
463 "show of her dirt": ibid. 176
463 "cat-piss": vii. 249
463 "whack of malaria": vii. 262
463 "sewing machine": ibid.
463 "castanets": vii. 260

463	"favorite fucker": vii. 179
463	"methodising shit-bag": vii. 309, 309 n. 1.
463	Aldington had observed: RA to Mr. Atkins, May 23, 1957 (Texas)
463	"look for one": vii. 284
463	do up a house in Italy: vii. 288
464	immigration barrier: vii. 288, 290
464	he was dying: vii. 295 n. 1, 298, 299, 318
464	"stringy bird": vii. 293
464	"feel perfectly awful": vii. 547
464	"animals are different": vii. 294
464	"dissonance" . . . not dying: ibid.
464	Dartington Hall: vii. 317
464	"last word about anything": vii. 322
464	He told his sister Emily: vii. 327
465	"unmixed colour": *Memoirs* 223
465	back to England: "1929 Ban on D. H. Lawrence's Nudes Lifted," Nigel Reynolds, *Daily Telegraph,* April 14, 1989; Channel 4 documentary, *Lost Lawrence,* March 12, 1991; "A Literary Curiosity, Not a Pretty Sight," *Daily Telegraph,* June 19, 1991
465	"self-expression": Trotter N iii. 333
465	"better not described": *Daily Express,* June 17, 1929
466	"dislike extremely": vii. 346
466	actively lesbian: Dunaway 71–72, 173
466	"women, women, women": vii. 356
466	"never writes": vii. 364
466	"little wooden cupboard": Hignett 203
467	"my chest sore": vii. 359
467	telegram from Orioli: vii. 8
467	"professional medicine": G. Smith 315
468	"nothing to be done": ibid. 313–14
468	being burned: vii. 371
468	"in the long run": vii. 370
468	burned four copies: "The D. H. Lawrence Paintings: Why They Were Seized," *Daily Telegraph,* August 9, 1929
468	"have leaves!": vii. 388–89
468	"strength, strength!": vii. 398
469	"to serve the hon. Dorothy": FL to DB, July 29, 1929 (Cincinnati)
469	"never be restored": ibid.
469	"quite a business-woman": vii. 392
470	"quite ignominously": FL to DB, August 20, 1929 (Cincinnati)
470	New York office: vii. 505
470	"mostly hatred for me": FL to DB, [n.d.; September 1929, from Bandol] (Cincinnati)
470	be recognized: FL to DB, August 12, 1920 (Cincinnati)
470	*"bores me stiff!!":* FL to DB, [n.d.; September 1929, from Bandol] (Cincinnati)
470	"ugly they can be!": vii. 384
471	"at least at present": vii. 459
471	swiftly sold out: vii. 440
471	"I dont see": vii. 515
471	was himself: vi. 205
471	"preposterous character": Mackenzie, National Sound Archive (BL)
472	"at once in prison": vii. 464
472	"makes one mad": vii. 461

472   "lovely it was! oh God": vii. 438
472   "it may be, really": Hilton N iii. 396–97
472   "magic of his life": Mohr N iii. 398
472   thought he was dead already: ibid. 397
473   "any lower": vii. 500
473   "not too late": vii. 495
473   "grow up overnight": Douglas N iii. 422
474   "on the razzle": vii. 614
474   "world was different": vii. 552
474   "let him live here": vii. 537
474   crossness out: FL to Caresse Crosby, September 29, 1929 (SIU)
474   "usual 'call' ": vii. 526
474   "seems to me": *Memoirs* 233
474   "*what* bores we are!!": ibid. 234
474   "vitamin B food": vii. 501
474   racing against time: Sagar (189) lists what Lawrence was working on
       in January 1930.
475   "an 'Irish' style": vii. 609
475   "high-school American": ibid.
475   "on the sea": vii. 523
475   Frederick Carter: His observations appear in Carter N iii. 414–15.
475   baked safely: vii. 571
475   instinct to kill fish: *Not I* 259
475   "you would let him": ibid. See also vii. 608.
475   attack him in the chest: Brewster N iii. 405–406
475   "horrid brown rocks": vii. 83
475   "was weird": vii. 552
475   "passport difficulties": vii. 575
475   "be what he may": ibid.
476   losses were small: vii. 547; Brewster N iii. 406; Worthen, *Literary Life*
       162
476   "understood bronchials!": vii. 575
476   "throw it away": E. and A. Brewster 308
476   "silver jar": vii. 601
476   "by no means lonely": vii. 590
476   "not the lungs": vii. 605
477   lemon tarts: A. Brewster N iii. 420

CHAPTER 20: UNFINISHED

478   "sanatorium": vii. 639
478   open lesion: Morland's findings are summed up in N iii. 423–25.
479   "nice lunch": vii. 626
479   "by the lung": vii. 624
479   quota: vii. 628
479   "afraid of *Lady C*.": vii. 636
479   he told Mabel: vii. 629
479   "Oh dear O!": vii. 630
479   "into the sea!": Barr N iii. 428
480   keep her balanced: vii. 632
480   to remain near him: Rudnick 295
480   "grumbles at me": vii. 628 n. 1
480   "*speak* of life": Moore and Montague 100
480   "to get well": EJ N iii. 426

480   "it was wrong": vii. 647
480   "go out and see them": vii. 633
480   "no worse": vii. 652
480   "get better": *Memoirs* 234
481   "6 years ago!": FL to MDL, [n.d. but clearly early 1930] (Yale)
481   "bury me here": Barr, Gerard interview (NCL)
481   "where he can get better": M. C. Chambers to MDL, February 10, 1930 (Yale)
482   he wrote Titus: vii. 648
482   "stupid to be ill": i. 334
482   "worst of being sick": vii. 646
482   "tonight to stay": Frieda N ii. 437
482   "stronger in me": *Not I* 264
482   "arguing in a pub": from review of *Art Nonsense and Other Essays*, P 393
482   "Does me no good": vii. 651
482   "for $2,250?": vii. 647
482   "Jew booksellers": vii. 647
483   mess of the kitchen: Bedford 226
483   exaggerated: Ada to Kot, March 5, 1930 (BL)
483   "Don't cry": *Not I* 264
483   "Look at *him*" . . . "let me die": Bedford 224
483   "Now I feel better": Barbara Barr to Kot, March [n.d.], 1930 (BL). Mrs. Barr later recalled his last words as "Wind my watch." BM interview, October 1989.
483   eighty-five pounds: vii. 646
483   "devotion": review of *Art Nonsense and Other Essays*, P 395

CHAPTER 21: IN HER OWN RIGHT

484   "wonder of things": FL to E. M. Forster, King's College Library
485   "specially with me": FL to MDL, May 5, 1930 (Berkeley)
485   "every way you know!": *Memoirs* 239–40
485   "lovely place for him": FL N iii. 467
485   do so again: FL papers, Ravagli papers (Berkeley)
485   "no worse": vii. 652
485   Ada poured her heart out: Ada to Kot, March 5, 1930 (BL)
485   "more or less expected": Rachel Hawk to MDL, April 3, 1930 (Yale)
485   "suit you better": MDL to UJ, June 3, 1931 (Berkeley)
486   clever at everything: Catherine Carswell N iii. 463
486   "obituary Press": Jackson 70
486   quotations from obituaries in *Daily Telegraph, Daily Mail, Evening Transcript:* Jackson, ibid.
486   quotations from obituaries in *The Times, Manchester Guardian, Glasgow Herald:* Draper 322–64
486   Dilys Powell: Jackson 52
486   "revealing, than his": H. Monroe in *Poetry*, vol. 36 (May 1930), 90
487   "princess cutting a thread": Autobiographical Sketch in "Assorted Articles," *PII* 593
487   sale of manuscripts and paintings: FL to Edward Titus, [n.d. but ca. March 15, 1930], Moore and Montague 4
487   body back to the ranch: *Memoirs* 235
487   "come here": Orioli to FL, [n.d.] (Berkeley)
487   hospitality: Angelo Ravagli to FL [n.d.] (Berkeley)

487 born the previous September: Federico Ravagli was born in Savona on September 2, 1929. Letter to BM and death certificate of Federico Ravagli from Commune di Spotorno, March 1, 1994.

487 in her honor: R. Lucas 254

488 month's furlough: Ravagli N iii. 449

488 be all right: Moore and Montague 43

488 leave from the army: Lucas 258

488 ranch together: Ravagli N iii. 450

488 chose to send her: Caresse Crosby to FL, [n.d.; 1930?] (SIU)

488 one of Frieda's hymns: Moore and Montague 40

488 "have ever known": G. Smith 332

488 Eliot: ibid. 334

489 refused to cooperate: ibid. 340n.

489 noncooperation: Zytaruk xxxiii–iv

489 "*perverse* in him!": MDL to UJ, dated July 2 [1931?] (Berkeley)

489 Frieda's needs in France: Lea 165

489 "fulfilment in love really meant": JMM to FL, July 12, 1953 (Texas)

490 "gave me back myself": JMM to FL, April 25, 1931 (UCLA)

490 "all my powers have been revitalized through you": Turner, 165

490 "all would be mine": Moore and Montague 8

490 "with half a dozen": William Lawrence, Gerard interview (NCL)

490 "the whole business": Montague Weekley to Nehls, February 1, 1954 (Texas)

491 get back together again: Moore and Montague 61

491 Barby's breakdown: A graphic description of the breakdown was given by MDL to UJ, July 15, 1931 (Berkeley).

491 bear no more: FL to Caresse Crosby, [n.d.] written from Villa Robermond, Vence (SIU)

491 an ingenious remedy: BM interview with Barbara Barr; also Lucas 257

491 "un mâle, madame": MDL to UJ, July 15, 1931 (Berkeley)

491 care administered: BM interview with Barbara Barr, October 1989

492 "affection & tenderness": *Memoirs* 238

492 "better than me": ibid. 239

492 Huxley called: G. Smith 352

493 "original edition": Draper 289; *Memoirs* 449

493 "chiffoné eyelids": Rudnick 294 (based on MDL to UJ, June 3, 1931 [Berkeley])

493 "*have* a man!": ibid.

493 in the making: Rudnick 291

494 La Salle: MD to UJ, June 3, 1931 (Berkeley)

494 "a miracle": Moore and Montague 50

494 One evening: described in MD to UJ, July 2, 1931 (Berkeley)

494 "what the hell is love?": DB to UJ, July 3, 1931 (Berkeley)

495 changed sides: Ada to Mrs. Crotch, in Moore and Montague 55

495 "future husbands": DB to UJ, July 3, 1931 (Berkeley)

495 "to the charm": G. Smith 364

495 Emile Delavenay: in "Making Another Lawrence: Frieda and the Lawrence Legend," *DHLR,* vol. 7, no. 1 (spring 1975), 84

495 "Ensample and a Mystery": Furbank 165

495 "smoking Woodbines": William E. Lawrence, Gerard interview (NCL)

496 considered that her counteroffer: Ada to Mrs. Crotch, Moore and Montague 59

496 to the contrary: Emily King to L. L. Pollinger, October 18, 1932 (Texas)

496   Frieda's position: Field Roscoe & Co. to JMM, November 26, 1931 (Texas)
496   judgment delivered: *The Times* (London), November 4, 1932, N iii. 477
496   lack of a child to be his heir: vii. 459
497   half her estate when she died: Lucas 262
497   left in a purse: "Italian Opera-Bouffe Lends Comic Relief to Taos Week of Tragedy and Misfortune," unidentified Taos newspaper, December [?] 1933, Jeffers collection (Berkeley)
497   safekeeping: Frieda's account of this episode appears as "And the Fullness Thereof" in *Memoirs* (32–33), and the drive to "catch the boat" as "On the Road," in *Memoirs* (34).
498   kept him in line: FL to Angelo Ravagli, *Memoirs* 255–56
498   found gold: Moore and Montague 50
498   hold Ravagli: Hignett 217
498   crush on any handsome male: MDL to UJ, *Letters*, May–July [1931] (Berkeley)
499   "gleamed yellow": "The Last Wish of D. H. Lawrence," *Daily Express,* March 15, 1935
499   organize the transport: Moore and Montague 69
499   ashes would do: Earl Brewster to FL, October 1934 (Texas)
499   handle it himself: Earl Brewster to Angelo Ravagli, January 1, 1934 [apparently misdated for 1935] (Texas)
499   agonized letters: Angelo Ravagli to Mrs. Crotch, Moore and Montague 71
500   ash from the fireplace: Hignett 224
500   left behind: Lucas 268–69
500   "the Angelino ménage": DB to UJ, September 14, 1935 (Berkeley)
500   scatter them over the desert: Lucas 269 credits Barby; *Memoirs* 137 credits a girl acquaintance with telling Frieda of the plot.
500   "the Angelino temple": MDL to WB, June 18, [n.d. 1935?] (Harvard)
500   local judge: Barr, "Memoir" 36
500   at sunset: Barr, "I Look Back," 257
500   victory over Mabel at last: Louis Untermeyer N iii. 485
501   "simple & beautiful": FL to UJ, [n.d.] (Berkeley)
501   "so Pan-like as Lawrence": DB to UJ, May 4, 1935 (Berkeley)
501   "no idea of what did happen": Hignett 224
501   convenient substitute: ibid. 270
501   Penguin Books did not seem to know: "Ten Titles by D. H. Lawrence," *New publications for 24 March 1950 and stock list,* Penguin Books Ltd, Harmondsworth, Middlesex
502   Bynner pleaded with Mabel: WB to MDL, November 4, 1955 (Harvard)
502   have a good time: *Memoirs* 274
502   "quite clearly": FL, unpublished fragment of essay on *Mein Kampf* (Texas)
503   "Führer": postcard, EJ to FL (Yale)
503   "in the world": *Memoirs* 275
503   Biddle: *Memoirs* 284
503   "debaucheries of sex": Re Frieda Lawrence Ravagli, Security Matter White Slave Traffic Act. Letter from [name deleted] to J. Edgar Hoover, July 15, 1944. FBI BU file 105–147-1 (hereinafter, "Hoover letter")
503   bad reputation "for immorals": FBI EP file 100–387-3
503   fig leaf: Hignett 218

503   code book: Hoover letter, 105–147-1
503   case should be closed: FBI BU file 105–147-3
504   represented by an attorney: El Paso, Texas, District Office of the U.S.
        Department of Justice, Immigration and Naturalization Service, to FL,
        April 19, 1945. File Number 2233-37 (Texas)
504   petition for citizenship: ibid., November 21, 1946; January 2, 1947;
        January 6, 1947
504   "I really liked her": Robinson 417
504   that rotten road: Lucas 273
504   "restless, uncertain": Tennessee Williams to FL, July 29, 1938 (Texas)
504   "like a firetruck": Tennessee Williams, *Memoirs* (London: W. H. Allen,
        1976) 104
505   "more powerful than men": FL N i. 182
505   "disbelieve in homosexuality": *Memoirs* 295
505   "Good wishes, Frieda Lawrence": FL to Eliot Fay, September 18, 1953
        (Texas)
505   "all your cleverness": *Memoirs* 277–78
505   "Mrs D H Lawrence": FL to Bennett Cerf, April 1, 1952 (Texas)
506   explained to Leavis: *Memoirs* 412
506   Leavises felt it proper: BM interview with A. Alvarez, October 19,
        1988
506   "creative quarreling": Valerie Grove, "Great Expectations of an Over-
        actress," *The Times Saturday Review,* June 15, 1991
506   "marvellous, scandalous grandmother": Alvarez 236
506   out of the water: *Memoirs* 436
506   "that Little Dorrit!": Barr, "I Look Back" 258
506   independent life: Hignett 242
507   "nothing but lip": Barr, Gerard interview (NCL)
507   "worse than complaining": Mori 39
507   "over his head": *Memoirs* 429
507   "at the school!": ibid. 349
507   marry him again: Moore, *Priest of Love* 508
507   sotto voce: unsigned memo of conversation with Prof. M. M. Lewis of
        the University of Nottingham, April 17, 1963 (Texas)
508   summer of their courtship: Barbara Barr to BM, June 30, 1989
508   "wanting you so badly": *Memoirs* 405
508   "hated most": ibid. 407
508   "could never have stood it all": ibid. 312
508   birthday party: Kraft 227
508   scold her: *Memoirs* 415
508   "beloved Frieda": ibid. 415–16
508   working for: Hignett 270
508   a fine funeral: T. M. Pearce N iii. 486–90, 736 n. 67
509   an advertisement: ibid. 490
509   "new ideas": *Memoirs* 460
510   "rather dumb": ibid. 293
510   "watered down Thomas Hardy": FL to UJ, October 10, 1936 (Berke-
        ley)
510   "nothing will stop it, Brett": FL to DB, August 12, 1930 (Cincinnati)
510   "if you can!": FL to Kot, August 4, 1934 (BL)

BIBLIOGRAPHY

MAJOR WORKS BY D. H. LAWRENCE

1911 *The White Peacock*, novel
1912 *The Trespasser*, novel
1913 *Love Poems and Others*
     Sons and Lovers, novel
1914 *The Widowing of Mrs Holroyd*, play
     The Prussian Officer and Other Stories
1915 *The Rainbow*, novel
1916 *Twilight in Italy*, travel
     Amores, poems
1917 *Look! We Have Come Through!*, poems
1918 *New Poems*
1919 *Bay*, poems
1920 *Touch and Go*, play
     Women in Love, novel
     The Lost Girl, novel
1921 *Movements in European History* (by "Lawrence H. Davison")
     Psychoanalysis and the Unconscious, essays
     Tortoises, poems
     Sea and Sardinia, travel
1922 *Aaron's Rod*, novel
     Fantasia of the Unconscious, essays
     England, My England, stories
1923 *The Ladybird*, tales including "The Fox" (in America, *The Captain's Doll*)
     Studies in Classic American Literature
     Kangaroo, novel
     Birds, Beasts and Flowers, poems
1924 *The Boy in the Bush*, novel (with M. L. Skinner)
1925 *St. Mawr*, together with "The Woman Who Rode Away" and "The Princess," stories
     Reflections on the Death of a Porcupine, essays
1926 *The Plumed Serpent*, novel
     David, play
     Sun, story
     Glad Ghosts, story
1927 *Mornings in Mexico*, travel
1928 *[Selected Poems]*, Augustan Books of Poetry series
     Rawdon's Roof, story
     The Woman Who Rode Away, stories
     Lady Chatterley's Lover, novel

The Collected Poems of D. H. Lawrence
Sun (unexpurgated edition)
1929 *Sex Locked Out*, essay
The Paintings of D. H. Lawrence (introduction by Lawrence)
Pansies, poems
My Skirmish with Jolly Roger, essay
The Escaped Cock, short novel (later called *The Man Who Died*)
Pornography and Obscenity, essay (expansion of *Jolly Roger*)
1930 *Nettles*, poems
Assorted Articles
À Propos of Lady Chatterley's Lover, essay
The Virgin and the Gipsy, novel
Love among the Haystacks, stories
1931 *Apocalypse*, essay
The Triumph of the Machine, poem
1932 *Lady Chatterley's Lover* (abridged edition)
Etruscan Places, essays
The Letters of D. H. Lawrence (ed., Aldous Huxley)
Last Poems
1933 *The Lovely Lady and Other Stories*
We Need One Another, essay
The Plays
The Tales
1934 *A Collier's Friday Night*, play
A Modern Lover, stories, including "The Old Adam"
1935 *The Spirit of Place*, prose anthology (ed., R. Aldington)
1936 Foreword to *Women in Love*
Phoenix, essays (ed., E. D. McDonald)
1940 *Fire and Other Poems*
1944 *The First Lady Chatterley*
1948 *Letters to Bertrand Russell* (ed., H. T. Moore)
1949 *A Prelude*, story
1956 *Eight Letters to Rachel Annand Taylor*
1957 *The Complete Poems*
1962 *The Collected Letters* (ed., H. T. Moore)
The Symbolic Meaning (early versions of the *American Literature* essays, ed., Armin Arnold)
1964 *The Complete Poems* (ed., V. de Sola Pinto and W. Roberts)
Paintings of D. H. Lawrence (ed., Mervyn Levy)
1965 *The Complete Plays* (first professionally edited edition)
1968 *Lawrence in Love* (letters to Louie Burrows, ed., James T. Boulton)
1968 *Phoenix II*, essays (ed., W. Roberts and H. T. Moore)
1970 *The Quest for Rananim* (letters to S. S. Koteliansky, ed., George J. Zytaruk)
1972 *John Thomas and Lady Jane* (second draft of *Lady Chatterley's Lover*)
1973 *The Escaped Cock* (ed. by Gerald Lacy, with new material)
1979–93 *The Letters of D. H. Lawrence* (Cambridge University Press)
1984 *Mr. Noon* (written in 1920–21)
1987 *Memoir of Maurice Magnus* (ed., Keith Cushman)

Reprints and pamphlets of only a few pages are usually not listed.

SECONDARY WORKS

Aberbach, David. "Screen Memories of Writers." *International Review of Psycho-Analysis* (1983), pp. 10, 47.

Adamowski, T. H. "Self/Body/Other: Orality and Ontology in Lawrence." *DHLR*, vol. 13, no. 3 (1980), pp. 193–208.

Albrow, Martin. *Max Weber's Construction of Social Theory.* London: Macmillan, 1990.

Aldington, Richard. *An Indiscretion.* London: Chatto & Windus, 1930.

———. *D. H. Lawrence: A Complete List of His Works, Together with a Critical Appreciation.* London: Heinemann, 1935.

———. *Life for Life's Sake.* New York: Viking, 1941. London: Cassell, 1968.

———. *Pinorman: Personal Recollections of Norman Douglas, Pino Orioli, and Charles Prentice.* London: Heinemann, 1954.

———. *Portrait of a Genius, But . . .* New York: Duell, Sloan and Pierce, 1950. London: Heinemann, 1950.

Alpers, Antony. *The Life of Katherine Mansfield.* New York: Viking, 1980.

Alvarez, A. *Life After Marriage.* London: Macmillan, 1982.

Annan, Noel. "Mission Impossible!" *New York Review of Books,* January 17, 1991, p. 15.

Anonymous. "Primal: A Burning Bay Stallion Incarnates Lawrentian Purity." *Time,* June 29, 1925.

Arnold, Armin. *Lawrence and America.* London: Linden Press, 1958.

———. "In D. H. Lawrence's Footsteps in Switzerland: Some New Biographical Material." *Texas Studies in Literature and Language,* iii (Summer 1961), pp. 184–88.

Asquith, Lady Cynthia. "D. H. Lawrence as I Knew Him." BBC Third Programme, September 7, 1949. BBC Written Archives, 14172–4.

———. *Remember and Be Glad.* London: James Barrie, 1952.

———. *Diaries: 1915–1918.* London: Hutchinson, 1968.

Balbert, Peter. *D. H. Lawrence and the Phallic Imagination.* New York: St. Martin's Press, 1989.

Balfour, A. J. "Creative Evolution and Philosophic Doubt." *The Hibbert Journal,* October 1911, pp. 1–23.

Bardswell, Noel Dean. *Advice to Consumptives: Home Treatment, After-Care and Prevention.* London: A. & C. Black, 1910.

Barlett, Norman. "D. H. Lawrence in Australia." *Australian National Review,* vol. 15 (May 1939), pp. 29–34.

Barnes, James Strachey. *Half a Life.* London: Eyre and Spottiswoode, 1933.

Baron, Carl E. "Two Hitherto Unknown Pieces by D. H. Lawrence" (including "With the Guns"). *Encounter,* August 1969, pp. 5–9.

Barr, Barbara. "I Look Back." *Twentieth Century,* no. 165 (1959), pp. 254–61.

———. "Memoir of D. H. Lawrence." In Spender, Stephen, *D. H. Lawrence: Prophet, Poet, Novelist.* London: Weidenfeld & Nicolson, 1973.

Bedford, Sybille. *Aldous Huxley: A Biography.* New York: Carroll & Graf, 1985.

Belford, Barbara. *Violet: The Story of the Irrepressible Violet Hunt and Her Circle of Lovers and Friends.* New York: Simon and Schuster, 1990.

Benkovitz, Miriam J., ed. *A Passionate Prodigality: Letters to Alan Bird from Richard Aldington, 1949–1962.* New York: New York Public Library and Readex Books, 1975.

Blanchard, Lydia. "Lawrence, Foucault, and the Language of Sexuality." In *D. H.*

Lawrence's "Lady": A New Look at Lady Chatterley's Lover. Michael Squires and Dennis Jackson, eds. Athens, Ga.: University of Georgia Press, 1985.

————. "Women Look at Lady Chatterley: Feminine Views of the Novel." *DHLR*, vol. 11, no. 3 (fall 1978), pp. 246–59.

Boulton, James, ed. *Lawrence in Love: Letters to Louie Burrows.* Nottingham, England: University of Nottingham, 1968.

Brett, Dorothy. *Lawrence and Brett.* Philadelphia: J. B. Lippincott, 1933.

————. *Lawrence and Brett.* With introduction, prologue, and epilogue by John Manchester. Santa Fe, N.M.: Sunstone Press, 1974.

Brewster, Earl, and Achsah Brewster. *D. H. Lawrence: Reminiscences and Correspondence.* London: Secker, 1934.

Britton, Derek. *Lady Chatterley: The Making of the Novel.* London: Unwin Hyman, 1988.

Brome, Vincent. *Ernest Jones: Freud's Alter Ego.* London: Caliban, 1982.

Brown, Keith, ed. *Rethinking Lawrence.* Milton Keynes, England: Open University Press, 1990.

Burke, Richard M. *An Historical Chronology of Tuberculosis.* Springfield, Ill.: Charles C. Thomas, 1955.

Burns, John. "On Consumption." *The New Age,* November 25, 1909, pp. 85–87.

Burwell, Rose Marie. "A Catalogue of D. H. Lawrence's Reading from Early Childhood." *DHLR,* vol. 3, no. 3 (fall 1970), pp. 93–324.

Bynner, Witter. *Journey with Genius: Recollections and Reflections Concerning the D. H. Lawrences.* New York: John Day, 1951.

Calvert, Peter. *Mexico.* London: Ernest Benn, 1973.

Cannan, Gilbert. *Mendel.* London: T. Fisher Unwin, 1916.

Carey, John. "Difficulties with Girls." *Sunday Times* (London), September 1, 1991 (review of John Worthen, *D. H. Lawrence: The Early Years*).

————. *The Intellectuals and the Masses.* London: Faber and Faber, 1992.

Carrington, Noel, ed. *Mark Gertler: Selected Letters.* London: Hart-Davis, 1965.

Carswell, Catherine. *The Savage Pilgrimage: A Narrative of D. H. Lawrence.* London: Martin Secker, 1932.

Carswell, John. *The Exile: A Life of Ivy Litvinov.* London and Boston: Faber, 1983.

Cavitch, David. *D. H. Lawrence and the New World.* New York: Oxford University Press, 1979.

Central Statistical Office, *Retail Prices 1914–1990.* Her Majesty's Stationery Office, April 1991.

Chambers, Jessie. *D. H. Lawrence: A Personal Record by E.T.* New York: Knight, 1936 (reprint, Cambridge, England: Cambridge University Press, 1980).

Clark, L. D. *The Minoan Distance: The Symbolism of Travel in D. H. Lawrence.* Tucson, Ariz.: University of Arizona Press, 1980.

Conan Doyle, Sir Arthur. "The Naval Treaty." In *Memoirs of Sherlock Holmes.* Christopher Roden, ed. London: Oxford University Press, 1993.

Concolo, Dominick P., ed. *D. H. Lawrence: The Rocking-Horse Winner.* Columbus, Ohio: Charles E. Merrill, 1969.

Copley, I. A. *A Turbulent Friendship: A Study of the Relationship between D. H. Lawrence and Philip Heseltine ("Peter Warlock").* London: Thames Publishing and the Peter Warlock Society, 1993.

Corke, Helen. *D. H. Lawrence: The Croydon Years.* Austin: University of Texas Press, 1965.

————. *In Our Infancy: An Autobiography, 1882—1912.* Cambridge, England: Cambridge University Press, 1975.

———. *Lawrence and Apocalypse*. London: Heinemann, 1933.

———. "The Writing of *The Trespasser*." *DHLR*, vol. 7, no. 3 (fall 1974), pp. 227–40.

Cowan, James C. *D. H. Lawrence's American Journey: A Study in Literature and Myth*. Cleveland: The Press of Case Western Reserve University, 1970.

Cox, Gary D. "D. H. Lawrence and F. M. Dostoevsky: Mirror Images of Murderous Aggression." *Modern Fiction Studies*, vol. 29, no. 2 (summer 1983), pp. 175–82.

Crichton, Kyle S. "D. H. Lawrence Lives at the Top of the World." *New York World*, October 11, 1925.

Cummins, Stevenson Lyle. *Tuberculosis in History*. London: Baillière, Tindall and Cox, 1949.

Cushman, Keith. "D. H. Lawrence at Work: 'The Shadow in the Rose Garden.' " *DHLR*, vol. 8, no. 1 (spring 1975), pp. 33–46.

———. *D. H. Lawrence at Work: The Emergence of the* Prussian Officer *Stories*. Brighton, Sussex, England: Harvester Press, 1978.

Dahlberg, Edward. "Lawrentian Analects." In *Samuel Beckett's Wake and Other Uncollected Prose*. Steven Moore, ed. Elmwood Park, Ill.: Dalkey Archive Press, 1989.

Darroch, Robert. *Lawrence in Australia*. Melbourne: Macmillan Australia, 1981.

Darroch, Sandra. *Ottoline: The Life of Lady Ottoline Morrell*. New York: Coward, McCann & Geoghegan, 1975.

Davies, Rhys. "D. H. Lawrence in Bandol." *Horizon*, October 1940, pp. 191–208.

———. *Print of a Hare's Foot*. London: Heinemann, 1969.

Davies, Rosemary Reeves. "The Mother as Destroyer: Psychic Division in the Writings of D. H. Lawrence." *DHLR*, vol. 13, no. 2 (summer 1980), pp. 220–38.

Davis, Joseph. *Lawrence at Thirroul*. Melbourne: Collins Australia, 1989.

De Almeida, Hermione. *Romantic Medicine and John Keats*. New York and Oxford: Oxford University Press, 1991.

De Beauvoir, Simone. "D. H. Lawrence and Phallic Pride." In *The Second Sex*. Harmondsworth: Penguin, 1972.

Delany, Paul. *D. H. Lawrence's Nightmare: The Writer and His Circle in the Years of the Great War*. New York: Basic Books, 1978.

———. "Men in Love" (review of the Cambridge University Press edition of *Women in Love* and *The Letters of D. H. Lawrence: Vol. IV, 1921–24*). *London Review of Books*, September 3, 1987, pp. 21–22.

———. *The Neo-Pagans: Friendship and Love in the Rupert Brooke Circle*. London: Macmillan, 1987.

———. "A Secret Riches": Postfeminism in *The Rainbow*. Unpublished.

———. "A Would-Be-Dirty Mind: D. H. Lawrence as an Enemy of Joyce." Unpublished paper delivered at James Joyce Symposium, Dublin, 1992.

Delavenay, Émile. *D. H. Lawrence. L'Homme et la genèse de son oeuvre: les années de formation, 1885–1919*. Two volumes. Paris: Librairie C. Klincksieck, 1969.

———. *Lawrence and Carpenter*. London: Heinemann, 1971.

———. *D. H. Lawrence. The Man and His Work: The Formative Years, 1885–1919*. Carbondale and Edwardsville, Ill.: Southern Illinois University Press, 1972.

———. "Making Another Lawrence: Frieda and the Lawrence Legend." *DHLR*, vol. 7, no. 1 (spring 1975), pp. 80–98.

Dervin, Daniel. "Play, Creativity and Matricide: The Implications of Lawrence's 'Smashed Doll' Episode." *Mosaic*, vol. 14, no. 3 (1981), pp. 81–94.

Doherty, Gerald. "The Greatest Show on Earth: D. H. Lawrence's *St. Mawr* and Antonin Artaud's Theatre of Cruelty." *DHLR*, vol. 22, no. 1 (spring 1990), pp. 3–22.

Doolittle, Hilda (H.D.). *Bid Me to Live*. New York: Grove, 1960.

———. *Tribute to Freud*. New York: New Directions, 1973.

Doyle, Charles. *Richard Aldington: A Biography*. London: Macmillan, 1989.

Draper, R. P., ed. *D. H. Lawrence: The Critical Heritage*. London: Routledge & Kegan Paul, 1970.

Dubos, René, and Jean Dubos. *The White Plague: Tuberculosis, Man and Society*. London: Gollancz, 1953.

Dunaway, David King. *Huxley in Hollywood*. New York: Harper and Row, 1989.

Eder, M. D. "Eugenics and Good Breeding." Thirteen-part series, *New Age*, May 9–July 25, 1908.

———. "A Case of Obsession and Hysteria Treated by the Freud Psycho-analytic Method." *British Medical Journal*, September 30, 1911, pp. 750–52.

——— (trans). *On Dreams: Only Authorized English Translation by Prof. Dr. Sigm. Freud*. London: Heinemann, 1913.

———. "The Present Position of Psycho-Analysis." *British Medical Journal*, November 8, 1913, p. 15.

———. *War-Shock: The Psycho-Neuroses in War Psychology and Treatment*. London: Heinemann, 1917.

Eliot, T. S. *After Strange Gods*. New York: Harcourt, Brace, 1934.

Ellmann, Richard. *James Joyce*. London: Oxford University Press, 1982.

Farjeon, Annabel. *Morning Has Broken: A Biography of Eleanor Farjeon*. London: Julia MacRae, 1986.

Finney, Brian. "D. H. Lawrence's Progress to Maturity: *The Prussian Officer*." *Studies in Bibliography*, vol. 28 (1975), pp. 321–32.

Firchow, Peter E. "Rico and Julia: The Hilda Doolittle–D. H. Lawrence Affair Reconsidered." *Journal of Modern Literature*, vol. 8 (1980), pp. 51–76.

Fisher, Dr. Mary Saleeby. Notebook, 1915. Unpublished. Texas.

Fitch, Noel Riley. *Sylvia Beach and the Lost Generation*. New York: Norton, 1983.

FitzGerald, Garret. *Garret FitzGerald: An Autobiography*. London: Macmillan, 1991.

Ford, George H. *Double Measure: A Study of the Novels and Stories of D. H. Lawrence*. New York: W. W. Norton, 1969 (originally published 1965).

Ford, Hugh. *Published in Paris: American and British Writers, Printers, and Publishers in Paris, 1920–1939*. London: Garnstone Press, 1975.

Forster, E. M. *Selected Letters*. See Lago, Mary, and P. N. Furbank, eds., *Selected Letters of E. M. Forster*.

Foster, Joseph. *Lawrence in Taos*. Albuquerque: University of New Mexico Press, 1972.

Fraser, Grace Crawford Lovat. *In the Days of My Youth*. Southampton, England: Camelot Press, 1970.

Furbank, P. N. *E. M. Forster: A Life*. Vol. 2, *Polycrates' Ring (1914–1970)*. London: Secker & Warburg, 1978.

Garnett, David. *Flowers of the Field*. London: Chatto & Windus, 1953.

———. *The Golden Echo*. New York: Harcourt, Brace and Company, 1954.

———. *Flowers of the Forest*. London: Chatto & Windus, 1955.

———. *Great Friends*. London: Macmillan, 1979.

Garnett, Richard. *Constance Garnett: A Heroic Life*. London: Sinclair-Stevenson, 1991.

Gathorne-Hardy, Robert, ed. *Ottoline at Garsington: Memoirs of Lady Ottoline Morrell, 1915–1918.* London: Faber, 1974.

Gay, Peter. *Freud: A Life for Our Time.* London: J. W. Dent, 1988.

Gerard, D. E., interviews for Nottinghamshire County Council Leisure Services, Oral History Collection, Nottingham (England) County Library.

Gibson, Arrell Morgan. *The Santa Fe & Taos Colonies: Age of the Muses, 1900–1942.* Norman, Okla.: University of Oklahoma Press, 1983.

Gilbert, Sandra M. *Acts of Attention: The Poems of D. H. Lawrence.* Ithaca, N.Y.: Cornell University Press, 1972.

———. "Feminism and D. H. Lawrence: Some Notes Toward a Vindication of His Rites." In *Acts of Attention: the Poems of D. H. Lawrence,* rev. ed. Carbondale and Edwardsville: Southern Illinois University Press, 1990, pp. 92–100.

Gilchrist, Susan. "D. H. Lawrence and E. M. Forster: A Failed Friendship," in "D. H. Lawrence. His Contemporaries and Europe," *Études Lawrenciennes,* vol. 9, 1993, pp. 123–39.

Glenavy, Beatrice. *Today We Will Only Gossip.* London: Constable, 1964.

Gloyne, F. Roodhouse. *Social Aspects of Tuberculosis.* London: Faber, 1944.

Golding, Douglas. *South Lodge.* London: Constable, 1943.

Goodhart, Eugene. *The Utopian Vision of D. H. Lawrence.* Chicago: University of Chicago, 1963.

Gray, Cecil. *Musical Chairs, or Between Two Stools.* London: Hogarth, 1985; first published in Great Britain by Home & Van Thal, 1948.

Green, Martin. *The Von Richthofen Sisters: The Triumphant and the Tragic Modes of Love.* New York: Basic Books, 1974; London: Weidenfeld and Nicolson, 1974.

———. *Children of the Sun: A Narrative of "Decadence" in England after 1918.* New York: Basic Books, 1976.

———. *Mountain of Truth: The Counter-Culture Begins, Ascona 1900–1920.* Hanover, N.H.: University of New England Press, 1986.

Greiff, Louis K. "Bittersweet Dreaming in D. H. Lawrence's 'The Fox.' " *Studies in Short Fiction,* vol. 20 (1983), pp. 7–16.

Guest, Barbara. *The Poet H.D. and Her World.* New York: Doubleday, 1984.

Hahn, Emily. *Lorenzo: D. H. Lawrence and the Women Who Loved Him.* Philadelphia and New York: J. B. Lippincott Co., 1975.

———. *Mabel: A Biography of Mabel Dodge Luhan.* Boston: Houghton Mifflin, 1977.

Hall, Richard, and John K. Ruffels. "Shipboard Talk: Did D. H. Lawrence Meet Father O'Reilly?" *Overland,* no. 117 (1990), pp. 11–14.

Hardy, George, and Nathaniel Harris. *A D. H. Lawrence Album.* Ashbourne, Derbyshire: Moorland, 1985.

Hassall, Christopher. *A Biography of Edward Marsh.* New York: Harcourt, Brace, 1959.

Haste, Cate. *Rules of Desire—Sex in Britain: World War I to the Present.* London: Chatto and Windus, 1992.

Healey, E. Claire, and Keith Cushman. *The Letters of D. H. Lawrence & Amy Lowell, 1914–1925.* Santa Rosa, Cal.: Black Sparrow, 1985.

Heilbrun, Carolyn G. *The Garnett Family.* London: Allen and Unwin, 1961.

———. *Toward a Recognition of Androgyny.* New York: Norton, 1982 (first published in New York: Knopf, 1973).

Heywood, Christopher, ed. *D. H. Lawrence: New Studies.* New York: St. Martin's Press, 1987.

Hignett, Sean. *Brett: From Bloomsbury to New York. A Biography*. London: Hodder & Stoughton, 1984.

Hilton, Enid Hopkin. "Alice Dax: D. H. Lawrence's 'Clara' in *Sons and Lovers*." *DHLR*, vol. 22, no. 3 (fall 1990), pp. 274–85.

Hobman, J. B. *David Eder: Memoirs of a Modern Pioneer*. With introduction by Sigmund Freud. London: Gollancz, 1945.

Holbrook, David. *The Quest for Love*. London: Methuen, 1964.

———. "Sons and Mothers: D. H. Lawrence and *Mr Noon*." *Encounter*, March 1988, pp. 44–54.

Holloway, Mark. *Norman Douglas*. London: Secker and Warburg, 1976.

Holmes, Richard. *Coleridge: Early Visions*. London: Hodder & Stoughton, 1989.

Holroyd, Michael. *George Bernard Shaw*, 3 vols. London: Chatto, 1988–91.

Howard, Michael S. *Jonathan Cape Publisher*. London: Cape, 1971.

Hough, Graham. *The Dark Sun: A Study of D. H. Lawrence*. London: Duckworth, 1956.

Howe, Marguerite Beede. *The Art of the Self in D. H. Lawrence*. Athens, Ohio: Ohio University Press, 1977.

Hunt, Violet. *The Flurried Years*. London: Hurst & Blackett, 1926.

Hyde, G. M. *D. H. Lawrence and the Art of Translation*. London: Macmillan, 1981.

Hyde, H. Montgomery. *The Lady Chatterley's Lover Trial*. London: Cape, 1990.

Ingersoll, Earl G. "The Pursuit of 'True Marriage': D. H. Lawrence's *Mr Noon* and *Lady Chatterley's Lover*." *Studies in the Humanities*, vol. 14, no. 1 (June 1987), pp. 32–45.

Jackson, Dennis. " 'The Stormy Petrel of Literature Is Dead': The World Press Reports D. H. Lawrence's Death." *DHLR*, vol. 14, no. 1 (spring 1981), pp. 33–72.

Jefferson, George. *Edward Garnett: A Life in Literature*. London: Cape, 1982.

Jones, Billy M. *Health-Seekers in the Southwest 1817–1900*. Norman, Okla.: University of Oklahoma Press, 1967.

Jones, Ernest. *The Life and Work of Sigmund Freud*. Three volumes. New York: Basic Books, 1953.

———. *Free Associations: Memories of a Psycho-analyst*. London: Hogarth, 1959.

Joost, Nicholas, and Alvin Sullivan. *D. H. Lawrence and The Dial*. Carbondale, Ill.: Southern Illinois University Press, 1970.

Judd, Alan. *Ford Madox Ford*. London: Grafton, 1990.

Kalnins, Mara, ed. *D. H. Lawrence Centenary Essays*. Bristol, England: Classical Press, 1986.

Keegan, Susan. *The Bride of the Wind: The Life of Alma Mahler*. London: Secker and Warburg, 1991.

Kiell, Norman, ed. *Psychoanalysis, Psychology and Literature: A Bibliography*. Supplement to the Second Edition. Metuchen, N.J., and London: The Scarecrow Press, 1990.

King, Francis. *E. M. Forster*. London: Thames and Hudson, 1978.

Kingsmill, Hugh. *D. H. Lawrence*. London: Methuen, 1938.

Kinkead-Weekes, Mark. "The Gringo Señora Who Rode Away." *DHLR*, vol. 22, no. 3 (fall 1990), pp. 251–65.

———. "The Sense of History in *The Rainbow*." In *D. H. Lawrence in the Modern World*. Peter Preston and Peter Hoare, eds. Cambridge, England: Cambridge University Press, 1989.

Knight, G. Wilson. "Lawrence, Joyce and Powys." In *Essays in Criticism*, vol. 2 (1961), pp. 403–17.

Kraft, James, ed. *The Works of Witter Bynner: Selected Letters.* New York: Farrar, Straus & Giroux, 1981.

Kuttner, Alfred Booth. "*Sons and Lovers*: A Freudian Appreciation." *Psychoanalytic Review,* no. 3 (1916), pp. 295–317.

Lacy, Gerald M., ed. *D. H. Lawrence: Letters to Thomas and Adele Seltzer.* Santa Rosa, Cal.: Black Sparrow Press, 1976.

Lago, Mary, and P. N. Furbank, eds. *Selected Letters of E. M. Forster.* London: Collins, 1981; Arena, 1985.

Laird, Holly A. *Self and Sequence: The Poetry of D. H. Lawrence.* Charlottesville, Va.: University Press of Virginia, 1988.

Larkin, Philip. "The Sanity of Lawrence." *Times Literary Supplement,* June 13, 1980.

Lawrence, Ada, and G. Stuart Gelder. *The Early Life of D. H. Lawrence.* London: Secker, 1932.

Lawrence, Frieda. *Not I, but the Wind . . .* London: Granada, 1983 (first published in Santa Fe: Rydal Press, 1934).

———. Introduction to D. H. Lawrence, *The First Lady Chatterley.* Harmondsworth: Penguin, 1973.

Lea, F. A. *The Life of John Middleton Murry.* London: Oxford University Press, 1939; New York: Oxford University Press, 1960.

Leavis, F. R. *The Common Pursuit.* London: Chatto & Windus, 1952.

———. *D. H. Lawrence: Novelist.* New York: Knopf, 1956.

———. *The Great Tradition.* London: Chatto & Windus, 1984.

Levy, Mervyn, ed. *The Paintings of D. H. Lawrence.* New York: Viking, 1964; London: Cory, Adams and Mackay, 1964.

Lodge, David. "Comedy of Eros." *The New Republic,* December 10, 1984, pp. 96–100.

Lucas, Barbara. "Apropos of 'England, My England.' " *Twentieth Century,* March 1961, pp. 288–93.

Lucas, Robert. *Frieda Lawrence: The Story of Frieda von Richthofen and D. H. Lawrence.* London: Secker, 1973.

McGregor, O. R. "The Social Position of Women in England, 1850–1914: A Bibliography." *The British Journal of Sociology,* vol. 6, no. 1 (March 1955), pp. 48–60.

Mackenzie, Compton. *My Life and Times: Octave Five, 1915–1923.* London: Chatto & Windus, 1966.

Mackenzie, Faith Compton. *More Than I Should.* London: Collins, 1949.

Macleod, Sheila. *Lawrence's Men & Women.* London: Paladin Books, 1987.

Maddox, Brenda. "Damagers of the Breast" (review of Margaret Storch's *Sons and Adversaries: Women in William Blake and D. H. Lawrence*). *Times Literary Supplement,* June 7, 1991.

Magnus, Maurice. *Memoirs of the Foreign Legion by M.M.* London: Secker, 1924.

Mailer, Norman. *The Prisoner of Sex.* London: Weidenfeld and Nicolson, 1971.

Masters, William H., and Virginia E. Johnson. *Human Sexual Response.* London: J. & A. Churchill, 1966.

Mehl, Dieter. "D. H. Lawrence in Waldbröl." *Notes and Queries,* no. 31 (March 1984), pp. 78–81.

Merrild, Knud. *A Poet and Two Painters: A Memoir of D. H. Lawrence.* New York: Viking, 1939.

Meyers, Jeffrey. "Memoirs of D. H. Lawrence: A Genre of the Thirties." *DHLR,* vol. 14, no. 1 (spring 1981), pp. 1–32.

———. *D. H. Lawrence: A Life.* New York: Knopf, 1990.

————."D. H. Lawrence and Homosexuality." In Spender, Stephen, *D. H. Lawrence: Poet, Prophet, Novelist*. London: Weidenfeld & Nicholson, 1973.

Meynell, Viola. *Alice Meynell: A Memoir*. London: Cape, 1929.

Millett, Kate. *Sexual Politics*. New York: Doubleday, 1970.

Milton, Colin. *Lawrence and Nietzsche*. Aberdeen, Scotland: Aberdeen University Press, 1987.

Moore, Harry T. *The Intelligent Heart*. New York: Farrar, Straus, and Young, 1954.

————. *Poste Restante: A Lawrence Travel Calendar*. Berkeley and Los Angeles: University of California Press, 1956.

————. "Richard Aldington in His Last Years." *Texas Quarterly,* Autumn 1963.

————. *The Priest of Love: A Life of D. H. Lawrence*. London: Heinemann, 1974.

Moore, Harry T., and Dale B. Montague. *Frieda Lawrence and Her Circle: Letters To, From and About Frieda Lawrence*. London: Macmillan, 1981.

Moorehead, Caroline. *Bertrand Russell*. London: Sinclair-Stevenson, 1992.

Mori, Haruhide, ed. *A Conversation on D. H. Lawrence, by Aldous Huxley, Frieda Lawrence Ravagli, Majl Ewing, Lawrence Clark Powell and Dorothy M. Conway*. Los Angeles: Friends of the UCLA Library, 1974.

Muggeridge, Malcolm. "Lawrence's Sons and Lovers." *The New Statesman and Nation,* April 23, 1955, pp. 581–82.

————. *Like It Was*. London: Collins, 1981.

Munro, Craig. "The D. H. Lawrence–P. R. Stephensen Letters." *Australian Literary Studies,* vol. 11 (May 1984), pp. 291–315.

Murry, Colin. *One Hand Clapping*. London: Gollancz, 1975.

Murry, J. Middleton. *Between Two Worlds*. London: Cape, 1935.

————. *Son of Woman: The Story of D. H. Lawrence*. London: Cape, 1931.

————. *Reminiscences of D. H. Lawrence*. London: Cape, 1933.

————, ed. *Journal of Katherine Mansfield, 1904–1922*. London: Constable, 1984 (first published 1927).

Murry, Katherine Middleton. *Beloved Quixote: The Unknown Life of John Middleton Murry*. London: Souvenir, 1986.

Nehamas, A. *Nietzsche: Life as Literature*. Cambridge, Mass.: Harvard University Press, 1985.

Nehls, Edward. *D. H. Lawrence: A Composite Biography*. Three volumes. Madison, Wisc.: University of Wisconsin Press, 1957–1959.

Neville, George H. *A Memoir of D. H. Lawrence (The Betrayal)*. Carl Baron, ed. Cambridge, England: Cambridge University Press, 1981.

Nixon, Cornelia. *D. H. Lawrence and the Turn Against Women*. Berkeley: University of California Press, 1988.

Nottingham Festival Committee. *Young Bert: An Exhibition of the Early Life of D. H. Lawrence, 8 July–20 August 1972*. Nottingham: Castle Museum, 1972.

Ober, Dr. William B. "Lady Chatterley's What?" In *Boswell's Clap and Other Essays*. Carbondale, Ill.: Southern Illinois Press, 1979.

Oliphant, Dave, and Thomas Zigal, eds. *The Library Chronicle of the University of Texas at Austin,* New Series no. 34 (issue on the D. H. Lawrence collections at Texas), 1986.

Orage, A. R. *Nietzsche in Outline and Aphorism*. Edinburgh and London: Foulis, 1907.

O'Sullivan, Vincent, ed., with Margaret Scott. *The Collected Letters of Katherine Mansfield*. Volume 1, 1903–1917; volume 2, 1918–1919. Oxford: Clarendon, 1984.

Page, Norman. *D. H. Lawrence Interviews and Recollections*. Two volumes. London: Macmillan, 1981.

Parmenter, Ross. *Lawrence in Oaxaca: A Quest for the Novelist in Mexico.* Salt Lake City: Peregrine Smith Books, 1984.

Patmore, Derek. *My Friends When Young: The Memoirs of Brigit Patmore.* London: Heinemann, 1968.

———. *D. H. Lawrence and the Dominant Male.* London: Covent Garden Press, 1970.

Pollak, Paulina S. "Anti-Semitism in the Works of D. H. Lawrence: Search for and Rejection of the Father." *Literature and Psychology,* vol. 32, no. 1 (1986), pp. 19–29.

Porter, Katherine Anne. "A Wreath for the Gamekeeper." *Encounter,* February 1960, pp. 69–77.

Potter, Stephen. *D. H. Lawrence.* London: Cape, 1930.

Preston, Peter, and Peter Hoare, eds. *D. H. Lawrence in the Modern World.* Cambridge, England: Cambridge University Press, 1989.

Price, A. Whigman. "D. H. Lawrence and Congregationalism." "Part I—The Background of Chapel and Home." "Part II—The Legacy of Congregationalism." *The Congregational Quarterly,* vol. 34, no. 3 (1956), pp. 242–52; vol. 34, no. 4 (1956), pp. 322–33.

Redman, Ben Ray. "But Why, Mr. Lawrence?" *New York Herald Tribune Books,* March 8, 1925.

Robinson, Roxana. *Georgia O'Keeffe: A Life.* London: Bloomsbury, 1990.

Rossman, Charles. "D. H. Lawrence and Mexico." In *D. H. Lawrence: A Centenary Celebration.* Peter Balbert and Philip L. Marcus, eds. Ithaca, N.Y.: Cornell University Press, 1985.

———. "Myth and Misunderstanding D. H. Lawrence." In *Twentieth-Century Poetry, Fiction, Theory.* Harry Garvin, ed. Lewisburg, Pa.: Bucknell University Press.

———. "You Are the Call and I Am the Answer: D. H. Lawrence and Women." *DHLR,* vol. 8, no. 3 (fall 1975), pp. 255–328.

———. Untitled review of *The Letters of D. H. Lawrence, Volume V; D. H. Lawrence: A Literary Life; The Challenge of D. H. Lawrence;* and *D. H. Lawrence in the Modern World. Modern Fiction Studies,* vol. 36, no. 4 (winter 1990), pp. 604–608.

Ruderman, Judith. *D. H. Lawrence and the Devouring Mother: The Search for a Patriarchal Ideal of Leadership.* Durham, N.C.: Duke University Press, 1984.

Rudnick, Lois P. *Mabel Dodge Luhan: New Woman, New Worlds.* Albuquerque: University of New Mexico Press, 1984.

Russell, Bertrand. *Portraits from Memory and Other Essays.* London: Allen & Unwin, 1956.

———. *Autobiography.* Volume 2, 1914–1944. London: Allen & Unwin, 1968.

Sagar, Keith. "Lawrence and the Wilkinsons." *Review of English Literature,* vol. 3, no. 4 (October 1962), pp. 62–75.

———. *D. H. Lawrence: A Calendar of His Works.* Manchester, England: Manchester University Press, 1979.

———. *The Life of D. H. Lawrence: An Illustrated Biography.* London: Eyre Methuen, 1980.

———. *D. H. Lawrence: Life into Art.* Athens, Ga.: University of Georgia Press, 1985.

Salgado, Gamini, and G. K. Das. *The Spirit of D. H. Lawrence: Centenary Studies.* Totowa, N.J.: Barnes & Noble, 1988.

Savage, Henry. *The Receding Shore.* London: Grayson & Co., 1933.

Schneider, Daniel J. *The Consciousness of D. H. Lawrence.* Lawrence, Kans.: University Press of Kansas, 1986.

Secker, Martin. *Letters from a Publisher: Martin Secker to D. H. Lawrence & Others, 1911–1929.* Iver, England: Enitharmon Press, 1970.

Seymour, Miranda. *Ottoline Morrell: Life on the Grand Scale.* London: Hodder and Stoughton, 1992.

Sharpe, Michael C. "The Genesis of D. H. Lawrence's *The Trespasser.*" *Essays in Criticism,* January 1961.

Sinyard, Neil. "Another Fine Mess: D. H. Lawrence and Thomas Hardy on Film." In *Filming Literature: The Art of Screen Adaptation.* Neil Sinyard, ed. London: Croom Helm, 1986.

Sitwell, Edith. *Taken Care Of.* London: Hutchinson, 1965.

Sitwell, Osbert. *Laughter in the Next Room.* London: Macmillan, 1949.

Skidelsky, Robert. *John Maynard Keynes: Hopes Betrayed, 1883–1920.* London: Macmillan, 1983.

Skinner, M.W.G. *Croydon's Railways.* Southampton, England: Kingfisher Railway Productions, 1985.

Smith, F. B. *The Retreat of Tuberculosis 1850–1952.* London: Croom Helm, 1988.

Smith, Grover, ed. *Letters of Aldous Huxley.* London: Chatto & Windus, 1969.

Sontag, Susan. *Illness as Metaphor.* New York: Farrar, Straus & Giroux, 1978. Harmondsworth: Penguin, 1983.

Sparrow, John. "*Regina v. Penguin Books Ltd:* An Undisclosed Element in the Case." *Encounter,* February 1962.

Spender, Stephen. *D. H. Lawrence: Prophet, Poet, Novelist.* London: Weidenfeld & Nicolson, 1973.

Spilka, Mark. *The Love Ethic of D. H. Lawrence.* Bloomington, Ind.: University of Indiana Press, 1955; London: Dennis Dobson, 1958.

———. "Lawrence and the Clitoris." In *The Challenge of D. H. Lawrence,* Michael Squires and Keith Cushman, eds. Madison, Wisc.: University of Wisconsin Press, 1990.

Squires, Michael, ed. *D. H. Lawrence Manuscripts: The Correspondence of Frieda Lawrence, Jake Zeitlin and Others.* New York: St. Martin's Press, 1991.

———, and Keith Cushman, eds. *The Challenge of D. H. Lawrence.* Madison, Wisc.: University of Wisconsin Press, 1990.

———, and Dennis Jackson, eds. *D. H. Lawrence's "Lady": A New Look at Lady Chatterley's Lover.* Athens, Ga.: University of Georgia Press, 1985.

Steele, Bruce. "*Kangaroo:* Fiction and Fact." *Meridian,* 1991, pp. 19–34.

Stevens, C. J. *Lawrence at Tregerthen.* Troy, N.Y.: Whitston, 1988.

Storch, Margaret. *Sons and Adversaries: Women in William Blake and D. H. Lawrence.* Knoxville: University of Tennessee Press, 1990.

Szeemann, Harald. *Monte Verità.* Milan: Electra, 1978.

Tacey, David. "On Not Crossing the Gap: Lawrence and our *Genius Loci.*" *Quadrant,* November 1990.

Tedlock, E. W., Jr. *Frieda Lawrence: The Memoirs and the Correspondence.* London: Heinemann, 1961 (revised and enlarged edition published in New York: Knopf, 1964).

Templeton, Mark. "D. H. Lawrence: Illness, Identity, and Writing." Unpublished paper delivered at Lawrence Conference, Ottawa, June 1993.

Thornycroft, Rosalind, and Chloë Baynes. *Time Which Spaces Us Apart.* Batcombe, Somerset, England: privately printed, 1991.

Tindall, William York. *D. H. Lawrence and Susan His Cow.* New York: Cooper Square Publishers, 1972; Columbia University Press, 1939.

———. *The Later D. H. Lawrence.* New York: Knopf, 1952.

Tomalin, Claire. *Katherine Mansfield, A Secret Life.* Harmondsworth: Penguin, 1988.

Tomlinson, H. M. *Norman Douglas.* London: Hutchinson, 1952.

Trail, G. W. "The Psychological Dynamics of D. H. Lawrence's 'Snake.' " *American Image,* vol. 36 (1979), pp. 345–56.

Trilling, Diana. "D. H. Lawrence in Love" (review of *Mr. Noon*). *New York Times Book Review,* December 16, 1984.

Tuchman, Barbara. *The Guns of August.* New York: Macmillan, 1962.

Turner, John, with Cornelia Rumpf-Worthen and Ruth Jenkins. "The Otto Gross–Frieda Weekley Correspondence." *DHLR,* vol. 22, no. 2 (summer 1990), pp. 137–227.

Tytell, John. *Ezra Pound: The Solitary Volcano.* London: Bloomsbury, 1987.

Watson, George. "D. H. Lawrence's Own Myth." *Encounter,* December 1976, pp. 29–34.

Weekley, Montague. "The Unexpected Stepfather." Interview with Hallam Tennyson, BBC Radio, September 27, 1970.

Weigle, Marta, and Kyle Fiore. *Santa Fe and Taos: The Writer's Era, 1916–1941.* Santa Fe: Ancient City Press, 1982.

Whelan, P. T. Untitled review of *Lawrence's Men and Women,* by Sheila MacLeod. *DHLR,* vol. 19, no. 1 (summer 1987), pp. 38–40.

Williams, Harley. *Requiem for a Great Killer.* London: Health Horizon, 1973.

Wolff, Geoffrey. *Black Sun: The Life of Harry Crosby.* New York: Random House, 1974.

Woodeson, John. *Mark Gertler.* London: Sidgwick & Jackson, 1972.

Woods, Greg. *Articulate Flesh: Male Homoeroticism and Poetry.* New Haven: Yale University Press, 1988; paperback, 1991.

Worthen, John. *D. H. Lawrence and the Idea of the Novel.* London: Macmillan, 1979.

———. *D. H. Lawrence: A Literary Life.* London: Macmillan, 1989.

———. *D. H. Lawrence: The Early Years, 1885–1912.* Cambridge, England: Cambridge University Press, 1991.

Zytaruk, George J. *The Quest for Rananim: D. H. Lawrence's Letters to S. S. Koteliansky 1914–1930.* Montreal: McGill University Press, 1970.

———. "The Collected Letters of Jessie Chambers." *DHLR,* vol. 12, nos. 1 and 2 (spring/summer 1979).

ACKNOWLEDGMENTS

MANY PEOPLE HELPED me take a fresh look at Lawrence. I am particularly grateful to those who invited me into their homes to talk about the Lawrence they knew: in Derbyshire, Margaret Needham and Joan King, with memories of their Uncle Bert; in Greatham, Sussex, Dr. Mary Saleeby Fisher, who showed me the room where Lawrence gave her lessons in 1915 and who allowed me to quote from the notebook she prepared under his tutelage; in London, Lady Juliette Huxley, who recalled the winter holiday with the Lawrences at Les Diablerets in 1928; in Florence, the late Sir Harold Acton, who told me of his visit to Scandicci in 1926 to see Lawrence's new paintings; and, in Tuscany, Lawrence's stepdaughter Barbara Weekley Barr. Her sharp wit, elegant bearing, and lively intelligence showed why Lawrence had been so fond of her. I was helped also by John Carswell, Anne Radford MacEwen, Chloë Baynes Green, and Bridget Baynes Coffey, who knew Lawrence as a friend of their parents. Mrs. Green's memoir of her mother, Rosalind Baynes, is a great addition to Lawrence studies.

For permission to quote from the unpublished works of D. H. and Frieda Lawrence and from certain copyrighted works, I would like to thank Gerald Pollinger and Laurence Pollinger Ltd. For permission to quote from the Witter Bynner Estate, I would like to thank the Witter Bynner Foundation for Poetry, and to use Bynner's excellent photographs, the University of Nottingham. Every effort has been made to trace copyright holders. I would be grateful to hear from any who have escaped notice.

For invaluable information about the history of the families concerned, I would like to express my thanks to Ian Weekley, Julia Weekley, Baron Hermann von Richthofen, and Freiherr Dr. Patrick von Richthofen.

I am greatly indebted to Professor Martin Green of Tufts University for allowing me to read the correspondence of Else Jaffe and Frieda Gross; also to Robin Whitworth, Myfanwy Thomas, and Elizabeth Jenkins for sending me copies of Lawrence letters in their possession.

Lawrence's life is so often treated in fragments because those writing about him are anchored to one spot. For their generous encouragement, I am indebted to my publishers, Christopher Sinclair-Stevenson in London and Frederic W. Hills of Simon & Schuster in New York. Not only did they make it possible for me to retrace much of Lawrence's global journey, they never flagged in their faith, like Lawrence's own, that there is no last word on anybody. Neil Taylor and Roger Cazalet of Sinclair-Stevenson, and Burton Beals of Simon & Schuster helped immeasurably by casting their experienced eyes on a long manuscript. My literary agents and friends, Hilary Rubinstein and Caradoc King of A. P. Watt Ltd. in London, and Ellen Levine in New York, have been a source of support throughout, in matters temporal and spiritual.

During research and travel, I have enjoyed much hospitality. I would like to thank Patricia Bleifer, Peter and Margaret Brooks, Ursula Barr Creagh, Joseph Davis, Paul and Helga Doty, Tom and Marguerite Jukes, Patrick Heron, Maureen Howard and

Mark Probst, Humphrey and Pamela Lewis, Nigel Lewis, Emily and Roderick Mac-Farquhar, Tom Mayer, David Norton, Mary Power, Peter Preston, Thomas and Carolyn Staley, Hugh and Barbara Witemeyer, and Dorothy Zinberg.

I am grateful also to my family: to Bruno Maddox for research, critical suggestions, and help in preparation of the manuscript; to John, Piers, and Bronwen Maddox, for long drives to out-of-the-way literary sites and help in solving the biographer's puzzles of renumbered and renamed streets and houses. My husband, John, contributed most of all, with years of patient listening.

For critical reading of parts of the manuscript I am indebted to the literary scholars Derek Britton, Keith Cushman, Paul Delany, Martin Green, Ira Nadel, Peter Preston, Charles Rossman, Bruce Steele, and Margaret Storch; also to Joseph Davis, Richard DuCann, Chloë Baynes Green, and Bernard McGinley. I also had the benefit of the kind suggestions and stimulating conversation of Lawrence's Cambridge biographers, John Worthen and Mark Kinkead-Weekes. What errors remain are my own. For translations from the German, my thanks go to Martin Albrow and Sophie von Rohr.

The Lawrence archive is necessarily far-flung. I would like to thank the following institutions for making their libraries or collections available to me and, in some cases, permitting me to reproduce photographs or letters or to quote from copyrighted material: BBC Written Archives Centre; Bancroft Library, University of California at Berkeley; British Council, Mexico City; British Library: Manuscript Room, Newspaper Collection, and National Sound Archive; British Medical Association; *British Medical Journal;* Witter Bynner Foundation for Poetry; Museo Casa Anatta, Monte Verità, Ascona; Central Statistical Office, London; Library of Congress; Croydon Local Studies Library; Archives of the British Psycho-Analytical Society; Israeli Psychoanalytic Institute; Institut für Zeitgeschichte, Munich; Archives and Rare Books Department, the University of Cincinnati Libraries; Eastwood, Notts. Public Library; Houghton Library, Harvard University; The London Library; Department of Special Collections, University Research Library of the University of California at Los Angeles; Zimmerman Library, University of New Mexico, and the university's D. H. Lawrence Ranch at San Cristobal; Berg Collection of the New York Public Library; Nottingham County Library; Manuscripts Department, Nottingham University Library; Reading University Library; Royal Literary Fund; Special Collections Room of the Morris Library at Southern Illinois University; Harry C. Ransom Humanities Research Center of the University of Texas at Austin; Thirroul, New South Wales, Public Library; Commune di Spotorno; Public Record Office of England and Wales; U.S. Embassy, London, Reference Library; U.S. Immigration and Naturalization Service; the U.S. National Archive; Wellcome Institute for the History of Medicine; the Friends of Wyewurk Committee; and the Beinecke Rare Book and Manuscript Library, Yale.

As a biographer, I have learned to trust the kindness of librarians. My particular thanks go to Vincent A. Giroud, curator of modern books and manuscripts at the Beinecke Library; Cathy Henderson of the Humanities Research Center; Michael Bott of Reading University Library; R. Russell Maylone of Northwestern University's Special Collections; the late Lola Szladits of the Berg Collection; Kay Bagshaw of the Wellcome Foundation Library; and, above all, for their constant friendliness and almost daily help, the staff of the admirable Central Library of the Royal Borough of Kensington and Chelsea.

I would like to thank also William Alfred, Al Alvarez, Annabel Farjeon Anrep, Albert L. Bearce, Sybille Bedford, Lydia Blanchard, Lord Bonham Carter, Rosalind Bowler, Melvyn Bragg, Moina Brown, Janet Byrne, David Callard, John Carey, George Chowdharay-Best, Dr. David E. Cooke, A. A. Crassweller, Robert and Sandra Darroch, Dilys Dawes, Steven Dickman, Noel Riley Fitch, Val Arnold Foster, Rosemary Friedman, Antonia Fritz, Richard Garnett, Walter Gratzer, John R. Green-smith, Lord Haden-Guest, Leo Hamalian, John R. Harrison, Mrs. Enriqueta Hawkins, Patrick Heron, S. J. Hills, David Holbrook, Richard Holmes, Michael Ivers, Elizabeth Jenkins, Saki Karavas, Mr. and Mrs. P. J. Kavanagh, Norman Kiell, Stuart and Shanie Kirkwood, Holly Laird, A. Walton Litz, Joan McCluskey, Nesta Macdonald, Lord McGregor, Barbara Miliaras, Lady Naomi Mitchison, Jane Mul-vagh, Margaret M. Mumford, Kay Needham-Hurst, Linda O'Shaughnessy, Vincent O'Sullivan, Norman Page, Christopher Pollnitz, Douglas Price-Williams, Sunetra Puri, Ginette Roy, Lois Rudnick, Dr. Merton Sandler, Colin and Elizabeth Shaw, Carla Shimeld, Erika Stegmann, Harald Szeemann, Mrs. Connie Windsor and the staff of Greasley Beauvale Infants School, John and Thérèse Wright, Caroline Zil-boorg, and George J. Zytaruk.

INDEX

PHOTO CREDITS

ABOUT THE AUTHOR

AUTHOR AND JOURNALIST BRENDA MADDOX was born in Massachusetts and took a degree in English literature at Harvard. She is a regular writer on the media in the British press and a frequent broadcaster on the BBC. Her widely acclaimed biography of James Joyce's wife, *Nora: The Real Life of Molly Bloom,* published in 1988, won the *Los Angeles Times* Book Award for biography, the British Silver P.E.N. award for nonfiction, and the French Prix du Meilleur Livre Etranger, was short-listed for the National Book Award and the Whitbread Biography Prize, and has been translated into eight languages. She lives in London and mid-Wales.